A TEXTBOOK OF PERSONNEL MANAGEMENT

George Thomason was born and brought up in the Lake District. He was educated at Sheffield and Toronto Universities and obtained his doctorate at University College, Cardiff, where he is now Montague Burton Professor of Industrial Relations, and Head of the Department of Industrial Relations and Management Studies.

He is a member of the Doctors' and Dentists' Pay Review Body and has previously served on a number of Wages Councils. He is a member of the Advisory Conciliation and Arbitration Service's panel of single arbitrators and has conducted over 300 arbitrations in the past 15 years.

For a time in the 1960s he was employed as Assistant to the Managing Director of Flex Fasteners Ltd and Porth Textiles Ltd. He also served for three years as a Deputy Principal of his present College in the mid-1970s.

He is married with two children. A Companion of the Institute of Personnel Management and a Fellow of the British Institute of Management, he is the author of a number of previous IPM titles: *Improving the Quality of Organization, Experiments in Participation, Job Evaluation: Objectives and Methods* and a companion volume to this present one, entitled *A Textbook of Industrial Relations Management* to be published in 1982. He is chief examiner for the IPM's examinations in Employee Relations, and for the Chartered Institute of Transport's examination in Manpower and Industrial Relations.

A Textbook of Personnel Management

Fourth edition

George F Thomason

Institute of Personnel Management

For my daughter
Sian Elizabeth

© *Institute of Personnel Management 1975, 1976, 1978 and 1981*
First published 1975
Second edition 1976
Reprinted 1977
Third edition 1978
Fourth edition 1981

Photoset, printed and bound in Great Britain by
REDWOOD BURN LIMITED
Trowbridge, Wiltshire

British Library Cataloguing in Publication Data

Thomason, George F.
  A textbook of personnel management.—
  4th ed.—(Management in perspective)
1. Personnel management
I. Title   II. Series
658.3   HF5549

ISBN 0–85292–301–5

Contents

Part two

Tables

Figures

Abbreviations used

ACAS	Advisory, Conciliation and Arbitration Service
All ER	All England Law Reports
APEX	Association of Professional, Executive, Clerical and Computer Staffs
ASLEF	Associated Society of Locomotive Engineers and Firemen
ASTMS	Association of Scientific, Technical and Managerial Staffs
AUEW	Amalgamated Union of Engineering Workers
BACIE	British Association for Commercial and Industrial Education
BIM	British Institute of Management
BISAKTA	British Iron, Steel and Kindred Trades' Association
CAC	Central Arbitration Committee (formerly the Industrial Court and the Industrial Arbitration Board (1972–4))
CAWU	Clerical and Administrative Workers' Union, now APEX
CBI	Confederation of British Industry
CIR	Commission on Industrial Relations
C of E Act	Contracts of Employment Act
COHSE	Confederation of Health Service Employees
COIT	Central Office of Industrial Tribunals
DE	Department of Employment
D & HA	Docks and Harbours Act
DHSS	Department of Health and Social Security
EEF	Engineering Employers' Federation
EEPTU	Electrical, Electronics, Telecommunication and Plumbing Trade Union (formerly ETU: Electrical Trades Union)
EP Act	Employment Protection Act
EP (C) Act	Employment Protection (Consolidation) Act, 1978
EPEA	Electrical Power Engineers' Association

GMWU	General and Municipal Workers Union
H & SWA	Health and Safety at Work etc Act
HMSO	Her Majesty's Stationery Office
ICR	Industrial Court Reports
IPM	Institute of Personnel Management
IRLR	Industrial Relations Law Reports
IR Act	Industrial Relations Act 1971
IT	Industrial Tribunal
ITB	Industrial Training Board
ITR	Industrial Tribunal Reports
MBO	Management-by-Objectives
MCB	Management Centre, Bradford.
NALGO	National and Local Government Officers' Association
NATSOPA	National Society of Operative Printers and Assistants
NEDO	National Economic Development Office
NGA	National Graphical Association
NIIP	National Institute of Industrial Psychology
NIRC	National Industrial Relations Court, 1972–4
NUBE	National Union of Bank Employees
NUPE	National Union of Public Employees
NUR	National Union of Railwaymen
OD	Organisational Development
PBR	Payment by Results
RCTUEA	Royal Commission on Trade Unions and Employers' Associations (the Donovan Commission)
RP Act	Redundancy Payments Act
SOGAT	Society of Graphical and Allied Trades
TASS	Technical and Supervisory Staffs Section of the AUEW
TGWU	Transport and General Workers Union
TUC	Trades Union Congress
TULR Act	Trade Union and Labour Relations Act, 1974; 1976
USDAW	Union of Shop, Distributive and Allied Workers

Preface to the fourth edition

In the 1970s, a good deal of attention has been focused on the world of work for many different reasons. Workers appear to have developed new expectations of it. Managers have tried to develop new methods of organizing and controlling it. Social scientists have offered new ideas and theories about it. Governments have adopted different postures in relation to it, either for reasons connected with 'the state of the economy' or because of a desire to 'harmonize with European practice'. The period has bubbled with change and people caught up in work have found themselves having to make some response to this.

Because much of the change has surrounded questions about the 'treatment' of workers in work, personnel managers have had to adjust to and accommodate it in the practice of their particular roles. Many different people and institutional representatives have offered them advice as to how the job of 'managing personnel' could and/or should be carried out. Trying to encapsulate all this in a book has led to this text running to three editions already, and the present one it is to be hoped will now serve for some longer period of time than the earlier ones.

What I have tried to do in this book is to produce a coherent summary of the position we have now reached in 'personnel management'. By this, I do not mean to imply that the field is not, still, full of different, even competing, values (suggesting what *should* be done) and ideas (implying what *could* be done). Indeed, the book would be both easier to write and to read if that were the case. But it is not, and I have tried to indicate some of the major differences whilst still trying to maintain a degree of coherence in the 'body of knowledge' associated with the practice.

I have also tried to present this body of knowledge in a way which will guide the student through the three main areas of the current Institute of Personnel Management examination syllabus. 'Employee resourcing' is treated mainly, but not exclusively, in part one; 'employee development' is discussed chiefly in part two but is followed up in some respects in part three; and 'employee relations' come in for consideration in part three, although some of the material in the two earlier parts (eg, on the contract of employment in chapter 4) is supportive of and relevant to this.

The organization of the different sections reflects a view which I take of the way in which people (whether they are personnel managers or anyone else) 'make things happen'. This is essentially a closed loop model of decision and action, which I adopt simply because it helps (heuristically, as is sometimes said) to organize our thinking about what is involved.

In so far as there is a starting point in this circle, it is with the *values* which that individual holds about things and events and which he or she uses to separate the good from the bad or the right from the wrong in a moral sense. In chapter 2, for example, some of the main values which are associated with personnel management and which have to do with the worth (worthiness) of people, are outlined. These values, as we see later, are commonly reflected in 'policies' which are adopted for undertakings or in the 'rules' which are applied to human conduct.

It is one thing to know what end a person wants to achieve (because it is a 'good' end) and another to know how to bring it about. The next major element in the model, therefore, is the concept of 'theory' which indicates a person's perspective of 'how things happen' or 'how ends might be brought about'. In the field of personnel management, there are all sorts of theories of this sort; there are theories of motivation and control (which are examined in chapters 10 and 11) or, more particularly, theories about the relationship of incentive to performance (chapter 13). A practitioner must have a *knowledge* of such theories and an *understanding* of the way things (may be made to) work which is one of the reasons why professional training and education emphasize the idea of 'knowledge' so much.

To know how a particular end might be brought about is not the same as having an ability to bring it about. Beyond knowledge and understanding, therefore, lie the *skills* of the practitioner. By these he or she effects some influence on those 'variables' which the theory suggests are important to the realization of the desired end. Many such skills in the personnel management area are 'social'; skills of communicating and influencing, or more particularly skills of training or negotiating, and a host of others which crop up in, for example, chapters 8, 9, 14, 15, 19 and 20. A textbook can indicate what the skills are, but it is not a good instrument for providing the learning opportunity required for their development. But they need to be learned before the individual can make things happen in the desired ways to achieve the desired ends.

The effect of applying whatever skills one may have to the situation is to produce an outcome. The question is, then, whether it is the outcome which one wants (according to one's values) or expected (according to the theory). The fourth element in the model is therefore that which entails assessment or evaluation of what is effected, and this is then fed back to influence one's conception of desirable ends and one's belief or understanding of method. This feeding back is what closes the loop or completes the circle. This 'model' we find cropping up all the way through personnel management, as for example, in connection with recruitment (chapter 9) or training (chapter 15). There are many others.

Readers will find, therefore, that there is a tendency in each separate part of the book for the sequence to run from value, through theory (or method) to the actual practices (to which the skills, as learnt, may be applied). Aspects of practice are kept as close as possible to the objectives and methods to which they relate, but it has to be said that some of the practices (such as communication which happens to be discussed in chapter 14) are more general in their application than their location in the book might signify. This pattern of organization also attempts to conform to the organizing principle behind the current IPM syllabus, in which in each separate area, the attempt is made to cover the full range of objective-and-policy-determination, planning-and-programming, and execution, as applied to them.

Two other short prefatory points might be made:

first, because the relevant body of knowledge is not 'settled' in personnel management, the text is deliberately sprinkled with texts which present alternative views and theories, so that the reader may readily find such alternatives when he or she wants them

secondly, because a textbook which tries to cover the whole spectrum must necessarily be limited in its treatment of any one aspect, a list of further reading which will supply greater depth is appended to each chapter.

In both cases, the references in the text itself are confined to the name, publication date and page reference and the full bibliography is given at the end of the book, pp 565–603.

Anyone who writes a book of this nature always owes a debt to many people—colleagues in work, colleagues in the profession and students—whose contributions cannot be acknowledged in textual reference. I have been particularly fortunate in having the help of such colleagues at various times as Michael Fogarty. Peter

Anthony, Ian Smith, David Dunkerley, Anne Crichton, Dave Simpson, John Bridge, Tom Keenoy, Kevin Wilson and Andrew Rix. Over the years many students on our diploma and masters degree programmes in personnel management in Cardiff have provided stimulation in tutorial and seminar discussions. Colleagues in the Institute and particularly those in the Cardiff and Newport Branch, have also contributed a great deal to my understanding of the subject. In the preparation of this edition, I have also had help from comments and suggestions made by course tutors and students, whose views were sought by the Institute of Personnel Management in 1980. I hope that those who contributed will notice where I have made changes in accordance with their suggestions.

To all of these people I express my gratitude, although I still accept full responsibility for what appears here. I would also like to thank Mrs B Clargo and Mrs M Price for their diligence and skill in transforming the script into a connected and readable typescript for the publisher, and Sally Herbert and the staff of the IPM's publications department for their patience and skill in making the actual book 'happen'.

Department of Industrial Relations *George F Thomason*
  and Management Studies *14 February 1981*
University College
Cardiff

Introduction
Personnel management in context

Personnel management in context

The setting of personnel management
This book is about personnel management. 'Personnel management' is a particular set of activities which acquire meaning from being purposively related to people at work. As the Institute of Personnel Management's definition puts it:

> Personnel Management is that part of management concerned with people at work and with their relationships within an enterprise. Its aim is to bring together and develop into an effective organization the men and women who make up an enterprise and, having regard for the well-being of the individual and of working groups, to enable them to make their best contribution to its success (IPM: *The Institute of Personnel Management*, August 1979)

This is a succinct and reasonable definition of something which does not have a meaning with which everyone would necessarily agree, and which is in any case both complex and still evolving. The rest of the book will put more flesh on these bare bones of definition, but this general statement will serve to launch us on the path we propose to tread.

Before moving far along that path, however, we need to note something about the 'setting' or the 'context' within which these activities occur. What we call 'personnel management' is, after all, a part of something much larger, and a good deal of the definition depends upon this larger thing. The concern is with 'people *at work*', their relationships within *an enterprise*, 'effective *organization*' and individual *well-being* (amongst other things) and all of these derive their meanings from the larger context. We therefore begin the discussion by noting briefly some of the main features of this context which will help to give meaning and structure to the particular activities which fall within the remit of the book.

Given the focus of personnel management activities upon *people* at work within work-providing enterprises, we may immediately distinguish three elements of the context:

(a) first, the people involved—not everyone, but those *at work* and therefore the ones who are themselves caught up in some purposive or 'co-ordinated' activity

(b) secondly, the enterprises involved—which, in a 'mixed economy' are oriented to a variety of purposes and are structured in a variety of ways in order to provide the employment of people with which personnel management is chiefly concerned

(c) thirdly, the relationships of individual and enterprise—which are themselves affected by the nature and requirements of the first two entities distinguished, *and also* by beliefs and principles which the wider society requires or expects both individual persons and individual enterprises to subscribe to.

The complexities of the context of personnel management are contained in a simple statement that it comprises people in relationships in enterprises within a social structure.

The complexities arise from the multiplicity of forms which these elements may take in combination and as a consequence of their interaction with one another. It is possible to state what is common in the whole situation which our practising personnel manager faces, as is done, for example, by Roethlisberger:

(1) organizations have *purposes*:
(2) to carry out purposes, *structure* is needed and *roles* have to be assigned. Also
(3) organizations are *peopled*, and
(4) people have *needs* (Roethlisberger, 1968, pp. 303–4).

As he continues, these are no longer matters to be discovered. . . . These are the givens from which to go on to ask more interesting . . . questions (*ibid*).

But these may be given at the level of principle. In practice purposes, structures, roles, people and human needs will reveal a great variety, both in isolation and in combination. A concept of 'setting' must therefore acknowledge that there will be variety on each of these dimensions and on the aggregated dimension. The 'problems' facing the personnel manager in such settings are therefore ones of effecting adequate diagnoses of what *exists*, discovering what is relevant *action* to take in them, and deciding what action is most appropriate in the light of the *values* which are to be applied in making the inherent choices.

In this first part of the book, therefore, we look at some of the main differences which are to be apprehended on these main dimensions singled out in Roethlisberger's statement, in order, simply to set the scene. Into this discussion, we then fit the conceptions of the particular set of activities which we refer to as 'personnel management'.

1 The context of personnel management

The locus of personnel management

As a 'part' of management (see above, p 3) personnel management is to be found wherever management is and therefore wherever there are people in employment whose activities call for co-ordination and control. As a 'specialist function' or specialist occupation, however, it tends to be found only in larger organizations in which there is a high degree of division of (managerial) labour. In the one framework, therefore, all managers might be said to 'qualify' as personnel managers in that they manage personnel as part of their general duties. In the other, the one which is usually in mind when 'personnel managers' are being counted, only those who carry out duties specifically labelled 'personnel' qualify for inclusion.

Examination of such evidence as we have of the location of specialist personnel managers suggests that they are usually to be found in the larger undertakings in both private industry and public service (and historically more often in the former than the latter). That evidence suggests that three statements might be made on location which relate the two conceptions (the part-of-general-management and the specialist-department of personnel management) which carry implications for the definition and structuring of the role itself.

First, that specialist personnel managers and departments have until recently been established in manufacturing industry (or perhaps more accurately the 'Index of Production Industries'), and in the larger undertakings within it (or them).

Secondly, such departments are not much to be found in smaller undertakings. Cuming, for example, makes the point that the conception of 'management of personnel' by the line managers themselves applies directly to small businesses (Cuming, 1975, p 2) and this was borne out by the surveys which were conducted by Collins in the 1960s (cf Collins, 1964, pp 3–5; Crichton,

6

1968, p 296).

Thirdly, Cuming also suggests that this other conception applies 'to those larger organizations, particularly in the public sector, where specialist personnel departments have not yet been established' (Cuming, 1975, p 2). In these organizations, there was, at this time, an 'establishment function' concerned largely with stocks and flows of manpower, but little else (cf Anthony & Crichton, 1969, p 157).

It may be hypothesized that this apparent fact of location will influence the conception of it. The present spread into the large-scale undertakings in the public sector might similarly be expected to exert some influence upon the definition of the ends and means associated with the specialist function. In fact, as we shall see in chapter 2, some of these locational aspects have left their mark on the occupation. But in the present chapter, we need to examine some of the features of the larger utilitarian and service undertakings which may have some influence.

But because 'the organization' is not the only variable in this relationship, we need also to take a first look at the 'people' involved, and at the kinds of pressure which this entity might conceivably exert on the role definition. It may be that 'people are people' wherever they are to be found. But we might keep open, for the moment, the question of whether people at work in large utilitarian and service undertakings are necessarily the same as people anywhere—at least in so far as they might influence the personnel management role. (That question will not really be answered until we reach the end of the book, but, here, to illustrate the reason why the question is worth keeping in mind, we might notice that, for example, the location of personnel managers in undertakings is quite well correlated with the incidence of trade union organization of workers. The interesting question therefore is whether 'trade unionists' are not to be differentiated from people in general in their demands upon the 'management of personnel'.)

Consequently, given the kinds of contextual factor which might bear on the personnel management role, this chapter is structured broadly in terms of the five concepts which Roethlisberger advances (above, p. 4). We give attention to the main forms of purpose, structure, role, people and human need in that order, and conclude by relating the two conceptions of personnel management to these differences.

Organizational purposes

Organizations are usually created by someone to pursue one or more purposes. Those with which we are concerned, that is the ones which are associated with the doing of remunerated work, usually have purposes related to the satisfaction of demand (in the economist's sense) or to the satisfaction of need. These two concepts of 'demand' and 'need' are quite often used loosely or interchangeably to express purpose, but they are used here to prepare the way for a categorization of organizations into private (demand) and public (need) sector undertakings. (There are some other organizations which may be separately distinguished, as by Blau and Scott (1963, pp 40–58) for example, but we will confine ourselves here to these two broad categories.)

Organizations in the private sector are more usefully referred to as 'business enterprises'. These may take the form of individual trading ventures, partnerships or companies, reflecting, generally speaking, the number of people involved in their founding and financing. These are 'private' in the particular sense that in the process of attempting to satisfy consumer demand they may make profits or losses in 'trading', and in principle these are acquired or suffered as the case may be, by the private citizens who contribute to their funding. They are the ones who, ultimately, bear the financial risks.

Organizations in the public sector may be identified as public service undertakings. These may take the form of central or local government departments or agencies and public corporations (like the nationalized industry boards) usually operating 'nationally'. They are 'public' in the sense that they are created by governments in the name of the public at large, usually to meet some need which is perceived to exist amongst the citizenry, and any losses or surpluses are usually borne by the public purse. Some of these services may be provided at no direct charge and some may involve trading in the same manner as applies to business enterprises. It cannot be said therefore that the public/private distinction equates with that between non-trading and trading activities (cf Rees, 1973). In this case, however, such risks or uncertainties as there might be are borne indirectly by the members of the society, not by 'private citizens' directly.

The purposes of business enterprise focus on the satisfaction of consumer demands.

> Looked at fundamentally, any and every unit (or firm) in this complex macrocosm of business enterprise takes its role from its setting and involvement therein, and it exists, in the last analysis, in order to provide something directly or indirectly for the benefit of the citizen-consumers. Each enterprise has, as it were,

a specific share in those general purposes, according to what has been determined for it by its founders, or their successors in the present day body of governors or directors. (Brech, 1975, p 23)

This, as Brech argues, is the prime purpose of business enterprise, not sensibly to be transposed with the objective of 'making money' or making profits. In the nature of private enterprise organization, however, 'the owners expect to reap remuneration on their investment or reward for their venture, in the form of profits' . . . out of the operations engaged in, in meeting the demand (*ibid*). This becomes a derivative objective.

The purposes of public service organizations involve the satisfaction of citizen need, regardless of whether the citizen can translate that need into effective demand or of whether any means can be found of charging directly for the service. This kind of undertaking acts to reduce needs which have been determined by the legislators to be ones to be met through public service arrangements. Consequently, their purposes and the conditions under which their services will be offered, are commonly specified in legislation although they may be varied by governmental or ministerial decisions promulgated through Regulations. These may require 'efficient' operation, but even in connection with the trading services where the avoidance of long-term losses may be enjoined as a spur to that efficiency, there is usually no question of an 'expectation of profit or surplus' (as in private enterprise).

Organizations within the private and public sectors are thus aimed at different purposes, distinguished by the terms demand and need, and their 'derivative objectives' are characterized differently. The way in which organizational purpose impinges upon those who work within them may be expected to vary as they seek to cope with the tasks which are derived from them.

Organizational objectives and structure
It is only to be anticipated that the basic purposes of organizations will exert some general influence upon both the manner in which they are structured and the expectations surrounding the roles of those who work within them. Commonsense suggests that private industry is not the same as public service in these respects. But the concept which may most helpfully link the notion of purpose and those of structure and role is that of 'objective' as employed by Woodward (1958). Faced with the problem of explaining the differences in her data on 100 firms in South East Essex, in terms of the firms' size, type of industry or histories or relative success, or of the personalities of the senior executives, she found an explanation

in the related concepts of objectives and technologies.

> While the firms were all manufacturing goods for sale, their detailed objectives depended on the nature of the product and the type of customer. Thus, some firms were in more competitive industries than others, some were making perishable goods that could not be stored, some produced for stock, and others to orders; in fact marketing conditions were different in every firm (Woodward, 1958, p 10).

This permitted a division of manufacturing establishments into categories according to the relationship with the customer (ranging from the personalization involved in bespoke work to the impersonality of continuous production for a mass market) and the length of production 'run' which could be developed in the market faced by the firm (from one-off, through small and large batches, to 'mass' or continuous production) (cf Saunders, 1952, pp 1–14; 86–98)

These differences tended to associate with production technologies: 'these differences in objectives controlled and limited the techniques of production that could be employed' (Woodward, 1958, p 10). For purposes of presenting her data, Woodward divides the field into 'unit and small-batch production', 'large-batch and mass production', and 'process production' categories, but for other purposes it would be possible to split each of the categories and to identify further subdivisions according to the nature and complexity of the product and its production process (*see* Woodward, 1958, p 11).

Woodward was then able to demonstrate that there were distinct differences in the firms' structures between the three broad categories: the extent and form of the division of labour in, and of the hierarchies of, management; the processes by which policy was evolved; the distribution of power to influence amongst members; and the nature and form of the formal and informal relationships amongst members, varied systematically between them. (*see* Woodward, 1958, pp 16–30). Additionally, the commercial success of firms appeared to be associated with the degree of conformity to the 'structural norms' for the sub-category rather than with the general rules or principles enunciated by the then-usual management textbook (cf Newstrom *et al*, 1975, pp 1–121).

The hypothesis that structure is contingent upon the nature of uncertainty stemming from the market, or that it is 'situationally influenced', may be applied to the public sector, by extension. The broad distinction drawn between the 'service' and 'commonweal' types of organization by Blau and Scott (1963, pp 74–81) might, in the absence of findings from comparably extensive surveys, serve to highlight the type of expectation which Woodward's research suggests.

In the service type of organization there is a distinguishing direct relationship with the public, usually in the form of identifiable 'clients' as in the cases of hospitals with patients, schools with pupils, employment exchanges or job centres with job seekers.

A service organization has been defined as one whose prime beneficiary is the part of the public in direct contact with the organization, with whom and on whom its members work—in short, an organization whose basic function is to serve clients (Blau and Scott, 1963, p 51).

The main contrast is offered with the 'commonweal' organization, whose distinguishing characteristic "is that the public at large is the prime beneficiary" (*ibid*, p 54). In the examples provided by the military or police forces, or the Foreign or Home Offices, individual clients are not much in evidence and where they are, there is almost a presumption that they should be discouraged from developing individual relationships. These may then be expected to influence the degrees of freedom which exist to structure the organizations serving such differently conceived needs.

The concept of policy
The 'purpose' of undertakings (the term 'undertaking' is used for the sake of convenience and brevity to subsume organizations in both the private and public, business and service sectors) is frequently associated in the literature with the concept of 'policy'. 'Policy', it might be said, mediates between purposes and roles and is an important influence on 'structure' in providing some guiding rules for conduct. It is not, however, a simple and well defined concept; rather it is a complex notion which has two main strands of meaning and which may be related to purposes and objectives in two distinct ways.

In one meaning it is used as an expression of the broad intention to achieve certain objectives (such as serving customers or making money) and may be couched in more general or more specific terms (cf Thomas, 1977, pp 79–93). In this form, it links with the concept of 'strategy', a term indicating a more detailed and systematic approach to the determination of the modus operandi of achieving objectives—the way in which we make our money, the methods by which we get the production out of the door, the steps in securing the employees we need, and so on. To identify this element of meaning, we might refer to it as a theoretical or techni-

11

cal component: it indicates the (theory behind the) method or means to be adopted to realize some goal.

It is possible to link the policy with the concept of objectives, as does Hawkins in identifying the purposes of industrial relations policies:

> First, 'to lay down the principles or settled rules of action to which operating management is subject' and
> Secondly, 'to define objectives ' (Hawkins, 1974, p 40).

This last statement could, however, as easily refer to policy in its other meaning: the indication of what in any given context, is to be taken as right and proper conduct to be adopted in moving towards the realization of objectives, ie how we treat our customers, or our workers, or our members, or how we behave towards those who are in some way opposed to or competitive with us. The distinction between this and the first element is highlighted by using terms like morals or ethics to indicate that the aim here is not the achievement of some concrete end (like production) but rather of a proper or civilized relationship between men.

Taylor offers a hint of this kind of association in his Introduction to Cuthbert and Hawkins' edition of *Company Industrial Relations Policies* (1974):

> Policy making is the last bastion of hunch management. Whereas production, marketing, finance (even human behaviour) have come to be regarded as fit subjects for scientific investigation, policy has acquired *a mystique previously reserved for theology* (Cuthbert and Hawkins, 1974, p ix) (italics added).

Because 'policy' is sometimes expressed as a code of conduct, the 'theological' connotation is perhaps not surprising.

In Brech's definition of the concept, both of these distinct meanings are to be discerned:

> the modes of thought and the body of principles laid down to underlie and to guide the activities of the firm (or other organization) towards declared or known objectives (Brech, 1975, p 37).

Although the two conceptions meld into one another in practice and in this composite definition, there is a clear sense in which the 'modes of thought' is the more directly associated with tangible objectives and the 'body of principles' with civilized conduct.

We will make more use of this distinction between the technical aspects of 'policy' (concerned with conduct to achieve tangible objectives by defined strategic means) and its moral aspects (concerned with proper or civilized conduct as this is defined within the

12

culture or sub-culture) in each of parts one to three. We shall also distinguish between the ethics which relate to trading (the commercial aspects of the undertaking's interchange with its market environment) and those which relate to employment (cf Brech, 1975, p 38) in part one, particularly.

At present, however, it is necessary to do no more than to give a meaning to the concept of policy (as above) and to note that all entities (state, undertakings, trade unions, etc) operate with some kind of policy, even if it is 'espoused' rather than 'explicit' (*see* Brewster, Gill and Richbell, 1981) or 'assumed' rather than manifest (*see* Brown, 1960, p 24), and that policy might cover all manner of human conduct (of which we will be concerned particularly with 'personnel policy').

In its nature, policy is unlikely to prescribe binding rules. Rather it seeks to offer guidance which represents the best that can be offered at this moment in time and in that situation. It may be of importance and significance to any organization, but its limits need to be fully understood. It might be said that it:

(a) represents a choice made by its initiators (whoever they may be) of some 'modes of thought' and some 'body of principles' (from a larger pool of them) selected on the grounds that they are, somehow, likely to realize the 'declared or known objectives' better than some others

(b) rests upon theories and theoretical models (modes of thought) relating to organizational and operational methods and techniques and upon ethical standards (eg the principles of fair trading or employment) which may be derived from the wider culture or from experience, or both

(c) exists either in written or other explicit form, or in the minds of those intended to be guided by it even without the necessity for its open expression, and is therefore a source of guidance to those intended to be guided by it

(d) is intended to guide, but not necessarily to prescribe or proscribe action, and is therefore aimed chiefly at constraining the members' discretion to decide or choose action when confronted with situations in which such discretion has to be exercised

(e) seeks to provide standards of action which will be as general and as standardized as they may be made, although recognizing that the 'facts of the situation' must present a comparable constraint upon the choice of action by those who are to be guided by the policy.

As such it is intended as a guide to best practice in both the technical and the moral senses. It serves to bolster the identity of the

13

undertaking as something distinct from others by virtue of its *particular* modes of thought and body of principles (cf Bennis, 1966, pp 50 & 55).

Public policy and undertaking policy
In the two preceding sections, we have proceeded on the assumption that in a 'free enterprise economy' undertakings (particularly the 'private' ones) are free to select their purposes and free to choose their objectives and policies without external constraint. Whilst this may appear to be 'less true' of the public sector, the principle of 'autonomy' appears to be given a degree of headroom there too, so that the public undertakings do not offer a complete contrast on this score.

The main contrast here is seen to centre on money making as an objective open to the private sector and (generally) closed or denied to the public sector. But even in this area, the real point of difference may be obscured by making that simple contrast.

There may be doubt as to whether 'making money' is a central purpose or a derived, secondary, or even displaced one, in the private sector, but it may provide a convenient criterion of success. Brech, for example, has suggested that the primary purpose of an enterprise is the making and selling of a given article or service, and profit-making and capital preservation become the main derived objectives (cf Brech, 1963, p 36); Cyriax put this in a moral context with his statement that:

> most of those concerned with senior management would agree that within the limits imposed by social obligations and the need to avoid a short-term viewpoint, a company's objective should be to maximize its profitability: this objective represents the distinctive standard imposed in business life (Cyriax, in *Financial Times*, 23 February, 1967).

As part of the same debate in the *Financial Times*, Lord Beeching suggested that where in private industry, there is a single, clear and unchanging primary objective, in the public sector, the objectives are 'more numerous, more ambiguous, and less distinguishable from qualifying conditions' (*Financial Times*, 26 February, 1967). Whatever other influences might be at work to influence structure, therefore, the greater uncertainty surrounding purpose could influence roles and role expectations and thereby, structure. But the distinction may be less clear cut than is often supposed.

Both private and public undertakings may be regarded as having 'social obligations'—meaning by this that they 'must' (as a duty) perform a function which society in the round (no doubt

14

acting through the agency of the state) considers desirable or necessary.

Broadly stated, society has an interest in the increase of wealth and its distribution through the population. That interest might be served in a number of ways; we choose at the moment to serve it through the mechanisms of the 'mixed economy'. In this some undertakings are given a considerable degree of autonomy to pursue their own chosen purposes and objectives (in the private sector) and some are subjected to greater constraint by the imposition of a wider range of conditions (as in the Beeching statement above on the public sector). But this is a matter of degree. The autonomy of the one may be constrained less directly and more 'at arm's length', but it is constrained nevertheless by the Companies Act in respect of its trading or commercial activities and by labour legislation in respect of its employment activities. The one relates most directly to the wealth creation process and the other to the benefit distribution process which is principally carried on through the wage system.

It may therefore be said that the primary purpose of any undertaking is to provide the goods and/or services which society through a market mechanism demands or through political decision establishes as a need to be met. But a necessarily concomitant purpose is the provision of employment (whether of land, capital or labour) by means of which distribution of wealth is effected (in rent, profit or wage/salary). However well or badly these societal interests are mobilized in order to state the conditions of licence for any employment providing undertaking, such conditions do exist for private and public undertakings, and because they do, the 'autonomy' with which we started the section is limited, by public policy articulated by the state and implemented chiefly through 'the law'.

In the past two decades, public policy related to trading and employment has changed appreciably. In respect of trading activity there has been less legislation, but in the Companies Acts of 1967 and 1980, new requirements of disclosure of information and new rules governing the use of inside information by those 'in the know', have appeared, effecting some change in the conditions under which businesses may trade and businessmen may conduct themselves (cf Gower, 1979).

In respect of employment activity, a much more elaborate platform of employee rights has been established, and rather more hesitantly a new status for trade unions as organizations of workers has been indicated (Rideout, 1979; Hepple, 1979). As practising personnel managers have appreciated from their experience over

15

this period, conformity to the new and changing requirements of public policy and the law in the establishment of policies and practices, has been an aspiration difficult to realize because of the sheer number of changes.

Nevertheless, many steps to conform to the requirements of the law (at least) have been taken. Policies are now increasingly made explicit by companies in response to the numerous exhortations to do so from the Donovan Commission Report (1968) onwards. These have frequently built in this principle of conformity to the law as a major requirement on managers' and supervisors' conduct, even when they also seek to develop best practice which is *not* enjoined by the law (cf Cuthbert and Hawkins, 1973, CIR Report, No 33, 1972). The *practices* in which companies engage in order to recruit and motivate employees in the realization of corporate objectives have also been reviewed against this same template. In fact, ensuring that practice throughout an undertaking at least conforms to the law has proved a compelling reason for developing guiding policies in many organizations.

Public policy and the law are not the only sources of pressure upon undertakings to establish or to change their policies in respect of people in employment. There are also general cultural norms which do not necessarily or explicitly figure in law—civilized and courteous treatment of human beings of whatever description may be supported by some of the requirements of the law, but there remains a good proportion of that iceberg which is below the water line. Some of these, and the more specific norms associated with different interest groups (such as those surrounding the categories of different stakeholders) may be more forcefully brought to bear upon management by, for example, the annual general meeting of shareholders, trade union representatives at the negotiating table, or the by-laws of the local community. 'The law' may function as a rather special kind of imperative, but it is by no means the only one, and it is in the nature of policy-making that it must take cognizance in due measure of them all.

The division of labour: roles
The accomplishment of any purpose and objective calls for action (or work) on the part of people. In some conception of a golden age perhaps any one individual might accomplish all his purposes and objectives by acting on his own carrying out all the contributory tasks. In the reality of modern organizations, however, work is not structured in anything like this integral fashion: it is characterized by division of labour which means the breaking down of the general task into a variety of specialized ones and their assignment to indi-

viduals as distinct roles (cf Trist *et al*, 1963, pp 20–8). The variations in discretion noted in the preceding section on policy are to be found in these individual roles.

This division occurs both horizontally and vertically. On the horizontal dimensions, the creative or productive work necessary to the accomplishment of purpose will be divided into specialized tasks; the most commonly quoted illustration is the production or assembly line in which the fractionalized tasks tend to be machine-paced and infinitely repetitive (cf Thomason, 1973, pp 62–72). A similar horizontal division occurs in management and supervision, particularly in the divisionalization, departmentalization or sectionalization of the production workers and therefore of their management (cf Dalton, 1959, p. 16).

On the vertical dimension, a division similar in principle is discernible. Where in the horizontal dimensions the underlying character of the division is between amounts of the total task assembled together in the job, in the vertical one, the basic principle involves the separation of decision taking from action taking so that vertical jobs are distinguished on the basis of the amount of discretion to decide (or the range of the decision) which is built into the role (cf Jacques, 1964). In broad categorial terms, there tend to be three main vertical divisions, both amongst managerial and amongst non-managerial work.

A variety of terms have been used to distinguish these. Chamberlain identifies the managerial divisions in descending order of discretion as directive (corporate), administrative and executive (Chamberlain, 1948, pp 20–7) and Paterson as policy making, programming and interpretive (Paterson, 1972, pp 25–6). The most common distinction drawn within non-managerial work is that between skilled, semi-skilled and unskilled (Leiserson, 1966, p 15). Consistently with his definition by decision-levels, however, Paterson distinguishes these by the titles of routine, automatic and defined decisions and/or actions (Paterson, *op cit*).

Within the broad structure in which managers are employed to decide and workers to act on those decisions, therefore, there exists a matrix or mould into which both deciding and acting roles are slotted. One dimension of this mould is given by the breadth of decision or discretion involved and the other by the extent of specialization of the productive tasks assigned to individuals. The matrix then establishes the broadest of the expectations which impinge upon the actual work performance of those engaged. It is frequently depicted in the form of an 'organization chart'.

The pictorial representation of this matrix in a management organization chart is always (implicitly if not explicitly) supported

17

and supplemented by a set of rules (which may be identifiable as position descriptions, policies, works rules, or whatever). Together these constitute the 'chart of expections' (Learned, Ulrich and Booze, 1951, pp 139–40, or the 'official map' (Dalton, 1959, p 17) which provides the basic understandings or guidance for action to those engaged in the work. In the midst of the uncertainty which surrounds all such action, they help to establish a greater degree of certainty about what is expected of the person in the role.

But whilst these charts and maps may be understood and accepted in these terms, they do 'not quite hold individuals to routine activity and assured compliance... In terms of daily working relations, a given chart seldom reflects less than what is possible, or more than an existing tendency' (Dalton, 1959, p 18). The actuality of behaviour is not to be completely explained simply by reference to *this* set of expectations, whether that behaviour is of the workers or of the managers: generally speaking, workers will comply with the rules and managers will conform to the policy guidelines. But there is still much variation possible at the level of the particular, as indeed Dalton's work demonstrates.

Managerial roles and their functions
In anything as large and as complex as the modern work organization, many opportunities exist for differentiating the types or categories of role to be found within them. One fundamental distinction which is often drawn (and which is particularly relevant to our subject) is that between managerial and non-managerial roles. Tannenbaum, for example, concludes a discussion of the services rendered by managers to organizations with the two statements that:

> managers are those who use formal authority to organize, direct, or control responsible subordinates (and therefore, indirectly, the groups or complexes which they may head) in order that all service contributions be co-ordinated in the attainment of an enterprise purpose

and

> an individual is not a manager, does not manage, unless he has and uses formal authority to organize, direct, or control responsible subordinates. Unless he conforms to this specification he is a non-manager (Tannenbaum, 1948; and in Tannenbaum, Weschler and Massarik, 1961, p 263).

18

Managers are the organizers, directors and controllers and workers or non-managers are the executants.

This same author, having reviewed the propositions advanced by a number of major authors in the field, also concludes that what managers uniquely contribute to the attainment of organizational purpose is to be described with the aid of three concepts: organization, direction and control.

The 'organization' function is defined by reference to the dictionary meaning of this word as indicating distinct parts or entities *and* the relationships existing between them.

> The managers must determine the degree and type of specialization to be effectuated within the enterprise, and they must determine the relationships that are to exist among the specialized units (Tannenbaum 1961, p 255)

This conception thus assigns a particular responsibility to managers for the determination of the structures and the roles referred to in the two preceding sections. Once this responsibility is discharged (although it is not to be seen as an initial, one-off, activity but as a continuous one) 'a mechanism for the attainment of purpose' is established (*ibid*, p 258).

Putting this 'mechanism' to work involves the other two functions distinguished, direction and control.

> Direction is the use of formal authority in order to guide subordinates. Direction involves devising the purposes of action and the methods or procedures to be followed in achieving them. The decisions to be made in connection with direction must answer the questions: 'What?' 'How?' 'When?' 'Where?' (*ibid*, p 258).

> Control is the use of formal authority to assure, to the extent possible, the attainment of the purposes of action by the methods and procedures which have been devised. The execution of this function involves the selection and training of individuals, the provision of incentives and the exercise of supervision (*ibid*, p 260).

Thus, the formal link of organizational purpose to these particular agency roles of managers is established: in order that organizational purposes may be attained, those whom we identify as managers are required, as a duty, to organize the instrument, steer it in certain directions along certain paths of their own determination and check progress along them.

As Tannenbaum himself makes clear (*ibid*, p 254) not all managers perform these functions in the same way or to the same extent. On the one hand, they apply their skills to the organization, direction and/or control of distinct tasks (eg, production, development, or marketing) according to their assignment within the horizontal division of labour. On the other, they may be responsible for the production of decisions in answer to the sequence of questions posed above which have about them a logic of time and a logic of dependency which are often reflected in a hierarchical structuring of the roles (cf Chamberlain, 1948, pp 20–7 and above, pp 17–18).

Thus all managers may be caught up in decision taking with these purposes or functions, but the extent to which they are involved in any of them will tend to be given by their position in the matrix demarcated by hierarchical level and task specialization. There are, to illustrate this somewhat over-simply, directors, administrators and executives (supervisors) in each of the specialisms of development, production and marketing and, indeed, in many more sub-specialisms.

Because of the nature of productive enterprise as involving the creation of something from a combination of capital and labour in a productive process, the accomplishment of the managerial tasks requires a concern with each of the three broad components:

first, with physical things, raw materials, plant and equipment, buildings and so on. These we often refer to under the label of 'technology' and consider to be of special relevance to technical people like engineers or chemists

secondly, with human beings, directors, managers and a variety of 'workers' in different job and occupational settings. These constitute the 'personnel' and sometimes they may be thought to be of particular relevance to 'personnel specialists' (cf IPM Jubilee Statement, and below, pp 28–30)

thirdly, with money, finance and valued resources or, more simply but more generally, with stocks and flows of value expressed in some tangible form. Referred to as 'finance' it is seen as of major concern to financial controllers, accountants and the like.

(This 'model' is exemplified in the structure of the German board of Directors, the Vorstand, which comprises a technical director, a labour (or personnel) director and a finance director.)

Any manager involved in tasks which are designed to contribute to the realization of organizational purposes and objectives will inevitably be involved in all three of these concerns to some (variable) degree. A technical manager in handling physical things is also handling valuable resources and is involved with personnel in so doing. A personnel manager or a purchasing officer must likewise reach beyond their area of immediate concern. Accomplishment of the 'task functions' of management (development, production, marketing) involves the manager in these 'element' functions based on concerns with the physical, the human and the financial (cf Woodward, 1965, ch 7).

The question of who is to handle each of these three 'elements' has to be answered. Also we need to know how the elements are to be handled. In the development of organization and management, the answers have changed over time, the one tending towards greater specialization and the other towards a greater rationality (itself partly assisted by the growth of specialization). Both of these are to be seen in the development of the handling of 'the people question'. On the one hand, a choice of perspective of 'people at work' has emerged more strongly. On the other, management has created a greater specialization in the 'personnel' field.

Introducing people

The elegance of the theories of organization and management functioning is somewhat deceptive in so far as what actually happens in practice is usually much less elegant and ordered. It is this gap or difference which, in essence, creates what becomes known as 'the personnel problem'. This is not to imply that there are no 'material' or 'technology', or even 'finance' problems within organizations. There are, but the present concern is with the people problem, that is with the differences which may be observed between what the mind conjures up as the ideal and what practice reveals.

The social scientific literature is replete with evidence on the subject of variation between prescribed and actual behaviours (cf Brown, 1960, p 24). It relates both to managerial roles (*see* Dalton, 1959; Gouldner, 1955; Burns and Stalker, 1961; Woodward, 1965 and 1970; Mintzberg, 1975) and to non-managerial ones (*see* Roethlisberger and Dickson, 1939; Sayles, 1959; Lupton, 1963; Crozier, 1964; Gouldner, 1955; Roy, 1954 and Cunnison, 1965).

In spite of the volume of this literature and evidence, however, it should also be stressed that these are variations on a theme, the theme being that most people for most of the time usually conform to the role specifications, the variations being mainly, if also importantly, at the margin (cf Argyris, 1953; Hyman, 1972, pp 33–4).

On the other dimension, the recruitment of compliance by organizational members has spawned a literature no less voluminous. Cartwright (in March, 1965, pp 1–47) has reviewed a good deal of this on the twin subjects of influence and control. These, as we have seen, form the twin props of the dynamics of management (*see above*, pp 18–19). Recruitment of compliance, loyalty, or consent, as Cartwright makes clear, is comparatively successful in some circumstances, but is never so completely successful nor so monopolized as to produce complete subservience or slavery. It becomes therefore a never ending as well as universal activity in all purposive organizations, regardless of the political ideologies which have structured them in their current form (cf Bendix, 1956).

The fact that people are never wholly compliant with the formal rules nor wholly persuaded by the moral exhortations to become so, may be taken to suggest that people are eternally 'struggling to be free'. A whole radical tradition of thought has developed on this foundation (cf Sabine, 1963, pp 755–883; Laidler, 1961; Allen, 1971; Banks, 1970; Anthony, 1977, pp 83–166) and it supports a broad category of ideologies which are counterpoised to the ideologies which support the managerial and efficiency ethics (cf Nichols, 1969; Hyman and Fryer, 1975; Anthony, 1977, pp 258–66).

This same phenomenon has also stimulated criticism of the classical views in a less radical vein. Here the main thrust of the criticism is towards the reform of organizations and of management approaches so that people are less 'coerced' by the discipline which flows from purpose and more able to realize some of their inherent humanity, even in work. In effect, this suggests a reduction in the reliance upon the conception of the people as instruments in the realization of undertaking purposes and more attention to man as a thinking reflective being. Consequently, a considerable literature has developed on 'the nature of man', both generally and particularly as a 'worker'.

Human needs, goals and purposes
In so far as 'enterprise purpose need not coincide with the ends which induce each individual to contribute his services' (Tannenbaum, *op cit* p 244) the gap may be seen to stem from either the distinction between man as a producer and man as a consumer or that between man as an instrument and man as an end in himself. The idiomatic expression of this is found in the double question as to whether man lives to work or works to live?

There have been many different thinkers who have taken quite distinct lines in answering these questions. On the one hand, there are those who have regarded work as a curse which none would assume lightly or voluntarily, but are compelled to do so simply because he who will not work will not eat (cf Anthony, 1977, pp 5–11). On the other, there are those who have regarded work as a 'be all and end all' of life to the extent that man is seen to realize himself only in and through work and that he is fatally diminished if he is prevented from so doing (cf Marx on the *German Ideology*; Marx and Engels, 1965, p 33; Veblen, 1899, 1953 edn p 29). Everyone, and particularly those who assume a duty of organizing, directing and controlling work, must make his or her own choice of position along this continuum.

The answer to such questions is not a matter of scientific proof. it cannot be demonstrated or proved either way. Consequently, it is a matter of faith or belief as to whether man should be regarded as needing to work in order to live or as needing to live in order to work. It becomes, then, a matter of perspective on the basis of which a person will approach the reality of human (including organizational) experience; believing one way may have quite different implications for the treatment of other human beings from believing another. This idea lies at the root of McGregor's distinction between the assumptions behind two quite distinct approaches to managing, for example, where he sets the assumption of man as the lazy, driven animal against that of man as disposed to responsible action (cf McGregor, 1960, pp 33–4 and 47–8 and below, pp 268–69).

What the social scientific literature offers in this area as an aid to selection of perspective is an attempt to identify the needs, drives or goals which might be associated with the human being. These tend to spread over a spectrum from physical or existence needs at the 'animal' end to spiritual or 'self-actualizing' or 'growth' needs at the more 'human' (in the sense of a reflective animal) end.

Maslow (1954, 1970) has put forward a two part theory. The first part offers a categorization of human needs, regarded as states of tension (physical or psychological) within the human being. The second offers an explanation of the way in which the being might be regarded as responding to these inner states in order to restore his equilibrium by reducing the tension.

First, he suggests that needs might be conveniently thought of in the following categories:

1 *Physiological needs* These are seen as the basic needs of the human organism, such as food, water, air, sleep, sex etc. The individual is seen to have needs, in other words, simply at the level of the animal organism which may be distinguished from needs which arise because he is also a socialized individual
2 *Safety needs* The emphasis here is upon the need of the individual person for a generally ordered existence in a stable environ-

ment freed from threats to the safety of the person as a person and threats to the opportunities which exist within that existence to satisfy various needs which he might have

3 *Love needs* These are seen as needs to develop relationships of affection with other individuals and the need for the individual to have some recognized place as a member of a group or a number of groups. The latter is often translated as a need to secure acceptance by the individual's peers or associates and might be described as a relatively low level example of the need for affection

4 *Esteem needs* The main point at issue here is that the individual needs to be able to satisfy himself by developing a firm basis for self evaluation. The need for self respect, self esteem and for the esteem of others depends to some extent upon the environment being relatively stable, but it also switches the emphasis away from environmental factors and towards a basis in the individual for developing a proper or stable evaluation of the self

5 *Self actualization needs* This conception of need moves the concept further forward and relates to the need for self fulfilment or the need to achieve full use of the individual's own capacity for doing things. The emphasis at this level is almost entirely upon realization of the human individuality or personality and although it depends upon a relatively stable and benign environment it is in itself nothing to do with that environment.

Secondly, he argues, these needs are hierarchically structured, and the individual will be disposed to reduce them serially, beginning with the lowest order, physiological, and moving upwards. This theory is expressable in three propositions:

1 The behaviour of any person will be dominated by the most basic category of need remaining unfulfilled at any particular time
2 The individual will seek to satisfy his needs systematically, beginning with the lower order ones and rising to the higher ones
3 The more basic needs will therefore be capable of description as being more 'prepotent' and will take precedence over the higher ones.

This represents one way of looking at the question of human needs and motivation. It has proved difficult to test the theory (*see* Porter, 1961–3; Hall and Nugaim, 1968; Wabha and Bridwell, 1975) but the researchers have had some limited success. The difficulty has, however, led to alternative suggestions being advanced.

Alderfer (1972) has, for example, suggested a modification in which he recognizes only three categories of need. Identified as an ERG theory, the three categories identified are: *existence* (close to

Maslow's lower order needs of a physiological and material nature), *relatedness* (close to the love and esteem levels in Maslow by virtue of their dependence on other persons) and *growth* (rather like the self-actualization in its emphasis on creativity and self-fulfilment). These he perceives to form a continuum rather than a hierarchy, thus permitting different personalities to 'fit' themselves at different points along it without presuming that the point of 'fit' must be better or worse than another's because it is 'higher'. His perspective also allows that some needs can be treated as persistent over time whilst others are more ephemeral and intermittent, and because any individual may be seeking to redress a number of different categories of need at any one time (according to his expectations of success in each or any) action which might appear inconsistent with long-run need satisfaction can be fitted into the view now taken of needs.

As Landy and Trumbo summarize the difference between these two theories, it amounts to this: 'The difference between Alderfer and Maslow can be described in both *content* and *process* terms. They differ in content terms—for Maslow there are five needs; for Alderfer there are three. They also differ in process terms—for Maslow the process is one of fulfilment-progression; for Alderfer, both fulfilment progression and frustration-regression are important dynamic elements' (Landy and Trumbo, 1976, p 300).

In some distinction from both Maslow's and Alderfer's views Herzberg (1966) has put forward a series of propositions which rest upon a two-level hierarchy. He sees all individuals as possessed of two categories of need only, the hygiene needs and the motivator needs. The first relate to the provision of a 'healthy', 'comfortable' or acceptable environment, whether for work or anything else, and are generally lower order needs in the Maslow hierarchy. In work these might include relative pay, security, fellow-worker relationships, authority relationships, general working conditions, rules and policies.

The second are high order, or growth, needs, and are assumed to be needs which pertain significantly to the *human* animal: these are met in independence of action, responsibility in work, and recognition of performance out of the ordinary. These are more usefully discussed when linked with goals of motivated behaviour but they do presuppose that the individual has certain innate characteristics which lead him to seek satisfaction at the 'purely animal' level (the hygiene area) and at the 'distinctly human' level. These relate to the inner need state as firmly as do Maslow's 'needs'.

Whatever the drives of the individual, it could be represented that the individual's motivation is to be explained in terms of what it is 'outside himself' that he wants, regardless of the 'reason' why he wants it. It might be represented, in other words, that observed behaviour may be explained teleologically by reference to what it is the individual establishes as his goals.

One interpretation of Herzberg's empirical study is that, whatever inner needs individuals may be regarded as responding to, they are able to articulate their perceptions and evaluations of work as a means of satisfying these in ways which suggest that there are 'environmental objects' to which they attach varying values. Whatever the 'kind' of person involved, and whatever his inner drive, there is a tendency to attach higher value to certain environmental objects and lower value to others. These in turn may be categorized into the two broad classes of motivators and hygiene factors, each with a different potential as a desired goal.

What this alternative representation does for us, therefore, is to open up the possibility that the individual may *learn* to attach values to the external objects (eg through 'socialization') almost regardless of his inner state. Human beings can, for example, act altruistically or 'against their immediate interest', and this may reflect a kind of learning process. It may therefore be as important to discover what external objects the individual attaches value to, as to discover what need or inner disequilibrium state may drive him to act. The consequences for action of making the choice of one view rather than the other are significant (*see below*, pp 262–93) which is what makes the choice itself important.

The choice is required of all those who are called upon to act as managers, whether they are personnel managers specifically or not, simply because in their acting they are called upon to pursue policies and practices which both depend upon and affect people at work. It is a choice which has to be made quite independently of whether managerial responsibility for relating organizational purposes and people's needs is discharged by generalists or specialists, both of whom exist within our field of concern.

The management of personnel
Simply because 'organizations are peopled' there is no escaping the necessity for any management to become involved in 'the management of personnel'. This is an *element* function of management, something which is inseparable from the definition of the management role, regardless of its other characteristics. Consequently, one conception of personnel management emphasizes this generality.

As a former head of the American Management Association (AMA) is reported to have said:

If management means getting results through people, then management is nothing more than personnel administration (Appley, quoted in Odiorne, 1963, and in Megginson, 1972, p 51).

Strauss and Sayles similarly declare that:

Personnel administration is the management of people. It is accomplished primarily through direct supervision and the development of official policies (Strauss and Sayles, 1967, p 1).

Pigors and Myers declare the central theme of their book to be the 'personnel responsibility of line management' (Pigors and Myers, 1973, p 3).

In the definition provided by Miner and Miner, however, this point is coupled with a recognition of the 'troika' conception of business enterprise with which we began this section:

... the process of developing, applying, and evaluating policies, procedures, methods and programs relating to the individual in the organization Essentially, the personnel function is concerned with the management of human resources of an organization in contrast to the material or financial resources (Miner and Miner, 1977, p 4).

Perhaps significantly, this definition also offers a trilogy of developing, applying and evaluating *policies*, etc. which bears resemblance to the business tasks of developing, producing and marketing *goods and services*.

This conception of personnel management as an element function is acknowledged in the definition offered by the leading professional body in this field in Britain, which says, in part:

Personnel management is that part of management concerned with people at work and with their relationships within an enterprise (Institute of Personnel Management (IPM) leaflet, August, 1969, p 1).

Since all managers, by definition, exercise a directive and control function in relation to other people, therefore, it is inescapable that they are involved in the 'management of people'. Indeed, it has been suggested recently that 'there is no managerial job in industry at any level which an intelligent person could not master in six weeks. Where the interest and skill comes in is in the practice of politics' (Mant, 1969, p 47). That skill does not however associate

27

only with personnel training even if it does imply one particular conception of this people managing function.

Nevertheless, for whatever reason in the particular case, many undertakings have taken the view that the adjustment and accommodation of organizational purposes and human needs are both sufficiently important and sufficiently complex processes and problems to make it desirable to have them handled or managed by specialists in the 'personnel' field and so the personnel manager as a specialist is born.

Personnel management as a specialist function

The IPM's Jubilee Statement on the nature of personnel management also included as part of the definition the statement that the term was 'a description of the work of those who are employed as specialists' (IPM, 1963, p 1). This did no more than recognize that whilst all managers were involved in the management of people, some had, by that date, became specialists, at the administrative or planning level.

One part of the reason for this is that there has been an apparently irreversible trend towards ever greater division of labour within the bureaucracy (cf Millerson, 1964, p 184) which led to an elaboration of the 'staff' element in the line and staff form of organization. The impetus to such development is usually regarded as lying in the need to secure ever greater, and therefore ever more specialist, expertise in the separate task and element functions of the management team (cf Urwick, 1959, pp 7–12).

But in the case of personnel management, it is possible to identify certain specific pressures which might account for the development of the specialism. Megginson, for example, argues that a whole range of factors (trade union power, extension of governmental involvement in enterprise, increasing organizational complexity and the growth of the behavioural sciences, amongst others) have tended to push the function into a specialist position in the management organization (Megginson, 1972, pp 99–128).

The emergence of this conception is clearly expressed in Northcott's discussion of the 'three essential relationships between the general structure of management and this specialized form of it' which had by then (1955) emerged from both debate and practice. He shows the derivation of the specialist function from general management, the allocation of an advisory (staff) authority and the organization of a distinct 'function':

1 'Personnel management is an extension of general management'

stressing management's 'second responsibility' of 'prompting and stimulating every employee to make his fullest contribution to the purpose of the business

2 'it is an advisory service ... and a staff activity' carrying 'no obvious authority except that which arises from its terms of reference and the knowledge and skill of the adviser'

3 'it becomes organized as a function, that is, a body of duties brought together as the responsibilities of one person and carried out wherever they occur in the establishment' (Northcott, 1955, 3rd edn p 12).

By about this date, personnel management as a specialist function *was* beginning to develop and acquire this kind of 'professional' stature in Britain (cf Niven, 1967, pp 135–63; Crichton, 1968, pp 293–300; Thomason, 1980, pp 26–37) but it was not without its traumas and difficulties nor did it have universal coverage.

In principle, this new specialist was supposed to exercise 'an advisory function, seeking to give practical help to line managers, but in no way detracting from their ultimate responsibility for controlling their subordinates' (Cuming, 1975, p 2). Because he was to be found in some work situations in this 'staff' conception, but not in others, it might be regarded as 'contingent' (cf Lawrence and Lorsch, 1967; 1970; Newstrom *et al*, 1975) upon the kind of situation which had developed in them. Thus in some, the simple fact of scale or numbers was often interpreted by managements as requiring special (and specialized) attention to the people problem and the task of securing compliance. In others, where the workers themselves had appreciated that the satisfaction of their needs and aspirations in work required them to establish a countervailing power to that exercised by management, the situation was interpreted to require specialist handlers of the 'union problem'.

But there were (and continue to be) situations in which the line managers considered themselves capable of handling the people question without such specialist expertise. Consequently, as Cuming indicates, some undertakings (usually the smaller ones) still resolve the compliance problem through the line management structure and personnel. In those situations, it is implied, those problems are easier to resolve through that mechanism. What it does not imply is that those managers are necessarily any less knowledgeable about or capable in dealing with people. They may not have formal training in handling people, and they may not possess formal knowledge about people or 'personnel management', but they may well have developed as a result of experience in situations which they could cope with, sufficient knowledge and understanding to enable them to go on coping.

This does not reduce the relevance of formalized knowledge on this subject, and whether personnel management is defined as a part of the general managerial requirement or as a specialized activity, it is desirable to attempt to codify our understanding of the ethics and the practically-technical aspects of the activity. Answering these relevant questions is the main aim of what follows. As we realize this aim progressively, however, we will have occasion to refer back to some of these features of the setting or context of personnel management.

Further reading

Indications of sources which students might consult on the subject matter of a particular chapter are provided at the end of each. These are given, as they are in the text, in abbreviated form and a bibliography is given at the end of the book in which the full reference is provided. On the varied subject matter of this first chapter, the following may prove useful:

On the general historical background to modern work organization and its management, see George (1972), Levy (1950), Florence (1961), Walker (1979), Pollard (1965).

On the structure and government of the economy and its work undertakings, see Brech (1975), Thomas (1976 and 1977), Thomson and Beaumont (1978), Gower (1979), Hepple (1979), Rideout (1979), Elliot (1978).

On people at work and at leisure, their needs, interests, goals and relationships, see Schein (1970), Warr (1978), Anthony (1976). Parker (1974), Anderson (1961), Dunkerley (1972).

On management functions and processes see Brech (1975), Tannenbaum, Wechsler and Massarik (1961), Koontz and O'Donnell, (1976) Likert (1967), Batty (1979), Woodward (1958 and 1965), Cuthbert and Hawkins (1974), Bridge (1981).

On personnel management in its context(s) see Crichton (1968), Legge, (1978), Price in Brech (1975), Anthony and Crichton (1969), Anthony (1977), Fowler (1980), Cuming (1971), Lyons (1971).

On the 'problem' of the relationship between line (executive) and staff (advisory) functions which appears to have beset the development of the personnel management occupation, see, Belasco and Arlutton (1969), Fisch (1961), Gardiner (1948), Logan (1966), Sampson (1955) and Dalton (1959).

2 Personnel management in Britain

Specialization

Specialization of those management tasks which are related to the political (in Mant's term) and personnel problems of modern organizations, has occurred along both the horizontal and vertical dimensions. We now observe differences between labour, industrial relations, welfare and training officers along the one, and personnel directors, managers and officers along the other.

Whether we speak of 'personnel management' or of 'the management of human resources' (in the more grandiose language of the Hayes Committee's Report), we subsume by such generic terms a host of specialist tasks, some historical, some modern.

To suggest that the development has been outwards and upwards from a relatively low level welfare role, appeals because it has a certain logic and rhythm about it. The evidence does not support it, however. Some of the early welfare officers carried a responsibility at corporate levels of undertakings, even if they were not directors, suggesting that development was not merely from the bottom up. Early labour and industrial relations officer roles have some claim to chronological precedence over welfare officer roles in some situations, suggesting that the horizontal development was not simply one of specialization from the latter.

If there is now a coherent conception of 'personnel management' this has not always been the case and the manner in which the occupation threaded its way into the interstices of scale-developing and bureaucratizing organizations has often made it a butt of many quips and jokes.

What the occupational group has always featured is a concern with people, a dependence upon 'social' skills, and a kind of mission to effect improvements or reforms. All of which have taken quite distinct *forms* from time to time. The big question was: Do these add up to a worthwhile job, or occupation? Often, the

31

answer presented was 'no'.

Drucker, for example, has commented trenchantly that:

> 'personnel administration . . . is largely a collection of incidental techniques without much internal cohesion'. Some wit once said maliciously that it puts together and calls personnel management 'all those things that do not deal with the work of people and that are not management. . . . As personnel administration conceives the job of managing worker and work, it is partly a file clerk's job, partly a social worker's job, partly fire-fighting to head off union trouble or to settle it . . . the things the personnel administrator is typically responsible for—safety and pension plans, the suggestion system, the employment office and union's grievances are necessary chores. . . . I doubt though that they should be put together in one department for they are a hodge-podge . . . They are neither one function by kinship of skills required to carry out the activities nor are they one function by being united together in the work process. . . .' (Drucker, 1961, p 243).

Crichton (1968) talks of the 'ambivalence' about the personnel specialist and refers to the allocation process as one entailing 'collecting together such odd jobs from management as they are prepared to give up'. McFarland (1968) refers to the personnel department as the chief executive's dumping ground for unwanted tasks.

This view is perhaps not surprising because the generality of early personnel work achieved its coherence largely by reference to 'people' (as the IPM Jubilee statement asserts) and therefore to those skills which might be most closely associated with 'people'—the skills of communication and consolation which manifest themselves in many different ways and forms within a complex work organization. Interviewing, explaining, consulting, persuading, suggesting, and even instructing, are all inter-personal skills rooted in communication, and they all have their particular forms of organizational connotation in selection, induction, training, consultation, counselling, motivating and even paying of employees.

Both the concern of the caring employer for the welfare of his employees, stemming from what Heller refers to as the 'twinges of social conscience' (Heller, 1961; in McFarland, 1971, p 31) *and* that of the system for efficiency in its employees when bureaucratic impersonality had replaced the personal touch of the owner, could be expressed through these media.

The welfare and the political connotations

Personnel managers are prone to trace their ancestry back to the welfare officers who were appointed around the turn of the last century. They are also liable to regard their present roles as much more centrally concerned with that special form of 'political' activity which is associated with trade unions and collective negotiations. There is more to the role than these two elements (*see* pp 39–46) but these two together do constitute one feature of it as it has developed in Britain. They link it with considerations of morality (as distinct from efficiency).

The origins of the welfare element lie in the juxtaposed awakening of the public conscience about industrial conditions a century ago and the changes then occurring in the size and structure of industry (cf Williams, 1924).

On the one hand, society, about that time, witnessed a good deal of 'political' and 'reformist' activity, both of which questioned the purposes of the 'system' as it was then constituted even if they offered different solutions to the problem as it was defined (cf Laidler, 1968, Chapters 17, 18 and 31; Hobsbawm, 1964). On the other, larger scale and more rationalized industrial organizations herded more workers together in ever more specialist (and usually 'semi-skilled') jobs, and placed a greater 'distance' between the boss and the worker as the managerial role developed in its particularly bureaucratic fashion (*see* pp 401–14).

Whether as a direct effect of these causes or not, there developed at about the same time the more militant trade union (the 'new unionism') concerned to increase the status and dignity of the worker-member, *and* the industrial welfare worker who was given the role of ameliorating the 'condition' of the employed worker (as distinct from the unemployed and the poor worker who had already attracted the attentions of charitable or 'outside' welfare workers). If the one was set in opposition to the employer's policies and practices, whilst the other was appointed on the employer's authority, they both, to an extent, focused upon a similar set of moral issues raised by modern industry. It is not, for instance, at all surprising that the early welfare worker organizations had to establish just what would be their relationship with the trade unions (cf Niven, 1967, p 51); in fact, they decided they would not aim to compete with or usurp the functions of the trade unions!

There is little doubt that the trade unions played their part in bringing about changes in attitudes amongst employers, but there is also a sense in which, at least for some employers, employee-welfare was a simple moral issue.

Cuming, for example, argues that the 'origins of personnel

management can be found wherever enlightened employers have tried over the years to improve the lot of their workers' (Cuming, 1975, p 4). Niven's historical account of the IPM asserts, in this same vein, that it was 'the plight of workers ... which was to mould the form welfare work was to take' (Niven, 1967, p 15). At this early stage in the development of what later became personnel management, it was often difficult to avoid the conclusion that the work was 'charitable' in the Lady Bountiful sense: indeed many of the first practitioners were women. Niven records that the first such woman appointed spent her first morning in the factory placing flowers in the workrooms.

A similar motivation might also be inferred in other later initiatives taken by employers to establish 'improved' work procedures (such as rest pauses, tea breaks and amenities) and improved communications procedures (such as joint consultative committees and suggestions schemes). The concern for employees' health and safety at work was also often one which developed from a general belief that the employer was in the status of the medieval lord and therefore ought as a duty to look after the general well-being of his 'subjects'. Many of these 'concerns' remain within the portfolio of the welfare officer or personnel manager—one of his tasks is still to attend the funerals of employees!—but it is perhaps important to recognize that the progressive evolution of these concerns has left the personnel officer capable of being described as Miller does, as 'the custodian of the corporate conscience' (Miller, 1975), a kind of corporate chaplain whose antecedents were also born of a Christian, authoritarian paternalism.

The secularization of this mission, in Britain at least, was a process which took place only after the second world war. At that time, the work of the social psychologists, particularly of the Hawthorne investigators in America, made its impact in our society. The Hawthorne studies themselves were fairly straightforward pieces of academic research and yielded a number of important generalizations, particularly about the place of 'the group' or 'the informal social structure' of work organizations, which had an important influence on the development of the academic discipline itself (*see* Homans, 1951). In addition, and initially in the hands of Elton Mayo (1933; 1945) but later of Stuart Chase (1950) the implications of these research findings (together with those of some other war-time researchers) were developed into what amounted to a new ideology.

In essence, this emphasized in a way in which traditional industrial practice and classical management texts had not the importance of people as people at work. The individual person was seen to have a primary anchorage in his own local group—whether in work (Roethlisberger and Dickson, 1939), in the community (Warner and Lunt, 1941; Katz and Lazarsfeld, 1955) or even in the army (Stouffer *et al*, 1949)—which in turn was necessary to the full development of his personality. If, then, the way in which work was organized denied this group space, the individual personality would be by so much denuded *and* industry would itself be the loser. However, this same point could be supported on more moral grounds, and it was argued that industry just could not be allowed to continue to be so 'inhuman'—it offended the canons of ortho-doxy in a democratic society. The basis of a new mission was thus established.

During the 1950s, therefore, we find this mission being pursued throughout management, under the banners which pro-claimed the need for 'better human relations in industry'. The evangelism was directed at management in general but inevitably those who occupied roles as personnel specialists found themselves enabled to assume 'expert' and change agent roles in this ethos.

Inevitably too the crusaders found that they could not succeed simply by appealing to morality and much effort was therefore devoted to hardening up the soft features of human relations, par-ticularly by trying to show that better human relations meant bigger profits, increased efficiency or a more contented labour force (and therefore a more comfortable life for the managers) (*see* Urwick and Brech, 1947). The movement made its impact on industry, and even when the fire died out of it, a sufficiently large trace was left behind to mark its passing.

The impact on the personnel managers themselves was even greater. In the same period, universities began to provide specific training programmes for them, and if the connection with social work and social science was close, a distinction nevertheless remained. But the close connection was there, partly because the 'welfare' function inside and outside industry was similar, and partly (and more importantly in the longer run) because the major training need of the personnel manager was in the applied social sciences (at this time mainly psychology and social psychology). The welfare worker's charitable concern for his or her fellow men or women now had a theoretical or scientific base to it which could improve practice, and the educational system was willing to perform the function of certifying competence. A far cry from simply arranging the flowers in the workroom, but still in the same tradition.

The industrial relations officer

Because the associations of welfare officers evolved into personnel management associations, welfare work has a distinct claim to ancestry of the modern conception of the function. But not all of the developments in this area a hundred years ago were so charitably motivated. There was also a development, partly inside organizations and partly through employers' associations, of the labour officer role, in which a strong motivation was that of resisting the claims of the trade unions to worker-employee loyalty and to recognition for bargaining purposes. If these roles appear to have been more closely associated with 'line management', so too (it should be remembered) were the early welfare roles. The specialization was within the generalist management framework itself in both cases, not in the form of a staff specialist and advisory function until much later.

The later development from this second characterization was also somewhat different. The early resisters of trade union pressures were turned by the tide of union development into what became known as the firefighters. Their role became not merely one of dealing with worker/union troubles when they appeared (pure fire-fighting) but seeking to impose procedural constraints upon the workers' organizations in order that the 'difficulties' could be contained as far as possible. The genesis of the now highly valued 'voluntary system of collective bargaining' (see Flanders, 1965; Donovan Commission, 1968) is to be found in this rather than the welfare officer stable, and it was animated by very different ideas from those associated with the Quaker firms. The latter-day industrial relations officer may believe that workers and managements have a single frame of reference, but his activities would suggest that he does not hold this belief in relation to the unions and management and, in *that* context, the notion of a corporate conscience is seemingly not very appropriate (Anthony and Crichton, 1969).

What is appropriate is the conception of personnel management as concerned with (initially) privileges or prerogatives and (later) rights. It would be idle to pretend that there was not about this strand of development a paternalism comparable to that associated with the welfare function, or that the initial reaction to the new unionism of the 1880s onwards was not one which emphasized the defence of the existing prerogatives of the employer.

But as this relationship developed, it became more one between 'equals' (at least to the extent that the trade union established an 'independent' role for 'the workers' collectively). Progressively, the simple prerogative question gave way to negotiations over the rules of work and, although the basic question reared its head from time to time, each party came to recognize that the other had rights which, whilst they did not necessarily balance, nevertheless allowed the process of joint regulation to proceed with fairness or justice.

It was this 'system of voluntary collective bargaining' (Flanders, 1965) which both underpinned the personnel manager's role (as well as that of the union officers) and brought into the personnel management ambit a different stock of knowledge from that required by the other strand in the function.

Because the personnel manager was concerned with negotiations, the material which was being produced by the industrial relations students and later by the sociologists in their examination of social conflict and social change, was brought into the training programmes to supplement that supplied by the individual and social psychologists. This incorporation of conflict studies of one type or another might be said to represent a rationalizing of the approach to protecting prerogatives and preserving a paternalistic order, equivalent to the secularization of the welfare mission.

An emerging ideology
In its origins and as it has developed, this stream of personnel activity has a strong ideological affinity with the 'welfare' stream, both of them being protectionist. The latter approach, aimed at the individual, sought to improve the lot of the worker and this as a consequence, whether intended or not, might make him more accepting of the system in which he was caught up; the former, aimed at aggregates and collectivities, sought to preserve a system which promised benefits of wealth for all or to adjust that system in an ordered way in order to effect improvements, some of which at least were suggested by the representative and associated state bodies.

If this began as a simple protecting role, it has since developed into an accommodating and adjusting role related to the organization as an entity, within which standards of fairness and equity have been redefined and developed. These two streams can then be covered by a single statement in the IPM's Jubilee definition:

> Personnel management aims to achieve both efficiency and justice, neither of which can be pursued successfully without the other. It seeks to bring together and develop into an effective organization the men and women who make up an enterprise, enabling each to make his own best contribution to its success both as an individual and as a member of a working group. It

seeks to provide fair terms and conditions of employment, and satisfying work for those employed (IPM, 1963).

This 'concern' with fairness and justice is first the modern expression of the dominant ideology of the welfare officer. It can be stated in a way which suggests its possible segmentation from the concern with efficiency. Thus Miller argues that the personnel management role is 'different from other staff jobs in that it has to serve not only the employer, but also act in the interests of employees as individual human beings, and by extension, the interests of society' (Miller, 1975). Similarly, Spates finds a conception of the personnel management role which provides a place for the goals and aspirations of the workers, to an extent which is perhaps not to be found in other conceptions. For him, the function of personnel administration is concerned with "organizing and treating individuals at work so that they will get the greatest possible realization of their intrinsic abilities, thus attaining maximum efficiency for themselves and their group and thereby giving to the concern of which they are part its determining competitive advantage and its optimum results" (Spates, 1964).

The concern with fairness etc has acquired new connotations in the light of major developments in the form of new conventions in the bargaining process itself and in a spate of legislation which began to flow in the 1960s. Both conventionally and statutorily, new rules are being imposed on the employment game, and these are not only changing what the personnel manager must do in pursuing his role, but threaten to make the older ideologies of a paternalistic sort impossible to hold. Instead of having privileges at the grace and favour of the employer, the worker has now either established by his collective power, or been granted through legislation, that these privileges are his by right.

The methods and procedures which were originally designed to secure order on the employer's terms are now established as a means of underpinning employees' rights, or of securing order on the *employees'* terms. Particularly with the appearance of the Industry and Employment Protection Acts in 1975, therefore, a number of commentators have been led to raise the question of what future exists for the personnel management function and role. Clearly, where that role is defined with reference to the need to establish control (Goodrich, 1921) in the employer interest, this question must arise when power shifts to the extent that recent legislation and the proposed legislation on participation indicate.

The attempt to preserve autonomy in this situation has led the personnel manager into embracing modern systems theories and the role of helping the organization as a whole to adjust to changes in the internal and external environments. The personnel manager is often recognized as uniquely fitted by his professional experience, ethic and training to develop this aspect, whether expressed in terms of securing more efficient organization or in terms of creating procedures for the conversion of inefficient conflict into more efficient agreement. This is found in the advocacy of Miner and Miner for example, who suggest that personnel managers ought to be concerned with 'strategies specifically tailored to changing demands from the outside world or to internal problems' (Miner and Miner, 1977, p 44). But this development makes efficiency more central to the emerging role.

The administrative staff function

In the conception of personnel management, there has always been another strand, different from those linked to welfare and industrial politics. This was the one concerned with the procurement of the right amounts of the right type of labour at the right time to meet the needs of the business. Sometimes, this was graced with the organizational title of 'employment office' or 'labour office' (Kelly, 1918), but whatever it was called in the particular case, it did perform a *managerial function* of an 'administrative' (or facilitating) kind in support of line management. Importantly, therefore, this strand was quite differently associated with what might be called 'pure task management', compared with the welfare and fire-fighting strands which were often seen as morally or ideologically necessary but necessarily reactive rather than proactive (cf Urwick, 1959, pp 8–10).

Quite early on in the development (cf Bloomfield and Willetts, 1916) this strand came to acquire a sort of identity associated with labour procurement tasks, even if some of the other, particularly welfare, ones were tacked on for the sake of convenience, or for the sake of giving them a home. Thus, Elbourne, in 1934, was already identifying the function in terms of six categories of involvement. These were associated with:

1 Personal relationships, including mutual consultation and individual guidance, where required, on employees' problems
2 Organization relationships, including definition of responsibilities and duties, the notification of appointments, transfers etc, and organized mechanisms for joint consultation and the dissemination of information

3 Employment procedures, including labour supply and the determination of conditions and regulations of employment
4 Education and training—operative staff (both factory and administrative), supervisors and executives
5 Physical working conditions, including matters of health, convenience and safety
6 Social services and amenities, internal and external to the firm; physical, educational, social or recreational.

These remain broadly indicative of the areas of application of the practitioner's skills to the facilitation of efficient *task* performance.

The skills themselves were generally those associated with interpersonal communication, and as applied to these areas, were regarded by Northcott, writing in 1955, as constituting 'a body of related duties which fit in so well with each other that they can suitably and effectively be made the responsibility of one executive and can be thought of structurally as a department of a business' (Northcott, 1955, p 213). This immediately establishes a link between the practice of the personnel specialist and the efficiency of the undertaking, and an involvement at the level of executive control in the classical conception of management (cf Tannenbaum, 1948 and 1961; and *see* above, p 19).

This association is preserved in some texts on personnel management, and it is highlighted in the IPM's Jubilee Statement (quoted above, p 37). French for example, talks of the 'personnel system process' as involving (in language reminiscent of both Fayol and Tannenbaum) 'the planning, co-ordinating and controlling of a network of organization-wide processes and facilitating systems, pertaining to the task of specialization, staffing, leadership, justice, determination, appraisal, compensation, collective bargaining, organizational training and development' (French, 1964, but see also French, 1974, ch 4 and especially p 53). Sayles and Strauss indicate a similar perspective in their statement that 'personnel administration is accomplished primarily through direct supervision' (Strauss and Sayles, 1960, p 1). Megginson is even more conceptually akin to Tannenbaum in his statement that 'the most significant aspect of personnel management is to be found through the direction and control of human resources of an organization in its daily operations' (Megginson, 1972).

The selection and incentive elements in the Tannenbaum definition are to be found in other texts. Thus Cuming, in common with a number of others, argues that the function is concerned with 'obtaining and retaining employees... getting and keeping workers ... and obtaining the best possible staff for any organization and having got them looking after them so that they will want to stay' (Cuming, 1968). Bakke also produces a similar conception wrapped around in social scientific terminology when he argues that 'personnel activities' are set in train to 'perpetuate people and their qualities' and that control activities are designed *inter alia* to 'reward and penalize or promise rewards or penalties for behaviour, or in the interest of making it conform to the type desired by the person or persons administering the rewards and penalties' and to 'review, appraise and rate performance, performers and results according to standards established, assign people (as well as other resources) to positions on scales pertaining to a number of dimensions (such as prestige, importance, power, ability, acceptability etc)' (Bakke, 1950).

Personnel practitioners, in this conception, therefore begin to look like any other manager in so far as their role becomes one related to organizational 'needs' or objectives. The simpler 'people' orientation of the welfare conception is replaced by an 'organizational' orientation in this one. The replacement helps to sweep away the foundation for the distinction between welfare officers tacked on to management and real managers.

Thus, Miner and Miner suggest that

> Another way to define personnel management is in terms of its goals, and in this sense the goals that personnel management seeks to achieve within the organization are the same as the goals of management in general. Although personnel managers carry out a unique set of activities having to do with the utilization of human resources, this work is done with a view to accomplishing exactly the same objective as is the work of other managers (Miner and Miner, 1977, p 4).

Here, therefore, the objectives of personnel management become those of developing and recommending strategies and procedures that will contribute to the organization's productivity goals and of maintaining the organization as an ongoing unit in the face of internal and external pressures and stress (Miner and Miner, 1977, p 5).

Or as Price argues, the task and purpose of the personnel manager become the planning and implementing of changes in the organization as the instrument for achieving the efficiency, productivity, or task goals of the enterprise. New skills are thus called for. The older 'social' skill (which never seemed to differentiate a personnel practitioner from any other normally endowed person, cf Wilensky, 1964, p 145) had to be supplemented if not supplanted by planning and decision taking skills of a different, more 'practical' order.

Now, like any other manager, he had to become proficient in objective setting and strategy formation for the 'personnel function' within the overall objectives of the enterprise, and with developing plans or strategies for the acquisition, development and deployment of human resources necessary to meet the needs of the undertaking. He thereby comes to be associated with 'administration' (in the Chamberlain conception of it as concerned with determining methods of goal achievement) and with the middle level bands in Paterson's schema, and not merely with the 'executive', lower level, activities associated with his former collection of people-oriented skills (see above, pp 16–18).

With this association with methods of controlling manpower, motivation (or morale), and performance levels attainable, personnel management became highly marketable as a skill. Firms were led to hire such people to allow a fund of strategic *and* tactical advice to be placed on tap, but not at this stage necessarily on *top* (Lyons, 1971). The focus of all this activity remained 'people', even if they must now be seen within a wider organizational framework, and the skills called for remained social or communications skills. What, particularly, changed about the role was the requirement that it should now orient itself to organizationally constructive solutions to people, inter-personal and organizational problems, rather than exclusively to the individually personal ones.

This development was also assisted by the coincidental development of the industrial relations role within organizations. As the changes in the labour procurement and labour negotiation roles came together, the 'organizational' emphasis was increased.

The role of the industrial relations specialist, in its earlier conceptions, was capable of being represented as that of protecting the enterprise from those consequences of trade union influence upon decisions which would, *inter alia*, reduce the 'freedom' of the employer to engage and deploy whatever labour he chose. Although essentially protectionist in conception, and although associated with a particular managerial ideology, it was nevertheless concerned to protect the efficiency 'ethic' as this was then defined. But to a considerable extent, the industrial relations officer role was less involved with technique and more with issues of will and judgement, often thought to be outside the scope of technique.

This was less the case with procurement activities in the labour market area, and here it was the change in the external circumstances which gave the nudge to practice. For as long as labour remained plentiful the personnel specialist had no strong foundation on which to develop from his 'low level of prestige in industry and commerce' (Wellman, 1972, p 32; see also Lawrence, 1973, p 5). When that condition changed, partly as a result of the greater general influence of trade unionism on decision taking at various levels inside and outside work institutions, this industrial relations, protectionist role could become linked with a new conception of the administered wage-effort bargain. The personnel manager now had a comparably 'protectionist' role based on the ability 'to present information regarding the enterprise in its labour market' which allowed him to become 'involved in high level strategic decision taking activities of the firm' in the manpower planning area (cf Wellman, 1972, p 32).

What is now expected of him is that, in the interchange between the organization and its environment of appropriate labour resources, the personnel manager shall recommend plans or strategies calculated to ensure that it has the right kind of labour resources in the right quantities at the appropriate time to enable it to meet its production objectives, or alternatively that its production objectives can be tailored in the light of such conclusions to fit the manpower situation.

Although, as Lawrence asserted in 1973, a good deal of manpower's planning occurs two levels below the head of the personnel department, the need for the undertaking to get its manpower interchange relationships right in a condition of full employment and more stringent control of labour movement by legislation and other governmental policies such as those concerned with incomes, helped to bring the top level of personnel management more closely into the corporate planning process.

A corporate personnel function

When these various strands of development came together the scene was set for the elevation of the 'personnel management specialism' to the corporate level in organizations. This developed first at the board level in private industry and later at the managing team level in some, at least, of the public service organizations.

The welfare/political strand had, by the 1960s, become more closely associated with employee (and trade union) rights rather than with paternalistically oriented propositions about employee welfare or well-being. Public expressions of concern about *both* conduct *and* performance in industry began to create a climate receptive to the proposition that something needed to be done. The Royal Commission on Trade Unions and Employers' Associations, 1965–68 (the Donovan Commission) added its weight to the idea

that industrial relations (at least amongst the personnel practitioner's concerns) should receive greater attention from directors
(Report, para 182, p 45).

The actions of governments from about the same period, particularly in legislating new rights for both individual workers and
trade unions, and in compelling new approaches to collective bargaining (cf Hepple and O'Higgins, 1979; Rideout, 1979; Cuthbert
and Hawkins, 1974; Thomason, 1980) provided a basis for an
increase in status and power to the personnel profession of which
something was made (cf Thomason, 1980, pp 26–37). Coupled with
a tight labour market, which continued through the 1970s, these
helped to involve personnel people 'in high level strategic decision-
taking activities of the firm' (Wellman, 1972, p 32) as well as in industrial relations policy-making.

In the public sector, this kind of development had to wait until
the 'labour problem' in that sector had impressed itself upon the
public attention in the 1970s. The preceding reorganizations had
prepared the way by creating space for personnel officers in the
new structures, but it was the experience of the 'winters of discon-
tent' which raised the status and standing of those who filled it,
allowing them to operate more directly with the management
teams.

The efficiency/productivity strand had also by about the same
time secured a better (or at least a more status enhancing) base.
This emerged via the research and training institutions which produced and disseminated to managers and potential managers much
more of the knowledge of man which the earlier practitioners had
hoped for. The whole of this development tended to acquire focus
with the developments in the educational sector in Britain in the
1960s, ie the Robbins expansion and the creation of the business
schools, often in new or elevated institutions. Although as Mant
commented, the numerical consequence of these developments
was relatively small in relation to the need, the qualitative or
fashion-creating effect was probably much greater. It probably
served to give the personnel management administrators a surer
theoretical or philosophical basis for their work and a more directly
attuned line management ear.

This general development had its effects upon the status and
power of personnel specialists. The long standing worry about low
status (eg Lawrence, 1973, p 5) because of the low 'level' of tasks
assigned and of abilities required by and applied to them, reflected
little more than that personnel practitioners were engaged in what
were essentially 'executive' tasks (cf Chamberlain, 1948, pp 23–4).
The general agitation within the occupational group to develop ad-

equate theories and training based on them (cf Crichton, 1968, p 223) sought and, generally speaking, succeeded in raising the level to that of administration in the Chamberlain (*ibid*, p 23) definition. But the subsequent developments enabled many more personnel people to move to the level of corporate direction (*ibid*, p 23) and encouraged the reformulation of the concept of personnel management.

Before the 1960s, it would have been not more than to express a professional hope to suggest that the specialist personnel management function could be equated with 'the management of human resources' in toto and without qualification. This expanded conception owes something to the Hayes Committee report which used this broader term to embrace the traditional concerns of both the personnel managers and the training officers. In their definition of it, it indicates a concern

> with the optimum deployment and development of people within an organization in order that the objectives of the organization may be met and effectively adapted to changing circumstances (Department of Employment, 1972, quoted by Price, 1975, p 555).

Consequently, Price, in the middle 1970s, can trace its evolution through three stages of:

(a) identifying activities proper to a specialist function
(b) developing a concern with aspects of personnel planning
(c) developing a change agent role in relation to the organization as a whole

to that where:

> the relationship between the 'line and staff' concept of the personnel role is becoming less rigid and the recognition that the whole personnel function is changing to one that is seen as being concerned with the management of the human resources of that organization (Price, 1975, pp 555–6).

Since 'line management' has usually been defined with reference to the technical or 'task' (development, production and marketing) functions of enterprise, this conclusion implies that the 'personnel' function may now to be set over and against the technical one, rather in the manner in which it is conceived in the German Vorstand, itself a 'team'.

In this conception therefore, personnel management becomes more clearly and emphatically involved in the planning of objectives and strategies by which the human organizational instrument may contribute to the task objectives of the enterprise or service organization. The goals of personnel management may then be said to become, 'the same as the goals of management in general', as Miner and Miner have it. They emphasize the tasks of developing and recommending strategies and procedures that will contribute to the organizations' productivity goals, and of maintaining the organization as an 'ongoing' unit in the face of internal and external pressures and stress (Miner and Miner, 1977, p 5). One way of listing these is presented in table 1 (p 50). The broad categories of task in the first column are related to the different demands likely to be generated by the corporate management and by the individual employees in the second and third columns to illustrate the sources of pressure upon the personnel specialist to effect reconciliation and/or compromise in pursuing the objectives.

The achievement of status

Specialist activities within bureaucratic organizations cannot remain outside the hierarchy of authority and power. Whatever their purpose and function, they must be fitted in at some point. So it is with the personnel management function and specialization. In the evolution of personnel practice, there has been a progression through these three 'levels' of management decision and action within undertakings, culminating in the present position where the personnel director stands as the apex of a hierarchy of personnel work of a directive, administrative and executive kind (cf Chamberlain, 1948, ch 1).

At the first, executive level the personnel practitioner operates at a managerial decision level not very different from that of the supervisor, and does so largely by applying his basic interpersonal and communications skills within a framework of directives and administrative methods laid down for him. At the second, administrative level he develops and recommends procedures and methods for others in the organization to follow in carrying out their roles, using his knowledge of theory in so doing, and operating largely within an advisory 'staff' role. At the third, directorial level, his chief task is to contribute to the establishment of objectives, overall policies and standards which shall govern conduct and the criteria which will be employed to evaluate success, and at this level, whilst the kinds of knowledge and skill applicable at lower levels are still relevant, the main abilities are likely to be more associated with 'judgement' (cf Vickers, 1965).

In this latest and broadest conception of personnel practice, therefore, there is a degree of protection for the whole gamut of

46

personnel work by virtue of the power and position of the top level of the function. It now becomes comparable in terms of domain, even if different in its range, from the general management function in organizations. The function as a whole must now, in accordance with normal 'systems thinking' (cf Miner and Miner, 1977),

(a) know where it is going and integrate its objectives with those of others in the organization as a foundation for all other action
(b) derive the guide lines and the criteria for action from such objectives
(c) decide upon strategies and tactics for realizing these objectives, calling upon such range of specialist expertise as is appropriate
(d) have (or be given) structural and procedural access to those parts of the system which it must necessarily influence
(e) develop and secure sanction for its own measurement/ assessment operations (which might require others to supply information) and
(f) constantly monitor the consequences of its own decisions as a basis for up-dating of objectives or methods.

Whilst this does offer a protection, it also provides a foundation for tension between this 'managerial' and 'efficiency' orientation and the archetypal 'professional' orientation.

Thus a personnel policy may be conceived as responding to the enterprise's need to secure adequate contributions from employees (the 'effort' part of the bargain) or as responding to the human aspiration to be treated with 'dignity' whilst at work (the 'wage' part of the bargain in the broadest sense of the term). Similarly, recruitment activity may be undertaken to secure employees who can make a required contribution at least cost to the enterprise, or aimed at providing individuals with full opportunities to make a contribution to society: whilst it can be argued that if either orientation is pursued 'properly' the other criteria will also be satisfied, such a happy outcome is by no means automatic in an imperfect world and the distinction remains worthy of recognition as a source of potential tension in the role.

This is a feature of the personnel management role which is particularly worthy of recognition in the light of changes made in social policy in Britain in the 1960s and 1970s. The opportunity which is provided by these twin orientations of the role to deprecate the manner in which the function is discharged, or to dismiss it as a hodge-podge of unrelated and unjustified activities, existed before these changes occurred. But the translation of welfare privileges into rights and the imposition of social as distinct from individual values at the aggregated level, by means of social policy borne by legislation in the 1960s and 1970s, throws the whole problem into new relief. On the one hand, the personnel officer now finds his activities prescribed by legislation, at one level, where he becomes the custodian of the means of discharging the employer's legal duties concerning personnel employed. (This process will be indicated in chapters 4 and 5 which seeks to show how the old 'welfare' concept has been underpinned by statutory conceptions of right and duty.) On the other, he now finds his skills deriving from his work with personnel aggregates being placed at a considerable premium as a result of the creation of new rights for labour in the aggregated sense. (These changes form part of the subject matter of chapters 6 and 7.) Where therefore he might have liked to think of himself somewhat whimsically in the past as a 'man in the middle' or as having a rather special and close relationship with the union officers (Anthony, 1977), the discussion of the role of the 'labour director' in schemes for employee participation, and the donation of new privileges to shop stewards in recent legislation, must raise questions about the place of the personnel officer in the scheme of things.

Nevertheless, thirdly, there is a focus to the role, and this occurs in the concern with 'people' in the system. However the role might have grown up, and in spite of the fact that it is sometimes concerned with individuals and sometimes with aggregates, it is concerned with the treatment or management of people in the enterprise, and not (to make the contrast) with the physical, inanimate elements of it. Making this broad general distinction between the management of the physical assets and the management of the human assets, allows the personnel officer to be aligned firmly and unequivocally with the second type of management to the virtual exclusion of the first. And what may be of more significance, the personnel officer is probably the only specialist in the enterprise who can be distinguished in this precise way: all his colleagues have some concern with the management of physical assets, but these are for the personnel manager little more than a component in the definition of the human *situation*.

It is perhaps for this reason that the personnel function as a specialist department of organization has survived (and indeed grown) in a soil which, if Drucker's 'trash-can' or Pigors' 'maid-of-all-work' strictures are to be accepted, could not be regarded as the most fertile. The personnel specialist's activities in relation to persons or aggregates vary widely; they make strange bed-fellows from the points of view of ends served and skills required; but they do acquire an integrity by reference to people. Further, it is this singularity of focus which justifies the separation of the function in spite of the fact that every other person in the enterprise must also be concerned with personnel, and which ensures its survival in a situation where the license of enterprise to 'use' people to realize its objectives is being subjected to new 'conditions'.

The current conception of the personnel function

The current conception of personnel management reflects its diverse origins and lines of development and the different levels or breadths of decisions taken with organizations.

There is, on the one hand, the role of the specialist who ensures the supply of labour to the undertaking. This stems from the development of a specialist role at the time when large scale enterprise found it increasingly difficult to secure adequate labour from purely local labour markets on the basis of the old methods of personnel contact. From this personnel specialist both developed skills in the 'employee resourcing' area and emphasized the development of the 'techniques' of the personnel practitioner. With the passage of time, and particularly during the tight labour markets of the period since the second world war, this kind of activity had to be gathered up in a more systematic fashion, and gave rise to the concept of 'manpower planning', in which personnel practitioners became more clearly identified with managerial as distinct from specialist practitioner activities.

On the other hand, the function of personnel management acquired two distinct ideological associations from the two kinds of custodian roles from which it also developed. The original welfare officer, as a kind of custodian of the corporate conscience, developed skills closely akin to those involved in employee resourcing, and gave them a meaning in individual welfare terms. The early negotiators, as custodians of the corporate identity, had also to acquire skills in the inter-personal, negotiating area, but also gave the function a meaning in terms of the corporate entity. In time these also came together to emphasize the general function of protecting the corporate undertaking as a concept, and also allowed the function's influence to be seen as relevant at the aggregated and disaggregated levels.

As all of these have come together in recent years, therefore, the personnel function has come to be regarded as distinct from the technical and financial functions (as identified above) and as having its own 'technology' (the logics of its relevant techniques) and its own 'ideologies' (generally bifurcated between the welfare of the individual employee and the welfare of the undertaking as a

49

Table 1
Personnel management activities

The textbook usually includes the following activities of personnel management	The enterprise usually requires action to provide the following	The individual usually demands action to create the following
1 Personnel policy formation (general)	A statement of objectives and standards to be followed by all acting in the name of the organization.	A perception of the organization's 'care' for its members, including a notion of justice and fairness.
1a Manpower policy and planning (dealing with the interface between enterprise and labour market)	A statement of how the enterprise projects itself into the future as an appropriately manned enterprise.	A perception of the organization's concern to maintain efficiency in manning consistent with security of those who have invested their working lives in it.
1b Policy and planning in respect of the work environment (welfare amenities, health and safety and services)	A costed statement of the conditions under which employment is offered in order to secure contributions required of employees at all levels.	A perception of the treatment offered by the employer to employees, including opportunities for personal development and growth.
2 Organization design (job analysis, communications, procedures, recognition)	An organization equipped with adequately defined roles and adequate communications channels to permit optimization of contribution.	An organization equipped with adequate structures and procedures to allow individual and sectional goals to be given due consideration.
2a Communications (disclosure, counselling and consultation)	A solution to the top-down and lateral communications problems of organizations.	A reasonable opportunity for all employees to be informed of problems, policies and projections.
2b Mutual influence (joint negotiating, disciplinary committees)	A bargaining structure which meets the demand consistently with time and money, costs of securing acceptance of policies etc.	An adequate opportunity to employees to exert their influence upon policies, practices, and projects.
3 Control of labour	Informed action on activities intended to secure appropriate labour: (i) recruitment and selection (ii) performance appraisal (iii) promotion etc (iv) training (v) reward package (vi) environmental climate	Fair and consistent actions intended to ensure the dignity of labour: (i) job opportunities (ii) recognition of worth (iii) development of person (iv) learning opportunity (v) fair rewards (vi) good treatment
4 Control of power	Definition of authority or discretion to decide, usually by tacit or open agreement manifest in: (i) job definitions (ii) rule books (iii) collective agreements	Acceptance of fair definitions of authority and discretion preferably by open discussion and joint agreement manifest in: (i) collective agreements (ii) union rule books (ii) joint decisions

whole). For similar reasons, it is concerned both with professional practice, associated with the application of inter-personal skills, and with managerial activity, defined in terms of decision-taking on behalf of the aggregate. These cross-currents at one and the same time help account for the differences which are found in the conceptions of personnel management throughout economic enterprises, and provide the foundations for the discernable tensions within the profession itself.

The major distinctions and the major tensions can be identified by setting, in the form of a matrix, the answer to the question of 'for whose benefit?' the activity is undertaken (enterprise or individual) against the level of decision involved, corporate (policy) administrative (method) and executive (control).

Personnel management, like any other brand of management, is concerned with the functions of planning, organizing and controlling. Related to the personnel element of the system, these are discharged through policy formation (indicating objectives and standards to apply generally, and particularly on the manning of the enterprise and the climate which it will create for working); through design and development of organization appropriate to the work to be done and to the goals, aspirations and values of those who will be called upon to do it (manifesting itself in appropriate definitions of roles and relationships and of the cultural values which will animate both); and through the control of the operation of the working arrangements to ensure adequate task performance and fair treatment to all concerned.

Further reading
On the history of the development of personnel management in Britain, see M M Niven (1967); A Crichton (1968); W Marks (1978).

On different perspectives of the growth of personnel management, see C H Northcott (1955); R R Hopkins (1955); P D Anthony and A Crichton (1969); D E McFarland (ed) (1968)

General textbooks on personnel management include M W Cuming (1975); T P Lyons (1971); and D Torrington and J Chapman (1979). American general texts most often used in Britain are L R Sayles and G Strauss (1967 second ed); P Pigors and C A Myers (1971); W French (1971); W French (1974); L C Megginson (1972); D S Beach (1975); J B Miner and M G Miner (1977).

(The distribution of chapter titles in these general texts is indicated in the table on the following page: it is based on chapter titles and does not therefore indicate content in detail nor does it include

Table 2
Textbook coverage of personnel management
(Main topics covered in major textbooks, identified from titles of chapters, and indicated in the table by chapter number)

Authors / Topic	Northcott 1955	Cuming 1968	Strauss & Sayles 1966	Pigors & Myers 1973	Beach 1975	French 1974	Miner 1977	Torrington & Chapman 1979
Objectives policy	2 & 3	2			3	9	1	
Organization of function	1 & 10	20, 21			4	30		32
Manpower planning								
Employment	12			15	11			6
Recruitment	11	4, 5	19	15	9, 10	11–13		5, 7
Wage determination		12				19, 20	10,11, 13	22
Termination				17	13			20
Employee records	12			12				32
Promotion		6	20	17	13	14		
Employee services	19		30		29		20	
Welfare		18						21
Health safety	18	19	29	22	28		17	
Employee development	17		22		15	17, 18	14	10
Interviewing/ counselling			10	10			12	7, 19
Resource control								
Standard setting			26					
Appraisal		8	23	16	12	15	8, 9	28
Training	14	10, 11	21, 24	16	14	16	15	9
Discipline/rules			13	18	23			
Motivation/ incentives	4, 5	3	5, 27–8	6, 21	17			
Wage and salary administration	15, 16	12, 13	25	20	25, 26		16	23–5
Supervision			6–8, 15	7		7	18	
Morale	17							
Industrial relations					5			3
Negotiations	8, 20	14, 15		13	6, 24	22–26	19	11, 14, 18
Joint consultation	9							
Procedures								12
Organizational development				3			6	
Job analysis				14	8	10	7	8, 27
Work groups	7		3		18–19			
Organizational analysis					7			2
Communications		9, 16	9, 14		22		21	29
OD				5	16–21			
Environment	6	18				27–28		

Note: where the chapter title does not include the noun in the left hand column (or one very close to it) a chapter number is not included: the book may however treat the substance indicated in another chapter with a different name or in a more generally titled chapter.

all the chapter heads in all of the books listed.)

Students in industrial undertakings will probably find the subject covered for their context in the books quoted above; more recently, a number of specialist books have appeared on personnel management in the public services and students in these fields in particular might find the following of relevance to their employment context:

Millard (1972) and Cuming (1971) on personnel management in the health services; Fowler (1980) on personnel management in the local government service; Armstrong (1971) on personnel management in central government organization; and Boella (1974) on personnel management in the hotel and catering industry.

On more specialist aspects of the function, students are referred to the ends of the various chapters.

3 Objectives, policies and practice

Organization and profession

If, now, we bring together the points which have been touched on in the two preceding chapters, we may establish a basis for considering the relationship between professional personnel practice and the purposes and objectives of the undertakings which employ the practitioners.

From the preceding discussion, it is reasonably clear that whilst the management of personnel is a task which every manager must carry out in whatever undertaking he is engaged, personnel management as a specialist activity is more often to be found associated with larger scale ones. What in the latter case is done by the specialist (whether directly or 'through' other people) is in the former carried out by the individual manager directly. What is requisite is the same in both cases, excepting only that the advisory staff element of the specialists' job definition is absent in the other.

We therefore make the assumption in the remainder of this book that what might be said about the requirements of the specialist role might also be said, *mutatis mutandis*, about the general personnel management function. When the function is discharged by general or line managers who do not have the support of staff specialists, some of the forms and processes will necessarily be modified, but the objectives and methods will remain broadly the same in both cases.

It is possible to say this in this way because undertakings do require the co-ordination of the activities of a variable number of personnel in order to achieve their objectives, and whoever's hands this may be placed in, it is the undertaking requirement which provides the basic definition of those tasks. The assumption in most organization and management theory and principle is, in fact, that what donates rationality to the tasks which both generalists and specialists carry out is the concept of undertaking purpose (which ever particular terms are used to identify it). The rationality of management of personnel and personnel management derives, on this assumption, from the pursuit of such purpose.

The specialist personnel practitioner's self-image is one which emphasizes the 'professionalism' of that role. In any context, the meaning of this concept is difficult to establish, but in that of management it is generally thought to be particularly so (cf Thomason, 1980). It is, in essence, just because the 'undertaking purpose' tends to define the rationality of managerial, as well as non-managerial, roles, that many see the local, sub-cultural (or undertaking) values thereby imposed, as preventing such occupations from adopting the cosmopolitan values commonly regarded as a *sine qua non* of professionalism. Whether personnel management qualifies as a profession is a question which will continue to be debated, within the more general discussion of whether any managerial occupation could qualify given the usual template applied.

What, however, personnel managers themselves usually mean by their use of the term professional is rather different from this. A professional, in this view,

> is a person expert in some field of activity who shares the responsibility for decisions, and gives a service to others in that part of their affairs to which the professional's expertise applies, bringing to bear in this participation, wider values than those whom he is advising may necessarily themselves consider relevant, ie supra-client values (Higgins, 1964, p 1).

Such can be established as a target for the individual to aim at, and such may be supported to the extent possible by a professional association, even if complete attainment is not realized in the event.

It is this conception of professional which both lies behind some of the statements about personnel management which have already been quoted, *and* which is set against the conception of undertaking purpose as discussed on the previous page.

It allows, in relation to employing undertakings, that in his or her specialist field of activity, the personnel manager accepts responsibility for his expert activities in the course of which he or she does bring to bear supra-client values which the 'undertaking' (or more strictly the people within it) might otherwise not consider relevant.

It also allows, in relation to the people within such undertakings, that the personnel professional will also apply his expertise responsibly in providing a service to them, in this area also bringing to bear supra client values. In both contexts, indeed, the values of 'the other' may form a part of the range which may be brought to bear, along with values which may be linked with neither but arise in the wider society.

The 'Man in the middle'

It is likely to be only in this particular sense that a personnel practitioner might be considered to be a 'man-in-the-middle'. Specifically, he is unlikely to be able so far to avoid the constraints imposed by employment in 'purposive' organizations, as to act as a kind of arbitrator or umpire who delivers a binding judgement or award. This would imply opportunity, not merely to share in responsibility for decisions in the process of bringing supra-client values to bear, but to impose them. In effect, therefore, the extent to which either the undertaking or the individual accepts such values as relevant will depend upon the power and authority available to the practitioner in the situation at the time (cf Legge, 1978).

In carrying out his or her role, the personnel manager will be involved in the influencing of immediate situations in which differences exist, and of continuing approaches made by the undertaking and its members to one another (which might also involve differences). Examples of the one are provided by such activities as selection interviewing, or grievance handling, and of the second by the concepts of policies and practices which are adopted on a continuing basis within the sub-culture. In so far as the first kind of situation is intended to be structured by the policies and procedures of the second, it is the second which is likely to prove the more significant and the more demanding of the personnel practitioner's expertise.

In this area of objective-setting, policy-formation, and practice-regulation in the personnel field, the specialist manager is the more likely to be able to adopt the 'man in the middle' role, as this is defined in the above paragraph. It is in these 'structural' devices, that the concept of *value* is most particularly to be seen: the values of the undertaking, the professional, or of someone somewhere must form the foundation of what is meant by 'policy' (*see* pp 11–14). As a statement of what should be done, and of how the doing of it should be approached, it is a statement of values. And because of this, it is at this 'level' of action within the undertaking that the personnel manager must aim to bring his supra-client values to bear.

To the extent that this proves to be possible (and it *does* depend upon relative power and authority, as has already been said), the personnel professional is placed in the position where his distinct values of 'efficiency' and 'human satisfaction' (as revealed in the IPM's conception, for example) may be brought to bear in contra-distinction from the values which individual or undertaking might otherwise take into account in the development of objectives, policies or practices.

56

The expert role

The power and authority issue in these regions is likely to depend greatly upon the extent to which the abilities of the personnel practitioners are seen to be relevant to the 'needs' of the undertaking. The latter may well become more pressing with increases in scale, higher rates of technological change, changes in human expectation and demand from work, and degree of organization amongst the workforce, and as a result, the demand for personnel services may increase. Personnel management may, in other words, thrive on the growth in incidence of undertaking problems in the human field.

But such changes by themselves are scarcely likely to assure those who call themselves personnel specialists a place in the undertaking's scheme of things. There must be a matching competence or expertise in the appropriate problems areas on the part of the personnel specialist. It is not unusual for the specialist competence of the personnel manager to be described in terms of social skills. There is a clear link between these and the value of human satisfactions at work, but they are notoriously difficult to 'package' as a basis for a distinct occupation or profession (cf Wilenski, 1964) and one would therefore expect there to be 'something more' than this in the conception of personnel management which might commend itself to managements which face problems of the above type.

It is, of course, often argued that the 'something more' is provided by the personnel manager's acceptance of the need to use his skills for the purposes of the undertaking, however these may, in the particular case, be defined. That 'something more' is one related to acceptable ends. But there is also something more at the level of means, and this is the significance of the noun 'management' in the specialist's title. As a manager, the personnel practitioner is concerned to use his or her skills in order to achieve ends deliberately and systematically.

In particular, this shows itself in the approach to problem-solving by the individual, which makes use of the concept of feedback. Given *some* end to be achieved (and regardless of whose end it may be) the manager seeks out means of solving the problem and applies that which is selected as most appropriate according to the criteria applied, *and* then deliberately measures or assesses the consequences of the chosen action in order to 'feed this information back' to allow comparison with the intention or the prediction on which the action was based in the first place. This is nothing more than a description of a closed-loop model of control, which, at the level of the individual, frequently provides a guide for organizing decision and action.

Consequently, we find running through any discussion of personnel management activities (or skills) a frequent use of some model of this type. Social skills may be the stock-in-trade of the personnel manager, but as these are applied to manpower planning, training, motivation, organization change, etc, they are fitted to a framework of a feedback loop. It is this which helps to distinguish what the personnel manager is about from the action of the amateur who is intent upon doing good but not disciplined in the planning and execution of it. When we speak of the expert role of the specialist in this area, therefore, it is of a role which is subjected to this kind of discipline, independently of whether the end sought is one dictated by the undertaking in some way, or by 'people at work', or by someone else. (For examples of this application in the text, see pp 128–30, 348–55, 372–75 and 525–37.)

Summary

A personnel management specialist, as a professional, is thus concerned with objectives, policies, plans and practices relating to or affecting people within work undertakings. In this 'concern' he or she seeks to influence the ends which are pursued, by bringing other and wider values to bear upon decisions taken in the name of the undertaking or its members, and by systematically deploying skilled methods of realizing them. The particular areas to which this concern is related may be subsumed as the 'people-problem' of undertakings (ie the problem of how the individual and the organization are to be related to one another). But it may be spelled out in more detail, and within the 'system' frame referred to by reference to employee resourcing (handling the interchange of people across the undertaking's boundary) which forms the subject-matter of part one; employee performance (contributing to more effective wealth-creation within undertakings) which forms the subject-matter of part two; and employee relations (developing the structure of the organization as a contribution to various ends) which forms the subject matter of part three.

In none of these areas is the personnel practitioner any more free of constraints than any other managers, and in each part we look first at the major constraints on the people-oriented role. The basis of the practitioner's authority to act in these situations depends, then, upon his understanding of the nature of the problems involved and of the solutions (methods) which might be adopted to reduce them. This forms the subject matter of the middle section of each part. On the basis of such understandings, the practitioner then becomes involved in a large number of particular actions (in application of methods and techniques) which call for the exercise of the particular social skills which have been mentioned; these appear in the last two chapters of each part.

Part one
The employment function

The employment function

Employment in a modern economy

In the United Kingdom economy, just over 26¼ million people (a little over 47 per cent of the total population) formed the working population in June, 1980 (see *Employment Gazette*, 88 (10), October, 1980, p S7). At that date, 1,660,000 of these 'workers' were without employment, leaving an 'employed labour force' of 24,618,000. The 'employees in employment' (taking off the 1,886,000 self-employed and the 323,000 members of HM Forces) numbered 22,409,000 (*ibid*, p S7).

This is no more than a simple 'snap photograph' of the position. The figures vary over time. Both the total in employment and the total unemployed at that date were appreciably above the totals 10 years earlier, for example. Masked within the figures, there are other changes. The number of men in employment had fallen and the number of women in employment had increased between the two dates, for example (*ibid*, p S7). Some of the changes reflect 'market changes' (world recession and the rest) and some changes in public policy (increased employment opportunities for women or lowered priority to the objective of maintaining full employment). The variations on these scores change the situations in which both individuals seeking work and undertakings seeking workers must reach decisions.

The employment which is available for people is provided either by undertakings which exist to 'trade' (to engage in the production, distribution and exchange of goods and/or services) or which, in the public sector, have been created to provide services to the public at large or to individual members of it (see above, pp 9–11). In so far as these undertakings require the labour of people to enable them to reach their objectives, to that extent they create employment and thereby provide both work and remuneration to people desirous of securing these.

Most of the employment available at any time is provided by undertakings in the private sector. The number of separate businesses is impossible to calculate accurately, chiefly because of the interlocking and overlapping arrangements which exist between them.

At the one end of the spectrum there are the, usually small, own-account and partnership forms of business. We know that there are about a million such self-employed persons who do not engage the services of employees to help them, and over half a million persons in the same business category who do engage labour. At the other end, there are the private and public companies which account for the bulk of employment in private enterprise undertakings. Of these, there are over half a million private companies (on the definitions applicable before the implementation of the Companies Act, 1980) and over 15,000 public companies. According to the report of the Bullock Committee on Industrial Democracy, the 'top 1,000' companies (usually public ones) provided employment for over seven million people in the middle 1970s, in a total private sector provision in excess of 17 millions (Bullock Committee Report, 1977, p 7).

The other large segment of employment is provided by undertakings in the public sector. This is usually defined to embrace central and local government undertakings and a miscellaneous group of industries and services run by 'public corporations' created by and in some fashion accountable to government ministers (cf Thomson and Beaumont, 1978, pp 3–6). The sub-categories are thus distinguishable largely on the basis of the directness of their relationship to the central government.

This sector in total provides employment for between six and seven million people; a majority of these are engaged in the three services represented by local government, education and health, and another one and a half million are to be found in the nationalized industries. Not by any means all of these are in 'Crown employment' (ie employed directly 'by the state' to contribute to public administration and defence), but they are all to a greater degree than could be true of employees in the private sector subject to more direct government influence.

Those undertakings which thus provide employment concomitantly with their pursuit of trading or service objectives, have a particular interest in the labour market. To realize their objectives, they require labour in certain quantities and qualities. If their objectives change, so too might the labour requirement, so that the demand might vary over time on both dimensions. The interest which stems from this is that of securing the appropriate amounts and quantities of labour when it is needed by the undertaking. The 'employment function' identified above (pp 39–43) recognizes the need of the undertaking to deal with this problem of taking in and giving out of labour; in the language of the 'system-theorists' it covers the activities associated with the interchange between the undertaking as system and its environment (which may be presented pictorially as in Figure 1).

But the 'labour' also has some interest in this interchange process. Labour is made up of those who are either at work or seeking it. The individuals concerned may seek employment, either because it establishes their title to a share of the wealth produced or because it is inherently interesting, or both. Since, in our economy, they have no 'right' to work, and therefore cannot demand work 'as of right', they are placed in the position where the individual's interest in the employment process is as particular as is that of the undertaking. He or she must take, for himself or herself, the decisions about the kind and location of employment which will be sought and accepted.

Both 'parties', the undertaking and the individual, are required to take decisions which affect the interchange process, and each is likely to pursue a 'particular' interest in taking them.

Clearing the market
The state has some interest in ensuring that all those persons who seek employment and all those persons or undertakings who seek employees will realize their aims. This is an interest over and above the interests of the individuals involved: persons want jobs and undertakings want employees, but neither is especially concerned that everyone else in their category should achieve their objective. This broader aim of 'clearing the labour market' (ie of ensuring that everyone seeking work secures it and that all undertakings seeking labour find it) is one peculiar to government. In the post-war period up to about 1966, 'full employment' was a major objective of government policy; after that date it has had somewhat lesser priority in relation to other objectives concerned with balance of international payments and price stabilization. The increases in levels of unemployment since then tend, in part, to reflect this change.

The question of how far the state should directly intervene in this process is a debated one. The poles in the debate are represented by the argument that the market mechanisms ought to be left in peace to do their own work of adjusting the price of labour to the level which will clear the market versus the argument that the state must interfere to co-ordinate the myriad of decisions which are involved in clearing the market because by themselves these will not achieve the objective because of the 'imperfections' of any free

66

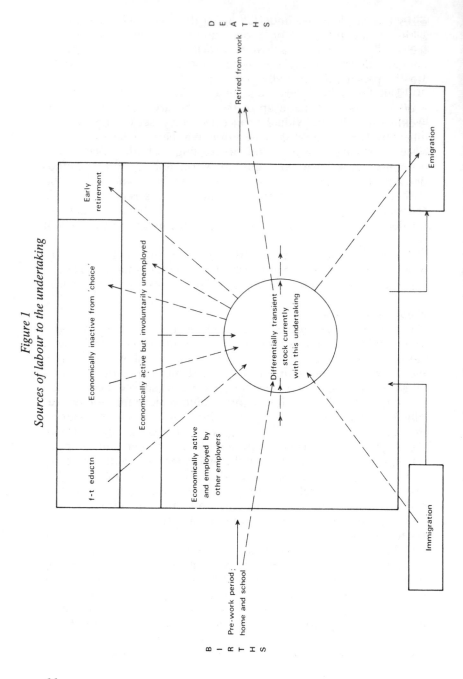

Figure 1
Sources of labour to the undertaking

market. Over the long term, governments have followed a meander path through the territory between these two polar positions.

The 'fact' of the present situation is, therefore, that governments to a greater or lesser extent 'interfere' with the processes of bringing employment-seeking workers and labour-seeking undertakings into a kind of accommodation. At one level, this process is facilitated by the provision of services such as jobcentres (formerly the 'employment exchanges'), employment subsidies and mobility allowances, sheltered employments, and rehabilitation and retraining programmes. At another, specific legal regulations govern the processes of interchange between the undertaking and the labour market, ranging from requirements in respect of employment of the registered disabled to proscriptions of certain types of discrimination in employment.

At a third, and somewhat 'deeper' level, the state (mainly through the edifice of law) supports the conventions and institutions of the culture which together structure the processes by which employment is made available and taken up. These are represented by the maintenance, through common and statute law, of the conceptions of employment as a contractual relationship between employer and employee voluntarily embarked upon by both, and of its regulation in the public interest as something to be devolved to a level as close to the decisions of the parties themselves as it is possible to decentralize it consistent with the achievement of both order and equitable terms.

Although, therefore, it is possible to refer to the manner in which employment is established and maintained as being something which is conceived in a kind of freedom to the parties to take their own decisions to suit themselves and their preferences, there are limits to this freedom stemming from both the market situation and from the superstructure of regulation which, in reflection of cultural values, surrounds it. Individuals and undertakings are not, and cannot be, completely 'free' to take self-interested decisions about employment in response to 'pure' market-derived data; they are also constrained by conventions, legal rules and cultural norms unheld by a host of institutions such as law or collective bargaining.

Managing the employment interchange

Managers of undertakings which employ people are involved in taking some of the vast number of decisions which go to make up the clearing of the labour market. The starting point in the decision making process is the determination of what amount of employment of what type is requisite to enable the undertaking to achieve the purposes which are set for it. The consequent decisions about how the labour force required will be attracted into association (and maintained in it for as long as it contributes to those purposes and objectives) fall within the domain of the personnel manager.

These will be constrained primarily by the need to establish a balance or equilibrium between the needs of the undertaking and the relevant 'labour market'. But they will also be constrained by the conventions and regulations which are imposed upon this equilibrium in the interests of securing more general balances or equilibria. The general manager and the personnel manager, involved in these kinds of decisions in the name of the undertaking, are not more free of constraint than anyone else. The objectives, policies and methods of recruitment and termination which they may opt for must take some account of both the surrounding structure of convention and law and the state of knowledge about how the interchange process operates, as these are brought into juxtaposition with the assessment of undertaking-need and 'labour market opportunity'.

In this part, therefore, we propose to look at these aspects of the process by which employment is established (and disestablished) within the undertaking, starting with the assumption that the personnel manager either represents the undertaking's interest in this process or is charged with realizing its objectives in the matter of recruiting, holding and terminating labour, or both.

In the next two chapters, opportunity is taken to review the major *constraints* upon the development of policies and approaches to recruitment and termination which arise particularly from the operation of law relating to employment. In chapters 5 and 6 we look at the *methods* which are available for forecasting the prospects of effecting an equilibrium of supply and demand at the level of the undertaking and for adjusting these two variables to achieve the desired balance. In chapters 7 and 8, we switch attention to the actual methods and techniques which may be used to *effect* employment on criteria derived from the perceived needs of the undertaking for labour of particular types and qualities.

4 The contract of employment

The law and employment
The undertaking usually requires labour services in order to achieve its objectives and as we have seen it is commonly a part of the personnel department's task to ensure that they are acquired in the amounts and of the quality required. But labour is no less a free agent than is capital (even if their respective power may vary) and there is no compulsion upon workers to take employment in a particular undertaking, just as there is none upon the undertaking to provide work. In effect, therefore, employment is established by 'agreement' between the two parties, employer and employee, and this agreement is identified by the particular term 'contract of employment'.

In the provision of employment, the undertaking performs a function which, if it did not do so, would have to be performed by someone else like the state. The state, therefore, has a kind of interest in this function, and has established a number of conditions to its discharge. Most of these are established through the law (in the form of both common law and legislation). Since most citizens (including employers and those who act on their behalf) tend to obey the law, we need to look at what these legal conditions attached to contracting in employment are. They serve as a first constraint on the freedom of the undertaking (or its agent) to contract or otherwise agree in employment, 'as it might wish' (that is, by responding to nothing more than its own requirements as developed from its own objectives).

This recognizes that 'the law' is a generally imperative force in our society. In Weber's terminology, it serves as an 'order' to which people are usually willing to orient their behaviour in the sense that they regard it as a duty to obey what it prescribes and proscribes (Weber, 1947). It is not uncommon, for example, to find undertakings stating in their written personnel polices that everyone acting in their name shall obey the law (cf Cuthbert and Hawkins, 1973).

Although we propose here to concentrate on what the law says must be obeyed, we should nevertheless note that the construction of policies may acknowledge other pressures and other ideas, in addition to law.

The workers' associations are also potent sources of pressure for change; their main reliance is upon the ability of their representatives to persuade representatives of undertakings to change their policies and practices, supported by the final sanction of withdrawing labour from the undertakings (cf McCarthy and Collier, 1973). The development of knowledge and understanding of human beings and the ways in which they interact with one another inside and outside work undertakings also operates as a source of pressure to change policy and practice (cf Gottschalk, 1973, p 33; Lupton, 1966).

All of these may be recognized as having some influence upon undertaking policies (whether these are explicit or simply espoused (see above p 3), and upon undertaking practice (cf Butteriss, 1975; Hawkins, 1978; Likert, 1967). This law is, however, treated separately here, partly because of its relative novelty in its present form and partly because of its transcendental importance for conduct within undertakings which do seek, at least, to conform to the requirements of law.

In this and the next chapter, therefore, it is proposed to review the major prescriptions and proscriptions of 'the law' as these affect the employment relationship between undertaking (employer) and worker (employee). Some of their implications for policy and practice are indicated although they are not the only ones which need to be recognized in its formulation, and will be taken up in later chapters.

The topic will be treated in two parts. In the remainder of this chapter, particular attention will be given to what some have referred to as 'the deep structure' of rules which govern the employment relationship (ie, the implied terms of the employment contract itself) and to the way in which recent legislation (mainly the Employment Protection (Consolidation) Act (the EP(C) Act in brief) of 1978, the Equal Pay Act of 1970, the Sex Discrimination Act of 1975, the Race Relations Act of 1976, and the Health and Safety at Work etc Act of 1974) has modified it in respect of the recruitment and continuing employment of employees.

In the following chapter, attention will be given to the same kind of issue but in respect of the permitted interruptions to the contract of employment and the restrictions placed upon its determination by the employer.

Recruitment to employment

Recruitment is a process through which the employment relationship (between employer and employee) is established. It is a process of mutual choice or selection: the employer chooses which employee(s) he will engage (and may use any or all of a number of devices to help in the selection process, *see* below, pp 206–17); and the employee similarly chooses the employer for whom he will work. The extent of choice, and the power to make it, are not necessarily equal for the two parties. There are usually more employees than there are employers in the labour market and the employer is usually less urgently in need of employees than employees are of employment. Nevertheless, as Kahn-Freund has suggested, the law proceeds on the twin assumptions that the parties are free to enter into these relationships or not as they choose, and that when they do so they approach one another as 'equals' in determining the terms of the contract which is established (Kahn-Freund, 1977, pp 1–17). This element of 'inequality' may, however, call for a policy response on the part of the employer (*see* below, pp. 86–87).

This contract which is deemed to be established by the parties, is conceived as a set of mutual promises which form the basis of a set of *rules* governing conduct in the employment relationship, although not by any means all of them are ever written down anywhere. These, in turn, determine what each party can and cannot, must and must not, do whilst the relationship exists. In this sense the relationship and the conduct within it become rule-bound and the basis of the status of the parties is thereby established: status derives from the rights and duties which the parties are deemed voluntarily to agree to in establishing the relationship and which are supported by these rules (cf Fox, 1974, pp 49–50).

To the extent that the status (and therefore the power) of the parties is important to them, it is important that the supporting rules should not be infringed by the other party and consequently that there should be a means whereby conformity of conduct to the rules can be enforced. One important means of this kind is that which depends upon the juxtaposition of the power of the employer and that of the trade union ('organized labour') in the 'collective bargaining' institution. Another older means lies in recourse to the courts to enforce promises and rules, but this mechanism is only available if in the contracting process five 'conditions' are met.

First, the persons or the parties making the agreement must be competent (in the eyes of the law) to make such agreements. There are limitations on 'competence' associated with age, mental condition, health or dependency, and there are differences in conditions attached to competence according to whether the contractor is a person (acting in his own right) or a corporation (a body which is 'given' a legal personality for convenience).

Secondly, the parties must clearly intend that the agreement shall constitute a legally-binding contract and give rise to obligations which might be enforced through the courts. Generally speaking social contracts are presumed not to be intended to create such obligations, whilst commercial and business contracts are presumed to be so intended.

Thirdly, the objects of the contract must themselves be legal, as the courts will not lend themselves to the enforcement of a contract (even if it would qualify on other grounds) which has as its object the achievement of some result which would be illegal or which identifies as the means of meeting the contract terms actions which would be illegal.

Fourthly, there must be both offer and acceptance in the same terms between the parties. An employer's offer of employment at a particular rate of pay, must be accepted by the employee in the terms of the offer, although it may be accepted (or indeed offered) by conduct rather than in words. A man who is invited to turn up to work on a Monday morning, and who is given work when he does, would be deemed to have had an offer and to have accepted it by reason of conduct.

Fifthly, in the employment contract context, the agreement on the terms of the offer must be supported by consideration of an identifiable and recognizable sort (usually of course a wage). Consideration has been defined as consisting 'either in some right, interest, profit or benefit accruing to one party, or some forebearance, detriment, loss or responsibility given, suffered, or undertaken by the other', or as requiring 'that something of material value shall be given or some other detriment shall be sustained by the recipient of a promise in order to make that promise enforceable (Mansfield Cooper and Wood, 1966 edn p 37).

Only if these requirements of the law are met, in the particular employment contract, can courts or tribunals recognize or enforce the agreement. These requirements are thus 'prior' to the establishment of a contract of employment.

Also prior to the establishment of the contract is the question of how far the opportunities of either party to establish a mutually-satisfactory contract depart from the normal. A prior decision by one party or the other constantly to deny the other the opportunity to enter upon a contract (even though in all other respects the other had capacity and competence) simply because of prejudice, could be anticipated to be against public policy because it destroys the public function served by employment. In recent years, specific legislation has sought to curb the operation of prejudices of this kind in respect of race and sex.

Non-discrimination in recruitment
Although the law may assume that the parties approach one another in the contracting process 'as equals', legislation enacted in recent years has attempted to outlaw selection of employees on the basis of criteria not related to the requirements of the job itself. Selection for employment is a process of discriminating amongst applicants; but the basis of that discrimination ought to be the fitness or suitability of the person to perform the duties expressed or implied in the contract. But, because there is more to a person than mere capacity or ability to perform, other attributes of the person might be used as a basis for selection; the law specifically singles out three of these and makes them unlawful criteria (*see*, Hepple, 1979, pp 169–89).

The first is the 'sex and marital status' attribute. The Sex Discrimination Act 1975, seeks to outlaw the preferment of one sex over another or of the single person over the married person as the basis for selection for employment (and for promotion, advancement, training, etc). The Act seeks to develop "a common strategy and philosophy, a parity of treatment approach and attitude" not only in respect of contractual terms, but also in "the whole range of intangible non-contractual relationships which arise when interviews take place, advertising occurs, selection is finally determined in the case of applications for jobs, promotion and the rest" (House of Commons, Official Report Standing Committee 8, 1 May 1975).

Discrimination against both men and women is covered, and so too is discrimination against married persons in favour of single ones. The Act applies to all employees of whatever age in Great Britain, unless excepted by the Act (and there are few exceptions) and to all employers with six or more employees (including any in associated employers' establishments), partnerships of six or more, trade unions, employers' associations, educational, training and qualifying bodies, advertisers, employment agencies and labour contractors.

The second is the racial attribute. The Race Relations Act 1976, seeks to outlaw preferment on grounds of 'colour, race, nationality or ethnic or national origin' as the basis for the same range of decisions, and Article 48 of the Treaty of Rome makes discrimination against nationals of the EEC unlawful.

The third is somewhat different from these and focuses on the question of membership or non-membership of a trade union. The Employment Act 1980, by imposing a duty upon a recognized trade union to act reasonably in admitting an applicant to membership, indirectly encourages an employer who is party to a union membership agreement, to offer employment to those who may not be union members at the time of application for employment.

The first two pieces of legislation affect recruitment in requiring the employer to avoid *direct* discrimination by advertising jobs for one sex or racial group rather than another; by short-listing interviewing or testing one rather than the other; and/or by offering a job on terms which discriminate between these categories. He must also ensure that such discrimination is avoided as between married persons and single persons, except that he may specifically treat married persons *more* favourably than single ones (but not less favourably). (SD Act 1975, s 3)

This kind of requirement is for the time being somewhat tempered by the possibility that the employer may still ask for qualifications for the job (provided that he can demonstrate their necessity) which are more likely to be possessed by men than by women. In the longer run, however, the other provisions of the Sex Discrimination and Race Relations Acts which are aimed at ensuring comparability of opportunity for education, training and qualification will tend to reduce this inherent disadvantage which may be suffered at the moment by women or by other groups. Certain occupations, very limited in number, are exempted from these provisions in the Sex Discrimination Act—mainly those where sex is required for authenticity (as in modelling or acting) or is desirable for reasons of public taste and decency (as with lavatory attendants) or where it would be unreasonable for the employer to provide facilities for both sexes in situations which have previously been single sex (as in the provision of sleeping or other accommodation on construction camps or lighthouses).

The employer must also bear in mind that, in situations in which the treatment actually accorded to persons may be non-discriminatory in itself, the consequences of the treatment may still be *indirectly* discriminatory. In connection with recruitment, for example, the proportions of the two sexes in a job or occupational category may be such as to discriminate against women, possibly because women are less likely to have the necessary qualifications or experience, and it will become progressively more important for the employer to be able to show that this result is not the result of discrimination. In both areas, race and sex, it will be necessary for the employer to develop positive employment policies, which, rather than accepting the world as it is, seek to effect changes which will demonstrate greater equality of both opportunity and treatment of the different sexes and the different races (cf Wainright, 1970).

The common law rules about contracting and the specific legislation outlawing certain types of discrimination in recruitment aim and serve to establish the rights of citizens to contract freely in employment, to reach agreements about what they will and will not do in this respect, *for themselves*, without hindrance from 'unlawful' barriers, erected prior to the contracting process itself.

In one other particular area, the law intervenes in the process of engagement, to require the employer to employ people who, without the support of law, would be likely to suffer disadvantage. Under the widely ignored Disabled Persons (Employment) Act 1944, a duty is imposed on the employer of 20 or more persons to employ a percentage of registered disabled persons (for whose voluntary registration the Act also made provision. S 9(1). The percentage currently applicable, by order and fixed after consultation, is three per cent, but it is believed that 60 per cent of private employers and a high proportion of public ones (the Crown is not bound by the Act but has agreed to observe its provisions) do not meet this quota figure *de jure*, even if many of them do so *de facto* by employing people who have not bothered to register as disabled. Failure to comply could lead to a fine or imprisonment or both, but only after review and report by District Advisory Committees and consequential legal action in the name of the Minister.

The sources of contract terms

A simple agreement between an employer and a potential employee to enter into an employment relationship (an agreement to 'give a person a start') does not by itself establish much in the way of the rights and obligations or the rules under which each will work. But such a simple agreement, which legally speaking 'establishes' the contract, imports into the relationship a whole host of rights and obligations and rules for their support, which would be recognized and enforced by the courts. They are usually unwritten in their full form, because they are so numerous. They are derived from four main sources, which supply the *express* and the *implied* terms of the employment contract:

First, what the parties explicitly agree to is one source of the 'contract terms'. But in employment relationships, what is agreed may be quite minimal—to work at a certain place for a wage—and a great deal more may be taken as agreed by the parties because of what is 'customarily' meant by such a simple reciprocal promise. Thus the question of what is 'really meant' and what is 'customary' may fall to be resolved at some stage in the relationship, if there is a difference of view about either. Historically, one of the roles of the trade union representative has been to try to influence the answers to these questions, and one of the roles of the common law has been to try to resolve these issues where they are brought before the courts. In both cases, it should be noted, a body of doctrines or understandings about *how* the questions should be resolved, have grown up.

Secondly, therefore, the contract terms are subject to influence, especially where the actual promises are minimal or silent on specific aspects, by 'custom' in the trade or in the employer's undertaking and by the understandings and agreements which have been developed in those circumstances between the employer (and his 'agents') and the worker (and his 'representatives'). It is in the nature of employment, that it is necessary as the relationship progresses through time for the details to be filled in to cope with the dynamic involved. The predilection of the worker over the past century or so has been to guide this process of filling in the details by 'collective bargaining': the evolution of guiding principles and precedents through discussion between the agents and representatives.

Thirdly, in distinction from this 'internal' process of evolving rules about how the questions about contract terms are to be answered, the common law has ever stood ready to do the same thing on the basis of its doctrines and rules. Where the collective bargaining process is sanctioned by lockouts and strikes and similar forms of industrial action, the common law processes are sanctioned by the penalties available to the courts. But the common law has developed its own notions of what is 'normal' or 'standard' in the relationship of the employment contract, and it has established its own rules as to what is recognizable and enforceable in the way of a contract of employment. Both of these influence what the parties do and agree to in contracting but it is often quite separate and distinct in its conceptions of what is right and wrong, or correct and incorrect conduct. This contains a potential for conflict between these two sets of influence upon the contract.

Fourthly, what the parties may agree individually or collectively (through agents and representatives) and what the common law may impute to the contract in accordance with its doctrines, are both subject to an overriding influence: that of specific legislation relating to both the processes of contracting in employment, and the terms and conditions which may be agreed or deemed to have been agreed. This has always been so in the modern industrial period but in the past two decades or so legislation has burgeoned to an extent which markedly affects the old assumption that contracts were 'freely' and 'voluntarily' entered into.

The important general consequence of this has been that, no matter what the parties may actually have agreed under certain headings in the contract, and no matter what, in accordance with the understandings and agreements of collective bargaining or with the doctrines of the common law, they may have been deemed to have agreed to, it is now to be presumed conclusively that they intended to agree to those terms (like minimum notice) which are stipulated in the legislation.

One way of looking at these various influences upon the employment contract is to see the first two as related to the worker's interest in preserving his only marketable asset (his labour power) in a way which will maximize his commercial advantage in hiring it out to employers, and the last two as concerned to preserve some 'balance of advantage' as between the parties to the process of contracting.

This notion of balance tends to be defined differently according to the cultural values which have applied in our society: by and large, the common law has developed its doctrines in response to a high value placed upon the enhancement of 'trade' from the middle ages onwards and tends therefore to define the balance of advantage in terms which favour trade over alternative objectives; but recent legislation has sought to shift the balance to favour the worker *as producer* rather than the worker *as consumer* whose interest the enhancement of trade might be expected to serve. In consequence, this shift has altered the status or rights and duties of the parties. (see also pp 154–58).

Because the contract terms may be varied in any or all of these ways, therefore, the actual agreement between individual employer and individual employee may not stand in law. What the parties may do, and what they may agree to, at the point of recruitment in particular is subject to close constraint in some respects by 'the law'.

This could be the case with agreements which might be made about the manner and form of remuneration to the worker. As we noted at the beginning of the chapter, remuneration serves a major 'public function' in effecting distribution of income, and this may be one of the reasons why legislation has for a very long time sought to control, not the amount, but the way in which wages are paid. How this operates is described in the next section.

The payment of wages

Generally speaking, Britain does not have 'minimum wage legislation' of the kind found in many other countries (cf Department of Employment, 1967) but there are a limited number of trades and industries (the so called 'Wages Council trades' and those where Statutory Joint Industrial Councils may have replaced the Wages Councils) in which payments of minimum amounts of remuneration are prescribed under Statute. A similar kind of requirement as to minimum remuneration is imposed upon contractors to central and local government under the Fair Wages Resolution of the House of Commons, but the extension of this idea by the Terms and Conditions of Employment Act 1959, and by S 98 and Sch 11 of the Employment Protection Act 1975, was repealed by the Employment Act 1980 (S 19).

Legislation imposes duties upon the employer, however, in relation to the manner and form of the payment of wages to workmen, under the Truck Acts 1831–96, the Payment of Wages Act 1960, and the Employment Protection (Consolidation) Act 1978 (Ss 8–10).

The Truck Acts prohibit the payment of workmen in goods or in kind except under special circumstances, *and* the deduction of fines or other amounts from wages for bad workmanship, except under special circumstances. The Payment of Wages Act made it possible to pay these classes of workmen by cheque, postal or money order, by consent, rather than in coin of the realm which was all that was allowed as the medium under the Truck Acts. The Employment Protection (Consolidation) Act stipulates the information to be given about payment.

At common law, the parties to an employment contract may agree between themselves as to the *form* of payment to be made, ie cash, kind, cheque, etc. The Truck Act, 1831, however, made 'illegal, null and void' any contract which provided for payment to any *manual worker* (other than domestic or menial employees) 'otherwise than in the current coin of the realm' (S 1) and further required (by S 3) that the employer was to pay the *entire* amount of wages due to the workman in this form (that is, without deduction). An employer in breach of these requirements commits a criminal offence (S 9). The basic right of this kind of 'workman' (but not of, for example, white-collar employees) is, thus, to be paid his entire wages in coin of the realm (Hepple and O'Higgins, 1979, pp 154–58).

It was this right which was modified by the Act of 1960. This allowed the employer to pay such workmen by money order, postal order, or cheque or directly into a bank account provided that certain conditions were first met. The workman must first make a request for payment in one of these forms and the employer must agree. The request from the employee may stipulate that he wishes the whole of his wages or only part to be paid in this fashion. The request will lapse if the employer does not answer the request within two weeks of receiving it; it would not then be possible for the employee to be paid in one of these ways unless the employee provided a seperate request for payment. Just as the employee is allowed to exercise his own discretion in this matter, so too the employer is not bound to make payments in the ways indicated simply because he has a request to do so from his employee. He may or may not do so but can stipulate that he will only do so at some date in the future (when he will have to notify the employee in writing) or he may give notice in writing to the employee that he refuses to accede to the request.

The employer must ensure that all cheques are made payable to the employee to whom the wages are due by name, or to his order: all payments into a bank account must be to the credit of the account specified in the written request. If either of these conditions is not fulfilled the employer is in breach of the Act. Similarly, the employer must not make any charge for wages paid in any one of the ways stipulated in the Act. Once both parties have agreed in writing to make payments in one of these ways, the arrangement will hold good until either party ends it by written notice. If notice is given it must amount to four weeks, although this period may be shortened at the mutual agreement of the two parties.

There are special provisions for paying wages to employees who are away from work through illness or personal injury, or through reasons connected with their work, who would otherwise be paid in cash. Provided the employee does not give notice to his employer that he does not want to be paid other than by cash, the employer is permitted under the Act to pay wages by postal order or money order (but not in any other ways allowed by the Act), even if he does not have the written request of the employed persons. Where the employer takes advantage of this permission under the Act, he must still meet the conditions about giving full particulars in the pay statement. Provision is also made in the Act for the individual employee, if he or she wishes, to authorize someone else (such as a trade union official, a lawyer, a bank manager, a relative or a friend) to act on the employee's behalf in either making or cancelling a request for payment of wages in one of the ways allowed by the Act.

79

Certain rights under the Truck Acts and the Payment of Wages Act of 1960 are generalized by the EP(C) Act, Ss 8–11. The employee must be given a written itemized pay statement before, or at the time when he is paid. The items required are:

(a) The *gross* amount of wages or salary (not component bonuses or commissions, for example)
(b) The amounts of any *variable* deductions where pay varies (such as income tax, graduated pension and national insurance contributions)
(c) The amounts of any fixed deductions (eg trade union contributions), which duty may be discharged either by listing the fixed deductions on the pay statement or by issuing annually a standing complete statement of fixed deductions showing amounts of each, the purpose of each, and the intervals at which deduction is made, and by giving written notice of amendments during the year if necessary
(d) The net amount of wages or salary payable (and if this net amount is paid in different ways, the amount and method of each part payment).

If any of this is not done, it gives rise to an 'unnotified deduction' which an industrial tribunal can require the employer to repay (on substantiated complaint) up to a maximum of 13 weeks at the amount 'unnotified'.

Payment for layoff and medical suspension

Although the employer does not usually have a duty to provide work to employees, he is under a duty to provide opportunity for them to earn their remuneration. Legislation places him under a duty to provide payment to them even when he is not able to provide work. The Employment Protection (Consolidation) Act, 1978, Ss 12–22, gives employees a right to payment when the employer does not provide work or when the employee cannot work for a reason outside his (the employee's) control. There are two circumstances:

First, an employee who has at least four weeks' continuous service and who is laid off temporarily for a whole day because of a temporary redundancy or other event which makes it impossible for the employer to give him or her work (other than a trade dispute involving his or her employer or associated employer) is entitled to payment for that day (subject to a maximum of £8.75 for the day) provided that such lay off has not already occurred on five days during the three month period calculated back from that day. In order to qualify, the individual must also not have refused an offer of suitable alternative employment and he or she must comply with all reasonable requirements imposed by the employer to ensure that he or she will be available to work should it become available.

The rationale of this is that if the fault does not lie with the employee or fellow employees (as for example in a strike situation) then he or she should receive payment. Thus, lack of supplies (eg raw materials or components) occasioned by a dispute elsewhere, or lack of fuel or power brought about by circumstances beyond the employer's control, do not absolve him from the duty to make these 'guarantee payments'.

Where a collective agreement provides for payment for layoff, it usually provides for a guaranteed *weekly* payment: now the employee is able to choose which scheme, contractual or statutory, is most beneficial to him, and the employer is not permitted to choose the cheapest of two parallel schemes. He can however attempt to arrange any layoffs to minimize cost to himself.

Provision is made for *all* parties to a collective agreement or wages order to apply to the Secretary of State for exemption from this requirement of guarantee payments. There is a proviso that the collective agreement must meet the criteria relating to appeals against non-payment, and it is likely that the terms of the collective agreement will have to be no less favourable to the employee than the statutory requirements before exemption will be granted.

An employee who feels he has not received the whole or part of his entitlement on this score will be able to present a complaint to an industrial tribunal within three months: the tribunal is empowered to order the employer to make the appropriate payment if the complaint is found well-founded. Whilst an employer probably needs to keep records of guarantee payments to groups of employees (eg departments affected) he probably does not need to keep separate records for each individual (assuming always that records of sickness, holidays, and so on are separately maintained).

Secondly, Ss 19 and 64 of the Same Act give the employee who is suspended from work on medical grounds (because of a requirement imposed under legislation or a Code of Practice) a right to payment by the employer whilst suspended for a period not exceeding 26 weeks. To qualify, the employee must have been employed for four weeks, must be fit (in health) for work, must not have unreasonably refused an offer of alternative work which is suitable, and must comply with any reasonable requirements of the employer designed to ensure that his services continue to be available. In the event of non-payment, the individual may complain to an industrial tribunal and, if the complaint is found to be substantiated, the tribunal may order the payment which it finds due to the individual. An employer who hires a replacement for the individual during the period of suspension may, if he informs that replacement that he or she is replacing someone on medical suspension and if he dismisses that replacement so that the suspended person may resume employment, so dismiss the replacement for good cause (*see* below, pp 114–16).

These are not the only occasions on which the employer is liable to pay the employee for periods when he or she is not working (*see* the 'time off' provisions, pp 103–6). A distinction may be drawn, however, between these payments above, where the payment recognizes the element of non-penalizing for something outside the individual's control, and those others which are related to continued payment to an individual whose time off is concerned (in most cases) with the 'facilitation' of the relationships between the contracted parties.

Anti-discrimination in remuneration
Just as discrimination in hiring, promoting and firing between sexes and races has been outlawed, so too has discrimination in the fixing of amounts of payment for the same or essentially similar work. *Whatever may be agreed in the individual contract or in the collective agreement, therefore, recent Statutes require non-discrimination in the actual payment.*

From the end of December 1975, the Equal Pay and the Sex Discrimination Acts must be read together. In broad terms, the Equal Pay Act attempts to eliminate discrimination in pay and other terms and conditions of employment, while the Sex Discrimination Act, as it applies to the servicing of employment, focusses particularly upon the access women are permitted (and particularly married women) to training courses, promotion and transfer and benefits, facilities and services. In many cases it will be necessary to review practices and procedures relating to issues like travelling expenses, flexible hours, clothing allowances, opportunities to work overtime and even provision of hairdressing facilities, as well as the more obvious questions of selection for training and promotion.

The main intention of the Equal Pay Act is to improve the terms and conditions of employment of females at work by bringing them to parity with those of men. The Act aims to do this in one of two ways:

(a) By establishing the right of the individual woman to equal treatment when she is employed either on work of the same or a broadly similar nature to that of men or in jobs which, although different from those carried out by men, have nevertheless been given the same value as men's jobs under a job evaluation exercise. (Equal Pay Act, S 1(1), 1(4) and 1(5))
(b) By providing for the Central Arbitration Committee to remove discrimination in collective agreements, employers' pay structures and statutory wages orders (where these contain any provisions applying specifically to men only or to women only) which have been referred to it.

It is provided that where the individual woman employee has a disagreement with her employer on her rights under the Act, she may refer the complaint to an industrial tribunal for a decision. Where the tribunal finds the complaint well founded, it may award arrears of remuneration (for up to two years before the date on which she referred the claim to the tribunal) and may also award damages in respect of non-cash benefits up to the same limit. It is also open both to an employer to refer the case to a tribunal and also for the Secretary of State for Employment to do so where it appears that a woman has a claim to equal treatment but that it is not reasonable to expect her to take the steps to make the reference herself. It is also provided that, where an equal pay question comes up in another court where an industrial tribunal is competent to decide the issue, the court may refer the question to a tribunal.

The individual rights granted by the Equal Pay Act apply to all persons employed under a contract of service or of apprenticeship, or a contract personally to execute any work or labour. The main exception concerns employment wholly or mainly outside Great Britain and the Act does not extend to Northern Ireland, but it does apply to workers of all ages.

It is not a requirement that a woman shall have terms and conditions of employment exactly equal to a man's. Certain matters are excepted, particularly where the employment of women is governed by legislation regulating the employment of women as, for example, under the Factories Acts; the Act does not preclude the unequal treatment of women in the terms and conditions of employment they may enjoy on the birth or expected birth of a child. Equal treatment is not required on terms and conditions concerning retirement, marriage or death or to any provision made in connection with retirement, marriage or death. The Act therefore carries implications for the statement of further particulars of the contract of employment which the employer is required to issue to his employees within 13 weeks of their engagement. From the few cases which have so far been taken to appeal on the Equal Pay Act, it is clear that permitted variations will be defined in a narrow fashion rather than a broad one, and this might be predicted to apply to the interpretation made in the Sex Discrimination Act, partly at least because conformity with Common Market practice here may force stricter interpretations than might originally have been intended in domestic legislation (see Wallington, 1978).

The Act seeks to define what is meant by the same or broadly similar work. Work qualifies in this way only if the differences between the woman's work and the work of men occur sufficiently often or if the nature and extent of the differences are themselves appreciable. If the differences between the work carried out by men and women are of practical importance in relation to the terms and conditions of employment, under S 1(4) the work would not be regarded as broadly similar. Thus if there were only three jobs in a factory, and men and women were employed interchangeably on one job but men were employed on job Y at a higher rate of pay, there would be no possibility of the woman comparing her job with job Y because the difference between job X and job Y would have practical importance in relation to the terms and conditions of employment (that is the difference is recognized in higher pay).

Where job evaluation has been carried out and the terms and conditions of employment are based on the results of job evaluation, and a job carried out by women has been given an equal value with a job carried out by men, in those circumstances both the men and the women concerned must receive the same terms and conditions of employment (S 1(1) (b)). For example, where a job evaluation using a points evaluation method had been carried out before the Act came into effect, and the number of points allocated to a woman's job equalled the number of points given to a man's job, the woman would have a claim to the same terms and conditions of employment as the man doing a different job, but which had been evaluated with the same number of points. The Act also makes it possible for a woman to claim the same terms and conditions of employment as the man when a job evaluation exercise has been carried out but not implemented (O'Brien and Others v Sim-Chem Ltd. HL, 30 July (1980) I WLR 1011 (HL)). The House of Lords in this case took the view that once the job evaluation exercise had revealed discrimination, the employer was in a position to take action to remove it. The intention of the Act (s 1 (2) (b) (ii)), was that such action should be taken at once when the fact of discrimination had been established; the mere fact that the employer had not implemented the restructuring of any wage rates on the basis of the 'voluntary study' was no reason for not doing so.

Furthermore, where it could be shown that the job evaluation itself was carried out with the intention of producing a different rate for men and women, the woman would have a claim for improved treatment. In Section 1(5) the Act requires the results of a job evaluation exercise carried out in this way to be adjusted so that, in so far as two jobs make the same demand of a worker, they would be evaluated equally. It should be made clear that the Act by itself makes no requirement for job evaluation to be done; these comments relate only to job evaluation which for other reasons has been carried out in the organization.

The Act also provides for making comparisons to determine whether this right has been infringed. The woman may draw comparisons with men or with men's jobs only where the men in question are employed by her employer or by an associated employer; even then the comparison would only be permitted if the terms and conditions of employment of the men in different locations or establishments of the same or associated employer were themselves common. If, for example, an employer had three separate factories and the men's terms and conditions in the three factories were all different, the woman who felt aggrieved about her terms and conditions of employment in comparison with those of men would only be able to draw comparisons with men in her own particular employing establishment and not across the three plants belonging to the one employer. It should be noted that for this purpose people are considered to be employed at an establishment, if they are employed either in the establishment or from the establishment (for example, travelling salesmen would be employed from an establishment in this sense (s 1(6) (b)). A ship is also treated as an establishment for this purpose, but certain restrictions do apply to the provisions of the Act in relation to people employed on aircraft, hovercraft or ships registered in Great Britain wholly outside the country.

It does not follow from this that no man may be paid more than a woman even when both are engaged on the same or broadly comparable work. Where this is so, it will be for the employer to show that the advantage enjoyed by the man (or the woman) is enjoyed because it is 'genuinely due to a material difference (other than the difference of sex)' between the woman's case and the man's. It is not, for example, uncommon to pay people differential rates because of length of service, level of output or for reasons connected with merit. Provided that such differences in payment do not discriminate between one sex and the other but simply between one individual worker and another regardless of sex, the Act does not require that the payment levels be brought into line. It follows that, if a woman has longer service with the employer than a man engaged in broadly comparable work, the system must allow her to receive higher payment. The principle upheld in the legislation is that the system of payment must not distinguish between men and women as classes; any difference that does exist must be genuinely due to material difference between the individual man's case and the individual woman's case.

Implications for hiring policy

Taken together, therefore, the legal influences upon the hiring of workers and upon the consideration offered in the establishment of contracts of employment, seek to serve the following objectives:

> first, to uphold the freedom of the parties to contract voluntarily in employment, by outlawing certain kinds of prejudice which might (on the historical evidence) affect the recruitment decisions and the consideration offered to the permanent detriment of some (categories of) citizen
>
> secondly, to uphold the 'wage system' as a mechanism of income distribution, both by outlawing the kinds of discrimination mentioned in the preceding paragraph and by protecting the principle that the worker should be entitled to remuneration for work done (or service rendered to the employer).

In these ways, the interventions of the law in this area may be justified.

From the standpoint of the employer, however, these principles are also worthy of being upheld. It is not in the long term interest of the employer that either the freedom of contract or the centrality of the wage system should be brought into disrepute amongst workers, by employer abuse.

To the extent, however, that the law interferes with the amount or level of remuneration offered and accepted in the contract, however, to that extent it might act against the short run interest of the employer. *That* interest is, however, largely composited from the terms of the competition which the employer faces; to the extent that competitors are caught by the same requirements, the individual employer's position is not adversely affected (but in international markets, of course, not all employers are caught by this kind of legislation).

As these requirements affect hiring policy, however, they are likely to prove unexceptionable to the good (or 'moral') employer. There will be a need for a policy statement to guide practice in recruitment which will at least uphold the principles established in law. But the employer who is concerned about his image as a good employer (whether for reasons of general morality or for the more practical reason that he wishes to be attractive to a potential labour force) will normally want to go beyond the bare legal requirements in establishing the policy.

In one other particular, the principle of *informing* employees (in the above case of the nature and composition of remuneration) may be regarded as acknowledging the desirability of treating employees as educated and intelligent beings. This has a deeper 'legal' dimension to which we now turn.

Communicating the main terms

Since a contract of employment may be 'established' with very little actually being said about the reciprocal rights and obligations of the parties, the law has stepped in to ensure that new employees are informed of at least the main terms and conditions. This requirement is imposed by S 1 of the Employment Protection (Consolidation) Act 1978, which carries forward the requirements of the Contracts of Employment Acts, 1963 and 1972.

The employer is required to make available to almost all new employees within 13 weeks of their commencement in the employment a written summary of the terms and conditions of that employment.

Certain categories of employee are excluded from these provisions. There are two broad types of exclusion, one by type of employment and the other related to working period.

(a) The individual is not entitled to *this* statement if he or she is a registered dock worker so engaged, if he or she is employed in the Merchant Navy or in the fishing fleets, if he or she is a Crown servant, where he or she is employed abroad and normally works abroad, and where the employee is a husband or wife of the employer.

(b) The employer may also ignore those engagements for a task not expected to last for more than 12 weeks (provided that the task does not last more than 12 weeks); and those engagements for less than 16 hours per week, unless the individual has already been working for that employer for 26 weeks for more than 16 hours per week and still works at least eight hours per week, or unless the individual has already been working for more than eight hours per week continuously for the employer for five years.

There are three ways in which the employer might discharge this duty:

(a) Where the terms of the employment contract are normally

expressed in written form, and the individual employee is either given a copy or has access to it in the course of his employment, this will meet the requirement provided that it contains the information detailed in (c) below.

(b) Where the particulars referred to in (c) below are contained in some document or documents which the individual employee has reasonable access to and reasonable opportunities to read in the course of his employment, the employer may refer the employee to this document(s) for any or all the particulars in (c) below. (In both these cases, it will also be necessary to issue the note referred to below and to keep the documents up to date.)

(c) Otherwise, the employer is required to give the employee a written statement containing the main terms, as stipulated. This may well accompany the letter of appointment, but it is not a requirement of the law that the new employee shall be issued with a written contract of employment and, strictly, the written statement does not constitute one. On the face of it, the legal requirement affects no more than practice and procedure. In fact, when it was introduced it forced employers to establish what policy and practice actually obtained in the undertaking.

Whichever method is used by the employer to discharge the duty, the written document given or otherwise made available to the employee must contain the following formation:

1 The identity of the parties to the employment contract
2 The date on which the employment began (and, if it is a contract for a fixed term, the date on which it will end)
3 A statement as to whether 'any employment with a previous employer counts as part of the employee's continuous period of employment with him, and if so, specifying the date on which the continuous period of employment began'
4 'The title of the job which the employee is employed to do' (a generic title might be employed instead of a specific one unless tribunals rule otherwise)
5 The terms of the contract as at a specified date not more than one week before the date on which the statement is given:
   (i)   the scale or rate of remuneration or the method of calculating remuneration
   (ii) the intervals at which remuneration is paid (ie whether weekly, monthly or by some other period)
   (iii) any terms and conditions relating to hours of work (includ-

ing any terms and conditions relating to normal working hours)

(iv) any terms and conditions relating to:

—entitlement to holidays, including public holidays, and holiday pay (the particulars given being sufficient to enable the employee's entitlement, including any entitlement to accrued holiday pay on termination of employment to be precisely calculated)

—incapacity for work due to sickness or injury, including any provisions for sick pay

—pensions and pension schemes (provided that these are not provided for in or under another Act of Parliament) and including a statement in most cases as to whether a contracting out certificate is in force

(v) the length of notice which the employee is obliged to give and entitled to receive to determine his contract of employment. If the employment contract is for a fixed term, the date when the contract is due to expire must also be stated.

If there are no particulars to be entered under any of these headings or sub-headings, this fact is to be stated. This must be accompanied by a note which:

1 Specifies 'any disciplinary rules applicable to the employee', or refers to a document which is reasonably accessible to the employee and which specifies such rules

2 Indicates to whom (person or committee) an employee 'can apply if he is dissatisfied with any disciplinary decision relating to him'—in other words, to whom he appeals—and what steps are open to him beyond the first level of appeal. (This need not embrace matters relating to health or safety at work)

3 Specifies the person (or position) to whom an employee can take a grievance relating to his employment to seek redress and the manner in which the application for redress shall be made

4 Either explains the steps consequent upon any such application or refers to a reasonably accessible document which explains those steps. (It is possible that there may not be any consequent steps within the organization, but compliance with the Code of Industrial Practice may require a grievance procedure to be negotiated).

If after the date to which the statement relates there is a change in any of these terms included in the statement, the employer has the duty to inform the employee of the change by a written statement; if the written statement is not left with the employee it has to be preserved and the employer must ensure that the employee has reasonable access to it and can read it in the course of his employment. This duty must be discharged within one month of the change being introduced. It is met if the employer uses the method (b) above and indicates initially that any changes will be entered into the document within one month of being introduced. It is also met if the method (a) above is used and if written statements of variations in the contract are issued to the employee from time to time as they are made (*see* EP (C) Act, 1978, Ss 1–7; Hepple, 1979 pp 97–106; Rideout, 1979, pp 30–32).

An immediate cause of these developments was the desire of the government to convince our national neighbours that we were good Europeans; to an extent these legal prescriptions help to harmonize our employment law with that of continental European countries. But a more general reason for them is the change which is taking place in workers' expectations of their employment not only as a source of material benefit but also as a support to human dignity. Nevertheless, what is now called for by the legislation remains a basic minimum, and an employer's conformity to the legal minima is unlikely to make him a highly respected figure in the eyes of his employees.

Originally, penalties were provided in the Contracts of Employment Act for failure to comply without reasonable excuse but these were removed in 1965. Failure to comply with these requirements in respect of information opens up the possibility of complaint by the individual to an industrial tribunal. The powers of the tribunal in the event of finding the complaint well founded are to state what the statement ought to have included. In order to establish what 'ought' to have been included, the tribunal must rely upon the express and implied terms of the individual's contract of employment. Implicitly, therefore, this acknowledges that the terms of the contract exist in some way and in some form apart from these stated ones.

Rights and duties

In fact, there are many such conditions which attach to an employment contract which do not appear in this mandatory statement. They are, nevertheless, extremely important in providing the parties with the authority for acting within the relationship. For example, they form the basis for the employer's actions in disciplining employees, or the basis for the employee's acceptance of the orders of managers and supervisors. Without them, the relationship could not continue in a co-operative and productive way.

Therefore, although they are not required in the statement referred to above, they need to be understood as the foundation of the employment relationship, *and* as the point from which most recent legislation takes off to establish new (usually 'employee') rights and (usually 'employer') duties.

These rights and duties are usually referred to as deriving from the common law and they will be implied by the courts in the absence of evidence to the contrary. The basic common law duties which the employer owes to the employee (and which therefore form the reciprocal basis of the employee's rights) are those of remuneration for work done or service rendered under the contract, of provision of opportunity to earn remuneration and to work (in a restricted range of circumstances) of taking reasonable care for the safety of the employee whilst in the employer's employment and to indemnify the employee for any loss sustained in service. In his useful tabulation of the duties, Rideout (1979, p 35) suggests that in addition, there may be a duty upon the employer to 'treat the employee with appropriate courtesy' which is the employer's 'contribution' to the sustenance of mutual trust and confidence between the parties to the contract (cf Courtaulds Northern Textiles Ltd v Andrew (1979) IRLR, p 84).

In 'return' for these, the employer obtains the right to expect service from the employee, to control the work conduct of the employee and to expect from the employee not only service in return for the remuneration, but conduct which will sustain mutual trust and confidence within the contractual relationship (see, *Post Office v Roberts* (1980) IRLR, p 347). But as these are translated into more specific 'duties' which the employee owes to the employer, they amount to a rather longer list than those owed by the employer, reflecting the nature of the relationship itself.

An employee may be said to owe to the employer the duties:

1 to be ready and willing to work
2 to offer personal service
3 to avoid wilful disruption of the employer's undertaking or, more simply, to co-operate with the employer and facilitate performance of the contract by both parties
4 to obey reasonable (or 'lawful') orders
5 to work only for the employer in the employer's time
6 to account for profits received
7 to respect the employer's trade secrets
8 to take reasonable care of the employer's property when it is entrusted to the employee
9 to take reasonable care in the employer's service.

In effect, these imply that the employee makes two distinct types of offer to the employer in embarking upon a contract. The first has to do with the individual's ability and motivation to perform the work which the employer is offering as available, and the other with the individual's willingness to work under the control of the employer; obeying his instructions and his rules.

In toto, therefore, what the employee contracts to do is to submit himself to the authority (or control) of an employer in all matters which might be said to come within the scope of the work he offers to carry out. Because of the inherent difficulty of defining the contractual terms with precision, the employer has relatively unrestricted power, exercised through his orders and the rules applicable in the employer's organization, and the employee has comparatively few safeguards or protections except in so far as he himself, or someone (whether union or state) acting in his interests, can curb that power. The history of the employment contract is one of progressive restriction of the employer's prerogatives and privileges in these ways, although he remains possessed of such authority and power (see chapter 10) over the employee's competence and conduct as has not yet been resticted either by collective bargaining or legislation.

The employee's rights

Because of the operation of both collective bargaining and specific legislation, the employee now secures 'in return for' the acceptance of these duties and responsibilities, a larger number and range of rights than were implied by the common law in years past. Between the two sets of rights, however, there is an important difference. Those established under collective agreements or common understandings between the employer and organized labour are both more varied (or less standardized) and subject to the trade union remaining able to mobilize adequate sanctions against the employer in the event of breach of the 'rule' establishing the right. But those established by legislation are relatively standardized (ie they apply to employees of a defined class regardless of other considerations) and are sanctioned by law.

The main employee rights in this category are:

1   a right not to be discriminated against in employer decisions in respect of engagement, treatment in employment or dismissal on the basis of sex, marital status (if the discrimination is against the married person) or ethnic origin
2   a right to be paid for work performed or service rendered, and if engaged in most manual occupations outside the public service,

to be paid in coin of the realm, unless he explicitly agrees otherwise

3 a right to belong to a trade union if he so wishes (but not a right not to belong) and to engage in its activities (in some circumstances with time off for the purpose) if he so wishes, although not necessarily at *any* time

4 a right to work in some very special cases, limited in number, or to compensation for lay off up to a certain limit

5 an embryonic right to adequate instruction and training for general purposes, but a more explicit right to instruction and training in safe methods of working

6 a right to expect the employer to exercise reasonable 'care' for the employee's health and safety at work

7 a right to basic information about the employment contract under which he works, about the way net pay is calculated and about the reason why his contract of employment is terminated

8 a right to question decisions by the employer which touch on his employment and to appeal against such decisions either to an outside adjudication tribunal or to an internal body which serves a similar function

9 a right to either a minimum amount of notice as provided for in statute law or the amount of notice either expressed in his employment contract or reasonable for the occupation and industry

10 a right not to be unfairly or wrongfully dismissed from his employment which implies a right to require the employer not to determine his contract in a discriminatory fashion or in breach of the contract terms themselves

11 a right, in certain industries (the Wages Council trades) to payment of wages at a rate which is laid down by regulation as a statutory minimum (cf O'Higgins, 1976).

The periods of continuous employment required of the employee as a condition of qualifying for these rights are listed in table 3 on page 94.

Although this list of 'rights' may be played down as being no more than the reciprocal of the employee's duties (a kind of *quid pro quo*) it is difficult to exaggerate their magnitude.

The changes which have taken place in the law of employment in the past 10 years or so ... represent the emergence of a complete new philosophy in the relationship which exists between employer and employed, with new standards to achieve in personnel policies. ... The traditional prerogative rights of management are being constantly eroded, for the law now imposes requirements which follow from the new concepts of equal partnership in employment matters. The old days of 'hire and fire' have been replaced by the doctrines of mutual respect and consideration, as the relationship of 'master and servant', servile in its implications, has altered beyond recognition. If some em-

Table 3

Minimum Periods of Continuous Employment to Qualify for Certain Individual Rights accorded by Legislation

Minimum period	Nature of the right	Source of right in law
1 No period	Not to be dismissed for trade union membership or activities	EPCA S58
2 No period	Not to be dismissed on racial grounds	RRA S4(2)
3 No period	Not to have action short of dismissal taken against him/her for trade union membership or activities	EPCA A 23
4 No period	To time off with pay for industrial relations activities or training therefor (officials)	EPCA S 27
5 No period	To time off without pay to take part in trade union activities	EPCA S 28
6 No period	To time off without pay to take part in public duties	EPCA S 29
7 No period	To payments (established under new legislation) in the event of employer insolvency	EPCA S 122
8 No period	To receive an itemized pay statement	EPCA S 8
9 4 weeks	To guarantee payments for lay off	EPCA S 12
10 4 weeks	To payments in event of medical suspension	EPCA S 19
11 4 weeks	Not to be dismissed because of a medical suspension.	EPCA S 64
12 4 weeks	To receive the notice prescribed by Statute as a minimum.	EPCA S 49
13 Within 13 weeks	To receive written statement of terms and conditions of employment. (If then changed, within four weeks).	EPCA S 1
14 52 weeks	Not to be unfairly dismissed for other reason (104 wks: where 20 employees or less in firm).	EPCA Ss 64 & 64A (Emp Act S 8)
15 52 weeks	To request and receive a written statement of reasons for any dismissal	EPCA S 53
16 2 years after age of 18 years	To redundancy payment in event of dismissal by reason of redundancy	EPCA S 81
17 2 years as above	To time off to look for work or to arrange retraining	EPCA S 31
18 2 years measured back from beginning	To maternity pay (six weeks) in event of pregnancy	EPCA S 34
19 of 11th week of confinement	To return to work after pregnancy	EPCA S 45

ployers bemoan the changing scene it is because they have not yet taken cognizance of the new style of employment law which is applicable to the last quarter of the present century. Industrial dinosaurs die hard (Selwyn's *Law of Employment*, Butterworth, 1976).

94

They begin the dismemberment of the older common law conception of respective rights and duties read into employment contracts through the doctrine of implied terms. We will have occasion to refer to various aspects of the change below (*see*, for example, pp 97–125, 239–61, and 434–49, where rights in respect of interruptions and termination of contracts, performance control and discipline, and association, are reviewed respectively). These are usually held to be the significant changes in so far as they restrict the employer's prerogatives and rights to control (both at work and by dismissing employees) and set up a countervailing power to his in the forms of protected trade unions and increased job security.

Further reading
On the current general requirement of 'the law' in relation to contracts, see Hepple and O'Higgins (1979); an alternative is Rideout (1979)

A more historical perspective is provided by Wedderburn (1971).

On the principles involved in contract see Kahn-Freund (1977) and Fox (1974)

Textbooks such as Hepple and O'Higgins (1979) or McGlynn (1977), summarize the position arrived at by the date of writing, but because of the newness of this field, they can go out of date very quickly on Court and tribunal interpretations. What might prove to be major and important decisions are often reported in non-law journals, as for example, by *Personnel Management* from time to time, but particular circumstances may require more detailed knowledge possessed only by legal practitioners or by managers who deliberately seek to keep up to date. It is therefore necessary for those in management confronted with the necessity of taking decisions in these matters to keep up to date with the main decisions taken by tribunals in their interpretation of what is requisite under statutory or delegated legislation. There are four main series of law reports in the employment field: Knight's Industrial Reports (now called Managerial Law), Industrial Tribunal Reports (HMSO), Industrial Court Reports (now called Industrial Cases Reports) and Industrial Relations Law Reports. Periodicals of relevance are *Industrial Law Journal, Industrial Relations Review and Report, Industrial Relations Legal Information Bulletin* and *Incomes Data Briefs*. The Department of Employment Gazette is the most useful source of statistical data on the use of and outcomes from cases before the industrial tribunals, information relevant to the assessment of the degrees of risk involved, either that such litigation will be employed or that penalties of certain types will be applied.

5 The law and contract termination

The power to terminate contracts

People do not enjoy a right to work in this country, in spite of the agitation to establish such a right in recent years. A right to work would require that anyone desirous of working could *demand* work from someone. Given our industrial structure this would mean that the demand would be made upon the 'employer'. If the one secured a right, the other would be placed under a duty to satisfy the demand. This is not yet the case. The assumption that employment is governed by a contract freely and voluntarily entered into remains operative. A major consequence which follows from the assumption that the establishment of the contract is free is that its determination must also be 'free' in order that the first principle will be upheld.

Both parties are thus able to end the relationship voluntarily and basically the only control upon this process is that 'due notice' shall be given to the other party. This rests upon the same assumption of equality between the parties as that which is assumed to exist in establishing the contract; but here again actual operation is affected by the greater capacity of the employer to bear the consequences of termination (cf above, p 71). It is this which has in the past, and currently to a lesser extent, supported the prerogative power of the employer or of managers in the employment relationship, as it also supports the 'freedom' of the worker from the kind of bondage associated with feudal structures.

The legislation which has been enacted during the 1960s and 1970s (see above, p 70) has, however, affected this position in a significant way. It has not provided the worker with a right to work in the sense of a right to establish contracts of employment. It has merely sought to outlaw certain kinds of discrimination as being immoral and to ensure that the worker is made more aware of what terms and conditions of employment he or she has agreed to. Nor has it provided that the employer shall not 'voluntarily' terminate contracts of employment when it suits him. What it has done is outlaw some of the reasons and some of the methods or processes which he might use to justify or effect termination.

It is, however, this aspect of the legislation which has effected most change from the previous position and which has caused most of the consternation amongst employers as well as the activity to review policies and practices in the employment area. It affects directly the prerogative power of the employer and enforces a change in the basis on which the employer may seek to 'discipline' employees (*see* below, pp 239–61) simply because a restriction of any sort on the employer's power to dismiss necessarily restricts his power to discipline in any way short of using this ultimate sanction.

In spite of this, the employer still has the right to expect an employee to be able and willing to serve in the terms of his or her contract, however this may be expressed in it (cf Rideout, 1979, pp 34–43). The law now, however, permits the employee to interrupt the continuity of his or her willingness to serve, without it being taken as sufficient grounds for dismissal. It also requires that the employer shall have good and sufficient reason for terminating the employment contract, even with notice, and shall also effect termination, even on sufficient ground, by a process which will give due regard to the principles of natural justice.

Failure to comply with these new requirements attracts penalties which are usually in the form of a compensation payment to the employee disadvantaged by the failure. It is the principle of visiting such penalties which provides the grounds for a change in the basis of policy from that which regarded employees as a variable direct cost to one in which employees are treated more as assets (*see* below, pp. 556–58).

In the following pages, we review the requirements of law in respect of:

(a) interruptions of the continuity of the contract of employment
(b) reasons for and methods of terminating employment contracts by the employer.

This is followed by a review of the penalties which apply in respect of established breach of the requirements, both as to their principle and their actual incidence.

Interruption of the contract of employment
The duty of the employee to make himself available for work when required by the employer is modified in the EP(C) Act in two main ways, both of which allow the individual employee in defined cir-

cumstances to interrupt the continuity of the contract without breaking it, and without thereby giving the employer the opportunity to determine the contract for good cause. Previously interruption was justifiable only on medical or trade dispute grounds, and/or with the prior permission of the employer. Now it is extended to cover, specifically, females who become pregnant whilst in employment and a number of other categories of employee who are given a right to time off from work for certain categories of activity. The employer is likely in these circumstances to develop new codes, in consultation with the trade unions, to govern the administration of these new rights.

Maternity pay and leave

The Employment Protection (Consolidation) Act 1978, as amended by the Employment Act 1980, makes it possible for a woman to interrupt her contract of employment when she becomes pregnant. She acquires three rights, to maternity pay, to maternity leave and to return to work after confinement, provided she has two years' service at the effective date and meets certain other conditions in respect of the second and third of them.

(a) Maternity pay is paid by the employer for a total of six weeks of absence (provided it falls after the beginning of the 11th week before the expected confinement). It is to be calculated at the rate of 90 per cent of a normal week's pay less the statutory maternity allowance (regardless of whether the woman is entitled to it) but is not to be paid *additionally* to any contractual remuneration due to her from the employer (EP(C) Act, 1978, Ss 33–5). It may be paid as a lump sum at the beginning of the 11th week prior to the expected confinement, or at the normal payment interval over the six weeks following (but not at the end of the period) and may be taxed in the usual way. The employer may recover the whole of the sum paid from the Maternity Fund financed from employers' National Insurance contributions; in appropriate circumstances, the employee herself may be paid directly from this Fund (EP(C) Act, 1978, Ss 37–42).

In order to qualify for maternity pay, the woman must meet certain requirements:

(i) that she has not resigned before the 11th week before the expected confinement (so that it will apply even if she is fairly dismissed before this date, and even if she is not actually at work immediately before the 11th week, provided that the contract of employment remains in existence)

(ii) that she has two years' continuous employment calculated back from the beginning of the 11th week before the expected date of confinement (with the same qualification as in brackets above)

(iii) that she notifies the employer orally (or in writing if requested to do so by the employer) at least three weeks before her absence begins (or as soon thereafter as is practicable if that is not reasonably practicable) that she will be absent because of pregnancy or confinement. The employer may request her to produce for inspection a certificate from a registered medical practitioner or registered midwife which will state the expected week of confinement, and the woman loses her rights to both pay and return if she does not comply with this request (EP(C) Act, 1978, S 33).

(b) A woman's entitlement to maternity leave is established by two stipulations:

(i) that dismissal will be treated as 'unfair' (*see* below pp 114–19) if the only or principal reason for it is that she is pregnant 'or any other reason connected with her pregnancy' unless in addition either the pregnancy has rendered her incapable of adequately doing the work she is employed to do or her continued employment in that work would contravene a duty or restriction imposed by or under any enactment (EP(C) Act, 1978, S 60). (For example, pregnant women are subject to a restriction of this sort in the Ionizing Radiations (Unsealed Radioactive Substances) Regulations, 1968). The 'any other reason' could cover a wide range of situations both before and after confinement and could be medical or social (cf. Hepple, 1979, pp 262–3).

(ii) that, provided she complies with the conditions laid down, she has a right to return to work after the period of confinement (EP(C) Act, 1978, S 33).

Placing these two together allows the concept of maternity leave to be conceived as a right. The woman must absent herself from work for the confinement, but she has a right to return to work and if she is dismissed because of her pregnancy alone that dismissal will be *prima facie* unfair and thereby compensatable.

This therefore creates the presumption that the woman who becomes pregnant will be allowed to continue working until her confinement, at her own job or in a suitable alternative job within the employment unit (EP(C) Act, 1978, S 60). If, in addition, she then seeks to return to work after the confinement, and does so in compliance with the requirements of the Act as to the actions to be taken to exercise this right, the period of absence may be treated as leave for maternity purposes, totalling 40 weeks (or 44 weeks with postponement). For purposes of calculating seniority, pension rights and other rights stemming from the employment itself, this period is treated as 'leave' and all of these begin to accumulate again from the date of resumption of work (EP(C) Act, 1978, S 45). (This is not the case with statutory entitlements—*see* below, p 102.)

Furthermore, if a suitable vacancy exists in the employment unit, the employer might be under a duty to offer such a vacancy to a pregnant employee or face a claim for unfair dismissal. The Act lays down criteria of suitability and, on the face of it, many vacancies might theoretically fall within this definition. This also applies where a pregnant woman is not permitted to return after maternity leave. She could similarly claim unfair dismissal.

The only real defence open to the employer here is that the job has become redundant in the interval but this will patently not be so if he hires a permanent or temporary replacement for her. The question of a suitable vacancy is relevant here as in the case of a woman becoming pregnant but, in the case of a woman returning, the employer has a duty to seek a suitable vacancy, not only in his own enterprise, but in associated employers' enterprises as well. Even if a suitable vacancy does not exist, it may be preferable, in the face of a potential claim to an industrial tribunal, to offer the returning employee the least unsuitable vacancy and allow her to make the decision, rather than the employer doing so (see Rubenstein 1975).

(c) A woman has a right to return to work with her original (or a successor) employer, at any time before the end of the period of 29 weeks calculated from the beginning of the week in which the confinement falls, unless redundancy intervenes (cf Hepple, 1979, p 264). The right is conditional upon the woman giving the same notice as is required for maternity pay and supplying the additional information that she intends to return to work and the date of the expected or actual confinement. Not earlier than 49 days after the beginning of week of the expected (or actual) confinement, the employer may also request written confirmation of her intention to return (provided that this is done in writing and informs her of the effect of the Section of the Act which restricts her right to return if she does not reply. The woman will lose her right to return 'unless she gives that confirmation within fourteen days of receiving the request or, if that is not reasonably practicable, as soon as reasonably practicable' (Employment Act, 1980, S 11).

In order to exercise her right, the woman must give written notice of her proposal to return to work on a particular day (the 'notified day of return') at least 21 days before that date. Both the employer and the employee may postpone the date of recommencement for four weeks, the employer for any reason and the woman for medical reasons. This in effect allows a basic 40 weeks of maternity leave which can be increased by postponement to 44 weeks.

The original right in the EP Act, 1975 (S 45) was to return to the job 'in which she was employed under the original contract of employment and on terms and conditions not less favourable than those which would have been applicable to her if she had not been so absent' (S 45 (1)). In the original, 'job' is defined strictly to mean the 'nature of the work which she is employed to do in accordance with her contract and the capacity and place in which she is so employed' (S 153), and this imputed a strict interpretation, tending to confine 'the job' to which the woman returned as 'the old job'.

Also in the original Act, 'terms and conditions not less favourable' is defined to mean 'as regards seniority, pension rights and other similar rights, that the period or periods of employment prior to the employee's absence shall be regarded as continuous with her employment following that absence' (EP(C) Act, 1978, S 45). In effect, therefore, the period of absence is not to count towards these although employment is assumed continuous, but for other purposes (redundancy, notice, unfair dismissal award entitlements) however, the absence does count as continuous employment.

This has, however, been 'softened' by the provisions of the Employment Act 1980, which provides that where it is not reasonably practicable for a reason other than redundancy to permit the woman to return to her actual old job, the employer (or successor employer) may avoid a dismissal claim (by reason of 'not permitting to return') on two conditions:

if he or an associated employer offers suitable and appropriate work under a contract whose terms and conditions are not *sub-*

stantially less favourable than those stipulated in Section 45 (1) of the EP(C) Act (above), *and*
if she either accepts or unreasonably refuses the offer.

It remains for the employer to show that the circumstances did not permit the offer of the 'old job back' and that the job offered was suitable, appropriate and subject to *substantially* the same terms and conditions. In the normal case, therefore, the stipulations of the original Act will apply, but there is now an escape route, both for the small employer (with less than six employees) who has to show only that he cannot offer any employment within the conditions laid down, and generally.

'Time off'
Legislation now provides that in certain circumstances, employees shall have a right to reasonable time off from work. This constitutes time off, not necessarily with pay, to engage in activities which are considered to be so necessary or desirable that the employee's engagement in them should not risk breach or interruption of the employment contract.

The right applies in the following circumstances; to pregnant women who have been professionally advised to attend during working hours any place for the purpose of receiving ante-natal care; any employee for purposes of performing certain public duties; any employee under notice of dismissal by reason of redundancy for purposes of finding alternative employment and/or arranging training; any employee who is a union member for purposes of taking part in certain union activities, and employees who are also union officials or representatives for purposes of engaging in industrial relations activities or of undergoing training for them. In each case, there are conditions which apply distinctly to each category, although only in the case of the employee under notice of dismissal is there a service qualification (two years in that case) (EP(C) Act, 1980, S 31).

(a) The pregnant woman advised to secure ante-natal care has the right not to be unreasonably refused time off during her working hours to keep the appointment, and to remuneration at her appropriate hourly rate for the time off (Employment Act, 1980, S 13). In order to secure this right, the woman must, if requested by the employer to do so, produce a certification from a registered medical practitioner, midwife or health visitor stating that she is pregnant. She must also produce, if requested, an appointment card or some other document showing that an appointment has been made, except when the request is for time off for a first appointment. If the employer refuses unreasonably or if he fails to pay the appropriate amount when time off is permitted, the woman may complain to an industrial tribunal within the usual three month period from the date of the appointment. The tribunal on finding the complaint substantiated may order the employer to pay the amount which would have been due had he not refused time off, or the amount due for the time taken off (EP(C) Act, 1978, S 31A, amended).

(b) The employee who is a justice of the peace, a member of a local authority, a member of any statutory tribunal, a member of an area or regional health authority (in England and Wales) or a Health Board (in Scotland), a member of a governing or managing body of an educational establishment or a member of a water authority, has a right *vis à vis* his employer to take time off for purposes of performing the duties of the office or a member. The employer is not, however, obliged to pay the employee for time off for these duties. The Act offers guidance on what would be considered a reasonable amount and frequency of time off for these purposes. What is reasonable, it is suggested, should have regard to the time required to perform the duties in general and on a particular occasion, the time the individual has already been permitted for this and trade union related purposes (*see* below, pp 105–6) the circumstances of the employer's business and the effect of the employee's absence upon the running of it (EP(C) Act 1978, S 29). Failure on the part of the employer to permit time off under this head, could give rise to a complaint to an industrial tribunal, which has power to make a declaration as to the facts and to award such compensation as it considers just and equitable in all the circumstances (EP(C) Act, 1978, S 30).

(c) The employee under notice of dismissal for redundancy, provided he has two years continuous employment with the employer, has a right to reasonable time off before the expiry of his notice at his appropriate hourly rate of payment to seek other employment or to make arrangements for training to fit himself for another job (although not to undergo it). Refusal to allow time off for these purposes may lead to a complaint to an industrial tribunal which has the power to order the employer to pay up to two-fifths of a week's pay appropriate to that employee (over and above any other contractual remuneration) if it finds the complaint substantiated (EP(C) Act, 1978, S 31).

The other two categories are related to trade union and industrial relations activities and are part of the 'drive' to improve industrial relations as much as to any concern simply to free employees from the duty to be ready and willing to serve the employer.

(d) Any member of a union recognized by the employer has a right to reasonable time off to take part in union activities or to represent the union, but the Act imposes no obligation on the employer to pay for time off for these purposes (EP(C) Act, 1978, S 28).

(e) Shop stewards and other officials of a trade union recognized by the employer for collective bargaining purposes have a right to be permitted reasonable time off *with pay* during working hours to enable them to carry out their duties as officials which are concerned with industrial relations affecting their employer (or associated employer) and to enable them to undergo industrial relations training (EP(C) Act, 1978, S 27).

As it was enjoined to do by S 6 of the Employment Protection Act, the ACAS has produced a Code of Practice which from 1978 has covered time off for lay officials and trade union members.

This code suggests that 'members should be permitted to take time off during working hours for such purposes as voting in union elections' . . . and to attend union meetings at times to be agreed which would involve least disruption of production (eg at the end of a working shift). In any agreement drawn up to guide such activities, provision might be made for time off for other activities where member participation might lead to the development of 'sound union structure at the workplace and effective communication and collective representation' (Code, p 3). Lay officials of the union are recognized to be in a special position in relation to trade union activities. The Code therefore suggests that they might need more time off for attendance at union policy-making meetings and conferences and at other meetings of external bodies where the official may represent the union. Guidance on both the time to be allowed off and on the kinds of activities which might be accorded relevance should also be the subject of agreement.

Otherwise, the Code suggests that officials should be allowed time off with pay, for industrial relations purposes, to engage in:

(a) collective bargaining with any level of management
(b) meetings with members called to inform them of the outcomes of negotiations or consultations with management
(c) meetings with other lay officials or full-time union officers to discuss business of an industrial relations nature

(d) interviews with and on behalf of union members on grievance and disciplinary matters
(e) appearing on behalf of constituents before an outside body on industrial relations matters
(f) explanations to new employees of the role of the union in the workplace industrial relations structure (Code, p 2).

In addition, given that the official needs training to perform his duties more satisfactorily, he should, it is recommended, be allowed time off with pay for initial basic training, arranged as soon after appointment as possible, and for subsequent training in specialist aspects of industrial relations where his duties change or where the situation changes to create a new need.

The courses of training should be relevant to the industrial relations functions performed, and should be approved by the Trades Union Congress or the official's own union, but each course will probably have to be considered on its merits because of the variations in need which are likely to exist. It is recommended that management and the representatives of recognized unions should draw up their own Codes to guide decisions and conduct, in particular to cover the problems likely to arise where the activities in which the official wishes to engage might be construed as both industrial relations and trade union activity.

Termination of the employment contract

The personnel practitioner's concern with the termination of the employment contract almost ante-dates the inception of the role itself. Early welfare workers concerned with the unemployed were scarcely to be distinguished from their colleagues 'brought into' companies to work with the employed. Those engaged to act as the Jimminy Crickets to the corporate Pinnochios were rarely involved directly in the firing process, which was reserved to the line management (as part of its 'prerogative') until much later. But they became more involved in the process as time passed and gradually came to participate in the formation of policy relating to termination, even before the legislation of the early 1970s compelled greater corporate attention to the question, as a matter of morality.

The personnel practitioners had, by this time, come to play a part in the development of practice and policy by way of demonstrating the economy of consistency in hiring and firing. Through the development of records and their (less frequent) analysis, they were enabled to show how much existing hiring and firing practices

106

were costing the organization. This was certainly a matter of concern in the generally tighter labour markets of the post-war period. By demonstrating the high cost of indiscriminate hiring and firing in relation to more positive (and more consistent) policies, they were put in the position where they could support arguments about the moral questions with hard 'practical' evidence. By the time that legislation imposed a specific price tag on terminations defined as 'unfair', therefore, personnel departments were already located in the right area to assist their organizations to cope with the new element.

When legislation, initially and indirectly in the Redundancy Payments Act 1965 and subsequently directly in the Industrial Relations Act 1971 (and its successors) made more coherent employment policies very highly desirable if not absolutely necessary, the personnel departments were well placed to advise on their content and form.

What was changed by the legislation was the degree of restriction placed upon the employer's unilateral exercise of power to determine the contract. On the same common law assumptions as were noted above (pp 71–73) either party to an employment contract could bring it to an end with 'due notice' (the notice expressed or implied in the contract itself) regardless of whether the 'reason' for so doing (ie the 'cause' in legal language) was a good one or not. The 'other party' had no recourse in law, unless the party determining the contract failed to honour the terms of the contract themselves (eg by failing to give due notice) when a remedy might be sought through the courts for 'wrongful dismissal'. For the same reasons as those above (pp 71–73) this tended to act 'inequitably' against the employee and it was this element of inequity which the legislation sought to redress.

This was attempted by creating the new concept of unfair dismissal, distinct from wrongful dismissal and by providing additional remedies for the employee to be administered by the industrial tribunals (ITs). What this change emphasizes is that termination of an employment contract by an employer must not only meet the requirements of the contract terms (eg as regards notice) but must also rest upon an adequate reason or 'cause' if it is to be regarded as 'fair'. It is important to note in this connection that this concept of 'cause' relates to the employer's unilateral exercise of his option to determine the contract: it does not introduce the concept of 'cause' *for the first time* since 'cause' has always lain behind the process whereby a contract might be terminated for reasons connected with external events or the actions of third parties.

In the development of policy and practice in this area, therefore, there are two major factors to be considered in relation to termination or dismissal, notice and cause, *both* of which have been affected by legislation in recent years.

Restrictions on 'due notice'

It has always been a requirement that contracts should (in the absence of flagrant breach by one party) be terminated with notice, the amount 'due' being established in the contract itself or by reference to what is customary in the situation. Recent legislation has not 'created' this principle, but it has sought to change the period of notice 'due' as a minimum in certain defined circumstances, regardless of what might be express or customary. The change was first introduced in the Contracts of Employment Act 1963, and is now enshrined in the EP(C) Act 1978, S 49. Its effect is to establish that the notice in an individual contract of employment shall be deemed to have been fixed by the parties at the minimum levels in the statute in the absence of express or customary provision for periods longer than these.

The general provision

First, an employee who has been in continuous employment for four weeks or more with one employer (or an associated employer) is required to give not less than one week's notice of his intention to terminate his contract. His actual contract of employment may of course require him to give more notice.

Secondly, an employer is required to give anyone who has been in continuous employment with him (or an associated employer) for four weeks or more not less than one week's notice (unless the individual is hired for a task which is not expected to last for more than 12 weeks and does not in fact do so), the week being counted (in this as in the previous case) from the day following the giving of the notice, subject to the stipulations of the contract of employment itself. This minimum applies to those employed for up to two years. Thereafter, the employee is entitled to one week's notice for each year of service up to a maximum of 12 weeks after 12 years' service.

Thirdly, these requirements now apply to employees working 16 hours per week or more; to employees working 16 hours per week or more but whose contracted hours are varied downwards to more than eight hours (until the reduced hours have been worked for 26 weeks or more); and to employees who work between eight and 16 hours per week after five years' (260 weeks) continuous employment.

Fourthly, where an employee is dismissed without notice or with inadequate notice, for purposes of calculating qualifying period of service and any unfair dismissal compensation, his service will be taken as running to the date on which the statutorily required notice would have expired. (This aims to stop employers dismissing employees before they qualify (at 52 weeks) to bring an unfair dismissal complaint.)

Fifthly, unfair dismissal complaints may be brought before a tribunal during the notice period. (This permits the tribunal to adjudicate before notice will expire in some cases, thus allowing an adjudication in well-founded complaints that notice be withdrawn, rather than that the employee be reinstated.)

Rights to waive notice and to accept payment in lieu of notice are not affected; the definition of continuous employment and methods of calculating it are contained in Schedule 13 of the 1978 Act, as amended.

The giving of due notice thus remains a necessary protection of the parties seeking to determine a contract of employment, but what constitutes due notice is defined as to its minimum by legislation for certain categories of employee identified above. The terms of an individual contract may still provide for longer periods of notice than those stipulated above, and these will remain enforceable (see Hill v C A Parsons and Co Ltd (1972) Ch 305; (1971) 3 All ER, 1345).

Special provisions

Certain special provisions in respect of notice apply to circumstances of redundancy or of a proposal to change the work of an individual employee.

In the case of redundancy, the EP Act 1975, S 99, provides that trade unions shall be informed of *any* redundancy at the 'earliest opportunity' and that consultation be initiated with the recognized independent trade unions at this time—on pain of a tribunal award of at least 28 days' pay to affected employees if this is not done.

Where an employer proposes to make 10 or more workers redundant he is required to consult representatives of recognized unions before implementing his proposals. (This applies regardless of whether the 10 or more work long or short hours, have long or short service (except the 12 weeks' category) or are members or non-members of the recognized union.) If consultation is not so initiated by the employer, the *trade union* may seek and secure a protective award from a tribunal. This requires the employer to pay the employees whom it was proposed to make redundant for a stipulated period at the discretion of the tribunal, and up to a maximum of 90 days' pay where the redundancy involved 100 or more employees within a 90 day period, 30 days' pay where the redundancies involved 10 or more employees in a 30 day period, and 28 days' pay in any other case.

An individual covered by a protective award is entitled to the appropriate pay, and can bring a claim before an industrial tribunal to recover it, but such an award to an individual and any contractual payments or pay in lieu of notice falling within the protected period will go towards discharging the employer's obligations under the protective award.

It is required that consultations begin at 'the earliest opportunity' with the recognized trade union, and time periods are laid down: 10 or more employees affected in one establishment must produce consultation at least 30 days before the first proposed redundancy, and the employer must therefore consider what to do about notice to individuals.

The safest procedure would be to give notice to individuals and invite consultation at the time (where the notice period is long enough to require this) because consultation will either confirm the redundancy and its date (in which case the notice will stand and long delays will be avoided) or it will reject or postpone the redundancy (in which case the employer can offer to withdraw the notice, and thus offer a reasonable defence to any subsequent claim).

A further constraint on the giving and receiving of notice in connection with redundancy occurs in the Employment Protection (Consolidation) Act S 84 in the requirement that, when an employee is faced with redundancy and/or a revised contract of employment, he has a right to try any alternative employment offered for a fixed period of four weeks, without in anyway foregoing his or her rights to a redundancy payment if at the end of that four week trial period he decides that the new job is not for him. The offer of new work does not have to be in writing: when a job is changed, it will be deemed that the individual is dismissed (technically); but if the individual stays on the new job for a four week trial period, he will be deemed to have accepted the new job and the employer will be deemed to have accepted him in it.

The trial period is not a matter of choice or election: when an employee starts on a new or changed job, 'there shall be a trial period'. It will normally be of four weeks, but the parties can agree in writing that it will be longer and when it will end, if it is for the purpose of 'retraining the employee for employment' under his new contract. If the employee decides to terminate during the trial period, he will be held to have been dismissed from his previous job, not that he had resigned from the new job. If the employee does not make out on the new job, the employer may also cut his losses, determine the contract and make redundancy payment, but in this case the reason must be connected with the new job (and not, for example, gross misconduct).

Legislative restrictions on 'sufficient reason'
This brings us to the question of what might constitute a sufficient reason for determining a contract of employment. Giving notice is a useful protection against possible common law actions but sometimes, as with gross misconduct, it may not be absolutely necessary.

Notice remains a useful defence in those situations where, however, the contract is brought to an end because it is 'frustrated' by external events, or by actions of third parties, which render it impossible to continue in the terms of the contract.

The main categories of example of frustration in the employment context are:

(a) termination by death of either party (or the compulsory winding up of a company) and in some circumstances the dissolution of a partnership or the appointment of a receiver
(b) termination by change of circumstances brought about by enactment (as in the passage of a law making the performance of a contract unlawful)
(c) termination by events which make it physically impossible for the contract to be performed (as in the case of a natural disaster or of illness of the employee which lasts or is likely to last for a long time)
(d) termination by a change which makes the performance of the contract no longer viable in commercial terms.

All of these have some relevance to the termination of employment contracts. The first is somewhat circumscribed by recent legislation in respect of employee rights related to the circumstances of insolvency and termination of partnerships, but this is only likely to affect small businesses, and the fourth is marginally affected by similar legislation.

The main provisions in this area (Ss 121–7 of the EP(C) Act) merely seek to protect the individual's entitlement to holiday pay, ordinary pay (up to eight weeks) and including pay relating to a period of notice, any payments for time off or due under the provisions for guarantee payments, remuneration for suspension on

111

medical grounds, or under a protective award, and any basic award for compensation for unfair dismissal, by making it possible for the Secretary of State to pay the amount he considers due from the Redundancy Fund, in circumstances where, for reasons of insolvency, that amount is not paid by the employer.

The third example, however, has a much wider domain than the others, and occurs particularly in connection with the illness of an employee as an 'external event' outside the volition of either party. The question comes to be whether illness can be taken as having frustrated the performance of the contract of employment to an extent sufficient to provide grounds for treating it as determined. It remains open to the employer to determine the contract, unilaterally, whether there is frustration or not, provided that he considers that he has grounds (cause) for so doing which would be regarded as fair, and provided that he gives the notice provided for in the contract.

In Marshall v Harland and Woollf Ltd (1972) 1 WLR, p 899), however, Sir John Donaldson provided guidance as to the factors which had to be taken into account in determining this question:

(a) *The terms of the contract, including the provisions as to sickness pay.* The whole basis of weekly employment may be destroyed more quickly than that of monthly employment and that in turn more quickly than annual employment. When the contract provides for sick pay, it is plain that the contract cannot be frustrated so long as the employee returns to work, or appears likely to return to work, within the period during which such sick pay is payable. But the converse is not necessarily true, for the right to sick pay may expire before the incapacity has gone on, or appears likely to go on, for so long as to make a return to work impossible or radically different from the obligations undertaken under the contract of employment.

(b) *How long the employment was likely to last in the absence of sickness.* The relationship is less likely to survive if the employment was inherently temporary in its nature or for the duration of a particular job, than if it was expected to be long term or even lifelong.

(c) *The nature of the employment.* Where the employee is one of many in the same category, the relationship is more likely to survive the period of incapacity than if he occupies a key post which must be filled on a permanent basis if his absence is prolonged.

(d) *The nature of the illness or injury and how long it has already continued and the prospects of recovery.* The greater the degree of incapacity and the longer the period over which it has persisted and is likely to persist, the more likely it is that the relationship has been destroyed.

(e) *The period of past employment.* A relationship which is of long standing is not so easily destroyed as one which has but a short history. This is good sense and, we think, no less good law, even if it involves some implied and scarcely detectable change in the contract of employment year by year as the duration of the relationship lengthens. The legal basis is that over a long period of service the parties must be assumed to have contemplated a longer period or periods of sickness than over a shorter period.

These factors are interrelated and cumulative, but are not necessarily exhaustive of those which have to be taken into account. The question is and remains: was the employee's incapacity, looked at before the purported dismissal, of such nature, or did it appear likely to continue for such a period, that further performance of his obligations in the future would either be impossible or would be a thing radically different from that undertaken by him and accepted by the employer under the agreed terms of his employment? Any other factors which bear on this issue must also be considered.

This offers sound guidance to the employer on the handling of long-term sickness, irrespective of whether he intends to rely upon 'frustration' or dismissal for cause, in bringing the contract to an end. It provides a judicial summary of the kinds of factors which the employer should take into account in coming to a decision. It does not, however, fully indicate the procedures desirable should the intention be to dismiss for cause.

In this connection, as in a number of others discussed below, the main principle to be followed is that which establishes two way communication between the employer and the employee. In this case this comes under the heading of 'consultation', where in others it is associated with 'warning'. Both indicate that the job is in jeopardy and allow the individual a chance to state his/her case and/or change the situation.

In sickness cases, consultation is emphasized in the leading case (*East Lindsey District Council v Daubney* (1977) IRLR 181), but a later case suggests that it is only required to ensure that proper consideration can be given to all the facts and factors (as in the quotation above) and not necessarily if it is unlikely to make any difference (*Taylorplan Catering (Scotland) Ltd v McInally* (1980) IRLR 53). The onus remains, however, upon the employer to show that the procedure followed did meet all the usual criteria of fairness.

Thus, the simplest course for the employer in most circumstances is to treat long term sickness as constituting potentially a sufficient 'cause' for dismissal, and to give it consideration in essentially the same fashion as any other 'cause'. This means paying main attention to the following of a proper procedure to ensure that he (the employer) takes adequate account of all the facts and factors, including the views of the person affected, in reaching the decision.

Dismissal for cause

The elevation of the concept of 'cause' in importance in the dismissal process is a relatively recent development. Until 1965, the law did not require the employer to have or to give a reason for dismissing an employee. Trade union pressure may have altered that position in fact in those situations where the unions had acquired sufficient strength. Otherwise, unless the employment contract made explicit stipulations about reason, or 'cause', for dismissal, the law would simply assume that it had been a proper one.

In the 1960s public policy changed, and implicitly recognized that the proper dismissal of an employee might nevertheless occasion him or her some loss of legitimate expectations and therefore ought to be compensated for. This principle was first applied to redundancy dismissal. The Redundancy Payments Act required the employer to provide additional compensation to the redundant employee for the loss of 'accrued property rights in the employment' since the reason for termination is not the fault of the employee. He is therefore entitled to notice, or to payment in lieu of notice; and although he may be fairly and correctly dismissed for this reason, the law now says that he should also receive a certain amount of monetary compensation over and above his notice to compensate him for such loss of seniority and similar rights and privileges as he might have acquired in his employment. This compensation is to be worked out on the basis of the time he has been in the employment and of his age, and at the maximum would amount to 30 weeks' pay (at weekly rates up to a maximum of £130) for 20 or more years' service over the age of 41 years.

In more recent years statutes have introduced the concept of unfair dismissal, by which it is intended to establish that the individual employee has a right to continue in his employment unless and until there is a good reason for its termination which does not depend upon an arbitrary exercise of private power by the employer. The law has intervened to require (a) that there should be an identifiable reason for termination, (b) that that reason should be sufficient to make it 'fair' (as defined), and (c) that it should be communicated to the employee at his request. In 1965, the Redundancy Payments Act established the presumption that every dismissed employee would be regarded as having been dismissed by reason of redundancy (and therefore entitled to redundancy compensation in addition to due notice unless the employer established that the reason was other than this). In 1971, the Industrial Relations Act established the concept of unfair dismissal and placed the onus of proof on the employer to show:

1 That the main or only reason for dismissal was a fair one by virtue of its being:

   (a) related to the capability or qualifications of the employee for performing work of a kind which he was employed by the employer to do, or
   (b) related to the conduct of the employee, or
   (c) that the employee was redundant, or
   (d) that the employee could not continue in work without causing either the employer or the employee to contravene a legal duty or restriction.

2 That he (the employer) had acted reasonably in treating that reason as sufficient to justify dismissal
3 That the decision to dismiss was taken on the substantial merits of the case and was equitable in its consequences.

This concept, and the right of the individual not to be unfairly dismissed, has been reinstated in the Trade Union and Labour Relations Acts 1974–76 and extended in the Employment Protection Act, 1975. In particular, an employee who has 26 weeks' continuous service with an employer may now demand a written statement of the reasons for his dismissal, and the employer is required to accede to the request within two weeks, on pain of having the tribunal award the employee a sum equivalent to two weeks' pay if it finds the complaint justified. This stipulation (now contained in S 53 of the EP(C) Act, 1978) was and is designed to help the dismissed employee determine whether he has been fairly or unfairly dismissed, and whether he therefore has a complaint which could be put to the tribunal. Thus, in 10 years, Statute law has changed the position from one in which the employer need never give reasons for dismissal to one in which written reasons must be supplied on request.

The unfair dismissal concept

Essentially, what makes a dismissal unfair is the exercise of the employer's power to determine the contract in either an arbitrary or a discriminatory fashion. Given the existence of good reasons for terminating an individual's employment (listed above), the employer would still be open to an action for unfair dismissal before a tribunal if he showed discrimination in selecting employees for dismissal.

Where the main or only reason for dismissal relates to the employee's capability (assessed by reference to skill, aptitude, health or any other physical or mental quality) or qualifications (represented by degrees, diplomas or other academic, technical or professional qualifications and/or experience relevant to the position held) the dismissal might still be unfair if comparable employees were treated differently, or if it could be sustained that the assessment was unreasonable. In the first category, it will probably be necessary to ensure that, for example, two employees with similar health or absence records are not treated differently with respect to termination; in the second, that a decision to dismiss for incompetence is not taken suddenly after many years of successful performance of the job. The greater cost of dismissing unsatisfactory employees must therefore focus attention on the improvement of selection and appraisal procedures and will probably make the need to reduce the well known tendency to leniency in most control arrangements in employment more urgent, if only to establish a foundation of consistency in treatment of employees.

Closely analogous to this, in some ways, is the situation when a woman in employment becomes pregnant. It will be fair to dismiss such a person if, before the effective termination date (ie the end of the twelfth week before the expected confinement) she is or must become incapable of performing the work she is employed to do; but it will become unfair if the employer fails to offer her the alternative of any suitable vacancy that may exist. Similarly, it will be fair not to offer re-engagement after maternity leave if in the meantime her job has become redundant (in which case she would qualify for redundancy compensation) but unfair if the employer did not offer re-engagement to perform suitable and appropriate work, at the same place and in a similar capacity and on similar terms and conditions, when a suitable vacancy existed in his or an associated employer's establishment. The link between this situ-

116

ation and the general one in the preceding paragraph is that pregnancy is not to be regarded as a sufficient cause of dismissal in itself, since no fault lies with the employee in relation to her contract terms.

Where the main or the only reason for dismissal is misconduct on the part of the employee, there are circumstances in which dismissal without notice is justifiable. But given the new requirement of the EP(C) Act and the recommendation of the Code of Practice that disciplinary rules and penalties are communicated to employees, departure from these will probably provide grounds for a complaint to the tribunal. Action is therefore called for to ensure that the organization's disciplinary rules are adequate to sustain as fair, decisions to dismiss employees on the ground of misconduct. In any event, peremptory dismissal, possibly in the heat of the moment, is in future likely to be at a considerable discount (see below, pp 119–25)

Where the main reason for dismissal is redundancy, discrimination in selecting any individual employee for redundancy, where that redundancy 'applied equally to one or more other employees in the same undertaking who held positions similar to that held by him and who have not been dismissed by the employer' and where the selection was made 'in contravention of a customary arrangement or agreed procedure relating to redundancy' and there were no good reasons for departing from it, would also provide a presumption that the dismissal was still unfair, attracting a compensatory award over and above the basic award for loss of job property rights.

In some ways comparable to this concept of discrimination in selection for redundancy is the discrimination in offering re-engagement to employees dismissed in the course of a strike or a lock-out. This could also lead to a successful complaint that the dismissal was unfair, where dismissal by way of a lock-out or for taking part in a strike is itself fair. The question here turns on whether only some of the class of employees involved were dismissed, or alternatively only some of them were offered reinstatement or re-engagement at the end of the action. The reason for dismissal in the latter case is then substituted as the reason for non-re-engagement (EP(C) Act, Ss 62 and 67).

Where, in the exercise of private power to dismiss, the employer breaks these new rules of fairness, the aggrieved may not only seek redress through his trade union (which may pressure the employer to change his decision) but may also take a complaint to an industrial tribunal. That tribunal is empowered to grant various remedies if the complaint is found to be substantiated, and it is in

117

these remedies that the curb on the employer's use of his power lies.

Where the main or only reason relates to contravention of a legal duty or restriction (which is predictably likely to arise most often in connection with duties on both employer and employee under the Health and Safety at Work Act) discrimination will again make a fair dismissal unfair. The main problems here will be either to ensure that *all* employees who refuse or fail to discharge the duty to cooperate with the employer in health and safety matters are treated in the same way, or to determine where the dividing line shall be drawn amongst degrees of cooperation/non-cooperation to justify dismissal on one side of the line or some lesser penalty on the other. The safest course here is likely to be to draw up an establishment code in cooperation with the safety representatives and apply it firmly, but equitably, through a joint committee.

The 'inadmissible reason'

Just as there are some forms of conduct which can place the employee outside the protection of the notice provisions of his or her contract, so there are some 'reasons' which the employer might have for dismissing an employee which are regarded as more than usually abhorrent, and as meriting a higher penalty if used. These are generally reasons connected with the kinds of discrimination which have been outlawed by legislation in recent years (*see* above, pp 73–75).

This concept of 'inadmissible reason' was introduced by the Trade Union and Labour Relations Act 1974, and is continued in the EP(C) Act, S 58(5). In this context, the inadmissible reason for dismissal is that the employee acted or proposed to act on behalf of an independent trade union, either by becoming a member or by taking part in its activities (including a refusal to take any part in a trade union which is not independent).

Discrimination against individual employees for refusing to join or take part in a union which is not independent, for joining or acting within an independent trade union, provides a presumption of unfairness and, if the tribunal so found, would produce a special higher level of compensation award if the employer did not reinstate or re-employ. It is also inadmissible to select an employee for redundancy on those same grounds (EP(C) Act, S 59).

Where a union membership agreement exists with the employer which requires all employees of the class in question to belong to one or another independent trade union, dismissal of the employee for refusing to join, or continue in membership of one or other of these unions, will, however, be regarded as fair unless the individual can establish genuine objection on ground of religious belief to being a member of any trade union whatsoever.

Dismissal of a person on ground of race or sex also comes into this category of dismissal for 'inadmissible reason' and the higher rate of compensation would similarly apply (SDA, S 65 (1) (b); RRA, S 58; EP(C) Act, Ss 75 and 76).

Every employee has the right not to be dismissed for an inadmissable reason or for the main or principal reason that the individual is of one sex or race rather than another. Only some categories of employee have the right not to be unfairly dismissed, some being excluded by the nature of their employment and some by their age and service characteristics.

Those in the first category who are excluded are registered dock workers engaged in dock work (EP(C) Act, S 145), workers engaged in the shipping fleets on a profit-sharing contract (EP(C) Act, S 144), the members of the police and defence forces and those who, not being merchant seamen, normally work in accordance with their contracts outside Britain (EP(C) Act, S 141).

Those in the second category who are excluded include those working under a one-year fixed term contract in certain conditions (EP(C) Act, Sch 15 para 10(1); S 142), those who at effective date have reached the normal retiring age for the class of employee or the age of 65 (in the case of men) or of 60 (women), (EP(C) Act, S 64), those who are spouses of their employer (EP(C) Act, S 146) and those who have not at the date of dismissal been employed for 52 weeks or more (EP(C) Act, S 64) (or 104 weeks in cases where the employer (together with associated employers) did not employ more than 20 persons during the qualifying period, (Employment Act, 1980, S 8).

The remedies

Any judicial body (whether court or tribunal) which finds a complaint of wrongful/unfair dismissal well founded, faces a choice of remedy. This lies between taking action either to secure the future performance of the contract or to provide compensation for any loss arising from future non-performance. Each of these takes a number of specific forms.

Even before the concept of unfair dismissal was invented in recent legislation, an individual who considered himself to have been dismissed in breach of the contract terms could take action in the civil courts for 'wrongful' dismissal. The court was (and, indeed, still is) in a position to consider one of three remedies, if it found the complaint well-founded. The first two look towards securing the future performance of the contract, and the third towards establishing compensation for its non-performance.

The first is the granting of an injunction to restrain the employer from acting in the way proposed (eg to dismiss) and could only apply if the legal action was commenced before the employment actually terminated.

The second is the order of specific performance by which the court could require the employer to remedy the breach itself by reinstating or re-engaging the employee.

Neither of these has been used much in the present century, the courts being reluctant to make either of these kinds of order, on two grounds:

first, that it would be difficult to supervise the enforcement of such an order even if in the first case there was time within which to make it

secondly, that it would mean ordering that two persons should maintain a personal relationship in circumstances where one or other might not wish this. In the words of Lord Justice Fry in the case of *De Francesco v Varnham* (1890), 'I think the Courts are bound to be jealous, lest they should turn contracts of service into contracts of slavery'. More recently this provided the reasoning behind the decision in *Rex v National Arbitration Tribunal ex parte Crowther* (1948), in which it was held, that the National Arbitration Tribunal had no jurisdiction to make an award directing the reinstatement of certain workers. This principle is also followed in cases which appear before the Central Arbitration Committee, although single arbitrators *have* awarded reinstatement

the third remedy, an award of damages or compensation for such loss as the individual could be shown to have suffered as a result of the employer's action, has therefore been the most common remedy employed by the courts in wrongful dismissal cases. Such actions are rarely undertaken, however, because the basic principle used to calculate damages limits the award to the amount given by multiplying the notice period by the relevant wage or salary as a maximum. Set against the costs of the action itself, therefore, the likely outcome is likely to provide little real remedy to the aggrieved individual.

Against this background, the new legislation of the past two decades has generally sought to make it easier and cheaper to take complaints to a judicial body and to provide new and additional grounds for them. Nevertheless, the spirit of the common law principles remains even though the industrial tribunal is enjoined to place most emphasis upon specific performance of the contract, if the complainant wishes it, in those cases where a complaint is well-founded. The statute provides that the preferred remedy shall be, as appropriate to the circumstances,

(a) withdrawal of notice (if the complaint is presented and heard during the notice period), or
(b) reinstatement, if the tribunal considers this most appropriate, or
(c) re-engagement. (EP(C) Act, Ss 68–71)

On finding a complaint well-founded, the tribunal is enjoined to explain to the complainant 'what orders for reinstatement or re-engagement may be made . . . and in what circumstances they may be made' and to 'ask him whether he wishes the tribunal to make such an order'. If he expresses such a wish, the tribunal may then make such an order. The tribunal is required to consider reinstatement before considering re-engagement, if the employee wishes. It must also consider whether such an order would be practicable (from the employer's point of view) and just (from the employee's point of view) even in circumstances where the individual caused or contributed to some extent to the dismissal.

An order for reinstatement requires the employer to treat the employee as if he had never been dismissed, and will include specifications of:

(a) any amount payable to the employee in arrears of pay (including bonuses) for the period between termination and reinstatement
(b) any rights and privileges, including seniority and pension rights, which must be restored to the employee
(c) the date by which the order must be complied with.

Furthermore, if the employee would have benefited from an improvement in his terms and conditions of employment had he not been dismissed, the order will require that he receive those benefits as if he had not been dismissed.

An order for re-engagement is an order that the employee be engaged by the employer, a successor employer or an associated employer, in employment comparable to that from which he was dismissed or in other suitable employment. The order will specify the identity of the employer, the nature of the employment, the remuneration for it, any amount payable by the employer in arrears

121

of pay (including bonuses) for the period between date of termination and re-engagement, any rights and privileges which must be restored to the employee and the date by which the order must be complied with. Approximately the same considerations apply here as with the reinstatement orders, except that the latter must be considered first and that, in considering contributory fault, the tribunal must seek to provide re-engagement on terms 'which so far as is reasonably practicable (are) as favourable' as those contained in any order for reinstatement.

In the case of both reinstatement and re-engagement orders, the tribunal is required, in considering both what is practicable and the amount of compensation which might be paid, to disregard the fact that the employer may have hired a permanent replacement of the employee dismissed, unless the employer shows that it was not practicable for him to have the work done without hiring such a replacement. When reinstatement or re-engagement is ordered, the calculation of arrears of pay will take into account any payments made by the employer (whether in lieu of notice or *ex gratia*) or by another employer, in employment or social security benefit, together with any other such benefits as the tribunal think appropriate in the circumstances.

The preference expressed in the legislation thus comes close to overturning the common law reluctance to order two 'free' agents to continue a contractual relationship which one may not wish to continue. It does not actually do so, however, because the complainant must first assent to such an order being considered by the tribunal and then the defendant employer retains the option to refuse to comply with it. When this happens, all that he (the employer) will suffer is an order for somewhat higher compensation than would otherwise be the case, even where the tribunal has come to the conclusion that continued employment would be feasible as well as just and equitable in the circumstances.

Thus, where such an order is either not made or not (fully) complied with, the alternative remedy open to the tribunal is that of a financial award in compensation for the loss of the job.

Awards for dismissal
An employee who is dismissed for good cause and with notice has no redress against the employer and, except in the case of dismissal because of redundancy, can claim no compensation. In the case of redundancy, it is considered that because this is not the fault of the individual he or she should receive some compensation for the loss of the job and the loss of the rights which go with it and accumulate (usually) with service with an employment. What the redundant

employee is entitled to is an amount of compensation which is determined by the amount of his weekly pay (up to a limit of £130) multiplied by the number of years he has been continuously employed weighted according to his age in the same way that a basic award for unfair dismissal is weighted. The maximum he could receive in accordance with statutory requirement would be (on the figures applicable from 1 February 1981) £3,900, although individual employers might award more than this and negotiated schemes for redundancy compensation agreed between employer and trade unions(s) might provide for more than this. The statutory requirement relates to the amount which an employer may recover from the Redundancy Fund (EPCA, 1978, S 104).

Where an industrial tribunal finds that an employee's complaint of unfair dismissal is well founded, it has the power to make an award in two or three parts, dependent upon whether an order for withdrawal of notice, reinstatement or re-engagement is made or not.

1 In all cases of unfair dismissal, the employee is entitled to a basic award, which will not amount to less than two weeks' pay (calculated according to a formula given in the Employment Protection (Consolidation) Act, (S. 73). A 'week's pay' is varied as to its *maximum* amount from time to time by Regulation; it is currently, from 1 February, 1981, set at £130 per week). This amount to be awarded in the particular case is based on the length of service and age of the individual at the effective date of dismissal with a maximum of 20 years worked backwards from the date.

An individual's entitlement in the event of either fair redundancy or unfair dismissal is computed from the 20 'weightiest' years of service based on the following formula:

$1\frac{1}{2}$ week's pay for each full year of employment between the ages of 41 and 65 years (60 in the case of women)
1 week's pay for each year between ages 22 and 41, and
$\frac{1}{2}$ week's pay for each year between 18 and 22 years.

The total possible, from 1 February, 1980, is therefore 20 years times $1\frac{1}{2}$ weeks @ £130 per week, or £3,900.
Redundancy payments due to the individual in a case of unfair dismissal coupled with redundancy will not be paid in addition to the basic award. The amount awarded will also be reduced if the individual is found to have contributed to his own dismissal.

2 A compensatory award based on any financial loss sustained by or threatened to the individual and any mitigation of it, may be

paid in the case of unfair dismissal, where the tribunal finds it just and equitable to do so (EP(C) Act, S 75). This is paid in addition to the basic award where unfairness is established but will be reduced by the amount of redundancy payment above the basic award in cases where both apply. The amount is also subject to deduction for contributory fault on the part of the dismissed individual. It is subject to a maximum of £6,250; the amount paid will be based on estimated loss, not by formula related to pay rate, age or length of service as in the case of the basic award. It can, therefore, vary from a zero award to the maximum figure according to circumstances but regardless of the individual's pay rate.

3 Where the employer fails to reinstate or re-engage an individual after the tribunal has made an order to this effect (and fails to show that it was not practicable for him to comply with the order) the tribunal may make a further (additional) award. In cases of unfair dismissal, this will be an amount judged just and equitable within the range of 13 to 26 week's pay (£1,690 – £3,380 and from 1 February, 1981); in those cases where the reason for dismissal is an inadmissable one (racial or sex discrimination or related to union membership or activity) the tribunal will fix this amount in the range of 26 to 52 weeks' pay (£3,380 – £6,760). Even where reinstatement or re-engagement takes place, failure to comply fully with the terms of the order may lead the tribunal to award up to this higher figure, having regard to the employee's loss.

The intention of this provision is that the employer will be encouraged to consider reinstatement or re-engagement as the first remedy in unfair dismissal cases, where the employee is willing to be reinstated or re-engaged and the tribunal considers this course to be fitting and feasible. But because of the long standing reluctance on the part of the courts to create contracts of 'slavery' this encouragement is supported by a qualified order of 'specific performance'.

In fact, reinstatement and re-engagement figure as remedies in only a small number of cases. In 1978, a total of 34,180 cases were recorded (*DE Gazette*, September, 1979, pp 866–7) of which about a third were withdrawn usually at the conciliation stage. Another third were conciliated, and of this 22,352, only 466 involved reinstatement or re-engagement. Of the remaining 11,828 cases, 72 per cent were dismissed by the IT, and only 106 involved reinstatement or re-engagement.

Compensation therefore remains the more frequent remedy adopted in 'successful' cases. Of the conciliated cases, 11,274 (33 per cent of the total in this category) involved compensation (other than redundancy payment) as did 2,477 (7.2 per cent of the total in the category) of those cases heard by the ITs. In so far as the new legislative provisions put pressure of a kind other than the purely moral upon the employer, therefore, it is mainly a monetary one.

However, the amount of compensation awarded in successful cases is really quite small. The possible figures given on preceding pages are rarely attained in practice. Of the cases heard at an IT, less than a third resulted in a finding of unfair dismissal. More than half the compensation awards made by them involved sums of less than £400 in 1978, the median (middle rank) award being £375. Only three per cent (61 cases) attracted compensation from ITs of £3,000 or more.

Of the conciliation cases resulting in compensation, almost half resulted in settlements of less than £200, the median being about £160. Only 168 cases resulted in agreed settlements at conciliation of £3,000 or more (1.5 per cent of the cases). The penalty upon the employer is not therefore large, and the cost in time in appearing at the IT to defend cases has been put much higher than the average or median award figures, suggesting that the time and trouble costs may be greater to the employer than the actual financial penalties for unfair dismissal.

Summary

Taking the material of these two chapters together, therefore, the position may be summarized in the following way:

1 The employer, as provider of employment, starts with a number of rights, given in law and supported by his greater power in the contracting process
2 The employee has no established right to employment in the sense that he or she can demand employment; the rights are to consideration and (in the general sense) to 'care'
3 The general effect of recent legislation has been to create marginal changes in these two positions:

   first, by making the employer's duties more explicit in detail in respect of remuneration, communication, facilitation and adjudication; second, by firming up the employee's rights in specific areas in respect of information, time off without interruption of contract, avoidance of prejudiced discrimination, and fair treatment and a hearing where the contract may be in jeopardy;

4 The employer has therefore been led to be 'more careful' in the

establishment and termination of contracts of employment. And to create more explicit policies and procedures in support of this end; the employee has been given a marginally greater protection, particularly in respect of the major abuses, but has not secured, through the law, rights to work or to employment security.

A great deal of discretion remains to the employer since, as often commented in employment cases, the law does not see its roles as acting in any way to the hindrance or detriment of commercial objectives where the choice has to be made (*see Hollister v The National Farmers' Union* (1979) IRLR, 238).

How the employer exercises that discretion is, however, constrained. In taking action to secure, retain and reject the employees necessary to the realization of commercial objectives, these constraints have to be taken into account. It is in this way that the approaches to manning and manpower planning have been affected by changes in the law.

Further reading

The major references are those given at the end of the preceding chapter. For reasons of space, however, I have not included a discussion of Industrial Tribunals and the manner of approaching them. On this topic, students might consult the Incomes Data Services' Handbook No 16 on 'Going to Tribunal' and Handbook No 17 on 'Appealing to EAT' which explain the procedures involved and the rights and powers of the various parties.

6 Getting the manpower estimates right

Growth of the employment function

The employment 'function', that part of the enterprise or organization specifically charged with the planning, control and execution of the entity's interchange with the labour market, has traditionally formed a part of the 'personnel function'. In some cases, the 'labour office' through which all applicants for employment and all whose employment was being terminated passed, was the starting point for what later grew into a personnel department. In Britain, the 'welfare function' appears to have had greater priority, although the redistribution of labour effected by call-up to the forces and 'dilution' in industry during the first world war, gave the employment office and function a greater urgency (cf Niven, 1967; Renold, 1950). The development of employment offices in American industry occurred at roughly this same time, for 'the more efficient handling of labour' (Nichols in Bloomfield and Willits, 1916, p 1) and although 'the employment office [usually became] the personnel department because its work necessitates such close relationship with the working force' (Bloomfield and Willits, 1916, p vii) there is a suggestion of greater emphasis upon efficiency in hiring and firing (Kelly, 1918) than upon 'welfare' *per se*.

In 1955, Northcott gave appreciable weight to the employment function in his *Principles and Practice of Personnel Management*. He saw 'the responsibilities of the employment department' as falling 'mainly under two headings, the supply and placement of workers and the maintenance and study of records' (of such phenomena as absence and labour turnover) but admitted that as a consequence of this involvement, 'some advice on employment policy is a responsibility' (Northcott, 1955, third edn p 226). By this date in Britain, this function had acquired a degree of coherence and systematization, the 'full employment' conditions of the post world war two epoch having lent some urgency to this development. As in the American experience, so in the British, this function developed into a broader 'personnel function', but still quite commonly at present members of personnel departments are involved in recruitment, selection, induction and initial training and in termination of employment processes, and still on this foundation offer advice on the undertaking of employment policy. But the 'function' may be said to have developed beyond executive tasks associated with these interchanges to the level of giving advice based on systematic diagnoses of present and future states of the undertaking in the labour market. These in turn called for different and more sophisticated methods and techniques of forecasting and planning.

For the purposes of this and the next chapter, we will proceed on the basis that 'employment' can be regarded rather impersonally (concerned with nothing more than the establishment or termination of an employment contract) and *can* be discussed in those terms. This neglects for the present that those who are caught up in the contract are people with many thoughts and feelings, which will not be brought into the discussion until chapter 11 although eventually their influence on the employment function will have to be acknowledged. But since we cannot discuss everything at once and still present a coherent account of the personnel function, this restriction is imposed in the present chapter. Employment is treated in impersonal 'system' terms to establish what methods are applicable to the development of plans and strategies for the securing of appropriate amounts of labour, or manpower, to meet the requirements of the enterprise or organization.

The 'system' model
In order to give a structure to the chapter we adopt a model of the enterprise as a 'system' seen to be interchanging with its environment over a boundary (cf Miner and Miner, 1977, ch 3; Buckley, 1967; Kast and Rosenzweig, 1970). The interchanges involve not only manpower but also components, products, money and many other things, although here we shall be directly concerned only with the first of these. The enterprise is seen to have a need both to attract labour from the environment and to return labour to it and the size of the need will vary with a number of internal and external circumstances at which we must look. That need will find expression as a *demand* for labour, which must take into account the *supply* of labour which exists in the environment. The relationship between these two concepts forms the foundation of the interchange. In order to carry out an 'employment function' effectively, we argue, those charged with doing so require a knowledge of both

internal demand and external supply, *and* a knowledge of how to interrelate these in the interests of the criteria established to define 'success' in this context. These criteria will usually be derived from the enterprise itself: the securing of the right number of the right people for employment in the enterprise at the right time as determined by the production etc objectives which the enterprise has set for itself (cf Silverman, 1970 pp 9–11).

They do not have to be derived in this way but other criteria are likely to be marginal in their effects upon manpower decisions, although impositions of some constraints by government, trade unions and professional associations may still prove important in some cases (eg in redundancy plans or in policies of engagement of labour by sex or colour).

It would not be outside the ideological remit of the personnel manager to conceive manpower planning in terms of employee satisfaction but it is common to see it in terms of performance. Thus models of manpower planning are usually constructed against an objective which is concerned to realize efficiency or secure 'performance' from all those engaged. Such models, of whichever type, will follow the normal distribution of steps: objective-setting, criterion-determining, predictor-calculating, assessment-making and decision-taking, followed by an evaluation process which will start the sequence over again. Where the objective is conceived in performance terms, the criteria, predictors, assessments etc will all be set up in terms of this dependent variable but, where satisfaction is taken to indicate purpose, the criteria etc would be established in these other terms.

If we make the assumption that we will in the rest of the chapter be concerned with 'performance',we might then recognize a number of relevant objectives, such as:

(a) the recruitment and retention of the amount of skill required to perform the work of the system
(b) the provision of sufficient flexibility in the manpower to permit system adaptability to changes in the internal or external environments
(c) the minimization of the costs of manpower planning itself consistent with these objectives and measuring costs in whatever terms are sanctioned by the norms of the system (eg 'social' costs might be included)
(d) the accomplishment of these objectives inside the framework of norms for any system of purposive activity (eg without resorting to slave or sweated labour conditions or infringing legal requirements).

129

As between these, priorities might well change as circumstances change, and therefore very different weights may be given to such objectives from time to time or from organization to organization. A high level of labour wastage which was proving costly, might well raise the priority of 'recruitment to reduce short stays' over the objective of securing the highest 'quality' of labour; poor work performance, for similar reasons might be expected to raise the importance of this objective relative to others. The establishment of objectives is therefore an important first step in developing any plan for manpower performance.

Manpower planning

'Manpower planning' may be defined as a process whereby courses of action are determined upon in advance, and continually updated, with the aim of ensuring that (a) the demands of an enterprise for labour (or manpower in any given sex-age-skill manifestation) are as accurately projected as possible and (b) that the supply of such labour to the enterprise is maintained in balance with those demands. This decision process does not take place in a vacuum, and it must therefore be carried out in relation to the environments in which the enterprise moves and on the basis of past, present and projected future information about enterprise demand and supply positions.

'Manpower planning', says Moss, 'is the attempt to explain, predict and influence manpower changes in relation to the changing economic, technical and social situation of establishments' (Moss, 1974, p 9). Patten quotes LeBreton and Henning (1961) to establish the general features of any plan: 'A plan of any type may be defined as a predetermined course of action. Every plan should have three characteristics: first, it should involve the future; second, it must involve action; and third, there should be an element of personal or organizational identification or causation, which means simply that the future course of action will be taken by the planner or someone designated by him within an organization or within society' (Patten, 1971, p 13). In other words, any plan includes object-setting, administrative decision and execution, thus linking predicted futures with calculated means and purposive action.

Bell provides a clear exposition of what is requisite in manpower planning which is consistent with these views. He treats it as 'the systematic analysis of the company's resources, the construction of a forecast of its future manpower requirements from this

130

base, with special concentration on the efficient use of manpower at both these stages, and the planning necessary to ensure that the manpower supply will match the forecast requirements.' The manpower plan thus becomes the consequence of reconciling, within the constraints imposed upon decision by the company's circumstances, the outcomes from (a) the analysis of manpower resources, (b) the forecasts of future demands or requirements and (c) the forecasts of probable internal and external supply of manpower (Bell, 1974, pp 9–10).

The plan itself will then have to cover areas of action which are relevant to the matching of expected needs with expected supply from various (internal and external) sources. It must say something about the expected performance of labour in order to indicate what marginal additions or subtractions will be required at various points in time to meet the productivity requirements; it must provide for action to recruit, transfer, promote or discharge labour in accordance with this estimation and in conformity with other constraints of legality and cost; it must reflect an assessment of the part which training and development of the existing labour force or new recruits might make to the achievement of the equilibrium between requirement and offer; and it must be set against a set of personnel policies, outside the manpower planning area strictly defined, which will provide appropriate backup for those actions which are more strictly to do with manpower planning. These elements are presented in diagrammatic form, based on Bell's own figures (1974, pp 10 and 12) in figure 2 on p 133.

The steps in the process of developing a plan of this kind are outlined by Stainer, who identifies:

(a) development of the criteria which will be employed in making judgements about the data
(b) determination of what data are relevant to the decisions required
(c) collection and collation of this data in order that it may be transmitted to those who must decide
(d) allocation of persons to decision-taking roles, on the basis of assumed competence to interpret the data
(e) taking of decisions about manpower, either unilaterally or in negotiations
(f) controlled implementation of the decisions thus taken, this implying that the process of feeding back data will also be involved (cf Stainer, 1971, pp 3 and 4).

131

These statements are apposite to manpower planning at whatever level it may be required within the economy:

(a) the macro level which embraces demand and supply components at the national or supra-national level
(b) the intermediate level where the concern is with stocks and flows in respect of whole industries or geographical regions or regional labour markets
(c) the micro level where the problem is defined in terms of balancing flows and stocks at the level of the corporation or undertaking.

At each of these levels, three components of estimation are required. These are (i) the level of demand representing the translation of employer need into effective demand upon the supplies available; (ii) the internal supply, representing the amount of the existing stock available to the entity in question which will remain available for and seeking continuing employment into the future; and (iii) the external supply composed of those not yet available to the entity for employment which may nevertheless be regarded as potentially available for the future (cf Bryant, 1972, pp 14–15).

Forecasting
Manpower planning thus aims to ensure that an organization so reacts to its internal and external environments that it has now, and will continue to have in the future, the numbers and qualities of people who will be required to enable the undertaking to achieve its output (whether of goods or of services) within whatever cultural constraints of efficiency may be imposed upon it. As with any other 'planning' process, therefore, it involves the forecasting of likely future situations with the object of identifying demand, and the determination of a series of actions which can be calculated to ensure that as far as possible those predicted needs will be met. No forecast of the future can be completely accurate but reasonable estimates of probability can be made on the basis of various hypotheses; therefore the value of the plan will always depend upon just how close such forecasts can be brought in relation to actual outturns in the future. No theory about what degree or kind of change in independent variables is necessary in order to produce a particular effect can be absolutely perfect; and therefore no plan can be perfect in its consequences even if the forecasts are accurate. But on both counts systematic analysis is likely to prove more useful, in a complex set of environments, than mere hunch or guesswork. It is the complexity of the environments which leads us to systematic

Figure 2
Elements of manpower planning and in the employment plan

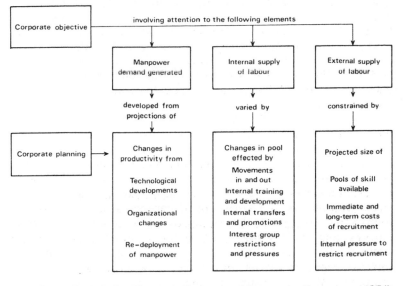

Based on: D J Bell: *Planning Corporate Manpower* (Longman, 1974), pp 10 and 12 (composited)

planning, not a fashionable supersession of 'hunch'.

Manpower planning, like any planning activity, rests upon forecasts and forecasts are frequently dismissed as being necessarily wrong. This, as Brech has argued (1975), is to mistake the nature and purpose of forecasting in management. 'Forecasting is the use of a numerate and logical system, incorporating judgement values, to evaluate the probabilities of future occurrences or outcomes. It is not a scientific method of prophecy, which implies knowing the future with certainty... It identifies possible outcomes and assigns them their relative probabilities. The logical structure is based on the known relationships and past experience ... and ... incorporates an assessment of how people or events are likely to react as judged from that experience, after allowing for known or probable changes in the environment' (Brech, 1975, third edn p 28). In effect this process of systematically forecasting can help increase understanding of uncertainties and converts them into 'risks' of more calculable dimensions. Any plan based upon forecasting in this sense may well turn out to be wrong, but the forecasting process helps to indicate something of the likelihood of

133

its being so or to inform the planner of the risk run by the plan.

It has to be recognized that the best information which is available to a decision taker in making any kind of forecast is that which relates to the situation (to which the decision is to be related) as it has developed in the past. The basis of most forecasting, in other words, is extrapolation from the known (past) to the unknown (future). But as Bell, amongst others, continually asserts in his discussion of the various kinds of forecasting required in manpower planning, the data required may not exist (because it has not been recorded at all, or not recorded in a useable form, or not kept over a long enough period of past time), so that the choice of forecasting method may be 'restricted by the availability of data' (Bell, 1974, p 19). It is this which makes the recording of data within the 'production system' as well as within the 'personnel system' of great importance from the standpoint of the manpower planner. Division of responsibilities between line management, management services departments and personnel departments, quite frequently renders 'bits' of separate data quite unsuitable for this (forecasting) purpose, and it is this which leads Bell to suggest that, even where adequate data does not exist at any one moment, a 'dummy run' forecast might be carried out if only to indicate what data are required and so to inform the minds of those concerned (Bell, 1974, p 19) and Bartholomew to argue that manpower planners must state what they need (Bartholomew, in Smith, 1970 see also p 138 below).

Where in the past the personnel management textbook concentrated on only two aspects of record keeping—the maintenance of fundamental personal information (like name, address, age, starting date, promotions, pay rate) and the collection of data which was thought to indicate something of the state of 'morale' in the enterprise (like time-keeping, absenteeism, labour turnover, discipline cases, dispute incidence), the greater involvement of personnel specialists in economic decisions about manpower has changed the pattern of data collection and the uses to which it is put (cf Stainer, 1971, ch 4). The data which was previously regarded as the province of production or wages departments are now necessary to manpower planning and employee resourcing processes and is therefore brought together more often. The predisposition of the personnel specialist to use his own data simply for purposes of divining the state of morale is complemented by its use for monitoring recruitment, selection and placement activities as well as for assessment of labour quality. In keeping with these changes, more systematic attention has been given to the record-keeping function (*see* Industrial Society, 1969; Butteriss, 1975). See also pp 221–3.

The kinds of data required for manpower planning purposes fall into two broad categories, the performance data and the stock and flow data. It is the first type which is most often associated with line management and management services responsibilities, and the second which is traditionally more the concern of the personnel department or employment office.

The first data are described as 'workload data' and may be derived in two quite different ways. In the one case, what is needed is some 'indicator' such as the level of demand for, say, the product or the service which the manpower in question will be concerned with making or providing. This will not always be discoverable for particular categories of labour but, where it is and where it can be given a value, it can be used to forecast demand for manpower, if there is a direct relationship between the indicator and the demand. A single shoe-repairer might provide an illustration: if the demand for shoe repairs (or for fitted heels) could be expected to double over the next year, and if the number of repairs or heel fittings thus predicted to be demanded linked directly with the number of units of manpower required, then a prediction of a requirement of two repairers at the end of the year would be reasonably made. But of course the relationships are not always so direct and so discernible (see Rowntree and Stewart, in Smith, 1976, pp 39–40). Bell refers to this approach as 'direct' analysis calling for the application of statistical methods of ratios and regression analysis (Bell, 1974, p 22), with which it is necessary to link analysis of productivity changes which might be expected with changes in volume (Bell, 1976, pp 28–40).

The alternative is to use the more conventional work performance data of the kind which manufacturing industry tends to amass in plenty (whether it presents it or uses it for manpower planning purposes or not). Essentially, this requires the development of data which indicate the performance of a standard unit of manpower in any given category—the performance of a 'trained operator working at standard pace in standard conditions' at either incentive or non-incentive rates as the case may be. These data are also not always derivable or available, dependent upon the kind of work which is being done but, where they are, they offer a basis in past fact for future forecast. If the standard or average performance of a semi-skilled machinist is known (in these terms) as a result of work study or more simply of calculated averages, it becomes possible to base estimates of future manpower demand upon this as related to expectations of changes in product demand. Bell discusses these methods more fully in terms of the development of inductive methods (managerial estimates) and of standard relationships based on work study (Bell, 1974, pp 26–8).

The data more likely to be available from the personnel department are those which relate to the stocks and flows of man-power within the organization. For purposes of internal forecasting, the data most readily usable are those which mean simply plotting numbers (stocks) of staff (in categories) against past time, fitting curves thereto and extrapolating the curve into the future. To do so demands statistics of numbers over a sufficient period to permit these operations to be carried out and sufficient numbers in homogeneous categories to make the calculations worthwhile. Both of these will restrict the opportunity in many instances. These data need eventually to be married with the other categories of data mentioned above, and that may mean bringing together data from two very different departmental sources (Rowntree and Stewart, in Smith, 1976, pp 37–8).

Flow information of a sort is also available in the personnel department, although quite often the data are collected for quite other purposes than manpower planning and for this reason are often not usable. The four main sub-categories of flow data which are required for this purpose are summarized by Butler and Rowntree (in Smith, 1976, p 54) as follows:

1 'out-movement from the organization for whatever reason, termed *wastage* [or labour turnover in many undertakings]—this covers voluntary resignation, retirement, death etc
2 'in-movement from outside the organization to any grade, termed *recruitment*
3 'movement between jobs leading to a change of grade. When this flow is upward within the hierarchy it is termed *promotion*; a movement in the opposite direction is termed *demotion*
4 'movement from job to job within the same grade' which may be referred to as *transfer*.

The value of these data for manpower planning purposes depends upon the possibility that exists for relating them to other information usually associated with the personnel record—such as age, date of starting, length of service, salary and wage position and de-velopment etc. If the information is to be used to predict what may happen in the future, it is in other words insufficient to know what the 'rate' of labour turnover is, but necessary to know how this relates to these variables of age, length of service etc and therefore what are the potentialities for flow in the next 'x' years in the exist-ing labour force (see Butler and Rowntree, in Smith, 1976, pp 54–77; and Bell, 1974, ch 4).

Differential availability and dispersed location of data are two related problems in this area. Another relates to the subjectivity of some information. Much of the basic information for forecasting purposes is 'only available *subjectively* from the appropriate manager' (Bartholomew, Hopes and Smith, 1976, p 6) (italics added); and 'success in manpower planning depends heavily on the formation of good judgements about the likely variations of parameters [and this] involves eliciting the managers' perceptions in a form suitable for analysis' (*ibid*, p 16). A third problem arises from the assumed necessity to use statistical methodology in order to carry out any manpower planning activity at all. It is true that the conversion of uncertainty into calculated risk, where this is possible at all, 'is an area where the statistician is presumed to be the expert' (*ibid*, p 6) but many useful exercises of manpower planning call for (and indeed can support no more than) a sensible calculation of future probabilities on quite limited data (cf Bell, 1974, p 19). In the more complex manning situation, the personnel manager will have some involvement in forecasting of internal demand, internal supply and external supply, and even if more specialist personnel are engaged on the actual statistical manipulation involved, he must have some appreciation of the processes involved.

Demand forecasting
Manpower demand forecasts start with 'the formulation of the organization's overall objectives' for the period over which the forecast is to be made. This, as Lawrence points out, is likely to be a very short period because of the uncertainties involved in long term forecasting and the high costs therefore likely to be associated with it in relation to minor benefits (Lawrence, 1973, p 15). For a similar reason, many organizations 'have little idea of what they want to be' (*ibid*) and therefore have no statement of forward objectives at all. Even where they do, 'it is not always easy to interpret a corporate plan into a set of manpower requirements' (*ibid*) within a framework of economic, social, political and technological change of which little is under the control of the undertaking itself.

The statements of objectives, where they do exist, may be stated in ways which have very different implications for manpower demand forecasts. The objectives may be stated as a 17 per cent return on capital, as the achievement of a market share of, say, 45 per cent, or as the sales of a stated number of product-units. These three statements have an increasing amount of direct relevance to manpower demand forecasting: the 'labour content' of a product unit is known and can be fed into the forecast directly even if it is varied by a factor representing estimates of either technological change or the effects of learning curves upon labour performance; the number of units to be sold multiplied by the labour content is likely to give an estimate of demand in which a certain confidence might be reposed and the same might be said of the effect of stating objectives in terms of market share. The statement of objectives merely in terms of a return on capital might leave much more room for change of the product mix in the light of changes in sales or pro-fitability of different lines, in which case the consequences in terms of labour content might be extremely difficult to predict with any confidence at all (Jones, Bell, Center and Coleman, 1967, pp 45–9).

These difficulties may help to account for the failure of corpor-ations to come to terms with the need to link manpower planning with more general corporate planning (cf Smith, 1971, p 49). Lawrence, noting this tendency, and the prevalence of system models offered to guide the necessary interlinking (see figure 7 on p 20 of Lawrence, 1973), suggests that 'typically the responsibility for manpower planning resides about two levels below the head of personnel (whence there are those who can achieve a great deal)' (*ibid*, p 21), but that it may still be sensible to develop the forecasts of the supply position (ie to deal with the tractable problems) and leave the plan 'flexible and responsive to the needs of the organiza-tion' on the demand side (*ibid*).

As Smith has summarized the position, demand forecasting 'in the mechanistic sense is the prediction of the future based on observed regularities in the past; and practical forecasting must make due allowance also for foreseeable changes in policy, organ-ization and technology which may break the established trends and relationships' (Smith, 1971, p 49). He also makes it clear that there is 'no ready-made methodology for forecasting manpower demand which can be taken off the peg by any organization coming new to manpower planning' (Smith, 1971, p 48). The firm must develop its own methods of calculation and extrapolation, and correlation to suit its own circumstances, employing the relevant statistical tech-niques where they are available, usable and useful, but bearing in mind that managerial knowledge of future 'facts' and judgement of likely future relationships are likely to be as important as the tech-niques themselves in increasing understanding and prediction(*ibid*, p 48).

The two main categories of statistical technique available for this purpose are 'single cell techniques' useful in relation to rela-tively stable situations and therefore to the short-run forecast, and 'matrix techniques' which allow the exploration of more complex interrelationships between skills and industries (Bosworth and

Evans, 1973). The first of these is particularly useful as a technique for extrapolating employment in a particular skill in a particular sector over a period and, with more sophisticated techniques, it can handle a long time series, which is more difficult to do in the matrix method. The single cell methods of making forecasts on the basis of a simple production gradient has some value: this says that manpower changes equal the product of (production × the gradient of change in production). To this can be added other factors such as technological change (cf Stainer, 1971, ch 6).

The matrix techniques are likely to be more useful to the undertaking seeking to make forecasts for a number of skills in a number of sectors or departments, where cells in the matrix can be considered to influence what may happen in other cells because of 'substitution' or 'productivity' effects (Leicester, 1968). What is 'predicted' by this method is the way in which the matrix might change as between two points in time, now and a date in the future. 'A matrix is set up in which the columns might represent the different activities or departments of an organization, and the rows the skills that are required. If this matrix can be prepared for two points in time, estimates can be made of the value of the row multipliers (r) and the column multipliers (s) that are necessary to describe the transition of the matrix over time' (Lawrence, 1973, p 19; see also Bosworth and Evans, 1973).

Forecasting internal supply
In order to meet estimated future demands for manpower, the undertaking must needs rely upon two main supply pools, one internal and the other external, but with the one forming a part of the other. The internal pool comprises those already employed, diminished by those who leave or are dismissed for a variety of reasons and increased by those who may be developed by training and experience. The external pool comprises those people who form the population of the country working or likely to be seeking work, modified by recruitment by competing organizations, and by additions to stock from the educational system, retraining programmes and redundancies elsewhere.

This aspect of forecasting is both more developed and more reliable largely because the data necessary are, in principle, more readily accessible to the forecasters and extrapolation of developments on the supply side is the more readily assessable by the managers who live with it. Forecasts of supply from internal sources start with the basic demographic data on the existing labour force, age, sex, length of service, capability (eg in terms of skills possessed or experience gained), which ought to be available in any personnel department. Projection of this population into the future will inevitably mean dropping off those who can be predicted to retire or quit in the period, say over 10 years. The modification of the existing stock by projections of labour turnover may be done crudely, using gross data (eg a simple variation at 10 per cent turnover per annum), or in a more sophisticated way based on calculation of turnover rates for age, sex and skill cohorts, and taking into account the predicted effects of changes in dismissal practice (eg under the Employment Protection Act) or changes in transferability of pension rights etc (see, particularly, Young, 1961 and 1965; Jones, Bell, Center and Coleman, 1967). No matter how sophisticated the method of forecasting, the resultant prediction will be no better than the assumptions fed in as to how changes are likely to make their presence felt in the future.

The long-standing involvement of the personnel people in gathering certain types of data on the labour force employed—the old 'employment function'—now acquires a new relevance and significance in the face of the need to make forecasts of the future. Statistics on labour turnover and on internal movement (by transfer, promotion etc) have usually been collected in detail and for many years where the employment function has been allowed to develop and these provide input data which can be extrapolated to inform predictions of how the existing labour force will diminish or change in the future.

Unfortunately, much of the data which is gathered and processed in personnel departments tends to be in a form which may allow very simplified predictions, but does not permit statistical analysis of the more complicated type. The basic distinction here is between the use of statistics in deterministic models and their use in stochastic models. The first model involves an abstraction from the complexities of the reality on the basis of averages—such as average age, average length of service or average rates of labour turnover etc. That it abstracts from the reality in this way is normal and natural, and necessary to the taking of decisions, because we cannot take decisions if we have to consider every individual event on its own. But the *kind* of abstraction, based on averages, does not permit the probability of a predicted outcome to be calculated and it is this—the calculation of probability—which is involved in stochastic models. These try to work out the probability or likelihood of some event or outcome coming about and, because of this, they are statistically more complex. But even the first kind of model can be linked across to allow probabilities to be calculated and, when that is done, when the uncertainty is reduced to statements about risk, these too become the more complicated as a consequence.

140

What these methods centre attention on are the dynamics of manpower populations and flows. In relation to internal supply forecasting, they demand analysis of the likelihood of people staying (being retained) in the undertaking (using labour turnover indexes of the British Institute of Management type, stability indexes for the whole or categories and the development of retention profiles) and of the probabilities of internal movements (from age or length of service categories to others, from grades to others, from salary levels to others, or any combination thereof) to give a prediction of structure on these dimensions at 'n' months or years into the future (according to the time horizon being used). It follows that in order to make these kinds of calculation the data required will have to be assembled in a usable form, and it is this which has not always been done in the past, because then either it was collected for other purposes or it was collected to inform a deterministic model rather than a stochastic one.

The point may be illustrated with reference to the old chestnut of personnel record keeping, labour turnover. This has usually been calculated in the form of a 'crude wastage rate', which may indicate how the undertaking is doing in comparison with other undertakings but does not of itself say much about what might happen to a cohort of new recruits taken on today in terms of stability or turnover (cf Lawrence, 1973, p 7). Some of the early work by the Tavistock Institute of Human Relations considered wastage in relation to length of service, on the hypothesis that leaving was a mathematical function of the length of service of the individual (Hill, 1951; Rice, 1951; Rice and Trist, 1952; Rice et al, 1950). This and the work of the National Coal Board in the early 1960s suggested that the relationship of labour wastage and length of service was log-normal; in effect, a given cohort of recruits will demonstrate high wastage initially and will then 'settle down' to a steady and diminishing rate of quitting. The NCB studies also showed a high correlation between wastage rate and the distance that miners had to travel to work (Tomlinson, 1964). Such studies thus offer an explanation and a model of labour wastage over a period and can be employed to structure forecasts of future internal supply (Bell, 1974, pp 43–55).

These early 'life expectancy' or actuarial' studies gave rise to various methods of profiling—the simple drawing of 'pictures' of a future structure of the labour force on such dimensions as age, length of service or expected grade in which located (Bell (1974) illustrates some of these on pp 63 and 64, as does Lawrence (1973) on p 10). One such profile, based on such actuarial calculations might be introduced in the diagram on p 66 above in place of the simple circle which is employed to indicate the nature of the boundary between an undertaking and its environment: the arrows showing entrance would then all lead to the 'base' of the profile and those indicating termination would take off from the survival graph. What is thus being depicted is only one step on from what is attempted in the production of 'back-up' charts in management succession planning, where the emphasis is usually upon individuals rather than 'cohorts' of entrants and upon individual promotability and promotion rather than probabilities of movement between grades. (See pp 145–48).

The developments from these early calculations during the 1950s and 1960s have sought to improve the predictions, where the data have been available, by the application of stochastic methods. Perhaps the most complicated and least easily understood approach, from the non-statistician's standpoint, is the use of the linear programming model (Purkiss, in Wilson, 1969, pp 67–78; Morgan, in Smith, 1970, pp 317–25) designed to estimate costs of policy variants in respect of recruitment and termination. The other two main variants are described by Lawrence in the following terms:

> The analytical models divide roughly into two sorts. The Markov or 'push' type assume that promotions are not dependent upon vacancies occurring, but instead are the result of management 'pushing' individuals along their career paths at fixed rates. These models are descriptive, technically comprehensible and computationally fairly simple. At the other extreme the renewal or 'pull' type models assume that all promotions are the result of vacancies occurring, as if employees are 'pulled' through the organization to fill gaps as they arise. Unfortunately, these models suffer from being computationally inconvenient and mathematically obscure to the non-technical person (Lawrence, 1973, p 14; see also, Bell, 1970, pp 57–62; Bartholomew, 1967).

These difficulties led the attempt to develop Markov models based upon the observation that promotions are the result of both push and pull factors and giving a result which was both 'more realistic in its assumptions and computationally attractive' (*ibid*). The model is made to represent any desired configuration of separate manpower groupings (grades, particular kinds of people within them, staff at different locations etc) and the required flows to and from the groupings, either between them, or to them from outside the system or from them to outside the system. The model is computerized and what is fed into the model is described by Lawrence (1973) as follows:

(a) current strength by grade and age
(b) wastage rates by grade and age
(c) age distributions of recruits into the system, specific for each recruitment grade
(d) grade-specific 'rules' for the selection of promotees. These are in terms of age bands from which specified proportions of total promotees from the grade, in a time period, are selected
(e) where there is more than one inward flow to a grade, the proportion of total vacancies in the grade to be filled by each
(f) where there is more than one outward flow from a grade (other than wastage, which the model treats as a first call on the strength), the order in which flows are to be treated
(g) the required future strength of each grade, usually expressed by a positive or negative growth factor. (Lawrence, 1973, p 14)

This data-input allows the computer to go through the process of filling vacancies created by wastage or promotion according to whether there is to be growth or contraction in the grouping concerned, and does this by external recruitment or promotion from below, taking into account the given age distribution for recruits, the promotion rules to be applied and the specified flow proportions. Shortfalls in recruitment are made up from those in other promotable age bands in proportion to their specified contributions to the total of promotees (Lawrence, 1973, p 14; Smith, 1976).

These more sophisticated exercises remain comparable in intention, although not form, to those which the personnel manager has often attempted in the past under the heading of manpower succession planning. This fits the one ideological orientation of personnel management, which emphasizes the inherent involvement with individual persons, but it tends to be applicable only where the category of labour concerned is not so large as to make individual predictions as to the future internal supply position impossible. In smaller undertakings, and on the subject of management succession planning, these 'individualistic' approaches may be all that is necessary and all that can be supported by the data which can be generated. (See below, pp 551–56).

Management succession planning
The approach usually made to management succession planning may be used to illustrate the affinity of manpower planning of a sort to the case work method (see below, pp 225–26). The affinity arises

Figure 3
Some stationary population models

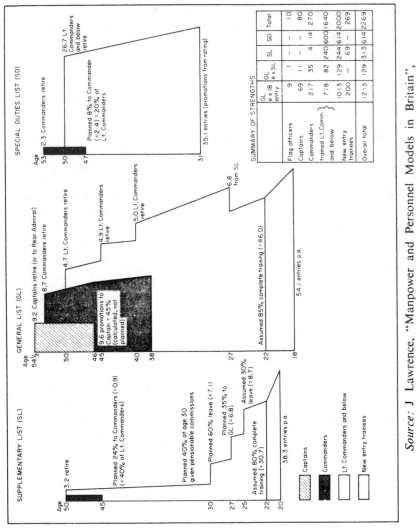

Source: J Lawrence, "Manpower and Personnel Models in Britain", *Personnel Review* Vol 2, No 3, Summer, 1973, p 10

144

partly because the vacancies to be filled in the future are individual and identifiable on a 'back-up' chart, and partly because it is considered that the qualities required in the manager are highly individualized and of a different nature from those needed in the manual or routine white collar worker. There is some reason to suppose that in some circumstances, at least, the approach to manpower planning may in future have to take on more of the caste of management succession planning than it has needed to do in the past. The more employing organizations come to regard recruitment to jobs in terms not merely of skills but in terms of securing matching of expectancies of individual and organization (Mumford, 1970, p 77), the more it becomes necessary to consider personal 'qualities' and position 'offers' in a framework of mutuality. For both of these reasons it is worth while to look at succession planning before examining the more general approach to manpower planning (cf Patten, 1971).

The problem of identifying possible 'successors' from within the undertaking (a measure of 'internal supply') is very often dealt with in association with procedures related to improving on the current job performance, to improving communication between the boss and subordinate and to providing data to allow testing of initial selection choices. 'Management appraisal' or 'management review' is a generic term which is used to apply, in various combinations, to these different problems and solutions but the effect is that, for all but the very top personnel, the approach to succession planning is wrapped around with other performance appraisal requirements. On its own, succession planning is usually stated to be concerned with the identification of more junior personnel with capacity and capability to move into more senior positions (usually with some development), in order that the organization has some appreciation at any one moment not only of what stock of trained manpower it has available for its current needs, but also what stock it has potentially to meet future exigencies, assuming that the future 'need' will replicate the current stock by number and skill (*see* above, pp 139–44).

Because of the association with performance review, some plans attempt to base assessments of future capacity and capability on current performance as predictors of that capability but in other cases a distinct set of criteria are postulated as relevant to the prediction of likely future promotion. In one company, whose plan was reported in the *Financial Times* some years ago, the aim was to identify 'managerial talents' in subordinate staff on the basis of their possession of (a) a sense of reality; (b) a power of analysis, (c) an ability to anticipate; (d) imagination, and (e) 'the helicopter quality'. Salaman and Bristow summarize the problem which arises when managers are invited to rate subordinates on a five point scale for such factors as diligence, application, job knowledge etc: 'Such a system presents a number of difficulties. The characteristics listed might be so vague as to be almost meaningless; they might be irrelevant to some or all of the people who are to be assessed; or they might be more important for some jobs than others. Sometimes it is not clear to those who are doing the job rating exactly what is meant by the characteristics that they are dealing with and they might not agree on what would constitute evidence of such a characteristic; this can increase the difference between ratings and make it impossible to compare them. Sometimes raters are asked to add their ratings to make a grand total, even when it should be clear that some of the characteristics are far more crucial to job success than others' (1970, p 37). Nevertheless such attempts at appraisal are perpetrated.

Once made and reported to the centre, these judgements are transferred to a back-up table or a back-up chart (*see* p 148 below) in order to show (a) which person(s) already engaged might stand as potential replacements for any listed manager, and (b) what is the likely prognosis for development and promotion of any of the charted personnel. Clearly, there are problems associated with the assessments themselves, where they are based upon 'dimensions of characteristics' of persons which psychologists would not claim to be able to measure and where, as is often the case, no or very little training is given to the assessors to enable them to establish norms and development motivation and ability to assess. It is probably in reflection, partially at least, of these problems that such back-up charts are often not employed when an actual vacancy occurs, the decision being taken at that point to throw the vacancy open to competition in the more normal fashion. This consideration led Browning (1963) to suggest that management succession planning was best done on a relatively informal basis without systematic annual trawling of superordinate's assessments of subordinates on this dimension.

A similar judgement is usually made about the generality of manpower in smaller undertakings where, by whatever methods, some judgement can be made of the likely availability of labour across the whole hierarchical spectrum. In these circumstances it is neither sensible from the point of view of the data base, nor economically profitable to engage in exercises which involve a set of sophisticated statistical techniques. Large organizations, and particular large tracts of the public service, may be able to develop these forecasting techniques with great advantage, but not the

Figure 4
Forward planning and replacement schedule (confidential)
Management record showing appraisals, anticipated position vacancies and probable back-up men

Division ....
Approved by ....
Date ....

PRESENT AND PROJECTED MANAGEMENT ORGANIZATION						PROBABLE BACK-UP MEN			
name	age	present and projected positions	performance appraisal summaries	recommended for	replacement estimated to take place	name	age	present position	estimated time required to qualify
						1			
						2			
						3			
						1			
						2			
						3			
						1			
						2			
						3			
						1			
						2			
						3			

147

small undertaking. But there is no reason, why the implications of these more sophisticated developments for the production of data should be ignored in the less complex situation of the smaller undertaking or labour category. A feasibility study might suggest that the more refined techniques were just not worth applying, but it might also suggest better methods of making judgements within the existing framework.

External supply forecasting
Such predictions must inevitably deal with only one part (and possibly even the smaller part in the longer term) of the total supply picture. To a greater or lesser extent an organization (even one which is not foreseeing expansion) will be dependent upon what happens to the pool outside the enterprise. This pool consists at any one time of a pool of actual and potential workers: the actual workers are those 'in employment'; the potential comprises those not in employment, whether because of unemployment or because, like many women, they choose not to work in those circumstances. The pool will be diminished in size by demise and retirement from the active labour force, and increased by those entering the labour market from the educational system or more simply from not working at all (again like the housewives). Clearly, the overall size of this pool will be affected by changes in the birth and death rates, by changes in school-leaving or retirement ages, and by changes in economic and social conditions (affecting the motivation of the 'non-working' groups to enter upon the labour market). At present, for example, there is some pressure to reduce the age of retirement and to vary the opportunities for young people to engage in further and higher education, both of which will, if implemented, affect the size of the available labour force, as will the post-war declining birth rate now affecting Britain.

Since the quantities in the wider external manpower pool are generally larger than those relating to internal demand and supply forecasting, it would be possible to make more probable forecastings of stocks and flows here, as indeed is achieved in national manpower forecasting although even here there is no determinancy. Nevertheless what may be expected to happen to the 'external pool' can usually be expressed with greater confidence than what may be expected for the internal one. The diagram of stocks and flows presented by the Edinburgh Group (at p 56) indicates the broad dimensions of this situation, although for the particular employer the addition of an 'output' to other employments might help to complete the picture (*see* Jones, Bell, Center and Coleman, 1967). That presented by Donald (1966) for the Health Service, is

Figure 5
Organization chart showing management potential

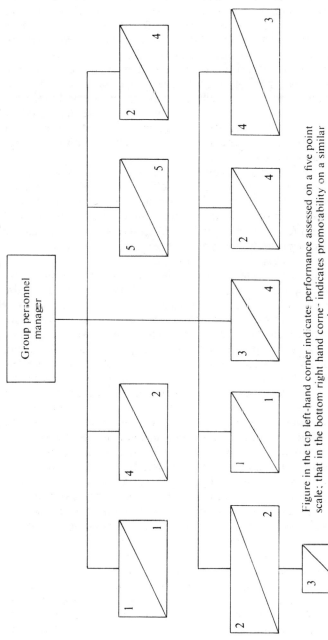

Figure in the top left-hand corner indicates performance assessed on a five point scale; that in the bottom right hand corner indicates promotability on a similar scale

1 Good all-round performance
2 Weak on technical aspects
3 Weak on control aspects
4 Weak on human relations
5 Weak on administration

1 Ready for promotion
2 Promotable with development
3 Doubtful promotable calibre
4 Impending retirement
5 Should be transferred

comparable but introduces certain other features peculiar to that kind of service industry. Such models alone will not indicate for the particular enterprise what part of this stock will be available to it, in varying circumstances of future demand. This calculation must be made in relation to likely conditions of competition for the available labour supply, which in turn has two components. First, how much competition from other undertakings can be expected in the particular labour market, which might reflect no more than mere numbers demanded. Secondly, how much can be expected in varying conditions of 'offer' by the enterprise and its competitors (eg whether the enterprise can create an image of being a 'better employer' than others).

The outputs of public manpower planning are of relevance at the undertaking level, particularly in so far as what is projected for the manpower in the economy as a whole will provide both constraint and relevant data for intra-enterprise decisions. In terms of a planning 'model', what happens in the environment (represented by national manpower planning) must be fed into the local model. In the British context at present this raises problems.

Although 'aggregate supply projections are the simplest and most commonly made' (Patten, 1971, p 47) they are made at the level of the economy and 'are limited almost exclusively to estimates of changes in the numbers of persons' (ibid), and more especially of persons by industry of employment and occupation, not skill. 'Skill' as a supply element is rarely projected at all, except in connection with specific formal training (eg the stocks and flows of scientists and engineers) in colleges and universities. In particular, the stock of skilled craftsmen, in engineering or electronics, is not and probably could not be calculated without a specific *ad hoc* study; consequently, in this major post-war shortage area, the projection which the undertaking's manpower planner would like to have is not available to him. Although there were high hopes of an improvement in manpower supply data, both in the 1960s (in association with the Industrial Training Act) and in the 1970s (with the establishment of the Manpower Services Commission and its specialized agencies for employment and training) these have not been realized by way of better information from public sources (cf Bell, 1974; and Dodge, 1977).

The problems associated with forecasting of external supply, are not so much associated with statistical techniques as with the availability of 'statistics' (data) and of knowledge of decided or possible developments within competitor undertakings. Particularly where manual and routine clerical labour is concerned, what the manpower planner is interested in is information about the

150

local labour market (in the case of managerial and professional labour, the 'local' labour market may be more closely identified with the 'national' market). This may be important where the purpose of the plan is to forecast likely situations to be encountered in relocation of plant or office.

As Bell says, 'the company manpower planner must make do with what information he can get' on this dimension (Bell, 1974, p 75). His own knowledge of what has happened and what might happen is unlikely to be supplemented by statistical data from official sources, except on a general national (and in a limited number of cases on an occupational) basis, where the very broad trends may be available to him from the Department of Employment *Gazettes*, the Monthly Abstract of Statistics, the particular Industry Training Board, and the special studies of some researchers. This is 'disappointing', says Bell (*ibid*, p 74), and his best advice is contained in the statement that 'a good manager keeps very closely in touch with all the employers in his area' (*ibid*, p 73).

The outcome of such an exercise will be to indicate how much manpower the enterprise can reasonably expect to be able to take up from the labour markets for the different categories of skill and experience which it considers on the basis of its demand analysis it will require. The general conclusion is likely to be that in future, for a variety of reasons, there will be greater pressure upon the enterprise itself to secure its manpower requirements less by recruitment directly from the labour market and more by redeployment following training and re-training of the existing labour force. Although the educational system, the main contributor of labour to employment, is currently subject to considerable pressures to change, any advantage to manning which might be expected from this source is likely to be outweighed, from the present point of view, by further restrictions on the employer's licence to manipulate labour to and from the labour market (*see* above, pp 69–126).

Conclusion

Clearly the very large organization is likely to derive benefit from the application of modern forecasting techniques applied to labour flows. The relatively small undertaking is less likely to do this and will remain more dependent upon data being supplied from external sources.

But in a tight labour market situation both large and small enterprises are likely to find their greatest scope for developing strategies in respect of internal supply. Even in a less than fully employed economy, there is no guarantee that quality of labour required will be available, a possibility likely to be increased with the onward march of technological change. More undertakings will be led to take in young labour and develop their own labour assets by training. The longer term trends are therefore likely to be in the direction of creating more of the so called 'internal' or 'segmented' labour markets (cf Doeringer and Piore, 1971; MacKay *et al*, 1971; Robinson, 1970; also pp 173–75 below).

Some undertakings will therefore face a future in which they will hope to rely upon a conventional interchange with the labour market, but some will increasingly rely upon this more novel form of interchange. There are implications in both situations for the development of an attracting and retaining payment structure and of policies relating to training and development, which are discussed in the following chapter.

Further reading
On the general approach to manpower planning, see Bell (1974) and Stainer (1971); more complex models and methods are to be found in Smith (1970 and 1976) and Bartholomew (1976). (Fuller bibliographies are to be found in the Department of Employment *Gazette*, July 1976, pp 722–6; November 1976, pp 1231–4; October 1977, pp 1093–6.)

7 Planning to influence labour supply

Elements of a plan

Systematic methods of forecasting help to provide data on which plans can be made; they do not form the plans themselves. What goes into the plans are chiefly strategies by which it is intended to alter the size and shape of the demand and supply variables as these are revealed in the forecasts. To bring what is forecast into line with what is desired, future actions have to be provided for. Some of these fall within the province of the personnel manager.

On the undertaking's demand side of the equation, proposed changes in the product/service mix and levels designed to meet changes expected in the market, and in the production and processing technologies intended to respond to expected developments in 'technology', tend to function as the independent variable. So the undertaking requires a quantity and quality of labour because of these proposed changes.

Because availability may prove to be a constraint on these other decisions, however, it may be sensible to integrate manpower planning with the development, production and marketing plans based on 'technological forecasts' (see OECD, 1967; Arnfield, 1969). This may involve a direct association of the personnel function with general planning processes, but not a direct involvement in them.

Such direct involvement is more likely to be associated with planning on the supply side, that is, with proposals for action to bring the dependent variable of 'labour supply' into line with the other proposals. The basic questions here are, 'What is it that the undertaking needs to do in order to ensure that the required amount of manpower will be available (supplied) in the quality necessary to meet the requirements?'; 'What does the undertaking need to offer in the labour market in order to secure the labour that it is projected to need?'. The first provides a basis for a plan for

153

change and the second indicates the probable content.

The worker's demands

The problem of attracting labour from the labour market into association with an undertaking is one of securing a match between what the worker demands of an employing undertaking as a condition of his joining and staying with it, and what the undertaking is able and willing to offer in order to attract the workers it wants. In very general terms, the question is what the worker perceives as a good employer.

Do we know what the worker wants of the employer? Or what criteria he adopts? We have had advice on both offered to us in plenty usually from one political position or another, and one's own predispositions on the political dimension will lead one to believe the one set or the other. A useful question (which is not in itself a-political) is that which asks what the answer to the above questions should be based on. It could be based on *a priori* reasoning, rooted in one conception of man or another (cf Herzberg, 1968; McGregor, 1960). It could be based on behaviour, what workers actually do (in the way of moving or staying according to the benefit characteristics of undertakings). It could be based on workers' actual statements made in response to systematic surveys (as in some of the cases reviewed below) or statements made on their behalf by their representatives (as in the course of negotiations).

The problem with all these, however, is that of trying to determine which hat the worker is wearing when he provides the behavioural or oral evidence. Workers, being human, occupy many different roles, and in the context of each, the conception of, for example, a good employer might be different. Some of these contexts are likely to be more relevant to the answering of our question than others. To illustrate the problem and to try to discover some useful answers, we will look at a small sub-set of them.

Goodrich (1921) has highlighted one such distinction when he poses four questions which might be of interest to the worker in his capacity as consumer (the first two) and as producer (the second two):

(a) how much the worker gets in the form of material resources to expend on consumption?
(b) what the production in which the worker engages is for, in the sense of whose ultimate benefit it most clearly serves?
(c) how is the worker treated in the system of production, in the

154

sense of how free or dependent he is made in carrying out his work?

(d) what does the worker actually do in the work situation, in the sense of how inherently simple or complex the work assigned to him may be?

A number of American surveys (designed to discover what workers wanted from working) suggested that workers could articulate both consumer and producer related answers.

In some early work by Morse and Weiss (1955) for example, the producer interest seemed paramount, since work seemed to provide workers with 'a feeling of being tied into the larger society, of having something to do, of having a purpose in life' (p 191). Their conclusions from a national sample survey were that workers could and did regard work as more than a means to an end and as sufficiently important to them for them to want to go on working even if they did not *have* to from sheer economic necessity.

Nevertheless, they found some 'class' differences in the replies (between, that is, manual and white collar workers) as did Dubin (1956) and Orzack (1959) in their attempts to discover what were the 'central life interests' of manual workers and nurses respectively in their work situations.

Dubin found that his manual workers did not usually (ie in three out of every four cases) regard work and the workplace as central life interests. Work was where they participated, and possibly found satisfaction, in organizational and technological concerns but it was not where they sought satisfaction in psychological and social terms: these satisfactions were sought and found ouside work. Orzack replicated this Dubin study with nurses (1959) and found that they 'overwhelmingly' preferred work to non-work or community settings for the satisfaction of a wide range of interests.

This 'class' distinction is supported in Lyman's conclusion based on a review of a wide range of comparable American studies: 'They agree beyond doubt that persons at the lower end of the socio-economic scale are more likely than those at the upper end to emphasize the economic aspects of work, whereas those at the upper end more typically stress the satisfaction they find in the work itself' (Lyman, 1955, p 138). This conclusion needs to be borne in mind in considering the conclusions reached by Herzberg in his 1959 study of engineers and accountants, on the distinction between motivators and hygiene factors (*see* chapter 1, above).

An instrumental orientation?

In Britain, Goldthorpe and a number of colleagues examined a closely related question in three factories in the Luton area, in order to discover 'something of the way in which workers order their wants and expectations relative to their employment'. They argue that 'until one knows what *meaning* work has for them—one is not in a position to understand what overall assessment of their job satisfaction may most appropriately be made in their case' (1968, p 36). This notion of an orientation to work refers to the manner in which the individual orders his expectancies of work and the work situation and rests upon his perspective of what it is sensible for him to expect from them (*see* also, below, pp 271–92).

It can be argued that all workers (or at least all employees) *must* sell their labour power, and have little choice in the matter. Therefore, as Goldthorpe *et al* argue, 'all work activity, in industrial society at least, tends to have a basically instrumental component' (1968, p 41) that it emphasizes that the work is a means (instrument) to some other end—like living—and can have chiefly 'expressive functions . . . only exceptionally' (1968, p 38). Nevertheless, variations in emphasis are clearly discernible, in casual observation as in research studies and the contrast which is most commonly seen is the one which appears in the American studies above, that between blue and white collar workers.

Goldthorpe *et al,* carrying out their studies at the time when the embourgement hypothesis was being widely discussed, could consider whether the worker's orientation was towards the consumer or the producer interest. Their conclusion was that these workers were 'particularly *motivated* to increase their power as consumers and their domestic standard of living, rather than their satisfaction as producers and the degree of their self-fulfilment in work' (1968, p 38) and that because of this peculiarity might be distinguished from other blue collar workers of a more 'traditional kind' (1968, p 38)

The dominant orientation of these workers in relation to their work is therefore a largely 'instrumental' one, work having meaning for them as a means to ends external to the work and the work situation itself. In so far as the worker may place major emphasis on this orientation, he will experience his work as 'labour', in which he feels involved only to a very limited extent, tend to act as an economic man in calculating whether it is worth his while in effort (cost)/reward (benefit) terms to remain in that job and, since he can find no great emotional involvement in his work because he does not see it as capable of yielding other kinds of satisfaction than the purely instrumentally-economic, he will tend to live a life which sharply dichotomizes between work and non-work (cf Anderson, 1961).

156

Alternative orientations

Such a finding as this implies that there might be other orientations applicable to workers. The producer-consumer distinction above offers the possibility that one such would be the producer, *homo faber,* orientation; but it is a part of the 'alienation' thesis that in capitalism and/or bureaucratic societies man is denied, by the conditions under which work is organized, the opportunity to experience his work as providing intrinsic satisfaction. In so far as this appears, it is argued, it becomes associated with a 'social' orientation, in which work as a source of human relationships of some kind comes to be valued for its associations rather than for itself.

In Goldthorpe's recognition of this alternative, therefore, work is experienced as a group activity, the group being either the enterprise (in which case involvement may be of a moral and positive kind) (Etzioni, 1961) or the work group, the trade union branch or the shop (in which cases involvement 'is likely to be to some extent alienative; that is, workers are likely to be in some degree negatively oriented towards the organization and to see their group as a source of power against their employer') (Goldthorpe *et al.* 1968, p 41). Because the person can involve himself in the work and work-generated relationships, work has 'much more meaning' for the individual with a solidaristic orientation, and may represent a 'central life interest' for him, helping to structure his extra-work relationships and activities (one graphic example of this is to be found in Dennis, Henriques and Slaughter, 1956).

White collar workers might also be regarded as having something of the instrumentalist orientation but, in their case, as in the case of the solidaristic blue collar workers, there is likely to be a difference in emphasis. Goldthorpe *et al* acknowledge two possible variants, the bureaucratic and the professional orientations. In both, the meaning attached to work is that it is a service, either to an organization (bureaucratic) or to a client (professional) each of which will provide a steadily increasing income, social status and security (ie a career). The worker therefore involves himself morally in the affairs of the organization or the client-system, rendering either 'faithful administration' or 'selfless service to the client' as the case may be 'in return for a relatively secure and privileged existence'. The worker's conception of himself must then become closely bound up with the work arrangement, amounting to a dependence of life-fate on the career, and ego-involvement is strong. In these circumstances, work and non-work may be extremely difficult to divide, the work providing the basis for a way of life, through which all relationships tend to be structured around

157

the work processes. Whilst work is not quite an end in itself, its interdependence is such that it must become nearly so (cf Hughes, 1958).

These constructs thus help to summarize the categories of meaning which, from various studies, various groups of workers seem to attach to their work. They help to crystallize and systematize the general observation that some workers have no interest or involvement in their work whereas others live, eat and sleep their work, whilst the majority fall at some point in between these extremes. The implication of much of the work is that these differences in emphasis occur systematically, as between classes, occupations and even enterprises and parts of the country. The answer to the question 'What work means for people who work?' is that actuarially speaking it means different things to different workers.

In effect, some, perhaps most, workers appear likely to put their interests as consumers first and therefore to demand of the work situation an adequate monetary reward (which they can then, as consumers, spend as they want). But others can be found who, whilst they still have a consumer interest to satisfy, will also seek to satisfy other interests of a social kind in work. The opportunities which such workers will seek of their (actual or potential) employers are therefore likely to be of a different kind, to be satisfied by different kinds of 'offer' from the employer.

The existence of different meanings and orientations amongst workers may then be expected to influence the nature of the offer which the undertaking might make to attract labour. The apparent dominance of the instrumental orientation (which may itself have been fostered by the offers made in the past) tends to justify the pre-eminence given to getting the money offers right, through administered pay policies or negotiation. This is, however, not the whole of the story, and many of the other 'welfare' concerns of personnel management ('human relations' is an obvious example) have a bearing. However, we will first look at the question of determining the 'consideration' offered (see p. 72 above) before turning to these other aspects.

Determining the 'consideration'

The main traditional emphasis in plans to influence labour supply has been upon determining what is the level of remuneration (or consideration) which must be offered to attract labour.

The wage or salary necessary to attract labour into a particular employment may not be influenced by quite the same factors as that necessary to retain it once it has joined (March and Simon, 1958, ch 4). Particularly, the hiring rate offered must overcome the individual's inertia which tends to keep him or her where he or she is (whether employed or not). This same factor will work to the employer's advantage in the fixing of 'retention rates' of pay.

The starting point for considering what constitutes the right level of consideration to attract labour is with the concept of the labour market. This has a classical and a modern conception. In the one, it was assumed (for purposes of analysis) that the market was freely competitive and that the operation of the market forces of supply and demand would tend to fix a (labour) price, as it were, autonomously, at which the market would be cleared (i.e. no one wanting work and no one wanting workers). In such a situation. were it to exist, manpower planning would be a fairly simple exercise of establishing the undertaking's demand for labour; supply and price would then 'determine themselves'.

At the present, the assumptions do not hold and manpower planning (to administer the interchange) and administered or negotiated pay rates (to establish the level of consideration) have themselves developed as ways of arriving at the decisions which are not to be assumed autonomously determined. In effect, therefore, there are now two competing, but mutually-interacting, rationalities which influence the ways in which it is intended that rates of pay to attract labour shall be fixed. The one is the 'employer's' rationality, which supports the administration of the wage and salary system; the other is the 'trade union's' rationality which supports the establishment of pay levels by collective bargaining.

The administered system
Once the employer realizes that he no longer faces a freely competitive market for labour, it becomes necessary to set up some principles which will govern his decision as to what is the correct level to offer and some mechanism by which these may then influence it. These are to be seen exemplified in conceptions of pay structures or systems and in the various 'survey methods' which have been adopted.

One aim of a wage system, from the standpoint of the employer, has been (a) to attract labour from the market and to retain it at the lowest rate consistent with securing enough in quantity to satisfy his production needs, and (b) to ensure that such labour will make a sufficient contribution to the enterprise's tasks to allow it to survive in its product market(s) at the prices he can secure.

The aims of salary systems are comparable in that they 'should *inter alia* influence suitable candidates in sufficient number to apply

159

for and accept employment in the undertaking, facilitate the deployment of employees in such a way as will conduce to the maximum efficiency of the undertaking, influence such people as are suitable to the current and future needs of the undertaking (and only such people) to remain in its employment, and be adequately related to the attainment and continuance of high performance by individuals' (NBPI, Report No 132, 1969, pp 7–8). Salary policy, says Bowley (1972), 'should help *inter alia* to attract staff of the right calibre, encourage staff to stay with the company (if it is in their own and the company's best interests) and facilitate movement of staff across departmental, divisional or sectional boundaries' (Bowley, 1972, p 6).

The objectives of salary policy for the higher echelons of management are generally not different from those pursued at lower levels. Such differences as do exist reflect mainly the different shape of this labour market (which will tend to be national at least and probably international in scope) and the different nature of the bonus or incentive payments generally regarded as applicable at this level. Additionally, determination of the 'compensation' package for this class of labour has in the past needed to pay close attention to remuneration in relationship to the incidence of taxation (although fiscal drag has more recently focused attention on this kind of problem for other wages and salaries). Nevertheless, when all such calculations have been made, the object of the compensation package is to attract and retain the senior managers etc required and to elicit their continued contribution to the health of the enterprise as a whole.

The conventional survey of pay rates
The personnel manager's involvement in realizing these objectives in the past was largely twofold. He had to assemble information (in discussion with fellow personnel managers or through local wage rate and salary surveys) on the rates being paid to classes (eg skilled, semi-skilled or unskilled) or categories (eg fitters and turners, machine operators or process workers) of labour in order either to determine what rates ought to be paid within his own establishment, or to fix the parameters for offer and settlement within a framework of negotiations with local trade union representatives on the structure of rates to apply in the company. He had also to engage in the actual bargaining processes themselves and, in so doing, had to secure acceptance not only of the particular rate of pay but also of the validity and applicability of certain underlying assumptions about what factors determined whether a rate was 'right' by comparison with other parts of the market considered rel-

160

evant. Success in both depended ultimately upon a sufficient stability in the structures of rates and in the assumptions underlying them in the environment of the company.

Where in the past there may have been a known or easily ascertainable 'supply price' for broad categories of labour (like skilled men or labourers) the task of the personnel practitioner in establishing what might be the expected price to be paid 'on the market' was less difficult than now, when even broad skill categories tend to be more closely identified with specific undertakings and their job requirements, from which more volatile rate structures have developed.

Because of this development, the calculation of a blue collar labour market price may call for more systematized techniques, based upon the concept of a wage or salary survey, described by Elliott (1960) as 'one of the most modern techniques at our disposal' which removed the 'obstacle to anyone who is interested in knowing what is generally paid for a particular type of man'.

The problem was seen then as essentially a technical one, that of getting the mix right. Thus Roy (1960), talking of surveys by professional institutions of the salaries of their own members, commented that they were suspect in that 'one is never sure that the cross-section or the sample conforms to the sample of technical staff and scientific staff in one's own company'. The real answer, he suggested, was to get companies to supply complete information on all their scientific staff in a scatter chart. 'If you get several companies common to that field, as we do (and we have selected surveys covering 6,000 scientists) they are only suspect in that your cross-section of scientific staff compares with the cross-section of these other companies. However, I think surely that that comparison will be closer than a comparison with institutions where they depend on the person willingly giving the information to that institution.'

More recently, Carvalho commented on what becomes a much more intractable problem when the rate of change increases: 'External equity is not established logically if historical data are used to 'update' a compensation program. Any updated compensation program is out of date before it is used simply because it requires time to update the program'. Time only becomes of the essence when either increased mobility deflects the direction of market forces, or an increased rate of wage settlement in inflationary conditions more quickly renders historical data obsolete. Since both these phenomena appear to be present in modern economics, they may help account for the pressure to find other methods of determining both general and differential levels of pay (Carvalho,

1971, pp 217–18).

In the case of managerial and professional compensation, the methods employed are different only in the form taken and the factors to be covered. A survey must give attention to a more diverse scatter of elements in the compensation programme, and quite often must spread over wider territory, for example, comparing executive compensation as a totality throughout Europe and/or North America. In this case too, comparison of like with like generally means controlling for the size of establishment or company, and distinguishing between public and private enterprise and, on the international level, making careful calculations as to the effects of taxation on the value of the compensation. Although such international comparisons are not confined to senior management compensation but also apply to various professional categories of employee, it is in the first area that the major problems of comparability lie, as compensation of scientists, engineers or doctors tends to be less ramified and related to more easily definable work roles.

In all three of these cases, wages, salaries and professional or executive compensation, what is sought is an indication of the right 'absolute' level of remuneration, and this is what essentially the survey (however shaped) is designed to provide. In all cases the data supplied in these ways will be historical data, and the need is for decisions about 'correct' future levels of remuneration. In general terms, two major problems arise for the personnel manager in the present context: (a) how far historical data offer a guide to future action, especially when—as may be the case currently in Britain—society may be passing through a period of change in its cultural values as these relate particularly to remuneration of different classes of labour? (b) how far action is possible to bring remuneration into line with either intra-national or international rates of compensation, when national remuneration policies and taxation systems are designed to effect outcomes which are clearly in opposition to achieving such comparability?

Systematizing comparisons
In order to provide a more systematic foundation for making inter-organizational comparisons of pay, Lupton and Bowey (1972–1973, ch 2; and Bowey and Lupton, 1973) have offered a method of comparing the characteristics of different jobs and the reward composition of different jobs. 'It is usual for employees to compare their earnings with those of persons doing similar work in other organizations. Much collective bargaining is based on claims for parity supported by such comparisons. If the employer resists the

162

claim on the ground that the work is not in fact similar or cites other comparisons unfavourable to the employee, then the appeal must be to some procedure that both claimants can accept' (Lupton and Bowey, 1973, p 50). The authors argue that job evaluation arrangements do not prevent unfavourable comparisons with pay in other organizations being made, and that the methods of *internal* job ranking are not suitable for inter-organizational comparisons, so that a distinct procedure is necessary.

In their view, comparisons of jobs in different organizations need to be based upon a systematic assessment and comparison of the selected jobs on the basis of skill, responsibility, mental effort, physical effort and working conditions, each of which can be broken down into sub-factors in order to ensure that jobs which are as nearly as possible the same as the one in the home organization can be identified. Since the individuals concerned and their representatives at the bargaining table will recognize that these factors and sub-factors will have different importance as a factor in wages, these can then be weighted; Lupton and Bowey indicate possible weights which have been applied, but do not regard them as sacrosanct (*ibid*, p 53).

A secondary weighting exercise is then carried out to ensure that widely different amounts of a particular and unimportant factor is not given overweight in the comparison and a method of conversion which reduces the scores on all factors in the comparison jobs to a plus or a minus by comparison with the zero score assigned to that factor in the bench-mark job in the home organization. (The scores are, however, all treated as positive (pluses) in order to avoid cancelling out.) The latter will thus end up with a score of zero, and the comparison jobs chosen will have variable positive scores on each of the factors and in total from which a conclusion can be drawn as to which 'other job' is closest in terms of its demands on the incumbent to the home organization job. This makes it possible to 'ensure that in comparing the pay of a benchmark job and a comparison job, one knows the extent to which one is comparing like with like' (Lupton and Bowey, 1973, p 64).

Comparing the 'closest' jobs in terms of pay means that the pay must be broken down into its component parts, in order to cope with the problem of variability of earnings from week to week. Average weekly earnings are divided into 'the part that is guaranteed (eg base rate, job rate), the part that is regular, although not guaranteed (eg the pay for regular overtime) and thirdly, the part that is sporadic and unreliable (such as very high bonus earnings or irregular and unpredictable overtime)'. To the first two, a figure for sporadic pay is then added, defined as the amount that can be relied upon for five weeks out of six, diminished by an amount equal to two-thirds of the deviation of sporadic pay: the formula: guaranteed earnings, plus regular overtime plus (sporadic pay minus two-thirds deviation of sporadic pay) then yields the 'compounded earnings'. This particular formula can be varied according to the desires of the calculator or the parties to negotiation of pay on the basis of comparisons.

In order to systematize the approach to inter-organizational comparison, Lupton and Bowey suggest a procedure within which four choices have to be made: of which jobs are to be compared, of what weights are to be used for factors, as to the limits to be set in 'secondary weighting', and of the rule to be used for comparing earnings (particularly in relation to the irregular elements). These decisions can be taken by the salary administrator to help discover what might keep the internal rates in line with those outside, or by the parties to negotiations, when they will form 'agreements' in the usual industrial relations sense of the term (Lupton and Bowey, 1973, p 71). The method can also be used either as it is or with modifications to take into account a different range of actors thought appropriate, to determine comparisons for white collar jobs in organizations, supplementing the salary surveys available which usually suffer from the same problem of determining what in the way of 'other jobs' is really comparable in terms of the demands which they make (Lupton and Bowey, 1973, p 122).

In this development, therefore, we may see the employer attempting to respond with an increasingly 'rational' approach to decisions about basic pay rates in the face of an increasingly non-autonomous labour market. As the customary or conventional structures of occupational pay rates, apparently associated with long term supply and demand effects broke down, the employer was increasingly drawn into more sophisticatedly rational planning to fix those rates which attracted the labour he needed. This has not, of course, been without challenge and the developments themselves are at least in part a response to the challenges made to this rationality.

The negotiated wage
The major challenge has come from 'organized labour' or the trade unions. As they developed, they have increasingly demanded two things: a higher level of remuneration for work done and a voice in the actual determination of the wage rates. Starting, historically, in roughly the same situation as the employer, they have sought to influence the otherwise assumedly-unimpeded effects of market

forces upon wage rates and employment. This attracted a similar kind of organization on the part of the employers, in the form of employers' associations, as they sought to protect, through solidarity or consensus, their competitive position *vis à vis* each other (cf Ross, 1948). What was then interposed between the 'market forces' was a structure of decision-taking which we have come to refer to as 'collective bargaining' a process in which the two parties seek, in agreement, a 'decision' about what the pay rate should be.

In Britain, in recent years, the traditional method of determining the wage rate, by negotiation between employer and trade union representatives, has been thrown into disarray by full employment, technological change and inflation. The first two have exerted their influence mainly upon the power of the worker (and his trade union) and the second has additionally effected significant changes in the composition of jobs themselves; but the third has, arguably, had the major effect in so far as it has caused bargaining to take place in conditions of greater uncertainty in which there are few devices for reducing this to a more calculable risk. Whether the cause of the inflation itself is external to the economy, and whether it is properly describable as demand pull or cost push inflation, attempts to deal with the uncertainty are themselves often contributory to the inflation because of the 'margins' which the negotiators seek to provide for in their settlements—in the absence of governmental restrictions on levels and forms of settlements (cf Jackson, Turner and Wilkinson, 1972).

Two main methods of dealing with this problem are discernible: the pursuit of an uncertainty-reducing 'round' of bargaining, and the search for a method of administering the external relativities in pay fixing (already discussed).

In the first, the pay fixing process is seen as beginning with a feeling on the part of workers of a sense of relative deprivation, either because their existing pay does not 'go as far as it did' or because they see some other more powerful group securing increases in pay whilst they stay still. This gives rise to claims which seek either a 'cost of living' addition to wages to make up for the inflation loss or restoration of relativity or comparability to put them back into their 'proper' place in the league table of pay. These feelings and the claims they give rise to are likely to be more powerful as stimulators of a new round of bargaining over pay than purely 'economic factors', such as those associated with productivity and mere ability to pay at the micro level or unemployment and balance of payments at the macro level.

From this point of initiation, bargaining in recent years has come increasingly to take the form of the development of 'rounds'.

165

In the 1960s, the idea of a 'round' of wage demands and wage increases began to gain ground (even though disguised to some extent by the prevalence of local bargaining in some industries) and progressively groups which were not originally in the 'rounds' were brought in, so that by the middle 1970s very few categories were left out.

During this period, too, except where government pay policies placed restrictions on the rounds, the tendency developed for the absolute level of increases to increase year by year, producing an escalator effect on inflation, and for the length of a round to shorten, with a similar effect compounded. Nevertheless by 1975 the idea of an annual round of pay bargaining had established itself and most groups of workers, from the lowest paid to the highest paid white collar workers had established their 'position' in the round, some coming in early and others late.

The importance of this concept of a 'round', viewed from the standpoint of planning wage rates for attraction and retention of labour at appropriate levels of efficiency, is that it lends itself to the practice of building in 'margins' to cover for the uncertainty expected to exist before the next round can be carried out. Where the situation is 'open,' particularly where it is not constrained by central pay policies of governments or labour market institutions (such as the 'social contract'), the negotiated rate is likely to contain explicit margins, in the form of automatic escalations made contingent upon inflationary changes or of re-opening provisions allowing renegotiation in similar circumstances. In the constrained situation the opportunity for negotiating such marginal protections may be denied and the same objective is therefore sought via other kinds of provision: the negotiation of fringe benefits which have value to the worker and are a cost on the employer but which have tended not to be accounted as a part of the wage settlement. All these have the general effect of protecting the worker against inflation to some extent, but they do not facilitate wage rate or wage cost forecasting by the employer.

Partly for this reason, employers have become keener to introduce systematic procedures for determining some elements of the wage and salary structures. These include attempts to 'abandon piece-work' as a control device because it tends, in a condition of inflation to associate itself with inflation of wage costs; attempts to abandon or at least restrict overtime working for comparable reasons; and plans to introduce job evaluation schemes in order to allow the differential position to be stabilized even if the minimum hiring rate might still be left to escalate.

All these help to increase the importance of company wide

negotiations at the expense of national bargaining, and focus more attention on the methods and techniques of wage and salary administration as within the competence of the personnel department. From the employers' standpoint, the development of such control methods and their containment within locally controllable negotiating frameworks offer some hope that the uncertainties inherent in the situation of change might be reduced to more predictable risks.

Overall, however, this approach to getting the money right is consistent with the instrumental view, in which both the undertaking and the worker are seen to engage in a relatively straightforward process of calculating the respective costs and benefits involved in the offer-demand situation. The negotiating process, involving representatives, is then seen to be a device for reducing the variety of separate decisions which would otherwise be called for and thus of achieving a degree of standardization in the 'offer-demand' position.

In the light of the earlier discussion, however, this must be regarded as a 'blunt instrument' in so far as it does not allow the subtleties and variations their due weight. In the past, some of these have been swept into the personnel manager's 'welfare' function, but the modern conception attempts to give this general concern a more rigorously analytical basis.

Beyond remuneration

Assuming that some resolution can be effected of the remuneration problem, we are left with what (for purposes of this discussion) may be referred to as the 'residual problem', ie what is demanded and what is to be offered 'beyond remuneration'. The 'problem' may be considered in two parts.

On the one hand, there is the issue of what the undertaking is actually seeking when it establishes the employment contract. At base it may be looking for a contribution of labour effort to the realization of the task objectives and for which 'consideration' will be given. But in addition, it usually seeks much more than this; this is usually identified by the concept of 'loyalty' and it usually means a constellation of attitudes which support the acceptance by the worker of employer's rules (see above, pp 90–95) *as an order or as a duty owed.*

Anthony, for example, suggests that

managers and employers have always required a high degree of involvement of workers in their work, and this commitment or moral involvement in work has a tradition of some two hundred years in which it has been emphasized as a duty (Anthony, 1977, p 174).

Fox's consideration of the concept of 'trust' in work (Fox, 1974, p 13) has similar connotations which he explores more fully in his book which is appropriately titled *Beyond Contract*. Recent studies by Gill (1978) and Gallie (1978) narrate the attempts by ICI and BP (respectively) to recruit loyalty and moral commitment amongst their employees by means which extend well beyond a simple material bargain.

For the undertaking, such loyalty, trust and commitment may have a high instrumental value which, in a highly competitive situation, may be difficult or impossible to acquire by simple transfer of consideration in the simple material sense. It is a part of Fox's argument that these contributions become more crucial to the undertaking's survival and success when the market position is difficult. But in the same circumstances, material value is more difficult to come by and other means of securing the contributions have to be found. Whether or not it is assumed that all workers want from work is money, therefore, there is a strong suggestion that the undertaking wants more from workers than (at least in some circumstances) it can actually purchase with this medium.

On the other hand, there is the question of what workers are willing and able to contribute to the organization. In Marchington's study of employees in a kitchen-furniture company, he found that the workers would probably use the criterion of how much pay as the main one in their decision (1980, pp 44–7) even though in talking about their existing jobs, they sought other benefits, ie opportunity to learn new skills, for recognition and advancement, even though they were usually not seen to be very forthcoming.

This offers the possibility of a mis-match. The argument runs that undertakings have taught workers to expect little but material reward; but undertakings must seek something more than can be bought in this way if they are to survive; and yet workers 'do not feel that they have to like their jobs or their employer' (Schein, 1965, p 46). The mis-match arises, therefore, because in that situation, business and industry is forced to try to 'establish new kinds of relationships' with workers based on normative conceptions (emphasizing loyalty, commitment, trust and the rest) rather than on the other utilitarian ones.

Members are increasingly expected to like their work, to become personally committed to organizational goals, and to become creative in the service of these goals (Schein, 1965, p 47).

But this, by itself, might result in the undertaking 'expecting workers to give more than it gives them' (*ibid,* p 46) and in order to re-establish some greater degree of matching, workers have to be 'given more influence in decision-making . . . in exchange' (*ibid.* p 47).

Schein's notion of a 'psychological contract' bringing together what is 'expected' by both employer and employee into a more general process of offering and accepting than that which is implied in the simple legal definition of contract helps to establish what kinds of match have to be made between offers and demands in the 'psychological labour market' and thus helps to guide planning activity in this area.

The basic idea of the psychological contract has been further developed by Mumford, as a way of indicating more particularly the dimensions of offer and acceptance which probably need to be covered in this process.

The variety of contractual elements
In her conception, the worker may be seen to make five distinct demands upon any undertaking in which he might be or become employed, and the undertaking to make five corresponding offers on these same dimensions. The ideal state would be one in which the two (demands and offers) would match each other. In so far as investigation suggests that they do not, the undertaking is given clues as to what might be changed in its present offer portfolio in order to effect the adjustment of labour supply and demand required by the proposals for future action. The conception, in other words, serves to direct management's attention to aspects of the employment contract in a systematic way (Mumford, 1972). Her five elements of the contract are:

1 The element of knowledge: the undertaking needs to establish what in the way of knowledge and skill it requires in its employees and which means (hiring in or development after engagement are two broad alternatives) are to be used to secure them, and to match these with what the worker expects (*see* table 4 on page 170).
2 The element of motivation: the undertaking needs to determine what psychological contribution it will expect of its employees (loyal service and high commitment to the solution of the organizational problems are alternative ways of expressing this) and what incentive offers it makes to secure it.
3 The element of efficiency: the undertaking has to set up the performance standards which it will expect of employees and to con-

169

Table 4
The nature of the employer–employee contracts

	The firm	The employee
1 The *knowledge* contract	Needs a certain level of skill and knowledge in its employees if it is to function efficiently	Needs the skills and knowledge he brings with him to be used and developed
2 The *psychological* contract	Needs motivated employees	Needs factors which will motivate him, eg achievement, recognition, responsibility, status
3 The *efficiency* contract	Needs to achieve set output and quality standards	Needs an equitable effort-reward bargain; needs controls, including supervisory ones, which are seen as acceptable
4 The *ethical* (social value) contract	Needs employees who will accept the firm's ethos and values	Needs to work for an employer whose values do not contravene his own
5 The *task structure* contract	Needs employees who will accept any technical contraints associated with their jobs	Needs a set of tasks which meets his requirements for variety, interest, targets, feedback, task identity and autonomy

Source: taken from E Mumford, Job Satisfaction: A Method of Analysis, *Personnel Review*, 1 (3) Summer, 1972, p 51

sider whether what is offered particularly in the way of material reward, forms the basis for an effort-reward bargain which will prove to be acceptable to employees given their expectations.
4 The element of commitment (ethics): what the undertaking has to work out here is how much of the human personality will be required to be committed to the pursuit of the undertaking's ends, and therefore just how big a demand it might have to make of the person in the way of adjusting his or her values to permit the individual to join and continue.
5 The element of interest (task structure): is the actual work being offered to the individual such that it will meet his expectations of it (whether those be for routine or for interesting or challenging work) when it is considered in the round, embracing both the set tasks and the setting (or structure) in which they are placed.

In the initial conception, these are distinguished from one another for purposes of making the analysis and setting out the 'check-list' of what needs to be considered. They may therefore be considered separately, but they do not stand in complete isolation from one another in practice. Gowler, for example, has suggested one way in

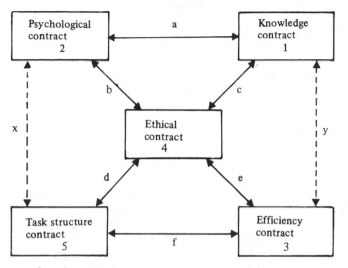

Figure 6
The relationships between employment contracts

Source: taken from D Gowler, Values, Contracts and Job Satisfaction, *Personnel Review*, 3 (4) Autumn, 1974, p 5

which the main relationships between them might be though of (Gowler, 1974, p 5; reproduced in figure 6 above.

Past experience in the personnel field has tended to emphasize some particular elements in this web (for example, the wage-effort bargain in No 3 and training and development in No 1) but for the rest has tended to sweep them all together in a conception of welfare policy which then carries the burden of the employer's offer on all dimensions other than (usually) the material reward element. The alternative inference to be drawn from Mumford's suggestion, therefore, is that the older general conception of welfare might in future be treated in this 'more clinical' fashion in order to improve the 'offer' position of the undertaking in the face of changing employee expectations of it.

This analysis bears upon questions relating to the actual performance of work once the contract of employment has been established, and aspects of it will be returned to later (*see* below, pp 218–21, 231–61, and 458–59). But if the third is the most directly concerned with the remuneration offer which we looked at in the first part of the chapter, there is always the other (effort) side of this bargain to be considered, and in Mumford's schema this is usually bound up closely with the knowledge-skill element in (1) and the

171

task-interest element in (5). We have already touched briefly upon the motivational/ethical aspects of (2) and (4) but the main discussion of these is left until we consider motivation in part two.

Work-effort-knowledge-skill

These other aspects, however, are likely, in combination, to have an important bearing on the recruitment/retention process. We have already noted the existence of some evidence which suggests that the worker has some interest in 'things-technological' (Dubin, 1956) even if his orientation is basically 'instrumental'.

The nature of the task structure within the undertaking is therefore likely to bear importantly upon his or her decision to join or stay. As a part of the response to the changing situation (noted above from Schein) undertakings have recently sought to change the trend towards greater fractionalization of work roles through the devices of job enlargement and job enrichment. This effectively changes the 'offer' position on this dimension, and when it is coupled with the concept of 'autonomous working group', it also conveys an impression of enhancing freedom or discretion for the worker. (This aspect is discussed more fully below, pp 341–43.)

The individual also expects to have to contribute effort to the achievement of work objectives and in return for the remuneration offered. The fact of an effort contribution is unlikely to be in doubt or dispute, but the comparative amount required in the particular case is. This implies that the offer made on this score should be based on a systematically and fairly derived standard and communicated effectively to the individual in order to reduce the uncertainties in the situation.

Usually the wage rate and bonuses will be computed and communicated with great precision, but the effort rate is vague and not communicated until day to day negotiations take place between the worker and either the trainer or the supervisor. (Some consideration is given to the question of standard setting on pp 195–98 and 298–311, below.)

The question, therefore, of what knowledge and skill the individual is required to possess or to acquire (and the opportunity offered to increase these) can only be answered by reference to these other two considerations (of task-structure and effort). To the extent that no information is available on those, the individual is unlikely to be able to be given any clear idea of what is either offered or demanded. But it is in this connection, in the provision of learning opportunities (or training) that all three of these tend to come together. On the other hand in so far as the undertaking makes offers beyond remuneration, it is most usually in the area of

172

training, simply because, in the attempt to influence the supply side of the interchange equation, training seems to offer a main means of increasing that supply.

Training to increase supply
'Training' may or may not fall into the same category as consideration, as something which the potential employee positively wants from the employer. In so far as the employer provides training, it is a cost to him just as the wage paid is a cost, but it is not necessarily perceived by the recipient as a benefit. The worker may view training as something which he or she has to undergo, even suffer, in order that the employer might secure the kind and amount of service which he wants.

Workers in this respect may be treated as differing between those (like the traditional craftsman) who want to preserve their independence from the employer in respect of their skill acquisition and development, and those who expect the employer to provide any skill training which 'he' needs. The first category is likely to include those whose career is conceived occupationally and therefore in terms of mobility between employers, and the second those whose career is conceived more in terms of remaining with any one employer for as long as possible and by doing such work as enables this objective to be realized.

The situation which generally workers now face is one which is likely to provide more opportunities for the second of these worker strategies than for the first. Marked reductions in product-lives and increases in the rate of change in production and process technologies are thought to pressure undertakings towards more training provision in order to secure the amounts and kinds of labour which the product-mixes and technologies seem to dictate to them.

This development is often associated with the growth of the so-called 'internal labour market' (a relatively new concept meant to indicate that the employer tends to recruit green labour at the bottom of the undertaking's skill hierarchies and to use training approaches to develop that labour to fill the vacancies occurring within them). The undertaking of the future may be predicted to depend much more upon a training approach to manning. Although there are still many employers who rely upon the kind of interchange with the external labour market of the type considered in the earlier section on manpower forecasting and planning, the belief is growing that with changes in commercial policies and technologies, this is a declining breed.

As between these two strategies and the situation which they create, the onus falls differently. Recruitment from the external market places the onus upon the worker, whilst internal recruitment places it upon the employer:

(a) a worker who applies for a specified job which calls for a specific amount, type or level of skill, in effect warrants that he or she has that skill; the employer would expect that, if hired, the employee would be able to discharge the requirements of the job. If that proved to be an unfounded expectation in the event, the employee would be open to dismissal on grounds of incompetence. This is by no means clear-cut, but the main onus is on the employee to demonstrate that he possesses the skills which he warrants he has
(b) an employer who hires an employee in order to train him or her in the skills required to perform the job is placed in the position where he has to select for 'trainability' and can ask the employee to warrant only that he or she is willing to undergo the training, not that he or she is necessarily 'trainable'. Failure to perform the actual job may be as much due to the quality of the training as to the capacity of the individual to learn. The employer may still have the option of dismissing the unsuccessful trainee at the end of the training period, but he cannot in so doing rely solely upon any kind of 'breach of warranty' on the part of the worker.

As is hinted at in these two statements, the law tends to support both of these positions, with common law having most to say on the first and recent legislation more on the second.

It is the first of these which, except in respect of professional and other high skill occupations, appears to be disappearing from a large part of the economy. With it therefore goes the convention that an employer can rely upon the labour market to supply his labour demands and contribute little more than a few apprenticeships to the maintenance of the pool of skill. Generalized ability may still be hired, but the jobs on offer are themselves so specific in their 'demands' upon the individual that the specific ability to cope with them has to be developed within the undertaking. In addition those demands may be increasingly complex and difficult to comprehend simply 'by experience' on which we have relied in the past, and formal training may be required as the only way of developing the ability. For these reasons a training strategy may be forced upon the employer; once adopted, it may then serve as a moral force in attracting at least one category of person.

The morality of providing training—perhaps to facilitate the mutual performance of the contract requirements—is something which has been increasingly argued in the 1960s and 1970s, but it has often been coupled with an argument that training would improve the productive performance of British industry. Both of these, the moral and the practical arguments, have been recognized in legislation designed to improve the amount and quality of industrial training generally within the economy.

External stimulation
The need for such advocacy by state and voluntary bodies was associated with the dearth of training for employment in Britain in the early part of the post-war period. Training was just not a habit of employing organizations, and where it was undertaken it was usually treated as a charitable donation which would be suspended when times were harder. In the full employment situation of the period, however, the chronic shortage of skilled labour was responded to by seeking ways to restrict the craft unions' control over entry to the trades, in order that some national programme of skill training might be developed to cope with the new technologies forecast. The training and re-training needs of other categories could and would be met by internal and on-the-job training methods, provided that employers were somehow protected from, or compensated for, the loss of their training investment as a result of poaching by other employers.

The Industrial Training Act of 1964 attempted to provide a framework for systematizing the various forms of training required, increasing its overall amount and spreading the cost equitably between employers. The Act required the Minister of Labour to set up a Central Training Council (CTC) and empowered him to establish Industry Training Boards (ITBs) composed on a tripartite basis and empowered to make levies on the firms in their industry to pay for the provision of training (some of which may occur within the same firms) and to provide or secure sufficient training for the industries' needs. After almost 10 years, dissatisfaction with the achievement of this levy-grant system led to a change to a levy and levy abatement arrangement under the Employment and Training Act 1973, which also placed the Manpower Services Commission (and its executive agency, the Training Services Agency (now Division)) between the government and the ITBs.

Neither the amount nor the value of training provided for workers in employment is capable of calculation in any precise way. Some major part of the costs of education must be included in it, and it might well be that the amount of training provided in employment undertakings themselves would represent a very small addition to this. But the schemes developed under the two Acts of Parliament were intended to increase the availability of training to workers at the beginning or during the course of their employment.

In spite of two decades of state intervention to do something about the situation, Britain remains, amongst the EEC countries, the one with the lowest proportion of apprenticeships and further education and training amongst young people. This may be altered by EEC proposals in the future, but at the moment it appears as if British workers may receive less training than their fellows in the EEC, in spite of attempts to encourage employers to do more of it by manipulating the incentives and disincentives under legislation. The level of levy income to the ITBs in 1978–79 was no more than £71.6 million, and the TSD's contribution to their operating costs in the following year was £42.5 million, with TSD contribution to training for skills etc adding another £40 million.

In its evidence to the MSC's 1978–80 Review of Employment and Training Act 1973, the TUC argued for an increase in the amount of training being carried on in industry, and for increases in levies and the number of ITBs to secure it. In their view, if it was necessary to achieve this end, this should be required by new statutory regulations which would bolster the national training programmes with both social and industrial aims (which they advanced as part of their alternative economic strategy).

In the CBI view, however, the operating costs of the ITBs are too high, and for this reason they would not be in favour of the government cutting the central fundings and requiring industry to foot the bill. Employers would prefer the national strategy to emphasize purely industrial and business objectives, and to be administered locally rather than through these centralized arrangements.

Clearly, there is little agreement between the two organizations as to the strategy to be adopted in respect of training.

The undertaking's plans
The manpower planner, in determining whether to incorporate a training plan in his overall scheme, will need to take into account both the objectives of workers and the nature of the 'demand' situation in the undertaking. The first helps establish whether he can expect the one or other category of labour to apply for the kinds of jobs which the undertaking will be offering. The second aids the decision as to whether training is an imperative if the demand and supply factors are to be brought into balance at the level of the undertaking. Even if the national bodies cannot agree on an overall training strategy for the country, the undertaking is likely to be

176

better placed to discover the limits to its own decision.

Whether training can contribute to the plan (in projection or in implementation) will depend upon its capacity to meet the needs revealed by the forecasts. Not all forecasts need training as a major element in the strategy, although the increased emphases upon employment stability and job property rights do suggest that the achievement of labour force flexibility will in future depend more so than in the past upon training.

From this point of view, training may be regarded as capable in appropriate circumstances of alleviating three difficulties, those of general skill requirement, specific skill (or limited role prescription) requirement, and (in a slightly more general context than manpower planning) motivational deficiency.

In the first category are those who enter the undertaking without skill (or skill of the needed kind) but are recruited for skilled work. The obvious example is the school leaver who enters upon an apprenticeship. Although undertakings might think it cheaper to recruit fully trained personnel, this cannot generally be done unless a public training service carries out this function; some organization somewhere must provide this 'basic' training that new entrants or job changers need in order to carry out their assigned roles. Where the 'external supply' pool is empty, it may therefore prove necessary to establish a formal programme of initial, skill training as a part of the overall strategy for manning the undertaking.

Training for future craftsmen usually takes the form of apprentice training, through which the skills are in some fashion transmitted to the young person who has decided to embark upon a craftsman's career. The fact that another employer may subsequently reap the benefit of this training does not alter the fact that employers in general must make adequate provision for training if the system of free recruitment is to work at all adequately. Non-craftsmen also require training and here it is more likely that the training will more often be given on-the-job because possibilities for transference of skill are less than in the case of craftsmen. To develop the appropriate amount and type of skill, therefore, formal training programmes are likely to be required.

Secondly, training may be incorporated in the strategy to improve or implant the skills which the individual will need in order to work within the particular organization. In certain occupational categories, the skills might already be present in the newly hired employee. Here the training process complements and completes the selection process. In an ideal world the organization might seek to recruit into its ranks those employees who came with the precise skills and the precise expectations that the organization requires of them.

Frequently this is not so and writers on organizations like Fayol and Urwick were therefore led to propose that management had a main responsibility to get the work patterns right, but should otherwise take what it could get in the way of people to carry out this work. It would tend to follow from this view that training would be necessary to ensure that new employees fully appreciated what skills they would be expected to develop in relation to their jobs, and what other expectations would surround their conduct within the organization.

Organizations will vary in the extent to which they can rely upon recruitment of this type. For example, the engineering or printing craftsman might reasonably be expected to have acquired the skills which would be required in his employment in any particular organization. On the other hand, the semi-skilled worker might enter the organization without ever having seen technology of that kind before, and might therefore be expected to have very little other than highly generalized skill to carry out semi-skilled work. It would therefore follow that in those circumstances the onus of training the individual to the level of skill required by the technology would fall upon the employer. In any case it could not be presumed that a new employee would know what the objectives, policies and standards of the organization were, so that even if the man arrived with a complete package of skills he would still need some element of induction training to ensure that he understood the context within which he would now be expected to work. In this sense of induction training in particular, therefore, one could refer to training as complementing the selection process.

Thirdly, training may also be used as a method of increasing the motivation of the employee either to work harder or to make a more effective contribution to the objectives of the employer. The argument here runs that if the individual understands what his work is all about in terms of the total set of activities which are carried out by the employer, then morale in the organization will be likely to be higher than otherwise and that because of the higher morale thus engendered the performance of people working within that organization will be increased. It must however be said that the attempts that have been made to uncover the relationship between morale and productivity have not been uni-directional in their conclusions; there is certainly no simple and direct relationship between morale and productivity as far as the evidence goes. Nevertheless, the belief is pervasive and most organizations would work on the assumption that training is one way by which the values as well as the aims of the organization can at least be explained to the employee in the hope at least that his performance will benefit from a knowledge of what these are.

The strategies and tactics of training will thus respond to these different objectives. Where, for example, a craftsman is hired into an organization as a craftsman, the training programme will necessarily emphasize the need for inducting the individual to the new organizational system. Where the new employee is hired to carry out semi-skilled work of which he has had no experience before, the training programme will have to cater not only for the induction of the employee but also the development of skills to an appropriate level and of an appropriate type. Since organizations are both different in the mix of skills that they require at any one time and in the extent to which they are affected by technological changes, it is unlikely that one-off training exercises will suffice to meet the problem faced by them. It is likely that different types of training programmes will be required for different categories or grades of labour so that the total training spectrum includes apprentice training, young person training in semi-skilled work, induction of new employees, and up-dating training for both hired-in craftsmen and for existing employees. But it is very likely that, with major changes in work method or changes in the underlying technology of the organization, the organization will have to establish a training programme which is oriented not so much to young or new employees as to the development and modification of skills that have already been acquired at some earlier stage in the individual's career. The total training package is not therefore likely to appear as a simple single process of training.

This, then, is the consideration which has to be set as the cost-bearing element against the benefit which training might bestow in helping to meet the manpower demand forecasts. These establish whether there is likely to be a shortfall and, if there is, how big it is likely to be. One role of training is to reduce the shortfall itself by providing, at a cost to the undertaking, the training which will require the necessary abilities to be 'grown' at home. Whether it is a worthwhile exercise is, however, to be determined very largely by the comparison of the costs and the benefits on the various dimensions (cf Thomas et al, 1969).

The provision of training can and does, in addition, serve to increase the attractiveness of the undertaking as a source of employment for those appropriately motivated, by virtue of the opportunity which it provides for personal growth and development. It helps to create the 'image of the good employer' in the minds of potential (as well as actual) employees. This element in the

179

equation cannot therefore be ignored, but it is better considered as a part of the total 'package' of advantages, other than the simple considerations of the wage-effort variety, which may influence the minds of those currently outside the undertaking.

This package is likely to include a large number of elements: from the challenge or otherwise of the work itself, through the attractiveness of the remuneration terms, to the fringe or welfare areas traditionally associated with personnel management. These may be examined in terms of their conventional outcrops in personnel management (see below pp 514–17) or in terms of the kinds of contract which Mumford identifies (above, pp 169–72). But it is pertinent to recognize that all of these, those discussed and those still to be examined, are likely to be people-contingent as well as contingent upon the undertaking's situation. In other words, people differ in the demands they make and therefore in the criteria which they employ to determine what is a good employer. In order to assist in the development of a recruitment strategy, the employer has some opportunity to ascertain something of these criteria.

Control of labour turnover

It is open to the employer to ascertain what his workers might want by asking them in some kind of survey (*see*, MacKenzie Davey, 1970; Palmer, 1977). It is also open to him to use the exit interview to discover what causes employees to leave. What individuals may say in either of these contexts may need to be treated with caution. The exit interview, however, is likely to be conducted mainly with those who have short service with the employer and the information which is obtained is likely to be relevant to the decision of a worker to join or not to join the undertaking.

The exit interview is unlikely to be particularly helpful unless it forms part of a broader strategy and policy relating to the control of labour turnover. This is a term used to identify the total movement of workers both into and out of the undertaking. Some of this turnover is unavoidable (as, for example, in the case of retirement), some of it is caused by decisions of the employer to terminate (for example, in cases for dismissal for cause), and some of it is 'voluntary' in the sense that it arises from decisions by the employee to terminate the employment. All three of these can be controlled although the main burden of it will be borne by the third.

Control depends upon an accurate measurement of the phenomenon. It is possible to calculate turnover rates for both joining and leaving but the employer's usual main interest is in the latter. This may be measured in one or all of three ways.

180

Firstly, it may be measured as:

$$\frac{\text{Number of separations during period}}{\text{Average number employed during period}} \times 100$$

This is, however, a crude measure and does not make the discriminations between newly hired workers and long service employees which are likely to prove more useful in developing controls.

Secondly, the phenomenon may be measured by means of a survival curve. This is based on the plotting of the incidence of leaving over time of an original cohort of workers hired into the organization. For example, if 136 workers are hired between January and March, their rate of leaving over the next two years can be plotted on a graph. All the evidence suggests that this curve will take a typical form of a high rate of leaving over the first year, followed by a steep decline in the rate of leaving in the second year and a levelling out over the subsequent period. The advantage of this calculation is that it produces data which are independent of the rate of expansion of the undertaking.

Thirdly, and in many ways similar to the survival curve, is the method of calculating a stability index. This is calculated as:

$$\frac{\text{Present no of employees with 1 year's service or over}}{\text{Total employed one year ago}} \times 100$$

This also discounts the influence of short service employees upon the index and consistently with the inference to be drawn from the survival graph it usually produces an index figure of about 80 per cent.

Thus the indices may be calculated for the labour force as a whole or for broad segments of it or for specific occupational and job groups within it. They indicate to the firm, by comparison with the rates for the appropriate industry (published regularly in the DE *Gazette*) whether the firm is succeeding in retaining employees or not. It therefore provides a first indication of whether action needs to be taken.

The second relevant set of data concerns the cost of labour turnover. The total cost is likely to be made up of:

(a) administrative costs in recruitment
(b) training costs including the cost of inducting the new employee and of providing any training necessary to enable the individual to start work
(c) costs arising from the loss of production and from extra overtime which might be necessary to compensate for it (it is likely to be the largest single item of cost)

(d) costs of damage whether to materials and equipment or to people themselves through accidents.

A number of publications are available which give guidance on making these calculations (BIM, 1959; Furness, 1950; Rubber EDC, 1968).

The third item of desirable information is that concerning causes which is what is likely to be contributed by the exit interview. The causes which are usually identifiable from the information obtained in such interviews are:

(a) inefficiencies in recruitment and selection procedures
(b) inadequate provision for induction of the new employee
(c) inadequate training to enable the individual to carry out the work required
(d) inadequate wage levels as the individual compares these
(e) physical conditions and the general amenity of work.

Armed with this information it is possible to develop a control strategy for labour turnover which, dependent upon the causes identified in the particular case, would emphasize improvement in the processes listed in the preceding paragraph. This, of course, implies that the products of the analyses are fed into the decision-making processes, and allowed to influence the decisions taken. Control is not to be equated with data-gathering and measurement, but to be seen as part of the decision process. Decisions about the offers to be made by the undertaking, both to get and to hold labour, require the information to be used constructively in strategic planning.

Summary
To help him plan to affect the labour supply variable, the personnel manager has both general ideas available to him to help shape his decisions and particular information (which can be generated within the undertaking) on the local situation to ensure greater situational relevance. Even if the demand side of the manning equation is taken as given there are methods which can be adopted to facilitate the manpower planning activities required.

It is inconceivable that workers will be completely non-instrumental in their calculation of benefits from work and a major element in the plan will be the remuneration offered in return for contribution. There are methods available to establish what level of remuneration is likely to prove attractive. But since in addition, the worker will demand some offer on the other dimensions of the contract (as categorized by Mumford) particularly as a condition of *staying* with the undertaking, attention will be needed to these other offer-demand features of the situation.

The methods or devices available in this other area are relatively new, and since they are more often related to 'performance' than to 'recruitment', the main discussion of them is deferred until later. But on the score of training (which has more frequently been associated with increasing labour supply in the past) the methods are now more refined than they were 20 years ago, largely because of the fillip given by the two Training Acts. It is therefore possible to be more systematic in planning this kind of action than has often been the case in the past, although training cannot be embarked upon systematically without much more attention to the task-structure, the contribution standards, and the motivational/attitudinal demands which the undertaking makes upon the worker.

Further reading
On the general ideas referred to in this chapter, see Schein (1965), Mumford (1972) and Marchington (1981).

Additional material on the ways of developing remuneration plans, see Lupton and Bowey (1974) and Bowey (1981). Some of the material in Thomason (1980) is also relevant.

Additional material on training is to be found in Singer (1969), Bass and Vaughan (1968) and Kenney, Donnelly and Reid (1979).

The preparation and uses of records are discussed more fully in Dyer, 1980, and Tavernier, 1971 and 1973; more dynamics aspects are considered in NIIP, 1964.

On the specific topic of labour turnover, see BIM (1959), Pettman (1973), Rice (1950). On the topic of absence and its control, see BIM (1961), Chadwick Jones *et al* (1973), Junes (1971).

8 Preparing for recruitment

Processes and activities

By itself manpower planning is sterile unless some action is taken in accordance with it. This action includes taking in needed labour and discharging it, and then deploying and re-deploying it within the undertaking as occasion may require. We need therefore, at this point in the development of the general theme of the book, to look at those processes and activities which are necessarily set in train in the execution of a manpower plan. There are naturally many of these, but for convenience of treatment it is proposed in this chapter to restrict consideration to those which can be related directly to the setting up and maintenance of the contract of employment.

This is a somewhat mechanistic approach to the general question of developing such relationships, but it does permit the bringing together of a number of activities and a number of related technical skills which have long stood as part of the stock-in-trade of the personnel specialist.

The general view is that, in carrying out a manpower plan, it is necessary to undertake actions related to recruitment, selection, engagement, transfer, advancement, promotion, termination, reinstatement and re-engagement, all of which entail some element of definition of the rights and duties of the parties to the employment contract. It does not follow that all of these elemental stages must have equal weight or equal applicability in the particular case; indeed, reinstatement and re-engagement are abnormal processes but for completeness they are included here. Taken together, they do permit us to review in one logical sequence the processes which might be associated with the implementation of manpower plans.

They also associate themselves with a set of inter-personal skills of the kind which the personnel specialist has usually been considered to possess as his main marketable commodity. At any and all of the elemental stages in this process as outlined, communication, structured in terms of the individual employee and the representative or agent of the employing undertaking, must take place. The individual employee both seeks and gives information and the agent does likewise, and each may be regarded as having his own set of criteria by which to decode that information and to evaluate it, for his own purposes, which will normally be quite different. The obvious examples of this are the selection interview or test and the interview for promotion. In these instances, the parties must exchange some information so that a decision can be reached. In many undertakings formal arrangements for exchanging information do not exist for some of the other processes identified (for example, transfers or termination). But however informal these processes may be, some exchange of information is necessary and the effect of recent legislation upon them is likely to be that of greater formalization of these activities in the future, as individuals become more conscious of 'their rights' established in this way.

Application of traditional inter-personal skills in the employment context must therefore take place within a framework of constraint derived from the sources of 'the terms and conditions' which have been identified in chapter 4 above: the common law, the collective agreement, the legislation applicable, as well as from the requirements of the undertaking itself as expressed in the manpower plan. A knowledge of the 'law', the terms of union agreements and of the intentions of the planners is thus a prerequisite of successful executive activity at this level. All these constraints are woven together to influence the directions taken by the activities of the specialists charged with securing and terminating employees.

We have already noted (above, pp 73–90) that legislation has restricted this activity in only a limited way (even if it is also an important one). The management is therefore still relatively free to establish the criteria which it will adopt to guide the selection process.

The information jungle
In order to be systematic about this, management needs to set up a conception of what work is required of individuals (defined by the patterns associated with it) if the undertaking is to realize its objectives in relation to it as well as a definition of the standards of performance or achievement to be associated with it. Thereafter it will be possible to derive a specification of the kind of person (by capability) required to perform to these standards *and* the predictors which will be used to guide the recruitment of such persons. All of these are a necessary part of the process of planning for recruitment, although they are not necessarily done, or done well in many organizations.

What actually exists in many work undertakings is a hodge-podge or a jungle of information about the work and what it calls for in the way of abilities from those called upon to do it. Some information exists on these scores in all situations, simply because without it, there could only be chaos. Managers and workers do know something about work, and they have usually formed some theories about what kind of person with what kinds of aptitudes is best able to carry it out. But rarely is this information systematically collected or collated and presented in a form which would enable the reader to form a view without further recourse to the actual worker and his job.

Commonly, undertakings move slowly and intermittently along the path of systematizing the information as they are nudged along by tight labour markets, trade union pressures, legislation or training board requirements, or simply 'fashion'.

For example, an undertaking may possess an organization chart, or it may have a flow diagram; it may have work study or synthetic data on performance standards; it may have some 'requirements' for new recruits expressed in terms of education or experience: it may have an appraisal system linked to salary review. All of these, and more, are involved in a manpower planning system, but if they are to be of any real value they must be related to and integrated with an overall plan and linked to one another in a systematic fashion.

The organization chart (usually more explicit in relation to managerial jobs than to manual jobs) offers a first identification of the separate jobs and offices which currently exist within the organization. It usually identifies the job by title and the present incumbent by name and, by virtue of the lines drawn between the positions, it indicates lines of authority, responsibility, communication and possibly work flow.

In spite of the book's frequent statement that the organization chart ought to be supported by a statement of duties and responsibilities, this is not frequently done. When it is, the description is usually in the form of a general statement of the incumbent's main activities. It tends to supplement the more cryptic information given on the chart itself, rather than stand in its own right. When it does so stand, it is often produced in occupational rather than job/task terms, referring to the occupation of ... fitter and turner, systems analyst, nurse etc, in which the occupational sub-cultural definition of the tasks is by implication all that is required for selection and, by extension, for planning purposes.

There is nothing inherently wrong with the production of a job description which is adequate for occupational purposes (and par-

186

ticularly so where recruitment—as in hospitals—is to a profession rather than to a service organization). However, the likelihood is that such a description will serve the organizational purposes inadequately. Most of the many reports on aspects of manpower for the hospital service are in fact couched in these terms: 'Cog-wheel on doctors'; 'Salmon on senior nurses'; 'Zuckerman on scientific and technical services'; 'Parish on building occupations'; 'Tyler on engineers'; and 'Lycett Green on administrative and clerical occupations'. Each of them might in fact be regarded as prevented by its terms of reference from looking at hospital manpower from a hospital standpoint.

Hospitals are not unique in this respect. Even outside professional organizations it is not all that usual to find an enterprise taking a total organizational view of its manpower. Questioning whether existing jobs are correctly divided or combined, whether descriptions of duties and responsibilities are sensible within the context of the whole, and whether present incumbents really match up to the criteria stated or implied, is not frequent. Consequently, the positive contribution which such data as exists might make is reduced by the likelihood that it is held in different parts of the enterprise and not brought together systematically. A personnel department may well hold data on the existing stock of manpower, for example, whilst the data on performance lie with a separate work study department.

It is to cut through this jungle of diversely developed and located information that a more systematic approach has been adopted to produce the 'job description' as the centre-piece supported by analysis of the job requirements.

The job description

The centre-piece in a systematic approach to managing the boundary exchange is the actual job of work to be done. From the undertaking's standpoint this is what has been determined to be necessary to the realization of objectives after careful analysis of need. From the individual's point of view, it is this which will offer him or her the kind of technical experience of work which some studies suggest is what is sought (Dubin, 1956) and supply the intrinsic satisfactions identified in others (Herzberg, 1968). This 'job' therefore has importance to both.

Such jobs are 'real', in the sense that they might be assumed to have 'objective' existence. But we can only appreciate that reality through a job description, through a use of words which describe the objective reality. Of course, it might be seen and described dif-

187

ferently by different people: by managers, by the workers doing the job, by uncommitted observers, etc. The way it is seen and described by management, however, will tend to reflect the purpose behind the attempt at description. Different purposes will lead to different descriptions because of the different emphasis which each interested describer will give.

The usual job description to be found in work undertakings is one which often has been much influenced by those with some kind of training orientation, but some attempt is made to prepare a composite description which will serve as a basis for a number of activities, including training:

(a) *recruitment*, in which case it should contain information which will make clear the qualities and qualifications needed in the person who will fill the job
(b) *training*, in which case it must contain the same information as (a) but with special attention to areas of likely difficulty or deficiency
(c) *manpower utilization*, in which case particular attention will have to be paid to the way in which tasks are combined in the job so that, for example, a re-division or re-combination could be worked out from the data provided
(d) *job evaluation*, in which case the description will need to contain information on whatever factors must or will be taken into account in devising a wage/salary structure on the basis of job content
(e) *productivity negotiation* for which it will be necessary to have indications in the job descriptions of standards of performance expected or required at a current rate for the job, so that variations can be readily traced.

Even so, it should not be assumed that a job description, however systematic its production, can indicate everything about a job. Every verbal description is an abstraction from a reality which is always more complicated than the abstract form of words which describes it. All that can be aspired to is a carefully carried out and controlled analysis and description of that which those involved or concerned would regard as the important elements of the job.

This means that the preparation of a job description will need to involve not only specialist job analysts, but also the man doing the job, his superior(s) and probably others like training officers who have a special insight into the work being carried on. No matter who is observed at work or consulted about it, the final result should represent a distillation of all the significant features. If the description is also to be used for evaluation it should be of a common form and constant length in order to minimize judgemental bias arising from variation on these points.

Since everything about a job cannot be included in the job description it is important to determine just what should be included. This decision can, of course, be based on hunch or can respond to fashion or custom. However, if it is to be more systematic, it is necessary to consider the criteria which will be adopted to assess for success or adequacy. In this area it is neither particularly easy to determine these criteria nor to construct a means of determining them. Refinement of job analysis tends to have this as a main objective.

Where selection processes are concerned, it is particularly important to know what one is selecting for. Normally it is for a particular job or a particular kind or level of performance in that job. This, by itself, implies that there will be some standard in mind when selecting, even if only one based on judgement of what a normal operator would produce in that job. The check-back on the worker in the job and on the supervisor's perception of the job, normally built into the job analysis, gives information for this but such conception of the normal is only one of many conceptions which may be employed.

Any individual might be assessed on any of the foundations (a–e) identified above. A management representative might well concentrate on (b) at the expense of the others; the man's colleagues might well employ different criteria.

To summarize any job description must include certain features:

1 *Identification of the job:* usually by stating the title of the job, the section or department in which it is found, and the level in the hierarchy at which it is placed (usually by identifying to whom the man doing it reports).

Some jobs are easily identified by title: everyone knows what is done by a nurse, a fitter or a cook. Others are less easy to identify in this way, and the job titles saggar-maker's bottom knocker or river or even systems analyst are not particularly helpful unless the reader happens to be in the industry concerned. Therefore, job descriptions usually amplify.

2 *Description of the job:* usually setting out in brief the main tasks which to go make up the job and indicating how this job differs from other jobs which may, superficially, appear similar.

For this purpose, it is important to develop and use a standardized and defined terminology to describe the purposes, functions or tasks involved. In this way the same word does not appear in different descriptions meaning different things because of the local language normally used and different words are not used to mean essentially the same thing for the same kind of reason. for the same kind of reason.

3 *Description of job content:* usually stated in a more detailed and expanded form as the body of the job description. In drawing up this part it is important to have the objectives very much in mind. A job description required merely for recruitment might be less rigorous than one to be used in evaluation. Nevertheless, it is sensible when preparing job descriptions to assume that they may be needed for any of the purposes identified on the previous page, and to prepare accordingly. Marrying the requirements of these various objectives leads to the following specification for a description of job content. It should include:

(a) *What is done?* This will include the person's activities, whether manual or mental (eg 'files', 'checks figures', 'plans activities for others', 'tends patients', 'diagnoses conditions' etc), and his main and subsidiary tasks. This ought to be a description of the job in its more 'mechanical' aspects such that an outsider can gain an understanding of what is involved for the job-holder.

(b) *How it is done?* Here the attempt is made to indicate whether the individual does the job alone and unaided or whether he has tools, equipment or organization to help him. This part of the description will show what 'things' and 'people' are needed for the job. Sometimes the things will include office equipment, measuring instruments, manuals and procedures, or complex plant (like computers); sometimes the job will depend upon getting a team to work as an integrated whole; sometimes the job will require little more than physical strength or stamina plus some intelligence or a capacity for exercising individual judgement. Such features vary from job to job, and even from task to task. They may also vary over time, and some attempt should therefore be made to indicate such variations.

(c) *Why the person does it?* The answers to this question focus on the context of the job in the work-flow sense. This part of the description will attempt to relate the one job to other jobs around or connected with it, and to link it to the overall objectives of the section, department or enterprise. This is an important element, particularly where the pattern of tasks is changing because of the possible introduction of new objec-

190

tives or technologies. Without this attempt to give meaning to the job by linking it to its work context, the necessary foundation for monitoring manpower utilization or changing relative evaluations will be lacking. The data for this part of the description is often collected by the management services organization, but the job description is prepared independently by the personnel department who have less information than the former on work flow patterns; in consequence this part of the description may be deficient.

(d) *What standard of performance is regarded as normal?* This is often left out of manual worker descriptions, but frequently included in managerial descriptions (where it appears in the guise of 'key results expected'). At manual levels, this requirement can be met by using work study data; at managerial levels it can embrace data produced in applications of management by objectives methods. Whether or not such standards are included openly, they are always implied in any job description: there is always some standard of performance which is regarded as normal even if different occupational groups may have different conceptions of this. One part of the function of work study at the manual level and of activity analysis at a managerial/professional level is to make them explicit. Although there is often prejudice against the statement of applicable standards in job descriptions, their omission leaves the way open for personalized and idiosyncratic review.

(e) *In what conditions is the work done?* This covers physical working conditions of the job at the time it is described. Such a description is necessary to prepare for job evaluation, selection or subsequent monitoring. To describe these conditions is, of course, to imply a normal, and normal will vary from situation to situation. What are normal conditions in a foundry are not normal conditions in a hospital, and what is normal on a ward is not necessarily normal in the kitchen. Consequently, the working conditions specified in this section will depart from a conception of the normal and will identify specific abnormalities. The most common items include the following:

dirt
heat or cold
necessity for protective
   clothing
monotony
noise or vibration
exposure to weather
   hazard or danger

work done in confined spaces
wetness of working environment
dust, fumes, gas hazards
exposure to infection or
   disease
other disagreeable conditions
   (eg smells)

191

Not all these will necessarily figure in any one job description.

4 *Special features:* This means the peculiar features of the job in question which, if point 3 (above) is carried out systematically ought to be covered already, but which might form the subject of a special section if only because they will probably have a particular influence upon the man specification. In this section a special note might be made, say, of the fact that a job requires operations using differential calculus, driving on a public highway or lengthy sessions with potentially difficult clients. Opportunity might also be taken here to indicate any special organizational features of the job—whether for example it is part of a promotion line or merely a dead-end job.

The criteria for different kinds of work also vary in the ease with which they can be established and accepted. The work of a clerk or a manual worker is often relatively easy to describe. This is because (a) it is relatively *stable* in its form and content, and (b) it is often concerned with a *rate* of output which can be measured fairly easily. With the development of more complex technologies, with consequent influences on job stability and manual control, this is likely to be less so in the future. There is still some variation in the performance of such workers on fairly stable jobs, in spite of trade union and informal group control of it, and this can be used to derive reliable criteria.

The work of a manger is usually more difficult to describe in spite of the work of the activity and job analysts, and its inherent complexity and fluidity are likely to perpetuate this problem. Criteria are less easy to determine. What makes for a good manager is less easy to describe than what makes for a good workman, because the inherent variety in the job itself masks the variations in performance even if we intuitively have some ideas on the existence of such variations. The development of criteria is therefore likely to prove more costly and difficult in consequence.

Job analysis
The job description, whilst it must be based on the actual job being (or to be) done, must also follow analysis of the situation to establish that what is being done (or proposed) is really necessary and that it is being done in the most economical or satisfying way. This first step involves the application of techniques of work study and/or organizational analysis, by which a systematic questioning of relevance and adequacy of jobs is carried out. If such questioning

produces negative answers, some degree of re-design is called for as a precursor to the job description (cf Carby, 1976).

Once this is done, however, there is a necessary job to be described. 'A job' in this sense is usually defined as a collection of tasks which are put together, mainly on the basis of convenience, to enable one person to be fully occupied whilst at work; he may have a main task, but will probably also have a number of ancillary tasks as well. In fact, a job which is composed of only one task is likely to be a highly repetitive and routine one; the grouping of a number of tasks adds variety and interest. At the same time it should be noted that it is correspondingly easier to describe a single-task job; covering all the side-tasks in a job description is always more difficult and time-consuming.

A systematic attempt to analyse the job will therefore proceed by breaking down the 'whole job' into its component or associated parts. The emphasis will be upon establishing which distinct parts exist and how they both differ and relate to the others. Such procedure makes it easy to dismember a job which for the person doing it may have some kind of integrity, and as Roff and Watson point out, care has to be taken in job analysis to ensure that both the 'job as a whole' and the 'job in relation to the total work flow' are given adequate attention. Without this putting together of what is otherwise broken down, the outcome will be nothing much more than a meagre description of a number of different activities divorced from the context which gives them meaning and the kind of rationality which is a necessary foundation for training or testing activity.

The development of the specific techniques of job and skills analysis has usually been associated with the need to understand jobs in order to provide training for them, but it has also served to supply the 'system' of the systematic approach needed to produce, as the first step, the necessary job description. The two are often subsumed in the one term, job analysis, but they do have somewhat different meanings. Job analysis in its more specific form, emphasizing analysis by activity, appears to stem from the early work of Viteles (1932) and the applications made by Tiffin and Rogers (1943). The other, emphasizing knowledge and skills required in work, was employed in the context of *Training Within Industry* (TWI) first in America (cf Dodd and Rice, 1942) and later in Britain (Ministry of Labour, 1962). Both have been continued since those days in the United Kingdom, and are now used in connection with different aspects of the learning/training process.

The first, now related to the part versus the whole job approach to training (*see* pp 173–80 above), manifests itself in the breaking

193

down of any given job or task into sections. These, as Seymour commented in 1949, 'may be sucessive, like the sections of a TWI job breakdown or a time study, or may be synchronous' (Seymour, 1949, p 175). Each section which is identified in this way may be associated with a particular skill or pattern of skills, but the emphasis is really upon the coherence of the task or tasks which comprise the section; different sections may, for example, call for similar skills and some transference may be possible from one section's learning to another, but ultimately there will be a need to progress through the sections in some order to give mastery of the whole job or task for which training is being provided.

Each 'part' or section may then be learnt in isolation from the whole job or task, with the advantages which have been demonstrated to flow from this method of training (see pp 380–90 below). But there are 'problems' about the part method, and 'special attention is given to the "connexions" between one section and the next, and trainees are taught to think of the whole operation as a connected structure of parts (*ibid*). Thus where the 'part' may be learned in isolation and out of sequence, there comes a time when the sequence has to be built up progressively until all the parts are related to their proper sequence or connection.

Where skills analysis is identified separately, it has the definition given by the Department of Employment:

> The identification and recording of the psycho-physiological characteristics of skilled performance and the determination of effector, receptor, and decision-making functions involved (Department of Employment, *Glossary of Training Terms*, 1971).

It manifests itself, therefore, in the identification of the 'underlying' human skills which are requisite for the accomplishment of the job or tasks—in whole or in part—which are isolated in the other process. As was noted in that connection, there is no necessary connection between a 'part' and a 'skill'; skills associated with parts are to be discovered by appropriate analysis, not assumed from the nature of the part-job or task itself.

In Seymour's original statement on this aspect, he suggested that the analysis required that the

> most difficult parts of the job are picked out and, where necessary, preliminary training exercises are designed to prepare the trainee for the actual job. These exercises may deal with the sensory or with the motor facts, or may deal with both (Seymour, 1949, p 175).

Outside the context of the mainly manual jobs to which he was then applying his analysis, however, there may be other kinds of skill in evidence, for example, the perceptual and the interactive.

Work measurement

If the application of these techniques of job and skills analysis provides a basis for describing what the job requires for its performance, a full job description also requires an indication of the level of performance which the undertaking requires of the person doing it. The setting of work standards by systematic methods has a somewhat longer history than the application of job analysis techniques, largely because measurement was seen as a more important managerial concern than was selection and training at some time in the past.

What is involved here is frequently described as a process of 'work measurement', but what is meant by this term is something quite different from what is involved in measuring the length of a piece of string. In the nature of what is to be 'measured', it is necessary to *assess* or *judge* what is possible or desirable by way of performance level, and it is the exercise of judgement which is mainly involved in spite of the reliance upon stop-watches or micro-motion cameras. The personnel manager's main involvement in this exercise (and therefore the call upon his skill which it makes) relates to the establishment of controls over the exercise of judgement in order to ensure consistency.

Manual and clerical work measurement usually proceeds by way of reducing the 'work content' of a job to a single measurement unit which is time. This on the face of it suggests that all that is necessary is to observe, and measure with a stop-watch, how long it takes a worker to carry out the job. But because there are individual and situational differences which might affect the time taken by the person who was actually observed and measured, some attempt has to be made to relate the observation to a 'norm'. It is this 'norm' rather than the final time standard which may be set for the job which falls within the purview of the personnel specialist.

The basic 'norm' here is that of the qualified operator (one who has the physical or mental skills and abilities to carry out the job) working at a normal pace in applying himself (ie without over-exertion) to the job over a normal working period. As Lockyer says, therefore,

an observer is thus required to have a very clear concept of the rate at which a worker who possesses the necessary physical and mental attributes, and the required skill, would satisfactorily

195

carry out the task under observation, safely, accurately at the correct speed and without undue strain (Lockyer, 1974, p. 162).

The 'basic' conceptions of what is 'normal' in these circumstances are conceptions of a person walking, without load, at a pace of three miles an hour (which is applied to body movement) and of a person dealing a deck of playing cards into four hands in 30 seconds, or half a deck in 15 seconds (applied to hand and eye movements). This standard rating point may then be expressed on a scale, and this on some scales is fixed at a 60 (the performance of the day-worker working without incentive) compared with an 80 (for a worker on incentive) and on others at 75 against 100 or as 100 against 133 (Lockyer, 1974, p 163). Practice in Britain is to rate this 'motivated' performance as a numerical value of 100 and to make no stipulation as to 'standard' unmotivated performance. Against this, actual performance can be related as a percentage (British Standards Institution, BS 3138, 1969).

These conceptions of the normal must then be translated into judgements of diverse patterns of body and arm-hand-eye motions. This can be done with practice under supervision of a trained rater. This is a special process which depends upon the expertise of the rater being accepted by the trainee as productive of 'correct' ratings—since there is no objective arbiter (like the standard imperial 'yard' in disputes about length of anything). It is now common to use film as a means of training, so that many more variations of movement in diverse patterns can be practice-rated in a similar context but the special nature of the influence process is not thereby removed.

Nor is it removed by the use of 'synthetic times'—work-factor system, methods time measurement, basic motion time-study or other similar variants. The earliest synthetics were developed by raters themselves, by the simple expedient of building up a data-bank of their own measurements, on which they could then draw for new jobs which included combinations of movements already timed and rated. The later, branded versions usually broke motions down into much smaller elements and used films in laboratory settings to amass data and derive standard times. This had the advantages of allowing motions too small or too quick for observations with the naked eye to be studied and measured, and of making possible the standardization of 'times' applied, provided that the trained analyst could break down any given job into its elemental motions and times. This has tended to standardize the rating or judgement factor, not eliminate it completely from the process of fixing standard times for work.

This same process of 'discovering' the acceptable standards of performance is to be found in connection with plans (such as the Clerical Work Improvement Programme, Group Capacity Assessment, or Variable Factor Programming) applied to clerical and related activities, even though this may not be called work or time study. Similar 'rating' and 'assessment' problems arise in this connection, and in somewhat different form in connection with job evaluation and merit rating plans. In all of these contexts, there is some probability that those who actually 'measure' are located in a different department from the personnel specialist, but the personnel specialist's contribution to this activity usually lies in the development of a capacity to establish consistent norms or criteria for rating and assessment purposes (cf Thomason, 1980, pp 125–79).

Criteria of judgement

It is somewhat paradoxical that these 'measurement techniques' are frequently applied unilaterally by management and as frequently challenged (for example, through the grievance machinery) by those to whose jobs they are applied, where different ones, allowing greater participation in the standard setting, are usually applied to more senior white collar (managerial and professional) activities.

The determination of the standards to be applied to this kind of work tends to remain the prerogative of the manager who is accountable for the work in question, but this process may well involve the personnel manager if it involves anyone else at all. The personnel department will either advise the managers on how to determine appropriate standards for this kind of work (ie in a general way, possibly using information obtained by the personnel department from other organizations) or it may be charged specifically with the responsibility for introducing a formal plan such as management by objectives (MbO) and for giving this the servicing needed to assure successful implementation. The latter part of the exercise would naturally include a full-scale programme of training and counselling as well as administration. The personnel department's degree of participation could well, under these circumstances, be much greater than in the cases already discussed.

What this approach and manner of organization highlights is that (whether it occurs through trade union challenge or through the greater participation allowed) the emergent standard of performance and associated criteria are likely to represent a compromise. In any situation, and regardless of how they are allowed to exert their influence, the standards to be applied in the judgement of whether a particular performance is correct or adequate may be founded on very different sets of sub-cultural values: those of the task-system itself, the organization, the occupation, or the informal group surrounding the task. Such distinctions are acknowledged in the literature, even if infrequently utilized in practical manpower planning exercises. Criteria for judging any job incumbent might be established in terms of variations in contribution to:

(a) the trade, occupation or profession as a simple task-system
(b) the section, department or enterprise
(c) the organized occupational group (trade union, profession)
(d) the informal work group, linked to a set of tasks.

Such criteria do exist and are used, if not deliberately or systematically. It remains open to any system to make them articulate, although it is more likely that the systems which will do so are the enterprise and the profession rather than the other two.

This requires us to recognize that criterion data are available in many organizations although they are infrequently used in a specific fashion. At the manual worker level they are found in work study data which are frequently seen as supports for an incentive bonus scheme, rather than as a basis for selection or promotion; at the white collar level they may appear in similar form, and in the higher echelons they may appear as criteria established in relation to key results areas. If, at the one level, the material is often difficult to employ because of formal or informal controls over variations in performance, at the other it is as frequently obscured by the apparent heterogeneity of jobs which renders comparisons difficult. Possibly for these reasons the data are often not employed consciously in devising a manpower plan.

What this means is that the likelihood that the basic data which it ought to be possible to derive from the job description is at best only imperfectly collated. To some extent those who are made responsible for selection (whether for employment, rotation or promotion) will therefore work with partial or inadequate criteria; where, say, both personnel department and line managers are familiar with these processes to different extents, they may well be working to different or even opposing criteria. The point is not to determine whether the one or the other ought to carry out the function, but rather to suggest that whoever does so, alone or in combination, ought to be in possession of as many of the facts as possible. Job analysis offers one way of assembling these facts, but it does not automatically ensure that they will be built into a comprehensive and integrated plan.

The person specification

Once it has been established what is required in the job in the way of activity and standard of performance, it is necessary to turn attention to the question of the kind of person required to perform it in the way described and to the standards set down. The question is whether it is possible to describe the kind of worker which is suggested by or derivable from the job description as this is developed. In so far as this is possible, the specification of the person is unlikely to indicate some of the vaguer 'qualities' of the individual which might, organizationally, be thought desirable (for example, those of 'co-operativeness', 'loyalty', 'industriousness' etc so favoured by the designers of merit-rating schemes) but is more likely to concentrate on straightforward abilities and attainments in past experience.

In other words, once the criteria have been established by the job description (pp 187–98, above) the next task is to derive the description of the person who might be expected (predicted) to satisfy these.

Obviously, different tasks will call for persons with 'individual' attributes which will 'precisely' fit that job, or for persons with general attributes which will broadly fit the job requirement: it by no means follows that for every job there is a single person who has the right combination of qualities and qualifications. There are, in other words, some jobs which in their generality call for a class or category of labour, and it becomes possible to specify the person required as simply one of a class—a skilled craftsman, a bookkeeper or a labourer. But there are also jobs which are much more individual in the person-attributes they appear to require, and for these it may be necessary to write the ideal man/woman specification which will match the job. Indeed, as more jobs become industry-specific and even enterprise-specific as a result of technological development, many of the old 'class' specifications may prove less adequate, and the pressure be on to develop personal specifications, of the sort indicated in the table on the following page, drawn from Plumbley (1976).

But whichever kind of result is produced by this kind of analysis, it is to be predicted that, in future, management will be led to give more attention to specifying the criteria of the person required as a basis for developing more adequate predictors. Because staff will probably prove to be more costly and difficult to dismiss in the future, it will become more necessary than before to translate the job requirement into a specification of kind of person thought most likely to be able to do it competently. It follows that the aspects of the person which are called in question in work must match up to the aspects of the job which make demands upon the person and, as Rodger has suggested, 'the requirements of an occupation (or job) must be described in the same terms as the attributes of the people who are being considered for it' (1952). The data on the job itself which have been discussed in the preceding section must now be stated in terms which will enable an individual or class of persons to be identified as willing and able to do the job which has thus been described. Such a description will then form the basis for selection of persons to fill jobs.

Table 5
The person specification

Physical make-up	Minimum height 5′ 4″
	Pleasant appearance
	Brisk, clear speech, free from impediments
Attainments	Essential to have evidence of application, concentration and capacity for detailed work
	Desirable to have some knowledge of technical drawing and of engineering terms
	Education should reflect academic or technical bias
	'O' levels or the equivalent are desirable
	Previous experience of record keeping in technical office or library is essential
	Experience of working with engineering drawings is desirable
General intelligence	Brisk reactions and an accurate memory are needed rather than ability to solve complex problems
Specialized aptitudes	Neat, quick and accurate at clerical work
Interests	Practical and social
Disposition	Self-reliant, helpful, friendly
Circumstances	Likely to stay for at least three years
Type of person	Traditionally this job has been done by a female but it could equally be done by a male. No restriction on race, colour or creed
Contra-indications	Obvious shyness.

Source: Philip Plumbley, *Recruitment and Selection* (IPM, London, 1976) pp 35–36

The question to which the person specification seeks to provide an answer is therefore what qualities and qualifications ought a person to have, if he is to do this particular job to the level of adequacy which is implicit in the criterion. These are minimum attributes, and not either average or maximum, and they could be determined in accordance with the values of the enterprise, the profession or any other sub-culture which might be associated with the job. They need in every case to be minimum, so that the size of the 'feedstock' for the job vacancy is made as large as possible.

Qualifications are usually more easily allocated than qualities. This is partly because qualifications have at least a superficial objectivity about them whereas qualities seem to be almost entirely subjective; moreover, qualifications seem to be more readily 'measurable' (eg as in examinations) where qualities appear to require complex psychological tests or equally complex interpersonal judgements. The effect of this is to distil the person specification down to the level of a statement of education, training and experience (the qualifications) required, and to supplement this with relatively vague statements about personal attributes. The criteria of the person are then often more vaguely defined than the criteria of the work.

The distinctions in objectivity or precision may be more apparent than real. If consideration is given to the qualifications associated with the job descriptions, for example, one might be forced to recognize that the requirement of a degree qualification might prove to be a rather blunt instrument of measurement in the face of the actual job of work to be done, and that on-the-job experience might in turn produce a very variable effect upon an individual in terms of qualification. In these senses a statement about apparently objective qualifications for a job may differ very little from statements to the effect that an individual must have a helpful, friendly and self-reliant disposition. This seeming precision of the one may be no less reliable than the seeming imprecision of the other.

Nevertheless, for most ordinary selection and promotion purposes, we might recognize that the *categories* of the variable, which might be expected to vary with performance on a job, can be identified quite readily. In the most general sense, these may be placed under three main headings:

(a) *Intellectual requirements* usually measured in terms of training and skill or experience. This part of the specification will deal with the previous experience of persons usually chosen to do the job, and the subsequent training they will require in order to do the job in a satisfactory way. If the person has to acquire any manual or mental dexterity to do the job at the speed at which the job is usually performed this will be noted.

(b) *Physical requirements* usually assessed by physical strength and health history. Sufficient information will be included under this heading to ensure that the reader can judge the muscular strength of the persons to do the work, and also the amount of effort they will normally expend when working without the incentive of a bonus. If the people who do the job must possess particular sensory qualities this will also be mentioned

(c) *Personality requirements* some of which are subsumed under the heading (a) above, but others of which creep in without the benefit of careful definition. Examples are:

good memory	ability to reason
speed of reaction	even temperament
cooperativeness	perseverance
mechanical sense	initiative
disparate attention	ability to visualize
sense of responsibility	

Of these three categories, the first two are of a rather different order from the third. They seem on the face of it to lend themselves to fairly precise and objective measurement, even if the measures are themselves normatively defined. A person of any age, sex and size who has no very acute physical handicap nor a history of poor health can be assumed capable of coping with most run-of-the-mill jobs that are available; and therefore only rather special job requirements are likely to call for the category of physical requirements in question, such as need for particular levels of vision or manual dexterity. A person of a given level of terminal education who has no history of physical or mental illness can also be assumed to have a capacity which is indicated by the level of educational attainment, which may in many cases be attested by the possession of some scrap of paper; experience which is 'certified' by some testimonial or reference may also be taken as indicative of capacity (on the legal constraints on references, see Hepple and O'Higgins, 1976, pp 512–13).

Such certifications are usually capable of predicting only generalized competence in a particular field: they usually say nothing about the more particular capabilities of the individual in working with this group on these particular problems or tasks in this particular organization. It is for this reason that such organizations as have organization-specific requirements of labour have been willing to explore the possibilities of developing their own independent criteria and predictors, some of them quite complex. Where the number of criteria which can be distinguished, especially if the organizational and occupational sub-cultures are both allowed to determine them, is large and their predictability varies appreciably, it may be necessary in recruitment to develop person specifications of great complexity. Taylor presents a list of 17 criteria for scientists arranged in descending order of their pre-

Table 6
Criteria of the success of a research scientist

9	Likeableness as a research team member (44%)	17	Supervisory rating of creativity (29%)
5	Scientific and professional society membership (43%)	16	Supervisory rating of drive-resourcefulness (25%)
13	Current organizational status (38%)	4*	Originality of written work (20%)
6*	Judged work output (35%)	10	Visibility (20%)
8*	Supervisory ratings on overall performance (35%)	11	Recognition for organizational contributions (17%)
15	Peer rankings on productivity (35%)	2	Recent publications (14%)
1*	Productivity in written work (32%)	14	Contrast monitoring load (11%)
7	Creative rating by laboratory chiefs (29%)	12*	Status seeking, 'organizational-man' tendencies (08%)
		3	Quality (without originality of research reports) (02%)

Source: Taylor, Smith, Ghiselin and Ellison, 1961

dictability from a number of test scores, rank being accorded by the percentage of significant validity coefficients above zero (the figure is given in parentheses). Although a degree of bias is introduced into this list, because of the particular method developed in the research (those affected are marked with an asterisk) this does not invalidate the rank nor does it detract from the point to be made here that the criteria are extremely varied in themselves. Perusal of the above list will show that, as it were, there are many ways in which the success of the scientist might be evaluated.

This may render it difficult to develop an adequate criterion strategy for jobs of this general type and pose the question whether it is worth it. What normally justifies this activity is the growth in the proportion of white collar occupations and therefore their relative cost compared with manual jobs. But if the job possesses these complex and multiple criterion characteristics, the development of adequate predictors will depend upon their adequate development.

Given the criteria, it may be asked what about the individual will permit us to predict any of these criteria—assuming for the moment that we have tests or other devices which will permit measurement of the variable identified. In a second part of this exercise, Taylor *et al* present data on which predictors were most useful (most highly correlated). These authors used a variety of

Table 7
Criterion 9: likeableness as a member of the research team

Nr	Predictor	r	Nr	Predictor	r
81	MSL Writing skills	.46	142	IB Intellectual thoroughness	.27
34	SR Discrimination of value	.41	28	SR Desire for discovery	.26
37	SR Creativity	.34	136	BIB Emotional restraint	.26
138	BIB Self-sufficiency	.34	141	BIB Liking to think	.25
31	SR Flexibility	.33	85	MSL Being well known	.24
145	BIB Modal response	.33	86	MSL Quantity of reports	.24
24	SR Cognition	.31	91	Apparatus test: total	.24
36	SR Intuition	.31	135	BIB Professional self-confidence	.23
139	BIB Inner directedness	.31	100	MAT Parents-home	.22
27	SR Desire for principles	.30	42	PRI Tolerance of ambiguity	.21
101	MAT Narcism (comfort)	.30	64	Match problems: Nr correct	.20
78	MSL Reading skills	.30	95	MAT Self-sentiment	.20
59	PRI Artistic (vs. practical)	.28	22	SR Math ability	.19
74	Visual imagery: % marked correct	.28	48	PRI Gregariousness	.20
79	MSL Speaking skills	.27	87	MSL Theoretical contributions	.19

The initials in the above table, and in table 11 (b), refer to test instruments, as follows:

BIB = Biographical Information Blank
MAT = Motivational Analysis Test
MSL = Minimum Satisfactory Level
PRI = Personality Research Inventory
SR = Self Ratings

(see Taylor *et al*, 1961: and Blum and Naylor, 1968)

tests to secure predictors (see foot of Table). In table 7 above they show the relative degrees to which their test results help to predict the first of the criteria in table 6 on page 203 likeableness as a research team member'. This is inserted here to *illustrate* the way in which such test results—which might uncover some of the 'less obvious' attributes of the person—can be related to the prediction of 'success' in the role for which selection is being undertaken. The fact that some test results are fair predictors and others rather poor ones ('r') also reveals that there is no reason to suppose that a normal battery of tests will produce results which remove the need to exercise human judgement in the selection process.

204

Conclusion

The broad import of the material in this chapter is that the personnel practitioner, in his executant role within the employment function, applies skills of analysis, judgement and communication to facilitate the development of a satisfactory or equilibrium relationship between the demands of the undertaking for labour and the supply of labour available. Those skills have to be addressed to both sides of the equation: there is a need for technical analysis of the work demands and of the offers represented by those who present themselves for vacancies, and there is a need to facilitate the exchange of information all along the line to enable the necessary judgements to be made.

Further reading
On the subject matter of this chapter students may find it useful to consult
Bramham (1975) on the practical aspects of manpower planning
Boydell (1970) on job analysis and Singer and Ramsden (1969) on skills analysis
Ray (1980) and Braithwaite and Pollock (1974) on advertising
Ungerson (1970) and Plumbley (1976) on recruitment and selection
Anstey and Mercer (1956) and Fraser (1971 and 1966) on selection and selection interviewing
Albright, Glennon and Smith (1963) and Miller (1975) on psychological testing.

9   Handling the interchange

System and humanity

There is, as this part has attempted to show, both a desire for, and means for effecting, a systematic approach to the whole business of bringing workers into association with an undertaking. As was suggested at the beginning, however, a depersonalized 'system' is unlikely to yield the consequences intended unless it is tempered by a certain humanity; one of the aims and purposes of 'policy' is therefore, to maintain some humanity in the approach by prescribing 'standards of conduct' as well as 'strategies for action'. The actual recruitment and termination of people bring together in the conduct of the person engaging in them, both the efficient pursuit of tangible objectives and the humane treatment of people (cf Weitz in Fleishman, 1961, pp 26–9).

Both of these processes of recruiting and terminating (deselecting is a term which has been used in some quarters for the latter) are now more closely constrained by specific legislation, in ways and to extents not present 20 years ago (see pp 69–126 above). Although the number of constraints in this area is not large, the main thrust of this pressure upon conduct has been in the realms of morality. For example proscription of discrimination and arbitrariness in decisions and prescription of more information to be given to the human beings on the 'receiving end'.

But the prescriptions of 'penalties' for breach of the new code has focused more attention on the technical processes adopted.

This in turn has led to more systematic (some would be prepared to say 'bureaucratic') procedures being adopted. There is both a paradox and a problem in this. The attempt to instil a more humane approach to the taking on and laying off of labour produces, as a consequence, a greater formality, about which there could easily develop connotations of depersonalization. Guarding against the overwhelming of the one by the burgeoning of the other is therefore a problem which a carefully developed policy might be expected to cope with.

206

The steps in recruitment

A discrete number of steps are involved in the recruitment of employees. At most of them, the opportunities for a systematic *and* humane approach exist. Some of them, however, achieve their humanity by performing the systematic part of the process properly and effectively.

The first step entails the preparation of a staff requisition form. This is usually completed by the departmental head in whose department a vacancy occurs, and transmitted to the personnel department for the next sequence of steps to be taken. It should give sufficient information about the vacancy to permit the personnel department to advertise it and carry out an initial screening of applicants. Information required includes department, job title (reference to establishment in appropriate cases), date new man required to start work, wage/salary range appropriate, and identification of the appropriate job description and person specification, assuming these to exist. Depending on economic circumstances and legislative constraints on hiring and firing, such a request should be checked against establishment (where this concept is used) or against the data on stocks and flows of manpower.

The next step is preparing and inserting an advertisement of the vacancy. This may be prepared by the departmental head and given to the personnel department or it may be prepared in the personnel department itself. But economies can be made by passing all advertisements through the personnel department, provided that it does evaluate its own advertising performance. The advertisement may be placed internally (usually by agreement with the unions), externally, or both, but ought in the latter case to be based upon some assessment of the effectiveness of advertising in a particular medium (Braithwaite and Pollock, 1974). When posted, a copy of the advertisement may be sent to the departmental head concerned to confirm that action has been taken and to indicate when future action will be required. The implicit centralization of this process reflects a prediction that such closer control will prove to be necessary both economically and politically.

Advertisements may draw enquiries from some of those who read them but enquiries may also come from individuals looking for certain types of job 'on spec'. The fortuitous appearance of an applicant when a vacancy exists could result in immediate processing and possible appointment if the criteria are met. In either case, the enquirer will have to complete an application form as a first

207

step in the procedure of informing the organization about a potential recruit; he will be given further particulars (ideally in the form of a job description) as a first step in informing him about the job; whilst the first part of this procedure is often done, the second is not.

When the personnel department receives the application form, it can screen applications to eliminate those who are unsuitable, given the requirements stipulated in the job description and person specification. In theory, the advertisement ought to have discouraged such applicants but in fact many people are willing to chance their arm in applying for jobs for which they may know they are marginally unqualified or unsuitable. This screening will result in a list of candidates whose references may then be taken up. In addition, the personnel department will be supplied incidentally with data on the local labour market for that type and class of labour; such information can be logged and used in developing manpower and recruitment strategies (see pp 53–83).

Whether references are taken up at all, or whether they are collected in writing or by telephone will usually depend upon the kind of vacancy and upon the state of the labour market for that particular grade. When they are sought in writing, the employing organization has a choice of simply asking for a written reference, usually a letter, or of inviting the referee to supply assessments on a standardized form which identifies qualities and qualifications deemed important in the job. The first will usually produce a statement which may or may not tell the potential employer what he would like to know; the second is often ignored or misinterpreted by the referee as being too complex for speedy completion.

Where references are taken up before interview, this makes a second screening possible: if the references are comprehensive, this can certainly be done but many are rather curious eulogies of doubtful validity and unlikely to be very useful. Whether or not such a secondary screening takes place, it is usual to invite applicants for interview. This may in some cases form a part of the secondary screening, for example, when it is carried out by the personnel staff in order to draw up a short-list for interview by departmental heads.

The stage then comes when the candidate will be interviewed with a view to final selection or rejection. This may concern only a departmental head or be undertaken by a panel drawn from, say, the personnel department, departmental heads etc. It may be undertaken as a straight interview designed to supplement information already available on the application form and references, or it may be supplemented by tests where validated ones are available for the vacancy in question; it should be borne in mind that few are so validated (see Anastasi, 1961; Albright, Glennon and Smith, 1963; Guion, 1965; Lawshe, 1948; Thorndike, 1949; Vernon, 1960; Wood, 1960). It may be structured or unstructured, ignoring or making use of interview methods and techniques which are now widely publicized (Anstey and Mercer, 1956; Fraser, 1966; Rodger, 1952; Sidney and Brown, 1961). The outcome will be a decision to appoint or to recommend appointment (where a higher vetting authority is given responsibility). It is normal for the departmental head to have final authority in the sense that none can be imposed upon him (although he may be denied the authority to appoint whom he prefers).

The personnel department can exercise its discretion in its role here, in the interests of improving practice. It has an essentially administrative or monitoring role in the whole sequence of recruiting and selecting for vacancies up to this point. In exercising it the department usually has the authority to ensure that establishments are not exceeded in requests for staff etc or that advertising is non-discriminatory as well as effective. Whether selection is done by interview or not or whether it involves the use of tests or not, the personnel department must not only possess the skills to carry out interviews or to administer tests, but must also seek to ensure that these are applied systematically by the other supervisors and/or managers who engage in recruiting. The personnel department's object is to achieve results which are at once efficient and fair, and which will also do least damage to the image of the employing organization in the minds of those who are put through the process.

In some industries and in many enterprises, this process is often badly botched, either because inadequate care is taken to establish the recruitment process, or because whim or fad leads to the employment of totally inappropriate methods. The increased cost of faulty recruitment (arising from the difficulty and cost of dismissing the mistakes) and the greater requirement for careful justification of the decisions taken (because of the possibility of complaints of unfair discrimination, for example) might between them help the personnel manager to ensure that more care is given to these activities in future.

Getting and giving information
The skills of the personnel practitioner in this area are associated with various aspects of communication. The selection process, assuming it conforms to the legislative and moral constraints, means the giving of information to the potential recruit—through ad-

vertisement of the job vacancy, through further particulars which might include the job description, through more general information which might be contained in an employee or staff handbook which describes the organization and sets out the rules to be observed and the benefits to be obtained from employment within it. Such specific information may be given at the interview at the request of the candidate and now, through the 'particulars of the employment contract', has to be given to the recruited applicant where he is not given an actual contract (or access to one) with the same information in it. It also means gathering information from the applicant to enable the selectors to make correct decisions against the criteria established for the job in question, through the application form when completed, through references where these are used, through the application of interviewing skills, through examinations (eg proficiency tests and medical examinations) and through the application of tests in special circumstances and for particular purposes where such tests are valid and reliable. Taken together, these two objectives should be pursued in such a way that a candidate is left with the 'feeling that he has had "a fair crack of the whip" and the "organization" with the feeling that it has secured the best candidate available in all the circumstances' (cf Cuming, 1968, p 66).

The personnel specialist normally has a responsibility in relation to this communication process which has two aspects; he must ensure that any part he plays in the process conforms to best practice in terms of method and skill; and he must ensure that others in the organization who are necessarily involved in the process also follow that practice. The discharge of both is facilitated by *proformae* and procedures which have been devised to guide the exercise, and this may be illustrated with reference to the central activity, the interview. A number of different 'guides' have been provided, the five-point and the seven-point plans being the best well-known (Fraser, 1966; Rodger, 1952)

The seven-point plan is a checklist of job requirements which have to be met in the person appointed to the job, and may be expressed as 'questions' and 'answers' which the interviewer might ask and hope to receive during the course of the interview: (p 211).

The five-point plan is in principle similar although it uses different 'check' headings: impact on other people, qualifications, brains and abilities, motivation and adjustment. Although in the particular case the precise form of the answers to the questions about the job requirement will vary, the important suggestion in these plans is that some systematic plan should be used by interviewers. Such a plan will impose a discipline, and will help to

1 *Physical make-up*
   Q What does the job demand in the way of general health, strength, appearance, manner, voice?
   A Has the candidate any defects of health or physique that may be of occupational importance? How agreeable are his appearance, bearing and speech?
2 *Attainments*
   Q What does it demand by way of general education, specialized training, and previous experience?
   A What type of education has he had, and how well has he done educationally? What occupational training and experience has he had already, and how well has he done in his previous jobs?
3 *General intelligence*
   Q What level is required to do the job (a) satisfactorily, (b) well?
   A How much intelligence can he display and does he ordinarily display? (This may be assessed by testing)
4 *Special aptitudes*
   Q Does the job involve any special dexterity—manual, verbal, musical, artistic etc?
   A Has he any marked mechanical aptitude? manual dexterity? verbal facility? artistic or musical ability? (Again, may be found by tests)
5 *Interests*
   Q How far does the job require a special interest in, for example, outdoor life, being with other people, artistic expression? Are any hobbies likely to be relevant?
   A To what extent are his interests intellectual? practical-constructional? physical-active? social? artistic?
6 *Disposition*
   Q Does the job call for any of the following qualities—leadership, acceptability to others, reliability, sense of responsibility, self-reliance?
   A How acceptable does he make himself to other people? Does he influence others? Is he steady and dependable? Is he self-reliant?
7 *Circumstances*
   Q How will the pay, prestige, status of job affect the worker's private life?
   A What are his domestic circumstances? How large a family? Does he own his house? Is he willing to travel? (Based on Cuming, 1968, pp 68–69).

reduce the likelihood of 'snap' judgements (which usually involve judging on stereotyping—the 'cloth cap' means ... —or on a 'halo' effect—a good looking blonde is probably good at typing) and, if initially following a plan tends to stilt the interviewers' approach, practice with a plan of some kind will probably overcome this and still lead to improved performance all round.

The interview may in some cases be the only source of information available to the selectors, but in most it will supplement the biographical information given on the application form (see Plumbley, 1976, pp 132–33 for an example of an application form). Some of the 'information' sought in systematic interview can be obtained from this form (even if it still requires supplementation at interview). Plumbley suggests that:

> it can provide some provisional evidence and clues concerning the applicant's
>
> biographical data and personal circumstances
> career pattern and attainments
> powers of self-expression
> range and depth of interests
> intelligence and special aptitudes
> behavioural patterns and preferences. (Plumbley, 1976, p 134)

On the basis of the factual information given and these 'clues' which can be gleaned, it may be possible to do a preliminary sort into definitely unsuitable, possible and probable categories. Translation of the last or the last two categories into successful applications may depend, in the general case, upon interview, and in the specific case upon interview and further tests.

The interview
The interview remains the most popular or common device for most selection purposes (ie whether it be selection for recruitment, training, promotion, transfer, discharge). This is so in spite of the fact that it can, in taking up employees' time, be quite costly and also so in spite of the likelihood that most people who conduct them have had no training in so doing. Ulrich and Trumbo (1965, p 114) suggest however, that at least part of the popularity may be due to the fact that it serves a number of different purposes at the same time: a tool of selection, a recruiting device, a public relations medium and a mechanism for disseminating information. Consequently, even if it were to be both costly and invalid as a selection tool (if used by itself) it might still be accorded value because of the other ends served.

The usual purpose of the interview in the selection context is that of permitting a better judgement to be made as to which candidate might best fit the requirements of the job for which a vacancy exists. Much doubt has been cast upon it as a valid instrument for this purpose in most of the research which has been conducted into it (cf Wagner, 1949; Mayfield, 1964; Ulrich and Trumbo, 1965). Doubt is also cast on its reliability when employed in isolation from other data (as may be available from the biographical information form, from references or from tests). Ulrich and Trumbo comment on the surprising lack of personnel management investigation of this universal instrument, and Dunnette and Bass have seen the profession's failure to do so as 'personnel management's prime problem' (Dunnette and Bass, 1963).

Such research as has been conducted into it by psychologists suggests that rarely are validity and reliability high for the interview alone, but both are raised where the interview is a supplement to other sources of data (as in the preceding paragraph). Both are improved also where the jobs for which the interviews are being held or the kind of candidates involved, are relatively 'standard'; a succession of single individual interviews for a variety of different jobs could be predicted to have low validity and reliability. There is some suggestion also that where they are appropriate, the results of tests, and the biographical information supplied on the application form, might well not only increase, but be necessary to increase, the validity and reliability of the judgements made by the interviewer on the basis of the data obtained from interview alone. On the point of the accuracy of the information obtained in the interview, the research suggests that this instrument usually attracts accurate data on the interviewee's experience of the recent past, but less accurate information on the more distant past.

Wagner concluded his summary of the research with the suggestion that it pointed to the need for greater standardization (both of the purposes and of the procedures followed), a more extensive use of ancillary sources of data (as above) and a narrower focus of the interviewer's questions. With this conclusion Ulrich and Trumbo see no reason to disagree on the basis of their later review. On the last suggestion (narrower focus) however, they offer their own suggestion that because other sources of data are more useful for other purposes, the interviewer should concentrate on securing answers to the questions 'What is the applicant's motivation to work?' and 'Will he adjust to the social context of the job?'. Neither of these are reliably answered in other ways, and yet the interview seems to inform the interviewer's judgement sufficiently for him or her to answer these kinds of question reasonably well.

213

The major problem about the interview is the assumption which most of us make that we are good judges of our fellow men in spite of the evidence that most of us are not good judges unless we have taken specific steps to learn about the norms applicable to judging and about the biases to which we are prone in the absence of controls (cf Thomason, 1980). Plumbley, for example, argues that:

> good selection can only derive from sympathetic training, ruthless self-criticism, and the attempt always to look at the process through the eyes of the candidate, as the only satisfactory ways to improve one's performance and skill (Plumbley, 1976, p 9).

There are, therefore, remedies for poor judgement in interview situations and there is now also an increasing amount of research data on what the candidate sees in interviews (Keenan, 1978; Alderfer and McCord, 1970; Schmitt and Coyle, 1976).

Tests

As the previous section suggests, data generated in tests are often both more valid and reliable in themselves than those obtained in the course of (especially unstructured) interviews and can be useful supports of those data when used in addition. Tests fall into two main categories:

Firstly, those which reveal attainments or typical performance, and applicable where the applicant is required to have, and represents himself as having, certain attainments and competences. In some cases an external 'certification', whether of apprenticeship, educational attainment or proficiency in skill, may be accepted in lieu of the first of these and they may be supplemented by test of normal or typical performance (eg the dictation of a letter to a shorthand typist applying for a job).

Where this is not so and yet it remains important to have a measure of attainment, it is possible to use attainment tests, although as Plumbley says:

> 'though laymen can devise attainment tests they are ill-advised to do so, unless they have a thorough understanding of the statistical concepts involved. For example, a battery of attainment tests for secretarial work will cover vocabulary, grammar, spelling, punctuation, arithmetic, etc. and within each aspect the items will be graded in order of difficulty, so that the battery will show the candidate's level of attainment and degree of accuracy' (Plumbley, 1976, p 163).

Secondly, three other categories of test which are also supplementary present different problems of administration because of their reliance upon psychological knowledge which may not always be perfectly present in the lay tester. These are intelligence tests, special aptitude tests, and personality tests, all of which are better not used unless the test results are vital to decision because of the job requirements, or unless there are trained testers available to administer and interpret them. In any event, consideration has to be given to the 'acceptability' of the tests to the applicant, since test results are often assigned a threat status by the testee, who, without careful handling may then reject the resultant offer because of what is imputed to the firm's agents as the intention of applying such tests (see Plumbley, 1976, p 164).

Taken together, these give appreciable amounts of information about the candidate to the selectors, who can then use it in reaching a decision about whom to appoint. It should be emphasized, however, that the candidate should also have been offered an opportunity to elicit a comparable amount and range of information, by one means or another, so that whether a job is offered or not that candidate would be able to decide whether to accept it or not. It may well be that the individual 'just wants a job, any job'; even in that case of 'no choice' the information given in the selection process ought to be sufficient to permit him or her to appreciate what, even in this no choice situation, he or she is taking on. The aim which should guide action here is indicated by recognizing, in Torrington's words, that in selection interviews, 'two people have to make a decision', the one in terms of the suitability of the applicant for the job, and the other in terms of the suitability of the job (and employer) for the applicant (Torrington, 1972, p 3).

Medical examination

The medical examination is a special kind of test which may be used to provide valid information for selection purposes, but it is also one which might in present circumstances offer some protection to the employer in health and safety claims. It has long been used in some special types of work (teaching and medical care, for example, where there are potential hazards in the work itself) but is now being increasingly used in general selection. A *proforma* covering the matters to be assessed in the examination is often provided, and appointment of otherwise successful candidates may be made conditional upon passing this examination. The completed medical examination form is then incorporated with the personal information contained in the employee's file.

The Health and Safety at Work Act makes it desirable for employers to ensure that anyone who is subjected not merely to hazard or to health risk but also to stress in the job, whether at a managerial level or on the shop floor, should undergo medical examination. If, for example, an employee suffers a heart attack and medical evidence suggests that this attack could have been prevented or at least predicted if the patient had known about it in advance, and if further the stress of the job carried out by the employee were to be alleged to have been a prime cause of the development of the condition or of the heart attack itself, the employer might well be open to prosecution for having failed to take such steps as were 'reasonably practicable' to safeguard the health of the individual concerned. But this policy on the part of the employer does not provide a complete answer to the problem that the employer might face.

If, for example, in the course of a compulsory medical examination an incipient heart condition is discovered, what does the employer do? He could take the diagnosis of the medical officer, relate it to the stress conditions of the job being carried out by the individual and draw the inference that the individual ought to be moved to a less stressful job. If the employer were to do this, the employee himself might not agree, more especially since the job offered would be likely to carry less income. The individual might therefore claim that the employer was engaging in the practice of 'constructive dismissal'; if the employee refused to take the new job offered, he might well appear before a tribunal seeking compensation for unfair dismissal. Again, the problem is only likely to be resolved when the matter has been tested by the courts. The employer is unlikely to be able to predict what action he might safely take in all these circumstances. What does seem reasonably clear is that, where there is reason to suppose that the conditions in which the individual works are likely to affect his health and welfare, the employer should make provision for a periodical medical examination if he is to ensure a reasonable defence.

A problem also arises under this same heading concerning the employment of disabled persons. Many employers have to employ a proportion of registered disabled persons. The Health and Safety at Work Act makes no distinction between the disabled and the normal person in imposing duties on the employer. It may well prove that the disabled person is exposed to much greater risk in some sense than the normal person. The discharge of the employer's duty on what would be reasonable or reasonably practicable for normal persons might prove insufficient for the registered disabled. Again, a matter of welfare policy is therefore called in question by this particular provision of the Act.

Those who have written on the new Act have frequently

offered employers a checklist which might help to provide them with an adequate defence if challenged and an example is provided by Mitchell (1974, pp 18–20).

Completion of the selection process

It could be represented that the selection process is never 'completed': like education it is a continuous process of re-selection on a mutual basis. The subsequent process of transfer, promotion and demotion and termination could also be said to reflect and rely upon similar methods and techniques to those which have just been touched upon when discussing initial recruitment. But for the sake of organizing material for this chapter, it may be suggested that the selection or recruitment process may be regarded as 'completed' by three further activities: the communication of the decision taken, together with any consequential information relevant thereto; the induction of the new employee; and the provision of any training which may have been judged necessary to bring the attainment of the individual into conformity with the job requirements.

The recruitment process proper is completed by (a) informing the unsuccessful candidates that the post has been filled (and in a tight labour market possibly offering to hold the application on file pending further vacancies), and (b) issuing a letter of appointment to the successful candidate(s) or informing the candidate of his appointment on the spot. Under the EP(C) Act, it is necessary to issue to almost all new employees within 13 weeks of starting work a summary of the terms and conditions of the appointment; in some cases, this will accompany the letter of appointment.

This required information for the new employee can only be the bare minimum. He or she is likely to require much more than this, if only because of the nature of the obligations which the employee assumes (or is deemed to assume) on taking up employment. Faithful service of the employer, in an agreed capacity and possibly based upon a warranted skill or competence will, *inter alia*, require the employee to obey those rules which are relevant to the employment and to apply his knowledge and skills in the way desired by the employer (see above pp 87–92).

It is therefore necessary for the new employee to acquire information and knowledge about the situation in which he now finds himself, and correspondingly necessary for the employer to make these available to him, usually through an induction and/or an induction training process and programme. By this means the new employee may be placed in the position where he can give the required service and do so in accordance with custom and practice

217

or the rules appertaining to the undertaking. This will not be 'the end of the process' of familiarizing the individual with the requirements of the role, because as we have already noted above the requirements are likely to change with the exigencies of the business, but it is an important beginning of it.

A second aspect of 'completion' is that which assures the undertaking a record of information about the successful applicant. A good deal of this information is contained on the application form itself, and this may be augmented by the information obtained in interview and from medical examination and tests. This can then provide the basis for the development of the employee's employment history; other items of information, such as job and pay changes, sickness and accident occurrences, training received and courses attended, will be added during the course of the employment. Many of these items of information are confidential, and some (like records of disciplinary action) may have only limited lives under agreements with the employee's trade union, and they need to be kept secure. But they need to be kept in order to provide a foundation for all manner of activities, from promotion to welfare counselling.

(Some commercial organizations, such as Formecon Services Limited, make complete packages of forms and records available which can be filed within an Employee Data Folder. Such packages will include application forms, employee interview record, statements of terms and conditions of employment, statements of company rules and disciplinary procedures, and induction checklists, which, together with the printed folder, covers all the information which most undertakings are likely to want to record or to present to the new employee at the point of establishing the contract. In addition, attendance and accident record forms are made available to complete the standard package, which is prepared in a fashion which conforms to the legal requirements extant at the time.)

Induction
Induction is conceived as a way of ensuring that the new employee, whether he/she is a young person or not, is adequately introduced to the job and the organization within which he/she will perform it. It is fairly obvious that the individual must somehow, and that fairly quickly, familiarize himself with the tasks he will be expected to perform. It may be less obvious that if he is to perform these tasks adequately he must have an adequate understanding of the organization within which those tasks occur and of the way in which he will be expected to perform them in conformity with custom and

practice and with the required standards. A failure to provide the individual with information about his job (which the individual himself would regard as of primary importance) might help to account for the high rate of labour turnover in the early months of engagement of new employees (see above pp 180–82).

The duties imposed upon the employer by the Contracts of Employment Act, the Trade Union and Labour Relations Acts, the Health and Safety at Work Act and the Employment Protection Act might be regarded as an attempt to distil best company practice in this particular respect into a set of duties which should be discharged by any employer, although in formalizing the duty in the legislation there is a mechanical consequence: the individual employee may be given further particulars of his contract within 13 weeks of his engagement. But the personnel manager must recognize that some at least of this kind of information is required by the employee at the beginning of his employment with the organization.

Giving information about the organization, its objectives, policies and standards might be seen as more in the interests of the employer than the employee (who might well regard this information as of less immediate relevance to him as a new employee). There is however a sense in which the individual employee will at some stage seek this kind of information in order to form a judgement as to the desirability of continuing to work for that employer. Although the immediacy of this information may therefore be lower, it is both normal and sensible to regard the giving of this information as part of the induction process.

The mistake is often made by employing organizations of assuming that *this* information is as important to the employee as it might seem to be to the employer, and the information is frequently given too soon and without later reinforcement so that the effect of providing such information is usually dissipated. A common method of *giving* such information is to present new employees with a booklet on the undertaking and an employee handbook. Effective communication calls for more than this, and this may be effected by *reinforcing* the messages of the printed word by discussion in induction or re-training sessions.

The way in which the induction programme is presented will probably call for the giving of information to the new employee on two different planes.

First, there is clearly a requirement for information about the organization as a whole and this is likely to be carried out fairly informally in the small organization by someone fairly senior in the management team. In the larger organization a more formal pro-

219

gramme might be arranged which would include a welcome to the organization by a member of corporate management who might spend some time talking about the development of the enterprise over the years, and who might support this with films about the firm's activities and by presenting visual data in the form of organization charts or charts showing sales or profitability or performance on other relevant dimensions.

The induction programme should include a tour of the buildings and departments so that the individual may have some feel for the general lay-out and activities which are carried on within that organization and this would provide a reasonable basis for informing new employees about the social and welfare facilities available. For example, the tour would include a visit to the pay office, which might provide an opportunity to tell the individual how he would be paid, and a tour of the sports and social facilities might provide a chance for someone to explain what facilities are available to the new employee on what conditions. Where the programme is as elaborate as this, there will be a tendency to put on the programme only when enough recruits have been assembled to warrant so much staff time.

The second plane of information referred to is that which focuses much more clearly on the actual job of work that the individual will have to do and the department or section within which he will be expected to do it. This information is probably best provided by the supervisor who has been trained to carry out the role. What is most often needed and provided is first a tour of the department, providing an opportunity to explain how each job within the department fits into the main flow of production or activity; secondly, the departmental rules about time-keeping, breaks for refreshment, health and safety rules, accident prevention, the issue of protective clothing, and any actions to be taken in the case of emergency, and explaining procedures on reporting sickness or other absence. It is also necessary here to tell the new worker what his rights are on union membership and activity and how he can process a grievance or put his views to management; this stage would ideally include some discussion of consultative arrangements in the organization and of suggestion schemes if they are run. If the organization recognizes trade unions, this would be an appropriate occasion on which to introduce the new employee to the shop representatives of the union and to anyone who has other representational functions within that particular section or department.

Certain matters still remain to be discussed with the individual employee by a member of the personnel department itself, such as information on the firm's policies and practices on helping individual employees with any private, financial or domestic problems, on the policies and practices on the development of the individual's qualifications and education, and, thirdly, information on remuneration policy and practice followed within the organization. At this stage information is usually given verbally. Legal requirements on giving further particulars of the contract in written form will doubtless be met later (see pp 87–90), but the individual needs some basic information immediately which must therefore be built into the induction programme at this early stage.

Monitoring selection

A further stage of the selection process is that of evaluating the selection processes and methods themselves.

The main problem of selection which any organization encounters is that which denies it the opportunity to check on the suitability of those who 'got away'. Unfortunately, this is often used as an excuse for not doing anything to check the validities and reliabilities of the methods which are employed in selection processes. To take this course is to miss the opportunities which the organization has for checking, using those who are selected and employed. Although these may be only a part-sample of the total feedstock, they are available for measurement operations, and productive of much more information than could be obtained in the selection process itself. If the appropriate assumption is made that they are a part-sample, and the better part of the sample if the selection processes are effective, data on them can be employed most effectively in checking on existing methods *and* existing objectives.

The success of selection can be evaluated, and it is not necessary that evaluation should proceed by way of 'sophisticated' techniques. Every piece of information can be evaluated against the performance of those selected. For example, age, length of experience, any test results and interviewer's opinion, can all be set against performance to indicate how successful they proved as predictors in selection. The determination of performance is difficult: supervisor's opinions or assessments of performance are frequently unreliable, and it is therefore better to use objective data (eg work results may be measured by bonus earnings—or length of stay with the company before voluntary departure).

Assessment of the success of selection procedures requires two sets of information to be set alongside one another. For example, the managers' opinions of a man at selection can be set against length of stay, these being plotted on a graph. If the selection procedure is a good (valid) one, the result of the plot will be a thin sausage-shape; the thinner it is, the better is the procedure. This requires that the manager scale his opinions, even if this is done only in terms of broad categories (eg very good, good, average, poor or very poor). Objective data may well lend itself to continuous plotting (eg length of stay in weeks). (See figure 7 below).

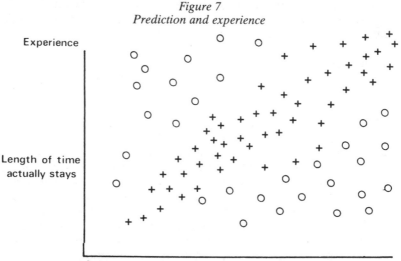

Figure 7
Prediction and experience

A quick and simple way of carrying out this evaluation is to divide both sets of data into two categories, such as the better half and the worse half, so that half the population is in each category. This information can then be placed in four boxes of the following table:

Table 8

Prediction and experience
Those who were predicted at selection to be

		in the better half	in the worse half
Those whose actual job performance is in	the better half of the performers	a	b
	the worse half of the performers	c	d

222

If each box has an appropriately equal number in it, then the selection procedure is no more valid than chance would allow, or than could be obtained by tossing a penny to determine what category a person shall fall into. A very good selection procedure would result in the population being divided more or less equally between boxes a and d.

This can be converted approximately into correlation by (i) working out an index: (a × d) divided by (b × c), and (ii) converting this index into the equivalent correlation from the table below:

Index	Equivalent correlation
35.0	0.9
15.5	0.8
8.9	0.7
5.8	0.6
4.0	0.5
2.9	0.4
2.2	0.3
1.7	0.2
1.3	0.1

The nearer the correlation to 1.0 the better the selection procedure.

This provides but one of many possible illustrations of the manner in which the personnel function is being wooed away from a possibly excessive interest in data as a basis for no more than morale considerations, and towards a use of data to monitor the personnel and manpower decision-processes.

Termination of contracts or deselection

It is to be expected that many employees who are secured in the manner indicated in this chapter will subsequently change their jobs within the enterprise. Sometimes this may result from voluntary transfer or promotion as the individual pursues a career within it, and sometimes because of the exigencies of the business which might reduce or eliminate the need for certain jobs or certain skills. Increasing restrictions on the employer's opportunity to discharge labour (see chapter 5 above) may lead to much more job changing within the undertaking than may have occurred in earlier years. During this process, both supervisors and personnel practitioners are likely to be involved in the tasks of selection and preparing people for the new jobs, following procedures and methods not too dissimilar from those discussed above.

Time, and the implementation of manpower plans in a changeable market, will also lead to terminations of the employment contract and the final 'de-selection' of the individual from the organization. Where the termination is voluntary on the part of the individual, he or she may cause no more than a small administrative action to effect the termination (giving of cards, tax statements and so on) and possibly, in a termination interview, to provide data which might be used in monitoring employment practice and policy within the undertaking. Where the 'voluntary leaving' is because of retirement, the personnel department may (as happens in an increasing number of undertakings) be drawn into a process of helping prepare the individual for the new status and condition. This may mean providing pre-retirement courses, frequently off the job, in which various experts (eg in health of the old, income and tax matters, or in welfare services and provision) may inform and advise or counsel the person retiring (and in some cases, even the spouse) about the likely problems they may encounter. Where death occurs in service, the personnel practitioners also often have to help the family to deal with the immediate and longer-term (eg pension or benefit) problems.

A number of terminations occur involuntarily from the employee's standpoint. Here, the activities imposed upon the personnel specialists are somewhat different.

In the first place, there is likely to be a responsibility upon the personnel department to see that procedures exist to support any decision by the employer to discharge an employee: this means, in effect, ensuring that there are procedures for monitoring the performance of the individual employee in a fair and equitable fashion, for applying known disciplinary and safety (etc) rules in a manner which accords with the principles of natural justice, and for allowing any redundancy which may be declared to be dealt with in a non-discriminatory and open manner as is required by legislation and (often) union-management agreement.

Secondly, it is often a responsibility of the personnel department to ensure that (in the interests of both the employer and the employee) these procedures are followed and that the principles of equity and natural justice are observed in doing so, in order both to avoid difficulties before tribunals or with the unions, and to help ensure that the individual(s) affected retains a reasonable amount of respect for the employer even when discharged. Where in spite of all the employer is taken before a tribunal about a dismissal, it will also often fall to the personnel specialist either to represent or support the representative of the employer in that context.

The personnel specialist will then find himself required to exercise a number of his basic skills in smoothing this de-selection process. He or she will need to design appropriate procedures, secure their adoption by others, police their operation, and become concerned in them in ways which will make use of his inter-personal and communication skills.

Counselling at termination

One major aspect of this involves counselling the individual, par-ticularly in cases where termination occurs because of retirement or redundancy. In such circumstances, the individual is often most apprehensive about the future, partly because of his lack of fore-knowledge and partly because of a fear of the change itself.

As that quite remarkable personal survival kit produced by the Newport and Gwent Industrial Mission for those made redundant puts it, to be told that one is redundant is likely to set in train a sequence of reactions which can be described as shock, defensive retreat, acknowledgement and adaptation. Whether the individual moves rapidly through this from the negative to the positive reac-tions, and thus adjusts to the situation in which he finds himself, will in many cases depend upon the help and emotional support he can obtain. Although not all this is likely to come from a personnel officer, some of it appropriately can.

In the retirement situation many similar cognitive and emo-tional problems are likely to arise for the individual. Many under-takings have now developed comprehensive pre-retirement 'courses' for their employees, in which the kinds of people who will be helpful to the individual after retirement are brought in to indi-cate what help they might give and what in their experience are the kinds of problems to be avoided by some element of forward plan-ning. In such situations, the factors of efficiency and concern clearly come together—a poorly organized course or other arrangement is not likely to succeed because a lot of concern is shown, and a lack of sensitivity by those providing a good course is not likely to produce effective results.

A first requirement upon anyone who would attempt to counsel in these circumstances is, therefore, that he or she should be sufficiently knowledgeable about the likely problems and possi-bilities. It is not likely to prove useful to the individual unless the personnel department can also mobilize experts from other ser-

225

vices such as the Employment Services Division, and possibly recruiters from other organizations to support the counselling activity, in cases of redundancy on a large scale. A second is that the counsellor develop and display sensitivity in approaching individuals. A third is rather different in that it calls for a history of effective and sympathetic counselling of the individual before the particular termination situation arises. Counselling is not likely to be effective if it is provided on an *ad hoc* basis. Unless the organization has consciously sought to develop a programme of career development for its employees, there is likely to be little data available to permit counselling in conditions of redundancy or leaving for other reasons.

Conclusion

At this point, therefore, the theme of this part comes full circle. The first problem considered is that of the undertaking in securing a sufficient quality and quantity of labour to realize its task objectives. The second is that of the individual worker, not only in securing the quantity and quality of employment to realize his or her objectives, but also of doing this in an environment in which 'employment' is not the paramount concern or objective of the 'system' which actually makes it available.

The undertaking's management has available to it an increasing number of methods and techniques by which the task-related problem may be reduced. Particularly those of manpower forecasting and planning, and of job description and person specification, when applied in the recruitment and deselection processes, help to effect the kind of local (undertaking-level) equilibrium which is sought. But these cannot be applied completely autonomously and unilaterally; at very least the proscriptions and prescriptions of the law have to be taken into account and in many situations those accepted as a result of trade union pressure exert a comparable influence upon policy and practice.

As human expectations of the work situation change, however, there is a pressure upon the undertaking in deciding policies and practices to take such normal considerations into account, almost regardless of what the law or the trade union agreements might say. In order to secure a sufficiently loyal and committed labour force, undertakings are increasingly drawn into the development of more complex kinds of contract than those acknowledged in the legal definitions. It is this problem and pressure which tends to support the modern conceptions of 'welfare' which emphasize the need to offer adequate tasks, training and organization, in addition to the basic 'consideration' of the legal contract, and which, in turn, draw the personnel manager into his involvement with individual cases (as in counselling) as well as into his association with stocks and flows in the aggregate.

The personnel manager, as executant, is involved in all of these processes at both the aggregate and individual levels. It is in this context that his skills of analysis, judgement and communication are called for, and that the conflict of ends first makes its presence felt.

Further reading
A number of general texts on personnel or industrial psychology cover the field considered in this chapter—for example, McCormick and Tiffin (1975) and Blum and Naylor (1968).

On the more specific aspects, see:
Bramham (1975) on the practical aspects of manpower planning
Boydell (1970) on job analysis and Singer and Ramsden (1969) on skills analysis
Ray (1971) and Braithwaite and Pollock (1974) on advertising
Ungerson (1970) and Plumbley (1976) on recruitment and selection
Anstey and Mercer (1956) and Fraser (1971 and 1966) on selection and selection interviewing
Albright, Glennon and Smith (1963) and Miller (1975) on psychological testing
Marks (1974) on induction.

Part two
Contributing to the production function

Contributing to the production function

People and production

Up to this point we have tried to stick to the assumption that certain aspects of the personnel manager's role can be discussed by regarding people 'in the mass', as stocks and flows of labour relevant to the undertaking's purposes. At this point, however, we need to relax this assumption in order to look at those parts of the role which relate to the person and his or her performance in the work situation.

We have already noted, (above, pp 3–5) that the personnel practitioner is disposed to see his or her main concern as being with people at work. But a concern with people, simply as people, is not quite the same as a concern with people 'at work'. The last two words indicate a concern with people as *workers*, as people engaged in making a livelihood (looked at from one standpoint) and people as instrumentalities in the production, distribution and exchange of wealth (seen from another).

This touches on the two perspectives of personnel practice which have run through its history.

The first perspective is associated with concepts of productivity and efficiency in the work process itself; the problem is that of ensuring that people, as human instruments of production, can and will perform efficiently, so that at the end of the day, their interest in the enjoyment of wealth as consumers can be satisfied (cf Goodrich, 1922).

The second is associated with concepts of satisfaction, or even happiness, not confined to the association with consumption of material wealth. The problem here is one of ensuring that people engaged in the wealth-creating process will be able to realize some of their essential humanity, to the point of getting direct satisfaction from engaging in that process, or even enjoying it.

As part of the management team, the personnel manager must

have some concern with the first (*see* above, pp 39–46), even if, professionally, he still seeks to demonstrate a concern with the second in acting out the role of 'conscience of the company' (above, pp (33–35).

It was a common aspiration of the students of human relations in industry to find an association between these two ends of working. Attempts to uncover it through empirical research usually proved abortive; the data had the awkward habit of suggesting that high productivity and high satisfaction might sometimes but by no means invariably go together (cf Kahn and Katz, 1953; Blauner, 1964). The lack of empirical demonstration of an association does not 'prove' that such a relationship does not or cannot exist, and it has not completely deterred those who continue to advocate better human relations or improved styles of management and supervision. But it does face management with having to choose between alternative ends, or of establishing the priorities between them.

This has often disconcerted the personnel managers during the history of their occupation. One example is provided by Fogarty's 'Independent Comment' on the IPM's Jubilee Statement, which begins with the assertion that 'the business of business is business: economic business, to create economic values and to minimize economic costs' and continues with the criticism that in the Statement:

> the business of personnel management appears on the face of it to be something else. The manifesto does, it is true, refer to 'efficiency' and to the fact that economic quantities such as wages and salaries come into the personnel manager's field. But I do not find it anywhere said squarely that the first concern of the personnel manager as of everyone else in a firm is with value for money or that a main consideration in the training of personnel managers should be to teach them to think in this way (Fogarty, 1963, p 23).

In the intervening period, it seems, personnel managers have moved more directly into this area of concern and have become more directly involved in the business of increasing efficiency in the undertakings in which they are employed (see above, pp 39–46). Their concern still retains the 'people' orientation, but it is (partly or perhaps substantially) an orientation towards people as instruments of production or efficiency. In this part we shall be concerned with this particular strand of personnel management—that which is related to performance and efficiency.

232

The personnel management dilemma

Achieving efficiency poses a fundamental dilemma for all those who would 'manage personnel', and it is crystallized in this debate within the personnel management profession. It is not simply the matter of confronting hard-nosed business management with some conception of morality (as in the 'conscience of the company'), although that is relevant. It is also a question of establishing the conditions of efficient management within our (societal) beliefs about human capacity and capability. In other words, there may be (indeed 'is') a question of morality in all management activity (cf Selekman, 1959) but there may also be a much more 'technically-practical' question to be answered about whether even hard-nosed, efficiency-oriented management has got right the relationship between human motivation and performance.

A manager whose experience or training might lead him or her to adopt certain beliefs about the way in which performance may be drawn out of the individual worker may well find himself or herself frustrated in an attempt to act upon these by the structure of relationships and expectations which surround the managerial role. This is not uncommon experience. It is not surprising, at least in the sense that no one enjoys the luxury of operating with a clean slate. Structures and conventions which support them exist 'prior to' the individual, and even if he or she would change them, they constitute a constraint upon action. No one is ever in a position to act upon individual beliefs independently of the structures which are already there (and without taking into account the 'effect' that experience of those structures may have had upon the individual). Many such 'structures' already exist, but in the next chapter it is proposed to look at two of these, the conception of the institution of management itself, and the structure of law which tends to support it.

In the classical formulation of management functions, prime emphasis is placed upon the imperative of securing the purposes and objectives of the undertaking through means which may be subsumed under the headings of 'direction and control' (cf Tannenbaum, 1958; 1961; and above, pp 18–21). The achievement of the objectives will be facilitated by the setting of a clear target *for* people to aim at in respect of both work performance and remuneration and by the supervision of their conduct whilst at work so that non-sanctioned (and non-contributory) behaviours may be changed by disciplining the individuals concerned.

This basic conception of the nature of the management's problem and function still holds good to a considerable extent. Furthermore it is focused most directly upon the role of the 'supervisor', in which the interface of management and non-management tends to lie. His planning and executive activities are directed to securing efficiency within his department or section and therefore to solving the problems of motivation and discipline.

Furthermore, this classical conception tends to be supported by the institution of civil law as it is applied to work organization. The supervisor does not operate in the kind of free situation in which he can simply reflect his own beliefs in the style he adopts or the way he seeks to achieve his production objectives. He both relies to a considerable extent upon the laws, conventions and rules which structure both his role and the roles of the people he supervises, and is in turn restricted in his opportunities for action by them. Fundamentally, these establish that there is in the situation 'a power to command and a duty to obey' (Kahn-Freund, 1972, p 9), which stems from the employment contract, but which is supported and reinforced by the institutions of work. This both supports the pursuit of productivity and constrains the strategies which are open to managements and supervisors to achieve it, placing the emphasis particularly upon the 'direction and control' strategies of the classical view.

Although personnel management has been seen as an historical outgrowth from this supervisor role (cf Crichton, 1968), the personnel practitioner has no continuing involvement in the role as such. He has a concern with the development of policy and practice which guides everyone's conduct in it. To that extent, the personnel manager is drawn into the dilemma of upholding 'the law' as it supports a conception of control and yet seeking to develop policies and practices which are valid and reliable even if these conflict with the assumptions of law as to the way in which performance by workers may be secured.

Stationary targets in human motivation

The 'problem' which calls for discussion in this context, however, is that of resolving what in the personnel manager's 'people' orientation contributes to the realization of this productivity/efficiency objective. In this as in most other areas of his concern, the personnel manager is not *directly* charged with 'getting the production out'; but consistently with the Fogarty-line above: he must make some contribution. The question is: what is it?

We might say that the personnel manager, by virtue of his training, has a greater understanding of 'people' and what makes them tick, than would be true of those who have not had the option of studying the subject as closely or for so long. This knowledge of 'people' might then form the base for his contribution to the undertaking which both employs him and is concerned to secure performance from those whom it employs. Since that performance can only come through people, how are those people to be brought to give the desired performance?

What the practising personnel manager often faces (and therefore what he often has to try to do something about) is an oversimplified view of the human being as a worker. In this view, 'workers' (as a class or category) are regarded as *all* (or with very few exceptions) cast in the same mould, tarred with the same brush—or some other statement which implies that there is a kind of 'stationary' worker-target for the endeavours of managers and supervisors. It follows that if workers are all the same, somehow what is called for by way of strategy is equally unitary: if it is true that all workers want from work is money, then getting the work out will be facilitated by making the opportunity to get more money conditional upon giving more work. All else would be cosmetic.

There is a very strong tendency for this kind of thinking to develop. The literature of the social sciences is replete with views of man which constantly throw up opposing, either/or, perspectives. Porter, Lawler and Hackman (1975, ch 2) argue that man has been seen in the following alternative frameworks:

1 As emotionally controlled at an often-unconscious level
   or As rationally oriented and therefore as essentially calculating

2 Behaviouristically, by which all behaviour is to be explained in terms of environmental control
   or Phenomenologically, by which all action is to be explained as a consequence of conscious thought.

3 As an economic animal or almost as a hedonistic one, consciously seeking material satisfaction and avoiding conditions like starvation
   or As a self-actualizing animal, in which personal growth and development provide stronger draws than mere money or materialism

4 As essentially passive or reflexive, responding only to that which cannot be avoided (as in the Theory X assumptions)
   or As essentially active and responsive, capable and willing to contribute to wider goals, provided the disposing condition is right (Theory Y).

These four categories emphasize different dimensions but through each of the two columns there runs a linking thread, one of passive or negative reaction to blind fate, and the other of active or positive response to a mutable environment. Each in turn demonstrates a consonance with perspectives of group and organizational behaviour, the one associated with 'system' perspectives in which the individual is seen as reacting, and the other with 'social action' perspectives in which the individual is seen as striving (at least) to respond.

It would seem, however, that both views could not be right simultaneously. Possibly some workers some of the time are in one camp, whilst other workers some of the time are in the other. But if the 'people' expert is to provide a solid foundation for strategies, something more than a simple 'either/or', 'some of the time this, some of the time that' propositions may be necessary. The something more may, however, lead us into even greater complexities, even if at the end of the day the complexity is reduced by the individual human mind to a much simpler *gestalt* model of human motivation (cf Johnson, 1972).

Moving targets in motivation

Human motivation is usually described in the textbooks as being both 'complex and highly individual' (McCormick and Tiffin, 1975, p 293). Generalizations about it are not easy, and certainly have not reached the stage where they command universal acceptance. Most of them are based upon an assumption that man has needs (or drives or desires) which he will be disposed to fulfil (or satisfy). The desire to satisfy these needs identifies his *motivation*.

Beyond that assumption, however, the approach divides. On the one hand, the individual in a state of need or of inner tension is viewed as disposed to act in a way which will reduce it. On the other, the individual is regarded as disposed to achieve or acquire something external to himself to yield him satisfaction. In other words, some theories, like that of Maslow (*see* above pp 22–25), emphasize the internal disequilibrium of the individual (the 'need') whilst others, like that of Herzberg (*see* above, pp 25–26) emphasize the external objective (the 'incentive' or 'goal').

Motivation may then be seen as need-driven or as goal-drawn, the one being more easily associated with fairly basic animal behaviour and the other with more complex (rational) human behaviour, and thus presenting a different kind of target for those concerned with 'motivating' or 'incentivating' (the term is mentioned as being more logically correct, but rejected, by Rothe, 1961) people at work.

In Maslow's (1970) and Alderfer's (1972) approaches to the

236

question, for example, the emphasis is upon the manner in which the general desires are ordered in the individual, upon how one might explain what it is the individual is trying to satisfy at any one time. In Herzberg's (1966) conception, on the other hand, the emphasis is upon the external job content and job context factors which might in predictable ways contribute to the individual's satisfaction, that is, upon what externally might be considered to contribute in what ways to the satisfaction of human needs.

Wolf has attempted to introduce a degree of order into these different conceptions and conclusions, by putting forward a number of hypotheses which might help to explain the differences perceived and derived by these students of the subject. In the abbreviated form given by McCormick and Tiffin, these read:

1 Persons whose lower level needs (as postulated by Maslow) are as yet ungratified, derive both their satisfaction and their dissatisfaction from the degree of gratification of their lower level needs (primarily the job context factors).
2 Persons whose lower level needs are conditionally gratified receive both their satisfaction and their dissatisfaction from the degree of gratification of their higher level needs (primarily job content factors), and their dissatisfaction also come when continued gratification of their lower level needs is disrupted or threatened.
3 Persons whose lower level needs are unconditionally gratified obtained both their satisfaction and their dissatisfaction from the degree of gratification of their higher level needs.
4 Dissatisfaction results from frustration of the gratification of an *active* need, and from interruption or threatened interruption of a previously gratified (lower level) need.
5 Satisfaction results from the gratification of any need (Wolf, 1970, pp 87–94, as quoted in McCormick and Tiffin, 1975, p 311).

This, then, has the merit of seeking to tie together a number of the strands of complexity which have been woven into the different approaches to the understanding of motivation. But because they are hypotheses, they serve to show that motivation is probably not to be understood in terms of a simple conception of sequenced hierarchies of need or of alternative sources of environmental satisfaction.

In effect, this suggests that individual differences will confound attempts to explain human behaviour and action in terms of some general conception of 'human nature' (cf Jahoda, 1958; Herzberg, 1966, pp 12–31). We are then led to seek the explanations in two relatively complex theories; the one relating to human learning as a source of behaviour and the other to human motivation as the trigger or stimulus to it. These are considered at greater length in chapter 11 in order to provide a foundation of understanding of the kind of 'motivational' contribution which the personnel department might make to those directly concerned with production.

10 The control assumptions

The centrality of control

To secure performance from a workforce demands purposive action guided by policies and strategies. Even if the personnel management function may have grown out of the supervisory role (cf Crichton, 1968) the personnel practitioner is not directly concerned, as is the supervisor, with drawing out the necessary performance, but he is indirectly concerned with the development of appropriate strategies and policies and their dissemination.

These, in turn, are likely to be based upon both the cultural values and the theories which, as a consequence of either training or experience, the personnel practitioner holds. The values directly applicable, as we have already noted in another context, are most likely to be expressed in those legal prescriptions which define the employer's duty. The theories are likely to reflect the conclusions of social scientific research (*see* chapter 11 below).

Between these there is likely to be some conflict because the assumptions about human behaviour which lie behind the law are very different from those which are emerging in the social sciences. In addition, the assumptions which underly work organizations and their management often reflect more of the former than they do of the latter (but see below, pp 394–426).

The 'problem' may be focused by suggesting (a) that the assumptions of the common law imply that people will perform in desirable ways only if they are subject to control; (b) that the definition of management functions emphasizes the centrality of this same control to be effected through selection, supervision and the provision of incentives; (c) that most social scientific theorizing now emphasizes the need for individuals to be provided with learning and growth opportunities if they are to perform at desirable levels and in necessary ways. The personnel practitioner's dilemma arises from this juxtaposition, and even though he or she may resolve the problem by throwing in his or her lot with the dominant cultural (legal) and sub-cultural (management) values for the sake of peace, the problem is just unlikely to go away.

The basic assumption of law
The problem presented to the personnel policy-maker by the common law is that which stems from the assumptions underlying the 'control test' which has been applied by the judges to determine (for purposes of the law) whether a worker is an employee or a self-employed person. In its original form, it sought to establish whether the person 'works under the control of another, not only as to *what* he must do but also how and when he must do it' (Hepple, 1979, p 57), which would indicate the existence of the employment contract.

Although never very precise, it served to define a relationship when the difference between the parties to it (say, a factory owner and an unskilled labourer) was considerable. It became less useful when applied to the relationship between, say, an airline and the captain of a jumbo jet or a health authority and a surgeon. It assumed, in Hepple's words 'that the employer is both a manager and a technical expert; in other words it reflects a stage of society in which the employer could be expected to be superior to the employee in skill and knowledge' (Hepple, 1979, p 58).

The 'simple' control test was therefore extended to include a question as to whether the person was 'part and parcel of an organization' in the performance of his work. As this was expressed by Lord Denning, who uses the older concept of 'contract of service' for the more modern 'contract of employment':

> Under a contract *of* service a man is employed as part of the business and his work is done as an integral part of the business; whereas under a contract *for* services his work, although done for the business, is not integrated into it but is only accessory to it (*Stevenson, Jordan and Harrison, Ltd v MacDonald and Evans* (1952) 1 TLR p 111).

The question thus became: 'Did the alleged servant form part of the alleged master's organization?' (Kahn-Freund, *Modern Law Review*, 1951, pp 505–6).

This has now been replaced by a rather more complicated, three stage test. The first stage entails establishing that there is agreement to provide a service to an employer by way of work or application of personal skill, and the third requires that the 'other' provisions of the contract should be consistent with there being a contract of employment, but the second stage still clings to the test of whether there is a sufficient degree of control exercised over the work to make the employer 'the master' (in the old-fashioned ter-

240

minology) (*Ready Mixed Concrete Ltd v Minister of Pensions* (1968) 2 QB, p 497). In all of the vicissitudes of this test, the assumption that control must exist 'in sufficient degree' to establish employee status is present.

The significance of this 'test' is that once the employee status is established in law by its application, it provides the employer with the legal foundation for the exercise of his prerogative or claimed right to make the rules governing work behaviour and to administer them through the 'disciplinary' machinery set up within the employing undertaking.

The managerial function

It does not matter much whether the common law doctrine or the managerially-claimed right 'came first': at the present time, both exist alongside one another. In the definitions of the management function, therefore, 'control' comes to be established alongside direction and organization as (in at least one characterization) part of the definition of what management is 'for' (*see* Tannenbaum, 1961, and above, pp 18–21). Managers, as Drucker has suggested, are the dynamic life-giving element in every business (Drucker, 1953, p 1) and they are so by virtue of their power, based on such rights, to organize, direct and control the use and application of resources, including the human ones.

This is then given expression in any treaty which may be drawn up between 'the management' and any group, such as the trade union(s), which seeks to challenge or share in the processes of decision taking. They are usually referred to as the prerogative clauses of collective (recognition) agreements, and they take the typical form of acknowledging the respective rights of the two parties. For example, Article 4 of an agreement of 7 March, 1980, between Inco Europe Ltd and three unions (UCATT, AUEW and EETPU) says, in part:

> Subject to the provisions of this Article and to the rights of the union and the employees as are expressly provided elsewhere in this Agreement, the company has the exclusive right to manage the business and direct all employees employed by it, including, but not limited to, the right to determine by whom, when, where and how work is to be performed and by whom work is to be supervised (p 4).

This may be rather more carefully worded than other recognition and status agreements, but it establishes an employer/management right in terms closely resembling those to be found in use in connection with the common law doctrines.

241

This 'right', claimed by the employer and usually accepted by the trade unions in negotiations, rests upon the same fundamental common law doctrines which we have already examined. Pressure from trade unions within industry and commerce has moved the actual frontier forward and a similar pressure upon government has brought the position in legislation closer to the actualities in recent years.

However, the basic position remains that the employer claims and the law generally upholds, the right of the employer to make the 'rules' which govern both performance behaviour and disciplinary conduct. The employer retains the right to manage his undertakings and to make such rules as are arguably relevant to the achievement of his objectives. Little or nothing in recent legislation has removed this. Consequently, the employer may determine the qualities and quantities of work required, the kind of conduct desired in the work situation, the penalties which might apply in each case to their breach, and the manner of proceeding in deciding whether penalties of any kind are appropriate to any given circumstances of breach.

The direction of legislative curb

What has been done in recent legislation is fix certain limits to the discretion of the employer to take these kinds of decision. Most of what has been done in this respect in recent enactments, stems from the concept of 'unfair dismissal' at which we have already looked. In so far as 'dismissal' is the ultimate sanction which the employer may apply to the individual worker for breach, to that extent any curbs upon that process will affect the whole disciplinary and performance-monitoring process. What has been done in this area, therefore, leaves the fundamental rights (in the preceding paragraph) alone at the level of principle, but curbs the arbitrary or disdainful exercise of those rights.

The right to make work and conduct rules (including health and safety conduct) remains, but the law now requires that such rules as are adopted shall be justifiable in terms of the needs of the business or in terms of facilitating the discharge by the employer of statutory duties. These overlap, but rules which may be justified are those relating to work performance, work conduct, health, safety and well-being and ordered relationships.

The right to prescribe (and apply) penalties and punishments also remains, but the law requires that a general indication of the relationship between transgressions and departures from the rules and the penalties and punishments which might apply, shall now be given to those subjected to the rules. This principle applies in all the substantive areas mentioned. From this, there develop other restrictions on the relevance of some categories of penalty to some categories of offence, the long-standing restrictions of this kind to be found in the Truck Acts being broadened for this purpose.

The right of the employer to administer the rules (and the disciplinary processes associated with them) remains, but the legislation imposes certain constraints in the interests of avoiding prejudice and arbitrary decisions, and the common law supports this by requiring that disciplinary processes should meet the general requirements of the law in respect of natural justice (essentially, the right of the accused person to hear the accusations and to receive a hearing on the matter).

In the general area of 'discipline' the effect of recent legislation has been to place curbs upon the employer's hitherto largely unrestricted freedom to decide these questions. It is these curbs which have attracted a good deal of attention, both by way of criticism and by way of policy and procedural responses.

The same is broadly true of the effects of legislation upon performance or capability, where the law has sought to reduce the likelihood of bias and arbitrariness influencing decision. Particularly in this area, but also to an extent in the conduct area, there are restrictions on the kind of penalty (eg avoidance of direct 'fines') which might be inflicted (see below pp 255–58).

In one other area, however, recent legislation has given a more direct boost to the employer's right to make and administer rules. This occurs in connection with the legislation on health and safety. The employer's common law *duty* of care is well established (cf Rideout, 1979, pp 46–8; Hepple, 1979, paras 227–81). For many years it has been supported and augmented by the provisions of the Factories Acts (from 1802) and more recently by the Shops and Offices Act. Together these enabled the employer to make rules (which might be justified on health and safety grounds) in order that he might the more effectively discharge the statutory duty.

Rules were clearly justifiable to protect the employee at work from sickness and hazard. But it has been said of the Factories (etc) Acts that they had become more successful in providing a set of rules for fixing compensation for injury etc, than in establishing rules which prevent the accidents or ill-health in the first place. The new legislation, following the recommendations of the Robens Committee (1970–72) Report, therefore sought to pin responsibility for rule making to prevent accidents more firmly and directly upon the employer (as well as others).

Preventing accidents and ill-health

The Committee expressed as a general principle that the responsibility for preventing industrial hazards and sickness be pinned squarely on those who create them. This meant that where industry was developing new products and new processes, it should assume and retain responsibility not only for the safety of those who were employed in its establishment but also for the safety of those who might advertently or inadvertently be brought into contact with them.

New legislation ought to replace the existing statutes (and regulations made under those statutes on particular hazards) by a new and more positive approach to the problem in which general duties would be imposed upon employers and specific regulations would be made within that framework. The new legislation was designed to place on the employer the onus of running his business with due regard to the health and safety of those he employed and those with whom the undertaking might establish some contact.

The thrust of this set of recommendations was accepted by government and embodied in the Health and Safety, etc at Work Act, 1974. This states the objectives to be:

first securing the health, safety and welfare of persons at work
secondly, protecting persons other than persons at work against risks to health or safety arising out of or in connection with the activities of persons at work
thirdly, controlling the keeping and use of explosives or highly inflammable or dangerous substances and preventing people from acquiring, possessing or illegally using such substances
fourthly, controlling the emission of noxious or offensive substances from any area.

The realization of these objectives imposes a duty, not only upon employers, but upon owners and controllers of premises. The employer is now more clearly under a duty to take such steps as are reasonable and practicable to prevent hazard to life and well-being. In the past, many employers have gone beyond the strict requirements of the law in developing their health and safety policies and practices. With the new Act what had previously been good practice, developed in response to moral imperatives on the part of the employer, became the basis for statutory duty.

Prosecution may be begun even if no accident has occurred, and actions may be begun against the employer, occupier, owner etc on the one part, against the employee who acts so as to risk or cause injury to himself or others, and against 'anyone' who interferes with or misuses 'anything provided in the interests of health, safety and welfare'. The Act also recognizes that there might be both criminal and civil liability. As Mitchell summarizes the situation (1975): 'anyone who after 1 April, 1975 does not take such steps as are reasonably practicable to ensure the health, safety and welfare at work of each employee may be sentenced to an unlimited fine and/or two years imprisonment' and, as he points out, the word welfare which occurs here is nowhere defined in the Act.

The statutory duty upon the employer is clear. He must provide any safety equipment or appliances that may be required, together with such plant, materials and appliances that the individual might need to carry out his work. The employer must also ensure that all machinery is properly guarded and that the employee is not exposed to any unnecessary risk in carrying out his work. If the employee fails to take precautions specified by the employer, the employer may well be held liable in whole or in part if the employee is injured or suffers damage to his health as a result, if the employer is unable to show that he has used all reasonable persuasion and propaganda 'to induce the employee to use any equipment provided or to so conduct himself as to avoid exposure to hazard.'

Under the Act, the employer's civil liability for the safety of his employees is converted into a criminal responsibility, so it is important that the employer does not render himself guilty of any 'consent', 'connivance' or 'neglect' which causes a breach of the Act. It is therefore incumbent upon the employer to persuade employees to take proper care of themselves. Even if they prefer not to use guards or equipment because this might interfere with their bonus earnings, because they find the equipment uncomfortable or clumsy or simply because they are lazy, it remains necessary for the employer to take every care to ensure that they will conform to company policies and practices on health and safety.

To meet the requirements of the Health and Safety at Work Act, recent writers on the subject have sought to provide a management checklist to ensure that the employer has a defence in cases where the employee contributes to his own accident or disease. The Industrial Society Guide to the Health and Safety at Work Act (1974) provides one. In his fuller treatment, Mitchell (1974) provides a much lengthier checklist, in which he seeks to provide defences not only for alleged breaches under the Health and Safety at Work Act but also against complaints of wrongful or unfair dismissal which might arise from action by an employer to attempt to ensure that employees conform to safety policy and practice within the company.

The employer must now take certain actions in order to fulfil his duties under the new legislation and, equally importantly, consider how he might do this without falling foul of other duties, such as the duty not to dismiss unfairly.

1 He must explain the manner in which plant or equipment is intended to be worked and seek by all reasonable steps to ensure that the employee knows both how to use it and what the potential hazards are and how to reduce them
2 He must take steps to ensure that employees understand the provisions of the Act, both in respect of employers' (and occupiers' etc) duties and of employees' duties, even to the extent of providing specific training. The main duty imposed upon the *employee* is that of cooperating with the employer in the provision and maintenance of a healthy and safe working environment. Disciplinary codes have to accommodate both rules and penalties consistent with this duty
3 He must communicate to employees information on all health and safety matters and state what health and safety policies and practices apply, and the names or designations of all with special responsibilities for (as in the case of safety officers) or concerns with (as in the case of trade union representatives on safety committees) health and safety
4 He must make provision for safety representatives appointed by recognized independent trade unions and, where a request from two such safety representatives is made, he must also provide for a safety committee with whom he must consult on health and safety matters, and whose help he must solicit in ensuring that health and safety policies and regulations are implemented (although such a committee is not given a statutory duty in any of these respects)
5 He must ensure that any employee breaking any rule or departing from any policy or practice is informed of this and requested to desist; in the case of repeated breaches or departures, the employer will be able to treat the matter as a disciplinary issue, although how it should then be handled will depend upon the disciplinary procedures in operation (*see* above pp 223–25)
6 He must provide for the full recording of both policies and programmes on safety, *and* of activities such as training consultation etc undertaken to ensure that the statutory duty is discharged. Any detected breaches of rules or departures from policy and practice together with subsequent action taken concerning them, should also be recorded.

These are likely to constitute reasonable steps in following the provisions of the new legislation, but differences in technology and situation may mean that either more or fewer than those mentioned may be necessary to avoid liability. In the present context, however, it is the general effect of these legal provisions upon the development and administration of rules which is important. By detailing the duty, the law fosters the employer's right (even if it also allows it to be discharged in negotiation) to make and implement the rules.

Requirements as to rules governing conduct

The right of the employer (or his agents) to make and administer the rules which will govern conduct at work is a long-standing and fundamental one. It provides, as we have seen, the basis for control by the employer, effected through a disciplinary process by which penalties may be visited upon employees for breach of these rules. Although recent legislation has affected the disciplinary process in a number of ways, it has, significantly, not removed this fundamental right; it remains the assumption that in order to trade successfully the employer must control and therefore must make the rules.

The employer has considerable latitude in the establishment of rules which are related to the requirements of the undertaking. Rules which are related to safety, production flow, or smooth relationships will generally satisfy the criteria. Rules about no smoking imposed in consequence of insurance stipulations or in order to secure lower premiums, by virtue of their relevance to commercial considerations, would tend to be acceptable in themselves. Rules concerning drunkenness or fighting might be held justified on grounds either of safety or smooth relationships.

Rules which appear to relate to 'the person', such as rules about dress or length of hair, may also be justified. But in *Greenslade v Hoveringham Gravels Ltd* (1975) IRLR 414, the tribunal stated that if the employer made demands as to the employee's manner of dress or appearance, it would still be unfair to dismiss the employee 'without making it clear beyond any doubt to him that he was in danger of dismissal if he failed to comply with the instructions given him as to the dress and appearance, whether they (the instructions) were reasonable or unreasonable'.

Similarly, the Glasgow Tribunal in *Talbot v Hugh M Fulton Ltd* (1975) IRLR 53 stated that an order to get a haircut could only be justified (and therefore constitute proper grounds for dismissal in the event of failure to comply) if the long hair was in fact a safety hazard and the length of hair which was acceptable was precisely specified; in that case they considered neither criterion to have been satisfied and held that Talbot had been unfairly dismissed.

What these interpretations limit are the rules themselves (by requiring that they be both reasonable and related to the requirements of the business) *and* the penalties which may be lawfully inflicted upon individuals for their breach (by requiring that the penalties should be appropriate in type and degree to the offence committed *and* that they should be made known to the offender in advance of their being imposed upon him). There are, in addition, some long-standing restrictions upon the employer's right to inflict financial penalties (see below pp 257–58).

This degree of curb upon the arbitrary exercise of private power in the interests of achieving some degree of natural justice in the operation of the employer's control function has, more recently, been generalized by later legislation, relating particularly to unfair dismissal (*see* above pp 106–25).

The changes that have now been effected are designed to ensure that:

(a) the rules are ones which are necessary to the conduct of the business, including those rules necessary to ensure healthy and safe working

(b) they are clearly stated and related to the penalties which might be incurred for breach of them

(c) they are made available in some form to those who will be subject to them

(d) they will be administered fairly and in accordance with the principles of natural justice.

These principles are, in themselves, such as any progressive employer who considered himself humane would seek to follow in the development of policy and practice in the area of employee relations. They were in fact often represented at the time of their introduction as being no more than a codification of best practice. But for those who had not already developed such policies, the new requirements did and do serve to compel a more careful approach to control and disciplinary practice.

The search for guiding principles
Confronted with such changes in the law, employers have sought to discover what principles guide the tribunals and the courts in determining whether the employer had acted fairly, or at best, what principles might be adopted as the basis for a positive employee relations policy which would incidentally secure the first objective.

Allowing always that anything new will take some time to become 'settled', there do exist some 'principles' of this kind which

248

help. They are to be found in the Codes of Practice (produced by the Advisory Conciliation and Arbitration Service (ACAS) under legislation) and in some of the decisions of the tribunals and (more particularly) the appeal tribunal and the courts. These do not provide simple answers to the simple questions, but they do guide. The employer seeking to establish positive or pro-active policies need not operate in a vacuum nor curse the inherent uncertainty of the external judicial environment.

The suggestions of the Code of Practice
The basic requirement of the EP(C)Act is supplemented and amplified in the Code of Practice, No 1, Disciplinary Practice and Procedures in Employment, issued pursuant to S 6 (1) and (8) of the Employment Protection Act 1975, and effective from 20 June 1977, by order. This offers guidance on 'rules' in the following terms

(a) ... When drawing up rules the aim should be to specify clearly and concisely those necessary for the efficient and safe performance of work and for the maintenance of satisfactory relations within the workforce and between the employees and management. Rules should not be so general as to be meaningless.
(b) Employees should be made aware of the likely consquences of breaking the rules and in particular they should be given a clear indication of the type of conduct which may warrant summary dismissal.
(c) Rules should be readily available and management should make every effort to ensure that employees know and understand them. This may be best achieved by giving every employee a copy of the rules and by explaining them orally. In the case of new employees this should form part of an induction programme (Code of Practice, No 1, 1977, paras 6-8).

It also offers guidance on the disciplinary procedures to be established. These, says the Code, should:

(a) be in writing
(b) specify the persons to whom they apply
(c) provide for matters to be dealt with quickly
(d) indicate the disciplinary actions which may be taken
(e) specify the levels of management which have the authority to take the various forms of disciplinary action
(f) provide for individuals to be informed of complaints against them and to be given an opportunity to state their case before decisions are reached

(g) give individuals a right to be accompanied by a trade union representative or by a fellow employee of their choice

(h) ensure that, except in cases of gross misconduct, no employee is dismissed for a first breach of the disciplinary code

    (i) for minor offences, a formal oral warning might be given (and noted, for future reference)

    (ii) for more serious offences, and for repetitions of minor offences, a formal written warning setting out the nature of the offence and the likely consequences of further offences of the same kind

    (iii) repetition of the misconduct might call for a final written warning which will state that a further breach will result in the appropriate penalty (eg suspension or dismissal or whatever) being applied.

At each stage, the individual must be informed of the 'stage' in procedure which is being involved or invoked; must be given a chance to state his case; and be informed of his rights, including that of being accompanied; any penalty imposed should be explained to the individual.

(i) provide for a right of appeal to be exercised by the individual and specify the procedure to be followed. It is common for the procedure to have the following form:

    (i) the complaint is first raised with the immediate supervisor, by the individual either alone or in company with his union representative or other employee of his choice

    (ii) if the matter is not satisfactorily resolved, the complaint may next be taken to the departmental manager, the individual usually being accompanied at this stage

    (iii) if the matter is not then settled, the procedure might provide for a final decision by, say, the General Manager and the full-time Officer of the appropriate union, with transfer to the grievance procedure if no resolution is possible at this stage.

Time limits may be placed on each and every stage in order that disciplinary complaints do not fester by reason of delays. Sometimes provision is made for independent arbitration of the matter by an outsider.

(j) the ACAS Code provides that disciplinary rules and procedures should be kept under review by management; it is not excluded that such review might involve the trade union representatives, as for example, in an annual negotiation of local

250

terms and conditions of employment, where such review might figure as one agenda item.

The operation of the common law
The requirements as laid down in legislation, even if supplemented by Codes, do not exhaust the requirements of the law. What the industrial tribunals, and more importantly, what the Employment Appeal Tribunal and the Higher (Appeal) Courts have upheld, constitutes part of the 'law' with which the employer is likely to try to comply. As the Code of Practice itself argues in justification of Disciplinary Practices and Procedures in Employment,

> the importance of disciplinary rules and procedures has also been recognized by the law relating to dismissals, since the grounds for dismissal, and the way in which the dismissal has been handled, can be challenged before an industrial tribunal. Where either of these is found by a tribunal to have been unfair, the employer may be ordered to reinstate or re-engage the employees concerned and may be liable to pay compensation to them (Code of Practice No 1, 1977, para 4).

But the Code of Practice is not, itself, law and there are circumstances in which what the law might require is opposed to the stipulations of the Code. In *Potter v W J Rich and Sons* (1975) IRLR 338, the IT, dealing with a case in which an employee, Potter, had been dismissed for allegedly driving a lorry 'at a fast speed' and 'badly', resulting in it being written off, found the dismissal to be fair because:

> in our judgement an employer who says that he cannot take this risk (that an employee will again act in such a way was to put members of the public in danger) is acting reasonably. The recommendations of this Code of Practice are not a rule of law, they are recommendations which responsible employers should consider in their dealings with their employees. But circumstances may arise where an employer can reasonably not implement them; and we consider that such is the case where an employer has a driver who has caused an accident in circumstances such as this, and decides it is not safe to risk continuing to employ the driver. . . .

Demands upon procedures
The Courts have established quite clearly that conformity with the advice specified in the Code is not a guarantee that the end result of

251

so doing will automatically be fair and that non-conformity must have the opposite effect. What is important is that the objective or the intention of the Code shall have been realized, even if the means of its achievement are different. This is to be found in the words of Sir Samuel Cooke, in *Neefjes v Crystal Products Co Ltd* (1972) IRLR, 118:

> ... we do not think that a failure to observe the detailed provisions of the Code of Practice is fatal to the employer in a claim for unfair dismissal, provided that the procedure which has in fact been followed is fair and equitable in the circumstances, and is one which enables the substantial merits of the case to be considered. That is the overall objective of the Code: and provided that that objective has been attained, we do not think that it matters that it has been attained without adherence to the detailed provisions of the Code.

This dictum has since been followed by the EAT in the case of *Littlewoods Organization Ltd v Engenti* (1976) ICR 516, where it overturned a tribunal decision for the reason that the latter had sought to apply the letter of the law in respect of 'warnings' and indications of possible sanctions for non-improvement of performance, whilst ignoring the effect of what was in fact done by issuing the employee with a 'plain indication that his work [was] not up to standard and a plain indication that it ought to be improved', two months before dismissing him. A similar consideration arises in *Cook v. Thomas Linnell and Sons* (1977) ICR 770, where it was held that it was not invariably the case that a failure to follow proper procedure must render a dismissal unfair.

On the other hand, in *Whitaker v. Milk Marketing Board* (1973) IRLR, 100, the IT made it clear that merely to go through the procedure as laid down in the Code without achieving an equitable result was in itself no guarantee that a tribunal must find the dismissal to have been fair. The Chairman stated that 'whilst the board might have appeared to have gone through an elaborate procedure very largely conforming to the requirements of the Code of Practice ... nevertheless, justice does not appear to have been done as a result of following that practice. It seemed something of a hollow shell.'

The conclusions of the tribunals and courts are often held by managers to place them in an impossible position, because they see no way by which they can predict in advance that their actions and practices will conform to the standards of conduct which the courts will set for them. But the alternative view is that, whilst there must always be some risk in these matters, a good deal of the uncertainty can be removed by accepting the objective of achieving a just and equitable consequence from whatever form of procedure and practice may be determined upon in the particular circumstances of the organization, rather than the simpler one of merely conforming to the letter of the law as this is revealed in legislation, regulation and code of conduct.

Specification of consequences of breach of rule
The Code of Practice recommendation in respect of specifying to employees the consequences of their breaking a rule is, in a particular sense, ambiguous. It is suggested that employees 'should be given a clear indication of the type of conduct which may warrant summary dismissal'. The clear intention of this recommendation is to inform employers that it is at least desirable that statements of rules should include indications of associated penalties. It is also likely that the most crucial aspect of this general advice is an indication of the circumstances in which summary dismissal might occur. But an employer who read the word 'may' in the Code's advice to mean that *he* could equally use this word in his statements, might well be in difficulty.

This may be illustrated from the two cases of *Dalton v Burton's Gold Medal Biscuit Co Ltd* (1974) IRLR, 45 (NIRC) and *Meridan Ltd v Gomersall* (1977) ICR, 597 (EAT).

In Dalton's case, it was reported that there was a prominent notice above the time clock, and a statement in the Employee's Handbook, to the effect that 'clocking irregularities would result in instant dismissal'. Dalton who clocked in for another employee, was interviewed on the matter the following morning and was dismissed immediately thereafter. The IT held this action not to amount to unfair dismissal, on the grounds that there were clear indications that in this situation clocking for another employee amounted to gross misconduct and that it would lead to summary dismissal in the absence of mitigating circumstances. The NIRC upheld the IT's finding.

In the Meridan case, the *Works Rules* stated that misusing the time clock would be regarded as a serious breach of the rules and would render the employee 'liable to dismissal'. There were also notices on display which informed employees that 'anyone found clocking cards on behalf of other personnel will render themselves liable to instant dismissal'. Miss Gomersall clocked in for herself and three other employees after a luncheon break and all four were dismissed. The IT held this to constitute unfair dismissal and on appeal by the company, the EAT upheld this finding, drawing the distinction between the Dalton case's certainty as to the consequence of irregular conduct and the Meridan case's possibility of (liability to) summary dismissal as a consequence of similar action. Mr Justice Kilner Brown observed: 'It seems to us that when the words 'liable to instant dismissal' are used, an employee might well reasonably take the view that to be caught out once, even if suspected of doing it previously, does not necessarily lead to an instant dismissal.'

This distinction has been maintained in other cases. But the problem for the employer seeking to comply with 'the law' in his employee relations practices is that which arises from the refusal of the Courts to lay down a definition of 'gross misconduct' which might then have general validity.

In *Connely v Liverpool Corporation* (1974) 9 ITR, 51, Sir Hugh Griffiths commented that 'this court declines to accept the invitation to attempt any legal definition of gross misconduct. What is or is not gross misconduct will be a question of fact depending upon the particular circumstances of each case'.

He repeated this view in *Dalton v Burton's Gold Medal Biscuit Co Ltd* (1974) IRLR, 45: 'It is not possible to provide any legal definition of gross misconduct which will fit the circumstances of every case. It would in each case be a matter of fact to consider whether it was gross misconduct or not.'

In *Grant v Luton and Hitchin Group Hospital*, the notice above the clock stipulated that any misuse of clock cards would lead to instant dismissal, but the conduct of Grant was held at the tribunal to have resulted from 'wrong thinking rather than intent to deceive' and on the facts of the case, the tribunal concluded that a warning that repetition would lead to dismissal would have sufficed, and found the dismissal to have been unfair.

In *Lilley v J Gimson and Co Ltd* (NIRC, 21 January, 1974) a notice 'threatened instant dismissal of anyone who clocked in for another employee' and at the IT it was admitted by the three employees dismissed that if they were guilty of the conduct alleged this would justify instant dismissal, and the NIRC took this to indicate clarity as to the relationship subsisting between the offence and its consequence in denying their appeal against unfair dismissal.

This kind of consideration could be held to apply to any rule and associated penalty, and not merely to clocking offences. In *Laws Stores Ltd v Oliphant* (1978) IRLR, 251 (EAT), it was reported that there was an explicit 'till procedure' and an agreement between the company and the trade union that any breach of this procedure 'was to be regarded as gross misconduct' which would 'normally result in immediate dismissal'. The IT and the EAT (which upheld the IT's decision) held that Mrs Oliphant, who had been in breach of this procedure, was nevertheless unfairly dismissed because she had been dismissed without an opportunity to state her case and therefore 'regardless of any explanation which she might make', which was not reasonable given that the penalty of instant dismissal was said to be 'normal', not 'automatic'.

Capable performance

Many of these same kinds of consideration arise in connection with decisions relating to an individual's capability in performing work. Legislation (on unfair dismissal) and decided cases have similarly (although not to the same extent) contributed a set of guiding principles governing employer decisions and procedures in this area. In effect, it might be said that the employer's right to make rules covers his right to establish standards of performance and from this point onwards the requirements are essentially the same.

There is, however, unlikely to be an equivalent situation in relation to capability as exists in relation to conduct under the heading of 'gross misconduct', unless it be that it is discovered after engagement that the individual falsely warranted his skill and capability. In the more usual case, it is the *level* of the individual's performance, in relation to the levels stipulated by the employer, which stimulates action.

In any and every such case, dismissal should be avoided until the individual has been (a) given direct and appropriate warnings that his performance is not of the standard required, and (b) allowed adequate time to try to demonstrate that he or she can perform at the required standard. An employer's decision to dismiss is unlikely, other things being equal, to be adjudged fair unless he can show that it was taken on the basis of performance *after* due and specific warnings had been given (see *Scottish Co-operative Wholesale Society v Lloyd* (1973) ICR, p 137).

Most of the 'problem cases' in this area tend to arise in the circumstances where an individual has been transferred or promoted from one job to another. The law does nothing to suggest that an employee has any right to expect that he or she can continue in the first job for which he or she may have been hired and that no changes in the tasks or duties will occur. An employer may change these, with the agreement of the individual, and provided that the employer's proposals are reasonable (in the sense of being within the competence of the employee) a refusal by the employee to undertake them might justify dismissal (see *Oliver v Sperry Vickers* (1975) IRLR, p 358). When such a change is made, therefore, the

255

performance of the individual subsequently might give rise to grounds for dismissal, provided that appropriate monitoring of progress and performance took place before the decision to dismiss on the grounds of post-change incapability was taken (see *Hedges v Phillips and Drew* (1975) ILR p 15).

The major policy questions which arise in these situations have to do with:

(a) the length of time in which it is reasonable for the individual to demonstrate his capability, once a warning has been given
(b) the action to be taken (ie whether dismissal or not) in the event that capability does not attain the level demanded.

Most guidance on the first of these is contained in the case of *Kendrick v Concrete Pumping Ltd* (1975) IRLR, p 83. Kendrick applied for a supervisor's job after it had been advertised internally, and although the employer had doubts about his suitability, he was given the position. He did not prove satisfactory and first resigned and then sought to withdraw the resignation. The employer allowed him to do so 'on the basis that he was to be on probation for three months'. Subsequently, however, he was dismissed. The tribunal found against Kendrick on his claim of unfair dismissal, and three principles articulated are relevant:

(a) that just because the company had some doubt about the employee's suitability at the time of promotion was not a ground for suggesting that it (the company) had a duty to secure the individual's future
(b) that the initial doubt did indicate that 'a somewhat longer time should be given for testing (suitability) than might normally be the case'
(c) that the initial doubt implied a 'higher duty to seek alternative employment for an employee promoted in such "doubtful" circumstances'.

The implication is that the employer's actions do not create any kind of absolute right or duty, but they may be contributory to the establishment of a relative duty.

The other major consideration in all this, associated with the third of these principles, is the duty on the employer to consider whether demotion or transfer might not be a more appropriate and 'reasonable' solution to the problem of unsuitability, either after promotion or following transfer or change of duties. In reaching a decision, the employer might be expected to take into account the circumstances in his own (and associated) establishments and in the local labour market as well as the extent and nature of the relation-

256

ship between the employer and employee concerned. What might be regarded as reasonable in one set of circumstances might be treated as not reasonable in another.

Bad workmanship and employer's loss

There is, in addition, one area which might be regarded as lying in the borderland between performance and (disciplinary) conduct. This is the area of bad workmanship, or that of conduct which results in damage to the employer's property (such as materials and plant) and thus in an actual loss. The fundamental question here is to what extent is the individual worker to be regarded as liable to recompense the employer for such consequences of his or her actions. The short answer is, only to the extent that such recompense is provided for in the contract of employment (and in a manner which conforms to legislative requirements) and even then, the liability is hedged around.

Since 1831, statue law has attempted through the Truck Acts to curb the employer's arbitrary use of his power to penalize workmen financially for breaking his (the employer's) rules. These Acts apply to 'workmen' (so defined as to cover both employees and the self-employed engaged in manual labour) and aim to prevent the employer from making deductions from their wages and from receiving cash payments from such employees, except in the cases of deductions for defective workmanship and of fines. Such deductions and fines may, however, only be made or imposed under certain strictly defined conditions, non-compliance rendering the employer liable to a fine.

In respect of fines for misconduct (which also applies to shop assistants) the Act prohibits the employer from (i) making a contract providing for such fines, and from (ii) making any such deduction or receiving any such payment by way of fine, unless:

(i) (a) the terms of the contract are contained in a notice kept constantly affixed at such place or places open to the workmen (or shop assistants) and in such position that it may be easily seen, read and copied by any person whom it affects; or the contract is in writing, signed by the workman (or shop assistant); and (b) the contract specifies the acts or omission in respect of which the fine may be imposed, and the amount of the fine or the particulars from which that amount may be ascertained; and (c) the fine imposed under the contract is in respect of some act or omission which causes or is likely to cause damage or loss to the employer, or interruption or hindrance to his business; and (d) the amount of the fine is fair and reasonable having regard to all the circumstances of the case; and

(ii) any deduction or payment which is effected is done in pursuance of, or in accordance with such a contract, *and* the workman or shop assistant is in each and every case supplied with written particulars showing the acts or omissions in respect of which the fine is imposed and the amount of fine involved, and a register of all such fines is kept.

The provisions in respect of deductions for bad workmanship are similar to these, excepting that paragraphs (b) and (c) above are replaced by the following:

(b) (c) the deductions or payment to be made under the contract do not exceed the actual or estimated damage or loss occasioned to the employer by the act or omission of the workman, or of some person over whom he has control, or for whom he has by the contract agreed to be responsible.

What is being regulated here is not to be confused with what is regulated by the conventional payment-by-results plan. An individual who (working under such a plan) does not achieve the target levels of performance, and who as a consequence does not *make* the target level of income, is not being 'fined' for inadequate performance or bad workmanship (even if 'bad pieces' are not counted). In such circumstances, the principle applied is that which regards the employee as not having established a 'right' to receive the payment in the first place, and therefore as not having the payment or part of it withheld as a fine or financial penalty.

In the general situation, therefore, the device of the fine for either bad workmanship or for undesirable conduct, is probably not worth adopting. The restrictions on the procedures, and the limitations upon the amounts which might be recovered in this way, make it likely that it will be more costly in direct financial terms as well as in goodwill than it was worth. Where questions arise in this area, therefore, the matter is most likely to be dealt with under the general procedures which stem from the unfair dismissal concept.

Meaningful policies

Such fleshing out of the bare-bones requirements of the statutes serves, on the one hand to confirm the guidance contained in the statement of principles on p 248 above, and on the other to indicate that the most meaningful policies and practices are likely to be those which seek to deal with the problems positively or proactively rather than by seeking merely to conform to the minimum requirements of the law.

A statement of policy in the matter of control and discipline might, for example, take one of the following forms, but consistently with the decided cases quoted above, it could be expected that the first of these would more likely fall foul of the legal requirements *and* more likely achieve less in the way of desirable conduct within the undertaking.

Thus a policy statement might provide that either:

(1) All those concerned in disciplinary activity, will ensure that their conduct is such that

   (i) the organization's rules are not broken with impunity by employees, but where they are,
   (ii) the procedures laid down for handling disciplinary matters are followed, in order that the organization is not embarrassed in any subsequent appearance before a tribunal.

or

(2) All those concerned in disciplinary activity will ensure that their conduct is such that:

   (i) employees know and understand the rules, the reasons for their existence, the opportunities existing for avoiding their breach and the penalties which might attach to their breach
   (ii) employees know and appreciate what procedures exist for handling disciplinary problems in such a way that both the employer and the employee may bring the matter to a satisfactory conclusion, in order that employer-employee relations may be maintained on a satisfactory basis.

Similar considerations arise in connection with capability as occur in respect of conduct. The personnel manager confronts the question of which policy should be adopted to ensure capability and qualification to the standard required. The decision cannot be taken in isolation from associated cost considerations, but the uncosted parameters of the problem may be indicated, and may be associated with the development of general employment policies (cf above, pp 173–80). One line of development might be to rely upon the warranting of skill, etc, by the individual employee, dismissing those who cannot or do not match their warrant by performance. An alternative involves the acceptance of some continuing responsibility of the kind which was no more than hinted at in Kendrick's case.

This presents the choice as one between relying upon bought-in capability as the basis for productive performance and developing a capable and committed labour force by a more pro-active reliance upon coaching and training within the undertaking. In the one case, the principle behind the policy is one of assuring simple conformity to the 'individualistic' proposition, by which the individual is regarded as performing adequately if the reward conditions are right. In the other, the principle is one which suggests that all methods of motivating required performance are relevant and will be brought to bear in attempting to solve the problems. The one is essentially reactive and the other pro-active.

In effect, the distinctions being advanced here in connection with both conduct and performance behaviour, are those on which the Robens Committee relied in advancing their proposals with regard to health and safety. Is the object of policy merely to provide a mechanism through which the employer's own performance and conduct can be protected, or is it rather to ensure that (in *their* field) employees have a healthy and safe working environment.

In all of these three areas which have been singled out here for discussion, a first response to the new legislative requirements has been the development of a greater bureaucracy to record events and happenings, against the possibility of such records being required to protect the management's position if ever a complaint is registered. In the longer term, however, it is at least to be hoped that the response will be the development of more pro-active policies, related to real objectives, within which adequate recording of events is undertaken as a guide to better policy and practice rather than for mere protection.

However, the achievement of that position may be seen to be limited by the limitations inherent in the concepts of control with which we commenced the chapter. The new legislation has not, as we have seen, moved very far away from this fundamental position; it creates opportunities but does not prescribe courses of 'positive' action. Securing a more pro-active approach must therefore depend very largely upon an acceptance of theories of human motivation of the kind discussed in the next chapter, together with the scenario which places workers of the future in an increasingly responsive and active position with regard to work.

Further reading
Some of the general principles alluded to in this chapter are discussed more fully by Fox (1974) and Child (1973). Questions of

'policy' are considered in Cuthbert and Hawkins (1974) and Hawkins (1978). The more specifically 'legal' aspects are covered by Mitchell (1974), Hepple, (1979) and Rideout (1979) and the more jurisprudential considerations by Kahn-Freund (1977).

Students should also consult the Codes of Practice published by the Advisory Conciliation and Arbitration Service (ACAS).

11 The motivational assumptions

The personnel manager and 'people'
The personnel manager's particular concern with people places him or her in the position where he must be willing and able to help with answers to people questions which arise in connection with performance. The classical view of management, supported by the common law doctrines, emphasizes the 'control' solution as a basis for getting the production out: most people, it is assumed, must be driven in some way if they are to produce!

There are at least two broad reasons why that proposition is being questioned as a basis for managerial action:

first, it has not, apparently, provided a firm foundation for action in the recent past, when productivity has not been developing at a rate which matches the consumer expectations of the population

secondly, it has been increasingly contradicted by the findings of empirical social science research and the moral philosophizing which has been added unto them, such that the suggestion emerges that it is both an inadequate theory and a questionable ethic.

The developing ethos, supported rather more than marginally by recent legislation, is one which emphasizes a different approach to motivation.

The personnel manager, given both his own history and the situation in which he is called upon to carry out his role, finds himself increasingly involved in the translation of the moral imperatives of each 'school of thought' to the other. On the basis that the future scenario is likely to be one which emphasizes the 'motivation' approach and discounts the simple 'control' model, he is likely to be increasingly involved in the development of motivational policies, strategies and practices.

In effect, this is likely to call for the development of an approach to securing performance which rests upon two sets of theory:

first, those theories which suggest that behaviour (and therefore, performance) is the product of learning, which is itself influenced by the nature of the experiences presented to the learner

secondly, those theories which purport to explain how (ie, by reference to which factors) the individual comes to determine just what kind and amount of 'performance' he will put out.

Motivation as a decided response

Instead of regarding motivation as something to do with a fixed state in the individual person, the modern tendency is to regard it as a relationship between the individual's repertoire of learned behavioural responses and the environment which provides the opportunity for their application. The modern view starts with the assumption that man has capacity for ordering his own life (and his work behaviours).

It postulates that man will respond to situations (or stimuli) in calculating or thinking ways—provided that the reinforcement received does not lead him to regress from this. It tends to play down the perspective of man as somehow inherently lazy and unresponsive, without, consistently with its own perspectives, denying such a person existence in the appropriate circumstances of socialization. This view may have developed in response to a new morality but it is one which is likely to have more relevance to the attempts to solve the problem of 'productivity' in a technologically-complex industrial system. The emphasis in developing a theory of motivation is therefore placed upon *how* the individual will decide upon the course of action to take in the circumstances of his own needs and goals and the capacity of the situation to meet them.

It is now generally accepted that man has relatively few instincts which lead him into an unthinking behavioural response to his situation. His basic anatomical and physiological make-up may influence him in what he can or cannot do; but what at any moment in time he does is seen as a product of 'learning'. It is now a psychological commonplace that practically all human behaviour (regardless of whether it is intellectual or not) develops from this (Bass and Vaughan, 1966, p.7). It is defined as to its process as one 'occurring within the human being which enables him to adopt to the changing demands of his environment' (King, 1964, p 109) and as to its effect as a 'relatively permanent change in behaviour that occurs as a result of practice or experience' (Bass and Vaughan, 1966, p 8).

On the one hand, therefore, we think that people learn to cope with their environment by coping with it, possibly in ways which build up from simpler to more complex experiences. On the other, we think that what the individual can and does do in any set of circumstances is what he has learned to do in such situations, regardless of whether it is appropriate or not on some criterion.

Thus to the extent that what is sought of people in their work roles is some kind of performance (action or behaviour), it is possible to see actual performance as a product of learning. To talk in these terms may imply that performance is a product of training, ie a deliberately structured set of experiences from which people might learn (*see* below, pp 370–91) and that they will be able to do what is required to the extent that they have been properly trained.

This, however, is too restricted a view to take of the problem. For example, the installation of a new payment system which is intended to act as an incentive to performance, is an act which calls for some kind of reaction (ie behaviour or action) on the part of the people to whom it is addressed. There may be no 'training scheme' for the incentive plan, but people will produce some behavioural response to it—we think on the basis of how they have learned (well or badly) to cope with such plans in the past. We don't provide 'training' because we rely upon the learned responses.

Disciplinary action offers another example. Work is in itself a kind of discipline and the institutions of work organizations have in the past tended to support a particular kind of approach to the maintenance of discipline. One might say that 'everyone knows' that work involves discipline and disciplinary procedures, and that *therefore* management can continue to rely upon what they 'know' or what they have learned. If, however, attitudes change towards discipline at work perhaps because of changes in attitude fostered outside work, the response to the internal disciplinary practices in work, may prove quite unsupportive of their continuation in their old (and 'known') form.

Taking on board the problem of controlling by securing commitment to a particular 'order' (whether represented by an incentive or a disciplinary régime) seems, therefore, to demand an appreciation of how the individual comes to possess the (learned) habits that he or she has, and how he or she is seen either to persist in these or to change them in changing circumstances. As we shall see, learning theory and motivation theory have recently displayed a certain convergence.

Learning theory
Learning theory, ie the ideas we hold about how people learn, may

therefore help us to explain some of the individual differences visible in performance at work or work behaviour. Some of our ideas about how learning occurs have been developed within laboratories using animals to test hypotheses, and some of them have been constructed from survey of and reflection upon what human beings may be observed to do in their everyday lives. Learning theory has, therefore, a foot in both the human-as-animal and human as reflective-being camps just as motivation theory does.

The description of the manner in which learning in human beings occurs is relatively complex. It relies upon four central concepts: stimulus, response, drive (or motivation) and reinforcement and it effects a complex theory on the building-block principle. At the base of the edifice there are thought to be some very basic processes of learning, identified as 'conditioning' theories, which have been derived from and developed in laboratory experimentation. They may not explain much of the eventual 'complexity' of learning, but they are regarded as foundation blocks for that explanation.

Omitting the differences between the various conditioning theories and the qualifications to them for present purposes, the basic process which is thought to occur may be expressed as follows.

First, individuals are presented with various stimuli to which they are called upon to make some response. A stimulus may be anything which calls forth a response: a feeling of hunger, a sense of social deprivation, the hearing of a buzzer, the sight of a man in difficulties. A response is what the individual does in reaction to that stimulus: eat, revolt, lift a phone, and either go to help or ignore by walking on, might form responses to the instanced stimuli.

In order to cope with these stimuli, the individual needs, Gagné suggests, to learn four things: how to recognize the signals, to understand them (in the sense of both attaching meaning to them *and* relating them to one another and to the rest of the environment) and to respond to them in ways which he finds appropriate and/or congenial. Although some responses are 'automatic' (the pupil of the eye automatically contracts if a light (stimulus) is shone into it) most require some element of learned response, and it is this last element which usually comes with practice or experience (to which formal training or instruction may contribute only a very small part of the total in the average human).

Problem solving
If we are disposed to see man as 'motivated' rather than 'driven' in the actions which he may be observed to engage in, we are also dis-

265

posed to regard his responses to stimuli or situations as considered rather than unthinkingly reactive. This predisposition helps to account for a reluctance to see human behaviour and human learning as adequately explained by the conditioning theories. Man, we feel, in much of his behaviour is acting in ways which he has thought out for himself as being appropriate for him in the circumstances, not in the ways which were induced in Pavlov's dogs and which are to be explained in those terms (see pp 525–29).

'Considered' responses are commonly associated with the concept of problem solving: the individual is seen to treat stimuli as problems to be solved, not as causes to be reacted to. Problem solving is then somehow at the apex of behaviours; Gagné, for example, makes it his eighth and last type of learning and sees it as requiring that all the other types have first been learned. It is normally not regarded as a different *kind* of behaviour or learning from those others which may be imputed, as by Gagné. In Duncan's words:

> . . . problem solving in human adults is a name for a diverse class of performances which differs, if it differs at all, only in degree from other classes of learning and performance, the degree of difference depending upon the extent to which problem solving demands location and integration of previously learned responses (Duncan, 1959, p 425).

One crucial factor or feature about this hierarchical structure of learning which emerges in the literature, however, is the element of language. This, in the sense of symbols with conceptual meaning, may not completely distinguish the human being from other animals, but in its development it is set far above them. All that Gagné has to say about 'signals' in his first four types of learning can therefore be focused particularly upon such symbols as signals which the individual learns to recognize, assign meaning to, sequence and code. But in order to cope with complex problem solving, Gagné suggests that in addition, the individual requires the building blocks of learning discriminations, concepts and rules (which, along with 'problem solving', comprise the other four types of learning which Gagné distinguishes) (Gagné, 1962).

The learning of discriminations is the process of learning how to distinguish different stimuli and associate them with different identifying responses (such as names to be assigned to individuals, whether persons or things in a class). As he sees it, the problem faced by the learner in this context is that of reducing or avoiding 'interference' with the retention (remembering) process. The solution involves some process of committing the characteristics of the

266

different stimuli to memory in some chain which allows him/her to recall the identifying response when confronted with the stimulus, even when that stimulus has many features in common with others.

Gagné's sixth type of learning, that of concept learning, might be defined as the process which achieves the opposite effect. 'Learning a concept means learning to classify stimulus situations in terms of abstracted properties like color, shape, position, number and others' so that the individual controls his behavioural responses 'not by particular stimuli that can be identified in specific physical terms, but by abstract properties of such stimuli' (Gagné, 1970, pp 51–2). Some of these concepts may indicate visual properties, as in the examples given in this quotation. Others may depend upon definitions which are themselves verbal manipulations; in the bargaining context defined concepts such as 'opponent' or 'team-member' might provide examples in so far as they refer to the nature of the person shaped by the context and not to the person himself or herself.

Once concepts have been learned, it becomes, in Gagné's view, possible to talk about the learning of rules each of which 'in a formal sense' constitutes 'a chain of two or more concepts' with chaining meaning what he suggests for it in his learning type three. Such rules might take the form of an expressed relationship, and thus qualify as theoretical propositions, of the 'if A, then B' type.

From this level and type of learning, the individual may move on to combine rules in novel ways to enable him or her to solve the problems confronting him or her. Problems as stimuli trigger off the process of thinking out a new rule that 'combines previously learned and relevant rules' in order that the individual can achieve his goal. But, as Gagné indicates, we know little about the actual process of combining. It seems reasonable to suppose that it must occur to permit the individual to achieve his goal.

Initiation and continuation
These ideas help to explain *how* learning occurs, but they do not by themselves explain *why* certain responses are made to some stimuli (and different ones or none at all to others). This is tackled in 'motivation' theory (which we will have more to say about below). Basically, the individual will initiate a response to a recognized stimulus because in some way and for some reason, he wants to. Sometimes he may be driven to do so for physiological reasons (causes) and sometimes he may choose a considered response which reflects or carries his preferences. As we noted in chapter 1, there are different conceptions of man in this respect, as well as different levels of stimulus and response which may be recognized.

It is a part of this conception, however, that the preferences, values or 'ends' of the individual, are themselves learned. We choose (in accordance with these values) what we are used to choosing or what we have been 'taught' we should choose in the circumstances. We are in a particular sense, creatures of habit, even if we are not slaves to it, and can always break the habit if we find good motivation and reason to do so. It is this aspect of persistence and change which draws in the fourth concept necessary to the conception, that of reinforcement.

Persistence of a behaviour (or a habit) is to be explained by reference to Thorndike's 'Law of Effect' (1911) which finds a place for reinforcement of a behaviour as a factor in its continuation.

A response evoked in the presence of a stimulus and followed closely by a reinforcing state of affairs will be strengthened, and the likelihood of the same response occurring to the same stimulus in the future is increased (Bass and Vaughan, 1966, p 12).

The individual is, thus, seen to 'learn' from that part of his experience which constitutes the positive or gratifying feedback of his own behavioural responses.

It is this conception which gives the concept of reinforcement such salience in the discussion of learning. Whether the reinforcement is appreciated consciously or not, it is thought to play a significant part in maintaining the dynamic of behaviour and behavioural modification.

A reinforcer is any object or event that serves to increase or maintain the strength of a response (Lewis, 1963, p 107).

The individual's perception of the effect of his or her own behavioural response to any stimulus becomes a major factor in the development of behaviour generally, and as we will note below (*see* pp 271–74) it plays a significant part in the development of our ideas about human motivation.

It is also in the nature of the model that the individual may be frustrated in his learning by the absence of adequate reinforcers. Repetitive success in reducing the stimulus is seen as a necessary encouragement of learning and of habit formation. The problem often seen to exist in work undertakings is that reinforcement may not only be absent, but actually negative, encouraging the individual to regress from the positive problem-solving behaviours of which he is capable.

This forms a major plank in McGregor's thesis; the lazy unresponsive individual is the individual whose experiences have encouraged him to respond to the situation in that way, whilst the

responsive one has reached his state by experiences of a more positively reinforcing kind. The implication is that what is provided to
the individual, advertently or inadvertently, during the course of
his work experience is likely to feedback to the individual as learning or as behaviour (cf Miller and Form, 1951, pp 519–786; Sayles,
1958; Lupton, 1963). In some cases his capacity will be increased
and in others decreased quite regardless of what his original stimulus or motivation might have been. What is perceived as 'human
nature' may then be no more than what is created by this pattern of
experience.

Learning and motivation as relationships
The individual differences which are to be observed in workers (as
indeed in any one else) may therefore be explained in terms of their
learning experience. Their capacities at any one time or in any one
place may vary in reflection of the kind and nature of the experience they have had.

Some men sometimes react to the situation in routinized ways,
acting, that is, with little conscious calculation of the response most
appropriate to felt needs in that situation. This, for example, is
often held to be the case where workers express their demands
upon industry simply and constantly in terms of money (cf Maslow,
1970, p 78; Brown, 1953, p 186). A similar example is provided by
Batstone, Boraston and Frenkel in their discussion of the way in
which, in different circumstances of union recognition, workers
will tend to use the most productive mechanism for securing the
redress of their complaints and grievances (Batstone, Boraston and
Frenkel, 1977, pp 10–11).

Others in the same or different situations may well respond
quite differently from this, more actively (or creatively) seeking to
match their response to both need state and the perceived potential
of the environment to reduce it. (This might also explain the first
kind of reaction; all depends upon whether the situation is read
consciously or not). Sayles' and Lupton's comparisons of patterns
of behaviour in different work environments tend to confirm that
these are not to be seen as simple and direct responses to 'need' in
the individuals, nor to the provision of incentive in the work environment, but from the two elements in some juxtaposition.

These differences in pattern or emphasis reflect, however, the
extent to which theories of human learning are married with
theories of motivation in seeking to explain observable behaviour.
In effect, what this marriage suggests is that motivation is to be understood as a relationship (between the individual's needs and the
environmental incentives potentially available) rather than as a

simple reaction on the part of the individual to either.

This notion is to be found in Rothe's suggestion that motivation is not to be considered in isolation from learning theories, and in the formulations of the expectancy model of motivation (*see* below, pp 271–92). It is also to be seen in Gellerman's discussion of the 'effects of work upon work' and of the 'effects of behaviour upon behaviour' (1974). This uses the notion of goal-seeking behaviour as something emanating from the individual but channelled by the opportunities presented by the environment. 'Most people', he suggests

> are capable of a wide variety of behaviour, and their actual conduct in any given situation will depend on the way in which environment draws upon their available 'inventory' of possible responses. Further, the 'environment' has to be understood more broadly: it not only includes working conditions, compensation and supervision (the main concerns of the 'benevolent' phase of personnel management) but also the experiences generated by doing the job and the web of communications in which the job is embedded. Recognizing that behaviour is usually a response, rather than an inevitable acting out of some inner drive, managers have become increasingly concerned with the extent to which they can deliberately shape the environment in which the response is made (p 41)

and 'behavioural scientists have become increasingly fascinated with the effect of behaviour itself upon behaviour: that is with the extent to which actions are largely explicable as *re*-actions to what other people do' (p 53).

If the individual may be conceived in social and work situations to respond in this fashion to what is presented to him, he may also be conceived as making no response to that which is not presented to him or not available to him as a stimulus. This in essence is the view taken by Lewin (1951) in his attempts to explain why people behave in the ways they do, particularly at the level of consumption conduct. His researches focused on the question of why people ate the food they did eat and why, when they had a choice of food, they would choose one food rather than another.

Motivated behaviour

From this kind of theorizing there emerge three propositions which are particularly important for the understanding of the opportunity which might exist for managers to draw forth the kind of performance at work which someone somewhere might consider desirable or necessary.

first, that what the individual wants from his work will reflect what he has learned (to want and to expect) might be obtained

secondly, that what the individual puts into his work is what he has learned to put in (work habits) and to expect to be demanded of him

thirdly, that, as a special case, both will probably be assessed against the values which he has learned to be appropriate to judgement of these two quantities of effort and reward.

The question of worker motivation, therefore, is now to be appreciated as a product of both learning theory, in the form in which it has just been expounded, and drive/motivation theory of the kind touched upon in chapter 1, but in the form developed by Tolman (1932), Lewin (1938), Vroom (1964) and Porter and Lawler (1968). In this form, it brings together, not only what people want but their expectations of getting what they want and the means through which they perceive their being able to do so.

Expectancy theory

The earlier conception developed by Vroom, in which behaviour was seen to reflect the relative attractiveness of different possible outcomes from different behaviours, helped to establish motivation theory as being something to do with 'considered responses' to environmental stimuli. This was then developed, particularly by Lawler (1968) and Porter and Lawler (1968) into an 'expectancy-instrumentality-valence' theory—or expectancy theory for short—which has been described by Landy and Trumbo as providing 'a comprehensive framework for dealing with complex industrial behaviour' (Landy and Trumbo, 1976, p 309).

In this theory, 'expectancies' are defined as a special category of belief or theory about the nature and dynamics of the environment and in this sense are to be regarded as important to perception, judgement and decision taking (or choice) by the individual. 'Expectancies are simply the beliefs that individuals hold about what leads to what in the environment. . . . Expectancies specify the relationships between what a person does and what outcomes he obtains in the organizational environment. How expectancies influence the voluntary behaviour of individuals in organizations' forms the 'problem' to be explained by expectancy theory (Porter, Lawler, Hackman, 1975, p 52). The use of the adjective 'voluntary' in this statement should be noted as suggesting a deliberate rejection of 'drive' theory from consideration, although as we shall see below, the concern of that set of theories with the content of motivation is still relevant to a part of expectancy theory.

The theory seeks to bring together a large number of separate factors which might be expected to influence the individual's expenditure of effort and his level of performance or achievement, these being the two related aspects of 'behaviour' to be explained. The factors thus identified as influential are the individual *perceptions* of these two factors and the link between them, and of the rewards and satisfactions available and likely to be allocated to him (together with the constraining factors upon performance, of skills and abilities and normative conceptions of that performance). The whole is encapsulated in a set of feedback loops which inform the perceptions of the individual, and which form a set of intervening and mediating variables between satisfaction-and-reward and effort-and-achievement. It is therefore essentially a decision-making model which seeks to link subjective factors and processes to environmental factors and processes (cf Simon, 1961; 1955) (see figure 8 on page 273.)

In its simplest form, the theory states that the individual's decision to expend effort will depend upon three perceptions or beliefs about the effort-receiving situation: first, that there are available rewards for *successful achievement* resulting from the effort to be expended and that these rewards have value or attractiveness for the individual; secondly, that the achievement of success as a result of expending the effort will in fact bring forth these rewards; and thirdly, that the expenditure of effort will result in successful achievement. It also states that successful performance (achievement) will depend not only upon this decision to expend effort but also upon the traits and skills or abilities of the individual (which set a boundary to potential achievement) and upon the role perceptions of the individual (which is essentially to be defined in terms of possession of appropriate standards or norms of 'success'). The theory allows that rewards associated with performance may be either 'intrinsic' (given by the individual to himself as a consequence of 'successful' performance) or 'extrinsic' (given to the individual by someone else in the same circumstances). It admits also that whatever these rewards may be they do not stand alone in the sense that both must conform to the individual's perception of what is 'fair and equitable' in the way of reward for that performance, which is in turn likely to involve comparisons. Those rewards, when evaluated, are the source of satisfaction to the individual, and this 'satisfaction' in turn influences the value which the individual will subsequently place on any reward.

272

Figure 8
The structure of expectancies

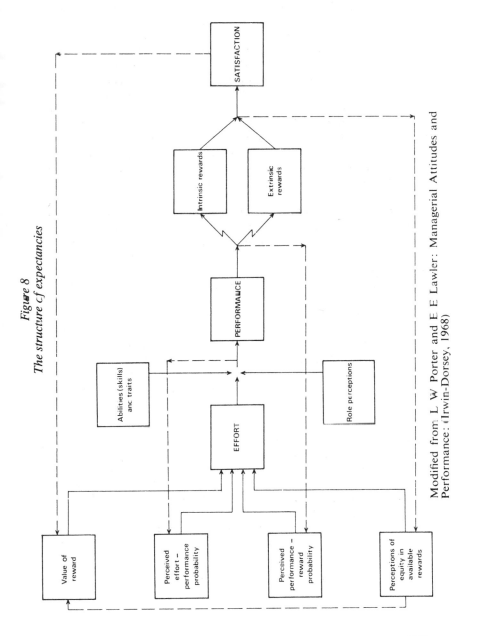

Modified from L W Porter and E E Lawler: Managerial Attitudes and Performance: (Irwin-Dorsey, 1968)

273

It appears to be worth changing the status of the factor 'perceived equitable rewards' in the Porter–Lawler model to permit this to be treated (along with the basic condition and the two types of expectancy) as a factor which will influence effort. In the original, it is seen to be derived from performance, since it is regarded as 'determined by the individual's perception concerning how well he fits the role requirements of the job, and his perceptions of how well he actually performs on the job' (Landy and Trumbo, 1976, p 308). Mediated by the factor of 'satisfaction' it is then seen to feed back on the basic condition, the perceived value of rewards, and this is clearly likely to be so. But to see its 'effect' as occurring by this route disallows the possibility that conceptions of 'equity' in rewards, or of what is 'fair', might have a direct effect on effort in some distinction from the perception of rewards as valued objects in so far as they give satisfaction. This is discussed further on pp 278–83 below.

The number of influential factors incorporated into the theory makes it impossible to argue that in the normal case, either the payment of more money will produce more performance (cf Brown, 1954, p 186) or the happy worker is a high producing worker (cf Landy and Trumbo, 1976, p 309). With so many influencing variables, a positive effect of one might easily be cancelled out by the negative effect of another. Simple statements of what in the way of rewards or satisfactions will motivate individuals to higher performance are, the theory suggests, not realistic. The value of the theory therefore does not lie in reducing the theoretical propositions to a few simple rule-of-thumb statements.

Its value lies rather in the relationships on which attention is to be focused in seeking to explain high or low achievement and/or to initiate action to improve it.

Satisfaction and reward value
What might be referred to as the 'end' and 'beginning' variables in this chain of causality are 'satisfaction' and 'value of reward'. Neither of them is explained or accounted for in the model, both being taken as facts which are related to one another in the sense that satisfaction experienced (or expected) is considered to have some influence upon the value of the reward (and therefore its valence or attractiveness) to the individual. 'Satisfaction' according to Porter, Lawler and Hackman,

> is determined by the difference between the amount of some valued outcome that a person receives and the amount of that outcome he feels he *should* receive. The larger the discrepancy

the greater the dissatisfaction. Moreover, the amount a person feels he should receive has been found to be strongly influenced by what he perceives others like himself are receiving (cf Lawler, 1971).

People seem to balance what they are putting into a work situation against what they feel they are getting out of it and then compare their own balance with that of other people. If this comparison reveals that their outcomes are inequitable in comparison with those of others, 'then dissatisfaction results' (Porter, Lawler and Hackman, 1975, pp 53–54).

This concept is then seen in the model to have some influence on the value of the reward, or the valence or attractiveness which it has for the individual. The model does not concern itself with an explanation of how outcomes come to have valence, it implies that that which satisfies (positively) will come to have a higher attractiveness for the individual. But at the same time, this can only be so if the individual wishes to obtain that 'kind' of satisfaction: a person entering a café to enjoy a cup of coffee is unlikely to want or appreciate the satisfaction which, in other circumstances, a cup of tea might be expected to yield. The question of what satisfactions the individual might want is, however, not regarded as the concern of this model and for answers to that question it is necessary to look to the 'drive' theorists (Maslow, 1954; Herzberg, 1970).

The model therefore invites us to consider these questions of satisfaction, reward value and their interrelation with reference to three questions which are not dealt with in the expectancy theory itself. First, the question of what outcomes exist as potential objects of value or valence? Secondly, that of what comparisons the individual is likely to make in order to establish that value or valence? And thirdly, the question of why (ie in the nature of the individual) different objects associate with different satisfactions?

The primary condition
The first condition stipulated for the explanation of behaviour in accordance with expectancy theory is that there are attractive rewards or benefits available to the actor for the accomplishment of the action. This focuses attention on the individual's scale of preferences in terms of reward, and upon the belief or theory as to the availability of benefits for distribution.

Expectancy theory displays a strong affinity with the notion of theory as advanced by Stinchcombe 'of how . . . activities can be organized to achieve the purpose of the organization' (Stinchcombe, 1967, p 156) where he defines theory as 'any set of ideas that allows people to make predictions about what will happen if some specified variables are changed' (*ibid*, p 157) and suggests that the theory must include four sub-categories, technical-costs, market, benefit-distribution and personnel theories. The first and third of these link with the Type I and Type II Expectancies (*see* below, pp 283 and 288), but the second and fourth appear to have some relevance to this 'first condition' established in the theory.

The first part of this 'condition' is that people must believe that there are rewards available; that, in another set of concepts, there is a 'supply' of rewards available in the environment which may (by whatever process) be brought into juxtaposition with the individual's needs or 'demands'. This therefore compares with the concept of a sub-category of 'market theory' in the Stinchcombe analysis, in which the ideas which link supply and demand variables are identified.

The second part of this condition, which is implicit rather than explicit in the notion of 'expectancy' itself is that not only must the individual *believe* that the rewards exist, but also that they will be available to him. Unless this is made to rest upon the assumption of an impersonal agency working to make these available, the effect of this is to imply, first, that availability will be the resultant of human decision or action (cf Lewin, 1953 and p 271 above), and secondly, that this human agency can be *trusted* to behave in a stable and predictable way—in accordance with the *expectation*, that is—in making the existing rewards available in appropriate circumstances (as described in the theory itself). It is this notion of 'trusting' other persons which lies at the root of Stinchcombe's third sub-theory: 'the theory that, under specified conditions and arrangements, we can trust certain people or groups of people ... is an essential component of all organizations' (Stinchcombe, 1967, p 159).

In expectancy theory, it is envisaged that any of a large number of objects might operate as rewards. Rewards then acquire attractiveness to the individual as a function of their ability to satisfy the person, and in this sense the question of whether any particular object has attractiveness as a reward will depend upon the nature of the individual and the cognitive and affective processes in which he or she subjectively engages. This therefore need not be inconsistent with the perspectives of the drive theorists. Valency and expectancy theorists do not regard it as necessary to the explanation of behaviour to impute any particular equilibrium-related theory as to how the individual deals with these processes. As in Vroom's theory, what is important is the preference which results from the calculation of relative valence.

Nevertheless, as Hackman makes clear in his development of Herzberg's views on the nature of the hygiene and motivator seekers, it is necessary to find some place in the theoretical construct for the psychologist's notion of 'individual differences' (Hackman, 1969). People are different in what they regard as attractive rewards. McClelland's identification of people with different drives related to affect, achievement, and power provides an example of one kind of directly-relevant difference which would be expected to influence attractiveness (McClelland, 1951); they are different also in how they set up the criteria of judgement of attractiveness. Riesman's distinctions between tradition-, inner-, and other-directed personality types presents an example which also carries import for the outcomes of evaluation of different rewards which might be available (Riesman, 1950). Such differences are not denied in expectancy theory, which postulates merely that whatever rewards are found attractive by the individual will prove influential in directing his effort.

What rewards are attractive to the individual may therefore be ascertained. The individual may be able to indicate what in the way of satisfaction he seeks, and therefore which rewards (which acquire valence according to their capacity to satisfy that individual) are attractive to him. For any given individual, therefore, the opportunity to earn more money may be more attractive than the opportunity to develop satisfactory relationships with fellow workers, or *vice versa*, but only the individual can say which way the balance of value (on the Vroom-type calculation) falls for him. That the individual will be able to make, and will in fact make, this kind of comparative evaluation is what is necessary to the theory as stated. How he does it is not stated, except only in the sense that satisfaction and attractiveness or value of the reward are linked. That people can and do indicate, when asked, what it is they *want* out of their work-effort is testified by many early studies of 'job satisfaction' (see Brown, 1954, pp 190–1). But why these people should want what they say they want may be a mystery to the observer applying his own values to work in the environment of, for example, an abattoir (*ibid*, pp 193–4).

We have already seen above, pp 155–58) that different workers, in different kinds of situation, may demand quite different things from work. In brief summary, we noted that some were in it for money, some for human (solidarist) relationships, some for career (or growth) opportunity. Just as their decision to join or stay within an undertaking might be taken in response to these orientations, so their decisions to perform or contribute might be influenced by them. Whether for the individual the primary condition is met in a particular situation will depend, therefore, on what orientation he or she has towards work. Similar considerations of situational influence thus apply here as in connection with decisions to join or stay.

The secondary condition
Whether, in the mind of the worker, the important relationship touching upon rewards is that between effort and reward or that between performance and reward, the evaluation of rewards as satisfiers needs to be considered not merely in relation to the 'inner' drives or feelings of the individual but also to their 'external' referents. An extrinsic material reward may, for example, be perceived to be available to satisfy a 'basic' need (in Maslow's conception) and an intrinsic reward may similarly be available to satisfy some higher order need such as 'recognition' (in Herzberg's schema); but whatever their potential for satisfaction of the individual in this 'direct' sense, they must also be evaluated against the rewards which others (taken as comparators) are perceived to receive for their efforts or performances. Thus a reward may be perceived to have a direct and individual value, and it may be conceived in the mind of the recipient to have an indirect and comparative value, which may be as significant in the chain of causality as the first perception.

This may then be thought of as concerned with the perceptions of the equity or fairness of the rewards available as distinct from the perceptions of the straightforward availability of rewards which may be expected to satisfy personal or inner needs. The recognition of this perception thus acknowledges that man's decisions about commitment of effort may not respond simply to inner drives, but may also respond to his perception of the comparative fairness which he detects in the way in which the distribution of benefits works in relation to him. It switches attention from the simple concept of a 'wage rate' to the more complex construct of a 'wage structure', or from rewards as affecting self-esteem to rewards affecting social esteem. Where the inexorable consequences of considering perceptions of reward availability lie in considerations of the 'incentive' opportunities and the manner of their perception, those of considering equity of reward allocation fall within the area of reward structure—with job evaluation rather than individual bonus practices.

The question now becomes, not which factor (effort or performance) does the worker consider to be rewarded but rather what he perceives as the foundation of equity as between his rate or reward with another. As Hyman and Brough (1975, p 1) argue,

278

although 'relations between managers and workers ... are commonly regarded as ... hard-headed and unsentimental ... the arguments of those involved in industrial relations are shot through with essentially *moral* terminology. In particular, appeals to the idea of fairness abound.' It therefore appears to call for a 'place' in motivation theory other than as a possibly discrete 'need' in a hierarchy of needs.

The psychologists have sought to deal with this aspect via 'equity theory' (Adams, 1965; Pritchard, 1969). It entails a construction of a relationship between the individual's perception of two variables, the input and the output. The individual will see himself putting so much into 'work' and getting so much out of it and these can be expressed as a ratio. Both inputs and outputs are to be defined, in the individual's terms, very broadly. A similar calculation can be made, by the individual of the perceived inputs and outputs of any 'other' whom the individual regards as significant for purposes of this kind of comparison. The two ratios may then be compared, and the result of doing so is that either there is no difference or there is a difference, which may be differently directed, as between the self and the other. The theory suggests that where there is a difference, of either kind, the individual will be placed in a state of tension and will be motivated to take action to reduce it.

When tested in an experimental situation, instructions to subjects have been used to create four 'conditions'—under-payment or over-payment on hourly rates, and under-payment or over-payment on piece rates—in each of which, the individual's attempts to reduce the tension are observed in terms of actions related to quantity and quality of performance. The findings of these studies have generally borne out the predictions that

(a) overpayment conditions will
    reduce the quantity of production on piece rate but increase the quality
    increase the quantity and the quality of production on time rates
whereas
(b) underpayment conditions will
    increase the quantity of production on piece rate but decrease the quality
    decrease the quantity and the quality of production on time rates

as the individual seeks to reduce the tension created by the instructions (cf Landy and Trumbo, 1976, pp 317–18).

This 'workshop' condition may be expected to produce such results but it would be expected, on the basis of reference group theory (Shibutani, 1962, p 168), that these directions of tension reduction would apply only where certain conditions of comparative reference obtained and where 'power' was such as to constrain other possible strategies in the withdrawal-aggression mould. The first of these is theoretically acknowledged in the expressions of equity theory, by the inclusion of the significant other, but in real life it would be expected that the 'level' at which individuals perceive such others would prove to be extremely important.

There are therefore two distinct features to this secondary condition which affect reward decisions. First, that any reward package or level must be capable of standing comparison with that of any other 'significant other' against whom the worker will compare himself. This comparison appears at different levels: the individual's satisfaction is likely to be affected by his comparisons with *his* comparators; the group's reactions to a given level of reward is likely to be based upon a comparison with another 'group' which may or may not include the individual's comparator; the bargaining agents may well introduce comparability arguments based on available data into negotiations and these may involve yet other comparators. Secondly, what constitutes appropriate comparators at any such level may well lose its direct relevance in the face of the sort of uncertainty generated by inflation or technological change; in such circumstances, the comparison may be made on the basis not of what the comparator is perceived to get in the way of reward, but rather of what the comparator is perceived as likely to secure within the period during which the individual's reward remains current. The condition of 'equitable' reward availability and distribution may thus be frustrated for either or both of these reasons.

The fact that such perceptions of fairness exist at different 'levels' of decision taking with respect to rewards is widely attested in the literature. In the workshop, the actions taken in response to variations in work in association with incentive payments (*see* above, p 279) reflect beliefs that it is unfair for individuals to receive a disproportionate share of either 'good' jobs or 'bad' jobs and that therefore in such circumstances the men are justified in 'gold-bricking', banking etc in accordance with their own norms (of both performance-reward *and* status) (cf Roethlisberger and Dickson, 1939; Lupton, 1963, ch 10). At the level of the 'bargaining unit', it is suggested by Jaques, there exist conceptions of what is 'fair' in the matter of differential rewards for those who are engaged in work whose character is understood by the respondents, this notion of fairness being characterized as having the quality of a continuing belief or value capable of being articulated and in fact used to determine what is equitable in the way of reward (Jaques, 1956, 1961, 1964).

Job evaluation methods in general rely upon similar notions, albeit at the more generalized level where they relate to cultural values: it is assumed that because such notions of 'proper' differentials exist in the culture, it is possible to discern them by these methods. Traditionally, people were thought to have assumptions on the relative worth or importance of different occupations, and that these could and would be associated with differentials in monetary reward. Caplow has provided one list of such assumptions:

(a) white collar work is superior to manual work
(b) self-employment is superior to employment by others
(c) clean occupations are superior to dirty ones
(d) the importance of business occupations depends upon the size of the business, but this is not true of agricultural occupations
(e) personal service is degrading, and it is better to be employed by an enterprise than to be employed in the same work by a person (Caplow, 1964, p 43).

To these might be added others; for example, that

(f) work which calls for higher skill, acquired by longer training, is superior to work which demands no or little training and skill
(g) work which requires the worker's intellectual competence to be certified (as by a grading examination) is superior to that which does not require such certification.

Nevertheless, whilst these assumptions tend to hold in society, the fixing of the absolute level and the differentials of rewards will remain relatively easy: there is at least some firm ground for the administrative or the bargaining decision.

Although these assumptions have some continuing validity, they are less sufficient as explanatory variables than they may have been in the past. The differentials implicit in them are now disappearing or at least blurring by overlapping to such an extent that it may be questioned whether 'white collar work still attracts more reward than manual work' etc. Changes in the pattern of differentials in the post-war period have led to suggestion that certain other assumptions, whilst they still do not have universal validity, may nevertheless serve as explanatory variables. For example, in place of or to supplement the above assumptions, it might now be possible to assert that

(a) workers with bargaining power based on solidarity will be paid more than those with less power or lower occupational solidarity
(b) workers in large manufacturing establishments will be paid more than those in small or service organizations
(c) workers who make up a significant voting category will be paid more than those who do not obviously comprise such a category.

These are variations on a single 'power' theme and could serve as explanatory variables in relation to *some* emergent differentials. They also have the implication that some of the 'ordered' arrangements which were based on the alternative historical assumptions would now have little relevance or acceptability, and therefore that new 'ordered arrangements' might have to be devised to meet the emergent expectations.

If in the longer run assumptions of the first order were to be replaced almost completely by assumptions of the second, then the foundations on which wage and salary plans would need to be based would have to be revamped completely. The resultant plans would also be very different.

This shows itself in current bargaining strategies of unions where it is associated with an ability to pay type of argument: where once this was concerned with the simple question of whether an employer could pay the traditional, comparable 'going rate' for a given class of labour, it has now become more associated with challenges to the traditional division of the product of industry as between the main factors of capital and labour. Analysis of the data on distribution in the 1960s, for example, suggests that there was a secular shift in the relative amounts distributed to capital and labour (Glynn and Sutcliffe, 1972); a variety of policy changes in the 1970s at the level of government control of the economy also suggest that, at this level too, there is support for the proposition that 'ability to pay' exists whenever profit beyond a certain minimum level is made or distributed (eg see the White Paper, *The Attack on Inflation*, 11 July 1975). These changes, in effect, derive their theoretical justification from a very different set of assumptions from those given above.

Briefly, these assumptions are changed at least to the extent that the 'superior' work identified there is now increasingly seen to bring its own inherent rewards (because, for example, it is more interesting or more responsible or more contributive to social well-

282

being, or cleaner etc) and therefore should not (as a value judgement) also attract higher pay. Therefore the economic distribution question can be resolved in totally other terms: everyone can be assured of a minimum amount of income (from whatever source) and the product necessary to maintain that minimum for the low paid or the pensioners can and should be taken from those who have previously had the biggest shares. In 1975, this emerged as the 'TUC-line' accepted by the Government as the foundation for its pay policy and only very few unions (the Electrical Power Engineers Association provides a significant exception in its paper to the Royal Commission on Income Distribution) are willing to express the contrary view that work ought to be rewarded according to its relative social value. In so far as this might then be taken as the new 'philosophy' of distribution in our society, it represents a distinctly different theory of 'benefit distribution' from the one which has served for the preceding century and a half.

The 'ability to pay' argument is therefore to be seen as one based on a particular conception of morality: it is not merely a matter of what 'can' occur but rather a question of what 'should' happen. At the simplest level, ability to pay may be determined by the answer to the question as to whether the firm has made a profit or not: if it has, then it 'can' find some money to pay more. This does not help in the determination of pay in the non-profit sector of the economy but there comparability can be adduced to maintain 'ordered progression'. At the next level of complexity, the argument becomes entwined with a social morality: even if a firm has not actually made a profit, there is still money to be found by narrowing the spread of differential payments to the staff, such that those at the top can give up some of their differential which can then be transferred to the lower paid. This is apparently where the present policies in pay determination are tending, with destabilizing consequences for conceptions of equity in relation to reward-distribution.

Type I expectancy
The first relationship about which expectancies form is that between effort and achievement, as this link is perceived by the individual. This is equivalent at the level of the individual to that part of organization theory which Stinchcombe identifies as 'technical-costs theory,' and which in his view must say, in effect, 'it is possible to achieve certain purposes by carrying out certain activities and in order to carry out the activities, we must have such and such resources' (Stinchcombe, 1967, p 157). In this view, developed in relation to organizations but applicable here too, there are com-

283

ponents on 'know-how' (technical) and cost (effort or energy expenditure), both necessary to the achievement of successful performance.

It by no means follows that increased effort must produce higher performance, and this is so even where the individual can be assumed or observed to have adequate norms of success and sufficient ability and skill. The case of the worker who works hard but ineffectively is well known. But in the context of British industry at present, a number of reasons why the *perception* of this relationship functions negatively might be hypothesized. One might be the perception of 'hard work' as a thing of the past in an age of 'automation' in which the machine could perform more highly than the human, with a much lower amount of human effort introduced into the equation. Another might be the comparative perception that, for whatever reason, no one else in a comparable position puts in the required amount of effort to secure the norm of achievement. A third might be that the effort expended at cost to the individual would be dissipated by, say, an imperfectly-operating machine or by other less competent persons which ruined the work. What all these have in common is that the individual perceiving this relationship between effort and performance is perceiving a relationship which is uncertain in its effects, because the worker is not in a position to control the consequences of his expenditure of effort.

It is a part of the theory that performance is also affected by abilities and skills on the one hand and role perceptions on the other. Given the perception of uncertainty, it is important to recognize that ability can be interpreted in two different ways, and that the distinction itself offers one potential source of reducing the uncertainty. Ability may refer to what an individual can do now, and what he can demonstrate his ability to do if he tries. An individual may have the actual ability (or the skill) to add 562 to 626, to lift a nine gallon firkin of beer or to prune his rose bushes 'properly', and may be able to demonstrate these actual abilities by satisfactorily completing appropriate tests.

Alternatively, an individual may, at this moment, have no ability to carry out any of these operations but the explanation may lie in the fact that he has never been shown or learned how to do so. Yet if he were shown he might quite well be able to master the skills or the methods and, later on, be capable of demonstrating his 'ability' to carry through the operations.

These two aspects of ability are identified, usually, by the concepts of *achievement*—what the individual can do and can demonstrate his ability to do—and *capacity*—what the individual could do with appropriate experience or training even though he cannot do so now. Both of these are finite: achievement identifies a discrete set of abilities or skills, theoretically capable of being identified and measured; capacity identifies another and additional set of abilities and skills, which also has its limits and which ought in principle to be capable of identification and measurement.

The process of converting capacity into achievement is referred to as learning, or more generally as socialization. Although the opportunities offered to individuals may differ in form and quantity for a wide variety of reasons, it is through handling such opportunities as are offered that individuals acquire their skills or 'achieve'; but it does not follow that two people will learn as much from the same form and amount of opportunity, so that individual differences in achievement will persist even if such constancy in the offers of opportunities is achieved (see Jensen, 1960). For this kind of reason, it is asserted that capacities are both limited and affected by both innate and acquired ability to learn. It is in this sense, and for this reason, that abilities are regarded as setting finite limits to successful performance.

This is also true of the third factor which is seen as influential upon performance: role perception. Role is usually defined by reference to a status, which is conceived as a set of rights and duties which when they are put into effect form the role. The rights and duties may in turn be translated into a set of expectations of what the person in that status will do or be guided to do, and the role 'perceptions' in this theory merely allude to the extent to which the individual in the status in question perceives these surrounding expectations correctly or incorrectly. These expectations are sometimes spoken of in terms of norms, ideas 'in the minds of the members of a group . . . that can be put in the form of a statement specifying what the members or other men should do, ought to do, are expected to do, under given circumstances' and which are associated with sanctions such that 'any departure . . . from the norm is followed by some punishment' (Homans, 1951, p 123). Small groups may well have mechanisms of sanctions, as Homans demonstrates, which are partly designed to ensure that unwritten norms are nevertheless known and understood, but in many situations the norms or the expectations are likely to be only imperfectly understood by those who might in their various roles be expected to live by them. In particular, the individual may not understand clearly what 'successful performance' means and, if so, no amount of effort or ability by itself will effect successful performance except accidentally. Its achievement deliberately requires a clear appreciation of what is expected of the person performing the role in question, and in particular demands a perception of what is 'expected' performance.

It should not be inferred from this that there is necessarily only one set of expectations, if only it could be stated and appreciated. There may well be a number of conflicting expectations, and failure of an individual to act in accordance with one set of expectations may reflect only that he chooses to act in accordance with another. Nor should it be supposed that what might be termed 'official' norms will always be accepted when they are perceived and understood. A comment by Leyland Cars to the National Enterprise Board on the problems facing the Company in 1977 illustrates this kind of problem in British industry: 'After a generation or more of people in manufacturing industry working gradually less hard, it is enormously difficult to reverse the trend. This is not purely a Leyland Cars problem' (see *Financial Times*, 3 November 1977, p 18). What may be postulated is that whatever may be taken to be the norm of performance will not be realized on the basis of effort allied to ability alone; it requires also appreciation of the norm itself.

Two studies of the role of manager-as-assessor in two different cultures may be used to illustrate this problem. In the first, Taft examined the conditions for successful performance appraisal by managers, and concluded that successful performance in judging others requires possession of appropriate judgement norms, ability to judge and motivation. Where a judge has a similar background to the subject, he is likely to have available for use appropriate norms for judging. Ability to judge seems to require both general intelligence and social intelligence, and possibly a factor of 'intuition'. 'But', says Taft:

> probably the most important area of all is that of motivation: if the judge is motivated to make accurate judgements about his subject and if he feels himself free to be objective, then he has a good chance of achieving his aim, provided that he has the ability and the appropriate judgemental norms. The act of judging one's self is a purposive piece of behaviour that involves not only conscious motivation but also ingrained attitudes towards social relationships, including the relationships inherent in the act of judging itself (Taft, 1962, p 48).

The three factors of expectancy theory appear in juxtaposition.

In the second study, undertaken by Rowe of the same kind of process in a number of British companies, the main discovery was that it was carried out quite haphazardly, spasmodically and therefore badly. Her explanation is similar in many ways to that advanced by Taft. There is some persuasive evidence in the study that appraisers are reluctant to appraise others, even when a set *pro forma* is given and an enjoinder imposed (ie when the norm is fairly clearly stated). The reasons for this reluctance might be put either in terms of the managers' inability or their unwillingness to judge. Rowe herself comes down in favour of unwillingness but this may make a too-easy assumption of managerial ability to judge, and a too-ready acceptance that everyone knows what is the standard in relation to which judgement is required.

Some of the reasons might be connected with the sheer mechanics of the appraisal system: for example, that the system pays so little heed to the results that managers feel it pointless to work hard at the appraisal procedures. Some might be connected with meaning and comprehension: some of Rowe's managers alluded in interviews to difficulties of understanding just what the term meant (in spite of training) and perhaps even greater problems associated with expressing oneself in appraisal in a way which would be understood correctly by a reader. Others are likely, in the light of this and other evidence on the skewness of these distributions, to be connected with standards or norms of judgement about many of the more vague concepts introduced, particularly on 'personal traits'. But behind all of these may lie a simple motivational reluctance which is often summed up in the moral imperative of our civilization: Judge not that ye be not judged!

Whatever may be the actual relationship between effort and performance, the perception of that relationship as one set in uncertainty is likely to have a dampening effect on performance. Anything which reduces the uncertainty perceived to surround this relationship might be expected to have a positive effect upon performance, other factors being assumed constant. This theoretical approach has provided one strand of justification for the movement towards job enlargement and job enrichment (or autonomous work groups) where one of the purposes to be served is to increase the amount of *control* which individuals (or the group) have over the relationship between effort and performance. It also, albeit more intuitively, forms a part of the support for the shop steward's demand for more consultation ('letting people know where they stand' and 'improving the quality of the machine performance') at the immediate shop level. This might also be postulated as the kind of reasoning which has produced two broad patterns of constraint on management decision in recent years, those of training (intended to reduce uncertainty by improving skills or competence) under the Industrial Training Act, and of consultation/participation (intended to increase appreciation of role requirements and standards of performance) under the Trade

Union and Labour Relations Acts and the Employment Protection Acts.

Type II expectancy

The second expectancy in the theoretical model focuses upon the relationship between performance and rewards. If performance is seen to be the resultant of 'the combined effects of effort expenditure, role perceptions, and ability and trait patterns' (Landy and Trumbo, 1976, p 307) rewards may be expected (or believed) to be the resultant of performance and *to that extent* draw forth the effort which gave rise to the performance. The expectancy necessary to the explanation, therefore, is that the successful achievement resulting from expenditure of effort will be inextricably associated with a benefit or advantage which will accrue to the individual. This is the equivalent of Stinchcombe's benefit-distribution theory, which might be paraphrased for present purposes from his original to state the idea that the rule governing distribution of benefits accruing from performance will operate in a way which is both predictable and beneficial to the one who has contributed the required effort (Stinchcombe, 1967, p 159).

The concept of 'reward' in this context has to be given its widest meaning—anything which the individual might draw from the successful performance to yield satisfaction is to be construed as a reward. In the latest formulation of the Porter-Lawler model, a broad distinction is made between intrinsic and extrinsic rewards.

Extrinsic rewards are rewards administered by an external agent such as the individual's immediate supervisor. This line is wavy due to the sporadic nature of the relationship between successful performance and extrinsic rewards. External rewards are not always provided when a task is successfully completed; the supervisor may not be aware of the successess or may not have the time or inclination to administer the appropriate reward. Intrinsic rewards are rewards which satisfy higher order needs (in the Maslow sense) and are administered by the individual to herself rather than by some external agent. The wavy-line connection in figure 8 (*see* p 273 above) implies that a direct relationship exists between performance and intrinsic rewards only when the job design is such that the worker believes that he felt challenged in the completion of job-related activities (Landy and Trumbo, 1976, pp 307–308).

As we have already seen, work organizations may be perceived to be differentiated by their capacities to provide these rewards. Manufacturing industry which generates wealth may have wealth available to it to distribute but it may not have as many intrinsic rewards available to it to allocate because, it is usually asserted, of the degree of division of labour practised there. Organizations not producing wealth may have few material rewards to distribute but may make up for this dearth by providing greater security or prestige, or even opportunity for the acquisition of intrinsic rewards. But this by itself does not necessarily imply that the individual will not develop expectations of satisfying any category of need in either situation nor, to the extent that the deficiencies in each are stable, that the individual will necessarily experience dissatisfaction because of them, if he embarked upon his employment in the full knowledge of what he might expect (cf Dubin, 1956; Goldthorpe, 1968). The importance of the 'gap' between expectation and experience as a source of dissatisfaction or of motivation to withdraw from situations has frequently been remarked (cf Revans, 1954; Brown, 1954; Cyert and March, 1963; March and Simon, 1958).

From these same studies we might also expect that the class or occupational status positions of the workers in question will affect the expectancy that they hold on the relationship which ought to exist between performance and reward. The traditional manner of looking at this question in relation to manual workers has been one which sees the expected relationship to be between effort and reward (enshrined, for example, in the notion of a wage-effort bargain) not mediated by 'performance' as an intervening concept carrying its own expectancies (see Baldamus, 1961). The introduction of this 'extra' variable, logical though this may be, may still reflect a 'middle class bias' in the conception of the model. This is hinted at by Landy and Trumbo, for example, in their summary of the Schuster, Clark and Rogers (1971) test of that portion of the Lawler-Porter model which concerns the perception of the relationship of pay to performance, which meant gathering data from 575 professional employees in an industrial setting. 'Their findings were generally supportive of the Porter-Lawler model, although ... they found that the professionals perceived *performance* as a more important determinant of pay than effort' (Landy and Trumbo, 1976, pp 308–309). Whether manual workers regard performance as an important determinant of pay is likely to depend upon how they respond, perceptually, to the development of 'automation' in industry.

In recent years, it is just this intervening factor of technological change which has diverted some of the thinking amongst managements and management theorists as to the assumptions that might be made about the worker's expectancies of the relationship between effort and reward. Part of Baldamus's argument is that effort and wages become almost inextricably fused together in the minds of both workers and managers: 'All judgements on effort values are a combination of effort and wage expectations: the evaluation of the right effort is inseparably fused into judgements on appropriate earnings' (Baldamus, 1961, p 99). The effect of this is, *inter alia*, that 'effort standards become more precise than they otherwise could be' (*ibid*). In addition, both management and workers are more certain in recognizing the wrong relation of effort to wages than the correct one: 'the various processes of adjustment (job-bargaining, job rotation, fiddling, rate-cutting, retiming, quota restriction, gold-bricking etc) are focused on effort values that are (from the worker's point of view) too high or too low. In other words, there is a margin within which job values may move up or down without provoking definite judgements and corrective adjustments' (Baldamus, 1961, p 99).

Because these two concepts are treated as one, at least in the sense of being assumed to move together, and because there is nevertheless a variable disparity between the two values (as is evidenced at the time of introducing new technologies), it remains possible to continue in the belief that wages are paid on the basis of effort but that the different interests of the worker and the employer are reflected in the tendency for both (in the view of the other) to get the relationship right. Behrend has therefore suggested that both managers and workers share (or collude in) a belief that if a worker works harder than is implied in the norm of a standard working day rewarded at a standard datal rate, he ought to be paid more for this. Bargaining about piece rates (and all the other adjustments listed by Baldamus) are then represented as explorations of the no-man's land to establish agreement on just how much extra effort should be drawn out by a given change in rewards (whether pay increases or bonus adjustments, or even 'self-financing productivity deals').

The traditional approach to incentives in industry, which has been carried over into measured day-work directly, has therefore been to conclude a 'wage-effort bargain' in the form of a 'financial incentive scheme' 'whereby workers agree to raise their standards of effort in exchange for higher earnings' (NBPI, No 65 S, 1968, p 4). Similarly, in Baldamus's view, 'the true purpose of time study is to guess these subjective effort standards as consistently as possible and then adjust the rates of pay to accord with them' (*ibid*, p 4). By implication, there are subjective effort standards to be guessed at, and there is a relationship to pay which will be accepted as according with them. It is, however, this assumption which may, as the quotation from British Leyland (above p 286) suggest, be untenable at present. The course of its decline may be charted.

First, although in the late 1960s it was still possible to argue that the principle of more effort deserving more reward was still relevant, doubts were already being cast upon this (cf NBPI, 1968, p 5). Two factors, technological development and changing cultural values, threatened to spell its doom. Consistently with their 'contingency approach' to the selection of payment plans, Lupton and Bowey (1974, p 79) suggest that such changes in the situation help us to understand

> the apparently conflicting prescriptions of people like R M Currie (1963) who advocated incentive bonus schemes of various kinds, and Wilfred Brown (1962) who recommends that piece-work be abandoned. They had each been observing situations in which the particular system they were proposing had been successful, but were not aware that there was something peculiar about those circumstances which contributed to the success of the scheme.

Thus, with Baldamus, they suggest that the production technology may correlate with type of plan.

Secondly, there is an increasing doubt being expressed about the underlying assumption because what people want out of work may be experiencing change. The Luton studies of Goldthorpe *et al* focus our attention on the instrumental orientation of the worker in which he is seen as willing, in Etzioni's term, to calculate the worth of a given reward against the required effort. But the Maslow and Herzberg perspectives of motivation suggest that either this is a special case or a passing phase (Maslow, 1954) or a highly dysfunctional conception because what is institutionalized as the manner of rewarding people is cosmetic (hygienic) and incapable of 'motivating' them (Herzberg, 1968). Although the empirical testing of this theory by Hinton (1968) particularly has cast some fundamental doubts upon it, it has produced offers of 'psychological' income instead of, or in addition to, money for increased contribution especially in high technology (Robertson, 1969; Paul and Robertson, 1970). In general terms, therefore, this change has altered the theoretical base to incorporate the prediction that man will not work by money alone! The package has therefore become much more complex as a result (see Schein, 1970; Mumford, 1972).

Thirdly, the definition by managers of the motivational problem has changed. Instead of seeking to explain motivation in relation to the wage-effort bargain itself, the problem is seen as one of effecting overall commitment to the objectives of the enterprise.

This, different authors suggest, may be brought about either by money mechanisms (the Scanlon Plan which provides a cash inducement on a plant-wide basis, offers one example) or by 'psychological' means (the emphasis on 'participation' in decision taking in which the prime emphasis is not upon the monetary reward which such participation might secure but rather upon modifications of meaning associated with work, offers the example in this area). This view is

> expressed by McKersie, who uses the concepts of participation, achievement and rewards to describe the essentials of an ideal incentive system. He sees participation as a mediating device for translating the primary goal of the employer—achievement— and the primary goal of the employee—rewards—into mutually shared goals. Advocates of this approach usually reject the beliefs and assumptions underlying direct incentive schemes (NBPI, No 65, p 5).

The logical culmination of this set of developments as it affects *monetary* rewards is that to be found in the discussion of 'value-added' bases of pay and pay increases (see Wilson, 1977, p 101). Since value added is in no way correlated with effort, the assumption that value added will prove an acceptable foundation for reward policy, must reflect the belief that the accepting workers appreciate a distinct and separate relationship between effort and performance and between performance and pay. Although value added does depend to a varying extent upon the technology employed as well as upon the bought-in cost of the materials (cf Wilson, 1977, p 102) as it affects the worker, it depends much more upon what he can achieve or upon his performance (with whatever capital assistance is appropriate) than it does upon his effort. The concepts of impairment and inurement, tedium and traction, weariness and contentment identified by Baldamus (1961, pp 51–80) as providing meaning to the concept of effort, remains relevant even if their form and incidents might change with technological development, but by managements pursuing value added concepts at least, the concept of performance as the direct link to pay is being substituted for effort. Whether the worker agrees is more problematical.

Conclusion
It is in something like this fashion that the developing ideas on human motivation challenge both the legal and the managerial assumptions about what leads workers to give work performance.

The picture which emerges is one in which the 'deep structure' provides for the subjection of the worker to an external authority as the main mechanism for achieving production, whilst the newly emergent theories imply that such productive performance is more likely to appear if the worker is encouraged to give it on his or her own authority. In the terms used above, the one implies a stationary motivational target and the other a moving (or at least diffuse) one.

The personnel manager's problem in helping to facilitate the production function of undertakings is that of developing adequate strategies based upon relevant theories, in a context which is largely structured by rules which are based on quite distinctly different beliefs and assumptions.

Consequently, an examination of current practice in the general area of performance motivation reveals considerable diversity. There are examples of plans for improving the efficacy of 'control' and of strategies which encourage new work habits on the basis of conviction (these often appearing under the general label of 'participation schemes'). There are examples of simple direct monetary incentive schemes (based on the assumption that all workers want is money) and of complex reward or satisfaction packages (based on the assumption that workers' priorities for reward vary and need to be negotiated on a broad front). In the development of the management-worker relationship, more diverse mechanisms of communication, which find a place for negotiation, consultation, discussion, mutual learning, and joint problem solving, may be seen to be replacing simpler devices for instruction which stem from the worker's 'duty to obey'.

Against the background of assumption reviewed in this and the preceding chapter, therefore, we now turn to consider the strategies and techniques which most directly fall into the 'production' area.

Further reading
On the general theme of this chapter, students might consult Herzberg (1968); Porter, Lawler and Hackman (1975, ch 2); McGregor (1960); and Landy and Trumbo (1976).

On the specific learning-training theme, Bass and Vaughan (1968); Gagné (1970) and Young and Findlater (1972) will be found to illuminate some of the main issues.

On the other specific theme of the expectancy theory of motivation and decision, see Porter, Lawler and Hackman (1975); Hackman, Lawler and Porter (1977) and Maslow (1970).

12 Performance control strategies

The concept of strategy

In order to realize its objectives, the undertaking must devise appropriate means. In the nature of the beast, some of these will be dependent upon inanimate objects (the plant and consumables) and some upon animate ones (people).

Although the inanimate means do not always perform in the manner stated on the manifest or expected by the purchaser, it is reasonable to generalize that, by and large, a machine, once installed will perform reasonably efficiently, if slavishly, provided it is fed and looked after. It may break down from time to time, but it doesn't usually reveal any will of its own by deciding to do something quite different from what it is designed to do.

The human means are different from this. They do, as persons, have wills of their own, and are quite *capable* of doing many things which are not called for in the employment. What is called for is what is covered by the employment contract and the job description and this requirement, this 'performance', is nothing more than a selected slice of the individual's potential. Furthermore, there is nothing about the human being that enables work 'performance' to be switched on, or the rest of the capability to be switched off, as he comes into work. Some other, less mechanical, method of securing a segregated performance has to be sought.

Part of the task which management sets itself is that of finding the way of doing this. A performance control strategy is just such a mechanism; it is a plan or a policy which, when implemented, will help to secure the performance which will best or most efficiently contribute to the realization of the undertaking's objectives. The criteria of 'best' or 'maximum efficiency' may well include some which reflect the moral imperatives of our society in respect of the treatment of people at work, but they will certainly include others which relate to the realization of undertaking purposes. A performance control strategy is not necessarily inhuman but it is a conception of what it is thought ought to be done to secure 'performance' of the kind demanded.

'What ought to be done' represents a decision which is taken on the basis of an idea or theory of how one best moves from the present reality to a desired future state. In the realms of personnel, part of the definition of the reality involves a conception of what human beings are like (or are capable of), and a major component of the 'theory' is that which links the nature of man with human performance.

In this way, our conceptions of man-as-worker (discussed above in chapters 7 and 11) and our ideas of the manner in which habits of work are formed and maintained (discussed in chapter 11) influence the kinds of strategy which are devised to secure performance at work. But the assumptions which lie behind the legal concept of the employment contract (chapters 4, 5 and 10) and behind the conception of the managerial role, may, in so far as these are at variance with learning and motivational theories, act against the creation of adaptive strategies. In considering performance strategies, therefore, we cannot ignore the dominance of the latter set of assumptions, nor the persuasiveness of the emergent theories. In this and subsequent chapters, therefore, we will adopt the device of considering the issues within a framework of the classical approach, bringing in at the appropriate points the challenges which the emergent theories offer to the traditional conceptions.

Even within the classical framework, however, the first question is: To what extent is there a choice of strategy?

The general view is that the management of an undertaking faces a choice of three broad strategies associated with the classical management definition of the control function. These are the strategies of selection, supervision, and incentives (or motivation). They do not and cannot exist in complete isolation from one another. The choice is therefore one of relative emphasis, not an absolute one.

Supervision and incentives

The development of the selection strategy has already been discussed, along with the personnel manager's involvement in it. Once this strategy has been decided and acted upon, therefore, the undertaking faces a choice of emphasizing supervisory or incentive strategies, and the personnel manager is comparably involved in these to the extent of recommending and perhaps also monitoring them. His involvement here, as in the first case, stems largely from the need for greater sophistication in planning which in turn arises from the changes in expectation.

Supervision and incentives have the same end of achieving controlled performance but offer foundations for different, even alternative, strategies. If in practice, they are never actual substitutes for each other, the principles underlying them appear to lend themselves to substitution.

Both demand that the undertaking shall establish performance norms appropriate to the objectives sought, and shall set up a means by which to measure, assess, appraise or review the actual performance of the individual against them. The *setting* of work standards on the shop floor is usually the prerogative of the supervisor or line manager who may in appropriate cases of payment by results scheme or measured daywork operation be assisted by work study engineers. The *monitoring* of performance against these standards is a task similarly assigned, although with incentive schemes the closeness of the supervisor's checking role will usually be reduced, at least until such time as the scheme has been 'mastered' by the working group. This is a common arrangement in manufacturing industry, leaving little scope for the personnel manager to interfere directly, except where he is involved in either the negotiation of regulatory agreements with the trade unions or the handling of grievances which may be processed under them.

The salience of the personal or 'official' authority involved differs between the two. In the case of 'supervision', the performer's immediate supervisor has the task of assuring through his personal influence the kinds and levels of performance which are established for the job in question. The supervisor relies upon his personal or 'given' authority and his skill in exercising influence. There is a clear (if also classical) relationship of superordination and subordination, which is supported by an allocation of different amounts of 'power' to the two parties. Simon (following Barnard, 1938, p 163) expresses the underlying relationship and the associated processes in the following way:

> Authority may be defined as the power to make decisions which guide the actions of another. It is a relationship between two individuals, one 'superior', the other 'subordinate'. The superior frames and transmits decisions with the expectation that they will be accepted by the subordinate. The subordinate expects such decisions and his conduct is determined by them . . .

and

> A subordinate is said to accept authority whenever he permits his behaviour to be guided by the decisions of a superior, without independently examining the merits of that decision. When exer-

cising authority the superior does not seek to convince the subordinate, but only to obtain his acquiescence. In actual practice, of course, authority is usually liberally admixed with suggestion and persuasion (Simon, 1953, p 11)

Simon recognizes a distinction between authority and 'influence', in the passage quoted. He goes on to make it even more explicit:

The relation of authority by no means comprehends all situations where the verbalizations of one person influence the behaviour of another. The verbs 'persuade', 'suggest' etc describe several kinds of influence which do not necessarily involve any relationship of authority . . ., a person who receives a suggestion accepts it as only one of the evidential bases for making his choice—but the choice he will make depends upon conviction. Persuasion, too, centres around the reasons for or against a course of action. Persuasion and suggestion result in a change in the evidential environment of choice which may, but need not, lead to conviction. Obedience, on the other hand, is an abdication of choice (Simon, 1953, pp 126–7).

Because of changing cultural values and new expectations of authority, the supervisor can now rely less upon the 'given' authority. Instead, he or she must rely more upon his skill in suggesting or persuading, or more simply upon his skill in influencing others. Given that the exercise of influence requires (cf Cartwright, in March, 1965) a power or authority *base*, the implication of this change is that the base is now likely to be more often one of *expertise* (superior knowledge and ability) or one of *identification* (conformity to the dominant values and norms of the group whose members are to be influenced, see below, pp 355–57). Nevertheless, the element of a 'personalized' authority remains, and will form the theme of the present chapter.

We might, however, note in passing that in an incentive strategy (see next chapter), this personalized element of authority is, in principle, removed. It is replaced by calculation and bargaining. The agents of the undertaking calculate what relationship between effort-performance-and-reward can be afforded in the situation faced by the undertaking. The individual workers, or their representatives in their behalf, calculate what is worth accepting in all the circumstances. In so far as the products of the two calculations are different, a process of individual or collective bargaining is engaged in to effect the adjustments necessary to establish a 'price' which is mutually acceptable (cf Flanders, 1969, ch 1).

This way of establishing levels of performance and reward pro-

297

mises to be less 'authoritarian' and to that extent more in keeping with current expectations. Whether it also results in a more willing acceptance of the standards is more open to doubt, although we would like to think that this would be the case. The evidence on the effects of 'styles' of supervising does not, however, point all in the same direction (Kahn and Katz, 1953), and the question of whether individual contracts or collective agreements constitute an 'order' which the parties will regard it as their 'duty' to obey, remains an open one (*see* below, chs 13 and 20).

The supervisor role
At base, a supervisory strategy focuses upon the supervisor's role. This calls for both setting standards and securing behavioural (performance) conformity with them. In practice, the realization of both is complicated and problematic and has been recognized to be so for a very long time (cf Dunkerley, 1975; Wray, 1949; Thurley and Widernius, 1973). Roethlisberger's diagram (see figure 9 on page 299) graphically sets it in its 'field of forces' which foster the complexity and the uncertainty.

The foundation is recognizable in the definition of this role:

> those in the first line of management who are responsible for achieving results through a work group . . . [who form] . . . management's direct contact with employees and [are] held responsible for the performance of a group of workers (CIR Report, No 34, 1973, para 70, p 18).

Much of the problem about the role is illustrated in the argument advanced by Wray that supervisors are required to be passive because the major decisions (eg about standards and conformity-inducing strategies) are taken by senior management either unilaterally or jointly with the workers' representatives. They are left with the limited task of trying to fit all these superordinate decisions to the reality of the working group and its environment (cf Child, 1975, p 6).

This is an important development. The original (if somewhat stereotyped) role of the first line supervisor was one which involved 'discovering' what performance standards were appropriate to the circumstances of his or her working group. Necessarily, this left the supervisor with a good deal of discretion. This has now been eroded. The setting of standards of shop floor performance has become a function undertaken by management services (see above pp 195–98).

The setting of managerial and professional standards has often been centralized through some plan of performance appraisal as-

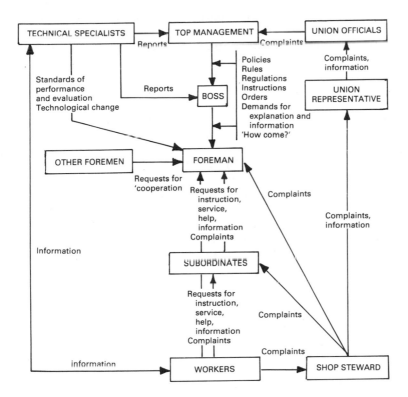

Figure 9
The forces impinging upon the foreman

This diagram shows only those forces impinging upon the foreman through the actions of other people. It is not designed to show the reaction of the foreman to these actions, either in terms of feelings or overt behavior, or to show the reactions of the workers to management's actions, which in turn become one of the chief forces acting upon the foreman. These reactions will be considered in the text.

Source: F J Roethlisberger: *Man in Organization* (Harvard University Press, 1968), p 40.

sociated often with the personnel department. In both cases, the 'results' of these decisions are handed down to the supervisor, with the enjoinder to operate to them in carrying out the role.

A good deal of evidence exists, however, to suggest that the supervisor is now often prevented from exercising the kind of judgement which the role demands, because he has no very real understanding of the criteria and the norms which have been employed by the staff specialists in arriving at their conclusions. This carries significant implications for the development of a 'supervisory strategy' and the problem created by this staff-line division may be illustrated by reference to studies which have been made of merit-rating and performance appraisal, each of which represents a specialist incursion into the formerly generalist approach adopted by the supervisor within his own patch. In both cases, the first line supervisor is asked to carry out assessments of the people in his working group on the basis of some criteria which are given to him 'in the plan', centrally-prepared. In both, he is required to exercise his judgement.

Merit rating

'Merit rating' is a term applied to the process of making judgements about the loyalty, commitment or cooperation displayed by employees generally, but usually it is the manual or routine clerical worker to whom such plans are applied. Staff appraisal may mean a similar kind of exercise but it is usually applied to more senior white collar personnel. Both tend to be treated with suspicion by both the raters and the rated. Merit rating is usually dismissed from unionized plants, if the unions are strong enough, and where it persists at all it is frequently little more than a way of assessing time-keeping and attendance as a basis for some kind of merit or bonus payment. Staff appraisal may still persist in white collar areas but there is a weight of evidence to suggest that the raters themselves are reluctant to rate or appraise in any very effective fashion, so that it too fails to hold to its original purposes and intentions. Here, however, the opportunity to link appraisal or rating norms to some apparently objective standard of performance is much less obvious.

Both the experts who design the plans, and the line managers who are expected to apply them, face the same kinds of problem in establishing the meaning of the dimensions set up for assessment and in determining what standards constitute the 'normal' on each of them. This is mainly because these plans usually invite the line managers to rate people in terms of personal qualities, instead of or in addition to, their actual work performance. The judgement

300

required is therefore of rather nebulous traits or qualities about whose definition and measurement most competent psychologists would display considerable doubt.

Nevertheless, in merit rating, it is common to find supervisors being expected to evaluate individual workers on traits as dubious as some of the following 12 drawn from one company's plan:

1	safety	7	industriousness
2	knowledge of job	8	initiative
3	versatility	9	judgement
4	accuracy	10	co-operation
5	productivity	11	personality
6	overall job performance	12	health

In one study, Bittner surveyed merit rating forms used in 18 companies. These showed that a 'total of 35 supposedly different traits were being used. The greatest number on any one form was 19, the smallest number was four, and the average was 10' (Bittner, in Dooher and Marquis, 1950, p 25).

The production of a list of words which 'sound' as if they are sophisticated may not help. Such words suggest that we have found a method of making articulate what was previously intuitive. This may, however, be far from the truth. We may merely produce a verbal sophistication which leaves the reality of judgement untouched.

So we may be doing no more than finding different words to identify what *in reality* may prove to be one thing. This is closely linked to the notion of judgemental norms, and is frequently referred to in rating as the halo effect. Evidence of the halo effect of generalized status is provided by Levine and Butler (1952) in their experiment to test the relative effectiveness of a lecture and a group decision in changing rating behaviour.

Their study involved 29 supervisors of 395 workers in a large manufacturing plant. The workers, who covered a wide range of skills, were paid an hourly rate according to the job class, in the spectrum of nine such classes determined by skill and training. Within each job grade three different hourly rates applied. The rate for a particular worker was determined by a performance rating carried out by the supervisor every six months. Rating scales were then established for five factors: accuracy, effective use of working time; output; application of job knowledge; and co-operation. The total score achieved by a worker on these five dimensions determined his rate for the following period.

The motivation for the study was that

the results of this rating system were not equal to expectations.
The foremen ... tended to overrate those working in the higher
job grades and to underrate those in the lower grades. This positive and negative halo effect resulted in the workers in the lower
grades of jobs receiving the lowest of their respective wage rates,
while the more highly skilled workers consistently received the
highest of their respective wage rates. Evidently the foremen
were not rating performance of the individual worker, but the
grade of the job as well.

Using an arbitrary division of the nine labour grades into high (top
five) and low (bottom five), the authors show the halo effect by the
mean difference in ratings of the two categories. (The table illustrates this for the three groups used in the experimental procedure.)

Group	A	B	C
Foremen	9	9	11
Supervising	120	123	152
Mean rating (low)	1.7	1.7	1.8
Mean rating (high)	2.0	2.0	2.4
Mean difference	0.35	0.33	0.63
Significance*	0.01	0.07	0.01

* The probability that a difference of this size or greater could have arisen simply
through errors of random sampling.

The halo effect might extend, not from job grade as in this case but
from the actual work contribution. In any organization there may
well be some norm, however well or ill-defined, relating to the
work contribution of the individual, but no norm relating to other
behavioural outputs or displays. It is therefore a distinct possibility
that an individual will be able to make some assessment of this, but
not of other attributes. If required by the system, he may still do so,
by allowing the norms relevant to work performance to apply to the
other factors as well.

Tiffin makes this point quite clearly.

Since there is a marked tendency to rate men at about the same
level on various traits—whatever these traits may be—a great
deal of time and effort can be saved by having the ratings made
on only one trait at the outset. Furthermore, most production
men will agree that job performance is the basic factor in determining any employee's value to the company, and that the

various other things such as cooperation, personality etc are worth considering only in so far as they contribute to the job performance. Rating on this basic characteristic is, therefore, made the foundation of this system (Tiffin, 1950, p 14).

Two observations need to be made about such studies as these. First, that the results obtained are indicators of what supervisors actually do. There is a tendency to read into the results the inference that somehow the supervisors have got the whole thing wrong. But perhaps it is the plan which has got the verbiage and the predictors wrong, and the supervisors are merely salvaging something from the central office's obfuscation of the whole issue.

Secondly that, regardless of whichever of these two inferences is drawn, a workable plan of appraisal is only likely to 'work' (on the specialists' or the supervisors' criteria of judgement) if it asks for judgements on aspects of performance or behaviour, not on personal qualities.

The supervisor of shop floor groups might be asked to assess on the dimensions of (a) accuracy of work, (b) effective use of working time, (c) output, (d) application of job knowledge and (e) cooperation. It is then usually assumed that the scores on each of these five scales can be totalled and that the total will give some correlative indication of the worker's total 'contribution' and can therefore be used to determine the pay he will receive in the next period. But in fact the halo effect may make such multiple ratings and their aggregations spurious and the common sense approach of the supervisor more intuitively correct.

If work contribution can serve as the main object of appraisal, it may, on the one hand, provide the real foundation for an overall judgement and, on the other, make it unnecessary to appraise on other factors. The use of a single factor in judgement would have the effect of eliminating double counting, but an organization may still require that both specific factor and overall judgements be undertaken simultaneously in order to make the latter more valid. The multiplication of factors may give the undertakings a spurious accuracy and may prove less accurate than rating on a single or overall factor, provided that the single factor was identified with the main purpose of activity for which norms are likely both to exist and be understood.

Such conclusions, can, however, be 'sold' to supervisors as indications of what they already do, not as something dreamed up in the central office. They offer guidance as to the kind of 'plan' which might be adopted (one which simply asks for judgement of performance) and as to the kind of 'training' which might be offered to supervisors (that which gives them a greater understanding of what it is that they already do). In this framework, the strategy would help to avoid the overselling of over-jargonized (and often wrong) schemes, themselves often seen as 'foreign' to the reality of the role.

Staff appraisal purposes

In the case of appraisal of staff performance, there is more tendency to be explicit about the assumption that managers must control in order to secure the necessary commitment to, or acceptance of, the performance standards 'required by the organization'.

Ghiselli, for example, identifies five distinct purposes which are served by assessments. These demonstrate how the 'organizational interest' is maintained as paramount in them:

1 Informing the person who is being assessed as to how he is doing, at least in the eyes of senior management
2 Stimulating the person to better performance if this is seen to be warranted by the current level of performance
3 Indicating which skills need improvement if the performance is to be improved
4 Cataloguing the capabilities of the manpower on an organizational basis—a memory bank of information on capacity
5 Indicating the strengths and weaknesses of the organization's initial selection procedures.

In this case, the immediate purposes of the appraisal process (to identify and rectify deficiencies in performance) are supplemented by the equally important total organizational purposes of building up an inventory of usable control information and using it to check on the effectiveness of other administrative procedures.

In individual company plans, it is not unusual to find that the stated objectives of the assessment plan include:

1 Improvement of the current performance of the manager on the job through the recognition of current strengths and weaknesses in performance, and the elimination or reduction of the latter through counselling or training, inside or outside the company
2 Guidance of the individual manager or professional person on what his strengths and weaknesses are, what he might do to capitalize on the one and reduce the other and where his future career path might appropriately lie
3 Identification of more junior personnel with capacity and capability to move into more senior positions, usually with some development within the enterprise, so that the organization has

some appreciation at any given time, of not only what stock of trained manpower it has available for its current needs but also of what potential stock it has to meet future requirements

4 Improvement of communications within the organization, particularly communications between the man and his manager (the son to father relationship) and frequently too between the man, his manager and his manager's manager (extending the relationship to embrace the grandfather). This applies particularly with schemes like MbO (see also below pp 503–506).

Three different things are being attempted in such plans. There is, first, the attempt to improve current performance (with the help of the man concerned); secondly, the aim to improve some aspects of organizational functioning, such as communications in the chain of command or manpower planning; and thirdly, the objective of producing data specifically for management succession planning. The first of these is a goal related to the short term, the second is one tied to the medium term, and the third is necessarily much longer term.

From a different standpoint, the objectives could be said to relate to the needs of the organization and also to the needs (or desires) of the individual. The distinction being between performance improvement and organizational planning on the one hand and career development for the individual on the other.

A plan of staff appraisal which seeks to have the line supervisor meet all these objectives within the confines of one appraisal plan is likely to confuse and inhibit him. Thus, in addition to the kind of obfuscation which long words have been shown to produce in merit rating plans (and which often applies here too) there is a different problem for the supervisor or manager to resolve.

As before, research suggests that supervisors (often, at this level, they have titles of manager) produce their own response to even the most sophisticated plans: namely that they don't apply them as the designer intended. A number of people (cf McGregor, 1972; Levinson, 1976; Teel, 1980) have questioned the concept of staff appraisal as a useful tool in its present form. Many others remain ready with answers on how to improve it.

The findings of the study by Rowe tend, however, to lead to similar conclusions as the work on merit rating already discussed. In her examination of 1,440 completed appraisal forms in six companies, carried out in 1964, she discovered that:

(a) appraisers did not always complete appraisal forms which they were required, as part of their job duties, to do

(b) they did not always complete every section of the form when required to do so
(c) they did not always acknowledge their authorship
(d) the content of the entries was often evasive.

Rowe concludes that this reveals a very low motivation on the part of managers to appraise, to discuss appraisals with subordinates and to initiate any follow-up action on the appraisals. So strong is this tripartite conclusion that it must mean that something is disabling about the appraisal plans themselves.

The problem of 'other people's standards'

What this and other researches suggest is that the appraiser feels himself or herself put on the spot in carrying out plans of this type. He is required, whatever his own perception of the subordinate's expectations, to confront the individual in an authoritarian setting and to prescribe courses of action for that subordinate on the basis of judgements which he may or may not understand or accept.

Investigations have shown that the appraisal interview, usually seen as a form of counselling, has generally been undertaken with reluctance by the appraisers. Thus Rowe found that

in three of the six schemes an interview was an integral part of the procedure, although one of them provided space on the form for giving reasons for not holding an interview. In another scheme interviews were considered highly desirable but were not insisted upon because of the newness of the scheme. In another, interviews were only considered desirable where written reports were required, depending on the performance grade given, but were not insisted upon and space was provided for giving reasons for not holding an interview. In the sixth scheme interviews were not an integral part of the procedure and were only required if an unsatisfactory grade was given for performance; no space was provided in the form for an interview report.

Randall *et al*, referring to Fisons, record that

many managers reported that they were uncomfortable in the interview situation and unsure of what was expected of them. This lack of skill had been confirmed by the training department, where managers attending a course on selection performance were asking for help and advice on how to conduct performance review interviews (Randall *et al*, 1974, p 64).

The authors found that managers were able to make assessments

306

and identify areas of weakness, but usually stopped at this point, partly because they felt diffident about trying to assess motivation and 'the reasons why' a particular performance was given, and had difficulty in exploring areas like intelligence or individual goals in an interview (*ibid*).

Such conclusions have to be seen against the situation in which these same reluctant appraisers, make, in the course of carrying out their 'ordinary' managerial and supervisory roles, many judgements which they do communicate to their subordinates in full confidence. They may not be the world's most brilliant judges, but they do have some ability, and they may well improve with practice as most people do.

We are therefore left with the conclusion that the reasons for so much failure (or reluctance) in this particular area may lie in the manager's lack of knowledge and understanding of the standards which he is being asked to apply, and in his lack of motivation to appraise at all or to appraise in this way on these foundations. These conclusions are also supported by the findings of research into the rating process.

Mahler has also pointed to some of the practical difficulties which affect the raters *ability* to make accurate and consistent judgements:

1 The extent of his opportunities for observing the performance of the employee to be rated
2 His consciousness of the need to rate performance during the period of observation
3 His experience and training in translating observations into judgements
4 His personal characteristics as these might affect rating ability
5 The facility with which the rating form permits him to record his judgements.

Mahler also identifies some of the practical difficulties in a rating situation which affect his *willingness* to rate:

1 His understanding of the entire rating programme
2 His acceptance of the stated purpose of the rating
3 His reflection of top management's attitude
4 His experience in applying the rating to employees under his jurisdiction and his assessment of how useful these are
   (Mahler, 1950, pp 51–2).

One general conclusion that is possible about all this, therefore, is that if supervisors are not to be left alone to do their own appraising of individual performance (and there are probably many good reasons why this is neither possible nor desirable) then the 'supervisory' strategy will need to include a major training component (to enable the managers concerned to learn the new norms, methods and reasons for their application) and will probably also need to be supplemented by other supportive strategies (such as that which we discuss in the next chapter under the heading of rewards).

Before the training strategy can be put into effect, however, it is likely that the purposes of appraisal will have to be rethought and the number of objectives which might be covered in one plan reconsidered. What is probably required here may be illustrated by the attempt by Cummings and Schwab (1973, ch 9) to order the chaos by producing a systematic conception of appraisal which allows three different programmes of appraisal to be employed for three distinct purposes, but with links between them which allow management to switch individuals from one to another as the situation permits or requires.

In the first, the *development action programme*, the emphasis is placed upon planning work and the whole focuses upon setting goals in work, self-control of performance and feedback of data to the employee himself on performance. In the second, the *maintenance action programme*, the emphasis is placed upon the definition of acceptable goals and levels of performance, and the whole focuses upon the establishment of a means of identifying and correcting departures from standard acceptable performance by the employee. In the third, the *remedial action programme*, the emphasis is upon providing an alternative to dismissal (or deselection) and the focus is upon providing communications between a superordinate and subordinate to establish why performance is below what is expected, and what might be done to bring it up to an acceptable level (and thus avoid termination).

Clearly these three programmes would be more applicable to different types of performance, sometimes occasioned by motivational differences on the part of the employee, sometimes by technological and job definitional constraints on the individual. Equally clearly, when the cause is motivational, an individual employee might move from one type of performance to another and the 'programme' might therefore have to change to be consistent.

Categorization of programmes in this fashion seeks to establish distinct objectives for the appraisal system which can be related to the kind of employee and the kind of work role involved. Failure to make such distinction in the past may well help to account for the generally unsatisfactory state of performance appraisals in any situation to which they have been applied, for there are relatively few situations in which considerable reliability and validity have been reported.

The individual performance audit

If these various arguments and research findings are put together, they suggest that perhaps the 'central office take-over' of the supervisor's discretion in respect of standard-setting and judgement of performance of their subordinates has probably proceeded too far. Certainly what we know about these processes should be brought to bear upon the task and its problems, but there is probably a need to accomplish this through general training for the tasks, not through detailed prescription of the manner of proceeding, as in a formal plan. The central office approach might well rest upon the following principles and conclusions:

1 An individual embarks upon employment in order to do a job and he expects to make some contribution to the achievement of the objectives of the organization.

2 Where he has the power to determine how his contribution will be judged (eg with strong unionization) he will (a) tend to throw out assessments based on rather vague personal qualities or on equally vague categories of general behaviour, and (b) will seek his assessment on the basis of the job/work performance itself.

3 Where an assessor is required to assess others, he too will tend to produce the same result as in 2, even if this is done less through organized power and more through a cautious approach to assessment which renders it worthless.

4 Where appraisal of performance can be related directly to output this ought to be done. Where it cannot, acceptable criteria directly related to contribution or performance should be agreed upon and used in the assessment process to the exclusion of any others in the final stage even if some prior, and more detailed analysis is carried out. This is to increase validity and reliability of the single overall assessment of contribution.

5 For a closely connected reason, appraisal schemes should have one objective; plans which seek to realize a number of different objectives should be avoided, especially those which seek to provide for succession and promotion in addition to assessment of current performance.

6 It would then tend to follow that the assessment process would be one which would directly concern only the assessor and the assessed, and the central personnel office or the countersigning officer (the grandfather) would come into process, if at all, only to monitor the fact that the appraisal had been carried out, and

not to engage in the appraisal process itself or to interfere with its outcome.

7 The role of the personnel manager in this area would then focus on the provision of adequate information and training for the three essential requirements of assessors: judgemental ability (an exercise in skill development), understanding of judgemental norms (an exercise in communication) and developed motivation to assess (an exercise in securing the enabling conditions—which might involve getting the 'system' right, as indicated in the above summary).

Such generalizations, about the plans and the response to them, must necessarily be related to the characteristics of the people and the situation to which they are to be applied. This is to suggest no more in effect than that any manager must apply diagnostic skills to situations and problems before applying general, off-the-peg solutions to them—the foundation of 'contingency' theories. In the field of managerial performance appraisal, this is not often done and a strong tendency remains towards application of a general plan as a means of pursuing greater central control.

However, to signal 'a contingency approach' as requisite in this area, is perhaps to learn only half the lesson which springs from these various pieces of research. The other half is concerned with the frequency with which the designer's intentions for plans are actively or tacitly ignored in their operation. Where the shop floor personnel are unionized, appraisal schemes are commonly thrown out in negotiations; in the (often-nonunionized) white collar area, a similar effect is achieved by a kind of collusive campaign of civil disobedience. This is the negative side of the conclusions.

On the more positive side, the adoption of such plans as Management by Objectives (MBO) in which the subordinate is placed in a position both to control the criteria of judgement and participate in the judgemental process, is often claimed (particularly in the white collar area) to work much more effectively. A more 'democratic' approach to standard setting and appraisal appears to give benefits. This is somewhat paradoxical, in that it is often 'within management' that the more democratic approach appears to be justified. However, this apparent paradox disappears if due attention is given to the benefits obtained in the era of productivity bargaining from a joint approach to shop floor standard setting and control (cf Thomason, 1971; Richbell, 1976). When these two features are placed together, they suggest that there may be some point to the theories which link participation to performance, and therefore to styles of supervision which (at whatever 'level' they are applied) devolve responsibilities for standard setting and performance to the lowest level possible.

Decision-taking and implementation

The second major element of the supervisor's 'people' role is that which concerns taking decisions about 'what ought to be done' and implementing them. The setting of standards and the measurement of performance against them is not something embarked upon for itself alone. It is done to indicate whether decisions are called for.

It does not however indicate necessarily what those decisions about action should be. These depend upon the supervisor's knowledge or 'practical theory' by which indications are obtained of what kind of change might lead to a desired result. Obviously, a good part of this knowledge and theory will relate to the technical and physical aspects of the supervisor's job; but there is a part which has to do specifically with people: what they are capable of doing and how they can be got to do it when occasion demands. It is this latter part with which we are primarily concerned here.

As the managerial representative most directly in contact with the working group (at whatever 'level' in the hierarchy it may be), the supervisor remains the person who must 'motivate' that group to produce whatever it is that they are there to produce. The 'motivation' problem is his. The question whether the personnel department can help him in this task, and if so how?

It is, of course, in the nature of the personnel manager's role that much of what is done there is supposedly contributory to this task. The whole area of employee resourcing (discussed in the preceding Part) is intended to produce the people with the skills and motivation to do the necessary work. In addition, the activities associated with training and development, remuneration-setting and administration, and the structuring of employee-relations procedures, are also intended to bring benefits to the supervisor in carrying out his role and meeting job objectives set for him. It is, however, in the nature of most of these developments that both the decisions and the monitoring are increasingly made or done at a more central level in the undertaking. There is the danger, therefore, that the supervisor, the man who must still implement action, is stripped of all effective power to influence those whom he supervises.

This occurs for many reasons on many of the dimensions of the supervisor's role. The problem may be illustrated by reference to training, and activity which was traditionally almost entirely within the purview of the immediate supervisor.

It is axiomatic that, in all undertakings, individual workers will learn from the jobs they are doing. Any individual brought into a work (social) situation which has novel features for him or her, must develop some perception of the expectations which surround the role, and in following out this imperative he or she will pick up information relevant to that role, whether anyone intends or orders it or not.

Increasingly, employers are now developing some policy and programme of training. This varies in its degree of formality according to many factors in the situation of which perhaps the most important are the size and technical complexity of the organization concerned, and the specificity of the skills required in the jobs available within it. At one extreme the training may mean no more than on-the-job instruction by a supervisor who attempts to show the individual how to carry out the particular job that he is hired to do. At the other extreme, organizations may establish elaborate policies and ramified programmes of training to cope with the whole spectrum of need for induction and technical training, training for personal development, and training for all aspects of supervision and management. Particularly when this last approach is adopted, the danger of taking discretion away from the supervisor arises, and tensions which detract from efficient operation develop.

At the one end of the spectrum of experience, a certain amount of training may be left to the supervisor to carry out on the job and, although it may therefore be necessary to give the supervisor some instruction in *how* to train, the extent to which the training process must be formalized to meet this particular requirement is perhaps quite limited. However, organizations will have to be mindful of the likelihood that individual employees will, willy-nilly, acquire their training whether it is deliberately provided or not, and that therefore the individual might learn practices and the values associated with them from his informal work group, from his formal work group (including from supervision) or from the trade union of which he might well be a member, and these practices and values may be inimicable with those required by the organization. Recognition of this possibility is likely to lead organizations to accept the view that even this kind of training ought to be formalized at least to some extent, possibly by giving supervisors deliberate and formal instruction in how to train and induct employees.

Where however the organization relies upon a large labour force of largely semi-skilled labour and where therefore it cannot rely upon recruiting fully trained people from the labour market, it might well prove advantageous to consider developing not only a

312

formal programme of training but a cadre of trainers to carry it out. In this case the trainers would be staff experts and would normally themselves have had at some stage some formal training in both how to devise training programmes and how to carry out the actual process of training in accordance with best principles derived from learning theory.

The major problem that now arises is simply a manifestation of a common tension between the staff specialists and the line management or supervision. Here the problem as seen by line management will be the problem that trainers displace the goals of training by making the training process itself an end which does not necessarily accord with the ends of production or selling or with whatever the line manager may be directly concerned. The problem as seen by the training expert is more likely to emphasize the undoing of the results of training by inefficient activities on the part of supervision and management whose attempt to pursue production objectives will very often undercut the achievements of the training department through its training programmes.

If the problem illustrated here by reference to training were to occur only in that area, it might not be serious. However, it has been seen and shown to occur in many other areas of the supervisor's task.

In respect of the work done, changes are determined upon within the corporate plan to change the product-mix or the production technology, and are 'given' to the supervisor. In addition, the developments which pass under the title of 'job enlargement' and 'job enrichment', usually spearheaded by job analysts or the management services department, tend to reduce the supervisor's discretion to vary work patterns, and may incidentally make it more difficult for him to train his workers in the new behaviours required.

In the related area of application to work, many of the changes which were introduced, on the initiative of personnel practitioners but with the agreement of shop stewards after negotiations, in the productivity bargaining era, also changed the rules of the game in such a way that the supervisor was left with less power and authority to trade work type or time off for application in order to facilitate the meeting of his job targets.

The general problem may, indeed, be illustrated by reference to the control of absenteeism, regarded as one form of withdrawal or non-application behaviour, which was traditionally under the direct control of the supervisor.

Absenteeism is seen usually as occurring at an unacceptably high rate (see eg the NEDO checklist for action by management

313

put out by the Economic Development Committee for the Food Manufacturing Industry in 1969 under the title of The Control of Absenteeism, p 5). For this reason it has attracted a good deal of attention, and as a result we think we can distinguish the likely 'causes' and some tactics for reducing it.

The CBI's pamphlet on the subject (January 1970) lists the most likely causes, for example, as higher earnings, excessive overtime working, limited commitment to work in the undertaking by youngsters and short service employees, variable incidence of spouse and family holidays, lack of personal motivation to work, and inadequate work relationships (pp 8–9). In addition, however, the 'attitudes of supervision' is listed as a causal factor, implying that this is an independent variable comparable in some way with others 'outside the control' of the undertaking and its management (p 9).

Similarly, the CBI's checklist addresses itself to 'the company', although the 'final word' does suggest that the 'questions asked may prompt managers, supervisors and employee representatives to think and act more positively about absenteeism' (p 10). One of the questions makes it clear that the checklist is not directly related to the supervisor as the main source of decision and action, however, since it asks:

> Are your supervisors aware that they are responsible for maintaining the standards of time-keeping and attendance of their staff? (p 6).

But many of the other questions relate to decisions which would certainly not be within the discretion of the supervisor. If, therefore, the control of absenteeism is to be effected by getting these decisions right, it is scarcely a matter which the supervisor could deal with adequately.

Comparably, the CBI's guidance as to possible solutions seeks to mobilize the welfare department (to visit house), the medical officer (to examine on return from sickness absence), the works council (to examine bad benefit cases) and the recruiters (to secure comment on absenteeism records in references). The supervisor figures only (if at all) in the issuing of warnings to persistent 'offenders' (p 11). At very least the co-ordination of action within a supervisory control strategy would appear to be difficult under these circumstances of diffusion of responsibilities.

In the area of discipline, also traditionally associated with the supervisory role, the more recent developments have stemmed largely from public policy and legislation. They have, however, had the effect of centralizing both the decisions and the procedures by

314

which they are to be reached, at levels above that of the immediate supervisor. This may have been influenced by trade union or shop steward pressure to eliminate the opportunities for favoured treatment of the blue-eyed boys and to increase the likelihood of equity in disciplinary decisions, but the consequence possesses many of the features of the other examples quoted.

These may be regarded as 'inevitable' developments arising from the situational complexity and the normal limits on the time and ability of any one person to deal effectively and fairly with all such issues. They may also be seen as indicative of a need for new conception of and skills in the performing of the supervisor's role, and initiatives have been taken on both of these scores, through organizational change (cf Roethlisberger, 1968) and through training (cf Thurley and Wirdenius, 1973). But at least as important, in the sense that without attention to this the other strategies are likely to fail, is the implication that the policies and strategies with which the personnel department is mainly concerned, must deliberately seek to bolster the influence of the supervisor in his working group, not detract from it.

The problem of the power base
It has recently become fashionable to characterize the supervisor's role as being one focused primarily upon task communications and motivational influence. This has, on occasion, been put forward as 'the secret' of the success of Japanese undertakings located in the United Kingdom. The emphasis is upon some kind of 'briefing session' in which the supervisor discusses what has been done by the work group, and what remains to be done, as well as how the group should tackle the doing of it.

This is, however, a surprising 'discovery' to make at this juncture, for two reasons. On the one hand, the empirical studies which have been made of what supervisors actually do at work, do rather suggest that this 'talking about work' is just what they appear to be engaged in, however well or badly they do it (on which question these studies tend to be silent).

Thurley and Hamblin, for example, conclude from their study that communication is in most cases the dominant activity engaged in by supervisors (Thurley and Hamblin, 1963). Dubin's review of a number of pieces of work carried out by others, however, concludes that foremen appear not to spend as much time in communication as do those above them in the hierarchy: 'it appears that foremen are much more likely to be doers rather than talkers' (Dublin, 1962, p 21). In addition, these same studies suggest that a lot of the communication in which they do engage is with peers

315

(other foremen, before and after them in the production sequences). Although on average, they seem to spend about half their time in communication, therefore, it might be concluded that not *enough* of that time is spent communicating with their own subordinates. But this evidence has been with us for some considerable time.

On the other hand, it is surprising because the general thrust of public and undertaking policy, aided and supported by trade union or shop stewards' policies, has been to 'by-pass' the supervisor as a matter of principle, leaving him with little more of a role than that of executing the plans and policies in the framing of which he or she had no voice. At the one level, this might be said to be the outcome of the main Donovan Commission recommendations (Donovan Report, 1968) and of the subsequent standardizing of rights by legislation (*see* above, ch 10). At the other, the development of plant or undertaking bargaining with the local union representatives has usually involved levels of management above that of the supervisors (cf Marsh, 1973; Beynon, 1973; Batstone *et al*, 1977).

These developments have been much discussed in terms of the changing *power* structure in work undertakings. But what is less frequently recognized in these general discussions is that in the course of any power redistribution which might be occurring it is the official leader of the work group who is losing most.

The problem arises because, in particular, such loss of power (even if it is only relative to others) threatens the power base, on which, so our theories suggest, all successful influence depends. 'Most theories of social influence assert that the ability of an agent to exert influence arises from the possession, or control, of valued resources' (Cartwright, in March, 1965, p 5). It does not follow that these resources must be material or economic ones, nor that they must take any one particular form; but it does follow that there must be some base, even if it is only the basis of the skill and ability of the individual agent to persuade others to act in one way rather than another.

The very removal of the supervisor's discretion to set standards and to determine the conditions for effecting conformity to them, and their allocation to staff specialists, may be the causes of the loss of adequate power base for this category of line manager.

This idea is supported by the obverse of the 'strategic contingencies' theory advanced by Hickson and others (1971). Briefly, this theory states that the power of a sub-unit (eg a section or department) and therefore of those whose roles are defined by reference to it, depends upon the opportunity which the *context* pro-

316

vides for it (or them) to reduce or otherwise cope with the uncertainties which have to be dealt with to ensure organizational survival and growth. The context, in turn, is to be seen as the organizational structure, through which both ownership of the uncertainties and opportunities to handle them, are assigned (cf Clegg, 1975, p 48). Applied to the supervisory role, this suggests that the structural context may be the factor which has reduced or removed the power base, and left the supervisor dependent upon those specialists whose roles have become more strategically powerful.

Figure 10
A section manager's role

The section manager's job is managerial in the full sense: he carries responsibilities for *engaging his operators* and supervisors, *setting standards* for them and *ensuring that standards are met*, and *rewarding* his subordinates with wages appropriate to the work they are doing. He is responsible for *training* his subordinates and ensuring that they have the skills needed to get his work done; for *planning* his production to meet his current and forward lead; and for *deploying* his men and machines in the most effective way. Line-shop activity is characterized by sudden changes in demand which must be coped with by equally rapid changes in plans to meet the new demands. The section manager is responsible for maintaining a high level of technical efficiency on his lines. He must continuously make decisions about production methods, interpreting manufacturing instructions where necessary. Although the development of production methods is normally the work of the production engineers, the manager has to see that the best possible methods are being used in production. He must meet standards of efficient operation set by his unit manager. His duties include the requisitioning of supplies and services needed to maintain his machines.

The section manager is responsible for establishing adequate relationships with his colleagues, with other section managers and with staff specialists of his unit manager. He must be able to contact and use the services of inspectors, personnel specialists, work engineers, the tool room and other staff in an effective manner. He must be able to work with representatives so that problems that arise are dealt with quickly and decisively. He has to carry out all his activities in conformity with established company and factory policy. He is responsible for establishing and maintaining on his section safe standards of work and a high standard of cleanliness and tidiness.

Source: J Kelly: *Is Scientific Management Possible?* (Faber and Faber, 1966), p 279

If, therefore, a supervisory strategy for securing performance is to be pursued (or emphasized) it may be necessary to re-examine and redefine the network of 'normative expectations and understandings' (Whitley, 1975) and the 'underlying rules' (Clegg, 1975) which together *structure* both the supervisor and the specialist-staff roles in the typical undertaking at the present time (cf Legge, 1978, pp 27–9).

This implies that the development of a strategy of supervision in the light of our understandings of human behaviour, may call not only for a simplistic kind of strategy (emphasizing, for example, the value of training supervisors to communicate or to use purely interactive skills) but for a more complex organizational-development type of response (which we discuss below, in chapter 19). The implication is that training which is based on an inadequate conception of the role is unlikely to prove effective in securing the kind of performance sought. The requirement may well be that the first-line manager's role may need to be de-specialized and de-fractionalized, as was done in the classic example in the IBM company. The job description provided by Kelly, (1966, p 279) for the section manager in the Glacier Company (given in figure 10 on page 317) indicates the kind of conception which might well emerge from this kind of re-structuring, to provide a better base for the exercise of a supervisory role focused on the reduction of uncertainties of production with the aid of people in all their motivational and attitudinal complexity.

With something like this structural foundation, the role might acquire an adequate power base, and training might be developed by way of job analysis and skills analysis to support its competent exercise. Without it, exhortation and training in human relations skills might prove dysfunctional in the extreme.

Further reading
On the foundation of the general theme of this chapter, see Simon (1953) and Cartwright (1965).

On the specific application to the supervisory role in undertakings, see Dunkerley (1975) and Thurley and Wirdenius (1973).

On merit rating and appraisal, see Randell (1974); Cummings and Schwab (1973).

The consequences of the above conclusions as they relate to the recruitment of commitment of workers to work tasks are further discussed in chapter 20 below.

13 Reward strategies

Control by incentive

The main alternative strategy open to the undertaking which wants to reduce the emphasis upon control through the exercise of personal authority, is that which centres on the offer of some incentive to draw out the desired response.

What may serve as incentive in this context may vary with both the objective and the subjective features of the situation.

On the one hand, a commercial undertaking (which is engaged in the exchange of valuable non-monetary objects for money value) is likely to be disposed to offer money value (or objects which may be readily purchased with it, as in the case of 'fringe benefits') as the main incentive. Non-commercial undertakings are unlikely to secure performance without offers of the same sort, but they may, in addition, be in better position to offer as incentives such objects as more interesting work, greater security of employment, opportunities to satisfy relatedness needs and so on. The distinction once illustrated in these broad category terms, it can be applied to different sub-categories which may be distinguished by their particular circumstances (cf Woodward, 1958; Orth, Bailey and Wolek, 1964; Scott Committee Report, 1981). Thus, the 'objective' situation might be expected to affect the incentive offer.

On the other hand, some of the researches at which we have already looked, suggest that people differ in what they demand of the work situation in the way of 'valued rewards'. Some workers place prime, possibly almost exclusive, weight upon the monetary rewards, as Goldthorpe's 'instrumental' workers appeared to do, whilst others may give greater weight, by addition, to other kinds of satisfaction—security, solidarist relationships, career growth, and so on (see above, pp 154–58). They may all 'learn' to want money as a substitute for these other kinds of satisfaction if, in accordance with learning theory, their experience persistently denies them such satisfactions (see above, pp 275–78). But no real situation is ever likely to present a simple black or white position on this dimension of ('subjective') demand.

In accordance with the theory advanced in chapter 11, therefore, the undertaking which seeks to develop 'incentive strategies' must first consider what valuable rewards or satisfactions are both available and demanded.

The second consideration concerns the perceptions of equity in the rewards (of whatever variety) which are available.

Such perceptions are not only those held by workers. The employer, facing a 'competitive' situation, holds views on whether what he is paying to his workers is equitable in comparison with what his competitors are paying. He often goes to some lengths to conduct surveys to secure data to inform those views. In recent years, the debate over the issue of company cars and other 'fringe benefits' versus index-linked pensions, has been joined between the private sector employers (who tend to provide the first) and the public sector employers (associated with the second), again in the interests of establishing what is equitable (cf Scott Committee Report, 1981).

That workers also have views on equity in rewards is, however, well established (cf Hyman and Brough, 1975; Thomason, 1980). These are frequently expressed in terms of 'internal relativities' (internal that is to the undertaking) and 'external comparability' (which has figured prominently in recent pay negotiations). The tensions and conflicts which often surround the introduction of job evaluation schemes (concerned with internal relativities) and annual pay negotiations (often at least partly concerned with external comparabilities) suggest that these questions are not treated lightly by either workers or their employers.

Nor should it be assumed that these conceptions of what is 'fair' by comparison are related only to monetary rewards, or only to what the individual takes home in the pay packet. Recent moves to achieve harmonization of terms and conditions of employment, or 'staff status' for all, including manual, workers, are concerned with many intangible (and certainly non-monetary) elements of the conditions under which people work and are rewarded. Developments such as those identified by the terms job enrichment or autonomous work groups may have some monetary connotations and spin-offs, but they are mainly concerned with non-monetary satisfactions from work.

Indeed, tutored by such advocates as Herzberg, many managements have come to the view that monetary rewards, important as they are, are not by themselves a sufficient source of 'incentive' in the present social situation. Various developments therefore seek to modify the 'offer' position accordingly. But as these take place, they heighten the workers' concern that these kinds of satisfaction, too, should be subjected to relativity and comparability considerations.

Control by incentive is not, therefore, to be conceived as a simple matter of getting the level of payment right. It involves that, of course, but also it involves setting monetary rewards in the appropriate setting of work satisfaction in the round and by reference to what may be perceived as equitable.

However, in terms of expectancy theory, reward policies within undertakings remain highly focused upon the central axis of effort-performance-reward. More than this, the factor of effort tends increasingly to be dealt with by assumption. In fact, the assumption is that there is a simple, direct, linear relationship between it and performance, and that therefore the reward of performance (whether by extrinsic or intrinsic means) is essentially all that is required of a reward policy. In other words, expectancy theory may provide a basis for developing a wide range of insights into what is requisite in the way of incentive, but practice frequently (indeed usually) focuses upon a particular sub-set of the elements which are there separately distinguished as relevant.

In this chapter, we will look at pay policy initially, and in so doing place main emphasis upon pay as incentive to *performance*, having already looked at some aspects of pay in relation to recruitment and retention (in chapter 7 above). We will also, for this purpose, disregard the questions of external comparability (considered also in chapter 7) and internal relativity (which will be considered in chapter 19 below). In the second half of the chapter, we turn to the question of other forms of incentive than the monetary ones. But given the realities of both offer and demand, we must first consider the question of 'pay as incentive'.

Pay policies for incentive effect

The notion of pay as incentive has attracted a great deal of conflicting argument as to its relevance and efficacy. The basic proposition is that more pay will tend to attract higher performance or productivity, although there is scant evidence of the truth or otherwise of this proposition as it appears not to have been much researched (*see* Opsahl, 1966).

The common effect of changing workers from day or time rates to incentive bonus or payment-by-results schemes, is to increase the quantity of output (cf Carroll, 1954). This seems to confirm the general proposition, although it tends to be silent on questions of quality. Also we know little of what might be expected of performance in situations where results are less amenable to measurement by some variant on the simple counting theme. The commonly observed phenomenon of 'decay' in the incentive power of such schemes however raises doubts about the longer-term effects of any such scheme which links money to performance.

Rothe's examination of such evidence as is available leads him to conclude that:

> ... while financial incentives do seem to result in greater productivity, their precise influence is impossible to determine. Productivity is clearly affected also by such factors as the size of the work group, the inherent nature of the task, the organization of the work, the nature of the incentive system itself, and perhaps the length of time involved... (Rothe, in Fleishman, 1961, p 254).

This in turn leads him to suggest that what is really attempted in the introduction of an incentive scheme is a change in employees' work behaviours and, more particularly, the introduction of a new habit. The intention to effect behavioural change, links the incentive plan to the conditions of effective learning (*see* above, pp 264–70). This link has been noted frequently in the context of those affected 'learning' to subvert the formal plan to their own advantage (Lupton, 1966, pp 70–5), but less often in that of developing new more positive or contributory habits.

Pay policies in undertakings
The normal pay strategy therefore is to rely upon the development of a structure or a system of wages and salaries which, on the basis of the fundamental principle mentioned above, will offer sufficient reward or remuneration to employees to draw out the level of contribution considered necessary. Statements about the purposes and objectives of pay policy or pay structure (whether in the particular case the reference is to wages or salaries) tend to reflect this fundamental assumption.

The National Board for Prices and Incomes (NBPI), for example, suggested that a salary system 'should facilitate the deployment of employees in such a way as will conduce to the maximum efficiency of the undertaking, be adequately related to the attainment and continuance of high performance by individuals and seek to achieve all these aims at the least cost to the undertaking' (NBPI, 1969). Bowley's 'aims of salary policy' include comparable statements:

Salary policy should help to: encourage staff to make full use of their abilities and develop their potential; and to strive to achieve the objectives of their jobs and of the company, facilitate movement of staff across departmental, divisional or sectional boundaries, and achieve these aims at minimum cost—a drift into overpayment must be avoided (Bowley, 1972).

From such statements, it is clear that pay policies and practices are expected to solve a large number of the undertaking's problems: those of securing and maintaining high contribution levels, encouraging individual growth and development, loyalty and mobility, and achieving competitive costs.

Pay policies do not necessarily achieve all of these objectives, where they are achieved at all, through the same or the single element.

Rewards related to performance
Theories of both motivation and incentive have changed markedly since the war, and the emphasis which is given to different methods of structuring the wage incentive (using the term in its broadest sense) has tended to vary in consequence. There are many particular plans available for structuring the pay side of the wage-effort bargain but these fall into a small number of general categories:

1 Straight time payment systems: simply a matter of paying so much per hour worked, and seen as satisfactory only where you can trust the individual to work hard or give his best or where the level of supervision is such that the same result is achieved. Recently, time payment systems have been linked to more specific controls in the form of 'measured day work' (cf Shimmin, 1966)
2 Direct incentive payment systems: this category covers systems (whether piecework or standard hour systems) in which more payment is offered for more effort on the part of the worker, and where effort is supposed to correlate with output. Problems arise here when variations in effort are difficult to measure in this way and when employees discover how to fiddle the rates
3 Indirect incentive payment systems: these usually take the form of lieu bonuses, or bonuses for one category of worker determined by the performance of another; frequently they reflect the need to provide some incentive when it is not possible to use simple measures of output as a means of indicating variations in effort
4 Similar in many ways are the bonuses which are of a profit-sharing or the Scanlon plan type, in which the total contribution of everyone is pooled and shared on some agreed basis, so that again the incentive is a very indirect one. Here the problems

323

which arise depend on how sensible it is to rely upon the assumption of a team spirit.

It may be said of any or all of them that the payment is related to the assumed effort involved but equally it may be suggested that what is actually paid for, as distinct from what is actually measured for the purpose, is the performance or the expected performance.

When the term incentive is used in its usual and narrow sense to apply to payment by results (PBR), the plans which are subsumed tend to relate payment to performance. It is usual to measure what is being paid for in units of time, even in straightforward piecework payments. This has the effect of focusing attention upon the assumption that time somehow measures effort, but particularly in the case of the piecework payment method, what is really being paid for are the 'pieces' or the performance. This is no less true of the schemes which work on the basis of payment (in some proportion) for time saved: the time saved correlates with pieces produced, even if it does encapsulate some assumptions about the relationship between time and effort (cf Lockyer, 1974, p 372).

These assumptions are dealt with in the application of time study, and in particular in the use of rating methods (see above, pp 195–98) but the incentive payment methods themselves *then* link the performance of the individual to the reward. It is the use of the rating methods which seeks to accomplish the objectives of the guessing game which Baldamus (see above, p 290) suggests has to take place. Thereafter, what he refers to as the consequential adjustment is effected by the negotiation of rates and by the policy allowance, 'the magnitude of which depends upon a managerial policy concerning the acceptable level of earnings of the grade of operator concerned' (Lockyer, 1974, p 165).

Once a time study standard has been set on the work in question, the one issue of how to set the ratio of bonus earnings to day-rate is dealt with by the policy allowance already mentioned, usually about 20–25 per cent. The other question of how to divide the element of time-saved is covered by the adoption of a payment by results plan (PBR) which permits the desired or negotiated division. Thus in a straight piecework scheme each piece is normally paid for at a constant 'piece' rate, although this could be varied. In the Halsey-Weir system, the division of the 'time-saved' is normally on a 50–50 basis between the worker and the company, but some other division could be substituted. In the Rowan scheme, the calculation of the division is more complicated but, essentially, this plan allows the split to increase in the employer's favour the higher the output achieved, a factor of importance, for example, where quality standards are important or work measurement difficult (cf Lockyer, *op cit*, pp 372–75).

Where a straight hourly, daily or weekly rate of pay is offered for 'work' whose amount and quality is notionally established in the employment contract, and supported by an implicit or explicit job description or statement of duties and responsibilities, it could be argued that the same principle of rewarding performance is involved. If the differential payments are worked out on the basis of job demands (as in the pay rate) there is at least a notional performance to be rewarded. This idea is carried forward more formally in the development of measured day work in which a datal rate is offered and paid for performance which is, again, established by the application of work measurement methods. Here the question of the standard of performance is neither notional nor implicit. In the variant, the premium pay plan (PPP) which is a stepped or graduated form of measured day work in which the individual can opt for whichever level of performance he wishes to work at in order to give him the particular rate of pay which he wants, the same idea is carried forward.

The tendency in all these plans to emphasize the linear relationship between effort and performance—by measuring through time-study the level of effort whilst rewarding through various individual or group plans the performance given—has led to a considerable amount of friction and 'abuse'. The friction shows itself in disputed rates and disputed payments which have been held to keep the supervisors away from their main tasks of ensuring work flow and performance; the abuse usually takes the form of what is often referred to as fiddling, whereby the workers themselves vary the formal rules and procedures to suit ends which were not intended by the plan and which results in loss of control of its operation. Taken together, these usually lead to management disenchantment and a replacement of the existing plan in order to re-establish some degree of management control. This is often achieved for a short time but over time workers frequently reassert their control (cf Lupton, 1963).

This common enough experience with such plans may be taken to support the arguments advanced in chapter 11 above on the manner in which habits are formed. A change of plan applied to an existing group of workers (whose 'needs' may be regarded as constant) so alters the environment in which needs may be reduced as to call for a different response on their part; in time, the most effective response is learned, and may well include a degree of autonomous regulation at the level of the job.

Undertaking-wide plans

With developments in technology and where managements have had difficulty with individual and small group plans, attempts have been made to develop plans which relate reward to overall profitability rather than individual performance. The necessity for considering these plans from the point of view of what needs to be provided in the way of supporting training activity is not removed or reduced just because the situation does not lend itself to solutions suggested as most efficacious by the Rothe-type analysis (see pp 329–30). The 'understanding' required in these cases has to emphasize the very factors of interdependence which give rise to the abandonment of simple and direct payment-by-results systems applied at the level of the individual and small group.

Plans related to overall efficiency and profitability

These plans are of two broad types, defined by reference to what is taken as the source of any extra payment—either the value of extra production or the profits which extra performance generate. In the first category are the Priestman, Scanlon and Rucker plans, and in the second the many profit-sharing and co-partnership schemes. It is generally true that these plans conceive of performance in a much wider frame than, say, conventional piecework. A better term might be 'contribution' rather than performance, as they all tend to emphasize a general commitment to the ends of the enterprise, only part of which is concerned with direct productive effort and some of which is certainly concerned with acceptance of change and flexibility and even avoidance of costly and time-wasting grievances over particular payments for particular efforts or achievements.

In the first category, employees all receive a guaranteed basic wage but in addition they are paid, as a group, an extra bonus based upon the increase in production beyond the standard set (Priestman) or upon the relative reduction in total labour cost (Scanlon). The Priestman scheme has a complex method of fixing the standard or base-line output where the undertaking is engaged in the making of more than one product, although it is fairly easy in the latter case. Even when by a points weighting process the base-line is arrived at, the offer of an x per cent increase in bonus for an x per cent increase in production above the base-line, the principle of a fixed relationship between reward for performance and the performance itself is established. In the Scanlon and Rucker plans, the same fixed relationship is established, usually by establishing as base-line the ratio of labour cost to total sales value, variations

326

from which then affect the bonus paid. This bonus may involve a straightforward payment of the saving as bonus to the group or some division, such as 75 per cent/25 per cent.

In all these plans the effect sought is a greater commitment to productivity, or at least to the reduction and solution of production problems and it is this which, as much as anything else is rewarded, *and* is claimed as the major advantage of the plan in question. They thus involve 'a philosophy of how to run a factory' over and above the actual method of calculating reward. They have had a limited acceptance on this side of the Atlantic and, as Lockyer says, 'as yet there is too little experience with [the Scanlon plan] outside the US to judge of its value in different employee/employer climates' (Lockyer, 1974, p 377; Butteris, 1977, pp 34–5 and 60–64; Bowey, 1981).

In the second category fall the straightforward profit-sharing plans. These are similar to the Scanlon-type plans in so far as they make available on an undertaking-wide basis a deferred bonus which is allocated from the profits earned during the year. In effect, these plans involve a decision to remunerate employees with 'something extra' over and above their ordinary rates and bonuses if at the end of the working/accounting year, there is a sufficiently large surplus of revenues over costs to warrant this.

The incentive effect is achieved, in so far as it is achieved at all, by holding out this possibility; the disadvantages of the plan are that the amount is uncertain because other factors than the worker's contribution may affect it and because the individual's contribution is difficult to relate to the bonus received. It is usually allocated on the basis of annual rates or earnings on the assumption that those who already earn more are the more likely to contribute to profit, but this may only hold good in a general, not a particular, sense.

The element of deferment to be found in such plans has also been built into share-option schemes which have been given a boost by tax concessions in the Finance Acts of 1978 and 1980. In these schemes, an amount of money (profit) may be allocated by the undertaking to purchase the company's shares which are then allocated to employees and qualify for dividend in the usual way. To this extent, the schemes are devices through which employees may secure a 'share of the profits' through dividends.

The problem to be overcome is that of persuading employees in the first place that any such sum of money as is available should be deployed to acquire shares on their behalf, rather than straightforwardly into the current-wage packet or annual bonus pay-out. This was attempted in the two Finance Acts by exempting the

327

employees' take up of share options from the tax liability which would otherwise apply, under certain conditions, one of which is that the 'realization' of the share value shall be deferred for five years (in the normal case, although there are exceptions). There are a number of other conditions and limitations, both in the general scheme and in the newer Save-as-you-Earn (SAYE) plan introduced in 1980 (cf Copeman, 1979, pp 36–39).

Although both of these types of plan involve a 'profit-sharing', the second (share option) scheme aims also at increasing the loyalty and commitment of employees to the undertaking, by virtue of the greater 'co-partnership' element which it imports (cf Copeman, 1975, p 148). The immediate performance incentive may, however, be relatively small and the value of the plans can only be assessed on multiple criteria related to the mutiple purposes which lie behind them.

The added-value concept

Both the undertaking-wide plans of bonus payments and the more mundane plans for determining pay levels on a continuous basis (as, for example, in the annual pay round) may be, and increasingly often are, rooted in the concept of added value as the method of determining what is in the 'kitty' for distribution in one way or another. In the case of responding to general wage claims, the intention is to determine what are the limits to settlements of wage claims or what kitty exists from which to meet wage and salary costs. It is a truism that wage and other factor costs must be met out of what is left from sales revenue after material and consumables costs have been met. The formal use of added value as a measure in this context is new. The Engineering Employers' Federation (EEF) provide a definition of added value which declares it to be the 'value added to materials and other purchased items which provides, as a result of productive activities in the firm, the sum out of which wages, salaries and administrative overhead expenses are paid, leaving any surplus as profit' (1972/1976, p 18). The EEF seeks to demonstrate that the use of this concept allows both comparisons to be made of labour productivity, and the derivation of an index of the amount of any increase in added value which can be devoted to the payment of wages etc and still provide a minimum percentage return on capital (*ibid*, p 30). In the present context this use of the value added concept suggests that there is a growing predisposition to attempt to fix rewards for work on the basis of performance, rather than on the basis of job demand or effort.

It is only at this end of the spectrum of incentive and bonus schemes that there is any deliberate attempt to influence directly the 'contribution' element in the expectancy model (see above, p 272). Job evaluation scheme place their emphasis on the job demand or effort inherent in the job's content, ordinary 'incentive schemes' place theirs upon the output or contribution as assumedly related to effort and thus seek to establish rewards by guessing at the underlying relationships. But co-partnership and profit-sharing schemes, and indeed the Scanlon-type plans, may be seen to focus upon what, in the work context, constitutes contribution as this may be measured at the end of the day. They seek, in other words, to establish rewards on a basis other than the customary one.

Monetary rewards and incentive
A wide variety of methods have, therefore, been developed to attempt to get the linkage right between the individual's demand for remuneration and the undertaking's demand for performance or contribution at a level which will maintain competitiveness. The ones already discussed may indeed be added to by recognizing, for example, the growth of attention to 'fringe payments' (such as free use of a company car, free medical insurance, subsidized lunches or housing assistance) and their extension from staff to hourly-paid workers with the growth of plans for giving everyone 'staff status' much of which has come about under the influence of 'incomes pol-icies' which constrained straightforward payments in wage rates and earnings.

The question of what a given management should do about re-muneration is, therefore, one which can be answered in any one or any combination of the ways which are touched on in the above review. The question is, which method of approaching payment might be expected to yield the greatest incentive effort.

Rothe has attempted an answer to this question by comparing a number of such different approaches on the dimension of how far the plan meets the need to inculcate *new work habits* in the indi-vidual worker. His approach is based on a conception of learning theory applied to this phenomenon; a given plan introduced to a group of workers must confront them with a need to learn new habits consistent with the changed expectations of reward and of the relationships between effort, performance and reward. He therefore argues that a new plan should deliberately aim to provide opportunities for learning new positive habits, and not be treated simply as another way of varying the simple wage-effort bargain. The relevance and efficacy of a plan can then be judged in advance on criteria derived from learning theory.

He submits that 'learning proceeds better . . . when:

1 The learner is motivated: when he has a need for some thing.
2 There is an incentive appropriate to the motive...
3 The learner intends to learn. The teacher should gratify his intention by keeping him informed of his progress. There must be an awareness of the relationship between the activity and its motive and incentive.
4 The learner understands what he is supposed to be learning: a principle that we implicitly recognize by instituting indoctrination programs.
5 The reward immediately and invariably follows the successful completion of the task, while failure is equally certain not to be rewarded' (Rothe, in Fleishman, 1961, p. 256).

Where, therefore, the intention is to introduce an incentive plan which will encourage positive habits of performance, he suggests, that plan must satisfy the criteria which can be derived from this model (Table 9 below). Two of the six criteria given by Rothe,

Table 9

How various types of financial incentives meet conditions required for increasing productivity

TYPE OF INCENTIVE	CONDITIONS REQUIRED FOR INCREASING PRODUCTIVITY			
	Appropriate to intent	Related to some behaviour	Immediate upon behaviour	Certain upon behaviour
Merit increase	possibly	possibly	possibly	possibly
Negotiated increases	possibly	no	no	no
General increases	no	no	no	no
Productivity increases	possibly	possibly	no	no
Cost-of-living increases	no	no	no	no
Length-of-service increases	no	no	no	no
Profit-sharing plans	possibly	possibly	no	no
Bonuses and commisions	yes	yes	possibly	yes
Individual incentive plans	yes	yes	yes	yes
Group incentive plans	yes	yes	yes	yes

Source: H. F. Rothe, Does Higher Pay Bring Higher Productivity? in Fleishman, E A: *Studies in Personnel and Industrial Psychology* (Dorsey Press, 1961 edn), p 257.

330

namely the presence of a motive (even if it is only the intention to learn) and an understanding of what is to be learnt, he sees as potentially applicable to all forms of payment system. Nevertheless, it will remain necessary for those who introduce such plans to ensure that adequate 'training' is provided to ensure that those affected are aware of the incentive possibilities and have an understanding of the intentions of the plan in respect of performance habits.

The other four criteria, are, however, only differentially satisfied by plans for providing incentive. Not all of the plans which he includes in his list are, strictly, performance-related plans, but they do cover the spectrum of plans for providing monetary incentives to those who work. The four criteria of appropriateness of the plan to the intention, its relatedness to action, the immediacy of its effect and the certainty of its application, are just not satisfied by plans which merely respond to custom and convention and (small) group incentive plans are regarded as satisfying all four of the criteria, whilst general, cost of living, and length of service related increases in wage rates are likely, in Rothe's view, to satisfy none of them. Where the intention is to inculcate more positive performance habits, therefore, the latter are unlikely to have much success.

A contingency approach

Whatever inherent incentive merits various plans may have, it is unlikely that managerial decision takers will be completely free to determine which to adopt simply on the merits of the plans as providers of incentive, or, indeed, on the basis of personal preference or whim (although no doubt this does happen).

Rather, it is thought that management will be 'constrained' in their decision by two, possibly related, sets of variables in the situation which they are managing. One set stems from the undertaking's own purposes, objectives and 'technology', ie in the senses in which these have been defined by Woodward and reviewed above, pp 9–11. What the undertaking is aiming for or trying to achieve and the methods which it has adopted in order to achieve it are seen to impose limits upon the choice open. The other stems from the kinds of orientation which the employees (both as a whole and as sub-sets) have towards work and what, in consequence, they demand from it, ie in the senses in which these have been expressed by Goldthorpe and his colleagues and reviewed above, pp 154–58).

Taken together, these begin to identify the 'contingency approach' to managerial decision taking (regardless, it might be said, whether that decision taking is unilateral on the part of management or joint with the workers' representatives, since the constraints are constraints on the decisional choice, not upon 'people' as such). In more old-fashioned terms, this is to say that decisions are to be taken after adequate diagnosis of the situation to which they are to be applied.

The 'objective' pressures

In broad terms, the effects of changes in objectives and technology upon the relevance of different payment systems may be illustrated from the history of PBR systems in the past 30 years. At the beginning of this period, the management textbook was usually most concerned to extol the virtues of such systems in securing the needed performance. Subsequently, they came in for a great deal of criticism, and their abandonment was cogently advocated (cf Brown, 1962). The growth in their use in the first half of the present century appears to have been reversed, although what little statistical evidence there is does not yet lead unerringly to this conclusion.

The apparent reasons for both the growth and the decline might themselves be indicative of the sort of pressures which are generated by a given type of market and technological system, although what is often referred to as fashion cannot be discounted entirely.

It can be argued that the growth of the mass production firm was the factor which sustained the development of PBR systems. This does not mean that PBR is only applicable to these kinds of firm. But there is reason to suppose that, if you are producing a standardized item for a mass market by relatively standardized means, first, the profit margins in a competitive situation will be cut (Allen, 1961) and therefore, secondly, there will be pressure upon unit labour costs. Labour is the only factor of production which is capable of variation in increased efficiency per unit—in the sense that once the machine is designed and built into a flow-line, there is little more to be got out of it beyond its fixed speed, unless labour's contribution is somehow enhanced, eg work faster, harder, on shifts or with more constant application during the work period. PBR systems seemed to have this kind of advantage to offer to the firm faced with this kind of market-plus-technology prospect.

It has recently been argued in line with this discussion of the efficacy of PBR systems that, where the mass production technology is carried through to a higher stage, so that the worker's direct influence upon rate of production is much reduced, the justification for the incentive scheme in that form disappears. To abandon piecework and comparable systems under these circumstances is then just as appropriate as their embrace at the lower level of technology. Nor does this mean that all oil and chemical

332

plants will immediately abandon these schemes, although many have, and some have carried productivity bargaining through to a higher level of sophistication than most engineering companies.

The small jobbing shop, or the small-batch producing unit usually avoids the simple, direct PBR system. Again, this is not clear cut but there is no reason why we should suppose that PBR systems are introduced merely for one reason in all cases. Similarly, and probably for similar reasons, the indirect element of a labour force, such as the maintenance crew or a yard gang, is often not subjected to PBR systems. But in these circumstances it is much less possible to measure that element in the situation which contributes to performance. Many different schemes have been tried, linking it to machine down-time or to time on a standardized maintenance job, but the kind of system which seems to be called for by the situation is different from that needed on the production line.

In fairly simple general terms therefore:

1 Unit and small batch producing units most commonly (ie modally) apply some type of straight time payment system
2 Manually-controlled line production of standardized products is usually linked with some form of PBR system
3 Automatically controlled line flow production systems (necessarily producing standard items) have commonly gone over to some newer system of payment, whether measured day work or more likely a productivity bargain type of payment system.

Fashion or whim can obviously affect the outcome, and so too can the element of panic or failure, in the sense that any firm which is failing by its existing methods of organizing effort could well seize upon a payments system straw to try to help itself. If there is a moral, it is perhaps that the market-plus production system that the plant or company has seems to exert some pressure towards one pattern of payment rather than another (cf Lupton and Bowey, 1974).

The 'subjective' pressures
Unless the assumption is made that the goals of the undertaking and those of the workers it employs, exactly match one another (cf Mumford 1972, and above, pp 169–72), a different set of pressures to limit the choice might be expected from the latter. Of course, as between individual workers, there are likely to be differences in demand for income (varying with the individual's age and circumstances, cf Lupton, 1963). But on the kind of evidence produced by Goldthorpe et al, (and reviewed on pp 154–58 above) and by Sayles

(1958), we should expect categories and groups of workers to exhibit differences in orientation which will have their effect. This is illustrated using Goldthorpe's categories:

(a) The instrumental group is more likely to demand a payment system which virtually guarantees high take home pay. The manner of its calculation is perhaps of secondary importance compared with its level relative to other pay packets, or with its constancy taking one period with another. These men are in it for the money and this is what they want out of work. Their manner of securing this may well vary according to the conditions of the labour market, and perhaps in particular of the local labour market. Where jobs are plentiful, the response to a low pay packet or to a fall in pay level will result in a tendency for the men to vote with their feet as they move into more lucrative jobs. Where jobs are not so easy to come by, or where there are no alternative jobs at anything like the same money, withdrawal is not a viable strategy but aggression towards the company to secure higher earnings becomes a stronger possibility.

(b) The solidarist group is more likely to be concerned with the side-effects of the payment system. Although its members are also interested in money, they will seek their money rewards on more stringent conditions. For example, a straight piecework or other direct incentive scheme, which will lead to a differentiation within the worker group itself, is likely to be either discouraged or, more likely from the evidence, to be used as a means of increasing group solidarity through some fiddle or other. This is really a way of ensuring that the worker group can offer cooperation to management in the bonus scheme without appearing to themselves to be accepting management's terms. The work will be 'banked' when a lot is done and only a fairly constant amount will be booked for payment purposes, so that the 'bank' exists as a buffer against the 'off-day'. Or again, any minor variation in the methods or conditions of the work will be used as an excuse for attempting to renegotiate the rate. For workers who have this general type of orientation, it might be suggested that the payment system will become just another aspect of the situation over which the worker group will seek to secure increased *control*.

This sort of distinction does not m rely affect incentive payment systems. Even with a straight day wage arrangement, the high-money men will tend to seek such extras as overtime and week-end

334

working, whilst the solidarist groups will be more concerned to ensure that there are arrangements within their control for sharing the available overtime working. Similarly, a solidaristically-oriented workforce is much more likely to organize and control arrangements for securing provisions at a discount (whether from the company from amongst its own materials or products, or by way of 'works' gardening, car maintenance, or photographic clubs) than is the more instrumentally-oriented one, and is likely to present fewer security or policing problems as a result.

There is also some suggestion that workers' reaction to methods of payment is partially determined by the sort of social system in which they have been brought up. One piece of research suggested, for example, that the rate busters on incentive are likely to have rural backgrounds, whilst the solidarist groups are more likely to have urban backgrounds (Whyte, 1955). The same research suggested that Catholics are more frequently found in the first category and Protestants in the second. In both cases, the standards of proper behaviour which are inculcated in the individual seem to make the difference.

There is also some suggestion that workers with different orientations will tend to select for themselves the sort of work and payment system which is most congenial to them; the rate busters will look for the system that will enable them to make big money and the solidarist groups will do the same, although in terms of their own orientation. If there are unlimited opportunities for employment, there could be a shake-out and a matching of expectation and experience.

It must be emphasized that such general propositions as those reviewed here are general or thought to be so. There is no reason to suppose that they must apply in particular situations, a point stressed by Lupton and Bowey in their reference to a contingency approach. This says, in essence, that no one payment scheme will meet *any* employer objectives or *any* worker objectives, and that the selection of a plan will demand close analysis of the given plan's properties in relation to the objectives and the situation in which it is to be applied. For this purpose, they offer the Lupton Gowler profile method of assessment, designed to meet the proviso indicated at the beginning of this paragraph. Use of this method of assessment places the problem of determining which payment system to employ in a given situation on the same footing as any other management decision: it necessitates adequate diagnosis of situation and adequate analysis of the properties of alternative courses of action, before the final choice is made (or the decision taken).

Rewarding by other means

Recognizing that money is likely to be an important requirement and incentive because of the necessary instrumentalism of work, it is also possible to recognize that there is more to work than money. There are 'other contracts' than the efficiency one, and other forms of 'consideration' than the monetary one. Indeed, what is 'offered' by an undertaking usually comprises a most complex and ramified mixture of benefits and advantages. Although there is little systematically collected evidence on the question, it is to be expected that the nature of this non-monetary reward package will reflect the same kinds of objective and subjective pressures as those noted earlier. A contingency approach might therefore be adopted in relation to them. However in the rest of this chapter some of the more common rewards, associated with Maslow's higher order needs, are simply reviewed without attempting to relate them situationally.

The security of reward

It is often suggested that one of the disadvantages of PBR systems, from the worker's standpoint, is the liability to fluctuation in earnings which they introduce, compared with the straight time wage. It is also recognized that workers often respond to this by 'banking' work done in good times and by drawing upon the bank when they have an off-day (Roethlisberger and Dickson, 1939; Lupton, 1963; Cunnison, 1965). One inference is that 'security' of earnings is a factor which workers recognize by their conduct.

Similarly, this same notion might be applied to the generality of rewards: the individual worker is interested not merely in the amount of reward he may happen to receive for his contribution (however it is computed) but also in the security with which he can earn it. It has been a feature of the employment structure over the period of the industrial revolution that contracts may be determined at very short notice, with the consequence that security of rewards has been extremely low for most of the period. This may have been mitigated by the paternalistic employer 'looking after' his own labour, and the personnel manager in his welfare role may have been somewhat instrumental in this. It may also have been varied marginally by recent legislation, but we still do not do a great deal to ensure the continuity and constancy of earnings of the worker. In so far as we do tackle this question, it has been through 'social security' provisions, ie, by provision outside the employment situation itself.

We are in Britain a long way from the life-time employment concept of Japan, and the rejection of paternalism by organized

Table 10
Pay and productivity in different situations

Type of work situation	Payment form	Productivity form	Worker orientation
Work situations with high discretion in the work role: problem solving			
1 Top management	High, secured by long contract	Creativity based on trust	Commitment to org objectives
2 R and D department	High, secured by professional career	Contribution to creativity	Commitment to creative tasks
3 Selling organization	High, secured by basic salary plus commission	Contributory to growth	Commitment to selling objectives
4 Supervision	Protected salary guaranteed by organization	Loyal execution of original directives	Loyalty to organization
Work situations with low discretion in work roles: execution			
5 Unit and small batch production	Day or piece rates guaranteed by the personal authority of boss	Flexible working on varied tasks	Expressive: work satisfies wide demands
6 Manually-controlled line production	Incentive payments secured by agreements	High and constant rates of production	Instrumental: work satisfies demand for money
7 Automatically-controlled line production	Pay and participation, secured by common commitment	Constant attention and intermittent action	Commitment to work tasks

labour in Britain is unlikely to allow such a concept to be similarly applied here. The donation of job property rights by legislation may help to bring the conception back into the game in another guise and, in so doing, force employers to consider the question of what kind of long-term 'career' they provide to their workers. If workers do have job property rights created by union agreements or legislation, they could well want to have more influence upon just what kind of situation they will be presented with in which they can enjoy those rights.

If we use the term 'career' to indicate what it is that thinking should be focused upon, we should not assume that this must necessarily mean a 'career' in the middle-class, professional sense from whence it sprang (Hughes, 1958). Rather we should perhaps think of this in terms of 'employee development' by which improvements may be achieved without necessarily implying progress upwards through a hierarchy of status and authority such as is found in a bureaucratic system. Instead, the improvements might accrue from planned (and agreed) training and movement (job rotation) which, whilst preserving economic status, still permits those who so wish to broaden their experiences and develop their skill (cf Gregson and Ruffle, 1980, pp 62–4).

Opportunities for growth

One extension of the concept of 'security' is that which sets it in the context of opportunity; not to stay as one is, but to grow as one progresses through life. Not everyone wants such opportunity; some prefer to stay put, re-experiencing the known and familiar. Others more actively seek chances of learning new things and experiencing new challenges. To meet these varying demands on the work organization as an environment for living, it may be necessary, as expectations of workers change, to think out new structures which offer opportunities for the development of different kinds of career for different kinds of people.

One such model has been put forward by Schein (1971) where he sees organizations as conical structures within which various types of career can be constructed. He defines career as

> a set of attributes and experiences of the *individual* who joins, moves through, and finally leaves an organization ... and as defined by the organization—a set of expectations held by individuals inside the organization which guide decisions about whom to move, when, how, and at what 'speed' (Schein, 1971, pp 401–2).

He depicts the organization for this purpose as a cone, in which rank or status is increased from bottom to top, centrality from the periphery to the centre (eg branch organization to headquarters), and separate divisions or functions are indicated by sections of the cone. Careers may therefore develop in one or a combination of three ways:

> vertically, by increasing or decreasing rank within the undertaking
> radially, by moving closer to the centre or further away from it
> circumferentially, by changing from one function or division to another.

Combinations might allow change of function with movement towards or away from the centre, or with movement upwards; and movement upwards with movement between periphery and centre; and in a complete combination, some variation on the spiralling theme. Equally, the possibilities for segmentation by boundaries on any of these same dimensions might well function as barriers to career development.

338

If this kind of conception is married to recent developments in the field of motivational theory as in job enrichment (*see* below, pp 341–43) the indicated solution is something more dynamic and wider-reaching than the mere provision of more challenging jobs (which are then equally as static as the ones they replace) or of 'autonomous work groups' (in which the individual members are made more subject to group pressures within the prison of the small working group). Now there is an indicated need to provide

Figure 11
The cone of organizational careers

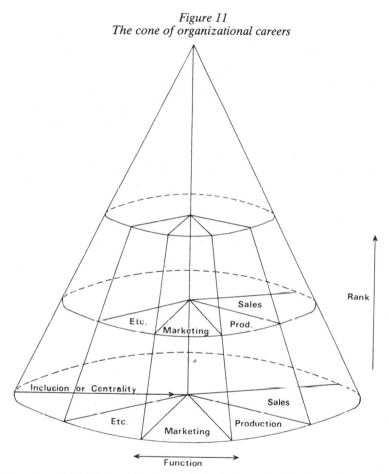

Based on: E H Schein: The Individual, the Organization and the Career, in *Journal of Applied Behavioural Sciences*, 7, 1971, pp 401–426. Figure 1: A Three-dimensional Model of an Organization, p 404.

for movement, up, across or around, so that individuals can at least perceive some opportunity of escape (should they wish to) and therefore some opportunity to plan their 'careers' within the organization. As yet this area is little affected directly by legislation, but some of the provisions relating to the offer of vacancies are tangentially relevant, and suggest some possible lines of future developments of policy on securing performance by more adequate structuring of the continuing environments of work.

Intrinsic satisfactions

The deliberate provision of opportunities for the development of a career may, therefore, be regarded as both security-enhancing and as challenge-providing for those who can, as a result, move from one job to another. There remains, however, the problem of the person whose 'career' could only at best be described as a flat one; even with guarantees of no-redundancy and annual wages many will, in the nature of the case, continue in the same job at the same relative level of earnings over most of their life. What is to be done about them?

This is a problem for management (either alone or in negotiation) to resolve. Such workers, through absenteeism, lateness, intermittent application to work, and other indications of 'withdrawal' from productive activity, constantly send messages to management that all is not well in the realms of work organization. Where an undertaking is equipped to monitor such conduct, what is fed back must cause management to consider whether the current 'offer' is the best that can be made.

The problem set for management is, as van Beek suggests, that rational methods ('job analysis permitting of dividing jobs into short cycle tasks which could be learned quickly and in which unskilled workers could reach a high level of proficiency, the assembly line promoting a regular flow of production and wage systems ensuring an equitable remuneration') may no longer provide an answer to some of the problems faced by managements. 'Extensive specialization' renders the production system vulnerable, sophisticated wage systems prove ineffective, better education and changed attitudes work against rigorous division, so that 'it is therefore highly necessary to study and reassess continually the organization of unskilled work' (van Beek, 1964, p 161).

Researches which we have briefly reviewed offer some guidance as to the lines of resolution. On the one hand, Dubin has suggested that, in addition to pay, workers want the work situation to offer them opportunity to apply their skills in a technologically and organizationally-developed environment (see above, p 340).

Herzberg has gone further and suggested that workers want the job itself to provide them with interest and challenge as well as opportunity for achievement and recognition, given that the pay and other environmentally-hygienic factors are adequate (see above, pp 25–26). On the other, a whole edifice of research stemming from the Hawthorne investigations has suggested that (in spite of Dubin's finding to the contrary) the work situation is one in which the satisfaction of 'relatedness' needs (Alderfer, 1972) may offer a kind of incentive in some circumstances.

These, in their time, have created their fashions in management action: better human relations, briefing groups, job enlargement and job rotation, job enrichment and autonomous working groups. Although the genesis of these forms of managerial response to their perceived problem may be associated with the names of main researchers, it was not the researchers who invented either the problem or the possible solutions. Their role was to collect, collate and organize the information which already existed, and *that* role is open to management to adopt, as indeed it has been adopted in a number of the experiments in job enrichment and the development of autonomous working groups.

Job enrichment

What has now come to be known generically as 'job enrichment' builds upon such knowledge as we have of the problems of work organization and motivation, and attempts to build more interest, variety and challenge into the work of those who are unlikely to secure an upward-moving career in modern work organization. Fundamentally, it attempts to increase the discretion which the individual worker has to determine his or her work patterns or pace, or, generally, how he or she will set about the job. It is, therefore, possible to give a salesman more discretion to negotiate prices and terms with customers, or an office worker to vary his routines to suit himself within wider constraints than he experienced before.

In many situations, the variation thus allowed to the individual would necessarily affect others in the section or department, and one variant on this theme therefore seeks to place the increased discretion in the hands of 'the group' rather than the individual. In that context, the notion of the autonomous work group merges with that of job enrichment. Some of the more widely known examples of job enrichment fall into this category; the 'grouping' of assembly-line operations in Phillips, Eindhoven, or in the Saab or Volvo plants in Sweden, for example. In these cases, the individual may benefit from the increased authority which is devolved to the work group but the group must itself 'take' the decisions for the sake of equity and co-ordination, so that the possibility exists that the group might be as constraining as the foreman might have been before. Consequently, in many of these experiments the attempt is made, via selection, to ensure that those who want to participate in this new arrangement are the ones who are given the opportunity whilst others who prefer to do so stay outside them: itself an attempt to allow increased discretion.

The changes in the structure of the work and the work groups which occur in these experiments indicate a reversal of a dominant trend in work fragmentation which has been with us over the whole of the period of the industrial revolution. For this reason if for no other, we should not expect that people will accept this change overnight. In fact, Walsh in his report on changes in the work of Electricity Board district offices (1969) indicates something of this where he points out (a) that *younger* people are more able to take this in their stride, whilst *older* people find it more difficult to adapt and to cope with the new situation, and (b) that supervisors experienced considerable *initial* difficulties in adopting the new role (revealed in anxiety) and that management in turn was within an ace of panicking in the *early stages* when performance fell off as people had to unlearn and relearn. By implication, the longer or the deeper the involvement in or commitment to the existing system, the greater the difficulty of adjustment revealed. Although Walsh infers from this that the first step ought therefore to be the selling of job enrichment to senior management, the point might be extended to suggest that selling will be more necessary the longer or the deeper the involvement of the category of person/status concerned.

This is helped by the existence of long term benefits:

(a) more contentment in the enriched sections
(b) less supervision, and lower costs, without deterioration in standards of work
(c) the development of a better attitude to the job and much more recognition of the importance of good customer relations
(d) finally, staff themselves say they have a better sense of participation in really worthwhile work. Their sense of achievement is greatly enhanced (*ibid*, p 44).

The emphasis here upon the 'long-term' is important, although others report shorter-term advantages.

Van Beek reports one of the earlier experiments, that of the work on assembly lines in Phillips' Eindhoven TV receiver factory started in 1960. The basis of this experiment was the modification of the organization of the line and the work associated with it, and measurement of the consequences of these changes was attempted in terms of output, quality and morale.

A complaint about the amount of waiting time on the line led to the division of one line of 104 workers into five distinct groups (ranging in size from 14–29 workers) separated by (a) inspection points and (b) buffer stocks amounting to the equivalent of an hour's work. This change was reported as reducing waiting time due to lack of material to 55 per cent, increasing earnings, heightening morale and reducing absenteeism. Further evaluating studies suggested that 'the shorter line with buffer stocks between adjacent workplaces offers the most favourable possibilities to achieve a good quality' (p 160).

Nevertheless, this is not achieved without cost and the investigators indicate some of these:

> The small group . . . also presents disadvantages. Small groups will for example require more space and increase the intermediate stocks. In some respects the small group may also make more demands on supervision. Where in the long line a member of individuals had to be dealt with, the small group constitutes a nucleus of informal organization, which will have to be guided into a positive direction (*ibid*, p 171).

Whilst one might still question, in line with modern systems theory, just what is meant by a 'positive direction' this makes it quite clear that there are problems for management. It is not merely a matter of changing the spatial layout to improve productivity and morale. It is also a question of learning how to cope with the consequent organizational and leadership problems which are effected coincidentally.

One of the more encouraging features of the movement towards autonomous work groups etc, has been just this blending of an economic realism, represented by management's willingness to experiment if the cost-benefit position is demonstrated to be correct, and the more reliable findings of empirical social research.

As Paul and Robertson (1969) express this point of view: 'At a time when there is a premium on individual effort, as labour becomes too costly to waste and concern about the underemployment of people in industry mounts, theory suggests that more attention to the motivators, a more critical look at the jobs themselves. . . . would pay dividends' (p 2). As managers have begun their own experiments in this field, and as more work has been done on costing what they yield, hard economic data is being produced to support the desirability of this kind of approach.

343

Conclusion

This explicit linking of performance problems and motivational theories as a basis for experimentation makes its appearance more often in the present climate. As it does so, it moves management practice beyond the simple reliance upon control assumptions and renders it a more complex phenomenon, difficult to describe and to understand in all its ramifications.

It may be suggested, however, on the basis of the material so far presented in part two, that performance-oriented strategies are becoming increasingly holistic. At very least they are developing in different ways interdependently.

For example, one development of the 'efficiency-contract' is that at which we have just looked, the proposal for 'job enrichment'. Its origins lie in the theoretical proposition that workers seek intrinsic (job related) satisfactions from work as part of the consideration required to elicit performance. But its consequences affect the components of both the remuneration and the supervisory strategies.

On the one hand, the increased discretion and responsibility introduced with job enrichment is unlikely to be accepted without some attention to monetary rewards, as many undertakings have discovered. As has been demonstrated with the aid of the examples quoted above, there are productivity and cost-saving advantages, and it is not conceivable that these will be allowed to accrue only to the undertaking. The jobs in question are usually enlarged as well as enriched, and in line with the usual considerations entering into job evaluation, the greater size is likely to be matched by demands for greater monetary reward. A programme of job enrichment cannot be embarked upon without attention to this other side of the contract.

On the other, the increased discretion is likely to affect the discretion of those (supervisors and associated staff specialists) who previously exercised it 'on behalf of the workers'. Without assuming that discretion constitutes a fixed sum within any particular work undertaking, it can neither be assumed that the distribution of discretion and power to exercise it will remain unaffected by this type of change. Unless this kind of development is to be allowed by default to reduce further the significance of the first-line supervisor, therefore, the roles of such persons have to be re-examined and re-defined. If the increased working group autonomy is to be 'offered' as a part of the total reward package, the demand within the supervisory strategy for compliance and obedience has to be altered. The job enrichment exercise cannot be undertaken without attention to the system of personal authority focused in the

344

supervisory role.

In addition, it is only to be expected that the consequences of such changes in response to altered expectations and theories which seek to explain them, will spread beyond these confines. The organizational climate or ethos, the roles of managers and workers, the policies and strategies adopted and the demands and offers made within the contract are unlikely to remain unaffected by such changes. In this sense, therefore, it is possible to conclude that the accommodation of Schein's concept of 'complex man' in managerial approaches will probably create a much more complex environment for work.

This will be manifest in changes at the level of the 'organization' as a whole (at which we look in part three) but for the present we may note that it is already manifest in the increasing complexity and interdependence of the control and motivational (incentivational?) strategies which may be seen in operation in the world about us, and which may be supported by the kinds of social scientific theory discussed above in Chapter 11.

One major consequence of all this, at which we must now look, is the impact upon communications structures and processes to be found in undertakings, and in even greater particular upon 'training' as a rather special form of communication

Further reading
The main texts which will prove useful in amplifying the material in this chapter are Lockyer (1974), Currie (1977), Husband (1976), Lupton and Bowey (1974), Bowey (1981) and Rock (1972).

The material in earlier chapters on motivation may usefully be supplemented by reference to Rothe (in Fleishman, 1961).

Specific pay plans are covered in the general references above, but Wilson (1977) and EEF (1976) are useful additions on value-added concepts, and reference might be made to van Beek (1964) and Paul and Robertson (1970) on specific experiments with job enrichment and to Wall and Lischeron (1977) on experiments with action planning groups.

Recent articles in *Personnel Management*, particularly that by Gregson and Ruffle (October, 1980) provide some support for the 'holistic' conclusion advanced. The main theoretic support for this view is to be found in Schein (1970).

14 Communications process and structure

The central position of communication

It is not difficult to find reasons why communication is regarded as 'vital' to the operation of work undertakings and, often, as a major problem to be overcome in them. Nor is it difficult to visualize the reasons why communication becomes a major skill which is required of managers.

The system theorists argue that 'information exchange' is as vital to organizational performance as 'energy exchange' is to electro-mechanical devices for performing work (cf Boulding, 1956; Buckley, 1967, pp 46–50). Simply because human performance within organizations must respond to the performance of others, it is seen as unavoidable that there should be adequate communication (and adequate influence as a result of that communication), to effect the requisite understanding (cf Jackson, 1962, p 407). Where it is necessary for changes to be brought about, communication is seen to be an inherent factor in this process (cf Jaques, 1951, p 301).

In addition, we have tended to use all occasions to convince ourselves that communication in and around work organizations is a major, and possibly intractable, problem. Society, through various agencies, has sought to establish that many of the current failings of British industry are to be laid at the door of inadequate attention to communications by managements and/or trade unions (cf Donovan Commission Report, 1968, pp 24–25; DE Code of Industrial Relations Practice, 1972, pp 14–16). Managerial spokesmen have also suggested that, for a variety of reasons, we are just not very good at communicating and that this might account for some of the differences in performance observed between our undertakings and those of other countries and cultures (cf Mant, 1977.

The personnel manager is involved in communication in two

346

main ways. First, he needs to be proficient in communication in order to realize the administrative and executive tasks of the role itself. Secondly, he needs a knowledge of communication in order to assist others to realize their ends. Both knowledge of and ability in communication are necessary to successful achievement. But this also depends, as will be shown below, upon an adequate structure of communications channels and upon access to them, and an additional requirement of the personnel manager is that he should play some part in developing both of these.

Such knowledge and skill is required on the one hand to enable the personnel specialist to carry out effectively the tasks of interviewing for any kind of appointment, inducting new employees, providing training, counselling, coaching, appraising performance, consultation and negotiation, which form some of the main areas which fall within the ambit of the specialism itself.

It is also required to enable the specialist to communicate his advice on any subject, including that of communication, to anyone else in the undertaking who may seek it. Advice on communication (whether in the simple form of counselling, or in the more structured form of policy-making and implementation) is frequently required to enable line management and supervision to handle their problems of discipline and grievance handling, consultation and negotiation, as well as the ordinary processes of 'instruction' and persuasion of the members of their teams and sections on whom the realization of their objectives ultimately depends.

Both generally and specifically within the role of the personnel specialist, therefore, there is sufficient reason to treat communications as important. In this chapter, it is proposed to look at the conceptions of communication which have been advanced as an aid to understanding of the processes and as a foundation for the development of skills.

There are, effectively, two levels on which the question might be considered. First, there is the level of communication as a very subjective process which occurs between two individuals, in which case the emphasis is upon a process linking people through communications media (speech, writing, etc) and dependent upon those particular 'codes' which people use to communicate and which is usually spoken of, simply, as language. Secondly, there is that of communications at the organizational level, occurring between what Hickson *et al* (1971) refer to as 'sub-units', being transmitted through 'channels' (lines of command or consultative structures) and involving 'messages' in some rather more formal sense than is implied at the first level. In fact, different textbooks on the subject make this kind of distinction, even though all of them may be concerned with the question of how meaning is communicated in order to influence others' thinking, feeling or behaviour, and all of them make use of a closed-loop model as the vehicle for understanding.

The closed loop model
Communication usually occurs when one person passes a message of some kind to another, who, in turn, is in some way affected by it at least to the extent of hearing or seeing it. Laswell (1969) has expressed this in the form of five questions: 'who ... says what ... in what way ... to whom ... with what effect?'. To answer these questions is to describe how communication takes place.

In this model there are therefore two processes which form the mirror image of each other. A *communicator* constructs a *form of message* which is *transmitted as the message* through some *medium* in order that it may be *interpreted* by another; that 'other', the *receiver*, in turn, constructs a *form of message* by reacting, and transmits this as the *return message* through some *medium* in order that it may be *interpreted* by the communicator. The one process is a process of feeding out a communication, and the other one of feeding back a reaction which is comparably 'a communication' which allows effect to be assessed. Following the approach adopted by Shannon and Weaver (1949) and Schramm (1963) these descriptive statements can be depicted in the form typical of the closed loop or feedback model:

Figure 12
Elements in a communications process

FEEDOUT

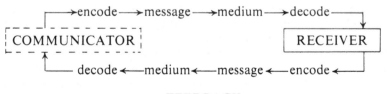

FEEDBACK

Something of the nature of each of these elements may be indicated in order to provide a foundation for consideration of more complex problems of communication in organizations.

1 *The communicator and receiver*   In our area of interest, the communicator and receiver are both *persons*; therefore anything which we might know about the nature of persons is relevant to our understanding of these two elements. But 'communicator' and 'receiver' are terms used to indicate two different roles in the communication process, and surrounding each there is a set of expectations about how the 'person' in question should act or behave in that role.

The communicator might be expected to engage in communication with certain intentions to influence another (or a number of them) and do so in accordance with his job requirements. A manager, for example, giving instructions to subordinates might be expected to conceive his communication role as defined by the prescribed need to get the production out; in following this prescription he might well act differently from the way he would communicate if he were simply 'being himself'. To the extent that he acts in this way, the way he frames his messages and the intentions behind doing this, will reflect his job prescription.

But the formal job requirements are not the only role constraints to which he responds. His occupational group (eg personnel managers), his peer group (his 'generation' of friends) or his work group (the department in which he works) all tend to present role expectations to him, and he will tend to respond to a varying extent to these according to how he establishes *his* reference groups for purposes of comparing or guiding his communicative behaviours (Dalton, 1959; Shibutani, 1962). Such considerations suggest that we should not regard communicators in formal organizations simply as persons: the role constraints responded to will bear upon how they approach the tasks (cf Rose, 1962).

The receiver is similarly encapsulated in a structure of role expectations. What may be said about group identities in the one case apply to the other. But consideration of the receiver role raises another question: whether the receiver should be treated as independent in the receiving? There may be two categories of receiver to be distinguished. The most convincing material on this aspect is to be found in the study of mass media by Katz and Lazarsfeld (1955).

The problem to which these researchers addressed themselves was that of how a message from a newspaper, radio or television (about politics, product advertising or whatever) 'got through' to people. A person might see an advertisement for Brand X on television and this, in one hypothesis, might represent an effective communication in the sense that the individual heard, saw and acted upon it. But such a person is probably also exposed to an advertisement for Brand Y at roughly the same time; the question arises as to how the individual selects between competing messages of this sort, because patently he does not rush out and buy everything that he is urged to buy or vote for every candidate who might solicit his vote.

The answer is contained in what emerged as a 'two-step' flow of communications. The seeing or hearing of the 'original' message is only step one; whether and how it gets translated into a verdict (which to buy or vote for) or an action (like buying or voting) depends on the other step, in which the content of such messages is mediated by a much more local and private group of friends or acquaintances. As Katz and Lazarsfeld uncovered these, they found them to consist of small networks of inter-personal relations within which there would probably be someone (whom they called an influential) who would play a major part in making up individual members minds and spurring them to some action or another. Thus there might be a fashion influential, a domestic chores influential, a political influential and so on.

This opinion would be given more weight than others, but also it might well prove to be a necessary preliminary to any of the members of the network taking any notice whatever of the content of the message. Only when this second step in the communications process had been taken could response to the message really be expected in the case of most people (although of course not all).

In a number of situations which arise in work organizations, something similar to this might be seen to happen. A notice on the noticeboard is read but not acted upon until it has been chewed over in this little group or that; even then it is often possible to discern that not only do individuals go about it in various ways, but quite often little groups of them will respond positively and others negatively as the group influence makes its presence known. It is therefore a hypothesis which is likely to help us explain some of the phenomena which we might see around us in such organizations.

For this kind of varying response to be feasible, we have to recognize that these groups are really going through an evaluation process in relation to the message and that, in doing so, they are measuring possible meanings against their own templates, standards or norms. This must be so if some groups come out of the exercise saying 'Yes' and others 'No' to the same message. It is this feature of the group as a repository of standards of comparison and standards of meaning which is the important variable and not merely the fact of group existence *per se*. Because the group is so equipped, it can help to define reality for the members, as suggested above. It is the values which are inherent in such standards which serve to refract communications and which yield varying interpretations of the same message.

2 *Encoding and decoding* Encoding and decoding are relatively technical operations: 'effectiveness is . . . dependent upon certain properties of the message transmitted. The possession of skill in constructing messages . . . is thus another base of influence', suggests Cartwright (1965, p 19). Equally, the possession of a skill in decoding or unscrambling them is an important skill for the recipient, possession of which permits a 'correct' response, whatever the criteria of correctness are in his particular case. In terms of skill the question of coding and decoding is likely to reflect upon 'individual differences'; the task of encoding or decoding call for attributes and abilities in the population involved which may be expected to be randomly distributed (cf Miner and Miner. 1977, p 61 *et seq*). Since, as Cartwright reports, 'much of the research on persuasion has been concerned with the problem of how to design effective messages' and has raised 'issues both of logic and rhetoric in the Aristotelian sense', both the cognitive and affective attainments and dispositions of the individual (communicator or receiver) are likely to be involved (Cartwright, 1965, p 19).

It is widely accepted that categories of person who are widely distanced from each other in terms of life styles are likely to have developed modes of thinking about the reality and a language to support these, which are widely different from one another, and communication between such categories is likely to present major encoding and decoding problems. Whilst this can be done—managers write one 'kind' of report for the board and another for the shop floor in order to deal with this kind of problem—it is more usual to attempt to meet the problem by a chain of translation. In this, the communicator transmits an encoded message to a receiver not far distant, who then re-codes it with further translation for transmission to one not far distant from himself and so on, until the finally translated messages reaches its 'final' destination. In effect this creates a potentially long chain of communication of the following form:

$$C \longrightarrow 1 \longrightarrow 2 \longrightarrow 3 \longrightarrow 4 \longrightarrow 5 \longrightarrow R$$

Hierarchical 'chains of command' are essentially of this nature, although they may not have been constructed solely to meet this problem of communication. They may have advantage of allowing suitable translation from one 'private language' to another but they are also likely to involve distortion: the first world war joke of the message being passed along the trenches from the young captain

351

(C) to headquarters (R) illustrates this. C asked, 'Send me re-inforcements, I'm going to advance', but R heard eventually 'Lend me three and fourpence, I'm going to a dance'.

Differing ability to encode and decode messages also has its consequences for the development of specialist translating and interpreting functions, which applies at both ends of the 'chain'. In management, for example, it is well established that some function-ally specialist roles are created to develop the organization's com-munications ability and effectiveness (cf Renold 1950 for one example of this kind of response). This often places message con-struction in the hands of 'staff' specialists, and yet leaves message transmission in the hands of the 'line' managers and supervisors. As Dalton's study of line and staff managers shows clearly, very real problems of 'communication' can develop between them which serve further to distort the messages which are transmitted (Dalton, 1959).

On the shop floor, the creation of formal positions of this kind may not be in evidence, but it is possible to interpret the findings of Katz and Lazarsfeld and some of the related small group studies in industrial organizations are revealing an informal 'staff' function surrounding the positions of the 'influentials' who mediate and monitor messages and meanings for their 'small groups'. These individuals are not necessarily and not always those who hold formal 'representative' roles within the work force (Sayles, 1958). But quite often such representatives do carry out this function for their constituents, and with similar consequences for the communi-cation of 'meaning' as were noted by Dalton.

This has led some undertakings to take action to try to elevate the first line supervisors into the role of 'influential' in relation to their sections, but with varying success: one of the more recent general attempts to achieve this was made with productivity bar-gaining in the 1960s, where it was found necessary to extend the volume of communication about desired changes passing through the supervisors on a 'cascading' principle (cf Thomason, 1971, pp 13 and 44; Richbell, 1976, pp 13–19).

3 *The media* The would-be communicators and receivers may present and receive messages through a number of media, most of which are relevant to communications within formal organizations. They may be classified in three broad categories, those of oral, written and situational communications.

1 *Oral communication* The essence of this category is that a would-be communicator speaks to one or more other members of

352

the organization. The recognizable sub-categories are distinguished in the nature of the relationship established between the communicator and those to whom he speaks:

(i)   the direct face to face communication in which one individual speaks with another, thus allowing direct check by the communicator on the reception of the communication (eg by perception of the demeanour of the recipient or by return communication in the form of question or comment)

(ii) the direct communication in which one individual speaks with another, but via electro-mechanical means (eg a telephone) allowing some check by the communicator on the effectiveness of his message but through a narrower range of perceptions than is possible in the direct face to face communication

(iii) the direct communication with the communicator speaking with a small group of people, which has similar characteristics to the first subtype, although with the added possibility of other influential communications being admitted to the process—whether functional or dysfunctional from the standpoint of the communicator's intentions

(iv) the direct communication with the communicator speaking to a large group of people (whether face to face as in a lecture, or on a non-face-to-face basis using one of the mass media) in which reverse communication from the audience is so limited (usually) as to be negligible, and in which therefore the construction of the first message is much more significant in terms of effective communication than in the other categories.

2 *Written communication*   The essence of this category is that the message of the would-be communicator is committed to a visible and readable form (whether in words or symbols) and in this form acquires greater permanence and therefore offers a greater opportunity for reader check and interpretation. It would be possible to recognize sub-types on the same kind of dimensions as with oral communication, although this would probably result in a degree of artificiality; it is more useful to recognize subtypes on the basis of both the size of the readership and the intended degree of permanence associated with the communication.

(i)   the inter-personal communication, best exemplified by a letter or a memorandum from one person to a named other (or a few named others) which may serve the same intention as 1(i) or 1(ii) above, although without the same opportunity for communicator check on the efficiency of his communication (except by supplementary means) but with some greater opportunity to effect permanence in the communication

(ii)   a more impersonal paper flow to those individuals on a distribution list, ranging all the way from circulation of a relevant journal carrying general information of assumed relevance to those on the list, to a work card which might pass through a whole sequence of operations (and therefore operators) informing each person through whose hands it passes of the decision/action required of him at the time when it does so

(iii) records and reports (to be distinguished only on the grounds of whether what is written remains stationary or is transmitted to others) which exist or are made available for reference purposes and therefore severe as a 'memory' function for the organization, capable of stimulating decisions or actions of a remedial or rectifying type; for this reason, these tend to have longish term consequences as well as permanence simply because they are in written form

(iv) manuals, whether of 'practice' or 'policies', which serve mainly as sources of reference and are therefore designed to have long-term relevance and effects, supporting such other organizational processes as training or induction of personnel.

These forms of written communication tend to be generally more supportive of centralized decision-taking than the oral communications above and vary in their intended permanence of influence upon the action of others.

3 *Situational communication*   The essence of this kind of communication is its existence largely independently of oral and written communications (although these may act as supplements or complements to it), communication taking place through example or contagion as the potential recipient perceives a message in the general behaviour of others or in the 'situation' in which he finds himself. The subtypes recognizable here are related to the extent to which the recipient of a message feels it is to be identifiable with a person or to be impersonally situational.

(i) Communication by example is a process which has been noted frequently and is often referred to as 'behavioural contagion' or 'emulation' (Cartwright, 1965, p 12). This underlies a good deal of reference group theory, in which a person is regarded as copying (a) 'significant other(s)' in forming his own behaviours.

Rose has summarized this concept as referring 'to the sources of values selected by an individual for the guidance of his behaviour, especially in cases where a choice has to be made. Reference

354

groups may be groups of which an individual is a member, but sometimes they may not. In all cases they provide direction for the behaviour of the individual concerned, and so constitute important sources of social control' (Rose, 1962, p 128). This meaning attached to the term is to be distinguished, as it is by Shibutani, from that other meaning which is sometimes attached to it, where it 'designates a group with which a person compares his fate' (or his wages!). For Shibutani, this is very different in import from the group 'whose presumed perspective is used by an actor as the frame of reference in the organization of his perceptual field' (Rose, 1962, pp 232–33).

(ii) Communication through experience which is essentially situational and non-verbal is also well recognized. In the language of people on the shop floor, 'the way they treat you', 'the pittance they pay you for sweating all week', 'the conditions they expect us to work in', are expressions which, by the attribution of causality to an unidentifiable 'they' (cf Hoggart, 1958, p 53) often serves to indicate the operation of these communications processes deriving simply from the situation. Important examples of these situational variables are the general expectations which exist as to standards of effort, contribution or performance, the appropriate levels and structures of reward, and the physical, social and psychological conditions within which people shall work. Often these are not expressed in any simple and coherent form, but, as was argued above (pp 274–92) they are vital perceptions in the context of motivation.

The role of the group
This, as well as the finding about the existence of 'influentials' in the Katz and Lazarsfeld study (above, pp 349–51), emphasizes the role of the 'group' in the communication process. The process of inference from the situation is not something which merely happens, as it were automatically. Giving definition to the reality is usually one of the purposes which the group serves for the individual member. It is not, therefore, simply that groups exist which complicates the communication process, but rather that the group performs certain functions in the course of which communication is effected.

This 'function' is but one of three main ones which are usually identified, covering, in turn, the areas of action, cognition and affect. Groups, generally, are thought:
(a) to have some kind of instrumental value for the individual, to satisfy some need which he perceives himself as having and

355

which he perceives identification with the group to be capable of helping him reduce

(b) to help the individual to assign meanings to things which do not have obvious meanings, and thus to help him to interpret various elements (like messages) in his environment in ways which may be special or peculiar to that group

(c) to support the individual socially and psychologically in conditions in which he might otherwise feel exposed and powerless, at the mercy of the cross-currents of life which bear upon him.

They enable the individual to achieve ends not otherwise open to him, they help him to make sense of the world about him, and they give him emotional support.

All of these are 'useful' to the individual, even if not absolutely necessary, and their utility, in this sense, is what renders it likely that the individual will 'conform' behaviourally, cognitively and affectively. It is hypothesized that the more useful the individual sees the particular group to be, the more he will conform on these dimensions. In respect of communication, therefore, the more 'useful' or important the group to the individual, the more likely that he will rely upon the group's (influential's) interpretations.

This, in turn, provides some measure of the imperviousness of the individual to influence by communication from 'outside' the group context. The greater the strength of the group attachment, the greater the power of the group to compel conformity to its ideas, values and actions, and the more cushioned will be the individual member from the direct influence of externally-originating messages. In this sense, therefore, the group is an important factor in communication.

In the context of work, many such groups exist. The extent to which they claim loyalty in the above sense will, however, vary tremendously.

On the one hand, there are the formal groups in the official organization. These are groups under different charge-hands or supervisors, on different shifts, in different rooms or sections or buildings and groups associated with different plant or materials. All such distinctions provide a basis for separate group identification. Each will then exist within a boundary which will serve to refract communication from outside. Just because they are 'officially-established' does not mean that the 'group-effect' on communication is absent when the communications are themselves 'official'.

356

On the other, there are many informal, free or voluntary groups which depart from the pattern of the official organization, even if 'proximity' is often a factor in their formation. An example of such variations in pattern is to be found in the bank wiring observation room in the Western Electric studies (Roethlisberger and Dickson, 1939). Some of these are to be found in Dalton's Milo study, differentiating the formally-educated from the experienced managers, and those who came up the hard way from those who walked in with a formal qualification well-documented (Dalton, 1959). Others are associated with different external experiences, such as a common area, town or country of origin in the case of mobile workers or common participation in leisure time activities (Lupton, 1963).

In addition, most work situations reveal other formal groups which have been established in opposition to or in competition with the formal organization. The main examples are the trade unions and the professional associations, which perform similar functions to those listed above, but which attempt to mobilize commitment and power by the use of more formal organizational means than usually applies at the level of the free, voluntary group of the informal kind.

A work situation may therefore be regarded as composed of a hierarchy of 'groups' which function as sources of alternative, competitive, or conflicting meanings, to those which may be intended in the 'official' communication processes and structure. Wherever people perceive a basis for 'difference' in self-identification, there may lie a foundation for group affiliation and loyalty. According to the importance of such affiliations, the resistance to, or distortion of, intended meaning may prove to be greater or lesser in the individual case. Facing such a situation, managements may have to work hard at establishing both structures and processes of communication through which intended meanings might be conveyed effectively (that is, in a manner which results in influence upon thinking, feeling or behaving). (See also below pp 511–13).

Overcoming barriers to communication

In the act of communication, this problem is commonly conceived as one of getting over the 'barriers' which are seen to exist at the level of the individual person, at the level of the technical processes of encoding and decoding, and at the level of the message form and content itself.

In the first category, the barriers natural to the persons are seen as linked to the existence of different 'frames of reference', themselves products of social experience. The individual's unique experiences will have influenced what he has learned about the meanings which might be associated with the surrounding reality and about the processes of coding and decoding. Since no two persons' experiences are exactly similar, two persons communicating can expect meaning to be expressed and perceived in more or less different ways according to the degree of variation between those experiences. Gibson *et al* develop this notion into two other linked concepts, of selective listening and value judgement: the first of these seems to be more usefully associated with cognitive processes in the sense that it involves an essentially cognitive response, whilst the second entails the assignment of worth to a message on the basis of the individual's pre-established preferences. Although these are treated by Gibson *et al* as three separately distinguishable barriers, they seem to 'belong together' as being three related conceptions of the individual's natural apparatus for communicating to or receiving meanings from his environment.

Secondly, the way in which each individual perceives and evaluates the other as communicator/recipient may be seen to serve as a potential influence upon the efficiency of the communication, in so far as it will affect both what is included in the message by the sender and what is abstracted from the message by the recipient. One side of this coin is represented by 'source credibility'— '. . . the trust, confidence, and faith the receiver has in the words and actions of the communicator'—and the other by 'filtering' in which the perception of the other is allowed to produce deliberately biased messages. The bias may be motivated by a perception of 'what is good for the recipient' because of a view taken of that recipient, or of 'what is good for the communicator' given the related perception of what the recipient might do if he received a 'complete' message. These may then be related to the concept of *social distance* as an influencing factor upon messages, this usually taking the form of authority or status difference within industrial organizations.

Thirdly, these differences link closely with the technical question of the form of the message transmitted or received. Messages may be transmitted in the form of symbols of many different types, words, numbers, facial expressions and gestures, displayed behaviour etc. Since any of these may be 'captured' by groups or subcultures and made their own, with their own special meanings, communications effected through any of these forms may be subjected to distortion because of this. At the 'individual' level, this form of barrier is usually thought of in terms of *semantic* problems (the way in which I express meaning in words may not be the way in which you find that meaning in such words), but this usually carries forward to embrace group and subcultural differences in use of language, so that a member of one subcultural group will be using his in-group language to convey to another in a different subcultural group a meaning different from that intended.

Finally, we may associate some problems with the operation of the communication system itself. Although these problems are within the control of the people concerned, there is a sense in which the problems are often seen to escape from this control. The main examples are the limitations of time in communication, which prevent the use of 'redundancy' (repetition in varied forms) as a means of conveying meaning more effectively, and the overloading of the communications process to the extent that adequate attention to communication or reception cannot be given. Both of these have opposites which may also be associated with communications problems: a plethora of time for communication is likely to lead to inefficient 'cycling' as the same messages go round and round with no added development of meaning, and an underloading of the channels is likely to result in atrophy and a suspicion (at least) that selective bias is being practised by the communicators.

Thus getting the balance right on all these dimensions is no simple task. Two nodes (linked by a channel designed to carry a specific kind of message) may be equal and opposite (or balanced with each other) so that the one is capable of conveying a meaning which is equally intelligible to the other, and the other is capable of receiving and interpreting it in the form in which it was intended by the one. The circumstances under which this kind of balance might be achieved in the context of inter-personal communication are likely to be few and far between, because node-capacities are likely to vary with all manner of factors like age, experience, education, class etc. In any one particular type of communication factors like differential status or authority distribution are also likely to produce an imbalance. In any purposive communication (ie one designed to influence in some way) it could be said that the fact that one person was the initiator and the other the intended recipient of the communication, might itself set up an element of imbalance because of the implicit dependency thereby introduced into the relationship (cf Kelley, 1951; Thibaut, 1950; Cartwright and Zander, 1953, pt IV).

In work organization there are two types of such 'dependency', one created by the flow of work through specialist jobs or 'stations', and the other by the structure of superordination-subordination developed for purposes of achieving co-ordination amongst such specialist activities. Given that specialization is unlikely to be eliminated, the twin needs of work-flow and co-ordination will remain, and might indeed be treated as 'permanent' features of the work system. It is this 'permanency' linked by some writers with the notions of domination and 'hegemony' (Clegg, 1976; Hyman, 1975) which may be associated with the communications problems usually identified. In the Kelley experiment, for example, the creation of 'permanently low status' and 'uncertain high status' positions in the 'game' used for the exercise appear to have been the main factors influencing the nature of the communications (ie influencing the choice of verbally or behaviourally-critical responses) and the directions which they took (Kelley, 1951). If this allows the conclusion that permanent dependency, or insecure independency must distort communications, and if these are necessary conditions of work organization, then the 'problem' of communications remains to be tackled in terms of both status and security.

Official messages in formal channels

All of these factors may be expected to affect those official communications which are transmitted through official channels in undertakings. Although, at this more formal level it might appear that the communications processes and problems are somehow different, they are nevertheless dependent upon human beings conveying and interpreting meaning. Whatever problems may be identified in the one framework are therefore likely to apply in the other.

The identification of the subject matter as 'official messages' does not by itself alter the basic nature of what is communicated. This other concept merely highlights the particular foundation of rationality from which the 'officiality' of the information stems, and the inference that messages are somehow not 'subjective' because they are derived from the undertaking's purposes.

Purposive organizations (as we noted in chapter 1) are seen to have an overriding purpose of converting something (whether raw materials or human skills) into something (whether products or services). Communication is then seen as the nervous system, through which those bits of information which are necessary to the coordination of activities behind the purpose are transmitted to the points in the system where they are needed. Like the human nervous system, therefore, the organization establishes fixed channels along which such information may flow, from one node or role to another.

The information which needs to flow along these channels to assist system operation is essentially of two broad types.

The one is composed of that information which is directly related to the tasks or the task objectives of the undertaking. Management (by virtue of its role) has a special interest in ensuring that this kind of official information flows efficiently, as only if it does so are its objectives likely to be realized. It does not follow that the *only* interest which the official flow serves is that of the undertaking as a whole; management, like any other category of people, has its own interests to serve as official messages may often respond to these as well as the task objectives. Nor does it follow that management is necessarily very efficient at establishing the information content of task-related messages or constructing the kinds of messages which will ensure their effective communication. Indeed, a considerable consultancy industry has grown up to sell managements improved approaches and methods of communicating this kind of information.

The second type of information is that which is related to the goals and interests of the people engaged in the tasks. In some perspectives, the information (eg about the consideration offered or the treatment afforded) is not seen as directly relevant to the realization of the task objectives. In others, however, it is regarded as just as relevant and vital, even though it may be related to the 'other side' of the wage-effort bargain. In either case, however, it is not to be avoided; it will flow whether management wills it or not and without an adequate acknowledgement of its inevitability might well swamp the communications channels or introduce so much 'noise' into the communication process, as to render effective communication on any topic impossible.

The recognition of these two categories of information may be regarded as a first step in developing an adequate perspective of what information ought to be communicated through what channels for what purpose. Recent legislation on disclosure of information (discussed on pp 446–52 below) has, for example, emphasized the desirability of communicating both types of information, but has associated it with the channels which have developed to carry information on 'consideration' rather than 'task' (that is the bargaining channels). The question of how task information should be communicated is left to managements themselves to answer, and by and large the answer is sought through improving communications within the 'chain of command' (for example, through briefing groups, quality circles, MBO and the rest).

The implication of making the distinction is that distinct channels might be necessary or appropriate to the different categories.

It may be that as Jaques has suggested that communication is concerned with the totality of 'feelings, attitudes and wishes' which have to be transmitted (consciously or unconsciously) through the organization's communication networks (Jaques, 1951, p 301). But as he goes on to suggest there may be a need in complex work organizations to establish distinct channels or networks to allow all of these to take place on a segmented basis. In his view, the aim should be to create

1 *A known and comprehensive communications structure.* In Glacier this was attempted in the establishment of what came to be distinguished as 'the executive, the consultative and the appeals channels' which were specified in the Company policy statement which represented an outcome of the long discussions in the Company undertaken with Jaques' assistance
2 *A code governing the relations* between people occupying various positions: in Glacier, this was attempted in the Company policy statement, the factory standing order on policy governing executive behaviour and by the largely unrecorded (informal) customs and procedures
3 *A quality of relationship* between people immediately connected with each other, such that 'adaptive segregation may be mutually agreed, and stresses worked at so that rigid segmentation becomes unnecessary'. In Glacier, the various discussions which were held with the various groups were either designed to produce this result or functioned to this end (Jaques, 1951, p 305).

But this aim may only be realized if there is a mechanism or machinery which facilitates its achievement. Such a mechanism will probably require the establishment of separate channels, as well as a 'code' which will govern the use made of them. Because of the way in which existing channels have developed, they are frequently seen as diametrically opposed as between negotiating and consultative channels, rather than as complementary to one another in enabling a segmentation of necessary communications. In consequence (using Jaques's distinction) communication tends to be segmented (non-complementary) not segregated (complementary although distinct).

Official channels
Historically, the undertaking's formal organization of managerial and worker roles was considered to be all that was necessary to carry the communications necessary. In Simon's terminology, these channels were designed to ensure that 'decisional premises'

considered necessary to the realization of task objectives would be 'transmitted from one member of the organization to another', mainly, of course, from management to workers (Simon, 1953, p 154).

They are usually depicted on the 'organization chart' of the undertaking, and commonly emphasize communication in the vertical dimension, ie instructions pass down and performance data pass up. Behind such charts lies the assumption that any and all necessary communications can and would be handled through the 'chains of command' which form their essential feature. Situationally, they belong to an era in which the degree of specialization (associated for example, with the growth of line and staff organization) was much less than typically it is at the present time. Line managers had generalist roles and were assumed to be able to handle all communications (*see* also below, pp 403–14). But now, doubt has been cast upon whether these channels really function in this way (cf Burns and Stalker, 1961).

In principle, this same chart aims to depict the horizontal channels and the nodes which feature in this other dimension. In this case, the channels are largely dictated not by personal authority considerations but by those of workflow. As a raw material is converted, it moves in a certain sequence and, as it does so, it passes through work stations which function also as nodes, and the work requirement at each needs to be stipulated. In its simplest form, the communications procedure here focuses upon something like the job card which moves with the work (or the patient's record in a hospital where the 'workers' visit the patient in one place). This seeks to ensure that the individual knows what has gone before, what is required of him and what action needs to be taken subsequently. The 'co-ordination' of this activity at a supervisory or managerial level also sets up a requirement of horizontal communication, and this is provided for (in channels) by the horizontial lines of the chart. The main distinction between the vertical and horizontal channels is that between the channels of authority in the usual managerial sense and those of work initiation in a work flow sense (see Klein, 1964).

In principle, these two sets of channels ought to be sufficient to carry all the communications necessary in the system. In practice, this is just not so. The view that communications occur in a simplistic fashion in the vertical and horizontal dimensions has been challenged by detailed studies of communications in managerial organization, such as those of Burns (1960) and Dalton (1959). Although these studies contain more ramified conclusions than these they respectively challenge, on grounds of the influence of authority difference and varied task demands, the traditional filter-amplifier conception of the node in the vertical channels and the simple mechanical conception of communication in the workflow channels between line managers and line and staff positions. Essentially, these conclusions are to the effect that communications do not (for whatever reason) conform to the pictorial image presented in the organization or work-flow charts.

The 'reasons' usually advanced are those which have already been identified as creating the barriers to inter-personal (and therefore intra-organizational) communication. The effect of these upon official communications is not, however, always recognized, largely because the management would like to cling to the unitary conception of organization and to the belief that all members of that organization are primarily or ultimately concerned with the pursuit of a single known and acceptable end. To act on such a belief is to endeavour to set up a number of separate channels of communication, all of them made 'official', in order to reach as many 'influentials' within these many groups as possible. This has been one of the traditional objects of 'joint consultation' in British industry and, from this point of view, it can therefore be regarded as an attempt to introduce multiple formal channelling of communications to supplement the formal hierarchial organization.

The intention in establishing 'better human relations' in work undertakings, by developing the relations between supervision and the informal 'group' structure of the workplace, was often similar to this. By 'bringing the informal into the formal' framework, yet another channel of communication was opened up. The development of effective communications through redundancy (in its technical communications sense) in communicating, appeared to be enhanced. Thus, in both these cases, one of the effects, intended or not, was to create alternative channels of communication which might, at least theoretically, supplement the formal and official channels of the organization chart.

The alternative channels
The theoretical possibilities thus opened up may not have been translated into actual achievements, at least in the majority of cases. The verdict on joint consultation, for example, is usually pretty damning (cf Guest and Fatchett, 1974, pp 33–6) and the contribution of the 'group' to communication efficiency is at least problematic (cf Batstone *et al*, 1977). What has achieved salience in the structure of the work situation is the set of channels which are usually subsumed under the title of collective bargaining but which are concerned with more than mere wage bargaining and include

channels for communicating dissatisfactions, complaints and down-right disputes (cf Donovan Commission Report, 1968; ACAS Code of Industrial Relations Practice; and below, chapters 17 and 18).

Whatever else might be said about these developments, they do establish alternative channels of communication which may be used by management either reactively (simply responding to initiatives taken by the trade union representatives) or pro-actively (regarding them, as in connection with a good deal of the 'produc tivity bargaining' activity of the 1960s, as two-way channels, cf North and Buckingham, 1969; Cliff, 1970). Under the influence of the various proposals for an extension of industrial democracy (cf Bullock Committee Report, 1977) a view emerges of these alternative channels as potentially available to consider (at least some) 'task' issues associated with, say, new products and new technologies. Nevertheless, the dominant perspective of them, supported by the recommendations of the existing Code of Industrial Relations Practice, is one which emphasizes their segmentation from such concerns and towards 'consideration' issues.

The development of collective bargaining appears also to have had two other adverse consequences for communications within organizations. First, it led many managements to treat joint consultation as a more amenable channel than that of collective bargaining, but one which was nevertheless concerned with similar issues, ie ones concerned primarily with consideration and treatment and hence the concentration on welfare and amenities. Secondly, it at least allowed, if it did not require, the by-passing of the official channels of communication on many issues, including those related to work allocation, and thus led to a deterioration in the power base of the supervisor (see above pp 315–18).

As a consequence, the one source of information relevant to immediate tasks and task-objectives was increasingly denied access to the main channels of communication, and the alternative channels of consultation were increasingly devoted to communications about consideration.

In this situation, therefore, it became necessary to re-invent channels of direct communication (under headings of MbO, quality circles, briefing groups, and the like) and to re-discover the necessity for talking to workers about their work (with, it seems, the help of Japanese managements operating in the UK).

Nevertheless, it cannot be inferred from this that managements have any real option in developing direct communication with workers about work to the exclusion of representatives from the channels concerned with consideration. The first inference to be drawn about practice is probably that (a) formal channels concerned with both task accomplishment and consideration for people are desirable for many reasons, but including the reason that they offer opportunity to communicate effectively, and (b) these channels need to be developed at both the macro- (undertaking) and micro- (working group) levels.

The important ideological or value premise behind this, however, is that communications policies and practices must acknowledge the realities of power in the present-day situation. Undertakings will increasingly be led to divert their communications strategies away from the rather paternalistic and interpersonal approach so much in evidence in the past and towards an engagement of the realities of differing values, differing objectives, different reference groups and different power/authority bases, and the consequential necessity for effective communications to be associated with (if not founded upon) a process of power bargaining rather than some effete form of consultation. This is the predictable direction of the solution to communications (and motivational) problems in the future and, if that solution is not yet much in evidence, the faltering steps taken since the late 1960s tend this way.

Principles governing channel construction

In spite of the criticisms which have usually emerged from experience with joint consultation and joint negotiation, there have been some successful ventures from which some lessons can be learned. Amongst these are the experiments in the Glacier Metal Company (reported chiefly by Jaques (1951) with joint consultation, and those in BP (cf Thomason, 1971; Richbell, 1976) and GKN-Shotton (GKN-Shotton, 1973) with joint negotiation. Because they cover both kinds of alternative channel (consultation and negotiation) the principles which their success appears to throw up may serve to indicate something of the way forward in establishing multiple channels. The broad principles may be stated as:

First, they acknowledge the fact of trade union existence and trade union attitudes, and seek deliberately to resolve the non-unionist issue either, as in the Glacier experiment by restricting representatives to trade union members or, as in the GKN-Shotton experiment by founding the whole exercise on the trade union representational and negotiating machinery (Jaques, 1951; GKN-Shotton, 1973).

Secondly, they define the subjects with some precision and make them matters for decision by the consultative bodies rather than simply for discussion. They do this by codifying the defini-

366

tive policy and the conditional policy decisions required, allocating the latter to the consultative machinery for decision (albeit with a proviso that decisions must be unanimous in order to prevent inconsistency in the two sets of decisions), or by defining in advance certain areas of bilateral interest which may range from trade union bargaining subjects of a traditional sort through safety, welfare and discipline to forward manpower planning (Thomason, 1971).

These two features help to avoid the complication of discussion by introducing resentments and rivalries which increase the noise and the resistance in communications, and the usually almost insuperable difficulty of making the subject matter sufficiently real for people to want to discuss them and communicate them further amongst their constituents. Although they could be justified on these grounds alone, an additional rationale for their introduction asserts that it is desirable, even necessary for management to give away its traditional prerogatives to control in these areas in order to assure greater order in the work situation (see Thomason, 1971).

In greater particular, what emerge as design principles for any such joint exercise—which we will refer to as 'joint consultation' for present purposes (but see below, pp 455–81)—are that in each case

1 an attempt is made to identify the *subject areas* for discussion in joint consultation, and these are then introduced as matters which the participants have a moral right to discuss
2 An attempt is made to make these subjects issues on which the committee must *decide*, even if this has to be done within what is a normal pattern of constraint on any decision, and in some cases there is an implicit or explicit *status quo* provision in the absence of such decisions in these committees
3 an attempt is made to ensure that decision-taking processes are informed, either by the presentation of information by management and (usually and perhaps more importantly) by the development of a working party structure by which matters for decision are worked through in more detail than a single committee meeting can normally aspire to
4 each situation acknowledges the actual distribution of loyalties amongst the people concerned: where the trade unions are well entrenched in the workplace, representatives must be trade unionists thus avoiding the tensions of trade unionists being required to sit alongside non-unionists from the same occupational category; also, foremen and middle managers are not left out or ignored
5 in each case, communications are seen to require a ramified

structure of representation which is not satisfied by the creation of a single committee: in the more extreme forms of communications structuring a deliberate attempt may be made to take the communications processes through to the far ends of the organization

6 in all cases, representatives are given some form of executive role—they have something to do, which is more than merely sitting and listening and talking—and the danger of producing a talking shop in the joint consultative committee is at least recognized in the structures established

7 finally, it might also be inferred that, whatever may be the attitude of individual managers towards joint consultative arrangements, in these examples the creation of rights and the redistribution of authority places the manager in the position where he must participate in order to carry out his role successfully.

These might well have more validity than the rather half-hearted suggestions of the ACAS Code of Practice, which recognizes that what is attempted in the way of multi-channelling will probably reflect the attitudes of managements towards trade unions and the strength of the trade unions themselves in the local situation. Whilst these are of relevance, they are perhaps less likely to effect improvements in communications or in performance through better communication, than the ones advanced above.

Nevertheless, they are unlikely by themselves to solve the fundamental communications problems. This, it might be suggested, on the evidence, is unlikely to be achieved unless (at the same time) action is taken to structure the role of the first line supervisor more adequately than the rather haphazard developments in the consultation/negotiation sphere in recent years have permitted. This aspect we return to below, pp 475–81 and 515–16.

But if that provides a more adequate base for the exercise of influence by giving the supervisor access to channels, it will demand in addition a willingness and an ability to communicate appropriate information on his or her part. The willingness might be expected to be affected by the way in which the role itself is structured within the overall organization. The ability may be increased by coaching or training aimed at increasing understanding of the communication process and skill in the actual construction (coding) and transmission of messages. Both motivation and ability, forming part of the power base, call for development along with the structural changes, if only to increase 'source credibility (p 358 above).

Communication and the personnel manager

Similar considerations arise in association with the tasks and task objectives of the personnel manager. He or she, like any other person in a managerial or supervisory position, is called upon to operate with a sub-set of immediate superordinates, peers and subordinates, and communications are most immediately directed towards them. What may be said about the generalized role of the supervisor can apply to this particular example. The personnel manager will communicate effectively only if he or she has an adequate (and adequately-defined) base which gives access to communications channels, a motivation to communicate the information required to influence others to act in ways appropriate to the realization of objectives, and an ability to structure the messages in terms of both their logic and their rhetoric which will assure the transfer of meaning.

The requirement is not different in principle when the focus is upon the advisory role. The major distinction between line executive and staff advisory roles in respect of communication is recognizable only if the one is seen to operate on the basis of 'instruction' and the other on the basis of suggestion and persuasion (*see above*, pp 295–98). In the realities of work organization, however, this distinction is usually blurred, as indeed, the above quotation from Simon suggests. The problem of communication is therefore not one of whether the individual is licensed by the role to instruct or to persuade, but whether, as was concluded above, he or she has an adequate base, motivation and ability. This conclusion may therefore be applied both to the personnel manager's role itself, and to the setting up of the objective which he or she works to in improving communications within the undertaking as a whole.

Further reading

On the process of communication, see Shannon and Weaver (1949), Gibson, Ivancevich and Donnelly (1976) and Simon (1953).

On the related subject of influence (purposive communication) see Cartwright, in March (1965) and Legge (1978).

On the structural aspects of communication in organizations see Jaques (1951), Brown (1961), Thomason (1971) and the Report of the Bullock Committee (1977).

Books with a more 'practical' orientation are Pigors (1949) and Irvine (1970).

15   Training and development

The changing situation

More emphasis has been placed upon training and development in industry and commerce in the past two decades than appears to have been the case previously. In seeking an explanation of this, one might attach significance to the Industrial Training Act of 1964 and the subsequent Employment and Training Act of 1973. Whilst these stimulated both discussion and provision of training, they were probably not the 'causes' of the changed emphasis so much as its instruments.

The 'causes' may lie more in the changing nature of both modern employment and workers' expectations of what it should provide. Changes in technology and production policies make work skills more 'industry-specific' and less likely to be developed externally to the work situation. Changes in human expectations may emphasize work as the source of development of the worker's capacity as well as of other satisfactions (cf Dubin, 1956; Orzack, 1959; Goldthorpe *et al*, 1968). Taken together, these appear to create a pressure towards more 'training by undertakings' and further than that, towards more 'domestication' of the actual training processes (that is, ignoring external sources). *Some* provision for training is therefore likely to be needed in all undertakings of any size, if only because reliance upon natural learning processes is unlikely to yield the levels of performance sought by management.

All of these different factors are therefore likely to influence the undertaking to develop more and more training of a formal kind in place of a reliance upon 'experience'. In the changing circumstances, it is, on the one hand, 'good business' to train and develop the workforce, and on the other, ethically supportable to do so to satisfy the expectations of the employees as to what a good employer should provide. (See also above pp 173–80).

Internal needs

It may prove difficult to arrive at a consensus strategy for training

370

for two reasons which are associated with the different circumstances of the various work undertakings in different sectors and industries.

First, training is not always the best or most reasonable means to adopt to solve local undertaking-level problems, since changes of structure, organization and policy might well effect more progress faster and training may then be consequential upon these changes taking place, a view taken by the Donovan Commission, for example.

Secondly, such demand as there may be locally for training (or for trained workers) may manifest itself in quite different ways, particularly as between the (often-small) undertaking which seeks qualified labour from the local labour market and the (usually larger and often technologically advanced) undertaking which as a matter of policy seeks green labour which will then be offered opportunities for training and development domestically (cf Robinson, in Cuthbert and Hawkins, 1973, pp 158–72).

In some undertakings, therefore, a specifically 'training' strategy might well have a low priority, whilst in others it is central to the whole approach to manpower planning and manning.

What the two relevant Acts have accomplished is a more systematic appraisal of the need for training and its place in the undertaking's approach to securing and retaining an adequately trained labour force. The conclusions from these diagnoses have not, however, necessarily supported the belief that more training must necessarily be a good thing for the undertaking. What it has done is highlight the need to establish:

(a) whether the behaviour (whether skilled work or negotiation, for example) is sufficiently well understood to enable its inherent rationality to be articulated for training purposes
(b) whether that rationality can be presented in an acceptable fashion within a training programme, either on or off the job, with some reasonable expectation that to do so will effect behavioural change
(c) whether the cost of doing so, either internally or externally, is justified or likely to be justified by the returns which might be expected to accrue from the changed behaviour.

The answers to these questions are likely to be found only if a systematic approach is made to understand and provide for the needs of the situation.

The diagnostic model

This idea of 'system' is incorporated in what is now taken as the standard definition of training:

> Training is the systematic development of the attitude/ knowledge/skill/behaviour pattern required by an individual in order to perform adequately a given task or job. This is often integrated or associated with further education. The use of learning experience to integrate the concept of training and education is increasingly common (Dept of Employment, 1971).

Consequently, training as a process is seen to rest upon the application of a 'system' model.

In fact, this model is used in two related ways. The differences in its conceptualization by different authors are usually traceable to whether they use the model as a diagnostic device (to determine *whether* training is relevant) or confine themselves to its use as a guide to the structuring of training operations themselves (that is, *assuming* training is relevant).

Thus, Kenney, Donnelly and Reid include as the first element in their model, that of 'identifying what training is needed' (1979, p 8) and Donaldson and Scannel make their first design step 'diagnosing problems to define the role of training' (1978, pp 13–23). Other authors have made a similar point (cf Singer, 1977, p 13).

In order to identify what the problems are and *whether* training might help to reduce them, it is necessary to find answers to a number of diagnostic questions:

1 What is the current level or kind of performance in the area in contention? How does this compare with the level or kind desired? What are the differences to be observed between these? Can they be described?
2 What changes are desirable? Can they be identified? Can they be described? Are they changes in structure, policy, procedure, practice or 'behaviour' on someone's part?
3 Are the desired changes ones which might be prepared for by training? Are they ones which might require training to effect them? Are they ones which might call for training *after* they have been decided upon? Is there a place for training in the change process?

Only if the outcome of the sequence of questioning is positive can a place be found for training. For these authors it cannot be taken as axiomatic that training has a role to perform.

But they, and those who do not build such diagnoses into their

372

formal models of 'training itself', then proceed (usually) to present a closed loop model of the training activity. This embraces the sequential processes of planning, implementing and evaluation (Kenney, Donnelly and Reid, 1979, p 8) in some form. The 'most systematic' presentation of these processes, which is followed by a number of other authors, is that offered by Eckstrand, who explicitly modifies the approach adopted in the development of a weapon system for his purpose (Eckstrand, 1964, pp 1–2).

The behaviour … men must exhibit on the job becomes the objective which must be achieved by the training system. The job of the training designer, then, is to select and sequence a series of learning experiences which will produce the desired behaviour. A testing evaluation phase is required to assure that the training program designed succeeds in producing men capable of performing as specified (Eckstrand, 1964, p 2).

Eckstrand presents seven steps in his model as follows:

1 Define training objectives.
2 Develop criterion measures for evaluating training.
3 Derive training content.
4 Design methods and training materials.
5 Integrate training program and trainees.
6 Compare graduates to criteria standards set up in step 2.
7 Modify steps 3 and 4 based on the results of step 6.

(The full diagrammatic representation of the approach applied to training is shown in figure 13 on p 274).

What, then, is meant by a 'systematic approach to training' is the analysis of the situation and the definition of the training aims and methods by following along the path indicated by this sequence of steps.

The assessment of training needs

This general system model is applied in the first instance to establish whether there are training needs (ie whether there are needs in the situation which training might conceivably reduce) and if so what they are. This is much easier to accomplish where the behaviour in question is one which has an accepted definition rooted in some conception of rationality, eg in a long-established and familiar routine job.

Consequently, where a 'job' exists and has been given definition in the form of a job description of the type referred to above (pp 187–95), it is possible to derive a conception of what is desirable

373

Figure 13
A systems approach to training

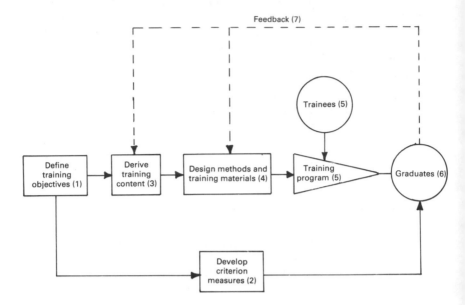

Feedback (7)

Define training objectives (1) → Derive training content (3) → Design methods and training materials (4) → Training program (5) → Graduates (6)

Trainees (5)

Develop criterion measures (2)

Source: GA Eckstrand, *Current Status of the Technology of Training* (AMRL Document Technical Report 64–86, September, 1964, p 3) *see also*: Stammers R and Patrick J, *The Pyschology of Training* (Methuen, 1975), p 19; Blum M L and Naylor J C, *Industrial Psychology: Its Theoretical and Social Foundations* (Harper and Row, 1965), p 253.

in the way of performance or behaviour. In the making of a training needs analysis it is then possible to:

> determine the gap between the present results of the way people learn their jobs, and the desirable results if the learning process were to be improved. [The training needs analysis] will indicate ... the type of training which is most appropriate for a specific operation, and whether systematized training can make an economic contribution towards the solution of an operating or production problem (Singer and Ramsden, 1969, p 16).

Where, however, this has not been done, it will be necessary to assemble information on the kinds of activities and tasks which people are required to carry out, the existing performance levels of those engaged in them, the length and cost of training under existing arrangements, and the difficulties which the present performers (or those who supervise them) experience in the course of learning the tasks and associated skills (Singer and Ramsden, 1969, pp 18–26).

This information will need to be collated *and* related to practice in other areas such as recruitment, production scheduling and control and manpower planning. As these authors point out, however, the object of this exercise is not to carry out an investigation of need for the sheer hell of it, but to provide a foundation for effecting improvements in training (*ibid*, p 18). The methods of job and skills analysis, already considered (above, pp 192–98) are usually applied to provide the necessary data to support these decisions.

On this basis, it is possible to establish 'the training need' by ascertaining whether a gap between the expected and the actual exists. If there is one, and if training is considered to be the means by which it is most effectively and economically reduced, then the 'training need' is determined.

Needs in diffuse activities
The problem is, however, more difficult to resolve where the work (or behaviour) is more diffuse, less structured and less easy to associate with measured standards of performance. Much managerial and professional white collar work falls into this category, but there are also examples of it on the shop floor. It is characterized by the probability that whilst many individual *tasks* may be amenable to measurement (in ways similar to those used in the previously-considered jobs) the *jobs* are composited from a variety of such tasks in variable combinations. Performance has as much to do with their 'proper' combination as with the efficient performance of any one of them. In a word, they are less standardized and therefore less amenable to simple measurement.

Under the influence of legislation and the Industrial Training Boards (ITBs), the emphasis on management and supervisory training in recent years has lead many undertakings to take a more systematic look at training as a support for manpower planning and employee resourcing in this area. Other legislation, particularly the Health and Safety at Work Act, has imposed the need for employers to look carefully at manual worker training outside the ordinary focus of skill training, and at training for other workers (white collar and managerial) to enable them to deal adequately with the discharge of the employer's various new obligations to his employees.

This kind of development faces the analyst who attempts to establish training needs of personnel performing these kinds of jobs with the problem of establishing training needs on the basis of subjective judgements made by superordinates. A human judgement of performance on some criteria (cf list of performance characteristics in table 11 on pages 378–79) which may be highly individual to the assessor, is substituted for more 'objective' measurement. Although attempts have been made to objectify this exercise of judgement, the weight of evidence suggests that the whole exercise remains problematic (cf Rowe, 1964; Randell, 1974).

There is as a result a dearth of information on what tasks are required of the individual and what skills are called for in the performance of them. It is not uncommon to find that 'needs' are expressed in terms of a blend of personal characteristics (cf attitude, emotional stability, and dependability in table 11) and job requirements (cf position knowledge, delegation and planning). The latter may indicate some relevant requisite skills in the same fashion that skills may be associated with parts of standardized jobs, but the former scarcely do so. At best they raise the question of whether training can or should be used to change attitudes to the job.

There are ways in which judgements may be improved (cf Thomason, 1980, pp 125–79), and it would be wrong to dismiss these as worthless. But they are little used in connection with personal and performance appraisal, and the analyst's problem of establishing the 'gap' between expected and actual performance on any basis other than the subjective judgement of the superordinate remains.

The question of whether this can be 'centralized' at all is therefore a very real one. It may be necessary to rest the identification of training needs amongst subordinates (with diffuse activity patterns) upon the superordinate's subjective judgement, even if it does lead to the usual uncertainty amongst trainees as to 'why they were sent on the course' (cf Thurley and Wirdenius, 1973). That problem, at least, might be tackled by improving boss-subordinate communications and by greater emphasis on on-the-job coaching and counselling.

The sources of learning
The acquisition of new behaviours and attitudes by the individual is something which comes through learning. It is largely because this 'natural learning process' does not produce the results sought either systematically or rapidly enough, that formal training is substituted for it. By this means a complete sequence of reinforced experience can be presented both systematically and relatively quickly, so that the lessons or the morals to be learned can be taken up quite speedily.

376

However, because training is, in one very important sense, no more than an extension of 'normal' learning activity, it would be quite wrong and pointless to assume that all 'learning' can be replaced by 'training' in a formal sense. However much or however little formal training is provided, an individual will continue to learn from his experiences, the vast majority of which will not be provided by the 'training programme'.

It is easy, however, to play down what an individual learns by positive or negative emulation of others (*see* above, pp 354–55). An individual seeing a boss or a respected peer doing something which he (the individual) considers worth copying may well add that action to his repertoire. Conversely, some observed actions may lead him to reject them from his own armoury. Thus, even before any deliberate and formal device is introduced to stimulate learning, a good deal of learning may go on.

But beyond this, undertakings which require purposive interaction between people will often *structure* learning opportunities all the way across the spectrum from informal contacts to formal off the job training programmes as is shown in the company checklist given in table 12 on page 381. This was drawn up to guide managers and supervisors as to the opportunities which exist for fostering learning, and as usual it reflects a concern to be thought a good employer and a concern to be a good business.

What is indicated by this table may be generalized to suggest that there are three broad categories of source of learning opportunity:

(a) informal development inside or outside the undertaking, dependent on superordinate and peer help with learning, and which may be given a degree of formalization through plans of performance appraisal, MbO, supervised project assignments, counselling, temporary replacement in more senior position, job rotation, and recommended reading of industry's journals or appropriate journals.

(b) Formal development, mainly within the company, including various types of formal course of instruction, possibly involving senior management, training staff or outsiders with relevant material to present. It should be noted that supervisors or managers cannot be expected to know how to carry out new policies or practices (eg performance appraisal) or to understand the workings of new plant, without some formal instruction.

(c) External formal development, making use of courses at universities, technical colleges or industry training situations, on such

377

Table 11
Development activity guide

The purpose of this development activity guide is to assist supervision in the selection of activities to meet the needs of the individual as determined during the performance appraisal of management personnel

Performances characteristics	Development activities which may be recommended
1 Position knowledge	Coaching or counselling by supervision Special assignments in areas where knowledge is available Position rotation in areas where individual is weak Special courses in field of activity Technical societies Reading in fields related to work Field trips or plant tours
2 Analytical ability and judgement	Coaching or counselling by supervision Opportunity to use more analytical ability and judgement Special courses (problem solving) Special assignments requiring the use of analytical adaptability and judgement Case studies
3 Planning	Coaching or counselling by supervision Opportunity to do more planning Special courses on subject Special assignment—where planning is required Special conferences on subject (BIM, IPM, IWM etc)
4 Initiative and acceptance of responsibility	Opportunity to accept responsibility and use initiative Special assignments—requiring use of initiative with responsibility for performance Chairman of committees or member, in and outside the company Officer of various organizations Coaching or counselling by supervisors
5 Dependability	Opportunity to perform with guidance, coaching and counselling Special assignments—difficult jobs stimulating and challenging—that will cause individual to extend himself—jobs that are important
6 Creative thinking	Opportunity to exercise this ability—encouraged and promoted by supervisor to do so Special assignments—where creative thinking is required—problem solving and development of new technique etc Institutional—special courses in creative thinking or other courses which require creative thinking Conference leadership Conferences—BIM, IPM, IWM etc Professional societies

378

Table 11 continued

Performance characteristics	Development activities which may be recommended
7 Delegation of responsibility and authority	Special courses in management techniques Practice of principle by supervisor and upper echelons of management Encouragement by supervisor to delegate responsibilities and authority Courses—human relations (industrial psychology)—principles of supervision, conference leadership—oral communications Special assignments that require delegation of authority and responsibility
8 Personnel handling and leadership	On-the-job coaching and counselling, opportunity to perform in this type of activity Outside reading Special courses 　Human relations (industrial psychology) 　Job training techniques 　Coaching—counselling—interviewing 　Conference leadership 　Oral communications Outside activities Organizations Management clubs 　Conferences Technical and professional societies
9 Relationship with others	Coaching and counselling by supervision Special courses 　Oral communications 　Conference leadership 　Human relations (industiral psychology)
10 Attitude	Opportunity to make decisions that affect operations Coaching and counselling by supervision Supervisor—subordinate relationship Outside reading—selected Opportunity to participate in company-sponsored activities
11 Emotional stability	Coaching and counselling by supervision Special institutional course (industrial psychology) Special assignments requiring person to work under pressure and difficult situations
12 Health	Check-up with company doctor
13 Self expression	Communication courses Speeded reading Oral communications Written communications Conference leadership

subjects as management, public speaking, quick reading or processes within the particular industry. Membership of external organizations, likely to apply more particularly at senior levels, also comes into this category as a means of development.

These broad categories can be expanded into more specific instances of training, as is done in the tabulation (p 381) which is based upon inventories from a small number of industrial and commercial companies. Whilst this does not claim to exhaust all possibilities, it does demonstrate the manner in which the personnel department, as advisor and custodian, might compile its own local inventory for distribution to managers who, in their supervisory capacity, might be called upon to decide upon training opportunities for subordinates. It is unlikely that this by itself will remove the problem identified by Rowe on the follow-up of appraisal, but it may prove to be a necessary if not a sufficient condition for its reduction.

The attempt illustrated in the *Development Activity Guide* to link the areas of weakness identified in the review and appraisal process, with possible means of overcoming them, may be more apposite to the personnel department's role. The left hand column lists what often appear in MbO as key result areas. Although some of these can be criticized for lack of definition (in the same sense that lists of personal qualities associated with selection processes or merit ratings can be questioned), they figure prominently and it is worth attempting to associate them (as training objectives) with the possible means to their achievement.

The approach to training
The 'system' which underlies the development of a training programme (and in the application of which the trainer might well be more expert than the trainee) can, and sometimes does, make the training itself a 'trainer-centred' experience. The trainer, having convinced himself or herself what is 'right' or 'best', proceeds to deliver this, confident that the outcome of doing so must be 'success'. But training, it has to be remembered, is expedited learning, and learning depends upon the relationship of the learner to the experience, not upon the brilliance of the trainer. In the actual delivery of training, therefore, the approach of the trainer must be one which pays adequate attention to the trainees' motivations and their appreciations of the situations encountered, and to the maintenance and development of these by reinforcing activities.

The first aspect is concerned with the question of the indi-

	Performance appraisal	On the job training	Counselling by superior	Temporary replacement for superior	Job rotation	Reading
Informal develepment	Annual review of performance and development needs	Under the guidance of trained instructor	Periodic discussions of progress	During vacations, illnesses, and other absences. Experience is gained for future promotion	Exposure to different jobs in department in order to gain broad technical knowledge	Supervisory and management journals

	Basic supervisory course	Personnel practices	Advanced counselling	Salary administration	Visitation programme
	To give an understanding of the scope of the supervisor's job, supervisory responsibilities, and training in supervisory skills. Methods of instruction—conferences, films	Understanding of supervisor's role in personnel policies of company. Visits to personnel department for orientation	Development of skill in obtaining facts identifying the problem, reaching a satisfactory decision in personal and job problem situations through use of instruction and case method	Understanding company salary policies and procedures	Knowledge of other department functions

	Administrative practices	Seminars—company development	Developmental reading	Performance appraisal
Formal development within company	A series of case discussions involving policy formulation and administration	Periodic meetings with senior officers to become acquainted with latest developments in the company	Understanding of reading process and development of reading skills	Practice in rating procedure and counselling

	Membership in organizations attendance at conventions	Courses at universities	Special management schools	Effective speaking	Industry courses and conferences
Development outside company working hours	Examples are: BIM; IPM; IWM; JCC. Will add technical knowledge	To further self-development, evening or extension courses at universities or correspondence courses may be suggested. Eventually Henley or business schools	Seminars in: operations research, increasing productivity in office-operations, managing punched-card systems, selection of office supervisors, etc	Preparing for public speaking engagements, sometimes representing company	To give broad knowledge of the industry

vidual's motivation to undergo training, which may itself be influenced by counselling. Such 'motivation' is not a simple concept: it cannot be taken as axiomatic that everyone will necessarily want to undergo training in order to improve his or her skills or even 'himself'/'herself'. Just because a training opportunity is offered is not by itself sufficient reason for thinking that everyone will want to use it. The redundant employee, for example, may well resent being placed in a position where he needs training in order to go on earning a living, and this resentment may influence very strongly the motivation which he brings to his training. It is therefore important for the employer in general and the trainer in particular to pay some attention to the motivation of the potential trainees.

This is because the student who is reluctant to undergo training, or who is indifferent to the training offered, is unlikely to learn much from an instructor, however brilliant. It is necessary thus for the trainer to take time to ensure that the individual is at least aware of the benefit which might accrue to him from the training he is being offered. It may well be that the individual who resents the system for forcing him to undergo training could, by counselling, be led to recognize that the training might in the long run place him in a much better position than before. If this kind of change in attitude towards training can be brought about, the individual's motivation may well develop to a level where the instruction given will be worthwhile.

There is a fine point of balance in motivation here which must be sought. A potential trainee who is over-motivated and who sees the whole of his future depending upon a notional success in the training process, may become so anxious about it that he will be prevented from learning: his own anxiety will introduce too much noise into the actual training process itself to permit him to work effectively. This often happens within the ordinary educational system, where passing examinations is given an excessively important significance in the life of the individual, so that he performs less well than he would had he attached less significance to examinations.

In training as in other activities, the motivation of the individual is likely to be affected by the rewards and penalties which are associated with performance in the training process. This is usually referred to here under the heading of reinforcement. It means simply that the individual must feel that there is some reward for him not only in the long but in the short run. It need not be a material reward and usually takes the form of encouragement by the trainer. The individual needs to develop some feeling that he is making progress through his training and the tutor's encouragement should be related to his performance and his progress in this way. Looked at from the trainer's viewpoint, this means that the training process has to be conceived in terms of some feedback system, whereby the performance of the individual is judged by the trainer and the results, with his reasons, must be communicated back to the individual trainee.

Again, as in the general case, such encouragement is likely to have a much more functional value than administering punishment or penalties when mistakes are made. This is not to say that when the individual makes a mistake the trainer should ignore it. The trainer has a duty to show the individual where he is going wrong. But this can be placed in the context of what is going right and indicating what needs further improvement or development, as part of the training process. It is important that the individual undergoing training should be able to develop knowledge about the results of his learning; this may be achieved by the supervisor forming judgements and communicating them or, in certain cases of technical training, by building into the mechanical system itself some devices (dials etc) which can tell the individual immediately how he is progressing.

The objectives which are established for the training must clearly be communicated to the trainee to provide him with the first piece of knowledge he needs to carry out some self-evaluation. But it is not uncommon for the trainer himself to have certain objectives for the training process but not to communicate them to the trainee, assuming that the trainee has his own objectives which must coincide with those of the trainer. It has been one of the major contributions of the industrial training boards that trainers have been led to establish programmes of training in which not only have they worked out objectives clearly, but they have made them explicit in formulating the training programme and have explained them to the individual trainees.

At one level the statement of objectives in training can and should be stated in general terms. For example, the object of a lathe operator's training ought to indicate just what capacity the individual ought to have to operate lathes at the end of his training. The steps aimed for during training must also be stated so that the individual has a hierarchy of sub-goals which he can seek to reach on the way to achieving the overall objective.

In this context too there is a point of balance to be attained. If very limited goals are set they will probably frustrate the individual who is probably more highly motivated to develop his skills to a reasonably high level, in which he and his future employer could repose confidence. Setting goals which are too high for the individual to attain at the outset, or in the early stages of training, is also likely to cause frustration: the individual will then tend to give up because the goals seem so far out of his reach at that moment. Thus goals are important in training and have an important bearing on the likely state of motivation on the part of the trainee.

Design of training content
In those cases where there is a basis for analysis of the tasks and skills involved in any job-element, the information generated by job and skills analysis provides the foundation for determining the content of a training programme. The objectives are already established by representing the gap between expected and actual performance, and the fixing of content must reflect the contribution which each job-part or each skill makes towards the difference.

The actual, 'real' content of a training programme will, obviously comprise the motions, the behaviours, the attitudes, etc, which it is intended that the individual should learn in this setting. In every particular case, there will be a particular content. Training for filing activity will involve filing 'in theory and practice', training for negotiatiating will involve negotiating in theory and practice, and so on. The problems of designing content are not to do with content at this level, but with the question of how the behaviours to be learned are to be presented, in form and sequence and with what repetition and rapidity, to the individual.

The starting point is the synthesis of what has emerged from the analyses. Gagné presents three 'basic principles' which govern this approach:

(a) identify the component tasks of a final performance
(b) insure that each of these component tasks is fully achieved
(c) arrange the total learning situation in a sequence which will ensure the optimal mediational effects from one component to another (Gagné, 1962, p 88)

The third of these, involving the concept of synthesis, is further explained by Singer and Ramsden:

Synthesis is the recombining of the identified facts, in such a way that the learning process is optimized by feeding new information to the learner in easily digested portions, rather than asking him to spend considerable time and effort in breaking up the total task, *by himself*, into digestible bits (Singer and Ramsden, 1969, p 52).

The emphasis in this is upon the concept of 'easily digestible bits',

384

which will tend to vary both with the task and with the capacity of the learner, and which are usually considered in the literature in the form of 'part' versus 'whole' task learning (*see* above, pp 373–76).

Naylor (1962) shares with Gagné (1962) the view that almost all tasks could be considered to be composited of a number of subtasks. But he takes the view that the extent of 'task complexity' and 'task organization', have important implications for the approach made to training (Naylor, 1962). The subtasks may, in themselves and viewed individually, be more or less difficult to carry out, and the degree of difficulty is what provides Naylor with his measure of 'task complexity'. They may also be more or less inter-related and inter-dependent or mutually-influential, and the measure of this provides him with an indication of 'task organization'. The total task may be regarded as more or less difficult to perform than the separated tasks. This, suggests Naylor, could be for one of three reasons: that the sub-tasks themselves are difficult; that they are so inter-related that the whole becomes difficult; or that the overall difficulty is a product of the measures of organization and complexity taken separately.

In his analysis of those training researches which had sought to evaluate the efficacy of part versus whole task approaches since 1930, Naylor tried to determine whether the characteristics of the task itself had any relevance to the findings. By producing a matrix in which the dimensions of task complexity and task organization could be related to the training approach (ie whole or part), he was able to demonstrate a relationship which he expressed in two propositions:

1 that in training for tasks with relatively high organization, whole task training appeared to become more efficient than part task methods as task complexity increased
2 that in training for tasks with relatively low organization, part methods appeared to become more efficient than whole task methods as task complexity increased.

This general conclusion that it is the degree of inter-dependence or inter-relatedness between the subtasks which influences the superiority of one approach over the other, was supported in later studies by the same researcher (Briggs and Naylor, 1962; Naylor and Briggs, 1963) and by the work of others (Bilodeau, 1954, 1955, 1957).

Presentation of learning opportunities
Consequently, a degree of skill is required in putting back together

385

the component elements into which a job may be broken down for purposes of analysis. Whether the part or the whole is presented as a learning experience, the trainer must first ensure a balance in the actual presentation. To break down the total task into very small elements is likely to prove frustrating to the individual and therefore to detract from his motivation to learn. If he repetitively attempts to master very small parts of the job he will quickly begin to supply his own context to the small part, and inadvertently learn contextual elements which he will later have to unlearn. Instead of breaking the job down into small fragments, a conscious attempt in training is therefore usually made to develop subcomponents of the total task, each of which has its own subobjectives which enable the individual to take a number of fragments in a meaningful context even if that context is not the whole of the job.

Secondly, it is clear that the individual undergoing training needs to know not only what to do but also some of the reasons why he should do it. This relates to the question of whether the trainee should be exposed to the theory or background of the set of tasks or techniques he is learning. The training of an electrician, for example, may not call for knowledge of quantum physics but he should probably understand why certain techniques are used in preference to others; a certain amount of theory about electricity is therefore necessary if he is to understand why he has been taught to do the job in a particular way.

Providing some theory in training has the advantage of helping the individual subsequently to transfer his skills without undergoing further training. If he is taught only a single technique, if the technology to which it is to be applied changes, he may have to be brought back for training in another technique. But if the individual has already been taught a certain amount of theory he may, on the basis of his own experience, be capable of transferring the technique originally learned into the new technology. This distinction is sometimes referred to as a distinction between logical training and rote training; although the latter may seem to involve less investment of time and money in actual training, it is likely that, with today's high rate of technological change, the logical method of training may prove in the longer run to be the more economical approach.

Thirdly, it is also clear from a great deal of research that the individual does not learn a great deal about required behaviours or skills simply by being told in the form of, say, a lecture, what those skills are. Wherever training is related to behaviours, whether technical or managerial, the individual must be allowed to become involved in the practice. This gives rise to the notion of learning by

386

doing rather than learning by listening.

There are neverthless problems about blending what above we have called theory and practice. Evidence supports the proposition that the individual will learn more rapidly if he is allowed to prac- tise the tasks or techniques in which he is being instructed. But to repeat a small part of practice *ad infinitum* is likely to prove less useful to the individual in learning than a spaced repetition of the task over a period. One of the advantages of traditional apprentice training was simply that it allowed the apprentice to develop his skills in a serial fashion and to repeat the particular skill in a spaced manner over a period. The actual involvement of the trainee in what he is learning can thus be made to contribute effectively to the learning process.

Beyond this approach to the structuring of the learning situ- ation in training, the trainer becomes involved in a process of com- munication. The training process involves the transmission of messages in appropriate codes through appropriate media with the intention of both conveying meaning and exerting influence as a consequence of so doing. What is therefore additionally relevant to the training process is all that is relevant to effective communication—adequate base, motivation (as revealed for example in enthusiasm) and ability (to construct acceptable mess- ages and to select appropriate media). On such a foundation is based the advice on the training of trainers: they require a knowl- edge and understanding of the efficacious learning/training struc- tures and a knowledge and understanding of the communication processes (cf CTC, 1968).

Evaluation

Training and development, like any other aspect of personnel man- agement, may be evaluated in terms of its effects upon the indi- vidual worker or in terms of its consequences for the enterprise.

In the first context, training consequences will link to the goals of the individual, whether these be immediate (as shown up in terms of greater job satisfaction, greater reward or greater job se- curity) or distant (related, for example, to his expectations of career development and long-term job security or equally long- term considerations of his self-concept).

In the second, training consequences will be assessed against the immediate contributions to improved job performance or im- mediate enhancement of the qualities of manpower required by the organization, and against the longer term opportunities which the training provides to avoid costly dismissal/recruitment exercises to effect adjustments between demand and supply. In both cases, there are costs incurred (by the individual who must take the trouble to unlearn some routine and acquire others; or by the enterprise which must expend money on the training and forego the individual's contribution whilst it is under way) and any benefits must therefore be calculated net of these.

It tends to follow from this that in a period of economic decline for the enterprise, the net benefit of training will tend to be small in the short run, since the main objective will then be retrenchment and the main constraint will be a shortage of revenue which will have the effect of making the cost relatively high and of discounting the longer term future benefits. Consequently, the enterprise will tend to cut its training activity in periods of recession.

Nor does it follow that the individual's conclusions from his calculation will be vastly different from this. Whilst the individual is employed in the enterprise, the main objective must be to secure his job-property rights, which tend to depend most closely on seniority in the job. In such circumstances, staying put and contributing at a level which is adjudged to be consistent with retention of employment, may prove a preferred strategy to undertaking training to improve some hypothetical future chances of employment or advancement. When the individual has no employment, this calculation may well produce a very different conclusion, as, indeed, it may do for those (such as apprentices and trainees) who are involved in a deliberate exercise of preparing for a future employment rather than in an established employment.

For such reasons, public policy has, in recent years, sought to meet the problem of preparing people for a changing employment pattern over the course of their careers by developing a programme of training for those in employment or recently out of it, in which the main initiatives are taken centrally, even if the cost of it remains partly borne by employers. In this respect the approach to training in public policy has something in common with the approach to the improvement of health and safety practices, although the training approach has not yet gone so far as to impose general or specific duties upon both employer and employee. But what has happened in this process is that training has become subject to more systematic planning and evaluation, with more attention paid to the setting of objectives, the establishment of relevant criteria, the development of technique and the evaluation of effects against the objectives set.

As Hamblin (1974) in particular has shown, however, the evaluation of a training process is fraught with difficulty because of the number of levels of effect which can be discerned. Objectives may be set, and effects may be measured, on the reaction of the individual trainee, the individual's learning of knowledge or application, the behaviour of the individual on the job, the performance of the organization as an entity, or the much longer term impact on individual or organizational performance or development. Measurement of success on these different levels may then be tackled by very different methods: reaction may be assessed in terms of trainees' opinions as to how interesting or relevant the training exercise was; learning by some form of test or examination; behaviour by before and after investigations at the behavioural level and so on.

Nevertheless, the further the evaluation moves away from the individual's reaction to the training exercise, the more difficult it is to establish that what is being measured is the consequence of the training exercise itself, rather than the consequence of some other variation whose occurrence cannot be controlled (eg a reorganization of the work or the department in which it occurs). In comparable fashion, the establishment of the objectives in training is fraught with similar difficulties, since any single objective which might be accomplished by a training exercise might also be brought about by other means (eg a reorganization of the work or the workers). Since even from the point of view of the enterprise it is difficult to carry out cost-benefit analysis (cf Thomas *et al,* 1969) it is therefore difficult to establish that training is the only or the best way to bring about a desired objective.

At the level of the individual case it is somewhat easier to evaluate the effects of training. The individual's reaction can be sought and obtained, a test can be administered, and behaviour can be observed before and after. Although, as Hamblin shows, there are problems of evaluation even at this level, some attempt can be made, and frequently is made by trainers.

But the main evaluation problem, here as in many other aspects of personnel work, is that of aggregating the case data: from the point of view of the management of the training function, is it realistic to add the reactions of the individual trainees and draw a managerial inference from this? The answer to this question is that such a datum could only be one possibly quite small part of the total data which would have to be taken into account in taking decisions about training programmes. What the trainer may properly use as his yardstick of success in training, may therefore prove an inappropriate one for use by the manager of the training function.

The manager with ultimate responsibility for the training function must take into account additionally the effects of training upon productivity and efficiency. Such efficiency need not be measured only in relation to actual 'products' sent out of the despatch bay; it could also include the measures of safety or labour stability, where expenditure was being incurred on training for these purposes. But there is always a nice calculation to be made as to how much difference training will make to the actual production and productivity of the enterprise, because so many other factors can enter into the determination of these consequences other than training. The training expenditure is one which in the short run often seems to be avoidable, even if in the longer term the costs of achieving productivity and production are actually increased as a consequence. Here, 'saving' on training costs may be not very different from 'saving' on cheaper but inferior components or raw materials and the consequences may be similar in the longer term. But only by including training as a part of the overall plan for performance, and regardless of what then the short-run decisions may be, can effective evaluations be made of its benefits in relation to its costs.

Further reading
On the general theme of training, there is an extensive literature. Amongst the more useful general texts are: Annett (1978), Barber (1968), Bass and Vaughan (1969), Craig and Bittell (1967), Gentles (1969), Holding (1965), Jaap and Watson (1970), Kenney, Donnelly and Reid (1979), King (1968), Mumford (1971), Singer (1978), Singleton (1968), Stokes (1966), Wellens (1963).

On methods involved in training (in addition to the above), see Stammers and Patrick (1975), Ward and Bird (1968), Boydell (1971), Gagné (1970), Hanson (1975), Mager (1962), Mills (1967), Rackham and Morgan (1977).

On management training, in its various manifestations, see Dept of Employment (1972c), Ellis *et al* (1968), Hague (1973), Burgoyne (1978), Leggatt (1974), Mant (1969), Thurley (1975), Smith and Delf (1978) and Foy (1978 and 1979).

On supervisory training, see Hamblin (1974), Meade and Greig (1966), Sykes (1962), Thurley *et al* (1973), Ward and Bird (1968).

On the subject of trade union officer and shop steward training, see Dept of Education and Science (1972), TUC (1968; 1975), Warren (1971a), Withnall (1972; 1973).

On the training of training officers and training managers, see CTC (1968), Finnigan (1970).

On industrial relations training, see Brewster and Connock (1980), BIM (1971), CIR (1972; 1973), Gill and Taylor (1976), IR Training Resource Centre (1978), Kettle (1972), Kilcourse (1977), Kniveton and Towers (1978), Leary (1975), NEDO (1975), Marsh (1976), Paper and Paper Products ITB (1973), Pedlar (1975),

390

Young and Findlater (1972).

On the specific topic of coaching and counselling, see Adams (1973), Megginson (1978), Moorby (1973).

On evaluation of training, see Hamblin (1974), Hesseling (1966), Warr, Bird and Rackham (1970), Whitelaw (1972). Williams (1976) and Cannon, chapter 5 (1979).

Part three
The organization function

The organization function

Organization as instrument or environment

A concern with 'people at work' may be manifest at many different levels and in many different ways. We have already looked at one manifestation as it affects the interchange of people across the boundary of the undertaking (in chapters 3 to 8) and at another as it relates to the securing of individual performance from people within the undertaking. However, as the personnel manager pursues his or her 'people-orientation' to the corporate level of undertakings, it is not possible to avoid involvement in the third manifestation, which is that with 'the organization' as an entity. The distinction here rests upon the view of an undertaking as a necessarily interacting and interdependent group which can be distinguished from both the environment and other groups as well as from the individuals as individuals.

The question of how sensible or useful it is to treat organizations as if they are entities has exercised many minds (cf Dunkerley, 1972). It is not axiomatic that organizations are 'things', and one of the problems which is to be discussed in this third part of the book, is that of securing the commitment of individuals to the ends of organized work—which suggests that it is problematic.

Nevertheless, we stand by the original proposition (*see* above, p 4 that organizations exist and attempt to pursue purposes. What we want to do is develop our understanding of how the pursuit is effected and what problems surround the process. We may accept for this purpose that organizations will, somehow, attempt to realize the purposes which are articulated in their name and that in appropriate circumstances, specific detailed objectives will be laid down for the participants. For example, in commercial organizations, the overall purpose of serving the needs of citizen consumers will, usually, be broken down (as Cyert and March (1963) suggest) into specific objectives in the areas of:

production (concerning level and its stability)
inventory (stock holding in all activity areas)

394

sales (again relating to level and its stability)
market share (linked to growth intentions)
profit (related to the expected demands of the major stakeholders).

There are other such lists in the literature, but these show one possible way in which purposes may be broken down in one category of undertaking.

Beyond this, the actual tasks of realizing such purposes and objectives have to be allocated to real people. It is certainly true that 'organizations' as such cannot *act*, but must act through people. In the process of that allocation of tasks as roles, the need for co-ordination arises. This co-ordination in turn needs structuring. The 'organization function' is the term then used to cover the allocating and structuring processes which necessarily occur within undertakings as they seek to realize purposes.

The function is not, however, merely focused upon some mechanical process of slotting docile 'parts' into depersonalized relationships, much as pieces are fitted into a jigsaw puzzle. It is true that the pieces may be odd shapes, reflecting the fact of individual differences, and that alone might make the task a complex one. But that is not the only cause of difficulty. Another major factor to be accommodated is that of 'uncertainty', a concept well recognized as relevant in many different disciplines (cf Shackle, 1970; Hickson *et al*, 1971).

For convenience, the sources of the uncertainty impinging upon people and their activities in organizations are put under two headings, to distinguish those uncertainties which stem from 'outside' (generated by the actions of others in the markets and the political (regulatory) structures within which the undertakings operate), and those which develop 'inside' the undertaking. The former cannot be ignored in our discussions (*see*, for example, below, pp 427–54) but our main emphasis in part three will be upon the latter.

Those which develop inside the undertaking occur at all levels: individual, sub-unit, and unit. At each level both 'official' and 'personal' sources of uncertainty may be recognized. For example, the individual has official tasks to perform but as a person he may 'want something more out of work' than merely the satisfaction of achieving the official goals. As he pursues both sets of goals by actions, the environment of decision and action for others is affected and often in a way which could increase *their* uncertainty. The same kinds of distinctions and effects may therebe recognized at other levels (cf Dalton, 1959).

At any and every level, therefore, the sheer fact of acting within an interdependent structure of action, is likely to generate uncertainty. This, in turn, is only likely to be reduced if action is determined upon in each and every case in accordance with some code which will serve as an 'order' to which as a matter of 'duty' individuals are prepared to conform. This 'code' is usually identified in the reality of organization by the term 'policy', although in the industrial relations area, under the influence of state initiatives in recent years, the term 'code' has itself begun to creep into everyday usage.

In addition, we must recognize that the goals and interests of individuals in the work situation have been organized around certain principles (of trade unionism, professionalism, or capitalism) and can be pursued or protected on a power-block basis. In this context, it is usual to identify the generality of such power blocks by the concept of stakeholder organization. This merely recognizes that some common interests may be combined around the 'stakes' which different categories (workers, shareholders, managers, customers, etc) hold in the enterprise or undertaking, in order to aggregate power to pursue or protect them. Action to protect or pursue interests is then undertaken on a 'collective' basis, instead of on an individual one, but the possibility that uncertainty will be generated by such action is not less than in the individual case.

The pluralist organization

The interaction which occurs, as each stakeholder seeks to achieve his objectives in the organizational environment, creates a condition of uncertainty for the others. What the one stakeholder may achieve is necessarily affected by what others may be doing to achieve their goals. Herein lies both the source of the uncertainty *and* the source of attempts to reduce it (temporarily or permanently) by structural arrangements.

This is essentially the foundation of the pluralist conception of organizations. This sees organizations as arenas within which the various stakeholders act out their goal-seeking behaviour and finds a 'statesman' role for the top management as the reconcilers of the varying demands made upon the undertaking. This permits 'it' to move forward *as if* there were a single, unitary objective to be pursued (cf Walton, 1967; Silverman, 1970). The achievement of this 'as if' position, in turn, depends upon the successful negotiation of a compromise agreement amongst the competing stakeholders. This is made possible by virtue of the uncertainty-reducing potential which such a compromise agreement possesses, but it can never move beyond certain limits without creating greater uncertainty for one or more stakeholders.

The pluralist conception is one which lends itself very little to absolutes: it is not one which depends much upon doctrine or dogma but one which proceeds largely on an empirical and pragmatic basis. This is one of the reasons why it seems to command support as a view of the organizational world in a culture which tends to emphasize the pragmatic in most things.

The challenges to it come from both the traditionalists and the radicals. There are those who argue that any entity must have a single objective and a single set of means for its realization, established by a single authority (such as the directorate or management) (cf Friedman, 1977, p 168; Wilson, 1980, pp 52–53). This is to continue the traditional, unitary conception of the enterprise, which secures support in law relating to corporations and to labour (*see* above, pp 69–96).

There are also those who would reject the 'mediating' role of the top management in reconciling divergent interests, in favour of some arrangement in which decisions would be taken in *direct* negotiation between the stakeholders. In some views this would be just some of them, ie one or more of the current stakeholders might be denied legitimacy and access. There are a number of different radical challenges to the pluralistic conception, but in essence they emphasize that such stakeholders as are accorded legitimacy should be treated as 'free-standing' and autonomous in the determination of the objectives and means to be pursued or employed. Decisions would therefore tend to emerge from 'power-bargaining' not from mediation by some supposedly third party.

These provide the cross-currents within which management (and, in the exercise of the 'organization function', particularly the personnel manager) must attempt to resolve the problem of accomplishing the various objectives which people impute to economic undertakings, including that of reducing the uncertainty surrounding work in complex organizations.

The organization function in context

The objectives served by the 'organization function' in undertakings may then be summarized as:

(a) securing the organization as a whole and in its parts against the uncertainty pressures which emanate from the external environment
(b) securing the individual members of the organization and their

397

sub-units against the uncertainties which are generated by their interaction in a co-operative arrangement aimed at 'mastering' the external and internal environments (cf Bennis, 1966, p 52).

The second of these is amplified by Selznick who suggests that what is imperatively required is:

(i) action to ensure that the organization as a whole and as a collective of individuals comes to a sufficiently common or consensual view of the purpose and meaning of the undertaking to allow enough concerted action to master the environment
(ii) action to ensure that the organization's policies (guiding conduct) and the sources of their determination are maintained in continuity, and that the formal and informal nodes and channels of communication are both adequate for their purpose and stable in their operation (Selznick, 1948, p 25).

The fact that such actions are called for from someone in the organization indicates that disciplined conduct behind the 'organization's' purposes is not something which occurs 'automatically'.

Realization of these objectives is unlikely to materialize from action by managements alone. Other stakeholders have an interest in the outcome, and power to influence it, so that it will not bear the stamp of managerial interest alone. But more than this, the reality of the work situation at the present time does not permit the organizational designer the luxury of relying upon a consensus about the sources of legitimacy of authority to act in this way.

There is here, as in connection with the other major functions identified previously, a dilemma occasioned by the different views taken by the interacting parties (and frequently highlighted in the participation/industrial democracy debate) of the nature of authority in organizations. On the one hand, there is a traditional conception of the organization as an instrument of the undertaking's purpose, and on the other, there is an emerging conception of the organization as a bargaining and influence system (cf Abel, 1975, pp 10–40). What differs between these conceptions is the manner in which authority, power and legitimation are regarded and treated.

In the one, authority and power are seen to flow from the concepts of ownership or entrepreneurship. Such authority is then legitimated by the principle that any individual has the fundamental right to do as he will with his own and particularly with his property in trade. Supported by the principle of free contract, the owner (or his agent) might then, legitimately, agree with others about the services they might provide to assist the development of enterprise or trade. By that contract, particularly by the contract in employment, individuals might become 'part of the organization' and 'subject to the control' of the owner/manager. The owner or his agents are then unquestioningly in the position to determine what tasks shall be allocated to whom, what standards of performance will be required of them in the performing of them, and what structure and rules should be imposed to serve this end. The organization is to be seen as an instrument of undertaking purpose (cf Abel 1975, p 10).

In the other, authority and power (whilst not unaffected by the historical facts of their distribution) are seen to be subject to negotiation and to be established at any one point in time by the bargains or truces struck to govern them. This also takes the concept of contract as a starting point, but carries it through to a more logically-consistent position in the scheme. The various types of resources which have been regarded as the bases or the supports of power (cf Bales, 1951, pp 73–80) are now seen to be capable of being exchanged or captured in the course of interaction within co-operative systems (cf Hickson *et al*, 1971; Cartwright, 1959 and 1967). Organizations may therefore remain 'instrumental' to some purpose or other, but they are also to be seen as 'complex mechanisms for arriving at *collective decisions* through bargaining and influence processes amongst a set of power- and influence-holding units' or as 'a bargaining and influence system' (Abel, 1975, p 11). In this perspective, therefore, the organization provides an environment or a site on which negotiation occurs.

However, little which has been discussed in this book so far suggests that anything ever happens 'automatically'. Structures may be designed to constrain behaviours, in the sense of making some more likely because people will learn from the feedback of the outcomes of action to adopt some rather than others. Processes of communication or training, rewarding or penalising, may either persuade people to act in some ways rather than others, or present negative and positive reinforcement in support of some actions rather than others. But in all of this, the individual still mediates the structural and processual influences, and it is his or her decision which ultimately determines the response to the variety of stimuli presented.

Consequently, it remains necessary to have someone to take steps to recruit human commitment to ends or purposes, regardless of how broadly or narrowly those ends may be defined.

In part three, therefore, we look at the main features of this organization-and-individual problem as it relates particularly to the role of the personnel specialist. We look at the 'kinds of organization' which lie on the cafeteria shelf (in chapter 16) and at the main organized challenge to the unilateral authority of management to select one of them (in chapter 17). In chapter 19, we look at the strategies of organizational change which are open to management to develop, on the assumption that it can still exercise initiative in this area, In chapter 18 we look at the structural arrangements which (in the form of 'collective agreement') seem to be emerging to contain the challenge in some orderly fashion. Chapter 20 then picks up some of the main tasks which have to be carried out in the area of 'negotiation' in order to bring about these changes, and which therefore begin to identify the skills which managers (including personnel managers) will need to carry out the 'organization function'.

16 The organization as instrument

Objective and form

At first glance the first objective to be achieved in an organization is that of ensuring that work tasks are assigned in such a manner that the best (most productive) use is made of human talent and skill. That people are enabled by the organization to do their own skilled thing without getting in the way of others and the others getting in their way. If it could be assumed that people would function as simple instruments of the undertaking's purposes, such first thought might be sufficient.

It is not quite true to suggest that this was the basis of organizational design in the past. We hear a good deal about people being regarded as cogs in a machine and this does suggest that this was the case. The reality, however, was rather more subtle than this implies. Rather, it was thought that people would, in pursuing their own best interests, accept a mechanistic definition of the work tasks in return for remuneration, and in accepting this 'contract' also accept that the organization's policies and rules, being rationally derived from its purposes, constituted an 'order' which it was their duty to obey. The development of bureaucratic organization and of scientific management rested chiefly upon this premise, although it was *not* thought that it would happen automatically (*see* below, pp 403–10).

More recently doubts have been voiced as to whether the concept of purpose is itself adequately conceived and, consequently, as to whether the organization is adequate to serve the emergent conceptions. A small facet of this debate has been quoted on p 396–97 above; its current focus is upon participation and industrial democracy (*see* Bullock Committee Report, 1977). Doubts about purpose reflect themselves, as Beeching indicated in the quotation (p 14), in increased uncertainty, which it then falls to the lot of someone to reduce. Questions about the legitimacy of traditional management authority, stimulate experiments with organizational structure undertaken with the intention of finding more adequate frameworks for both the development of acceptable purposes and for the reduction of debilitating uncertainties at the level of work tasks themselves.

Research studies in recent years have suggested that the bureaucratic organization, aligned with scientific management, does not necessarily exhaust all the major possibilities of organizational structure which may be found to exist, even within a single sector such as manufacturing industry (cf Woodward, 1958; Burns and Stalker, 1961; Trist *et al*, 1963). Consequently, undertakings facing a particular external environment may have some degree of choice in the organizational form which they might adopt to cope with uncertainty.

Other studies have thrown doubt on the belief that bureaucracy, allied with scientific management, could solve the motivation and commitment problem in undertakings (*see*, Gouldner, 1955; Blau, 1955; Crozier, 1964; Dalton, 1959). The monocratic bureaucracy, at one time seemingly set fair to become the 'universal' model of large-scale work organization, came to be seen as a rather special case relevant to certain purposes and environmental conditions. Other forms which varied in the flexibility which they permitted in the establishment of 'order', were discovered and measured for their efficiency (*see*, Burns and Stalker, 1961; Trist *et al*, 1963).

These doubts and discoveries were then caught up in discussions of the desirability of 'democratizing' work, for either moral (ie, the simple democratic imperative of the EEC Green Paper on *Employee Participation and Company Structure*, and of the Bullock Committee Report, p 25) or efficiency reasons (ie the pragmatic conclusion that efficiency will only increase if workers participate in the decisions affecting them and their work). In response to one or both of these, proposals for reorganization have been advanced (eg by the Bullock Committee) and experiments conducted (*see* Blum, 1968; Guest and Fatchett, 1974) to develop participation at the level of the work tasks (eg, through 'autonomous working groups') or at the level of representative systems (as in the case of the Bullock proposal for a unitary board of directors composed of worker, shareholder and 'independent' representatives).

Consequently, the organizational designer now faces a range of choice of organizational forms which have different capacities for handling the motivational and efficiency problems which confront undertakings. In this chapter we look at some of the main variants and at some of the developments in thinking about organizational design and purpose.

402

Bureaucratic organization

In spite of all the proposals and experiments, it remains true that at the present time the main organizational means adopted in undertakings, private or public, which have attained a certain minimum size (cf Urwick, 1949; Renold, 1950) is that of 'the bureaucracy'. This concept is used to distinguish the manner in which control is attempted in modern organizations on the basis of rationally-developed rules administered by 'office-holders' who achieve their positions through their demonstrated competence. In its pure form, it stands in distinction from familial and communal forms of organization, although in practice complete 'purity' may not manifest itself. It has nevertheless served as an exemplar or template against which particular organizational arrangements may be compared.

'Bureaucracy' in the meaning given to the term by Weber (1947) is therefore to be seen as an organizational instrument or vehicle for the application of rational-legal authority to the solution of work problems. He was little concerned with the precise or detailed manner in which modern undertakings were to be organized, and such questions were left to be tackled by the exponents of scientific management, like Taylor. Weber's interest was in the much more fundamental question of how it could be that people who were not related to one another (by kinship), who were not necessarily known to one another through neighbourly association (as in the traditional community) and who therefore might be thought of as strangers to one another, were nevertheless willing to allow themselves to be welded into a highly-efficient, cooperative entity, which was how he saw the modern bureaucracy. His description of the bureaucracy was therefore merely an attempt to answer this question, not to say in any detail how it actually worked.

What set the bureaucracy apart from other forms of organization for Weber (in addition to the distinction of its efficiency) were five characteristics

(a) the *division* of the total task into specific jobs or specialized offices which could then be defined with some precision
(b) the reliance upon a *hierarchy* of such offices to make coordination of the diverse tasks possible
(c) the animation of the office-holder's position in accordance with a well-developed set of abstract *rules and procedures*
(d) the avoidance of personal biases and favouritism by concentrating the office-holder's performance upon an *impersonal*

approach to clients and problems

(e) the organization of the offices in such a way that an individual could be motivated to accept the conditions of employment in a bureaucracy by the creation of a legitimate expectation of a 'career' within it.

Together, as Weber saw them, these defined the individual member's role (both in tasks and in terms of dependency), offered him the incentive of personal progression in career terms and ensured that both aspects would be developed within a framework of equity (guaranteed by the formalistic impersonality of science or rationality).

Certain things inevitably followed from these characteristics:

First, that the bureaucracy must take care to ensure that the way in which work is divided up into official duties rests upon a kind of rationality which the individual himself could understand and appreciate (and not, for example, upon incomprehensible whim or fancy). The care taken to describe jobs in modern organizations is one manifestation of this (*see* chapter 8 above).

Secondly, that the bureaucracy must also take care to ensure that those who are given these 'offices' are competent to carry out the official duties, the competence in turn being treated in the same 'rational' way as the definition of duties so that the individual can determine it for himself (and so acquire it by education or experience): the emphasis on qualification and training in modern organizations is a manifestation of this (*see* chapter 8 above).

Thirdly, that the bureaucracy must ensure that the necessary exercise of authority within the arrangement shall be subject to and limited by a set of rules, rationally-founded, and certainly not arbitrary (*see* chapter 10 above and chapter 18 below).

Fourthly, the organization would, in order to serve the interests of this same rationality, have to establish a coherent 'personality' of its own, so that it would have identity and integrity as a 'rational' entity. This manifests itself in structures which, *inter alia*, admit the possibility of adjudication of issues in terms of doctrines of rationality (cf Brown, 1951) and elaborated in processes of recording, reporting and storing information about the activities of the entity, so that no matter who happens to stay or leave, the undertaking has a 'memory' of its own which can be used and appealed to in the interests of consistency (cf Hahlo and Trebilcock, 1977, p 42 *et seq*; and above, pp 239–60).

These imperatives of organization (cf Selznick, 1964) arise from the 'rationality' as expressed in rules, to which the members will in all probability orient their behaviour. It is because of this probability that the 'strangers' allow themselves to be influenced by the rules.

This has many implications but two are particularly relevant to this discussion. First, that there is no certainty, even in Weber's original characterization, that people *will* so orient their behaviours and indeed a large number of studies have been made of organizations which show just how limited may be the probability (cf March and Simon, 1958, ch 3, and in Pugh, 1971, ch 2). Secondly, that issue apart, there is nothing automatic about the orientation of the modern individual to the rationality of the modern organization: somebody, somewhere, has a task of effecting the kind of consequence which Weber is describing and analysing and thereby of increasing 'the probability'.

Structuring organizations for commitment

The question of what could and should be done to foster the commitment necessary to organization operation attracted the interest of a number of managers who put their conclusions from experience on paper. The main contributors in this category are Taylor, Urwick and Fayol as the exponents of 'scientific management' (in which 'scientific' has similar connotations to the 'rationality' of Weber). Thus where Weber merely sought to answer the question 'what are the distinguishing characteristics of these modern organizations?', these other writers sought to indicate what it is that 'management' must do if it is to be efficient and 'rational'.

Taylor's main contribution to organization theory lay in his attempt to define competence in modern complex organizations. In his view, the main problem with large organizations was that management had not fully recognized what role was required of it and as a consequence was inefficient in managing modern enterprises. It was therefore necessary for managers to make systematic studies of the tasks that were required and, on the basis of such studies, to develop criteria and standards by which they could exercise their real functions of directing and controlling the activities of the workers. It was this which led him into his main preoccupation with work study and to develop his various theories of 'scientific management'.

But these activities were essentially subservient to the general aim of defining not only the work which the individual worker

405

would have to do but also that of the manager. Once these were known, it would be possible to define the required types and amounts of competence that both the managers and the workers needed. Where Weber had concerned himself with a simple description of how organizations achieved efficiency, Taylor set about prescribing the manner in which efficiency in modern organizations might be improved. The principles on which competence should be defined were virtually incidental to the realization of this particular objective.

In deriving these principles, like his co-founders of the scientific management school and like Weber himself, Taylor tended to base his deductions upon a mechanical system analogy. An organization ought, if it was managed 'properly', to run like a machine.

Urwick makes this quite clear in his argument that it is necessary to use an engineering design analogy in his prescription of organizational principles, simply because men are just not sophisticated enough to understand and develop organizations on the basis of an organic or chemical analogy. In his view, it is largely a matter of determining what the relationship shall be between line and staff or what the relationship shall be in a numerical sense between supervisors and supervised, and on the basis of this to put together the pieces of a jigsaw. If in the end the jigsaw is a rather loose one this must be accepted, because although one can make the formal organizational definition fairly precise on these sorts of principles, one cannot equally machine the individuals who will have to carry out the formal duties which are thus defined.

The classical definition of management as it emerged therefore emphasizes that what distinguished managers was their use of authority to organize, direct and control the activities of non-managers (*see* above pp 18–21). What emerged as the function of the non-manager was essentially to work at the behest of the manager who would automatically define the type and amount of work that the non-manager would be required to do.

The possibility that this division of the activity in modern organizations might in itself lead to tension between the managers and the non-managers was not a matter to which Taylor gave a great deal of thought. For him it was self-evident that the efficient organization, run along these lines, would be as much in the interests of the workers as the managers or owners, and when once it had been explained to the workers it would be accepted by them in this spirit.

The scientific management approach as this came to be called was therefore prone to condemn conflict whether verbal or behavioural as somehow aberrational and, for Taylor, who was highly critical of what he called 'systematic soldiering', such reaction on

406

the part of workers could be expected in those circumstances where management did not have proper control. This in turn for him meant that *management* was not competent and was not performing its 'official duties', as these might have been described by Weber.

In the work of these two men there is an implicit or explicit assumption that the adjustment of the individual to the role which he is given or acquires in organization will be effected through the mechanisms of the bureaucracy itself. That is, the individual will be enabled to adjust to his role according to the extent to which the organization defines the work role itself in a rational fashion and equally rationally defines the skill or competence that the individual requires for it and, thirdly, determines the system of rewards and punishments which will be applied to encourage the individual to behave in the required fashion. Whether this assumption would hold in practice was not questioned.

Control by structure
The burden of the argument of these authors is therefore that organizations must ensure, as far as is humanly possible to do so, that the purely formal (that is the non-human) aspects of organizations shall be as precisely defined as possible. Only in this way can the organization hope to move towards efficiency. Since it would rely on similarities between human beings to ensure the efficiency for the organization, then the organization must in turn seek to define roles within itself, so precisely as to ensure as much efficiency on this score as possible.

This led these writers to look in particular at two problems. First, that of finding a place for experts in organizations whose administration really called for people with *generalized* ability to supervise. They thus followed Taylor in making a distinction between the 'brainwork' and the 'supervision' of production. They also recognized that they could not have in the supervisors of production the same degree of expertise across the whole range that they might find if they hired specialists in each particular field. Therefore the problem became one of finding some organizational accommodation of both generalist supervisors and specialist experts. Their solution was the 'line and staff' organization.

The line part of this is made up of those who have authority over those who carry out the many specialist roles into which the production work tasks have been divided. The four people, the owner and the sales, financial and factory managers, together with their respective foremen and supervisors, are the examples in figure 14(a). Their authority and their responsibility for the co-ordination of these tasks therefore tends to be general. The staff part of the organization, on the other hand, will be made up of those who have expertness in particular areas. They appear in figure 14(b) as cost accountant, chief estimator, maintenance engineer and personnel manager. These people cannot be directly placed in the line management as the whole exercise would then tend to become confused. Therefore they are given a less direct and specialist relationship to the line organization, whose roles they are supposed to supplement.

The second problem to which the writers on formal organizations addressed themselves is the problem of the span of control. Here again their view was that people are so variable in themselves and therefore so variable in the competence which they would have to supervise in other people, that the organization must give careful attention to the definition of the number of people they should be expected to control and co-ordinate. Examination of a large number of organizations suggested that a span of control of between six and 10 people seemed to be in the competence which they would possess to supervise other people. Certain other writers have suggested that the span of control can be worked out precisely on the basis of a mathematical formula. In order to do so, it is necessary to gather data on the features of organization explored by these writers. First, the precise definition of the work roles, supported by work study data and adequate competent instruction of the worker in his duties, which would indicate how much work there was and, from the supervisor's point of view, how varied it might be. Secondly, the precise delimitation of the extent of the co-ordination problem for the supervisor, the data on this being capable of presentation on the basis of line-of-balance charts, showing not only roles but also sequences and even the points at which other departments might become involved (*see* figure 15).

The suggestion in this is therefore at one with the idea that the organization's responsibility in these matters is to be precise in the definition of official duties (of which supervision is a part) and to leave the question of whether individuals can perfectly cope with this precise definition for consequential consideration. The effect is to suggest a principle on which the organizational designer might work. He now has an apparently precise relationship established which he can incorporate into organizational design decisions.

Between them, these various writers provided a basic justification of this manner of organizing authority and a fairly detailed blueprint for designing it. We are provided with both basic principles and formulae. Both are illustrated in Dale's *Ten Commandments of Good Organization* (Dale, 1952, p 155) which are shown

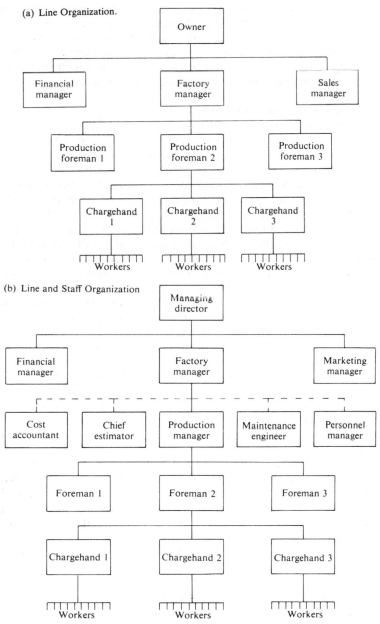

Figure 14
Basic patterns of organization

(a) Line Organization.

(b) Line and Staff Organization

409

on p 411 in table 13. From this, the bureaucracy could then be constructed and in principle it ought to have ensured efficient organization of authority, efficient co-ordination and control, efficient communications and influence (Belasco and Arlutton, 1969).

The more modern view, reflecting both academic research and managerial experimentation, is that the bureaucracy, both in concept and in manifestation, is a relatively blunt instrument for the achievement of undertaking and member objectives.

Dysfunctionality and contingency
The general thrust of the analysis and argument of these writers on bureaucracy and scientific management is that an organization structured in this (bureaucratic) way and run by managers properly fulfilling their roles, may be predicted to be efficient. The emphasis is upon the *functionality* of this kind of organization and this kind of management; they produce 'consequences which make for the adaptation or adjustment of a given system' (Merton, 1957, p 51).

But, as Merton himself pointed out, any item (for example, division of labour, hierarchy, etc) might have both functional and dysfunctional consequences, where the concept of dysfunction is defined as observable 'consequences which lessen the adaptation or adjustment of the system' (*ibid*). At one and the same time, therefore, a bureaucratic organization may be seen to contribute both to the efficiency which Weber highlighted and to inefficiency in coping with the internal and external problems presented to it.

At the particular level, the 'abstract rules and procedures' (as one distinguishing characteristic) might help it to cope with problems and at the same time create problems of adaptation and accommodation of the kind referred to in popular usage as 'red tape'. A manager rigorously following out the requirements of his role might contribute to efficient performance and at the same time create other, often unintended, consequences which detract from that efficiency (cf Gouldner, 1955).

This perspective offers, at least, a caveat against the adoption of the belief that, because bureaucracy may be observed to be more efficient than some of the organizational forms which preceded it in history, an increase in bureaucratization (for example by developing the division of labour, hierarchy, etc) must lead to even greater efficiency.

In addition, as more modern research indicates (cf Woodward, 1958; Burns and Stalker, 1961) there may be circumstances in which a decrease in bureaucratization (defined as in the previous paragraph) might increase efficiency. Burns and Stalker, for example, suggested that in conditions of environmental uncer-

410

Table 13
Ten commandments of good organization

---

1 Definite and clear-cut responsibilities should be assigned to each executive.
2 Responsibility should always be coupled with corresponding authority.
3 No change should be made in the scope or responsibilities of a position without a definite understanding to that effect on the part of all persons concerned.
4 No executive or employee, occupying a single position in the organization, should be subject to definite orders from more than one source. (This should not interfere with functional direction exercised by staff specialist departments, such as accounting, personnel, purchasing).
5 Orders should never be given to subordinates over the head of a responsible executive.
6 Criticisms of subordinates should, whenever possible, be made privately, and in no case should a subordinate be criticized in the presence of executives or employees of equal or lower rank.
7 No dispute or difference between executives or employees as to authority or responsibilities should be considered too trivial for prompt and careful adjudication.
8 Promotions, wage changes, and disciplinary action should always be approved by the executive immediately superior to the one directly responsible.
9 No executive or employee should ever be required, or expected, to be at the same time an assistant to, and critic of, another.
10 Any executive whose work is subject to regular inspection, should, whenever practicable, be given the assistance and facilities necessary to enable him to maintain an independent check of the quality of his work.

Source: Put out by AMA, quoted in Ernest Dale, *Planning and Developing the Company Organization Structure* (AMA, New York, 1952), p 155.

Figure 15

A process chart, developed (A) Figure 15 in conventional form, and (B) to show movement between departments and division of work among operators

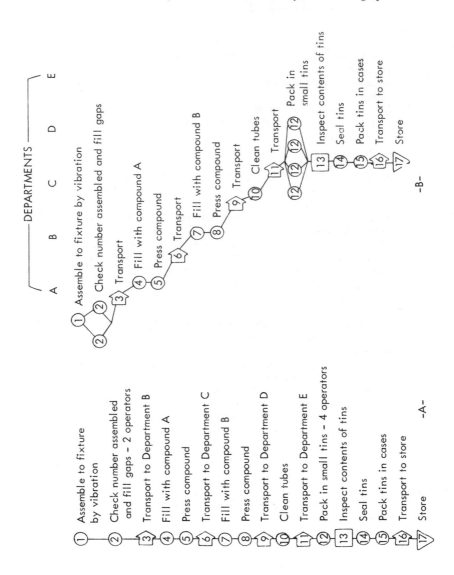

DEPARTMENTS

A   B   C   D   E

1 Assemble to fixture by vibration
2 Check number assembled and fill gaps
3 Transport
4 Fill with compound A
5 Press compound
6 Transport
7 Fill with compound B
8 Press compound
9 Transport
10 Clean tubes
11 Transport
12 Pack in small tins
13 Inspect contents of tins
14 Seal tins
15 Pack tins in cases
16 Transport to store
17 Store

-B-

1 Assemble to fixture by vibration
2 Check number assembled and fill gaps – 2 operators
3 Transport to Department B
4 Fill with compound A
5 Press compound
6 Transport to Department C
7 Fill with compound B
8 Press compound
9 Transport to Department D
10 Clean tubes
11 Transport to Department E
12 Pack in small tins – 4 operators
13 Inspect contents of tins
14 Seal tins
15 Pack tins in cases
16 Transport to store
17 Store

-A-

Source: H B Maynard, *Industrial Engineering Handbook*, McGraw Hill, 1967, p 2–60 (reproduced with permission by McGraw Hill)

412

tainty associated with new products and processes, it might be imperative (that is, almost against the wishes and intentions of the managerial actors) to develop a much looser (if still rationally-based) structure of organization in order to cope with it at all. All the distinguishing characteristics may still be identifiable, but the form which they take is quite different from that usually assumed to be indicated by the bureaucratic model.

Burns presents his observations in the form of a polarity between 'mechanistic' systems (appropriate to stable conditions and strongly resembling the formal functional model of bureau-cracy) and 'organic' systems (appropriate to changing conditions in which the problems presented cannot be simply bundled up and allocated as defined rights and duties) (cf Burns and Stalker, 1961, pp 119–22).

The main distinguishing features of the latter are: the empha-sis upon roles defined by the organizational tasks and emphasizing expert contributions from individuals rather than the fulfilling of the duties of a defined 'office'; the stratification of the population on the dimension of senior to junior (greater to lesser expertise) rather than the hierarchy of positions; the development of action rules and criteria of judgement from the task concerns of the under-taking rather than from the body of established rules; procedures established over time and as a result of past experiences; a ten-dency to replace a simple personalized loyalty to the undertaking ('as a person') by a commitment to the undertaking's tasks (as problems to be solved).

One inference to be drawn from this is that where the external environment generates its own uncertainties, those within the undertaking who must respond to them are likely to develop their own patterns of response which enables them to live with, if not necessary to reduce, their uncertainties.

The organic form, by departing from the familiar clarity and fixity of the hierarchic structure, is often experienced by the indi-vidual manager as an uneasy, embarrassed, or chronically anxious quest for knowledge about what he should be doing, or what is expected of him, and similar apprehensiveness about what others are doing. . . . This kind of response is necessary if the organic form of organization is to work effectively. Under-standably, such anxiety finds expression in resentment when the apparent confusion besetting him is not explained. In these cir-cumstances, all managers some of the time, and many managers all of the time, yearn for more definition and structure (Burns and Stalker, 1961, pp 122–23).

413

By implication, the intentions of many managers might be to revert to the mechanistic structure, but the constraints of the 'objective' situation prevent this happening. What then presents itself to the eye as the structure of this kind of undertaking might therefore be said to be reflective of, or contingent upon, the nature of that objective situation.

Accommodating discretion

But if the external environment may be regarded as limiting the scope for choice in organizational structure, so too may the internal one. In the case of Burns and Stalker's electronics firms in Scotland, the nature of the market appeared to impose limits upon what was possible in the way of organizing activity. But the effect of the limitation was, generally speaking, to impose flexibility and high discretion upon the managerial roles which formed the focus of the study. The inference is that because the market had the form it had, managers could not retreat into their precisely-defined roles, but had to absorb a good deal of the uncertainty in the situation in much more fluid ones.

There are, however, a large number of studies which have been made of work roles, which, for whatever reason, involve relatively high discretion. Examples are the studies of professionals in research and development departments (cf Orth, Bailey and Wolek, 1964; Barnes, 1963), production managers in changing production and processing situations (eg Burns and Stalker, 1961; Gouldner, 1955; Ronken and Lawrence, 1952) and professional workers in such service fields as health and social work (eg Algie, 1970; Rowbottom, 1973; Thomason, 1969; Heisler, 1977) or education (cf Hughes, 1970).

In these situations, it appears that the bureaucratic structure fits ill and infrequently in its pure form. Although it may be that all organizational theories and forms in modern society are but footnotes to Weber (Katz, 1964, p 431), a number of quite distinct forms, justified on somewhat different theories from the bureaucratic, have made their appearance in these same kinds of situation.

Research and development departments have experimented with 'dual hierarchies' (Shepard, in Orth, Bailey and Wolek, 1964); in social work, Rowbottom (*op cit*) has proposed a modified conception of bureaucratic organization; Algie (1970) a polyarchic structure; in medicine, Hunter (1967) has advocated an arena pattern of organization in 'self-run hospitals'; in the health, social service and local government services, a group of official reports relating to 'reorganization' all stressed the desirability of team or consensus management (cf Brunel University working papers on health service reorganization, 1973).

These various proposals and experiments appear to have been derived as much from considerations of limitations internal to the undertakings, as from those relating to the external environment. In some cases, the 'workers' demands for highly discretionary work roles in order to serve clients (and thus cope with the external environment) may have defeated any attempt to impose a monocratic bureaucracy upon the undertaking, but the possibility of making such demands stick derives from the internal authority system as much as from the demands of the environment.

Once attention had been focused, by research or by proposed new designs, upon such an apparently diverse range of options, it was relatively quickly perceived that the classical writers on organization and management had offered alternative models which were not, at the time, taken up or developed.

Weber for example identified as one of the historical forms of administration, what he referred to as 'collegial administration'. This derived from the situation in which administration was carried out jointly by equal or near-equal colleagues, and has given rise to the modern concept of 'collegism' (as used on page 418, for example). Admittedly, this was based on the early organization of Italian mercantile cities, but in essence it provided for the various 'members' of the organization to contribute to the collective running of the system, each according—it might be said—to his ability to do so. The emphasis in the administrative process was therefore on a contribution from a 'specialist' base to a 'collective' administration.

In his turn, Taylor recognized that one possible way to take advantage of managerial expertise was to establish a 'functional organization'. In this arrangement, each highly trained specialist manager would concern himself throughout the enterprise with his special and limited function, contributing this, as it were, to the general need to run the totality as expertly as possible. In this conception, there would be no *general* manager or supervisor who would have general authority and responsibility for sections of the whole on an individual basis, but merely specialist (expert) managers who would have specialized authority and responsibility over the whole domain. Consequently, integrity of operation would only be achieved if the specialists saw themselves as required to achieve a 'consensus' amongst themselves, to use a term which has suddenly become currency in the service organizations following recent changes (see Brunel University, working papers on the

Reorganization of the NHS, 1973).

Weber himself did not place much emphasis on his collegial administration, and his disciples have tended to ignore it (*see* Albrow, 1970). Taylor saw functional administration as somewhat idealistic and industry certainly did not take it up with anything like the fervour with which it adopted the other parts of his main thesis (Urwick and Brech, 1947). Nor for the most part have the recent discussions on new models of organization for scientific bodies, social work agencies, health care units or educational establishments reached back into the literature to develop an ancestry for their proposals. They have instead tended to adopt a more pragmatic approach to the problem, seeking immediate solutions to emergent problems which appeared with increase in scale of operation.

Segmentation

In practice, one of the main variants on the worker-organizing theme in situations where high work-role discretion is found, is that of the matrix organization. This is depicted in figure 16 on p 417, in the form adopted in a BP-subsidiary computer soft-ware undertaking. It is based on the idea that work-task organization can and should be separated from people (or 'consideration') organization.

In the diagram the 'numbered' managers bring together groups of staff for varying periods of time to engage in projects of work, whilst the 'lettered' managers hold these same staff in groups defined by reference to qualifications and competence. The latter are primarily concerned with staff welfare and development and the former with completion of projects. The major advantage claimed for this kind of structure is that the people questions can be dealt with in separation from project questions, so that the one can be segmented (*see* above, pp 360–62) from the other, thus avoiding 'interference'.

The main significance of this development, which stops far short of functional organization in Taylor's sense, lies in its confounding of many of the 'commandments' of good organization which stem from the classical conception (*see* above, p 411). Although it has so far made its appearance mainly in 'professional' organizations (including hospitals which have had approximately this kind of project organization for many years) it appears to offer the prospect of seeking to organize people in such a way that the task and people concerned may be segmented with some advantage to the prosecution of both.

The general effect of these changes has, however, been to shift the emphasis from unitary and somewhat authoritarian structures towards pluralistic and somewhat more federalist arrangements,

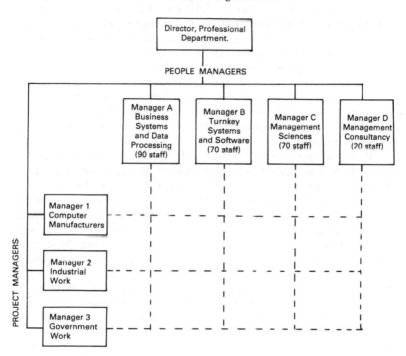

Figure 16
Scicon's matrix organization

A matrix organization is designed to split the roles of managing people and managing projects. People managers run the careers of their staff. Project managers must bid for use of these staff as and when they need them. Scicon's 250 professional staff, therefore, usually have two lines of responsibility. They report vertically to their functional boss, and horizontally to their project boss.

Source: David Palmer in *Financial Times* (29 December, 1970)

417

certainly at this 'managerial/professional' end of organization.

These terms are drawn from the continuum of organizational forms presented by Rice and Bishoprick (1971, p 202) which ranges from autocracy at one extreme to egalitarianism at the other. In between they recognize bureaucracy, systems, decentralization, collegism and federation as providing identifiable points along the continuum. Most of the current debate on this subject of structure tends to cluster around the middle of this range, stressing the differences between relatively closed or mechanistic organizations of essentially the bureaucratic/systems type, and the relatively open or organic organizations of the decentralized/collegist type. As the Burns and Stalker study in particular shows (see the descriptions of the mechanistic and organic structure offered on their pp 119–22) there are very real and significant differences on the dimension of the discretion sanctioned over this relatively narrow range along the full continuum.

It seems unnecessary to assume that this development must be confined to managerial and professional levels of organization. Where, for example, workers of any description have the power to refuse to accept bureaucratic authority, as the professionals tend to do because of the nature of the work they do, a similar structural consequence might be expected to follow. In other words, changing socio-cultural values and attitudes in themselves may be admitted to the list of factors which might force a structural modification.

At 'lower' levels of organization, changes of this attitudinal kind appear to have occurred and to be pressuring for consequential changes in the form of organization. At the present time, this pressure is contained within the actions related to 'participation', but in terms of the development of thinking on the subject of organization, the present position has been reached after a long process of 'discovering people' in organizations (cf Katz and Lazarsfeld, 1955) which owes a good deal to the work of psychologists.

The human relations studies
The findings of researchers in social psychology were to effect some changes, if not in the basic structure of organizations, at least in their textures. Much of the work done in the 1930s, 1940s and 1950s in this area effected changes in the place accorded to the small group in formal organizations, although the experiments with the autonomous working groups (as a kind of logical conclusion of these developments) were relatively slow in appearing (*see* above, pp 341–43). But this kind of research also opened up some important questions about worker commitment and loyalty to work (*cf* Lupton, 1963) and helped prepare the ground for new theories of

418

motivation (*see* above, pp 262–93).

This came about mainly because the early researches were based on assumptions not unlike those of the exponents of 'scientific management' and because as the work progressed it became clear that those assumptions would not hold.

The early work in this field sought to determine the capability of the individual to exercise the roles which organizations were prone to assign to them. In Britain the work of the Industrial Fatigue Research Board (later the Industrial Health Research Board) followed in the mainstream of psychology at that time, which was mainly concerned with explaining and measuring the differences between individuals. They were not particularly concerned with organizational design. The kind of problems that were thrown up by the first world war, and which tended to structure the approach of British scientists to industrial problems, were essentially the sort which scientific management was quite ready to recognize. These were the problems of how long an individual worker could work without undue fatigue, of the effect various physical variables at work might have on work performance, and so on.

This approach was also to be found in the United States and the earlier Hawthorne experiments conducted under the auspices of the Western Electric Company in the 1920s adopted a very similar approach even though ultimately the outcome of this research was to be significantly different. Although therefore the psychologists addressed themselves to rather different questions from those which interested Taylor and the other scientific management proponents, they were nevertheless concerned to supply answers to a similar kind of question, namely just what an organization could expect of an individual under definable conditions.

The assumption here was that if the physical conditions of lighting, ventilation, heating and timespan were adequately controlled, improvements in productivity might be expected. It is true that some at least of this psychological experimentation was concerned to answer the question of what effect variation in the physical environment had upon the health or well-being of the workers, and not with the simple question of improved efficiency.

The main later contribution of these studies, however, was in showing that small free groups were a prevalent feature of the work situation, cutting across the formal patterns of organization designed to co-ordinate and control work activities; that they possessed significant structures which equipped them with leadership and discipline; that they frequently possessed distinct norms or standards of conduct against which proper group behaviour might be assessed; and that the sanctioned thoughts, feelings and be-

419

haviours might or might not accord with their counterparts in the official organization (cf Homans, 1951; Cartwright and Zander, 1953 and 1960; Sprott, 1958).

It was only somewhat later that the parallels between these free and voluntary *informal* groups and the structures of local union organization in the workshop were noted (*see* Sayles, 1959; Batstone, Boraston and Frankel, 1977). However, even before this, the potentialities of the informal structures for either co-operation or conflict with official policies and practices were recognized, and, as in the Bank Wiring Observation Room studies at Hawthorne, actually charted (Roethlisberger and Dickson, 1939; Roy, 1954; Lupton, 1963). Phenomena such as 'restriction of output' and 'resistance to change' became explicable by reference to such groups, even when no organized union had made its appearance (*see* Coch and French, 1948, and in Cartwright and Zander, 1953 and 1960; Mathewson, 1931).

These conclusions thus challenged the simple premises of scientific management which saw the worker as essentially an individual, and, by offering management an explanatory theory, paved the way for management action to incorporate 'informal groups' into the 'formal' or official structure. The informal leadership and communications structures became new and additional channels of effective shop floor communication, and the disciplinary arrangements within these groups might, by persuasion, be brought to support management's rules and standards of conduct (cf Margerison, 1973; Heller, 1971).

These 'changes' were, however, concerned with issues of management (or leadership) style in organizations which nevertheless maintained their essential structure. They relied upon the training of those who already held formal managerial and supervisory positions to operate in such a way that they both took account of this 'group texture' in their formal conduct and sought to use the structures for 'official' goal-seeking ends (cf Blake and Mouton, 1964; Ellis *et al*, 1968). The findings of this type of research did not, however, directly impact upon the formal organizational patterns, although by creating an awareness of an underlying informal culture, it might be said to have prepared the ground.

The power question
What this prepared the way for, was an acceptance of the idea that people on the shop or office floor might well have both aspirations for other ends than those assumed to be there in the 'official' conception and mechanisms by which they might either achieve these

or at least protect their position. Consequently, with the growth of shop steward organization in many undertakings (particularly in manufacturing industry) in the post-war period and the full-employment situation, there was a predisposition to accept this as a legitimate force. The fact of an informal 'culture' having been dis-covered, it was not so surprising that workers would seek to develop this more positively and pro-actively once their 'power' was enhanced (as it was seen to be by full-employment and (later) by employment protection legislation (*see* above, pp 69–126)).

In some ways it is perhaps unfortunate that this development has attracted the label of the 'informal system of industrial re-lations' (as a result of the Donovan Commission's analysis) but in other ways it is not without its significance that it should attract the same adjective as the free groups' culture. It remains an 'informal' structure, but becomes one with the 'power' of the trade union around it, able as a result to develop informal agreements and understandings with management which served either to protect that culture or to develop it. In the area of 'custom and practice' as Brown (1973 and 1972) has shown, this relatively new and more powerful representative force of the local shop stewards' organiza-tion was able to exert an influence upon decisions about work which had hitherto been considered for management to take unila-terally, whether in fixing standards or determining conduct.

This development helped to establish the worker's goals as having comparable legitimacy to those of the 'undertaking' or of management acting in its behalf, and to do so on the basis of a sanc-tioning power which helped to guarantee it. In so far as these goals involved different productivity targets and alternative loyalties from those traditionally set by management, they confronted man-agement with a challenge to which they had to make some response. This called for a 'new look industrial relations' (Oldfield, 1966) and a 'coming to terms with trade unions' (McCarthy, 1973) and for the incorporation of these new, relatively free-standing shop steward organizations within the constitutions of the local undertaking, as recommended by the Donovan Commission and the Bullock Committee.

The Donovan Commission's proposals were for the reform of collective bargaining (Report, 1968, pp 38–53 and 262–64) by which they meant mainly the constitutionalization of industrial re-lations at the factory (or company in multi-plant undertakings) level. This emphasized the finding of a place for workplace repres-entatives in the local decision-taking processes, the review by direc-tors of industrial relations policies, structures and practices, and the development of a set of joint agreements which would govern conduct on a wide range of issues (*see* para 1022, p 263). This suggestion for the incorporation of the informal system did not, however, imply a major revolution in industrial relations, but rather its 'reform' in the interests of securing order (para 1019, p 262) (*see also* below, pp 442–49 and 458–61).

The Bullock Committee proposals

The Bullock Committee's proposals went much further than this, and suggested a federal structure for industrial governance (*see* Rice and Bishoprick, 1971; and above p 418). The Committee's brief was to consider how (ie not whether) 'a radical extension of industrial democracy' involving the trade unions 'can best be achieved' taking into account the proposals of the TUC, and experience in both Britain and the EEC. The conclusions and proposals (which have not been implemented) are of interest in the present context in that they offer a new design formula for industrial government in which the 'partnership' idea is developed in a way which still looks towards a 'unitary' conception of objectives and means.

The Committee recommended that initially all large (2,000 or more employees) companies should be required by legislation to provide an opportunity for all employees to vote on whether they wanted an extension of 'industrial democracy' in the undertaking, and if the outcome of that was positive, to establish a single-tier board of directors with elected or appointed representatives from both the trade unions and the shareholders upon it. This proposal thus rejected the more common European practice of establishing a two-tier board, one concerned with direction and management, and the other with its supervision, on only the second of which are the employee representatives to be found.

The formula adopted for the unitary board is one which retains the element of 'mediation' of conflicting interests (*see above*, pp 396–97) in the form of a small group of agreed independents. It is expressed as a board composed of $2x + y$, where x equals a number of shareholder or employee directors, and y equals a number of other directors who shall be an odd number greater than one and less than a third of the total number of directors. 'We propose that in companies where all the conditions for the introduction of employee representation are met, the boards should be reconstituted to be composed of three elements—an equal number of employee and shareholder representatives, plus a third group of co-opted directors.' These additional directors should be co-opted with the agreement of a majority of the other two groups of representatives, and will normally number three or five persons according to the size of the board which the parties would want to establish (ie one of 11 or 17 on the application of the formula).

The majority of the Committee think that in principle:

> all directors should have the same legal duties and liabilities. We propose that there should be some changes in the law regarding director's duties to ensure that the employee representatives are able to carry out their normal and reasonable functions as representatives of the workforce. We recommend that all directors should continue to be required to act in the best interests of the company, but that in doing so they should take into account the interests of the company's employees as well as its shareholders.

The majority of the Committee seek legislative division of the functions of the shareholders and the board to permit some matters to fall within the purview of the new board, even if others could be delegated to management. They draw a distinction between the attributed functions and the non-attributed. The first set, on which the board will have the exclusive right to submit a resolution for consideration at a shareholders' meeting, are:

(a) winding up of the company
(b) changes in the memorandum and articles of association
(c) recommendations to shareholders on payment of dividends
(d) changes in the capital structure of a company (eg on the relationship between the board and the shareholders, a reduction or increase in the authorized share capital; as regards the relationship between the board and the senior management, the issue of securities on a take-over or merger)
(e) disposal of a substantial part of the undertaking.

The non-attributed functions are listed as:

(i) the allocation and disposition of resources to the extent not covered by (a) to (e) above, and to the extent to which they are not delegated to management
(ii) the appointment, removal, control and remuneration of senior management, whether members of the board or not in their capacity as executives or employees. Within these limits, no restrictions on delegation are envisaged, and existing rights and obligations in dealings with third parties, the shareholders' power to appoint auditors or to compel a Board of Trade investigation, or to appoint or recall the shareholder directors are not to be altered.

The objective in *attributing* functions to the board is to ensure that the body on which the trade union representatives sit shall have some kind of 'right' in these matters. But on the face of it their attribution takes away from the shareholders' meeting their existing right (whether they in fact exercise it or not in the particular case) to have the final say where the existing Articles provide for this.

It is not absolutely clear whether this 'ultimate' authority is to be removed. On the one hand, 'it is for serious consideration whether our proposals should apply to all companies irrespective of board level representation, or only to those with employee representatives on their board' (Bullock 1977, p 77). On the other, they suggest that on the attributed functions, the 'right to take a final decision would rest with the board of directors' *and* that 'the shareholders' meeting would retain a right to approve or reject the board's proposals in certain specified circumstances' which are not indicated or specified (*ibid*).

Later (p 81) the board is given 'the exclusive right to convene a meeting (of shareholders) for the purpose of considering resolutions in these areas' and the shareholders' meeting 'the right to decide whether to pass the resolutions or not', thus implying that the shareholders' meeting has power to refer back but not alter resolutions on the attributed functions with which it does not agree. How many times it may exercise this power before a terminus is reached will no doubt require a conscious decision by the legislators.

This attribution is, quite explicitly, recommended in order to allow the trade union representatives to act as representatives of their constituencies. The obligations of directors will be varied to allow other interests than those of the shareholders to be taken into account, but that said the trade union directors will then have the same obligations as other directors. But they will be answerable to their constituencies, not to the shareholders' meeting, a proposal clearly in accord with the 'democratic imperative'.

However, the determination to clarify this 'representative' role, places the shareholder directors in the same 'representative' capacity. The shareholders' meeting, instead of retaining an authority role on decisions about the government and operation of the company, will itself become a constituency with powers of recall and reappointment (or re-election). The removal of the modicum of authority to influence the Board's decisions as they may now have (see *Scott v Scott* (1943) 1 All E R p 582) ostensibly gives more power to the directors. Since the directors would now include the workers' directors, they too would presumably share in this greater power and greater freedom to decide. But whether *their* constituency would be content to exercise the same limited powers as the shareholders' meeting might be doubted; these constituents have, after all, a sanction in the form of industrial action which could be used against *any* Board decision, including those in which their own representatives had acquiesced.

By clear implication, therefore, this kind of proposal for change in the structure of the government of work undertakings must lead to a federal type of organization (*see* above, p 118). The Board would embrace two sets of directors, each separately powered by their constituencies, and for this reason meeting as independent 'persons' to negotiate the resolution of problems presented to the undertaking by the nature of the internal and external environments. The principle of unity which animates the autocratic and monocratic bureaucratic forms of organization would necessarily be replaced by a principle of pluralism in both this and the collegial forms. As the necessary legislation was passed to bring about such a change, the 'voluntary' pluralism inherent in recognition of and negotiation with independent trade unions would come to be supplemented or replaced by a legal pluralism. If this has so far been conceived as a pluralism embracing capital and labour (plus a few 'independents') only, the organizational ramifications of the duality or plurality could be expected to be extensive.

Conclusion

From the purely technical point of view (simply organizing interdependent tasks) there are problems for the organizational designer. The main form of organization on the cafeteria shelf, the bureaucracy, has (one presumes from its ubiquity) considerable advantages for the organization of tasks; but it has also been shown to have disadvantages. It is possible to suggest, as is implicit in the work of the pioneers of scientific management, that the defects stem from the failure of management to accept their 'duty' to define, measure and arrange the work tasks. But this is, in principle, the same view as that taken of the 'worker' who fails in his duty to serve the ends of the undertaking in a completely committed way, and perhaps the problem is, therefore, that it is 'people' who cause the disadvantages.

Attempts to find a solution have generally tackled the problem from the point of view that what is 'wrong' is the amount of discretion which divided work roles allow to human beings. Consequently, new organizational forms and structures might be created which either 'protect' the discretion already there (as in many 'professional organizations' such as those in health and social work fields) or 'compensate' for low discretion in actual work tasks by providing opportunity to exercise choice at superordinate decision-taking levels (as in proposals for increased participation). In the event that neither of these is possible, some attempt might be made, as in matrix organizations, to segment the concerns into task and people divisions, so that each does not hinder the other. All three developments do something to diminish the 'unitary' nature of authority.

But these are proposals which need to be translated into a reality by the actions of the same actors as those 'for' whom the accommodation is being sought. It is in the nature of the situation that they will have some interest, not merely in the outcome, ie the form of organization adopted, but also in the manner of reaching it. In the main area of our concern, workers have views on both questions, and in the following chapter, therefore, we look at their associations from the standpoint of their aims and the power which they might have acquired to realize them.

Further reading
On the main topic of this chapter, bureaucracy and its variations, see Albrow, 1979; Dunkerley, 1972; Burns and Stalker, 1961; and Etzioni, 1961.

On the associated theme of authority and power, see Cartwright in March (1965) and Clegg, S (1975).

Proposals for organizing in various contexts are to be found in Rice and Bishoprick, 1971; Thomason, 1973; the Bullock Committee Report, 1977.

17 Trade unions: objectives and control

Trade unions and the personnel manager

For part of their history, trade unions and personnel managers have developed somewhat similar concerns with changing working conditions in parallel with one another (cf Niven, 1967; Beaumont, 1980; and above, pp 36–7), sometimes on the same side and sometimes in opposition across the bargaining table. This has left behind at least two perspectives of the personnel specialist role: those of the linkman or the honest broker between labour and capital, and of the corporate industrial relations manager.

However, their sources of legitimacy are distinct: the trade union developed largely against the authority of management, whilst the personnel manager acquired and maintains his position on the authority base which is shared by all managers. Whether their objectives are shared or opposed, however, the personnel manager cannot avoid a relationship with trade unions, nor the necessity in his official position, for developing ways of coming to terms with them.

The two major questions which arise are: What is it that the management or the undertaking has to come to terms with and how is such adjustment and accommodation to be conceived?

The first of these questions, which will form our concern in this chapter, is to be answered not only by reference to the fact of trade union presence in work undertakings and the form which it takes there, but also by the deeper question of trade union objectives and power in the wider as well as the narrower (undertaking) context.

The trade unions, whatever view may be taken of them, are a very present fact of the current work scene. They are 'facts' which all managers have to adjust to or accommodate as they seek to realize their objectives. Numerically, these 'facts' are significant.

At the last count (end of 1979) there were 454 autonomous trade unions in the United Kingdom (including 13 with headquarters in Northern Ireland). (The higher figure reported by the Certification Officer, whilst it excludes trade unions in Northern Ireland, also includes 'sections' of unions where the Department of Employment's figures (quoted here) include only the 'parent' bodies.) The total membership of these unions was about 13½ million workers organized in branches within the UK, or about half of the employed labour force. Just over 80 per cent of these were members of the 27 unions whose membership was 100,000 or more, and almost two-thirds of the 11 unions with a membership of a quarter of a million or more. For most of the past decade, the number of trade unions has been steadily decreasing (as a result mainly of merger and amalgamation) and the number of members steadily increasing (cf *Employment Gazette,* January, 1981, pp 22–24).

A number of different ways have been adopted to classify them as 'national' associations. Because of the historical tendency towards organization according to skill category of members, one classification emphasizes this organizing principle; amongst both manual and white collar workers there are horizontal associations based on high and low skill (cf Flanders, 1952; Clegg, 1979; Farnham and Pimlott, 1979). Because of the presence of rules which in some cases open the union to almost anyone in an industry or group of them and in others restrict it to those with defined prior qualifications, another classification has distinguished the open and closed associations (Turner, 1962, and in McCarthy, 1972, pp 100–1).

The value of such classifications lies in their capacity for allowing prediction of some other variable. The one classification helps to distinguish unions according to their pursuit of occupational, industrial or general political objectives as being consistent with their organizational bases and the sources of their power to achieve them. The other has certain predictive power in relation to attitudes and policies towards jurisdictional and demarcation questions and ultimately towards the closed shop issue. In similar vein, distinctions based on membership or non-membership of the Trades Union Congress (TUC) may explain differences in attitudes and behaviours.

But whilst the 'kind' of union which is organized in the particular workplace is a factor of some significance to the manager, the issue of the number recognized and the relationships which exist between them in the local undertaking, is likely to assume greater significance. Multiple unionism in the workplace, reflecting the past policies of union organization and employer recognition, is a well-established phenomenon in British industrial relations.

428

With the growth in power of the local shop representative system in the full employment condition of the post-war period (cf Donovan Commission Report, 1968, pp 25–9) both the significance of the national types, and the number of them recognized, in the local situation, came to possess lesser significance than the bargaining arrangements developed locally.

By the 1960s, in some of the major industries at least, it was already clear that effective trade union action was being channelled through this local, workplace organization centred on the role of the shop steward as representative. Although not all unions recognized stewards (by this or any other title) managements (and particularly personnel managers) found themselves increasingly involved in local negotiations with local representatives, and opportunities developed for conducting such negotiations with representatives of a number of different unions in the workplace simultaneously. At the company level in some industries, notably engineering, these 'combined' stewards developed more formal 'combine committees' to co-ordinate approaches to negotiation in the separate plants of multi-plant companies.

As a consequence of this kind of development, the managerially-defined problem of multiple unionism at the workplace level, was often reduced as a practical issue. Also as a consequence, the national union organizations saw themselves with a 'dual' trade union structure developing alongside the traditional hierarchical arrangements. Noting these, the Donovan Commission Report recommended the formal incorporation of the dual, shop-steward-based arrangements into both the local collective bargaining structure and the formal trade union organization, as a means of improving industrial relations, reducing wages drift and avoiding fractional disruptions to the even flow of relations (Donovan Commission Report, 1968, pp 86–88).

This kind of development is not to be taken to mean that local union organization is, as a consequence, something less than or other than trade unionism. Shop stewards are primarily trade unionists and managements are required to cope with the phenomenon in these terms. In effecting adjustments and accommodations, therefore, the salient factors for consideration, remain the purposes and objectives which trade unions attempt to pursue and the power which they have available to do so.

Trade union purposes
Trade unions have largely developed spontaneously in response to needs felt by workers to mobilize power to protect or advance their

work-related interests *vis-à-vis* both the employer and the state (cf Milne-Bailey, 1929, p 1). From time to time, principles, doctrines and dogmas have been advanced to guide the organization of workers, but generally it is taken that trade unions have appeared, grown and developed their organization pragmatically (cf Flanders, 1952, p 24). Their development has been a slow and gradual process, and the conceptions which both trade unionists and others have held of these associations have certainly changed over time and will no doubt go on doing so (cf Hughes, 1966, p 64).

In their history, trade unions have been defined in many different ways, although two which emphasize purpose are generally used at the present time.

Firstly, there is the definition given by the Webbs, who saw trade unions as 'a continuous association of wage earners for the purposes of maintaining or improving the conditions of their working lives' (S and B Webb, 1920, p 1). This is clearly rooted in the historical period in which they were writing. It emphasizes the 'class' relationship of the trade unions of the time and it implies a generalized political mission for the trade union (a point to which we return below). Secondly, the definition of the law, as contained in S 28 of the Trade Union and Labour Relations Act:

> . . . 'trade union' means an organization (whether permanent or temporary) which either
> (a) consists wholly or mainly of workers of one or more descriptions and is an organization whose principal purposes include the regulation of relations between workers of that description or those descriptions and employers or employers' associations; or
> (b) consists wholly or mainly of
>   (i) constituent or affiliated organizations which fulfil the conditions specified in paragraph (a) above (or themselves consist wholly or mainly of constituent or affiliated organizations which fulfil those conditions), or
>   (ii) representatives of such constituent or affiliated organizations:
>   and in either case is an organization whose principal purposes include the regulation of relations between workers and employers or between workers and employers' associations, or include the regulation of relations between its constituent or affiliated organizations.

This has to be read in conjunction with the definition of worker in S 30 which is made to include anyone with employee status, except those in the armed and police services but not those with professional clients. Since 1977 this definition has been employed by the Department of Employment for administrative, data-collection purposes, in which trade unions are defined as 'organizations which appear to satisfy the statutory definition' whether registered, certified or not. This new definition excludes some organizations previously included in the figures (31 organizations with 167,000 in 1977—half in the police service) on the ground that they had nego tiation as a central objective.

Of these definitions of trade unions, the difference which exists between that provided by the Webbs and that found in legislation is quite often ignored in public and undertaking policy-formation. We tend to assume that trade unions are exclusively, or at least primarily, concerned with the objectives associated with collective bargaining which, in turn, guided by Flanders (1965) and Dunlop (1958), we have come to think of as 'job regulation' a process of converting the disagreements about the rules which should apply to work, in the workplace, into agreements. It is this assumed objective which is given prominence in the administrative and legal definitions of trade unions, although they do not exclude the possibility of others existing. It is also the characterization of trade union objectives which has recently been strongly derided by some writers on the subject of trade unions (see eg Hyman and Fryer, 1975, pp 170–82). Three other objectives are ignored or understressed in this characterization.

First, the objective of improving the conditions of members working lives by self-help, what the Webbs referred to as the 'method of mutual insurance'. This was always a method more associated wth the craft and skilled-worker unions than with those of the semi- and un-skilled, and this remains broadly the position. (In the area of white collar worker association, it is similarly more associated with the professional associations than with the white collar unions.) Currently, however, this is not a very significant objective for many worker associations in relation to material improvement, but self-help through education and training is often engaged in.

Secondly, the objective of bringing about improvements by regulating competition amongst workers in the labour market through the adoption of common rules and common standards of labour market conduct. *This* was the objective which placed the early trade unions outside the law. It depended upon workers establishing for themselves (and therefore upon their 'conspiring' in the language of the law) the minimum terms and conditions upon which they would offer their labour to employers. It was this agreement, not the approach to the employer to negotiate terms and conditions with him (which up to a point was legal at the time) which made trade unions unlawful combinations by virtue of their 'purposes' being 'in restraint of trade' (the term then used to subsume competition in the market).

It is not implied by this that the restriction of competition was not aimed at securing improved wages. Any action which restricted the labour supply, even plague and pestilence, could be expected to increase prices. Trade unionists merely adopted this principle and sought to place a restriction upon the supply through the common rule and through what came to be known as the attempt to 'impose the union rule book' (embodying these agreements *inter se*) upon the employers.

Thirdly, the objective of effecting improvements in conditions inside and outside work through political action aimed at securing more sympathetic legislation. The petitioning of Parliament was a mechanism known to labour for longer than they had known what came to be called 'collective bargaining'. From the second half of the eighteenth century, it was one which, though used, was of little avail. But political agitation to change the policies and approaches of the legislature and the judiciary, during the first three quarters of the nineteenth century, was not as novel a mechanism as was the collective bargaining method adopted in relatively malign circumstances by the 'new model' (mainly craft) unions around the middle of the century.

The changes sought (and eventually obtained) in the law were ones which would provide the worker with more rights in the employment relationship and the trade union with both fundamental legitimacy (it was by legal definition necessarily an 'illegal body') and power to (at least attempt to) impose the common rule upon the employer. Although there have arisen from time to time, political ideologies which emphasized the desirability of changes in the structure of industry itself, and although some of these (eg, the ideology supporting public ownership of the means of production) have had some success, the dominant stance taken by British unions has been one rooted in pragmatism in both industrial and political areas of concern.

Over time, there have been changes in the form of these objectives and in their relative emphasis. At the present time, however, they remain relevant both to 'the trade unions' as national associations and to the branch, lodge, chapel, office or workship organization within them. The major emphasis may now be upon 'collective bargaining' and 'control of competition' at the local level, and the form taken at that level by both of these may differ

432

quite markedly from that found a hundred years ago, but the broad generalization holds. It is not sensible or realistic to ignore the other objectives of national and local union organizations simply because, for administrative convenience, a formal definition gives prominence to just one.

Trade union power

The realization of the trade union's purposes, as with the realization of any objectives by anyone, calls for the acquisition and deployment of 'power'. 'Trade union power' is a topic of which we have heard much in recent years, usually in the vein that 'trade unions now have too much power'. The basis of this observation has usually been the incidence of strikes in the British economy in the post-war period, something associated with 'the challenge from below' (Flanders, 1965, p 39) or 'the new militancy' (Hawkins, 1978, p 11).

Strikes as such are no new trade union phenomenon; even before the law was willing to concede legitimacy to this form of worker sanction, workers' organizations were using this 'concerted refusal to work on the offered terms' as their main weapon to compel employer compliance with some trade union demand. But such concerted refusals have recently taken on both a higher degree of complexity, and have been deployed on a fragmented or disaggregated basis by the unions' local organizations at the level of the workplace, and it is this which has tended to foster the perspective quoted. The whole aspect is succinctly summarized by Cuthbert in the following way:

Strikes are by no means the only available sanction in the hands of shop stewards. 'Cut price' direct action in the form of the go-slow, work to rule and overtime ban can sometimes be equally damaging, apart from the operation of various restrictive labour practices, including work-spreading to obtain premium overtime earnings. Strikes, however, are the form of work group sanction which claims the most attention. The Donovan Commission declared that the prevalence of unofficial strikes and their tendency (outside coalmining) to increase have such serious economic implications that measures to deal with them were urgently necessary. Further such unofficial and unconstitutional strikes comprised the great majority of all strikes, about 95 per cent (Donovan Commission Report, 1968, p 19) (Cuthbert in Cuthbert and Hawkins, 1973, pp 4–5).

Whether these sanctions are most effectively deployed to secure the living standards of members, generally or domestically, may be questioned in the light of the comparison of British standards with those elsewhere in the industrialized world, but these weapons are used, comparatively speaking, with *medium* frequency in Britain, at least to protect what are interpreted as the workers' interests in management decisions. This may reflect the influence of the state through the law.

State protection of the trade union

At least until about a hundred years ago, most employers were unwilling to allow trade unions any influence in the determination of the main terms and conditions of employment of their members/ employees, and in this they were usually supported by the exercise of state power through the law.

When the early trade unions sought either to 'impose the union rule-book' on the workshop or to negotiate terms and conditions with the employer, their representatives and spokesmen were as often shown the door as invited in. In the more strident cases of employer opposition to this (as the employer saw it) 'dual' organization, he could and frequently did resort to the law for protection.

This was possible for two main reasons: first, the common law, with its doctrines supportive of 'individualism', denied combination, collusion, or association any place in the taking of economic and political decisions of the kind of interest to trade unionists; secondly, and for much of this time, legislation (particularly, the Combination Acts from 1799 until their repeal in 1824, and the repeal Acts of 1824 and 1825 thereafter) was either expressly prohibitive of trade union existence or (after 1825) highly restrictive of trade union activities. The fear of the 'mob' as a factor in the political life of the nation, also restricted the opportunities of citizens in general to engage in political pressuring during this same period.

By the third quarter of the century, however, attitudes were beginning to show some movement, under the influence of the observable conduct of the new model unions, and with a further extension of the franchise, legislation was enacted (particularly in the 1870s) to remove some of the common law disabilities suffered by the trade unions. At that time, in the nature of the situation, what was required primarily (and what was largely secured) in the Trade Union Act of 1871, the Conspiracy and Protection of Property Act of 1875, and the Trade Union Act of 1876 was a protection of the trade union from the penalties which might be inflicted upon them by the courts because of their (illegal) objects and their (unlawful) methods of realizing them. The protection was not

434

'complete' until the Trade Disputes Act of 1906 added some immunities from civil actions to the immunities from criminal prosecution, but these Acts taken together really provided the foundation of trade union protection in law.

The essentials of this legal protection remain today, although marginal changes are made from time to time the latest being in the Employment Act, 1980. They are contained in Ss 2 (5), 13 and 14 of the Trade Union and Labour Relations Act, 1974, as amended by the Employment Act, 1980 (which adds sections covering picketing (S 16), secondary action (S 17) and actions to compel trade union membership, as being outside the general provision of S 13 of the main Act). By S 2 (5) the trade union is protected as to its purposes.

The purposes of any trade union . . . shall not, by reason only that they are in restraint of trade, be unlawful so as—
(a) to make any member of the trade union liable to criminal proceedings for conspiracy or otherwise
(b) to make any agreement or trust void or voidable nor shall any rule of a trade union . . . be unlawful or unenforceable by reason only that it is in restraint of trade.

By Ss 13 and 14, the trade union is protected as to its actions taken in pursuit of its (lawful) objectives. These free the trade union as a body and its members or officers from actions in tort which might otherwise apply because of actions taken by or in the name of the trade union (provided that these do not involve negligence resulting in personal injury or breach of duty arising out of ownership or use of property) or actions done in connection with the regulation of relations between employers and workers (S 14). They also give immunity to persons from actions in tort which might otherwise arise if the grounds are merely that the person induced or threatened to induce a breach of an employment contract or threatened to break such a contract, in circumstances where the actions specified were done in contemplation or furtherance of a trade dispute (S 13). (The full statements are given in table 14, p 436.)

What is introduced by Ss 16–18 of the Employment Act, 1980, is a set of restrictions on this general immunity under S 13 of the main Act. The first (S 16, which substitutes a new S 15 in the main Act) removes the immunity from persons who may meet all the other conditions, where they engage in picketing which is not declared lawful by the provisions of this new section. The second removes the immunity where the breach involved is of a contract other than a contract of employment *and* where there is involvement in 'secondary action' of the kind not satisfying the requirements of the law as to its legality.

Table 14
Restrictions on legal liability and legal proceedings

Trade Union and Labour Relations Act, 1974, as amended

Section 13 Acts in contemplation or furtherance of trade disputes

(1) An Act done by a person in contemplation or furtherance of a trade dispute shall not be actionable in tort on the ground only—
   (a) that it induces another person to break a contract of employment: or interferes or induces any other person to interfere with its performance; or
   (b) that it consists in his threatening that a contract of employment (whether one to which he is a party or not) will be broken or that he will induce another person to break a contract of employment to which that other person is a party

(2) For the avoidance of doubt it is hereby declared that an act done by a person in contemplation or furtherance of a trade dispute is not actionable in tort on the ground only that it is an interference with the trade, business or employment of another person, or with the right of another person to dispose of his capital or his labour as he wills

(3) Repealed 1980

(4) An agreement or combination by two or more persons to do or procure the doing of any act in contemplation or furtherance of a trade dispute shall not be actionable in tort if the act is one which, if done without any such agreement or combination, would not be actionable in tort

Section 14 Immunity of trade unions and employers' associations to actions in tort

(1) Subject to subsection (2) below, no action in tort shall lie in respect of any act—
   (a) alleged to have been done by or on behalf of a trade union which is not a special register body or by or on behalf of an unincorporated employers' association; or
   (b) alleged to have been done, in connection with the regulation of relations between employers or employers' associations and workers or trade unions, by or on behalf of a trade union which is a special register body or by or on behalf of an employers' association which is a body corporate; or
   (c) alleged to be threatened or to be intended to be done as mentioned in paragraph (a) or (b) above
   against the union or association in its own name, or against the trustees of the union or association, or against any members or officials of the union or association on behalf of themselves and all other members of the union or association

(2) Subsection (1) above shall not affect the liability of a trade union or employers' association to be sued in respect of the following, if not arising from an act done in contemplation or furtherance of a trade dispute, that is to say—
   (a) any negligence, nuisance or breach of duty (whether imposed on them by any rule of law or by or under any enactment) resulting in personal injury to any person; or
   (b) without prejudice to paragraph (a) above, breach of any duty so imposed in connection with the ownership, occupation, possession, control or use of property (whether real or personal or, in Scotland, heritable or moveable)

(3) In this section, 'personal injury' includes any disease and any impairment of a person's physical or mental condition.

436

The third removes the immunity where the breach in question involves a contract whether of employment or not, and the action was undertaken by the person in order to compel a worker or workers to become members of some union, in the circumstances where none of those workers are employees of the same employer as the person so acting.

These recent changes were intended to, and did in fact, reduce the power of the trade unions to act in pursuit of their purposes and objectives. They were brought in at the end of a decade in which picketing, secondary action, and pressure upon employers and some workers to establish closed shops, had attracted a good deal of public attention and discussion. They were resented and opposed by the trade unions as being regressive, but they do little more than return the immunities of trade unions and trade union-ists to the position obtaining at the time when the Donovan Com-mission was set up (1965). It is still possible to assert that the state still affords considerable protection to the trade unions in their attempts to realize their assumedly-central economic objectives as-sociated with collective bargaining. This, as much as their 'inherent' strength based on solidarity, helps to ensure that employers will feel a pressure to come to terms with them.

State pressures on performance

This class of legislation is, from the trade unions' standpoint, 'per-missive': it allows them existence and status but compels neither the unions nor the employers to any course of action. There is, however, another category of legislation which is designed to at least encourage some courses of action rather than others. This is generally of later origin than the legislation for trade union protec-tion, and that part of it which gave positive rights to trade unions *vis-à-vis* the employer (to information, to recognition, and to be consulted) is very recent indeed (and, it might be said, also hesitant and incomplete).

It stems from the fact that, once trade unions (with some help from the law) had established themselves, the pursuit of their objectives necessarily led them into decision-taking (albeit on a 'joint' basis) about economic and political problems confronting their members. For this reason, they came to perform what Kahn-Freund has referred to as 'public functions'—the mobilization and communication of worker attitudes and aspirations and the deter-mination of terms and conditions of employment (in conjunction with the employer). The performance of these functions then came

437

to be subject to an increasing degree of public control through legislation and government economic policies.

The first and more obvious of these public functions was that which occurred through 'collective bargaining'. This process required (and still requires) the assent of the employer before it could be established, but where the trade union was strong enough to attempt to impose its own rules upon the workshop, the almost inevitable next stage was that of negotiation of the rules to be applied as the employer made his response to the attempt. The employer interest in preserving as much as possible of his interest in rule-making led him to negotiate a new 'frontier of control' (Goodrich, 1920) and it is consequently possible to regard the growth of 'collective bargaining' as something arising from *both* the trade union's pursuit of its interest and the employer's protection of his (cf Clegg, 1979, p 65).

Had the trade unions (and the employers) not developed this collective bargaining institution as a mechanism for deciding pay and conditions of employment, it might well have fallen to the government itself to establish a mechanism. This was the case with the 'sweated trades' and later the 'unorganized trades', distinguished chiefly by their low levels of remuneration and the absence of both worker and employer organization concerned with pay determination, where the state established the so-called 'trade boards' (Trade Boards Act, 1909) and 'wages councils' on a tripartite basis to perform these same function (IR Handbook, 1980, pp 29–34). Something similar was discernible in the attempt to develop a broad-based Whitley Council structure (*ibid*, pp 15–16) although this had neither the same statutory base nor the same impact, at least outside the public service.

Over a progressively larger segment of employment, therefore, the main mechanism established to perform this function was that of 'voluntary' collective bargaining. The first state interventions to structure performance were therefore intended to foster, guide and facilitate this 'voluntary' activity. The first main examples of this approach are the Conciliation Act of 1896 (which sought to encourage voluntary collective bargaining but made provision for a public service of conciliation, arbitration and advice of the kind now associated with the Advisory, Conciliation and Arbitration Service) and the Industrial Courts Act of 1919 (which complemented this provision by adding a standing 'industrial court' whose present-day equivalent is the Central Arbitration Committee). Essentially, these statutes aimed at facilitating the parties to avoid open disputes by providing avenues for their speedy and external resolution.

It is, however, not without its significance that the first stated purpose of the 1896 Act was that of encouraging the parties to set up conciliation agreements voluntarily for themselves (as had already occurred in many organized trades). This general principle of seeking to foster voluntarism—or at least avoiding its destruction—runs through the gamut of labour legislation in this country.

Even the Industrial Relations Act of 1971, which many regarded as an attempt to substitute a high degree of state regulation in the industrial relations area, commenced with a statement of certain general guiding principles to be observed by all whose roles were established by legislation and concerned industrial relations affairs (ie bodies like the Commission on Industrial Relations and the National Industrial Relations Court and individuals like the Chief Registrar of Trade Unions), which also genuflected in this direction. Two of these, for example, read:

(a) the principle of collective bargaining freely conducted on behalf of workers and employers. . . .
(c) the principle of free association of workers in independent trade unions, and of employers in employers' associations, so organized as to be representative, responsible and effective bodies for regulating relations between employers and workers (IR Act, 1971, S 1).

Of similar effect is the provision in later legislation which sought to provide more positive rights and privileges in collective bargaining relations, under which that which the parties may agree to amongst themselves may, in appropriate circumstances be substituted for that which is statutorily required. The circumstances are, generally, that the agreement shall provide workers with rights or benefits at least as high as stipulated in the legislation as the minimum. The main example is that which gives the negotiating parties the right to seek to have a dismissal agreement made between them substituted by order in place of the unfair dismissal provisions of the Trade Union and Labour Relations Act, 1974 (Ss 1(2) and Sch 1 Part II).

Thus, both at the level of principle and at that of practice, legislation seeks to preserve the idea that collective bargaining is, and is best left as, voluntary.

The role of ACAS

The public service which now provides this 'facilitation' of voluntary collective bargaining is the Advisory, Conciliation and Arbitration Service (ACAS). This is supplemented and complemented by the Central Arbitration Committee in so far as that body is concerned with voluntary arbitration (its role in relation to the new rights accorded to independent trade unions is considered on pp 449–50, below). In both cases, the service offered is made available on the consent of the parties, and it is this which distinguishes them from the adjudication role associated with the Industrial Tribunals and the Employment Appeal Tribunal and exercised in respect of the new rights accorded to individuals by the legislation.

Although ACAS had been formally established in 1974, the Employment Protection Act 1975 provided the statutory foundation for its activities and generally served to codify the arrangements. The 'independence' of ACAS of the Government was effected by making it a corporate body, with a chairman and up to three deputy chairmen, drawn from the ranks of the 'independents', and three council members appointed by the Secretary of State from nominees from each of the trade unions and the employers' associations. The general duty imposed upon the ACAS is that of promoting improvement in industrial relations, particularly through the encouragement of an extension of collective bargaining, and the development (and if necessary the reform) of collective bargaining machinery. The functions of the new body bring together those which had previously been developed in the Department of Employment or in various other recently established *ad hoc* bodies, like the Commission on Industrial Relations. Five functions can be identified.

1 The service is empowered to provide a conciliation service. Where a trade dispute is apprehended or in existence, the Service may either offer its assistance as a conciliator or provide such assistance at the request of one or more parties. The conciliators may be officers of the Service or independent persons: their role is to be to encourage the parties to reach a settlement by using any agreed procedures and, whether such procedures exist or not, to help them to come to a resolution of their differences by 'conciliation or by any other means'. In extension of this general conciliation role, the Service is empowered to designate some officers to perform the functions of conciliation officers in matters which are or could be the subject of proceedings before an industrial tribunal (S 2).

2 The Service is empowered to provide a service of arbitration. Where a trade dispute is apprehended or in existence, the Service may provide arbitration 'at the request of one or more parties to the dispute and with the consent of all the parties' to it,

either by reference to a single arbitrator or a board of arbitration (made up of persons who are not officers or servants of the Service) or by reference to the Central Arbitration Committee. This power is restricted to those circumstances in which procedures are ascertained to have been exhausted and in which conciliation is judged not to be capable of resulting in a settlement, provided only that there are no 'special reasons' which justify arbitration even though the procedures have not been exhausted. This section continues provisions of the earlier legislation but by S 3(4) provision is made for publication of awards of arbitrators or boards of arbitration 'if the Service so decided and all the parties consent', and a firmer basis for establishing precedent in arbitration awards is thus established (S 3).

3 The Service is empowered if it thinks fit, 'to enquire into any question relating to industrial relations generally or to industrial relations in any particular industry or in any particular undertaking or part of an undertaking'. The Service is given powers to publish the findings of any such enquiry, together with its advice based on these findings, if the Service thinks that publication would help improve industrial relations, generally or specifically and after submitting a draft to, and taking note of the views of, the parties concerned with the inquiry. This Section continues the powers previously enjoyed by the Commission on Industrial Relations (S 5).

4 The Service is given powers to offer advice on industrial relations or employment policies, whether this is requested or not, to employers, employers' associations, workers and trade unions, and it may also publish general advice on these same matters. The Act offers a list of matters which are considered to be within the scope of this provision:

(a) the organization of workers or employers for the purpose of collective bargaining
(b) the recognition of trade unions by employers
(c) machinery for the negotiation of terms and conditions of employment, and for joint consultation
(d) procedures for avoiding and settling disputes and workers' grievances
(d) questions relating to communications between employers and workers
(f) facilities for officials of trade unions
(g) procedures relating to the termination of employment
(h) disciplinary matters
(i) manpower planning, labour turnover and absenteeism

441

(j) recruitment, retention, promotion and vocational training of workers

(k) payment systems, including job evaluation and equal pay (S 4).

These provisions also continue the functions previously performed by the Advisory Service of the Department of Employment and the Commission on Industrial Relations.

5 The Service is given a permissive power to issue Codes of Practice.

Performance-related rights and privileges

Where this provision merely permitted the use of a facility, the second category of state interventions was both more positive and later. These were based on the recognition of the trade unions' function of mobilizing and focusing worker attitudes and opinions. At the national level, from the first world war onwards, governments had recognized the value of drawing trade union leaders and representatives into consultation on national policies, *de facto* if not *de jure*, and organized employers over the same period came to see the value of this same kind of consultation and negotiation. At the domestic (undertaking) level, however, recognition of this same function by the employer was still 'voluntary'. As the 'national system' of collective bargaining yielded place to the domestic or 'informal system' (cf Donovan Commission Report, 1968, pp 36–37) in the period after the second world war, the pressure to guide and control this 'voluntary' response increased, and became focused in the recommendations of the Donovan Commission Report.

The legislation which followed in the 1970s (Industrial Relations Act 1971; Trade Union and Labour Relations Acts 1974 and 1976; Employment Protection Act 1975; Employment Protection (Consolidation) Act 1978; and the Employment Act 1980) attempts different statutorily-guided solutions to the 'problem' of securing more responsible and more effective collective bargaining at the domestic level. Both the trade unions and the employers were seen to be defective in their approach to the securing of this end, and a good deal of support for the proposition that some of the defects might be removed by appropriate legislation to guide or control collective bargaining performance was generated.

The fundamental question in the debate focuses upon the extent to which the employer should be compelled by law to recognize trade unions as representative of the worker interest in work, and to facilitate them in their function of influencing decisions *in* that interest. The main alternative to this is seen to be to leave the employer free to determine these issues 'voluntarily' in circumstances where the trade unions continue to enjoy certain 'privileges' (essentially those represented by the 'immunities' referred to above) which enhance *their* power to 'compel' employers to give such recognition and facilitation. The legislation of the 1970s has been rooted in both of these perspectives, with the IR Act and the Employment Act emphasizing the second alternative and the other statutes, the first.

Without debating here whether what has emerged in this legislation should properly be treated as a right or a privilege (but *see* Barnard, 1946, pp 207–43; Thomason, 1978, pp 10–18 what has emerged has generally been cast in terms of a kind of trade union right which imposes a kind of duty upon the employer. If, for the sake of brevity, we refer to these simply as 'rights', the legislation of the decade from 1971 has offered a conception of legislative control over the performance of the parties to industrial relations which highlights the value of recognition, facilitation, and consultation by the employer. Whilst it is true that the Employment Act 1980 removed some of these pre-existing 'rights', the conception remains a valid factor to be taken into account in the employer's decisions about how to approach industrial relations at the undertaking level.

1 Recognition

The Employment Protection Act gave trade unions a limited right to recognition by the employer, supported by the sanction of appeal to the CAC through ACAS where the conditions for claiming the right were met but the employer refused recognition (S 11). This right was removed by S 19 (b) of the Employment Act, 1980, but since the intentions behind Ss 11–16 of the EP Act had not really materialized in practice, this removal was, in itself, no great practical loss. The employer's problem of deciding how to respond to a recognition claim from an independent trade union remains, however, to be decided by calculating the advantage of dealing with representatives of a concerted worker interest against the disadvantage of admitting, or even encouraging, a dual loyalty.

The other removal of the Employment Act (S. 19 (c)), that of the qualified right of the independent trade union to claim an extension of recognized or general terms and conditions of employment to undertakings in which the employer had not conceded recognition (given in the EP Act, S 98), removes what could serve as an important sanction to be deployed by the trade union in seeking recognition of an employer. This repeal could, therefore, be seen as an attempt to return the employer's decision to the pre-existing 'voluntary' position. However, certain restrictions in the Employment Act, S 18, upon the applicability of immunities where acts are committed to compel trade union membership of employees of another employer or engaged elsewhere, goes somewhat beyond the pre-existing position, and effects a reduction in the sanctioning power of the trade union in the matter of compelling recognition.

2 Consultation

The law does not uphold directly the right of a trade union to negotiate with the employer, even when recognition has been secured (by whatever avenue). This decision is, again, voluntary, with the consequence that unions may be recognized by employers for consultation and negotiation over a considerable range of issues or subjects. There are, however, some exceptions to the general proposition in so far as the law prescribes 'consultation' with recognized independent trade unions in certain circumstances.

The Acts which nationalized various industries enjoin consultation upon the employer, and in this case, 'consultation' is usually interpreted to mean 'negotiation' where there are already recognized trade unions, *and* consultation through mechanisms distinct from those of collective bargaining.

More recent legislation requires consultation with recognized independent trade unions in connection with both health and safety and redundancy. By this, trade unions are offered

> a right to appoint safety representatives with whom the employer must consult on health and safety matters, and who may request the establishment of a health and safety committee (Health and Safety at Work Act 1974, S 2 (4) and (7) and Health and Safety at Work Regulation, R 2(1) and Sch 1) a right to be consulted by the employer about redundancy (S 99) and to complain about an employer's failure to consult and secure a protective award (S 101, EP Act).

Additionally, the Social Security Pensions Act 1975, requires companies to consult recognized unions on occupational pensions schemes.

Important though these areas may be, they cover only a very restricted area of the conditions under which people are employed. In practice, many recognized trade unions in many different undertakings have secured the 'right' to be consulted about and to negotiate a much wider range of issues. These rights have usually been secured, as the trade unionist might put it, by 'struggle', that is by deploying their collective power based on the sanction of in-

444

dustrial action, to secure the 'voluntary' assent of the employer to negotiate over an increasingly wide range of subjects (cf Roberts and Gennard, 1970).

The other aspect of 'negotiation' which has been extensively debated in the 1970s is that which now passes under the title of industrial democracy and/or participation. The main proposition here is that worker representatives should be afforded opportunity to participate in a wider range of industrial decisions than those which have hitherto fallen within the subject range of 'collective bargaining'. The focal point in this debate was the Report of the Bullock Committee on Industrial Democracy (1977) which recommended the restructuring of the Board of Directors to admit equal representation of shareholders and workers in association with a small group of independent outsiders. This found little favour and has not been acted upon by governments. But the question of the future extent of worker participation in industrial government still awaits an answer, and this may well be found through the development of practices within undertakings (*see* below, pp 475–78). For the moment, however, no imposition of a minimum standard from the centre has materialized.

3 Facilitation

On the other hand, a centrally-imposed minimum standard of facilitation of trade unions in their collective bargaining role has been imposed (and has survived the amending of these rights in the Employment Act of 1980). There are, essentially, two categories of right in this area, one requiring a general disclosure of information relevant to collective bargaining, and the other an accord of time off from actual working to allow union officers and members to participate in collective bargaining (and training) processes. There is, therefore, a general right to trade unions (which are recognized) to have disclosed to them by the employer, such information as might be calculated to facilitate collective bargaining (S 11, EP Acts) which is supported by the opportunity to present a complaint to ACAS and the CAC in respect of an employer's failure to disclose (S 19). There is, also, a right accorded to trade unionists to time off to take part in industrial relations, including trade union and IR training, activities (*see* above, pp 104–6). These are supported by the recommendation of the Codes of Industrial Relations Practice, which also indicate the kinds of facilities in the way of office space and access to telephones, which might be agreed locally in support of these statutory rights.

A rather different order of 'facility' is that which focuses upon the granting to the trade union (by the employer) of an exclusive

445

jurisdiction as a basis for establishing and maintaining a trade union 'discipline' amongst employees in a given undertaking or industry. The union membership agreement (UMA) by which some degree of exclusive jurisdiction is accorded to independent recognized unions (singly or plurally) is in itself lawful, but is to be secured, if at all, by voluntary agreement of the parties. The effect of legislation is, however, to allow the employer fairly to dismiss those who refuse to join the union(s) specified if the grounds of the refusal are other than ones of conscience or religion or those who cease to be members after a lawful UMA has been lawfully brought into existence (EP(C) Act, as amended, S 58). The legislation also provides that new UMAs will only achieve legality if they comply with certain requirements with respect to the proportions signifying assent to such an arrangement in a ballot (S 58A, EP (C) Act, as amended by the Employment Act 1980, S 7). Thus, although the UMA may be said to facilitate the trade union in its concern to present a common and disciplined front to the employer in collective bargaining, the effect of the legislation is primarily to hedge about the attempt to acquire this kind of union security with a number of legal restrictions designed to safeguard the rights of the individual *vis-à-vis* the trade union and *vis-à-vis* the agreements which may be made between it and the employer.

Thus, taken together, this category of legislation, in contrast to the first (pp 438–42 above), seeks to compel the parties to industrial relations to certain courses of action in their collective dealings. These two categories are not so exclusive as to be uninfluencing of each other (for example, the union security aspects of the second category have much to do with union protection) but the second *is* developed primarily in the interests of securing good or improved industrial relations, and for that reason may be distinguished from the first. Taken together they do support the trade union's power to sanction but the second category provides an extra source of sanction to that which the unions might otherwise command. As a consequence, therefore, the employer, in determining policies and practices in the area of collective relations is confronted not merely by trade union demands, in isolation, as it were, but also by obligations which are either imposed or at least supported by the law.

Disclosure of information and the ACAS/CAC role
With the donation of certain positive rights to independent trade unions in the EP Act of 1975, particularly those relating to recognition (S 11), information disclosure (S 19) and extension of recognized terms and conditions of employment (S 98 and Sch 11), both

ACAS and the CAC acquired adjudicatory roles and the power to impose a limited kind of sanction upon employers who refused to accept their recommendations on these questions. Two of these rights were removed in the Employment Act of 1980, leaving only information disclosure of the original trinity. The disclosure requirement and the manner in which ACAS and the CAC become involved in the claims of independent trade unions in respect of it, are discussed in this section to illustrate the variation of role which this kind of right imposes upon these two bodies.

The basic duty imposed on the employer in connection with disclosure is that of supplying information to recognized independent trade unions, on request and where it can be established that the information is both available and relevant to collective bargaining. Thus, this duty is additional to the long-standing requirement upon companies under Companies legislation to publicize certain information of interest to shareholders, investors and creditors, and to the more recent requirement (Companies Act 1967) to make available certain information considered to be in the 'public interest' or necessary for public planning (Industry Act 1975).

Disclosure to employees

Disclosure to employees and their trade unions of information about the current state and future plans of an enterprise is something which trade unions have often sought in negotiations in the past: the view was taken that information was a basis for power and control, and that its retention by management provided the foundation for the exercise of a management prerogative. The TUC's 1974 Report of the General Council to Congress shows the direction of thinking: 'The provision of information on the operations of the enterprise—whether public or private—to the employees and their representatives is an essential background against which extensions to industrial democracy can occur on a rational and informed basis.' Already the 1970 TUC Report had given a shopping list of information to be sought for the facilitation of collective bargaining. This list included financial information, cost information and remuneration data, together with information on prospects and plans in the financial investment, marketing and manpower areas. What the trade union movement wants, and what it wants it for, is thus spelled out.

Disclosure of this general type of information entered the realms of public policy through the recommendations of the Donovan Commission for the development of orderly and effective industrial relations in British industry. The Commission argued that boards of companies would have to 'collect systematic information on which to base action in [such matters as recruitment, promotion, training and retraining] and to make available to workers' representatives such information as they may reasonably require.' This was taken up and extended by the Labour Government's policy statement *In Place of Strife* and by its Industrial Relations Bill of 1970. It was also taken up by the Conservative Government, and promulgated in the Industrial Relations Act of 1971: by S 56 the employer was required to supply information to a trade union (or its representatives) where it could be shown that this information was necessary for the furtherance of collective bargaining at any and every stage, or that its non-disclosure would be detrimental to good industrial relations practice. This part of this Act was never implemented, but it did provide the basis for the CIR investigation into disclosure which appeared as a report, *Disclosure of Information,* in 1972.

The CIR placed main emphasis in its report on the desirability of securing an agreed policy on disclosure and then set out two categories of guideline, one on Types of Information and the other on Conditions and Methods. The report was conservative in its suggestions, arguing that it did no more than indicate what might be included in disclosed information where the circumstances were right and the parties agreed. It did not pretend to be exhaustive in either range or depth and did not suggest that in all undertakings information on all items should necessarily be given.

The Employment Protection Act 1975, S 17, reinstates the duty upon the employer to disclose information, originating in S 56 of the repealed Industrial Relations Act. The general duty is to disclose to recognized independent trade unions, on request by them (in writing if the employer so requires) 'all such information relating to his undertaking as is in his possession, or that of any assocated employer, and is both—

(a) information without which the trade union representatives would be to a material extent impeded in carrying on with him such collective bargaining, and
(b) information which it would be in accordance with good industrial relations practice that he should disclose to them for the purposes of collective bargaining'

and at the request of the union representatives this information may be required in writing.

The general duty is restricted by certain other provisions of the Act, in addition to the above restriction that both conditions (a) and (b) shall be present. Information against the interests of

448

national security, which would contravene a legal prohibition, which is obtained in confidence or which relates to an individual, or which was obtained in connection with legal proceedings, need not be disclosed. Nor need information 'the disclosure of which would cause substantial injury to the employer's undertaking for reasons other than its effect on collective bargaining' (EP Act, S 18(1)). Nor is the employer under a duty to show or copy any document, other than that prepared by him to meet the request of the union representatives, or to compile or assemble information where to do so would mean an amount of work or expenditure out of reasonable proportion to the value of the information in the conduct of collective bargaining (S 18(2)).

The CAC role

Where an employer, after receiving a proper request for information, does not give it or does not confirm it in writing when requested, an independent trade union is enabled to complain to the Central Arbitration Committee. The CAC may then refer the matter to ACAS if it is of the opinion that the issue might be resolved by conciliation. Otherwise, and where conciliation does not result in a settlement, the CAC is empowered to hear the complaint, and thereafter to state whether it finds the complaint in whole or in part well-founded along with its reasons for the finding. The declaration must indicate the information in respect of which the complaint was found to be well founded, the date on which the employer refused or failed to disclose or confirm, and a period (not shorter than a week) within which the employer ought to disclose or confirm.

Thereafter, at the expiry of the stated period, the trade union may present a 'further complaint' that the employer has not disclosed or confirmed the information in the statement. If, following the same procedure as before, the CAC concludes that this further complaint is well founded, it is empowered to say so. Once this is done, the trade union in question may present a claim to the CAC that the contracts of employment of a named group of employees should include the terms and conditions which the union specifies in the claim presented. Provided that the employer does not disclose or confirm in the interim or that the claim is not withdrawn, the CAC is empowered to hear the parties, and to award either the claim or such other terms and conditions as it considers appropriate from a date at its discretion provided it is not earlier than the date specified in the original complaint. The specified terms and conditions of the award shall then be observed by the employer as part

449

of the contract of employment of the employees in respect of whom the claim was made, until such time as they are superseded or varied by a subsequent award or agreement (EP Act, Ss 19–21).

In so far as it may, on finding such complaints well founded, impose new terms and conditions of employment, against the wishes of the employer, the CAC is thus given a powerful role.

The ACAS role
The main continuing role of ACAS in this area is that of conciliating the issue, where the CAC considers that this course might prove fruitful. But the Service's main contribution in this area is represented by the Code of Practice issued under the provisions of the legislation.

The guidance which this offers to employers is in many ways similar to that offered by the earlier CIR Report (No 31, 1972), particularly in its cautious statements and its list of suitable items of information for disclosure. Like all the other Codes this does not impose any legal obligation upon the employer, but the extent to which its guidance has been followed may be entered in proceedings under the EP Act in support of a claim or counterclaim. The Code therefore makes it clear that what is to be disclosed in the particular case shall depend upon local circumstances and requirements and shall reflect the general criteria of 'necessity' in those circumstances and 'good industrial relations' conducted voluntarily. It is also intended that the Code shall be read as stating a minimum standard of good practice which such collective bargaining could well extend.

The Code therefore lists some examples under broad category headings of the information which might in appropriate bargaining circumstances be disclosed, and points out that the main weight of responsibility for showing that any item of such information is necessary or desirable really falls upon the trade union representatives, who will have to identify their precise needs clearly and early in the proceedings. Similarly, the Code places the onus upon the trade unions to ensure that, by training or any other means, the representatives are in a position to define their need and to make use of the information when they have received it. Many companies have already developed policies on information disclosure which take their practice well beyond what is suggested in the Code itself, and the point of the Code's list of examples is therefore to offer broad and general guidance to those which still have to develop relevant policies (cf Smith, 1977, Management Survey Report No 31, BIM).

450

The Code lists:

1 Pay and benefits: principles and structure of payment systems; job evaluation systems and grading criteria; earnings and hours analysed according to work group, grade, plant, sex, outworkers and homeworkers, department or division, giving where appropriate, distributions and make up of pay showing any additions to basic rate or salary; total pay bill; details of fringe benefits and non-wage labour costs

2 Conditions of service: policies on recruitment, redeployment, redundancy, training, equal opportunity, and promotion; appraisal systems; health, welfare and safety matters

3 Manpower: numbers employed analysed according to grade, department, location, age and sex; labour turnover; absenteeism; overtime and short-time; manning standards; planned changes in work methods, materials, equipment or organization; available manpower plans; investment plans

4 Performance: productivity and efficiency data; savings from increased productivity and output; return on capital invested; sales and state of order book

5 Financial: cost structures; gross and net profits; sources of earnings; assets; liabilities; allocation of profits; details of government financial assistance; transfer prices; loans to parent or subsidiary companies and interest charged.

The Code strongly urges employers and their recognized independent trade unions to work out and agree their general and longer-term information needs, as a foundation for the development of a systematic relationship in bargaining. Such an information agreement might conceivably develop from a review of what information is currently available or disclosed and what might be desirable if it could be made available. It would then seek to establish the form in which information might be presented, when and to whom this should be done, regularly or as required, generally to employees or specifically to bargainers. This would have to make some provision for the treatment of some information as confidential, particularly in the eartly stages of negotiation, for the protection of both 'sides' in the negotiating process. The agreement might also make provision for elucidation of information, after disclosure, a mechanism being agreed to allow this to happen, possibly outside the negotiating process itself. It would also be necessary to establish a similar mechanism for resolving disputes about what should be made available, or whether what had been agreed as capable of disclosure had in fact been disclosed as agreed.

Such information agreements might also form a part of the general disclosure or informing policy of the undertaking. This policy would need to take account not merely of the information to be disclosed for purposes of collective bargaining under S 17 of the Employment Protection Act, but also of the disclosure required by the Employment Protection (Consolidation) Act in respect of terms and conditions of employment to new employees (*see* above, pp 87–90) and of the information to be communicated to union representatives in respect of redundancy proposals (*see* above, pp 109–11). As and when the harmonization with European practice in respect of 'participation' is effected through legislation, there will doubtless be more information to be disclosed, and therefore more to be incorporated in a comprehensive agreement. (This aspect is taken up in connection with the development of a 'pluralist constitution' below, pp 471–78).

Conclusion

It is, perhaps, not surprising that the personnel management occupation has blossomed during the last two decades coincidentally with the development of the local trade union organization and of undertaking-wide negotiations. The two grew out of similar conditions in work undertakings, and if they have now polarized to some greater extent than formerly, they now exist together in a significant relationship cemented by the existence of plant negotiations as a dominant feature of the present situation.

The trade union is, however, a factor which has to be reckoned with in the development of work organization. Once local bargaining had established itself, the way was open for the worker representatives to influence directly the contours of the total work situation. This did not depend upon the Donovan Commission recognizing the informal system, nor upon the law giving workers and their trade unions 'rights' to recognition and negotiation; the simple fact that the local situation was now structured to allow or encourage *domestic* negotiations was probably sufficient to increase the scope of joint-decision-taking within undertakings. Both the Donovan Commission and (to some extent) the subsequent legislation merely recognized and helped to codify the extant pattern.

But the Donovan Commission did make certain recommendations and the law has subsequently been modified. The presumption is created in public morality that local, domestic negotiations will take place, and the power of worker representatives to compel them to do so has been increased (even if there has been some degree of back-tracking on this in the Employment Act, 1980). Union purposes in relation to industry and legal enactment remain and are generally sanctioned in law, even if there are still some curbs upon the manner in which their power may be exercised in their pursuit. The standing of the trade union and its local representatives, in law, is pretty well assured and even though there is no compulsion upon the individual employer to recognize and negotiate, there remains a strong presumption in these directions, and few employers are likely to avoid negotiation as a dominant requirement of much decision-taking in the future.

In fact, much of this kind of pressure is probably not to be associated simply with a trade union morality or simply with a legal requirement. Behind it, and what may permit us to regard this pressure as stemming from a cultural imperative of our society, is the probability that workers demand that management take more notice of their goals and aspirations. If that is the origin, negotiations or collective bargaining in the conventional mould becomes an economic mechanism to use to ensure that that 'notice' is taken. In so far as trade union organization recruits conformity to the pursuit of certain goals in a priority order, to that extent the employer is enabled to 'take notice' of something that is reasonably coherent. The alternative to representation in this way might well be to carry out surveys to find out what values are dominant amongst a group of workers (*see* above pp 179–80).

In spite of current discussions on trade union immunities and of doubts about the extent to which industrial democracy might be compelled by legislation, the future is likely to lie with negotiation as the main mechanism through which people-problems are to be solved and through which commitment to the organization and its purposes is to be achieved.

However, all of this requires human action to bring about any future which may be forecast as likely. In the next three chapters, therefore, we look at the possible directions in which this 'negotiation' strategy might move and at the methods and tasks which might be associated with them. In the next chapter, we look at the structural aspects, under the heading of the 'pluralist' constitution, and in the following chapter at the methods and techniques which have been advanced as relevant to bringing about organizational changes of the kind envisaged in this and the preceding chapter. In chapter 20, we then look at the main features of the process by which commitment may be mobilized through negotiating processes.

Further reading
A vast literature exists on trade unions, but the following might be used to illuminate some of the themes of this chapter: McCarthy, 1972; Hyman and Fryer, 1975; Barrett, Rhodes and Beishon, 1975; Batstone *et al,* 1977 and 1978; Marchington, 1980.

On the specifically legal aspects, *see* Hepple, 1979; the Bullock Report, 1977.

On the contextual aspects, *see* Elliott, 1978 and Clegg, 1979.

18 The pluralist constitution

The wind of change

In the form of the Memorandum and Articles of Association, the commercial company provides itself with a constitution. Legislation usually provides a similar set of principles to guide the running of undertakings in the public sector which are not registered under the Companies Acts. Unlike British society as a whole, these subordinate bodies *are* governed by written constitutions (cf Padfield, 1972).

The history of British industrial relations since the first Companies Act appeared, has been one of growth in trade unionism and in union recognition (by employers for purposes of negotiation, etc). At the present time, therefore, about half of the working population are trade unionists (as well as employees) and about three quarters have terms and conditions of employment which have been fixed in negotiations (even if not, in every case, by *direct* negotiation between the parties themselves). Industrial relations might therefore be characterized as largely the product of 'collective bargaining' between trade union representatives and employer representatives (cf Flanders, 1965; 1967; 1969).

Collective bargaining could also be said to produce many different outcomes, ranging from understandings to strikes and other forms of industrial action. But the predominant one is the collective agreement, a written embodiment of the accords and understandings reached.

In the nature of the history of trade unionism and collective bargaining, this collective agreement has only gradually and grudgingly been accorded status and standing. For many employers, it was something 'forced' upon them by the growing power of organized labour, and something to be tolerated only at the minimum that had to be accepted. It was not something which could or should be regarded as a positive force or instrument in the regulation of employment relations.

This attitude is now changed and changing. More employers

455

are coming to see positive advantage in coming to terms with trade union objectives and in developing the collective agreement as a mutually accepted and acceptable instrument of regulation of conduct in the work situation. At company and plant level, there has been a response to the Donovan Commission's exhortation to develop more, and more comprehensive, agreements. At the public policy level, however, there has, as yet, been no legislative response to the Bullock Committee's recommendation that trade union representatives should, by law, be given a place on the governing Board of Directors of (at least) larger companies; nevertheless, the pressure to temper the wind of the company's Articles to the shorn lamb of trade unionism remains.

In the search for a strategy for coming to terms with trade unions, therefore, managements are likely to face the need to move towards the constitutionalization of the relationships between organized capital and organized labour, as the two most powerful stakeholders in modern undertakings.

At its simplest level, such constitutional development is likely to continue the trend associated with the response to Donovan: more comprehensive and more integrated collective agreements are likely to appear as a mechanism of what Flanders called 'job regulation'. In the longer term, it is likely to generate a new conception of 'the Articles' which, no doubt guided by enabling legislation, will find a more constitutional position for what has hitherto been described, with some truth, as a 'permanent opposition' in industry, namely the trade unions (cf Clegg, 1951, p 24).

If that is the shape of the future, the organization of work undertakings may change radically. At very least it would tend to move it in the direction of a federal structure at the level of industrial government. In the shorter run, however, the response to current pressures is likely to emphasize the development of more comprehensive collective agreements of the kind we have known for some time.

Collective agreements

The concept of a collective agreement is used to identify two distinct kinds of accord reached between employer(s) and representatives of 'organized labour'. One such is the product of a kind of bargaining over the substantive terms and conditions which the employer for his part is willing to observe and which the trade unionists for their collective part are willing to accept as the 'consideration' in their individual contracts.

The other is the outcome of a negotiating process through

which is developed a more or less complex set of rules which will govern the conduct of the parties jointly and severally in those circumstances where they may find themselves in disagreement over the appropriate manner of maintaining or developing their relationships in either the 'production system' or the 'industrial relations system' (cf Flanders, 1969, pp 11–41; Dunlop, 1958).

The concept has developed from that of 'collective bargaining' coined by Beatrice Webb in 1891 to identify what engaged the attentions of organized labour and employers.

The agreement became the embodiment of what emerged from the bargaining. Flanders has challenged the idea that this process is to be seen as a collective equivalent of individual bargaining (*op cit*) and has sought to build on the distinction between 'substantive' and 'procedural' agreements, to suggest that the process is one concerned with rule-making or 'job regulation', following Dunlop (cf Flanders, 1965 and 1967).

It may be useful to rest the distinction upon collective bargaining as a process of establishing common terms (such as wage rates, premiums, hours, holidays, etc) and collective negotiation as a process of creating a treaty of rules governing the main forms of interaction between the parties in both their aggregated and disaggregated forms.

Collective bargaining/negotiation has also been represented as a process of converting disagreements into agreements. These disagreements might well arise over both substantive and procedural matters and might well be 'converted' into agreements in the form of bargains or treaties. Such disagreements might develop over any facet of the relationships in the production or industrial relations systems, but it is common to see them as being focused on these same two categories of issue, the substantive and the procedural.

Disagreements about substance will then focus upon the two sides of the 'how much' equation: 'how much' work for 'how much' remuneration. The worker's standards of a fair day's pay for a fair day's work might well differ from those of the employer, and a constant source of disagreement may be found in this difference. A common resolution is to be found in annual agreements as to wage rates and associated premiums, but where payment-by-results systems are in operation, there is usually a source of continual disagreement and continual bargaining leading to frequent, if temporary, agreements (cf Brown, 1973).

Disagreements about the procedures in operation in association with the contract of employment will, on the other hand, focus upon *how* each (other) party treats any matter in which the one might have an interest. The individual certainly has an interest in the 'how much' questions, but apart from those, there are matters to do with the nature of the work situation itself in which he is likely to be interested. In fact, one might use as a checklist, the factors identified in, say, Maslow's hierarchy of prepotency of need (*see* above, pp 22–25) to show that actions by the other to change the offers of security, inter-personal interaction, esteem, or growth opportunity, might be predicted to produce disagreements. These disagreements are less easy to formulate (unless by a sleight of hand they are converted to money) and for this reason less easy to resolve.

What therefore tends to happen is that agreements are reached on 'procedures' to be followed, on the assumption that if an agreed procedure is followed, the chances of securing a 'fair' and 'acceptable' outcome are enhanced. This is similar to the assumptions in law that substantive justice is more likely to be achieved if the rules of natural justice (themselves procedural) are followed (cf above, pp 251–53).

Thus, in the industrial relations area, two distinct sets of procedures have been developed to handle this type of issue. On the one hand, there are the procedures which apply to issues which might arise between the negotiating parties themselves (claims, disputes, and consultative procedures, for example). On the other, there are the procedures (which may well overlap with the first ones) which apply to issues which arise between single or small groups of individuals within the 'production system' (disciplinary appeal, grievance and complaints procedures, for example). Although both categories may be negotiated by the same representatives, the distinction is worth maintaining.

Collective agreements and the law
One reason for maintaining the distinction is that, both historically and currently, the supports for these three different kinds of agreement are different (*see* above pp 88–89).

Substantive agreements
Until the beginning of last century (at least officially, even if the rules were as much honoured in the breach as in the observance) the substantive elements of the master-servant contract were fixed annually by the magistrates—as to the hours to be worked and the wages to be paid. Thereafter, (at least officially, even if the power to fix lay largely with the master or employer) these quanta were to be decided in individual bargaining to establish the terms of the individual contract of employment. If, currently, these quantities are

most often determined in 'collective bargaining' between trade union and employer representatives, and if the power to influence these rests upon the collective sanctions which might be brought to bear, they are still deemed to be effective by being imported into these same individual contracts. The minimum wages, etc fixed in the Wages Councils are similarly deemed to be imported into the individual contracts (Kahn-Freund, 1972, p 34; 1977, p 31).

But a collective agreement is not, itself, recognized in law as a contract, because the Trade Union Act of 1871 prohibited the entertainment by the courts of any actions to enforce agreements between trade unions, and this has ever since, been taken to exclude such jurisdiction.

The 'fiction' of recognizing the substantive terms of the agreement through the individual contract is not automatic. Two conditions are laid down.

> First, the representatives bargaining in behalf of the workers must be in an explicit agency relationship to them. Mere membership of the same trade union is insufficient. There must either be a Union Rule which makes the agency relationship express or the individual members must expressly authorize the representatives to act on their behalf (cf *Rookes v Barnard* (1964), AC p 1129).
>
> Secondly, the individual contract of employment must expressly provide for the incorporation of the collective terms (*National Coal Board v Galley* (1958) 1 All ER, p 91) or such incorporation must be capable of being construed as an implied term (eg by custom). Even then, incorporation might fail if the terms were not clear enough to indicate the intention and effect.

Where all of these conditions are met, therefore, there are two supports for the substantive terms of the collective agreement, those of trade union sanction and legal sanction applicable to actions in contract. Where they are not, only the first is available.

Agreements on collective procedures

The attitude of the law to the procedural aspects of these collective agreements in so far as they regulate the relations between the negotiating parties themselves is quite different. These bind only those who make the agreements and no one else, and they are binding 'in honour only' (ie, they are legally unenforceable 'gentlemen's agreements'). No 'fiction' rescues these agreements from the limbo to which inter-union agreements were assigned by the 1871 Act and the embargo on entertaining actions on agreements

459

between unions and employers' associations (defined as trade unions for this purpose) has so far been extended to cover *any* such procedural agreement which involves a trade union.

Both statute and common law had little interest in this area before 1971. It was left to the parties to establish their own rules and procedures to govern their collective relations. Initially, towards the end of last century, it was usually the employers (or their associations) which sought to establish procedures—like the famous agreement contained in the York Memorandum (*see* Marsh, 1973, ch 3) which was originally imposed on the engineering unions. In the post-war period, the national unions, seeing the growth of relatively uncontrolled shop stewards organization, became more interested in the development of such agreements. But it was left to the Donovan Commission to present the strongest arguments in favour of domestic procedural agreements that have yet appeared (Donovan Commission Report, 1968, paras 182 and 191–6).

The Donovan Commission saw the public interest as best served by the development of more explicit agreements on procedures. It framed its recommendations, therefore:

(a) to emphasize the responsibility of the board of directors for the conduct of industrial relations within a concern and for the framework of collective agreements within which those relations are conducted; and
(b) to highlight those aspects of industrial relations which the public interest required should be covered wherever possible by clear and firm company and factory agreements (paras 191–196, pp 47–48).

The Commission's specific charge upon the board of directors was that it should develop a series of agreements with the workers' representatives to provide procedures for both the industrial relations and the production systems, specifically:

1 to develop, together with trade unions representative of their employees, comprehensive and authoritative collective bargaining machinery to deal at company and/or factory level with the terms and conditions of employment
2 to develop, together with unions representative of their employees, joint procedures for the rapid and equitable settlement of grievances in a manner consistent with the relevant collective agreements
3 to conclude with unions representative of their employees, agreements regulating the position of shop stewards in matters

such as: facilities for holding elections; numbers and constituencies; recognition of credentials; facilities to consult and
report back to their members; facilities to meet other stewards;
the responsibilities of the chief shop steward (if any); pay while
functioning as steward in working hours; day release with pay for
training

4 to conclude agreements covering the handling of redundancy
5 to adopt effective rules and procedures governing disciplinary
  matters, including dismissal with provision for appeals
6 to ensure regular joint discussion of measures to promote safety
  at work.

However, at the present time, the law does not require that procedures governing collective relationships shall be developed. In the
interim period—between the Donovan Commission Report and
1981—there have been statutory provisions relating to recognition,
consultation and negotiation, but the only vestiges of these which
now remain concern information disclosure (*see* above, pp 446–49)
and consultation in connection with redundancy (pp 109–11) and
health and safety matters (pp 444–45). In that period, however,
many undertakings developed new procedures and procedural
agreements, under some pressure from the statutory requirements.

But at the moment, what is likely to keep them in existence
(apart from inertia and the power of the unions to prevent them
being abandoned) are the recommendations contained in the
various Codes of Practice. These do not have the force of law, but
whether the employer has followed the recommendations is a
matter which might be alluded to in any tribunal or court action
which is founded on some other substantial cause, and might
influence the outcome. Broadly speaking, therefore, and apart
from this rather mild pressure upon employers to conclude procedural agreements with their recognized independent trade unions
as is found in the Codes, the question of collective procedures is
once again left largely to the wishes of the collective parties.

Constitutionalizing collective agreements

The pervasive impact of legislation in recent years upon the rules
and procedures governing collective and individual relations in
industry makes it easy to forget that most of these rules and procedures were developed 'voluntarily' through collective bargaining.
The guiding spirit in the legislation was that which sought to
generalize best practice in the unionized sector of the economy, not

461

one which sought to create new approaches unknown to industry before that time.

One effect of this was to create a situation in which there was considerable variety of practice, and in which new and specific agreements appeared in a piecemeal fashion in any particular undertaking. The general impact of legislation and supporting government exhortation has been sudden in the sense that much of what was required was introduced within 15 to 20 years. But even that grew bit by bit, and with some false starts and some backtracking, so that undertakings which responded speedily to new law, also found themselves with new arrangements which were developed piecemeal and *ad hoc*. Since the voluntary system has by no means been ousted by the legal requirements, there is additionally the probability that some new elements will continue to be added because of what the unions can compel.

It is now not unusual for larger undertakings to have between 10 and 20 major procedural agreements and a similar number of procedures governing negotiation of claims, settlement of disputes, handling of both discipline and grievances, securing of information for bargaining purposes, consulting on general or specific questions, dealing with redundancies, introducing and maintaining job evaluation plans, introducing new technologies and consequential changes of job, and probably a number of others. *Taken together*, these might be read as forming a constitution governing a whole range of decision-making processes. But often they reveal overlap and lacunae and whilst both parties are often reluctant to re-examine procedural agreements because to do so might result in some regression, there is some concern to systematize them, possibly along the lines indicated by the ACAS general Code of Industrial Relations Practice as supplemented by later specialized Codes.

The main elements which go to make up the 'constitution' may, however, be identified.

1 The Status agreement

A status agreement is one which attempts 'to establish rights and obligations, which together define status' (Flanders, 1965, p 11). Status is thus composited from agreement to recognize each named party as having capacity to negotiate and as having 'rights' to carry out certain named functions in so doing. Status also extends to a recognition of the capacity and 'rights' of the representatives. In a rather special extension of status, the agreement may also provide for a degree of 'union security' focused upon the question of how far the employer is willing to go in giving rights exclusively to one union (or a small group of them) in respect of a named category (or categories) of employee.

(a)   Recognition

With the removal of the clauses governing recognition in recent legislation (*see* above, pp 443–44), this question now falls to be decided by the employer 'freely' in the light of the strength of the union concerned within the undertaking and the advantage of dealing with the workforce on a range of matters through representatives. The issue is more likely to arise in the future in the realms of white collar employment than on the shop floor where the union recognition question is, for the most part, already settled (cf Bain, 1970; Bullock Committee Report, 1977; Clegg, 1979).

The kinds of consideration which the employer may want to take into account in reaching a decision are those which were attended to in the 'recognition' exercises carried out by the CIR (see Second General Report, 1971). The first question is whether the union seeking recognition is adequately representative of the category of employee in respect of which the union seeks standing. (Adequacy is ultimately a matter of judgement, but it might be informed by the results of a ballot on whom the employees wish to have represent them, and this might be conducted along the lines laid down by the CIR.) The second (and more difficult) question is whether the union is adequately equipped to represent these employees. From the employer point of view, this is not merely a question of 'what kind' of shop stewards might be available but rather whether the union concerned has adequate back-up resources and facilities (eg, availability of full-time officers or of training for shop stewards) to service the relationship once it is established.

Once a union is recognized, it does then acquire rights under extant legislation (usually if it also meets the condition of being independent, as all TUC-affiliates are (in law) and as others may be certified to be on application to the Certification Officer). Apart, therefore, from what the employer may agree with the union on recognition, the union may also claim certain rights to consultation, information disclosure, and facilities for its officers and members, under the law. At the point of agreeing recognition and status, therefore, the employer might also sensibly seek to incorporate agreements relating to these.

What is agreed at this point of recognition is likely also to take into account the existing recognition and negotiating structure of the undertaking. In many, if not most, undertakings there is now some form and degree of unionization, and the recognition of another union as having capacity to represent an additional category of personnel, might well affect the existent arrangements. The employer will therefore need to consider what problems might arise in this area.

The most likely major problem centres on the structure of the bargaining unit: simply which unions will be prepared to sit down in negotiations with which others. In many service undertakings and in the white collar staff areas of others, tensions of this kind were increased as a consequence of the different responses made to the registration provisions of the Industrial Relations Act 1971, and these continue to divide employee associations which may have established their 'independence' in different ways.

With the growth of white collar unionization in the 1970s, some have appeared which approach negotiation with ideologies which reject the strike weapon as part of the attempt to maintain a professional position and posture. This, too, might be anticipated to lead to difficulties in securing a joint-union approach to negotiation.

These factors are also likely to affect the prospects of the employer securing (what might be called) 'standard-form' procedural agreements with the various unions recognized. From the employer's position, it is clearly advantageous to have one form of procedure covering any aspects of the relationship—claims, grievances, or whatever. This can be, and is, attempted even where the unions concerned are not prepared to negotiate jointly with the employer, but individual union ideologies and rule-books may present difficulties in the way of securing this outcome in particular cases.

Once the decision to recognize has been taken, its nature and form should be established in an agreement. At minimum, this should identify the 'parties' entering into the agreement and the 'constituencies' which they will be recognized as representing. For example,

> The ABC Company hereby agrees to recognize the following (named) craft unions as representing for purposes of negotiation of terms and conditions of employment, those of the Company's employees who are employed in the Engineering Department of the Company's XYZ Plant located at Soggy Bottom.
>
> The (named) Unions hereby agree to use their best endeavours to represent those categories and grades of employee listed against the name of each union below in any differences which may arise between the employees concerned and the

Company and which are not resolved in discussions between them and their immediate supervisors.

Other clauses may then establish whether the employer will represent himself in negotiations or whether he will be represented in some or all of them by officers of an employers' association to which the company may belong. Similarly, the manner in which the relevant employees will be represented by internal or external (to the plant) officers in any or all of these negotiations, will be established.

(b) Status and the extent of recognition

The next question to be determined is 'what the recognition is *for*?' Historically, the unions have extended the number of 'subjects' which may be negotiated with employers, and in doing so have reduced the number which remain for unilateral determination by the employer (or, technically, by the employer in individual bargaining with the employee). Agreements, consequently, seek to establish (albeit often rather vaguely and generally) where the 'frontier of control' lies in the undertaking at the particular time. This is usually done by inserting a clause which agrees 'mutual status', or the 'rights' of the respective parties.

These rights usually include a 'right to manage' in some form: the trade unions recognize the right of the company to manage its affairs, including its right to take steps to maintain or improve efficiency and to maintain order and discipline within the undertaking. In recent years, trade union pressure to have a *status quo* clause introduced into procedural agreements has tended to limit management's discretion here. It usually provides that where management seeks to change an existing practice and this is challenged, the *status quo* shall be maintained until the matter has been resolved in 'procedure'; this is frequently stated to imply the continuation of the practice in question and a continuation of 'normal working' by employees during the period (Incomes Data Service, *Status Quo*, April 1971).

The rights of the trade unions are also acknowledged in this section. Minimally, this entails recognizing the right of the named unions to represent their members' (or the relevant class of employees') interests.

This right may be restricted to accompanying members whenever they have a complaint or grievance or whenever they become involved in a disciplinary process. Beyond this, the right may extend to the negotiation of a shorter or longer list of terms and conditions, beginning with the basic pay rate but potentially extending to cover all terms and conditions. This right may

465

however be restricted to negotiation on behalf of the actual membership or negotiation on behalf of a category of worker regardless of whether they are all union members or not. In future, it is possible that the right to participate as a recognized union in the areas covered by 'participation agreements' (*see* below, pp 477–78) may be offered or withheld in a similar fashion according to the strength of the union concerned and the determination of the management to structure its own bargaining and participation units.

The other question of status which falls to be resolved is the extent to which the employer is willing to support the union(s) in its (their) representative role. This is frequently subsumed by the term 'union security', but it is often spoken of loosely as being to do with some variation on the 'closed shop' theme. This too may be established to very different degrees through a range of options, dependent on similar considerations to those mentioned above.

At base, the employer may agree to inform all new employees that the union is recognized in respect of their category, or even to encourage them to belong to the union, ie to join and to remain in membership. The employer may also agree to facilitate the union by checking-off union dues from pay under certain conditions. The offer may be, for example, to deduct union dues on receipt of individual authorization (as required for all deductions by the Trunk Acts) but not to recover any arrears or to repay any dues refundable, provided that the union undertakes to distribute and collect authorizations for transmission to the accounts office (see, Ramsay and Hill, 1974, pp 9–13).

Beyond this degree of encouragement and facilitation, there is a choice of union security options which the employer may be asked to select from. The two main ones are the post-entry closed shop (whereby all new employees may be required to join one or other of the specified unions, as a condition, subject to the requirements of law, of continued employment) and the pre-entry closed shop (whereby the employer undertakes to employ only those who are or become members of the specified union *before* commencing employment—again subject to the requirements of law). (*See* EP(C) Act, 1978, Ss 58 and 58A, and above, pp 434–37.)

Whether the employer should accede to any request for a degree of union security entails balancing on the one hand, the morality of restricting the freedom of the individual worker and the efficacy of restricting his own future discretion to vary the shape of the bargaining unit, against, on the other, the morality of recognizing that individual freedom as the kind of fiction referred to by Kahn-Freund (1977, pp 12–15) and the efficacy of strengthening the power of the union(s) to discipline their own members. Whatever decision is arrived at in this respect, however, there is some advantage in expressing the agreement and intention clearly in the status agreement.

(c)   Recognizing representatives
It is pertinent to indicate in the agreement how the employer will be represented in his dealings with the union (and with employees who may seek union assistance and support in disciplinary and grievance matters). The basic choices are between being represented in whole or in part by officers of an employers' association or by 'himself' and in the latter case where multi-plant undertakings are involved, between head office and local management. The role identity of the representatives on management's side (eg General Manager, Personnel Manager, etc) may be indicated, and is virtually requisite under the law in respect of the early stages of disciplinary and grievance procedures (*see* above, pp 87–90).

The recognition of trade union representatives was one of the subjects on which the Donovan Commission had a good deal to say. It argued both for their more explicit recognition as representatives and for their facilitation. Action on both has generally followed, and both legislation (regulating 'time-off') and Codes (on time-off and facilities) have served to structure and guide this.

Provision is usually made, now, in the local procedural agreement, for a defined number of shop or office representatives to be recognized by management after election by the union members on a constituency basis which may also be agreed. The agreement is also likely to stipulate what duties such representatives will undertake during working periods, these duties reflecting partly what is contained in the union rule-book and partly what management in the local circumstances would expect such representatives to do as a *quid pro quo* for recognition by management. The procedure will often also make provision for the manner of electing these representatives, with constituencies indicated along with any service qualifications which management would expect a candidate to have as a condition of recognition if elected. In some cases, an increasing number under the stimulus of the Code of Practice issued by ACAS, the management will agree to make facilities available for voting to take place smoothly during working hours.

Once elected, the shop steward is commonly issued with credentials signed by duly authorized officers of the trade union and of management, thus formally establishing his status in industrial relations activities rather than merely as an officer of the trade union. It is also normal practice for unions with large numbers of members in particular companies or undertakings to appoint a convenor of shop stewards from amongst their numbers. Managements have often (and again increasingly often under the stimulus of the new Code) not only recognized such a convenor as the key representative of the union's members, but have given him freedom of access (within limits) to any part of the works and to the other shop stewards and to management and office and telephone facilities.

One area which remains more contentious concerns the provision of training for shop stewards. Management is usually anxious that shop stewards receive training and, whilst management may be willing to provide it, the trade unions usually prefer that such training should be given by their own agencies (such as the TUC or the individual union college). The compromise most often adopted is that management gives the shop steward time off for training of defined types, and the unions arrange the actual training programme. This too is now subject to the Code governing time off for union officers (see, for an example of such agreements, Ramsay and Hill, 1974).

Such developments may therefore be seen to change the old order in which shop stewards were often tolerated but scarcely helped in many organizations. Under the impact of the various Codes of Practice a more constitutionally founded status is developing for shop representatives. The emergent *de facto* practice in many large undertakings in the 1950s and 1960s has thus been made more standardized.

The mutual recognition and facilitation thus built into the procedural agreement at local level is intended by both the parties themselves, and the State agencies charged with advising on industrial relations matters, to provide a foundation for cooperation to resolve differences over matters of interest or matters of right that might arise in the working situation. This is also normally acknowledged in the preamble to the agreement, with statements recording that the parties agree that greater mutual benefit will be obtained through cooperation to ensure that differences are resolved 'through procedure' rather than through precipitate 'industrial action' by one party or the other.

2 The coverage of negotiations

Because the present pattern of collective bargaining at local level is something which has usually developed out of a national, industry-wide pattern, the coverage of the negotiations is not something which has been established by deliberate decision in the domestic situation. The Codes of Practice suggest that once status has been determined, thought should be given to the question of what is to be negotiated and at what level.

This brings together two distinct issues. What should be negotiated nationally, at company-level or within the individual undertaking, and what substantive terms and conditions in the employment contract shall at any or all of these levels be negotiable subjects.

The two questions are clearly related, and one of the difficulties which arises in the attempt to develop adequate local constitutions occurs because national agreements frequently pre-empt negotiation of some issues at the local level. This is essentially what was intended in a situation which was highly supportive of national, industry-wide negotiations; but as full employment and changing cultural values appear to support more local autonomy in these matters, the continuation of these stipulations limit the range of opportunity available locally to effect changes.

Flanders suggested in 1967, that collective bargaining suffered from a 'poverty of subject matter' largely because of what the Donovan Report or Commission later branded as 'the two systems' of industrial relations. The restricting influence of national arrangements for bargaining upon the development of coverage at the domestic level was already breaking down at this date, and Flanders concluded that there was therefore 'considerable scope for further growth' (Flanders, 1967, p 15). Some of this 'growth' has occurred, as the parties adjusted to the 'two systems' perspective and the subsequent enactments affecting industrial relations.

However, undertakings face the need to make two kinds of adjustment, one in relation to the national structures centred on the negotiations between employers' associations and trade unions, and the other in relation to the domestic situation within companies which operated through a number of plants or offices.

Centralization versus decentralization

The problem created by the 'two systems' for domestic negotiations was the limitation which the national system imposed on coverage and discretion at the local level. It gave a mixture of rates and conditions and a mixture of procedures and procedural agreements (*see* Munns, 1967). In highly centralized bargaining, many basic terms and conditions may be fixed and little discretion allowed to the local bargainers; in decentralized or looser arrangements, general guidelines might come from the national negotiators and the substance and range of coverage be left for local determination. Where the pattern of demand for negotiated terms and conditions is changing, employers face the need to decide which pattern they favour in all the circumstances of legislative constraint and shop floor volatility.

This requires the local management to review its relationships with its employers' association on the one hand. Should it, at one extreme seek to retain all power to negotiate on all subjects with employees in the unit, or should it forego some of the discretion to a central employers' association to attempt to secure a common front in the face of union demands? The company's decision on this question is not necessarily unconstrained: the wishes of the employees have some part to play in determining the outcome. A number of other options are open to the individual employer: he might well decide not to join an employers' association or a national/district joint negotiating exercise, but nevertheless follow the terms and conditions of employment determined in this way in his trade or industry; alternatively, he might decide to join in such an exercise but accept in advance only some part of the total package of outcomes, retaining to himself the opportunity to negotiate locally on others.

This is not a once and for all decision. As the pattern has developed, the two parallel systems of the Donovan analysis provide opportunities for determining one standardized set of conditions at the national or district level so maintaining a basic control over competitiveness, and another set of less standardized conditions at the company/plant level, giving a more specific control and more flexibility for cooperation.

A similar kind of question calls for consideration at the level of the multi-plant company. Although this plant *versus* company question was little considered by the Donovan Commission in reaching its recommendations about local bargaining, there are currently a number of very different options available to the multi-unit undertaking and different ones have been selected. It is possible to distinguish, for example,

1 The situation where all unit issues are decided domestically within the unit: this is a more common practice in the USA than in the UK, where the tradition of centralized bargaining has tended to militate against it, and where employers are more liable to fear the leap-frogging type of claim. On the other hand, the development of the fragmentation of bargaining in the post-war period has helped to bring this about even here
2 The situation where the unit has similar autonomy but where local discretion must be contained within an overall budget for the unit which may be laid down by a higher authority, but which refrains from interfering with the unit bargaining processes themselves. In recent years this kind of situation has often been subjected to pressures from the trade unions whose itinerant offi-

470

cers are often able to deploy a more universal knowledge of practice to good effect (cf Ramsay, 1971)

3 The situation in which unit negotiations are conducted within the unit's own structure of relationships but where negotiations from the employer's side are either conducted or directly supervised by managers from the centre. This is the obverse from the previous situation, in the sense that management seeks to deploy the more universal knowledge of practice to its advantage in the negotiations, and is likely to create pressures from the union side for a similar arrangement which might then turn the situation into one in which enterprise wide bargaining (as distinct from unit bargaining) was practised (cf McCarthy, 1971)

4 The situation, logically arising before company wide bargaining, where some subjects are negotiated at unit level and some at company level. In effect this is likely to divide subjects in a manner similar to that practised in the Donovan Commission's two systems: wage rates, hours, and holidays may be centrally negotiated, whilst piecework prices, shiftwork arrangements and grievance procedures and grievances themselves are left for determination at the unit level (cf Hawkins, 1971)

5 The situation in which all bargaining is conducted at the centre by centre managers, so that local unit management has no discretion but to refer all such matters upwards. With the greater volume of controlling legislation present in Britain, strong pressure may be expected upon managements in Britain to centralize their bargaining, at least for some time, as new standards and procedures are evolved to cope with the situation (cf Baker and France, 1954).

Similar considerations arise between the centre of public services, such as the Health Service or nationalized undertakings, and their local units (eg, hospitals or local collieries). It is broadly true that the power of the centre in bargaining here has remained much greater than in the generality of private industry in recent years. Although this reflects the structure of the respective enterprises, there remains some reason to suppose that the monolithic structures (such as that of the Whitley Council machinery in the National Health Service) may be under strong threat of change from the trade union side as they seek an alternative strategy to secure members' interests in a period of rapid inflation and of government economies (cf McCarthy, 1977).

Specified subjects
Collective bargaining in the industry-wide mode tended to estab-

lish that the process was concerned primarily and almost exclusively with that which was readily quantifiable on the reward side of the reward-effort bargain. The amounts of basic wage, piece-working and shift premiums, holidays and holiday pay, could be determined at that level to establish the minimum standards of reward which would apply throughout the industry. On the other side of the coin, however, only the hours of work, and perhaps the standard of effort required under the operation of PBR schemes, were fixed on the effort side, and, as the Donovan Commission pointed out, most of the control of this side of the bargain was left for local management and supervision to achieve.

With the development of domestic bargaining at the undertaking level, however, more of what had previously been reserved as management prerogative, became exposed to negotiation. The whole conception of productivity bargaining, for example, with its emphasis upon the effort side of the bargain, was made possible largely by the development of localized bargaining, and indeed, led a number of private undertakings to withdraw from employers' associations and national bargaining arrangements in order to carry it out. But a good deal on the wage side which had previously been covered by local understandings between supervisors and departmental managers and their shop leaders on the union side, was also exposed to more formalized (and increasingly centralized) bargaining once this change-over occurred. The subject matter of local bargaining came to be both fuller and more balanced as a consequence.

Once the locus of bargaining and negotiation is to be found within the undertaking, the 'management' process and problems immediately become the main source of subject matter. Thus justifying, it might be said, the early characterization of 'collective bargaining' by Chamberlain (1951, p 121) as a 'method of management'. Since local managements must necessarily manage the work as well as the rewards for it, and since workers/trade unionists have an interest in both, anything which relates to the imperative of the one and the interest of the other, becomes a matter which might be negotiated.

It is not therefore surprising that undertakings which engage in domestic bargaining will find themselves involved in bargaining about and in developing procedures to cover such managerial questions as the introduction of job evaluation schemes, the determination of piecework prices, the handling of redundancies, or the control of productivity levels and standards. In some of these, the procedures and the structures developed to support them may be similar or parallel to the main claims and grievance procedures and structures, but in other cases quite different and *ad hoc* (cf Thomason, 1971).

Another source of extension was found in the subjects which had hitherto (in the protective cocoon of the two systems) been associated with joint consultation. This being seen as a part of the management's prerogative power, it had frequently dealt with subjects such as production and productivity, health and safety, suggestion schemes, pensions and profit-sharing arrangements, amenities and welfare matters. Some of these related to the effort side of the bargain, although at the level of ideology and rules, and some to the reward side, albeit in respect of those aspects which were regarded as non-negotiable and to do with 'policy'.

Yet a third source of extension of subject coverage arose indirectly from the public debate about participation which developed as a consequence of the EEC's Fifth Directive. One of the topics in this debate concerned what representatives of the workers might participate in, in the way of undertaking decisions. But some trade union leaders (and somewhat more eclectically, the TUC) were prepared to argue that whatever a 'supervisory board' (which at that time appeared to be the main structural device for developing participation) might discuss, could equally well be debated within the framework of domestic negotiations.

The TUC, for example, argued that the idea of a supervisory board would bring 'a wide range of fundamental managerial decisions' within the control of work people, but that the extension of this control locally would 'require an extension of collective bargaining'. It is therefore advocated that collective bargaining should be freed from the strait jacket of wage determination and extended to embrace a long list of subjects, including manning, training, recruitment, speed of work, work-sharing, discipline and dismissals. This in turn would require more information to be given to negotiators and improved procedures, but it would lead to greater 'joint control over the immediate work situation' (TUC Congress, 1974).

Consequently, by the end of the 1970s, the question of what subjects were proper for consideration within the framework of collective bargaining, had been answered (by some, although not necessarily accepted by many employers) by reference to what was negotiated within the executive system (ie between shop representatives and manager), what was traditionally regarded as negotiable within the industry-wide bargaining system, what had hitherto been reserved for discussion within joint consultative (production) committees, and what was being proposed as the subject matter for decision within new participatory arrangements.

In the particular undertaking, however, what is a proper subject for negotiation remains to be determined in the local circumstances of history and predilections of the parties (as well as their power). The embodiment of this decision in a procedural agreement is usually likely to be resisted (as being hand-tying) by both parties, unless the statement appears in a very general form. In other words, this aspect, it might be predicted, is likely to remain a question which will be answered only in terms of custom and practice and understandings, rather than in terms of precise formal definitions. (But see, GKN-Shotton, Charter, 1973; INCO Europe Limited, Agreements with Craft Unions, 1980.)

3 Procedures and structures

Whatever may, therefore, be the 'content' of negotiations, and however general may be its identification in agreements, there will be a stronger incentive to establish:

(a) what procedures will be followed in their discussion and consideration
(b) what structures will be established to permit these to take place.

The main incentive here, lies in the greater certainty for both parties which known procedures impart, and the greater probability that the negotiations will be ordered if they are subjected to procedural control where they are themselves the outcome of joint agreement. The incentive effect is such that most larger undertakings now have such procedures based on agreements.

It is not uncommon to make some distinction in procedures between those claims which seek to establish (by agreement) some new right for the employees or the trade union (claims of interest) and those which rest upon the belief (to be tested through the procedure) that some existing right has been denied to the worker (claims of right). In addition, the agreement reached may provide for a different procedure to be followed (perhaps also through different formal machinery) where the employer is proposing to make a change in work methods or performance standards, from that applicable where the claim is being made by the union representatives on behalf of members or some of them. This last seeks to preserve the 'right' of the employer to manage his business efficiently, and represents the other side of the coin from the union's attempt to secure a *status quo* agreement, so that all claims may be dealt with in one procedural framework (*see* above, p 465).

The general position is that a procedure for processing claims, disputes or grievances, will attempt to provide a sequence of stages through which the matter may be processed with a degree of expedition. The number of stages to be built into the procedure will vary with the type of establishment and the type of bargaining arrangements applicable. The procedure can state:

(i) that the matter should first be raised by the employee representatives with the level of management directly responsible, or by the management with the level of employee representation most directly concerned according to union procedure
(ii) what is the next stage of appeal in the procedure
(iii) what further stages will be involved, even to the extent of appeal to an industry-wide arrangement
(iv) whether the appeals machinery should terminate within the establishment, at industry level or with a reference to ACAS, and whether the parties agree to be bound, in advance, by any award made there.

At each such stage as may be identified, there is usually a provision which governs how quickly it shall be commenced and terminated (in the absence of an agreement between the parties to vary this) and who, on either side, will normally be involved in dealing with the stage. On the management side, the stages will move up the formal management hierarchy, and on the union side up the hierarchy of union officers, firstly within the undertaking and later outside it.

In spite of the care which is taken in drawing up such agreements to make them realistic in respect of the time necessary at each stage and the likely availability of members of the respective hierarchies, in practice there is often appreciably longer delay than is provided for because of non-availability of *all* the named officers on a particular day. Sometimes delaying tactics are deliberately employed, usually by adjourning meetings which started within the procedural calendar. Where this is done, however, it is usually perceived for what it is, and goodwill towards the procedure is dissipated. When this occurs, the main purpose of the procedures is rendered nugatory and of no effect, and the wildcat industrial action comes to be regarded as the more effective method open to the workers to secure redress of their grievances, complaints and claims.

Communication, consultation, negotiation, and participation
The variety of channels and procedures for handling differences and conflicts within modern, larger-scale work undertakings may often prove irksome to those who feel themselves under pressure to

475

decide and act in order to realize the undertaking's objectives. They demand the investment of time and skill which might be deployed in other 'productive' directions. They are justified, however, in terms of the expectations of people at work, which are commonly characterized as supporting the need for conviction to precede commitment to work tasks. The multiple channels of communication which are created are regarded as creating a functional and desirable redundancy in communication within what have become highly complex organizations (*see* above, pp 364–68).

This same idea tends to justify the maintenance of distinct channels of consultation and negotiation although the division may be maintained, also, for quite other reasons. The legal obligation to consult and to inform (in some situations) is already established, and a legal obligation to develop arrangements for 'participation' may lie in the not too distant future as further harmonization with European practice is developed. As yet there is no very real consensus, either within or between the parties to collective bargaining, as to the form that this participation might take (cf Bullock Committee Report, 1977).

But there is an employer view which would seek to develop participation on the model of 'joint consultation' rather than via 'an extension of collective bargaining'. The CBI, for example, in its evidence to the Bullock Committee of Inquiry on Industrial Democracy offered this model as relevant:

> Many large and small companies already successfully operate formal, but voluntary consultative arrangements. The CBI favours this approach, and therefore proposes that the establishment of deliberative bodies representative of all employees, should be actively encouraged in all firms of a size where they would be practicable and where the need for increasing participation is felt (paragraph 19).

Some trade unions, on the other hand, would see this as but an attempt to continue into the era of 'participation' the same kinds of management prerogatives as were upheld by those approaches to joint consultation which were motivated by a desire to avoid negotiation with the unions. For them, the alternatives lie between extending collective bargaining in the manner proposed by the EEPTU in evidence (Bullock Committee Report, pp 39–40) and the deliberate institution of industrial democracy by a power shift of the kind envisaged by the Bullock Committee itself in its majority report (1977, pp 71–91).

The actual proposals of the Bullock Committee have not attracted a great deal of enthusiastic support from any quarter, and

476

it looks unlikely that government will take the steps necessary to bring about such a change. It is therefore the more likely that participation will be developed, in so far as it is developed at all, through negotiation of new treaties between the trade unions and managements. By default, it might be said, participation will probably occur by extending collective bargaining.

This being the case, the main demand expressed to the Bullock Committee, that participation ought to be tailored to the circumstances of the undertaking, is likely to be met in many cases.

The CBI evidence lists (paragraph 24) the kinds of structure which the Confederation thinks ought to be open to establishment within the compass of such agreements. These include:

'company councils; plant or subsidiary councils, with or without a company council, for multi-plant or groups of companies; non-executive directors to whom employee representatives have special access; trustee advisory 'boards; direct employee representation on either unitary or supervisory boards, with a suitable representative structure beneath this level; and other variations and combinations.'

This list is then consistent with what the CBI sees as a major principle to be followed: namely, that the parties in the company itself should have maximum flexibility under any legislation to adopt whatever structure is most congenial to them.

'A fundamental principle on which proposals for greater employee involvement in company affairs must be based, is that participative arrangements must be designed to fit a company structure, and not vice versa. Moreover, such participative arrangements must be sufficiently flexible to accommodate the various forms of participation already in operation successfully, and to the satisfaction of all the parties, in a number of companies' (paragraph 13) and 'It is vital that employers and employees retain freedom of action to develop a form of participation which can reflect their wishes and the structure of their particular organization. A standard system applied to all companies, large or small, centralized or decentralized, could not possibly be suitable to meet the needs of employees and companies' (paragraph 9).

What is thus proposed in substitution of legislative compulsion based on something like the Bullock Committee's proposals, is a local, undertaking-level 'participation agreement' or 'constitution' which would in most cases necessarily have to find a settled and secure place for trade unions and their representatives (if only to acknowledge the 'facts of industrial relations life') and a way of defining 'constitutionally' what was intended by the parties:

First, a definition of structure, of the kind advanced by the CBI in evidence to Bullock, but spelling out in more detail the nature of constituencies and the composition and relationships of committees and councils to be established.

Secondly, a definition of subject matter for each 'part' of the system, which in effect would indicate what subjects (as for example, in the Bullock recommendations) would be for joint decision, and what subjects (as advocated in calls for extensions of collective bargaining) would be for management decision and union challenge.

Thirdly, a definition of the procedure to be followed in *both* these areas, including the important voting procedures required in joint decision bodies but embracing procedures governing challenge of those decisions which are to be taken by the joint board.

In the development of such a participation agreement, there is opportunity to constitutionalize the 'collective bargaining relationships' along the lines suggested above, to give a foundation for the ordered resolution of differences. There is also opportunity to develop participation in decision-taking on other subjects in which these same parties may have different interests but also some concern that they be reconciled in convergent rather than divergent problem-solving. This, in turn, would need to be based on the lessons of 'good practice' in consultation, and not be allowed to serve as an excuse for inaction.

The relevant principles
Based on past good experience, it may be suggested, a number of principles may be articulated to guide this kind of exercise in constitution-building. Successful outcomes are likely to demand:

(a) a definition of the problems faced by the parties (not just one)
(b) a discussion and agreement on the principles which will be applied to the negotiations of their solution
(c) a spread of awareness, involvement and agreement throughout the departments or branches of the undertaking, so that all (management and workers) likely to be affected have a chance to express their views before a formal plan is made
(d) a gathering together of these views with the principles and the analyses of the problem, in the form of a plan which can be discussed and amended before the final negotiating sessions

(e) a formal negotiation on the 'equity' of the final solution as depicted in the plan.

In this approach, two important new principles are established in:

(a) the evolution of a new discussive—consultative—bargaining relationship out of the traditional bargaining framework
(b) the growth in the time-investment required to secure solution and acceptance before 'agreement' (*see* below pp 494–96).

These changes do allow more emotional commitment on the part of the managers and the workers likely to be affected by any final agreement, and allow criticisms which are often voiced after agreements have been arrived at to be put before the negotiation takes place, the greater time commitment to communications and discussion in these approaches is justified on the ground that it is easier to modify plans whilst they are still being made than after they have been agreed between the parties.

In this approach too, both the conception of learning and training, and its place in the development of an acceptable constitution are changed. In effect, both communication and training become so interwoven that it is difficult to separate them. This was most clearly visible in some of the more sophisticated developments of productivity bargaining (*see also* below, pp 522–24).

The general point is made by Harris in her discussion of this topic:

> The preparation and planning which must precede productivity bargaining cannot be done until management and all others involved have an adequate understanding of the basic economics of production and the means of measuring productivity: an appreciation of its financial implications is also needed . . . The intensive consultation that must precede plant bargaining and the negotiation that ensues must involve many managers, supervisors, employees and employee representatives. This communication will not be effective unless it is conducted with understanding, skill and conviction by all concerned. Training in the objectives and methods to be pursued may therefore be as important for effective communication and negotiation as for preliminary planning. This may mean training employee representatives as well as management and supervision in basic production economics (Harris, 1968, p 18).

The practical illustration of the same interweaving is provided in a number of actual exercises of productivity bargaining. In the experience of BP Plastics, for example, both 'communication' and 'learning' developed through an elaborate cascade of discussions on productivity issues, which ran through the whole undertaking. In each case, reliance was placed upon the line supervisor running his/her own discussions and securing his/her own staff's contributions to the debate. Initially, with the help of a consultant, the process was applied to the managerial staffs on the following basis:

> First, the consultant briefed the top management in pairs. Then each pair of managers took the next level in pairs, and so on down the line. Discussions were held with pairs of managers so that they could provide support and help to each other. Shop stewards were attracted by what they were hearing of these discussions and asked if similar sessions could be arranged for them. To maintain the objectivity of these discussions, the consultant led a similar series of discussions with the shop stewards. The objective at this stage was to achieve a complete understanding of what obstacles lay in the way of improving productivity. Both sides were asked to list the obstacles involved and these were found to be virtually identical when compared. It is important to see this as a general orientation exercise concerned with problems and principles. It was put forward that there would be some sort of productivity deal, but the *content* was not considered at this stage.

This 'orientation' exercise, which preceded the drawing out and testing of productivity improvement ideas in teams under supervision, therefore had a great deal in common with what is often intended in training. Subsequently, the discussions between the supervisors and their section members to identify possible ideas and to test them out as feasible with the aid of staff specialists (accountants, work study personnel, etc), who acted as consultants on request, provided another kind of learning opportunity for those concerned. Thus even before the negotiations began with the union representatives on any formal basis, many people in the undertaking had already been provided with the opportunity to engage in a new experience, with learning potential built into it, from which they could derive (if they so wished) some of the advantages which are normally regarded as accruing from formal training.

By implication, therefore, the process of establishing new constitutions of rules governing productive and moral conduct within undertakings is unlikely to be a matter simply of writing words on paper. It will also require the development of supporting attitudes and policies in which the emphasis is clearly and firmly placed upon an 'organic' solution, ie the development and deployment of effective communication and learning opportunities in support of the development of the new understandings which represent the real objective of developing them.

Further reading
On the formal constitutions, represented by the Articles of Association of the company, see Gower (1979) and Charlesworth and Cain (1977). A useful discussion of some of the issues raised by the Bullock Committee's proposals for these relationships is contained in Sullivan (1977).

On collective understandings and agreements, *see* Flanders (1969), Brown (1973) and Ramsay and Hill (1974) and on the legal aspects, Hepple (1979).

The public policy aspects of this subject are discussed in the Reports of the Donovan Commission (1968) and the Bullock Committee (1977).

19 Organizational and management development

Making things happen

In *Rise and Fall of the British Manager* (1977), Alistair Mant suggests that one of the major problems in British industry is the inability—for reasons which he discusses—of managers to make things happen within the productive system. He is not alone in this: not long before the publication of his book, *Der Spiegel* had had some unkind things to say about the British manager. The English disease, so well known to outside observers but usually not regarded as fatal by inside ones, is often attributed to similar deficiencies in management. These deficiencies may be expressed in the language of theories of class and status consciousness strongly reminiscent of Veblen's earlier strictures on the 'cultural survivals' and the dead hand of the 'business men' (who kept the engineers from solving the problems of the economic world). But they generally amount to the single charge of inability to make things happen—whether because of lack of motivation, lack of knowledge or lack of know-how (or 'technology' in its stricter sense).

Everyone engaged in work, in whatever capacity, is necessarily concerned with making something happen. This is the essence of the conversion process in the production of goods and services from physical and human resources. The toolmaker may make a particular shape 'happen' in working on a piece of metal; the cleaner may make a cleaner, safer and healthier workplace 'happen' by deploying his or her equipment and skills; the production manager may enable co-ordination of diverse activities to 'happen' by his or her actions; and so on. All the way across the piece, people are engaged in causing happenings. Whether they, any of them, are somehow deficient in the way they do it, is a question which many continue to debate. But all of them require for effective performance that the situation in which they work shall be supportive.

The manager's involvement in this process is a particular one. As Drucker's opening statement in his *Practice of Management* suggests, managers have a 'dynamic, life-giving' role and one which they exercise by getting other people to make happen those things which are considered requisite by those who have the right to establish objectives. The personnel manager's involvement is even more specialized. It entails not only carrying out certain executive tasks as a service to other roles, but also the development of structures and processes by means of which those others are facilitated in realizing the objectives which their roles establish for them. In so far as there is a concern with structure, the role of the specialist is focused on the 'organization' and in so far as there is a concern with process it is directed towards individuals. These form the usual twin concerns of the personnel specialist as he pursues a role which is both managerial and people-oriented.

In the present context, they come together in an organizational-level approach to the creation of the (structural and personal) conditions which will facilitate the achievement of the objectives, whether these be of the organization or of the individual. This approach has now been 'packaged' and 'labelled' and it is convenient to establish at the outset the nature of the proffered commodity.

Organizational and management development
The label applied most consistently to this is organizational development (or OD), a concept and an approach which may either subsume or exist in distinction from, management development (or MD). The options here tend to reflect the way in which the relationship between manager and system is perceived.

On the one hand, the manager may be seen as dependent upon the environment (the system) within which he has to work in his achievement. On the other, the system may be regarded as no more than the aggregated consequence of managers exercising their roles to the best of their ability in a social context, and thus as dependent upon the managers' abilities. In the early development of OD and MD, the two dependencies were often confused, but there was some recognition of the distinction. Thus, Burke suggested that

> the primary reason for using OD is a need to improve some or all of the *systems*/that constitute the total organization. . . . The main reason for using some form of MD is a need to improve some aspect of the *manager* (Burke, 1971, pp 571 and 573).

483

The two might therefore be assigned a distinct and separate existence, but they must remain complementary.

OD may then be defined as

> a long-range effort to improve an organization's problem-solving and renewal process, particularly through a more effective and collaborative management of organization culture—with special emphasis on the culture of formal work terms—with the assistance of a change agent, or catalyst, and the use of the theory and technology of applied behavioural science, including action research (French and Bell, 1978 edn p 14).

MD, alternatively, may be aimed somewhat differently. Jarman assigns five objectives:

(a) to improve the job performance of the managers currently in the post
(b) to provide adequate 'cover' in the event of unexpected short-term changes . . .
(c) to raise the general level of management thinking and understanding
(d) to provide a supply of managerial talent which will meet the anticipated needs of the future development of the organization in terms of commercial change, growth and increased technological and managerial expertise
(e) to extend the frontiers of knowledge in the understanding of the management function (Jarman, in Torrington and Sutton, 1973, pp 5–6).

It is, however, possible to adopt the view that either may subsume the other. MD appears to continue in use in Britain (Thakur, 1974; Easterby-Smith *et al*, 1980; MSC, 1979; Burgoyne and Stuart, 1978) where it appears to receive more scant attention in US literature (Alderfer, 1977).

Miner has offered what might prove to be the explanation of this apparent difference:

> OD that results in a total restructuring of the organization handles the training need by eliminating it; the organization is changed to fit its members. In contrast, the MD approach takes the existing structure, policies and procedures as given, and attempts to change people to make them more effective in meeting the requirements of the organization as currently constituted (Miner, 1973, p 35).

This is a feasible explanation if only because of the strong association of OD, in its early exposition, with a total educational

484

process, similar to the total training conception advanced by Young and Findlater (1973). This is particularly clear in Bennis's early definition, where he describes OD as:

(a) an educational strategy adopted to bring about planned organizational change, in which the change agent is always external to the organization and is a professional behavioural scientist who seeks to develop a collaborative relationship with the client system based on mutual trust; (for a discussion of the forms of collaborative relationship, see Mangham, 1968)

(b) an attempt to meet some current exigency faced by the organization, through which the educational and planned change processes can be developed in the form of a strategy which relies heavily upon experience behaviour (as distinct from book learning) to generate publicly shared data via such methods as sensitivity training, data feedback and confrontation meetings

(c) the change agents share a social philosophy and normative goals which are consistent with the developing perspective of organizations which attributes to them certain analogous characteristics to those of the organism (see Bennis, 1969, p 16).

Theoretical underpinning of 'organizational' roles

Behind this conception lies a belief that modern organizations (or client systems) may be treated as if they were human organisms with capacity or health problems. An organizational doctor role is created for the consultant change agent, and an assumption made that, as in the doctor-patient relationship, there will be high-trust between change-agent and the client-system.

Because most consultants are called in by managements, the model is worked out in these terms. There would seem, in principle, however, to be no reason why the same client-system might not be treated by any other 'doctor', including the trade union representatives, provided that the problem of generating the necessary level of trust between client and change-agent can be overcome in the particular case. Indeed there are examples of this happening although they tend not to attract the same labels to describe the exercises (cf GKN-Shotton: Charter, 1973; Thomason, 1971; Gregson and Ruffle, 1980).

What distinguishes the approach is not the form which consultancy may commonly take, but the development and allocation of three specific change-oriented roles in association with the client system, based on the belief that the client system can be thought of as amenable to treatment and that these defined roles can competently achieve this end.

The foundation of the whole exercise consists of the idea that up to a point, an organization may be thought of and treated as if it were a living organism, or at least an ecological system, with something that can be thought about as a life of its own. The system may then be thought of as having periods of growth and development or maturation between a succession of crisis points. In this view, therefore, there is a conception of successive maturation as crises are successfully surmounted, although in 'organizational life' terms it may be that failure to cope with a crisis results in a kind of regression which could not happen to a living thing (see Lippitt, 1969). The relevance of this theory to OD lies in the implication that the management of change must rest upon an awareness of the phase or crisis point in the life cycle, reached by the enterprise: management decisions, here as elsewhere, call for correct assessment of where we are and where we should be going.

Following on from this is a theory about how change can be effected within complex organizations. In fact, there are many distinct theories of 'change' in social systems (cf Smelser, 1967, ch 12) but OD selects one. This is the theory that organizational change can be brought about by the influence of some external agency (ie externally supported and powered) where it can establish a partnership based on a sufficient degree of trust with the client-organization. The theory, in other words, finds a particular place for human influence in the change process. The capacity of that agency is then seen to be limited by the 'organic' condition of the client organization; the stage-phase of organizational growth and development reached imposes some kind of constraint on what is possible in the way of effective treatment (cf Lippitt, 1969).

Given this conception of the role of agency in change, the approach must then establish a number of individual roles, each with a different part to play in the process, which must then be associated carefully within an overall strategy. Three such roles, those of change-agent, catalyst and pacemaker are usually distinguished, as in the following terms by Jones (1969, pp 60–61):

(a) a change agent may be a person, a group or an organization, but in any case 'includes the property of professionalism', and adopts a role which involves 'the stimulation, guidance, and stabilization of change in organizations' essentially as a 'helper', a 'mover' or a 'doer' (pp 19–20)
(b) a change catalyst is 'any agent that causes, speeds up or slows down change (catalysis) in the organizational system' without undergoing any change itself, and may in the extreme case

486

have no more complex role than that of simply bringing the change agent and the client system together, although it is a characteristic of this role that the effect of the role tends to be disproportionately great in relation to the input (pp 45–46)

(c) a pacemaker, like the change agent, may be an individual, a group or an organization but is seen as 'powered' by a source of energy which is external to the client system ('professional knowledge' would offer one illustration) and functions to stimulate and control the change process itself (pp 60–61).

In Jones's view, the change agent and the client system are to be regarded as the two principal 'actors' in planned change and the catalyst and the pacemaker as secondary ones. On the other hand, the client system and the catalyst are often regarded as 'internal' to the organization-as-client, and the change agent and the pacemaker as 'external', at least in the sense of having external bases of power which enable them to exert influence. It is in this sense that there is a significant point in the conception of OD as a partnership between an external agency and the client system: when attempted entirely from within the client system, it is difficult to ensure that the necessary 'energy' or power required to stimulate and control change will be guaranteed to the internal actors for the period of time required (see Jaques, 1951, and above, p 361). Provided that the whole exercise remains conceived as a learning experience for all concerned in it, there seems to be no reason in principle why the initiative should not be taken from within the undertaking itself, and therefore why change agents should not be internal ones. This would presuppose that there was already sufficient flexibility in the organization to allow the necessary roles to be assumed (Burns and Stalker, 1961).

This general conception of OD allows a number of quite different role allocations from those associated with the common consultant-client-system model, although they are infrequently made and when they are they are often not acknowledged in these terms. There is for example a strong tendency to assume that the 'mutual trust' mentioned by Bennis (above, p 486) will only be present where the client system is a managerial system and the consultants are 'management' or 'business' consultants.

It may be, as Fox suggests (1973) that many client systems, defined to include the employees, are characterized by low-trust relationships but there are many situations where (at least) 'adequate-trust' relationships could be developed for the purposes of ensuring planned organizational change. A broader conception of the 'client-system' might thus admit to the discussion, the trade union representatives as change-agents, catalysts or pacemakers. (They have, after all, an external referent and external sources of power.) What is problematical about this conception is the potential for sufficient 'mutual trust' in the exercise, but there are examples on record of planned change being carried through on this basis and with sufficient mutual trust, particularly in productivity bargaining.

This does rather suggest that what is important about the OD concept is not whether outside consultants are available and can be afforded, but the principles which animate the whole approach. These principles stem from an appreciation that change will tend to be resisted by anyone when they do not understand it, when their basic securities are threatened by it and when they have change imposed upon them. They emphasize the need for action by someone, alone or in partnership to remove the 'causes' of these resistances and to ensure that change occurs in a controlled fashion.

The OD approach therefore presents itself as a package because it presupposes a particular view of the organization as a client system in need of treatment. It also emphasizes the role of perceived need for change as the trigger or prime mover and this is located in the relationship of client system to change-agent. In distinction from this, MD implies that the individual will probably be the best judge of the need for 'change' in the self, but that this judgement will be helped by a supportive organization and that action on the judgement may actually require organizational facilitation. But in a number of packaged approaches, these two conceptions are often brought together, although not always deliberately or with the degree of clarity which might be desirable.

Harmonization of conditions

A currently prevalent example of 'organizational development' (and one which relates more to the 'people' element in the equation than to the task element) is that which might be identified initially by the terms 'staff status' and 'harmonization of conditions'. These are, however, inadequate terms to identify what is discernible as a general (strategic) development in organizations aimed at reducing the interference of unresolved people problems with attempts to resolve external (eg market-derived) problems. No simple generalization will cover the variety of developments, but they may be regarded as aimed at meeting the expectations which people have of equitable rewards for working, not merely in relation to gross or take-home pay, but across the whole spectrum of material and non-material satisfactions.

Within that framework, the harmonization of conditions is but one part of the process. It tends in practice to equate with the development of 'staff status' for manual employees, because what is often effected by such harmonization is no more than the granting of similar conditions to manual or hourly-rated employees as are already enjoyed by white-collar or weekly- and monthly rated employees. This was a process which secured its major impetus from the productivity bargaining exercises of the late 1960s, but it has continued beyond that decade and has now become much more common.

What is commonly involved is action to grant to all such groups of workers the same conditions as respects the calculation of rates (eg, on a weekly basis or per annum), the control of work time (eg, flexi-time arrangements for staff may 'put them on the clock' along with manual workers), the entitlements to holidays and other time off (eg, all with the same age and service qualifications being entitled to the same period of holiday), the coverage by sickness or pension schemes (eg, with age and service being the only varying conditions) and access to facilities and amenities (eg, as related to use of canteens or parking space). In the particular case, there may be either additions or subtractions to this list, but behind all is to be seen the same principle: that employees shall be treated alike in respect of such conditions, regardless of whether they happen to occupy staff or non-staff positions (*see* Butteris, 1975).

Behind the changes there is a recognition that such discrimination is both productive of individual tensions and structural distortions, and is difficult or impossible to defend when, as frequently happens in negotiations, management is called upon to defend it.

Equitable pay

Such harmonization does not extend to actual amounts of payment made, nor necessarily or usually, to other quantifiable benefits (such as holidays). In the one case, different rates continue to be paid and in the other different entitlements operate. What is removed is discrimination and distinction on indefensible grounds. Pay, etc, can be defended as something which carries differentials, not simply because it may be customary or traditional that such differentials have existed, but because different rates of pay reward different degrees of skill or contribution or responsibility or whatever else is considered important in the individual's work contribution.

But pay is also a factor which is subjected to judgement in terms of what might be considered equitable. Such judgements are often exposed in negotiations and one researcher has claimed to have secured evidence that people have very clear and detailed conceptions of what is fair or equitable pay for their kind of work in comparison with others (*see* Jaques, 1956, 1961, 1964)—although the grounds for the claim have been disputed (cf Paterson, 1972). Nevertheless, it has been thought for a long time, that in broad category terms pay differentials have been generally accepted as equitable; the problem has usually been associated with the new and changed job which had no customary 'position' in the scheme of things (cf Thomason, 1980).

In this area in recent years there have been two major developments. First, in the face of more frequent and more fundamental changes in the nature of work tasks (eg because of changes in technology), the old customary foundations for acceptable differentials have been removed and bickering over what is the appropriate relativity has therefore increased. This has led many more undertakings, through their remuneration managers, to substitute 'job evaluation' plans for the traditional methods of determining differentials.

Secondly, and for very similar reasons, there has been pressure to allow individuals to progress in payment terms beyond the boundaries erected by traditional divisions between unskilled, semi-skilled and skilled or process (production) and maintenance work as means of containing pay levels. This is leading a number of undertakings to couple job evaluation plans with proposals to develop remuneration bands across the whole of the labour force in such a fashion that no adjacent group of workers is necessarily held above or below the rate applicable to its neighbours (cf Gregson and Ruffle, 1980).

In both cases, the aim may be to reduce the sources of tension and therefore of dissatisfaction that exist over terms and conditions of employment, in much the same way that the other forms of harmonization aimed to do. But, in addition, the development of job evaluation, alone or in combination with 'continuous grading' (cf Gregson and Ruffle, 1980, p 63) seeks to effect a kind of 'harmonization' by seeking to relate differential payment to differential job demands (or job content), and *only* to these. Job evaluation plans come in many different shapes and sizes, but this is a constant objective: to relate job payment to the job demand.

Basic plans
Where plans vary from one another, it is in the method which is

adopted to identify the job demands or content and in the control arrangements which are developed to guide the process of judging between them for purposes of establishing a rank order (cf Thomason, 1980)

The most basic distinction is between the relatively simple 'whole job' ranking or classification plans and the relatively complex 'job factor' points rating and factor comparison plans. These are combined and permuted in various ways, particularly in order to give 'optimum fit' to different circumstances of their application, as in relation to white collar workers generally or managerial and professional staffs in particular. It is generally considered that the development of complexity reflects the decline in 'whole job' familiarity with technological change and the increase in 'new jobs' without as yet familiar conceptions, brought about by the same process. In effect, this development has tended to introduce into the essentially simpler plans some element of factor analysis, and it is these factors (which are thus becoming more universal in these plans) which indicate the association of job evaluation not only with effort—but also with the skills/abilities and role perceptions factors in expectancy theory.

In the two analytical schemes of job evaluation, points rating and factor comparison, the first step involves the determination of which factors will be taken into account in assessing relative worth of the jobs in the job family or enterprise. These are usually fewer in number than those identified by Lupton and Bowey in their procedure for making inter-organizational pay comparison (Lupton and Bowey, 1974, ch 2; and above, pp 162–64), but they are similar in many ways. The number of factors included in any particular points rating scheme may vary tremendously, although they may be cut down to about six: training; experience; mental application; physical application (or effort); responsibility; and working conditions. This list is usually varied in response to what are seen as local circumstances.

The factor comparison method of job evaluation is an extension of the points rating method, but one which takes into account the research finding that rating suffers from certain halo problems. For this reason factor comparison concentrates on five factors (usually): mental effort; skill; physical effort; responsibility; and working conditions. Concentrating on these, the problems of carry over and overlapping in the rating process are reduced. In both of these sets of plans, therefore, the element of effort or application, coupled with skill and ability, is obvious. In addition, the element of 'responsibility' appears and gives some inkling of the importance of the role prescription within which the job itself is done, just as

491

the 'working conditions' factor acknowledges that the physical environment of the job may call for some compensation.

The two originally simpler methods of job evaluation gave more weight to the determination of relative money worth on the basis of general comparison. Both job ranking and job classification dealt with the job as a whole, but depended upon the raters having appreciable familiarity either with all the jobs (in job ranking) or with the bench-mark jobs (in job classification). The difference between these two methods lies in the order of proceeding but both of them *could* be concerned either with 'difficulty' (and therefore with 'effort') or with 'value to the firm' (and therefore with 'performance') although the practice in the determination of the criteria varies from scheme to scheme. Nevertheless, it cannot be argued that they are concerned even in the appropriate case, purely with performance criteria, as both depend for their success upon the possibility existing that ranking can be achieved on the basis of broad skill categories such as skilled, semi-skilled and unskilled (cf Stieber, 1959; Thomason, 1980).

As Raimon has argued (1953, p 181), this kind of broad categorization has become obsolete in many instances and it is this that has led to the increase in the use of points evaluation and factor comparison plans, *and* also (and in association often with joint approaches to evaluation) led to the introduction of elements of points rating into these simpler methods. The two main categories of development from these simpler schemes are the direct consensus method and the job profile method both of which broaden the judgemental base and both of which bring these schemes more directly into line with plans which rest upon skill, effort and role prescriptions as the elements on which the differential reward will ultimately be based (cf Edwards and Paul, 1977).

White collar plans

Plans of job evaluation for white collar jobs are not necessarily different from these and the same basic distinctions tend to apply. But such plans are more often 'tailored' to the different nature of the work and the different concepts used to identify it.

The Institute of Administrative Management plan, for example, is a non-analytical one which avoids the use of factors and points. Nevertheless, it deliberately seeks to reconcile the type of work (clerical) with the degree of difficulty, knowledge, skill and responsibility involved in it. New and more complex white collar jobs tend to attract points rating or factor comparison plans (NBPI, Report No 83, 1968) and the factors which are then singled out for attention tend to be differently labelled and weighted from those used in manual plans, in order to demonstrate relevance and appropriateness (cf Cuthbert and Paterson, 1966).

The different kind of work performed by managerial and professional staffs (ie decision-taking work) has produced plans which are based upon some theory or model of information-exchange or decision-taking. A number of apparently very different tailor-made or consultant-branded plans could thus be linked together under this heading.

The rationale of many such plans is as follows: managers and others who do not necessarily have this title, take decisions; they also implement them; the work therefore calls for skills related to these; and it is this skill as much as anything which must therefore be brought into the plan. It is also true that this work is carried out in a context which might vary in the way in which working conditions vary for the manual worker; that it entails varying responsibilities; and that it calls for different levels of education and experience. These factors do not set the work apart from any other (except in the sense of having different relative values). But the skills and the 'raw material' to which they are applied do appear to be very different, and differentials ought therefore to reflect this. But what provides the 'bed' of the approach are the different role prescriptions which apply to them.

This may best be illustrated by the former BBC plan described by Doulton and Hay (1962). Essentially a grading scheme, it also seeks to provide a basis for analysis of the complex sets of variables included in work tasks at the managerial and professional level. It specifies three steps in problem-solving, which is held to be the main characteristic distinguishing this broad class of jobs. The steps are:

(a) the selection of the best possible solution, which requires the collection of all relevant facts and information, the determination of possible courses of action and the assessment of their advantages and disadvantages
(b) the taking of a decision, involving the use of judgement
(c) the implementation of the decision.

In order to analyse 'all the essential mental activities associated with solving problems of every type' they employ three factors related to step (a) and one related to each of the other two steps, together with a final additional difficulty factor:

(a) (i) application of specialized knowledge and experience

(ii) exercise of powers of evaluation or reasoning (judgement)

(iii) the production of new ideas in adapting or devising an unusual course of action (or creative thought)

(b) decisions—the extent to which the job holder commits the use of the organization's resources; by spending money, allocating facilities for activity, selecting staff for work tasks, undertaking new work programmes, and engaging in publicity

(c) man-management—the ability to handle other people in a manner which enables the job holder to achieve his aim

(d) interpretative performance, a factor used where the different elements of the job are inextricably mingled and the physical qualities could not be assessed adequately by themselves.

Each of these factors is assessed in terms of five grades which are offered in the plan, and the final grading of the job is based upon the 'highest' grade achieved on any factor (ie, there is no attempt at summing or averaging the scores).

Enough examples have probably been given to support the contention that job evaluation plans seek to establish differential rates of payment on the basis—not merely of job content, as the textbooks have it—but of the demands which are made upon the individual by the job. Those aspects of the job demand which are constant for all work (or all work in the class or family under consideration) tend to be ignored as not contributing anything to the 'differentials', but for the rest it is what the job calls for in the individual which is assessed by one or other of these methods. Thus the performance of the individual—what he or she achieves in doing the job—is not in contention, since it is assumed that the job itself makes a necessary or minimum demand upon the person and it is this which is to be assessed to provide a foundation for a structure of differential basic rates.

A single integrated reward structure

This becomes a defensible basis upon which to base differentials. That advantage is often, however, dissipated because quite different plans are adopted to fix the differentials of different staff categories. In effect, artificial barriers to pay progression are erected by the use of different plans, with the result that the plans' credibility is denuded.

In order to overcome such problems, Alcan Sheet Limited, after many years of discussion of these kinds of question, instituted a single-status pay and conditions structure. Previously, different methods of measurement had been used to fix differentials for different levels of job, and each set was therefore kept distinct from all the others. The new single integrated reward structure (SIRS) is described as featuring:

1 Continuous grading of pay against size of job
2 A common system of measuring jobs—job evaluation
3 Harmonization of non-pay conditions
4 Less barriers to individual advancement
5 Joint negotiation by all unions (Gregson and Ruffle, 1980, p 63)

But it is in the advantages claimed for the achievement that the factor of clearing away the clogging undergrowth of soluble problems is most apparent. The authors list the 'highlights' of SIRS as:

1 There is now one main agreement covering all employees on site, including senior managers
2 There is a joint council that negotiates with the company on behalf of all employees
3 There is a salary scale with 14 grades covering all employees
4 There are no staff and hourly paid; all are employees paid an annual salary which does not vary
5 There is no overtime. Rather employees are committed to do in their normal week what they took overtime to do previously
6 There is one sick pay scheme based on the principles that no one should loose money while sick, gain money while sick, or abuse the scheme
7 All employees clock in and out and there is a system of work handovers and staggered breaks to ensure that machines or tasks do not stop
8 There is a productivity scheme linked to output so that employees can share in improvements (Gregson and Ruffle, 1980, p 64).

These might constitute a list of desirable management objectives for any proposal for organizational development. In this particular case, the adoption of a total system perspective of the basic 'people problems' and the persistent discussion of possible futures, the undertaking secured the kind of outcome which many others are still prospecting for.

This case provides, *inter alia*, an illustration of what is meant in the literature by the development of an adequate people orientation in addition to, or in supplementation of, the necessary task orientation. It emphasizes that just as 'production problems' may be tackled systematically and in the long term, so too may the remuneration and industrial relations problems. A great deal of effort has been put into securing in recent years managerial recog-

495

nition of this complementarity, and we turn to discuss this now under the heading of management development.

Management development

Changing expectations of a wide variety of people of the managerial role (cf Hawkins, 1978) have tended to invalidate those conceptions of it which date from the Victorian and paternalistic era. Changes in markets and technologies (cf Burns and Stalker, 1961) have helped to foster new role conceptions in practice, even if their theoretical rationales have not yet appeared. Managers are therefore expected to behave differently within their roles but are less likely to derive the comfort from understanding what is required of the cost accountant, the production manager or even the general foreman, in the new circumstances.

In this situation, there has developed not merely a managerial demand for 'training' in the limited sense of being directed towards the acquisition of knowledge and technique associated with traditionally defined occupations, but a need for exposure to new understandings of what managers are supposed to be all about. This is not to be equated (quite) with role conceptions such as those used above, ie change agent, catalyst and pace-maker, although these indicate something of the direction. The point is perhaps more clearly indicated in the expression used by Burns and Stalker in connection with their 'organic' organization, in which they saw knowledge and know-how as something which was being 'contributed' to the solution of the team's problems rather than as something wrapped up and associated with a traditional bureaucratic 'office' or occupation.

The underlying perspectives of the processes involved in this are provided by the theories of leadership which have emerged from social psychology. Indeed, it might be said that this provides the main contribution which the work in the human relations field has made to management. It might also be said that we have not yet worked through and applied all the implications of these theories. One example, is provided by the rediscovery of the advantage of discussing work with workers in spite of the existence (and wide acceptance) of a task-oriented theory of leadership.

One of the problems with this, however, is the tendency of students of leadership to adopt obscure concepts to describe the differences discerned. Far too often these leadership studies have tended to polarize 'leadership styles' between open, democratic, missioner, 'people-oriented' styles and closed, autocratic, bureaucratic, production-oriented styles. Within each of these sets there may well be subtle differences but the wide variety of terms used by

496

researchers and consultants to present their ideas tends to be dysfunctional from the point of view of understanding the central message. It was in some reflection of this problem, that McGregor (1960) gave his two 'style' theories, the titles of X and Y, and to avoid association with terms like democratic and autocratic.

In the development of thinking about 'leadership' as a phenomenon, psychologists have moved through three quite distinct conceptions of what constitutes leadership.

First, leadership was seen to be something to do with the leader himself or herself—there were traits or personal characteristics which distinguished the leader from others. (This proved difficult to sustain, although some fairly constant traits were discovered, and the basic conception remains of some relevance to the selection process.)

Secondly, leadership was seen to have something to do with the group of people who were being led or who accepted the leadership—there were universal group processes which would ensure that leadership would be conferred, even if not always on the person who looked as if he/she ought to be the official leader. (This also did not quite 'jell' with experience and study although the importance of the group in legitimating leaders is not to be discounted) (cf Homans, 1953, chs VI and VIII.)

Thirdly, leadership was seen to be something which emerged out of the task to be done, the work to be performed, or the problem to be solved, in the particular setting, and in particular out of the interaction of the task demands, the perceived needs or aspirations of the group, and the abilities and motivation of the leader to respond to these—which, in a sense, brings together some of the basic ideas of the first two approaches with the technical component of the group's task. (It is this perspective which underlies the grid training now widely used in management, Blake and Mouton, 1964; Reddin, 1964; Mangham, 1968.)

It is the third of these conceptions which is relevant to our present theme. Effective leadership is perceived as having to do with:

(a) the task set for the section or group supervised and its setting
(b) the orientations of the people in the section or group, and
(c) the skill and motivation of the supervisor.

Any leadership role, managerial or supervisory, union official or shop steward, comes then to be seen as associated with task achievement on the one hand and with the mobilization of group commitment on the other. But, by clear implication, people do not have to be born to lead: they can learn (the skills) and develop (the motivation) to do so (as the many approaches to managerial and supervisory training have assumed as the basic premise).

But a part of that learning process is, consistently with the theory, concerned with the recognition of situational differences, both in respect of task objectives and in respect of human orientations. The leadership styles and skills called for in a particular case are then seen to be task-contingent and people-contingent, even though they can be learned along with the appropriate diagnostic ability to establish relevance.

The response of 'grid-training'

The attempt to meet the need which managers feel they have for a new appreciation of what is involved in their roles in changing organizational structures, has produced training packages in the form of group dynamics, T-Group training and Grid-Training. There are many branded offers within these categories, but it might be noted that the first two are largely focused on the 'people' aspect of the problem (on the assumption that managers are already aware of the requirements of the task aspects) and the third on both in some combination (*see* Mangham, 1968; Blake and Mouton, 1964; Reddin, 1964).

All three, but particularly the first two, are based upon the rationale that work is essentially social in form and context, and that leadership in it must be based upon a full appreciation of the mutual impact of different roles and particularly of one's own role upon others. This kind of training therefore seeks to hold up a mirror to the manager's own behaviour in a social context, in order that he may the better appreciate both his image and his impact. Grid training also, more explicitly, relates role impact to expectations in others and forces the manager to make choices between orienting his role to the achievement of tasks and orienting it to people (*see* McGregor, 1960). Grid training attempts not to force a manager to adopt the role (or 'style' in the language used) which balances these two concerns, most of them tend to assume that this 'middle-way' must, for reasons to do with our cultural values, be the best and therefore the one to be aimed at. This normative conception has more recently been challenged in the contingency model advanced by Vroom and Yetton (1973).

Blake's grid is the creation of Robert R Blake whose writings on group dynamics, T-group and management training are prolific and figure as essential reading for those who go through the grid training exercise. He is currently a consultant, trading as Scientific Methods Inc of Austin, Texas, whose object is to sell the grid in the form of a six phase training package to any interested management

498

group. An important part of the marketing exercise is that there are no 'part-packages': the package must be swallowed whole or not at all.

Reddin's three-dimension grid is an extension from this. Reddin develops his concept from a criticism of both McGregor and Blake, centring largely on the place of 'effectiveness' in the scheme of things. His grid approach has been applied by him in a number of firms in Canada and abroad. In both cases, an aim is to develop a greater awareness of roles, both about the opportunities or choices open and the constraints imposed by the organizational purposes, at the level of the individual manager—a preparation for the adoption of those roles (like change agent or catalyst) which are requisite to organizational change.

The prime purpose of the grid approach is to secure managerial commitment to the aims and methods of the organization. In this it goes well beyond the group dynamics/T-group training approach, in which the object is to provide an unstructured problem-solving situation in which people can learn in interaction with others what their personal impact on others is like and, on the basis of this heightened knowledge, develop a greater awareness of both themselves and others and thus acquire a more positive foundation for understanding and communication. The grid uses these methods but in a more definitely structured situation, in which the structure is aligned to the prime object of recruiting commitment.

The starting point for this is the simple premise that an organization is both a production unit and a social organism. All organizations are seen to have two intertwined sets of objectives, one concerned with the development of a satisfactory relationship with the external environment (eg production for sale in a commercial company), and the other relating to the internal environment (eg the maintenance of a healthy, functioning production/selling organization). Much of the pre-seminar reading which participants in the exercise are required to do is related to this simple understanding.

Blake and Mouton have erected on this premise a simple chart on which managerial attitudes and performances can be measured. The two axes of the graph are identified as 'concern for production' (horizontal) and 'concern for people' (vertical). Each is scaled from 1–9, the numbers being merely gradations from low to high concern. The resultant matrix presents a theoretical 81 co-ordinates but for practical purposes only the four corner boxes and the middle of the graph box are employed. In effect, therefore, the grid employs the categories of 'low-low', 'low-high', 'high-low', intermediate and 'high-high' as the relevant and workable categories. A scale of 1–3 on each axis would therefore serve the practical purposes as well as the 1–9 scales now used, and it would still be possible to use the term 'grid' for it.

The grid itself is the basic device which provides the invitation to managers to move into the more acceptable and more desirable corner of the graph. As is illustrated in the chart below, the scale numbers become the shorthand jargon expressions for the identification of the 'position' of the manager. Since only the 9.9 or high-high position is perceived to be acceptable or desirable this is the obvious place for any manager worth his salt, hence the pressure to move towards it. In all the other (four) positions, the manager is found wanting on one or both scores to some degree (ie 1.1 means that he is completely wanting on both, 5.5. that he is partly wanting on both, and 1.9 and 9.1 that he is wanting on one or the other).

The social scientist will readily see the theoretical bases of this grid. First, it depends upon the achievement/maintenance distinction of the natural system theorist and of the recent understandings of leadership as a cluster of actions appropriate to system functioning. Secondly, it depicts in modified terminology the compliance relationships identified by Etzioni and locates Whyte's 'organization man' on the 5.5 management square; it attempts a modified synthesis of McGregor's Theory X and Theory Y approaches to management.

Reddin has criticized the ultra-simplicity of Blake's two-dimensional grid in terms similar to those which he levels against the basic McGregor dimensions. His main point is that where McGregor sees the pure relationship orientation as optimal, Blake brands this as ineffective because he sees effectiveness as possible only with a *combination* of the relationship and production concerns (ie the 9.9 management style). Reddin replaces the production concern by a task orientation; he puts forward a *three* dimensional grid which admits as a separate dimension the variable of effectiveness, and then assigns Blake's four 'ineffective' positions to the plane of ineffectiveness and his 9.9 style to that of effectiveness, which is then expanded to include other degrees of effectiveness but on *both* other planes.

He thus sees some possibility of retaining the underlying ideas of both McGregor and Blake in his new three dimensional grid but argues that the 'assumptions' of the one and the 'concerns' of the other must be recast as orientations and linked with a third dimension of effectiveness. Where Blake uses the terms 'concerns for production' and 'concerns for relationships' he substitutes 'orientations' (as being more behavioural and less intellectual) first to 'task' and secondly to 'relationships' respectively and argues that

Figure 17
Main dimensions of Blake's and Reddin's Grids
(for details see, Blake, R R and Mouton, J S, The Managerial Grid, Gulf
Publishing, 1964, p 10; and Reddin, W J, The Tri-dimensional Grid,
Training Directors' Journal, July, 1964, p 18)

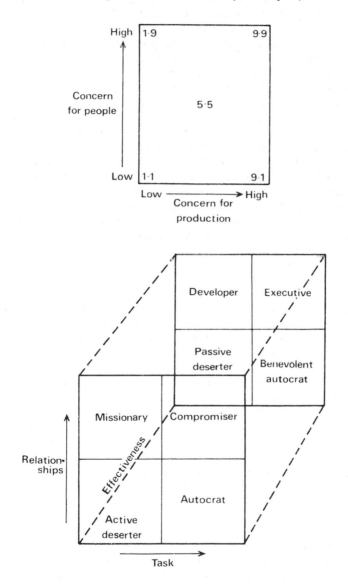

501

either can be implemented effectively or ineffectively with 'effectiveness' defined in terms of 'long-run production'. Movement along the 'X' (task) and 'Y' (relationship) axes, he then refers to as indicating an increasing commitment to, or amount of, each oriented behaviour and that along the 'Z' (effectiveness) axis as 'resulting eventually in optimum production' (Reddin, 1964, p 14).

Reddin depicts his grid in the form on p 501, in which four combinations of task- and relationships-orientations are indicated for each of the two planes of effectiveness and ineffectiveness. The terms used to indicate these are derived from current North American stereotypes of managerial style.

In spite of the distinction introduced by these two consultants between the descriptions of their various axes, there is a hint at least that both wish to draw a distinction between affective and cognitive concerns or orientations. Given the past tendency to emphasize the (cognitive) rationality of the work organization, the modification of this to take account of (affective) relationships in managerial style, can be viewed as no more than an attempt to redress the balance—and then to train a new cadre of managers to operate in this more balanced way. It is distinctly possible that the depicting of the choices in the form of a two- or three-dimensional grid is a useful way of communicating the essentials. But it is also possible that the maintenance of the cognitive/affective distinction helps to continue the belief that the two aspects must remain separate—that task orientations reflect the 'hard' or 'real' interest of the organization and its management, and that relationship orientations represent a 'soft' and somehow 'unreal' interest. The challenges to authority (or domination) which we have noted in chapter 12 may call for a new synthesis of such conceptions of real or proper interest in management: this may indeed prove to be the direction in which the new 'rules' which may be established on the changed power base may be leading.

Thus training indicated by these grid approaches may prove advantageous in setting the limits of choice facing management which seeks to re-establish its authority in a changed environment of cultural value and changed allocation of power, but the *outcome* of that training may have to be a capacity to put together some answers to the real, cognitive and affective, problems facing work organizations at present. There are a number of categories of answer in this sense, applicable at different levels of organizational existence. For example, job enrichment (see above, pp 341–3) involves an initiative at the level of the individual worker, and productivity bargaining (see below, pp 522–4) at that of the group. More specifically, however, in the area of the managerial role, a major initiative focuses on the method of managing by objectives, in which the attempt is made to ensure that managers communicate more effectively about their own work.

Tackling the motivation problem: MBO

Changing managerial attitudes to the role is but one part of the problem. In addition, it is necessary that a manager should be motivated to tackle the tasks, and in this respect he is no different from any one else. Formal training on or off the job may effect necessary changes in attitude and ability, but motivation is unlikely to be increased by these means alone. Unless the role structure within which he must operate is sufficiently benign to allow him to secure reinforcement of the learned behaviours, he or she is unlikely to develop high motivation to put them into effect. Enhancement of motivation is therefore likely to require attention to the organization's structure.

The problem to be resolved is whether a manager would think it worthwhile to 'contribute' in the kind of organizational climate which exists. Is it worth his while to appraise the performance of subordinates, discuss their performance with them in order to improve it, make suggestions as to how improvements might be brought about and take action to facilitate this? The discussion of expectancy theory (in chapter 11) suggests that this is not a set of questions whose answers will stem merely from the individual person, but one which will depend upon the individual-organization relationship. Therefore, the solution is likely to focus upon the relationship, rather than the individual or the organization.

The main illustration of the attempt to resolve this kind of problem in this way is provided by MBO. The term, management by objectives (MBO), is now used to cover a wide variety of different forms of the approach, but what is emphasized by the approach as a whole is just this attempt to tackle the relationship problem.

As originally put forward by Drucker (1955) and pursued by many others since, this approach emphasizes the need for undertakings to find some method of so legitimating objectives that people will feel both able and willing to pursue them in the organizational context. This need is met by making objective-setting a deliberately joint exercise, between boss and subordinate.

The latter is given the opportunity to indicate not only what he considers he could do but also what he thinks he should do. In this way, the individual has some opportunity to secure legitimacy for his 'dissatisfactions' with what is current and for his 'theories' as to

503

what might be done. It requires the 'boss' as the significant other in the exercise to adopt his co-ordinating role in relation to all subordinates, by urging the wider considerations which must constrain the one individual in his role but to do so within a framework of provision of opportunities.

This perspective is clear enough in Drucker's original outline of the approach. Management by objectives, he argues 'requires each manager to develop and set the objectives of his unit himself' even if at the same time 'higher management must reserve the power to approve or disapprove these objectives'. 'Their development' remains 'part of a manager's responsibility' and furthermore 'every manager should responsibly participate in the development of the objectives of the higher unit of which his is a part' (Drucker, 1961, p 111).

This not only gives the individual manager an opportunity to say his piece, under certain constraints, but also puts the more senior manager on the spot by exposing him to criticism (actual or potential) and by requiring of him the special efforts to ensure that not only are all his subordinate managers *au fait* with the overall objectives of the larger unit but that they are also freed from the encumbrances of misdirection (arising out of casual comments and suggestions or intermittent inspections).

Raia's detailed study of a 'goals and controls' programme in the Purex Corporation in 1961–62, was conceived as a systematic evaluation of the kind of approach advocated by Drucker. The programme had three main ingredients:

goal setting by the individual manager under the guidance of his immediate supervisor

control by the individual on his own initiative in response to control information supplied to him as well as superiors

periodic review in relation to established goals with an aim of removing identifiable obstacles to their attainment (Raia, 1965, p 157).

Raia gathered both 'objective' data on performance (such as the effects on goal attainment and on the introduction of new goals on the individual's initiative) and on perceptions and attitudes (through an interview programme). On the first, he found that productivity improved in most plants as a result of the programme and appeared to maintain the improvement. On the second, he found 'relatively highly favourable attitudes in all of the 15 plants in the company' and indications of higher motivation 'to improve performance'. Most thought that authority and communications had been improved, and there was some evidence to support the latter perception (Raia, 1965).

Thus the general effect is one of improvement from most of the points of view that managers or anyone else would regard as the relevant and important ones. Performance, productivity, organization and satisfaction seem to be higher in most cases, suggesting that everyone with an interest in the operation of the system might be getting something out of it. On the other hand, Raia is realistic in reporting snags which had not been ironed out. In particular he is able to show interview data on who participates in goal setting and who does not, and that whilst plant managers met their supervisors regularly, at the two lower levels of management 'only a proportion reported that they attended regular scheduled meetings with their immediate superiors', suggesting that the programme was not being fully implemented at lower levels. He goes on to suggest that 'there is considerable evidence that the company philosophy of growth for the individual has not yet permeated throughout the entire organization. There appears to be some distortion, particularly at the lower levels' and this may in turn account for the failure to achieve fuller implementation of participation.

It may be concluded from this study that this kind of more open approach to the solution of 'task' related problems in the organization, which simultaneously sought to allow more involvement of the individual's feelings and preferences, is that it produced some efficiency and some satisfaction benefits and some disadvantages on both scores. This might be expected on the *a priori* grounds that (a) people do differ in their perception of and reaction to any given environmental stimulus, and (b) people used to one kind of work environment will not necessarily 'take to' a change of this sort just because it has been introduced (even with their consent). But at the same time it is possible to detect in the replies of managers in the interviews some willingness to calculate the benefits and drawbacks of the new arrangement and, depending on the outcome, to give it a go if it promised some longer-term satisfaction—for task or maintenance reasons.

A number of organizations are now experimenting with changes of approach or style in which some of these same general features are to be found. Many of them are confined, as in the above case study, to relatively senior managerial personnel. We have already noted that managers (as a manifestation of white collar or professional workers as a class) are likely to attach particular meaning to their work: we might therefore expect them to be particularly receptive to a proposal so to change the framework of organization as to improve their independent performance.

On the other hand, given the arguments which have been

advanced about human motivation in general, we might expect this conclusion to apply generally, or at least in those circumstances where the re-inforcement presented by work within organizations did not cause the kind of regression noted on p 268 above. If, therefore, some conception of management by objectives can be shown to work at the 'managerial' levels, there is at least some presumption that a similar proposal might tap motivation at other levels. But the organizational development problem there might, in many cases, require a fundamental reconsideration of what 'reinforcement' experience does offer the individual or the group. The main example of that reconsideration which we have in our experience is that which is associated with job enrichment and autonomous work groups, already discussed (pp 341–43 above).

Further reading
On the concepts of OD and MD, students might consult Alderfer (1977); Burke (1971); French and Bell (1978); Bennis (1966 and 1969); Lippitt (1969); Jones (1969); and Miner (1973).

On the various aspects of 'harmonization', see Butteris (1975); Gregson and Ruffle (1980); Thomason (1980).

On management development in the context of training, see Reddin (1970); Blake and Mouton (1964); King (1968); Mangham (1968); Ellis *et al* (1968).

On MBO, see Raia (1974); Drucker (1961); Humble (1970 and 1973); Odiorne (1965; 1968; 1970; and 1971); Schaffer (1964); and Varney (1976).

20   The mobilization of commitment

Individual and organization

The relationship of the individual to the organization is seen as constituting a characteristic problem in modern society (cf Argyris, 1964; Dunkerley, 1972; Albrow, 1979). Much effort is expended in both attempting to understand its dimensions and seeking adjustments and accommodations which might reduce it.

There is certainly no agreement on how the problem should be defined. But one common perspective which has developed is that which regards the sheer scale of modern organization and the 'power' which that scale gives to those who act in its name, as confronting the individual with a fact or thing which he or she (as an individual) is powerless to influence. The condition of individual powerlessness is then evaluated as diminishing the human personality unless the individual can somehow acquire power by some other, non-organizationally-dependent means.

Although the argument may be expressed in many different forms of words, this analysis and evaluation then becomes the basis for justifying either pluralist or radical alternatives to the present conception of unitary or monolithic organization. In particular, and within the personnel manager's main sphere of interest, this kind of argument is used to justify the support for trade union existence and 'recognition' both generally within the culture and specifically through enabling legislation. The trade union represents one of a number of independent associational forms (along with, for example, professional associations) which might accrete power to challenge the unitary organization in the interests of the individual worker within it. Given the definition of the problem, association around such objectives, becomes a mechanism which, it is argued, should receive support from the state—as, of course, it does (*see* above, pp 434–52).

Nothing in the culture nor in the specific legislation, however, has seriously diminished the demand made upon employment organizations to 'produce' wealth, or to act efficiently in the consumer or citizen interest (*see* above, pp 14–17).

These organizations continue to be oriented towards ends which are essentially consumer-oriented. In some cases, consumers have associated themselves in order to defend their interests in the face of both organizational scale and the apparently greater emphasis of recent times upon the producer interest. But whatever may be the position with regard to 'producer power' (as a consequence of full employment or because of the trade union's 'privileges' under the law) the consumer generally tends to remain sovereign and to make demands on employment organizations which remain dominant over those of organized labour.

Herein lies the management dilemma. Management is charged with securing efficient consumer-oriented performance, and, increasingly, with giving greater attention to the producer interest in the pursuit of those objectives. The problem for management then becomes one of discovering how to cope with this new pattern of constraint stemming from the organization of the main stakeholders and supported by the law, when most of its available structures and methods are based on the idea that the corporate body (from which the management derives its authority) will be better organized and more powerful than any interest group associated with it.

We have already noted that one answer which has been put forward is one which involves the development of a new structural or constitutional arrangement which will then serve as an 'order' to which people (including work people) will the more readily orient their behaviour (see above, pp 422–25).

Our understanding of learning theory must, however, lead us to realize that this orientation is not likely to occur 'automatically', nor, indeed, that such structural solutions will themselves happen without human agency. The second element in the managerial dilemma at the present time is, therefore, that the solution to the main problem is not something which management can (unilaterally) impose upon the situation; the solution of the problem of commitment to the ends of working may be one of establishing some kind of joint-decision-taking and joint-execution, but that solution may itself have to emerge from joint-decision-taking and joint-execution (cf Schattschneider, 1975).

The essence of this, as it is conceived in public policy, is that the problem of commitment to the ends of working in organizations is to be resolved by jointly setting up mechanisms for joint resolution of the problem. In a word, the emphasis is upon negotiated solutions to the whole hierarchy of 'problems'.

One might, therefore, suggest that the paradox associated

with these problems and these dilemmas is that managements will be called upon to 'lead' in the development of new structures and processes and at the same time 'accept' the constraint that these must emerge from joint-decision and find a place for joint-development. In the 'new' situation, created by changing cultural values and supported by state action in the legislative field, management remains involved in a process of mobilizing commitment to the task objectives of the undertaking.

It is in recognition of this that this present chapter aims to consider 'influence' in organizational settings. By influence we choose to mean the process whereby one person (say a manager or a shop steward) successfully induces a change in the behaviour of another by a means which would generally be accorded legitimacy in our culture, and in order to serve an end which would also be culturally sanctioned.

We also acknowledge that what has most markedly changed in this area in recent years is the constraint which is imposed upon managers (and others) in their choice of the means by which they effect this influence. In the specifically employment context, that constraint has emphasized the desirability of avoiding authoritarian and unilateral decisions and action, in favour of negotiating strategies, policies, methods related to the achievement of undertaking purposes. Such 'negotiation' is not, however, confined to formal collective negotiations with trade unions; there is, indeed, a longer cultural predisposition towards negotiation at the interpersonal level than there is towards negotiation at the trade union level. Our aim is therefore to review the likely directions of the development of 'influence' in modern organizations in the context that it is increasingly likely to be 'influence through negotiation'.

In order to identify the kinds of activity which are necessary to secure the appropriate accommodation of the individual in the organization, we will make some use of the Walton and McKersie characterization of the different processes of 'bargaining' (although we will use the term negotiation for the most part in order to emphasize more the 'treaty-formation' aspect of influence). The hypothesis guiding this approach is that tasks will tend to vary systematically according to whether the negotiations are between 'individuals' or focused upon these authors' processes of distributive, integrative, or intra-organizational bargaining or attitudinal structuring.

Inter-personal negotiation
Negotiation between two individuals to establish an agreement or consensus to a course of action is common, not to say universal. In

fact, it is so much a part of the warp and woof of social activity, that it is difficult to establish that it ought to be considered as a part of the general process of negotiation. However, consistently with the view taken by Simon of authority and influence (*see above*, pp 296–98), we should recognize that suggestion and persuasion, and even 'instruction' itself in so far as it depends upon an acceptance of a superordinate's right to give instructions, represent types of negotiation. The exchange theorists would go further, and suggest that all of them represent a kind of bargaining in so far as some valued resource is exchanged as a basis for the mutual acceptance.

In that perspective all management interaction might be referred to as negotiation. Unless there is a situation in which one, a manager, has some kind of absolute power to compel compliance by another, say, a worker, the exercise of authority and/or influence may be seen as a process of give and take, shift and shift-about, until a mutually-acceptable outcome is achieved. In the usual case, what is involved is something between the absolute positions of complete dependence and complete independence, and the usual representation is therefore one of a process of influence which depends to a degree upon the possession and acceptance of power (cf Cartwright, 1965). The two-way process of communication (*see above*, pp 348–55) then becomes the mechanism through which the 'persuasion' process, leading to agreement, takes place.

The 'normal' position tends therefore to be one in which control and compliance is brought about by 'influence'. As Gilman has expressed this:

> positive control of performance down the line is possible only because one can influence, when and if necessary, the behaviour of the subordinate in such a way that he acts on the basis of his superior's judgement rather than his own (Gilman, 1962, pp 106–107).

In this sense, 'influence' may be treated as a rather special example of causality in the sense that it attempts and achieves the modification of one person's behaviour by another. Influence is thus merely another 'determinant' of human behaviour, which competes with other determinants in any particular case.

'Personal' influence is but one amongst a number of methods of influence which may be separately distinguished as available in any organizational setting. It is common to distinguish at least three methods, those of physical coercion, economic (utilitarian) manipulation, and symbolic manipulation (cf Etzioni, 1961, pp 4–8) and influence of the kind with which we are here concerned falls

510

within this third category. Symbolic manipulation based upon a capacity to manipulate both the symbols used to convey meaning and the symbols of prestige, esteem, recognition and the rest, is primarily what is involved in inter-personal influence. In the work situation, it often relies upon a degree of physical restriction (obedience to the clocking rules and acceptance of 'position' in the workflow sequence) and upon manipulation of utilities (through the payment structures). It is therefore often a 'residual' process by which the other is got to act in a way which he might not otherwise do.

Influence as exercised at the inter-personal level depends, in the usual conception, upon the would-be influencer having a 'power base', which is usually defined as ownership or control of resources (including access to channels of communications) which can be deployed in any influence attempt. The existence of such a power base may itself play a part in 'influence'. Here the fact that a supervisor's position rests upon there already being in existence and operation, a contractual relationship, a structure of remuneration, a pattern of organization and an established work-flow system, enables the supervisor's persuasion, suggestion and instruction to take place in a receptive context. This 'nesting' of overt authority in an underlying-structure of 'power' is frequently observed in treatises on the subject of power and authority (cf Lukes, 1974).

But such influence is also seen to be dependent upon the existence of congruent (or matching) attitudes and predispositions on the part of the person who is to be influenced in these attempts. Such influence might be expected to 'work' only if the influencee is willing to be influenced by the method and by the person in question. This is often spoken of in terms of 'acceptance of authority' (Simon, 1953) or of 'legitimation of authority' (cf Lukes, 1974). In addition, it also depends upon the capacity (or ability) of the influencee, in the sense that he must be able to interpret (decode in the language of communication theory) the intention of the influence attempt before it could have any promise of being effective (*see* above, pp 351–52).

It is because we think that the underlying conditions have changed in recent years, that we also regard the exercise of inter-personal influence as being now more difficult than in some golden age of the past.

'Technology' and behaviour

However, it cannot be assumed that there was a golden age in which workers were always amenable to influence by their immediate superordinates, nor that practice will be standardized by legislative or collective prescriptions in the future.

Evidence from different situations, suggests that a much more potent effect upon the opportunities to exercise styles and methods of influence at the inter-personal, immediate-supervisor-to-worker level is exerted by what has been referred to as technology. This is perhaps not merely the physical means extant in the workplace, but subsumes the supposition that a defined type of work task will tend to attract an identifiable type of work attitude and behaviour into association with it. For something like *this* reason, situational and group differences may be observed.

Likert, for example, has suggested that distinct situations are visible in American industry. One he identifies as the kind of situation in which the technology imposes upon the workers highly routine, short-cycle tasks which allow very little discretion to the worker, and in which the *control* environment emphasizes reward related to performance (which may also correlate closely with effort) and close supervision. An example is the large office carrying out standardized tasks on a mass basis, or the assembly and production line industries with similar characteristics. He contrasts this with the situation in which the technology offers opportunity for variety of tasks and discretion in carrying them out to the worker, and in which the control environment emphasizes self-control and high-trust relations (cf Fox, 1974) with the management and supervision. Examples are drawn from tool rooms and research and development departments.

In the one situation, because of the way in which the mutual selection process works out, the workers tend to display a low range of attitudes (they are, to put it over-simply, relatively alienated) and such attitudes do not matter from the production point of view because of the efficacy of control. In the other, however, the jobs and the workers also seek one another out: those who want to have high discretion jobs go for them and gatekeepers of the undertaking tend to select those whom they consider will cope successfully with such jobs and develop the right kinds of attitudes towards them. Here attitudes do matter (cf Herzberg, 1959) and those who enter the undertaking tend to be those who want attitudes to matter in work (cf Dubin, 1958; Orzack, 1959). In the two polar types of situation, therefore, there is a happy correlation between need and between the criteria of their satisfaction (*see* also above, p 169).

Sayles conducted a more detailed study of the relationship between work-group grieving activity and the technology (1958). He identified four types of group on this dimension, the apathetic (which never engaged in this activity), the erratic (which engaged in it only spasmodically), the strategic (which was usually 'at the very centre of most of the really important grievances'), and the conservative (which engaged in grievances only rarely and with notice).

In his actual study he associated each of these groups with a number of specific jobs in identified sections. He generalizes that the degree of activity tends to be associated with:

1 the relative position on the promotional ladders of the plant
2 the relative size and importance of the group
3 the similarity of the jobs within the group
4 the degree to which the job is indispensable in the functioning of the plant or the department
5 the precision with which management can measure workload and pace.
(Sayles, 1958, p 69)

On the other hand he found that the repetitiveness of the task, the hours of work, the ratio of men to machines,and the sex distribution within the group were much less important in explaining differences in behaviour.

The suggestion is that the 'technology' is a relevant factor predisposing groups to engage in grievance activity. But as Sayles argues, the technological factors are no more than enabling conditions. As such they can be mediated by the official and unofficial leadership (cf Sayles, 1958, pp 98–99). This point has also been made by a number of other studies, particularly in some of the Warwick studies of the roles of shop representatives (*see* Batstone, Boraston and Frenkel, 1977 and 1978).

The major implication of this is, therefore, that although there are predisposing conditions (as in what we have referred to as 'technology') there is scope both for individual differences of response in general, and for individual (eg supervisor or shop steward) influence as a form of causality in modifying the response.

Intra-organizational bargaining

Walton and McKersie use the term 'intra-organizational bargaining' to refer to the process of securing agreement within a 'side' in negotiations as to the course of action which should be followed in coping with the other side (Walton and McKersie, 1965, p 4). The process thus identified may be considered to have a broader context than this in that it frequently happens that managers (or for that matter union leaders) have to secure commitment from their colleagues to a course of action, which, whilst it may have a great deal to do with industrial relations, is not directly concerned with formal negotiations.

In the management context, for example, it frequently happens that such commitment must be sought and found to strategic plans and policies, as without this, they could not 'succeed'. Frequently, such commitment is not forthcoming, possibly because there is a lack of understanding of what is intended, and possibly because those whose commitment is needed are not persuaded that the objective or the means is a correct one. An example is provided in some of the studies quoted above on responses to plans of performance appraisal (*see* pp 304–8). On the other hand, it may be that negotiators more readily and quickly appreciate the need for solidarity in negotiation and respond accordingly. But it must remain the case, that such accord may be problematic, and intra-organizational negotiation may be necessary to secure it.

The accord sought is, essentially, one to the effect that an objective, a plan or a policy is the right one to adopt in the circumstances, and therefore one to which the individuals will be prepared to commit themselves. The most fundamental question of this sort which arises in the employee relations area is that which focuses upon how far the undertaking as a whole ought to go in developing collective bargaining or perhaps some other form of 'joint' approach, given that the major alternative is to continue with an individually-oriented, possibly paternalistic and welfare approach to the whole question.

The first question in this, and one with particular relevance to the personnel manager, is how far the welfare approach is still a viable alternative. The second is how far along the road of collective bargaining is it necessary or desirable to move, given the various positions which exist, and the constraints existing in the particular case.

Welfare and its metamorphosis

On the first question, the problem appears to be that although the welfare approach might have been a useful and congruent one in the past, the development of a new 'rights-based' conception of human dignity in work (whether supported by trade union sanctions or legislative penalties) has cast some doubt on its future viability as a strategy for encouraging loyalty and commitment in the modern large-scale undertaking.

The traditional conception of 'welfare' had a good deal to do

514

with ethics. Some employers see themselves as having a moral duty to care for their employees at work, over and above that assumed in the 'consideration' elements in the employment contract, and developed a welfare office to help discharge it. It is not necessary to assume that such employers had a mercenary view of the process, in order to suggest that what was offered to employees under this heading also served to influence them in their attitudes towards the employer or towards the employment and in their commitment and loyalty to the undertaking and its tasks.

Traditionally, the conception of 'care' as a duty owed by the employer to his workers, was translated into a mixed bag of provisions related to the environment of the work or the work contract. The contents were then associated with the welfare officer or the personnel manager, who often assumed direct line or executive responsibility for their provision. Included amongst the contents are usually:

1 canteen facilities
2 recreational facilities (including sports clubs and facilities, rest rooms and library facilities
3 amenities (including washrooms, cloakrooms, nurseries, housing transport, sick clubs, benevolent funds, long-service grants, savings and pensions)
4 information services (including certain forms of counselling, the provision of legal aid and advice, and help with holiday travel)
5 further education facilities
6 medical services.

What distinguishes these is, perhaps, that they are outside the normal channels of 'consideration' central to the functioning of the undertaking. Rather, to paraphrase a thought which can trace its ancestry back to Aristotle, one might say that the enterprise comes into existence equipped with methods of planning manpower, rewarding contributions, monitoring performance etc in order that it can function and these become the substance of the contract of employment. But it then proliferates other activities and provisions in order that the members might live better within its context, and these come to be considered only peripherally. If many of these provisions were made within a spirit of paternalism, they continued in existence because some people some of the time derived some advantage or satisfaction from them.

Because these were seen in this way they were treated as fit subjects for discussion with employee representatives in a way which would help ensure that the right lessons were learned from them. This was effected through 'joint consultation', in the course of which the employer invited views from employees on how the 'welfare' fund which he was willing to make available should be allocated as between the alternative uses, but also took occasion to discuss performance questions as a basis for influencing commitment.

Taken together, these various strands of welfare provision amounted to a conception of what, originally, the employer considered would cause him to be thought 'a good employer'. With the passage of time, many of the strands have been reshaped, by trade union pressure and legislative requirement, into a structure of minimum rights for workers, thus providing a new standard for those who want to be considered 'good' in the above sense to match or improve on (*see* above, p 168).

With the progressive development of collective bargaining, the subjects reserved for joint consultation were rendered even more peripheral to the mainstream. Whenever any welfare benefits were placed under threat, the trade union with power would tend to bring the topic within the ambit of negotiation; whenever legislation or incomes policies choked off the opportunities for movement on the main 'consideration' questions, the strong trade union would switch attention to these other questions. Participation in joint consultation might itself be used as a weapon in negotiations, the union representatives threatening to withdraw should their demands not be met (cf Anthony, in Balfour 3a).

If this began a process of metamorphosing welfare, recent developments in legislative prescription have continued it. The 'rights' legislation of the 1960s and 1970s taking their cues from the 'good practice' in collective agreements, have brought within a new framework of law, a good deal of what could be described as policy or practice touching on the 'treatment' of employees—on notice of termination, information about conditions of the contract, compensation for peremptory dismissal or discrimination.

The Health and Safety at Work Act is more directly relevant in that it provides in part that the employer shall have a duty 'to provide and maintain a working environment ... that is, so far as is reasonably practicable, safe, without risk to health, and *adequate as regards facilities and arrangements for ... welfare at work*' (italics added). The concept of welfare is nowhere defined in the Act, although one might presume, in advance of court interpretation or definition in regulations or Codes of Practice under the Act, that it is to be defined in terms of provision of adequate air conditioning, lighting, fume eradication, facilities for rest pauses and meal breaks, and protection from inclement weather etc which affect the employee's physical well-being.

If this is the kind of meaning intended, it does not admittedly go as far as the term welfare in the personnel management context. If this merely represents a 'catching up' of 'welfare' provision under the Act, there remains scope for the development of policies in this area. It *could* be interpreted more broadly than this and represent an attempt to standardize a good deal of what was previously idiosyncratic provision in the field of welfare. In the face of this, there may be less scope for more individual variation, and therefore for a new look at the old welfare function, as Kenny has suggested (1975).

A 'right' conception of collective bargaining

On the other hand, there is *more* scope, not to say pressure, in many situations, for the development of some form of collective bargaining or joint regulation of many features of the work relationship. Whatever the correct posture on welfare provision and approaches, therefore, managements face a choice of how far to develop their joint approaches to these issues. The element of choice arises because there are a number of ways of conceiving collective bargaining, each of which imports quite distinct degrees of difference in the amount of negotiation which is likely to be given legitimacy.

A number of distinct cognitive models are offered in the literature. One of the main classifications is provided by Chamberlain who in his 1951 edition (he changed it slightly in the later editions) suggests that collective bargaining may be so structured and developed as to present any one of three mechanisms:

1 a means of contracting for the sale of labour
2 a form of industrial government
3 a method of management. (1951, p 121)

These may then be labelled marketing, governmental and managerial theories of collective bargaining. The first is essentially the theory developed by the Webbs, but followed in essentials by Dunlop (1944) in his approach to wage determination and by Fischer (1971) who also sees the trade union in the position of a labour cartel. In this view bargaining is confined to the consideration elements of the employment contract and does not get into areas of decision about task objectives.

The second is comparable to Flanders' theory of job regulation but the rule-making process is extended to embrace what Leiserson has called the setting up, definition and limitation of organs of government and the provision of 'agencies for making, executing and interpreting laws for the industry and means for their enforcement' (Leiserson, 1922, p 61). In Chamberlain's own view, this conception involves both a sharing of industrial sovereignity (ie as between management and trade unions) *and* a joint defence by both parties of the autonomy of the two parties acting together (Chamberlain, 1951, pp 128–9).

In the Leiserson conception, it is a little difficult to draw an adequate dividing line between collective bargaining as a means of industrial government and as a method of management, because of his incorporation of agencies for *executing* the laws jointly made. Chamberlain's own argument on this aspect is that because employers and unions combine 'in reaching decisions on matters in which both have vital interests', the usual union disclaimer of any interest in usurping management's function can itself be discounted because 'collective bargaining', by its very nature involves [them] in the managerial role and they are 'actually *de facto* managers' (Chamberlain, 1951, pp 137, 130 and 198).

But this view is based upon the management function being seen as (simply) that of *deciding* on behalf of the undertaking, whereas in Chamberlain's own analysis of that function he also recognizes a three-level hierarchy of such decision taking which is variously attacked or influenced by union activity (Chamberlain, 1948, ch 2). If we are to distinguish the method of government as concerned with some aspect of industrial decision taking, it might be preferable to define the method of management in terms of subordinate decision functions of administration (deciding how the 'top-level' decisions are to be carried out) and execution (seeing to it that these decisions are implemented 'correctly' and 'appropriately'). This would remain consistent with the Chamberlain view that collective bargaining helps to make management (as distinct from industrial government) more 'democratic' (cf Flanders, 1969, p 33).

Given these three distinct views both managements and trade unions are called upon to make a choice as to which they will prefer over the others, and this makes attitudinal problems salient to the negotiating approach and structure.

Attitudinal structuring
It may be suggested that the crucial negotiation in which managements of undertakings engage with their employees at the present time is that which relates to attitudes. The attitudes most in contention here are those which people within an undertaking adopt and hold in respect of the legitimacy of the actions taken by others. In the face of the many changes which have taken place in relation to

the rights and obligations of the parties both to the individual contract of employment (*see* above, pp 69–126) and the collective agreement (*see* above, pp 434–54) it is not surprising that the question of what is legitimate and what not is unresolved.

The most deep-seated aspect of attitudes is that which focuses upon the values held by the parties as to the legitimacy of the other's power. Ought management to have the power it has, or ought the trade union to have the power it has, are questions of value which are answered quite differently. Because managements and unions may hold quite distinct values on this dimension, assessment of the underlying position is often a starting point for the development of any strategy in this area of collective bargaining.

It is possible to visualize that a range of value positions may be found on either side of the bargaining table. At one extreme there may be complete acceptance of the values of 'capitalism' and at the other complete rejection of these values and a desire to set up a society based on quite other values. In the nature of industrial relationships, parties with different values and different derived objectives do face one another in the production or employment situation and, when this happens, the common characterization of collective bargaining as cooperative may prove inapplicable or inept.

This idea is to be found in Walton and McKersie's attempt to identify different relationship patterns in industrial relations, which they label: 'conflict, containment-aggression, accommodation, cooperation and collusion' (Selekman, Selekman and Fuller, 1958, pp 4–8: quoted in Walton and McKersie, 1965, p 185). This categorization indicates that there might be five quite different sets of relationship, supported by five quite different perspectives and scales of preferences. But Walton and McKersie associated these with different situations of relationship, thus implying that the parties to the relationship share the objectives and values which these labels suggest. Equally possible is the conclusion that the separate parties might approach the relationship from any of the five positions so that, whilst there may be pressure to adopt consensual positions, there might still be a considerable possibility of mismatching.

Thus on either side of the bargaining table, there are at least five such salient value positions to be recognized. In table 15 on page 520, these values are set against each other in a way which, reading along the horizontal lines, might yield the kinds of 'relationship pattern' identified by Walton and McKersie. In this table, I have suggested, in the central column, terms which might the more appropriately indicate the nature of the relationship

Table 15
Spectrum of salient values in industrial relationships with indications of types of guiding philosophy adopted by the parties

The corporate (employer) philosophy	The salient value of either party to the relationship	The trade union (worker) philosophy
Individualism F (unfettered by R organization E of power) E	REVOLUTION	F Overthrow unionism A in one of its many I manifestations R
Boulwarism* and similar abrasive employer philosophies	REBELLION	Unionism in the mould of a permanent and critical opposition
Demotivated abdication Pursuit of No change or *status quo*	a) ACCEPTANCE (passive) b) CONSTRUCTIVE TOLERANCE	A pathetic acceptance of what is Preservation of what is thought to have been achieved
Constitutionalism: proceduralization of the relationship	CO-ORDINATION	Aggressive business unionism
Socially F responsible A I R	COOPERATION	F Non-affiliated R unionism (or E non-political E unionism)

*For explanation, see Walton and McKersie, p 187 (cf Walton and McKersie, 1975, p 189, from which this has been developed)

which might be expected to develop over a rather wider spectrum of value (and associated philosophy or ideology) than that indicated in the Walton and McKersie statement. There are, for example, situations in which the employer attitude of completely unfettered individualism juxtaposed with an ideology which completely rejects existing forms of organization on the part of the workers or their organization, could yield little more than a revolutionary situation. In others, an employer attitude which emphasized his responsibilities to the workers or to workers-plus-other-groups, brought into association with a politically non-aligned workforce or unionism, might effect a high level of cooperation between the parties. In between these two situations, a number of intermediate positions can be distinguished, yielding relationships of rebellion, passive acceptance or constructive tolerance, or co-ordination. But the possibility must exist that in the short-run (and therefore for shorter or longer periods within an ongoing relationship) the values and objectives of the parties must diverge, and so create situations in which one party (with one value based objective) must react to the other party who is intent upon some other type of value-based objective. Conceived in this way, the assumptions that relationships are 'normally' to be found in the lower half of the spectrum and to be congruent with one another across the light are thrown into question. And, equally importantly, some of the 'extreme' relationships indicated on this chart may not qualify for the title of a 'collective bargaining' relationship at all.

Nevertheless, there is little doubt that in Britain and some other countries this relationship is predominantly one which *can* be characterized as one of 'collective bargaining'. There are some who think the term might be felicitously altered (for example to job regulation) and some who regard it as only one of a number of different types of relationship which might be established, even if it is the one to which most principals and representatives appear to orient themselves in these societies.

But it is important to recognize that were they not to do so in the particular case, a collective bargaining relationship of the kind which might produce agreements as to rules, could not exist. Nor, it might be said for the sake of completeness, could other congruent relationships exist where the values and attitudes of the one party were not matched by those of the other party in the horizontal plane.

Consequently, where any of these incongruities exist, there is likely to be pressure on some one acting in the name of the one organization or the other, to try to resolve the question by action to change the attitudes of the 'other', particularly those towards the legitimacy of the 'other's' position.

This is an example of what Walton and McKersie had in mind in their use of the term 'attitudinal structuring', although as they see it, it is not a distinct and discrete set of activities, but a part of the continuous bargaining relationship. In their view a process of distributive bargaining does not merely concern a division of the economic product and the rules under which it will be made, but in addition both relies upon and effects changes in 'the attitudes which the negotiating parties hold and adopt towards each other's actions. The reliance is indicated in their statement that the attitudes of each party towards the other, taken together, define the relationship between them' (Walton and McKersie, 1965, p 184). These are themselves a product of the past relationship, and the 'on-going' processes of bargaining will produce both intended and unintended effects upon the attitudes.

This kind of problem arose, in Britain, in connection with the development of local (undertaking-wide) bargaining in the post-war period, and more particularly in connection with productivity-bargaining in the 1960s. In the one, the question of what was legitimate for local managements to propose and do arose when they adopted a more proactive response to shop steward organization and demands for negotiating rights, inside or outside the confines of the national agreement. In the other, the question of how far managements should go in suggesting and securing agreements to changes in (trade union supported) working practices, presented the union negotiators with a need to reconsider their attitudes towards what was locally negotiable and what was not.

In effect, managements had to decide, first, whether they were going to take initiatives in negotiating changes with the trade union representatives in the work place, and secondly, if they were to do so to decide on the extent to which they were going to adopt a plan or a position which they would then, simply, seek to realize in power bargaining in a traditional fashion. In other words, were there matters traditionally regarded as within management's pre-rogative power that they would now open up to negotiation, and, if there were, were these to be treated as occasions on which management's intentions would be simply to protect and preserve that power in its traditional form.

Similarly, local trade union representatives had to decide, first, whether they in their trade union roles had already or could acquire an authority to accept such proposals put forward by management for change, and secondly, if they had, on the extent to which they would allow themselves to 'become involved' in the actual decision taking process. Against a trade union attitude which traditionally emphasized the 'permanent opposition' position, and the view that it was for management to propose and the trade union to challenge, the shop stewards were presented with difficult attitudinal questions concerning legitimacy.

Productive bargaining
In a number of approaches made in the 1960s to the local bargaining problem, some fairly novel resolutions were effected, although frequently, the advances were choked off in the early 1970s with the reimposition of incomes policies which denied local negotiators

522

the flexibility which they needed if they were to continue. Such changes as were made, however, illustrate the second of the above propositions, to the effect that a change in approach will tend to produce a change in attitude towards what is legitimate action. This came about largely because a deliberate break was made, usually on the initiative of management (although not always) with the traditional approach to bargaining.

The traditional approach was generally one in which management, having engaged in analysis and planning before the negotiations, sought in those negotiations to secure agreement to the plan or something as near to it as the exigencies of the bargaining situation would permit. From the beginning, productivity bargaining began to open up the situation at the bargaining table by interposing novel stages. A plan might be arrived at but before it was put into negotiation soundings were taken and the plan modified in the light of them; only then was the bargaining process begun. This was the kind of approach associated with the Fawley agreement and also that in Alcan. Another variant of this was the production of a 'part plan' which was discussed in part, before the whole plan was formulated for introduction into bargaining, as happened with the ICI and Electricity Supply bargains in the middle 1960s (NBPI, Report No 36, 1968) (see Table 16, p 524).

These might be regarded as tentative moves to open up the bargaining situation to a degree of problem-solving in advance of an actual bargaining process being undertaken. The problem foreseen, was that building sufficient trust to achieve this end might prove difficult. This is indicated in McKersie's statement that 'one side needs to expose itself—it runs the risk of being victimized, but it also creates the possibility of having the trusting overture reinforced by a similar gesture' (McKersie, 1966, p vii).

The NBPI Report on Productivity Agreements suggested that the risk might be worth taking 'in the light of this varied experience' and that

> the advantage lies with joint discussion of principles with the unions before the presentation of formal proposals and with early discussions at workshop level. This view is supported by the contrast between the patchy reception of the ICI proposals and the reluctance of some of the men on the trial sites to go ahead; and, on the other hand, the ease with which British Oxygen's final agreement went through, was accepted and applied (NBPI, 36, p 33).

In the British Oxygen and Mobil Oil approaches to this problem, even more stages were introduced into the process in order to give more opportunity for discussion of general principles and criteria before plans were formulated and negotiated.

Distributive and integrative bargaining

Productivity bargaining of this type is frequently quoted as an example of what Walton and McKersie call 'integrative bargaining', a process through which the parties are enabled to 'find common or complementary interests and solve problems confronting both parties' (Walton and McKersie, 1965, p 5). In many productivity bargaining exercises, the 'competition' was frequently set up as the common enemy, and the returns to the stakeholders were seen to be dependent upon the skill with which the negotiators could deploy their resources jointly. The search for productivity improvements was often justified in this way.

Table 16
The evolution of productivity bargaining

		Stages in evolution		
Step	Traditional	Esso Alcan	ICI Elect. Supply	British Oxygen Mobil Oil
1	Plan	Plan	Part plan	Definite problems
2	Imposition in bargain	Surroundings	Discuss	Discuss and agree principles
3	—	Modification of plan	Full plan	Local consultation and agreement
4	—	Imposition in bargain	Imposition in bargain	Formal proposals
5	—	—	—	Agreement to joint solution

But there was not necessarily a suggestion in this approach that it constituted an alternative approach to that which Walton and McKersie refer to as 'distributive bargaining', a term which they use to refer to what most people have in mind when they use the phrase collective bargaining in its usual everyday sense. These authors acknowledge that distributive bargaining is 'central to labour negotiations and is usually regarded as the dominant activity in the union-management relationship' (*ibid*, p 11). Its function is to resolve what they call 'pure conflicts of interest' (*ibid*, p 4) which most commonly centre on the distribution of the product of work activity. For this reason, distributive bargaining usually succeeded any exercises of integrative bargaining.

In much the same way, that integrative bargaining which occurs when the parties agree to seek an appropriate set of proce-

524

dures to guide the various aspects of their relationship, is often followed by distributive bargaining, if only by virtue of the fact that the procedures themselves may be agreed in order to make the distributive bargaining a more orderly and possibly even more 'efficient' affair.

Although all four processes are distinguished separately, and although they appear to be capable of characterization as different conceptions of bargaining, Walton and McKersie stress that they are inter-related and indeed may be discerned in any one single sequence of bargaining behaviour. They are concerned to demonstrate that each is associated with different motives, different objectives and therefore with different strategies, tactics and behaviours, which may place the actors in dilemmas during the bargaining process itself. What for the moment we wish to draw from this characterization is merely that, as distinguishable sub-processes, these four help to extend the conception of collective bargaining to embrace a number of quite distinct tasks or activities which have to be carried out by those who are involved in them.

An attempt to identify the tasks involved in the mainstream types of bargaining must be based upon two main pieces of work in this field, those of Walton and McKersie (1965) and Morley and Stephenson (1977). The one uses a method of retroduction and is based largely upon the American experience and the other that of induction founded largely upon experiment and simulation.

The assumption in all this is that collective bargaining can be regarded as a special (and specially structured) case of 'influence' (Cartwright in March, 1965, ch 1). It may therefore be deduced that certain types of task will be common to all bargaining. These tasks are derivable from general statements about the nature of the process of determining objectives, strategies and tactics, in the light of the situation in which the bargaining will take place, and of establishing adequate arrangements for control via feedback or information-gathering mechanisms. Such statements are thus based upon the generalized notion of decision taking as a process which relies upon open or closed-loop procedures (cf Buckley, 1967).

1 Situation evaluation

The first such task entails an assessment of both the internal and the external environments of the matter to be resolved in bargaining, and a definition of 'the matter' to which attention must be addressed.

One part of this process involves a two-level assessment of the position of the 'other' characterized for this purpose as constituting the external position. The first 'level' is the 'immediate' one. Thus a shop steward may raise a matter for consideration jointly, and in so doing may define or describe the 'matter' in question; similarly, a foreman may initiate a discussion with the shop representative about a 'matter' which concerns him in his role and he too will give it some definition. Each receptor is immediately faced with the need to form a view on the nature of the issue or problem thus raised, and this may or may not mean acceptance of the definition presented by the initiator. This will therefore call for processes of comprehension of the message, and evaluation of its importance, leading to a definition of 'the problem' or 'the issue' and ultimately decision as to action required.

All three of these processes will be affected not merely by the 'matter' itself as a separate item conceived in a vacuum but will also be structured by a much wider comprehension, evaluation and experience of action. This is alluded to by Parsons in his assertion that social action 'does not consist only of *ad hoc* 'responses' to particular situational 'stimuli' but that the actor develops a system of 'expectations' relative to the various objects of the situation' (Parsons, 1951, p 5). It is consistent with Parsons' further amplification of this point to suggest that a party confronted with a particular stimulus will comprehend, evaluate and decide to act not merely in the light of that stimulus but in the light of experience or knowledge of the other party's objectives, values and likely action around the consideration of the issue. Thus this level of response may be differentiated from the 'immediate' level (cf Coddington, 1968, p 1).

Because these two 'levels' of appreciation interact and are likely to be interdependent, the 'definition' of the issue or problem cannot be considered in relation to the first communication alone. It takes the practical form: 'X raised the matter of Y but what is really behind it?' The way in which this question is answered demands the development of an intelligence of the kind that is implicit in the value positions taken up by the sides.

Thus any one stimulus which can be identified may arise in the form of a problem or an issue. This rests on the distinction which Walton and McKersie make and, having made, associate with integrative and distributive bargaining respectively. 'The agenda item appropriate for distributive bargaining is an *issue* ... The fixed sum, variable share pay-off structure is our point of departure for defining an issue. It describes a situation in which there is some fixed value available to the parties, but in which they may influence shares which go to each. As such there is a fundamental and complete conflict of interests' (1965, p 13). The agenda items 'appropriately handled by integrative bargaining are *problems* (p 13).... Problems are agenda items which contain possibilities for greater or lesser amounts of value which can be made available to the two parties' (1965, p 127). The first estimation required therefore is whether the motive of the raiser of the item is to define an issue or a problem.

In addition, it follows from this that what is behind the creation of the stimulus will tend to reflect the dominant value position of the raiser. To raise a matter as an issue is to imply a particular approach to the relationship, to emphasize the conflict of interests seen as inherent in the relationship, and thus to presume that the action and response will be held in a relationship which will link the parties in the upper half of the chart on p 520 above. To raise a matter as a problem similarly presupposes a particular kind of relationship, to be found in the lower part of the diagram, and emphasizes some possibility of cooperation between the parties.

It then also follows that a first consideration to be given to the stimulus is whether to respond in the 'same vein' as that implied in the raising, or whether to engage in a deliberate process of attitudinal structuring, before or during the course of the negotiations, in order to effect a change of expectations and a different relationship pattern as an intended consequence. This was what happened frequently in the 1960s as managements in particular began to respond to the criticism that they were too often merely reacting to trade union demands and on the trade union's own terms (Anthony and Crichton, 1969, p 107). To the extent that, as Walton and McKersie demonstrate, attitudinal structuring calls for different tasks from other forms of bargaining, the answer to this kind of question will call for more or less of the tasks associated by them with attitudinal structuring.

A second part of this process requires a comparable evaluation of the position of the 'self' (and the self's side, where the self can be regarded as having a representative position). This assessment can be thought of as involving two 'levels' of appreciation which are also inter-dependent. At the level of the self, the individual is faced with the necessity to consider what he is 'prepared' (ie willing and able) to do (ie to believe, to accept, to report, to act upon etc) in all the circumstances of the issue. This response may, as Parsons says in the same context as previously quoted, 'be structured only relative to his own-need dispositions and the probabilities of gratification or deprivation contingent on the various alternatives of action which he may undertake' (Parsons, 1951, p 5). It may also respond to the expectations held of the 'other' as we saw above (p 526).

It will also tend to respond to the expectations of the reactions

527

and responses of those others who constitute the self's-side, when the individual finds or feels himself to be in a representative position of some kind (which is normal for any and all who get involved in bargaining processes whether at a formal or informal level). The individual will therefore additionally tend to make his assessment of what he is prepared to do, in the light of his expectations of the consequences for him of his own side's reactions and responses. For him, this relates to the external environment, but to the extent that he is representative, it must be considered as a part of his 'internal environment' of assessment and response. This places the individual in the position of the 'involved' person in Donne's famous and much quoted passage (from his *Devotions* (1724), p 17) but it is possible, as indeed is done by Coddington (1968, p 15) to represent this individual as if he were a non-involved entity treating the external environment as composed of *all* others regardless of the 'side' to which they belong.

The definition by the individual of what Barnard has called the 'occasion for decision' can thus be expected to respond to both of these kinds of perception of the internal situation. It takes the typical form: 'What would I do in this case, *and* what would I be permitted to do (or 'get away with')?'

The objective sought and served by this part of the task is thus two-fold: On the one hand, it serves to define the nature of the 'problem' which the self may be called upon to resolve and, on the other, it serves to indicate the directions in which that self will have to look in order to find solutions to it, acceptable to both the self and those others in the situation whom he must treat as concerned referents. If the tasks were to be carried out systematically and in detail it would result in a schedule defining the 'problem' at different but interrelated levels of abstraction and it would yield a statement of the parameters to or constraints upon the possible lines of resolution.

In so far as the perception of the self and the expectations of others are different, there is scope for the initiation of intra-organizational bargaining. This depends upon taking a particular view of the representative role. It may be seen as that of a 'servant' of the side to which it relates,or it may be seen as that of a 'leader' of the side. In the one case, the assessment of the expectations held by the principals will lead to a conclusion on the expected action of the representative, in the determination of which he has little autonomy. In the other, the assessment may lead to a conclusion that, in all the circumstances, these expectations held by the principals are wrong or incorrect, and need to be changed by an exercise of influence initiated by the representative. This whichever role conception is held there might or might not be scope for engagement in a deliberate exercise of intra-organizational bargaining (cf Coser, 1956 pp 111–19).

Where the conception of the role does permit this, the assessment of the internal environment of the side may point the direction of action in intra-organizational bargaining required, in addition to any other considerations of objectives which may be sparked by it. Whether that bargaining is undertaken before or during the course of the development of a response to the stimulus in interaction with the other side is a matter of judgement and opportunity; but this part of the prior assessment process does throw up indications of the directions of this kind of action as may be required. The question is important for the company side in circumstances where specialist negotiators are engaged in preference to having such negotiations conducted by the top management; it has significance of a particular stamp for the trade union side in circumstances where full-time officials may be brought into negotiations.

2 Objective setting
The second task is directed towards the establishment of objectives in bargaining: given the stimulus and the need to make some response, what ought to be the outcome of that response? In any bargaining situation, this 'outcome' is never likely to be singular; even a simple response like a pay increase is likely to have implications for other features of the relationship. Objectives are therefore likely to be cast in terms of achieving 'this settlement' plus a degree of maintenance of the relationship or a degree of attitudinal structuring. This aspect might therefore be extended to embrace not merely a simple, possibly quantifiable objective responding to the immediate level of definition of the issue, but also a bargaining character objective, in which a deliberate decision is made as to what kind of bargaining exercise will be sought or engaged in in order to resolve the issue as presented. For example, using the Walton and McKersie categories in an over-simple fashion, one might think of the situation in which management decided to respond to a simple wage claim (conceived in distributive bargaining terms by the 'other') with an attempt at integrative bargaining (as indeed was often done in the productivity bargaining era of the late 1960s) (cf Oldfield, 1966).

Much has been written about objectives in bargaining, usually at a relatively high level of abstraction and in respect of distributive bargaining (Dunlop, 1944 and 1966; Ross, 1948; Fisher, 1971; Flanders, 1969). For present purposes, we are interested less in objec-

529

tives in this sense than in the process of objective-setting within the framework of any particular negotiation, and much less has been written about this (see Anthony, 1977). The first question to be dealt with, given some external stimulus, is what kind of bargaining character response is to be made to it. Here it is worthwhile considering the Walton and McKersie distinction between issues and problems as a first step. If it is chosen to treat the matter as an issue, when it is raised, it will follow that the bargaining exercise will be characterized in win-lose terms, and each side will therefore be concerned to keep its own end up and, eventually, win or secure enough to prevent loss of face. If it is chosen to regard any matter raised as a problem, there will be a presumption that the exercise will be one of problem-solving, jointly and that both parties will 'win' only if they can, together, reach a satisfactory resolution of the matter so presented, but will both 'lose' if this outcome proves to be impossible. A decision is thus required on whether the stimulus is to be taken as a cue for issue resolution or problem solving for distributive or integrative bargaining attempts.

In a related fashion, decisions are called for on the dimension of what effect is to be aimed for, either in respect of the relationship pattern between the parties itself (the attitudinal structuring process) or in relation to the solidarity of one's own side (the intra-organizational bargaining process). Whatever the decision about how to treat the stimulus, these considerations of pattern maintenance must enter into the calculations about what to go for and how to go for it. Whether these considerations are treated as 'objectives' or as constraints upon objectives or the means to their attainment, they enter into the process of 'objective setting'.

It is not unusual to suggest, on the subject of distributive bargaining, that both parties do have objectives which have been set in advance. These are commonly regarded as having a target and a resistance point, and possibly a fall-back position. As Walton and McKersie argue, 'negotiations involve a series of decisions interspersed with performance activities' and the negotiator needs something to aim at (a target) which is not a once-and-for-all or 'optimum bid' on which all negotiations would then turn, and a notion of a point below or above which it would prove preferable to lock-out or strike rather than settle. In distributive bargaining these will tend not to be disclosed, until in the judgement of the negotiator their disclosure would help his case, and therefore opening bids will tend to differ from either of these, allowing the negotiator to fall back to another position as his judgement suggests this might be appropriate to the case he is hoping to win. In Walton and McKersie's model, the target and resistance points

530

which indicate complete or minimum success for the two parties, set limits to a range of 'settlements', which may be either positive (where those of the two parties overlap) or negative (where they fall outside each other's range) (Walton and McKersie, 1965, pp 41–45).

In Anthony and Crichton's (1969) discussion of distributive bargaining they include determination of objectives as part of the 'preparation for bargaining (including the determination of negotiating objectives and the assembly of the agenda)' (p 106). But they go on to suggest that, although British industrial relations has been criticized because management allows the unions to take the initiative in establishing objectives, the same complaint is often heard from the union side that 'the unions are entirely controlled by the strategies and initiatives of management' (p 107). They also contend that objective setting is probably carried out by the 'professional negotiators'—those who actually meet each other across the bargaining table—rather than by the 'sides' as entities (p 107). This is seen as happening in a non-conspiratorial fashion but nevertheless as responding to the professional role-self needs of the negotiators. The reluctance of management to specify its objectives ('targets and resistance points') on which these authors comment may then respond to this semi-covert process of fixing them and be aimed to avoid one's own side realizing just what they are as much as to prevent the other side from learning of them too quickly or clearly (*ibid*, p 108).

The serial process of objective setting on distributive bargaining is well authenticated in the literature. Objective setting on other types of bargaining is less well understood. There is some tendency to assume that integrative bargaining for example is simply concerned with problem-solving, and it is enough to say that the solution of the problem is a sufficient statement of the objective. The examples of objectives which might lend themselves to this kind of bargaining quoted by Walton and McKersie and others are job and union security, institutional security, including the control of various types of withdrawal behaviour (whether in the form of wild-cat strikes or absenteeism and labour turnover), payment structures, and health and safety measures (cf Walton and McKersie, 1965, pp 127–37; Gouldner, 1955, pp 157–228). However, in a bargaining context, it has to be remembered that an objective of both parties must be to increase the size of the cake (whether that cake be an economic, a political or a social one, or any other variety). Thus '. . . the parties are exploring a problem in which it is *inherent* that some (low) amount of sacrifice by one will be associated with (considerable) gain on the part of the other . . . and there will be evident tendencies to disagree about problem definition, criteria for settlement, the alternatives to be considered, and the information to be divulged. There may well be differences in motivation to engage in integrative bargaining' (Walton and McKersie, 1965, p 140). Such differences may be what qualifies this as 'bargaining', but the fact of their existence does indicate that different objectives may be recognized in it, and that therefore decisions on objectives are as relevant here as in distributive bargaining.

The objectives in attitudinal structuring are open and articulated but are expressed in general terms. This may be because 'the relationships and the attitudes which define them have implications for the parties and their joint dealings' no matter whether these joint dealings are cast as distributive or integrative (Walton and McKersie, 1965, p 190). Therefore 'a party's preference for a particular relationship pattern may become an important objective of that party. Some ... relationship patterns, such as accommodation, will presumably seem more appropriate as a goal than others, such as conflict, but sometimes a party will prefer a more conflictual pattern, perhaps for purposes of preserving internal cohesion' (*ibid*, p 190).

The objectives in intra-organizational bargaining may for similar reasons be summarized equally briefly: the objective is always to effect solidarity, consensus or the end to role-conflict arising out of different perceptions and/or expectations of the principals and their representatives. The targets are generalized—the bringing of 'the expectations of his constituent group into alignment with his own' either 'before the fact of settlement or afterward, or if perceived achievement is brought into alignment with expectations' (Walton and McKersie, 1965, p 303).

3 Deciding upon strategy

The development of strategies for the attainment of these objectives—the third stage of the process of preparation for collective bargaining—is also likely to produce discrete alternatives according to the objective chosen for attainment and the vehicle determined upon for this purpose. The resolution of a relative-shares issue by means of distributive bargaining will tend to call forth one range of strategies with subsidiaries linked to attitudinal structuring and intra-organizational bargaining; and the solving of a quantity-available problem via integrative bargaining will most likely call for very different strategies, albeit with its own distinct subsidiaries for attitudinal structuring and intra-organizational bargaining. In this area, a number of very different approaches have been developed to characterize the strategies possible, and these draw their philosophies and justifications from very different conceptions of competitive and cooperative interaction.

Thus distinct sets of theories attempt to explain and predict what forces are most influential upon the outcomes of bargaining, and these include the 'purely economic' theories such as that of Dunlop (1944) and the 'augmented economic' theories such as that of Levinson (1966), together with the psychiatric theories such as that of Douglas (1962). Other theories restrict themselves more to explaining what happens in the process, such as those based on game theories (Pen, 1952) or on problem-solving theories (Deutsch, 1973) or on straightforward social psychological theories (Cooper, 1975). Other researches are directed more to the determination of what skills appear to be influential in bargaining, and these tend to be based on simulation exercises (Morley and Stephenson, 1977). Generally speaking, although these may all prove relevant to the process, they do not complement one another since the questions asked by the students themselves are usually very different ones. But importantly each of these distinct sets of theories serves to throw up ideas as to strategies and tactics, which may be adopted in bargaining.

For reasons which are perhaps obvious (eg it relates to 'the basic rationale for conducting labour negotiations' (Walton and McKersie, 1965, p 126)) distributive bargaining has attracted the greatest attention from the point of view of determining strategies (see Anthony, 1977, p 229 *et seq*). Building on the theories of the economists, the institutionalists and the game theory exponents, Atkinson (1975) has distinguished 'four broad categories of strategies which are most likely to be common to the majority of situations discussed' together with two others relating to the agenda and the bargaining situation itself. The basic four he identifies as strategies of

(a) the opening moves
(b) the zero movement position
(c) the sanction
(d) increasing bargaining power (Atkinson, 1975, pp 46–69).

The first of these rests upon the convention that the original demand and offer positions will be abandoned during the course of a negotiation, so that it becomes important initially to establish starting positions which can be departed from with least cost. Once the demand and offer are put into play, however, the basic shape of the negotiation becomes determinable; for example, whether the side making the demand seeks a high or a low settlement or a confrontation of some sort for other reasons. Where important matters of principle may be seen to be at stake, the opening move may be one which allows little subsequent movement, so that the plan may have to allow for the attracting of other demands or offers in order to give some opportunity for movement, and thus for working towards a settlement without compromise to the principle. Alternatively, it may be possible to change the relative bargaining power by delaying the negotiations (or speeding them up) or by bringing in other issues which have importance for the other side, but which give added power to one's own side or detract from that of the other's side. The question of whether sanctions will be threatened or used in the negotiation is also one which can be considered in advance, and particularly once the opening moves have been made known.

All such plans for developing the negotiation will inevitably be affected by two other aspects: first, the strength or weakness of the case itself, in the determination of which relative rather than absolute considerations are likely to prove important; secondly, the situation in which the negotiations occur, the crucial factors in this being the kind of relationship which the other party has come to expect of the first side. In the first of these, what is likely to be significant in influencing the ease or difficulty of the negotiation is the extent to which the other perceives the first side to be acting in conformity with common, normal or good practice—on both the offer or the demand and the manner of making, defending and modifying it. In the second, the history of the relationship as it has developed is likely to prove one indicator of the likely course of action, but a change of personalities (on either side) can upset this and lead to 'sudden' changes in the manner of address between the sides.

It would therefore tend to follow that, in preparing plans for negotiation, each side will have to consider in the circumstances of the matter arising what the relationship is likely to bear in the way of both conflict and agreement (or cooperation), what immediate and longer-term sub-goals are feasible and sensible, according to the strength of the respective cases, and in what sequence the moves will be made in response to the other side.

This strategic planning is likely to be guided by two considerations, however. There is the fact of possible gain or loss in a zero sum game to be considered: the employer might concede too much in the way of a wage increase if he does not plan ahead of the negotiation. There is also the equally important fact that whatever the outcome in these terms, the negotiation might disrupt the existing 'balance of power' between the parties in a way which will disrupt

534

the relations, not only in the industrial relations system but also in the production system. (This kind of disruption is certainly not confined to the outbreak of industrial action, and indeed could arise without any such action occurring.) The likelihood of these *two* factors playing their part in determination of strategies is attested in the analyses of Walton and McKersie (1965) and Anthony (1977, ch 9), both of whom draw attention to the 'power' issue as a separate but equally important consideration in any plan for negotiations.

For this kind of reason, it is not sensible to consider the tactical moves of bargaining simply in terms of 'problem-solving' which can be analysed in terms of some instrument like interaction process analysis (Bales, 1951) and trained for in terms of inter-personal and communications skills. This problem is acknowledged by those who have sought to apply social psychological methods of analysis to the negotiating situation as, for example, by Morley and Stephenson (1977). They developed the instrument of conference process analysis to try to overcome the 'difficulty of recording and analysing the interaction between negotiators' (Gottschalk, 1973, p 52), but make modest claims only for it. It remains a major problem in the construction of training courses for negotiators on either side that our knowledge of what activities are to be woven into the skein of collective negotiation is still rudimentary (CIR, Report Nos 33 and 33A, 1973), although the categories used in conference process analysis are useful here. What can be hypothesized, however, is that the interpersonal or communications activities 'obviously visible' in negotiations only assume tactical (and therefore purposive) significance in association with the exercise of skilful judgement (a factor to which some reference has already been made in chapter 12). There are numerous references in the literature to the need to guess the other's next move, his resistance point or his fall back position, for example. All these allude in some fashion to the need for developed judgement in addition to a knowledge of 'the game' and its rules. The major problem for training in this area is therefore that associated with the development of judgement: a knowledge of strategic and tactical concepts (as in Atkinson, Walton and McKersie, or Gottschalk) may be necessary to the understanding of the negotiation processes, but it is not by itself likely to develop judgement in those who are caught up in them.

Judgement in negotiations

Judgement in negotiations may be treated as focused upon two quite distinct features of the situation: first, upon the dynamics external to the persons involved; and secondly upon the dynamics internal to them. This dual focus may contribute to the peculiarity of the negotiating process and contribute to the difficulties faced by those who seek to analyse it.

The making of judgements about the 'objective facts' of the situation is not a process which distinguishes bargaining from any other kind of decisional activity. The assessment of the 'reality' (as Vickers, 1965, identifies it) is a common enough experience. It demands in this context an understanding of the movements or the trends or the developments in the bargaining field: are differentials between blue-collar and white-collar workers increasing or decreasing, what are the new and fashionable subjects for negotiation, what is the level of settlement being reached or likely to be reached in this industry, what is happening to labour cost as a result? All such questions may be partly answered by information, but they require some assessment of the meaning of the facts for full answer. The assessment of what might be done in a given bargaining situation (the exercise of 'action' judgement) also calls for facts and evaluations: what objectives and strategies might be pursued in this context? The choice of a preferred alternative is then a matter of comparing each such answer against the appropriate scales of value.

The making of judgements about the human dynamics of the bargaining situation itself and of the constituencies behind it is an equally important and necessary part of bargaining. The reality is represented by the aims and strategies adopted or likely to be adopted, both by the representative and by his constituency, and there is no reason to suppose that these two must always be in accord. The questions of what the negotiators are really up to or what the men really want are frequently on the lips of managerial negotiators, because the discovery of answers to these questions about the negotiating reality is important to their approach. Since in the nature of the bargaining 'game' information is a resource to be manipulated, answers are not to be found simply in such data, but are to be inferred (judged) from impressions and understandings. The question of what action is to be taken in this inadequately revealed reality is then the more difficult to answer and the onus is more fully placed upon judgement. Choosing a best or optimum course of action must then become almost exclusively a matter of 'sheer' judgement.

Both processes are then complicated by the distinct probability that the scales of preferences or values adopted by the confronting parties will be very different from one another. This is almost a

536

part of the definition of the collective bargaining process. Consequently, the understanding of the other side's objectives and conduct in the negotiation requires a suspension of one's own values and the assumption of his, whilst the determination of one's own objectives and strategies calls for a firm grasp and application of one's own values and the dismissal of his as being inappropriate or irrelevant. This kind of dilemma for the bargainers (regardless of which side he may be on) is indicated, although not perhaps fully described, in the use of such terms as bluff and double-bluff, threat and counter-threat etc. It is sometimes difficult in all this to appreciate what is true or correct and what is untrue and incorrect, and sorting out the two is one of the major skills which negotiators must develop. To this extent, therefore, negotiation calls for skills over and above 'mere' communications skills, and for an understanding of values and judgement criteria which belong to the production system as well as those of the negotiating or industrial relations system itself.

Further reading
On the constraints upon the negotiating process as these have developed in recent years, see the various Government White Papers on the Social Contract and Incomes Policy; Glyn and Sutcliffe (1972); Balfour (1972).

On the processes of negotiation, see Anthony (1977); Walton and McKersie (1965); Morley and Stephenson (1977); and Atkinson (1975).

On aspects of training for negotiation, see Commission on Industrial Relations Reports Nos 33 and 33A (1972/3); National Economic Development Office (1973); Kettle (in Torrington, 1972); Kniveton and Towers (1978); and Sisson (1977).

21 Future conditional

A number of writers on the subject of personnel management have predicted a future for the occupation which emphasizes growth in numbers and significance, and an end to the trash-can/maid-of-all work image. This is discernible in the assessment by Helier (see McFarland, 1971, pp 30–43) although the main burden of the argument is that such a future depends upon a greater use of theoretical knowledge and the assertion of greater independence of the professional group. It is more clearly spelled out by Fischer (*ibid* pp 21–29) in his four predictive propositions:

The personnel function will assume a more important role in the management of the business.
The personnel function will become more creative, less mechanistic.
The personnel function will be responsible for furthering the organization, not just maintaining it.
Top management will become more directly involved in the deployment and development of human resources.

Although these propositions emerge mainly from American experience, where the history of the function is different, they have been accepted as having comparable relevance to Britain.

This came about because the occupation seemed to take off in the 1950s and 1960s. It freed itself from its case-work and paternalistic-welfare connotations, and became acceptable to enterprises as a part of the specialist management competence in *man*-management (as distinct from technical and product management). This seemed to suggest that what personnel managers were engaged to do was something that society wanted doing. The numbers involved were large enough to produce a strong occupational association, which came to give advice to society and to government on how the function should be developed. The coincidental growth in the output of the social sciences served to provide a more solid theoretical foundation for much of the personnel specialist's activities, and formal training increasingly embraced this kind of knowledge. Apparently assured of an economic future because of the demand for specialists, the occupation seemed to be poised to secure a charter from society as a profession—if only it could overcome the long-standing problem of securing independence (cf Kenny, 1976).

For those who would seek assurance about the future, therefore, there is much that would seem to supply it, although awkward questions do raise their heads from time to time.

The changes effected by public policy and legislation in the 1970s have, at one and the same time, increased the demand for people with this kind of competence, and have so altered the structure of power and authority associated with the role that further adjustments and accommodations appear to be called for. The occupational group itself and the enterprises which sustain it are therefore called upon to review once again the nature and future shape of the role of the personnel specialist.

The predictive statements which have been quoted above rest upon certain limited demographic and technological forecasts: the decline in the proportion of the producers in future society and the emergence of a new relationship between man and machine (usually subsumed in discussions of automation). But there are a number of other forecasts which can be made about work in the developing society, and it is upon these that a prediction of what will happen to the personnel function must rest. These merely provide the constraints upon the choices open to personnel specialists and their employers as to the kind of policies and practices which will be relevant to the emergent structure of work contributions and rewards. It is, however, worth outlining the future which can be reasonably foreseen, in order to provide some kind of foundation for discussion of the future shape of the personnel function.

What forecasts might be made?
What can be predicted as the future role of the personnel specialist depends primarily upon the view one takes of the situation in which it will be discharged. That situation will be composited of perspectives of the future performance and shape of the economy, of the directions of change in cultural value and their consequences for the institutions of British society, and of the attitudes which people develop in all these evolving circumstances. Nevertheless, some forecasts are likely to have a keener and more direct consequence for the personnel specialist role.

It might, for example, be predicted that the British economy must take some note of the changed terms of trade and of the loss of Commonwealth trading relationships, and that this adjustment will be so influenced by changing demographic structure as to make productivity increases more necessary than may have been the case in the past. Such a prediction would then offer a major constraint to decisions about living standards and welfare benefits which the society and its constituent elements (such as firms or public service enterprises) might aim to provide. Nevertheless, changes in this area are likely to affect the future role of the personnel specialist generally rather than specifically.

It might similarly be predicted that the British society will change the conditions under which it seeks to solve the economic problem. After a short post-war honeymoon with a mixed economy and a welfare state, we may be moving into a new situation in which the private or individualistic element of the mixture is further diminished and the social or consensual element correspondingly increased. This might imply a development of corporatism (developing the Galbraith/Winkler theses) or it might suggest little more than an extension of the new cultural imperative that trade unions be more fully integrated into the decision-structure, which will itself increasingly emphasize team-decisions and consultation (following the Bains/Ogden/Brunel University propositions for public service management). Whatever the particular outcome of these trends in modern society, their general consequence will be such as to directly affect the condition in which a personnel role will be carried out.

It might also be argued about this changing future that low profitability, low investment and low confidence on the part of both investors and workers, yield an unsatisfactory situation in which to experiment with changes in institutions of the society: that, in a word, we cannot afford participative management at the present juncture. This argument cannot be ignored or completely discounted, because it is likely to affect human predispositions to accept or reject the existing pattern or the future projection: unless people can see some positive relationship between change and their own well-being (whether they be investors or workers) they may well opt for the *status quo* but, unless the current arrangements are seen to hold sufficient promise of improvement in well-being, people may well opt for change. How attitudes will develop on this dimension is extremely difficult to forecast: recent history seems to suggest a willingness to support the change-agents in many areas of life, and this may provide a foundation for simple extrapolation. On the other hand, it can be suggested that much more dialogue must take place on how much of the idealism can be reduced to realism in terms of popular support for radical programmes, and that therefore simple extrapolation is not a sensible ploy to adopt. Nevertheless, formation of a view or a guess as to the way in which attitudes are likely to move is material to any comment on what the personnel specialist will be called upon to do in the future.

Certain extrapolations can however be made with some confidence. Certain changes are discernible in social and cultural values which have already revealed an influence upon patterns of behaviour in society, and which are likely to continue without reversal even if at different rates:

(a) The output of the educational system will in future place greater emphasis upon the free abilities—to think, to create, to argue—than upon the rather mechanical abilities often spoken of as the three Rs, because of the approaches to the creation of learning opportunities in the educational institutions as much as because of the actual subjects taught: mechanical ability in reading, writing and arithmetic may well continue to fall away, but the capability to exploit the novel and the untried and traditional is likely to be much more in evidence amongst new workers

(b) The authority of the individual (whether in the form of a capitalist or of a manager or indeed of an influential leader of men) is likely to be undermined increasingly, and to produce the predictable consequence that those with responsibility will seek security in association with others in reaching decisions, or in consensus management

(c) The condition of dependency—of workers, or the poor or any other category—is likely to be further relieved both by transfer payments outside the strict employment context and by the donation of rights both outside and inside work, so that individuals will be better able to take an independent line than in the past

(d) The greater emphasis upon a kind of equality or fairness in social relationships is likely to support demands for a more formal and less personalized approach to their development; more concretely, relationships will be progressively subject to a kind of audit, which will emphasize the formally impersonalistic conception of the ideal type bureaucracy, and this will spawn a demand for more recording of inter-personal events occurring during the working period.

Some of these developments have almost direct counterparts in the predictable developments within the work context itself and related to the context in which work is to be carried out in the future. Thus the organizational context provided by the employer (eg (a) below) or by the workers (eg (b) below) at once reflects both cause and effect of change in cultural values; comparably, changes in societal norms of treatment of people ((c) below) or of distribution of rewards ((d) below) respond more directly to changed values in society generally but find their application more particularly in the industrial context:

(a) The scale of enterprise is unlikely to reduce the tendencies towards oligopoly in private industry and commercial operations and towards larger scale public service organization, both supported by central government, being unlikely to reverse.

(b) The extent to which society will rely upon organization of major categories of citizens (as in trade unions) to contribute to policy *and* to monitor its implementation is likely to increase dramatically and particularly for white collar employees, although this change is likely to exact its toll in the form of co-operation and conformity.

(c) The imposition of minimum conditions of treatment of employees by legislation is likely to increase in volume, even if only marginally in the next few years, since no government is now likely to unravel the structure of welfare rights already in existence.

(d) The material incentives available for managers and other supporting white-collar staff are likely to continue to decrease in comparison with those available to blue-collar workers, because the benefit-distribution system will itself continue to change in a direction which emphasizes the diminution of the significance of the wage system as the sole method of distributing title to material possessions amongst workers.

These predictive statements alone (and there are others which might be included) impute certain inevitable influences upon the personnel function.

Those changes which have already occurred in public policy require executive *action* to be taken. This might respond directly to the legislative prescriptions or it might be refined and extended through developed policies which seek to encompass them in a more forward reaching fashion.

Those changes which have occurred, or which will probably occur as a consequence of changing attitudes towards dependency

542

and authority and towards distribution of rewards in society, will require some reformation of methods and techniques of assuring the appropriate levels of contribution. In this case there can be little question of a purely mechanistic reaction to requirements of the culture and a degree of creativity will be necessary to get the measures right.

The changes in the formal organizational or power structure will in turn call for a much more fundamental re-thinking of the nature of the decision process as it relates to man-management in modern large scale enterprises and as it responds to the organization of the members of the enterprise under the benevolent eye of the government. In this case it will be difficult to escape the need for developing new and more radical policies touching on the nature of the enterprise and the licence it enjoys to operate and make use of labour.

Indications of the likely changes in the role of the personnel manager, which may follow from these predictions, may thus be given under three headings which indicate three distinct levels of decision taking within organizations.

First, at the lowest or executive level, the future is likely to lie with the implementation of those policies and prescriptions as to rights and duties which are contained in both legislation and collective agreements. These can be set together, first because what has entered into social policy via legislation in recent years frequently (but not always— see the Health and Safety at Work etc Act) generalizes the best practice which has emerged from joint decision and which has formed the substance of collective agreements and, secondly, because legislation has also recently increased the legal standing of collective agreements as influencers of the individual contract of employment (although they still remain unenforceable in themselves).

Both therefore give rights to the individual employee, and impose duties which the employer must discharge, on pain of judicial sanction or industrial action by organized labour, or possibly both. Just as the shop stewards and other union officers can and do police this system in the interest of members whom they may advise and help, so too can and do the personnel officers advise and help the employer to discharge the duties imposed. This is not a matter which can be fully dealt with by personnel specialists, since anyone acting in the name of the enterprise in such a way as to manage labour must cooperate in the discharge of these duties. For this reason, therefore, the personnel specialist must also police the execution of policies of this sort.

The main point about this kind of activity is that it responds to a given set of policies, and in this sense involves executive action. The personnel specialist will therefore most probably function as

(a) a repository of knowledge as to the rules which must apply
(b) adviser or trainer of line management in the application of these rules
(c) monitor of the actual application of the rules, which must in turn emphasize careful record keeping.

At this level the personnel department of the future will be concerned, *inter alia*, with the constant up-dating of information, with its effective dissemination to other members of the organization and with continuous check on its implementation (see above chapters 4, 5, 10 and 17).

Secondly, at the intermediate or administrative level, the future is likely to call for the development of more sophisticated (or perhaps even just more complex) methods and techniques for ensuring the continued cooperation of the total work force in the realization of the objectives of both the enterprise and its sectional members. It is possible to argue that the objectives of the enterprise ought to embrace both the economic goals of production and the goals of those brought into association with it, but the distinction is worth maintaining if only to signal that in future more attention may have to be given to the latter than has usually been true in the past. The conditions under which commitment to any of these objectives is to be secured are likely to be different in the future, and to that extent new methods and techniques for securing it may well be called for—from the personnel specialist.

Here, the personnel function will increasingly be called upon to create (or help in creating) new methods and techniques of handling three types of problem. First, the securing of abilities required, at all levels and in all functions. (This will focus upon the development of adequate stocks and flows of manpower through such recognizable processes as recruitment, development, and de-selection and discharge, all of which are now more narrowly constrained by cost-bearing limitations upon discretion than was true in the past.)

Secondly, the securing of the understanding or comprehension required to permit people to form adequate perspectives of their working environment. (This will demand attention to channels and methods of communication within the organization. Some new legislative requirements touch on the surface of this problem, but the main problem of effective communication is not tackled by 'idiots' guides' to the accounts or statements of contract particulars, and requires more detailed action of the type being developed in such organizations as BP Plastics, Smiths Industries or Reed Corrugated Cases.)

Thirdly, the development of commitment to the common tasks of the enterprise—usually discussed in terms of motivation in the management literature. (This will probably require the evolution of new conceptions of reward from work which, whilst they can scarcely seek to diminish the significance of material rewards in hard cash, will nevertheless seek to extend the notion of consideration in the formal contract in return for an extension of contribution as required in that contract: this will bring together what currently goes under the headings of pay and fringe benefits, and benefits which are currently thought of under the heading of psychological income from work—including growth and development, training, job enrichment and the rest.)

It is mainly at this level of decision taking that the personnel specialist will be expected to base his contribution upon adequate theories. Theories in this context must be defined in similar terms to those used by Stinchcombe, to mean propositions which so explain a relationship between two variables as to permit the prediction of how the dependent variable will alter if and when a given change is made in the independent variable. These theories are the stock-in-trade of the manager, whether he recognizes this or not. For example, a statement that an increase in effort or contribution will follow from an increase in the pay offered, or a statement that the provision by a company of a sports and social club will increase the likelihood of employees staying in the employment of the firm, are essentially statements of a relationship between two variables which are used to make predictions and as a foundation for decisions.

There is some evidence to suggest that:

(a) personnel specialists require *more* and more sophisticated theories to sustain them in their emergent roles in administrative decision-taking. (These may be identified as theories about individual behaviour in groups or organizations) and

(b) personnel specialists need theories about different variables from those which have traditionally concerned them. (In particular, theories about clients-as-individuals now require extension into theories about the action or behaviour of human aggregates such as organizations, associations or power-groups) (cf Fox, 1971).

In one sense these differently focused theories come together in role theory, in which theories about the person meet those about the individual-in-organization but the separate sets of theory are necessary supports to comprehension of the synthesis. The concern with people and the concern with work organization, which we noted as part of the definition of the personnel function in the Introduction, might be replaced by a concern with roles, but understanding of persons and organizations is a pre-requisite of understanding roles (cf McKinlay, 1975).

Two further points might be made on this aspect of the personnel specialist's requirement in the future. First, the theories most appropriate to the function are so-called 'applied theories' (but cf Goldsmith and MacKay, 1966); the universalistic conception of human behaviour and relationships must be given a situational relevance, for example.

Secondly, the theories themselves are of little value or use to the specialist unless he also has sufficient facility in applying them, both at the individual level (the so-called social skills) and at the aggregate level (the so-called skills in numeracy).

At this level, therefore, the personnel department will be expected to be creative of new methods, approaches and techniques which, whilst they will be applied to the aggregate of the workforce, will nevertheless focus upon the individual member of it. New methods etc will require legitimation as policies,but their efficacy will remain assessable at the level of the individual, and for that reason a knowledge of the individual (and of individual differences) will be a prerequisite.

Thirdly, at the highest or corporate level, the future will tend to emphasize the need for a more fundamental re-thinking of what enterprise is all about. This debate has already begun, most commonly under the twin titles of the social responsibilities of industry and employee participation, but it has not yet either reached a realistic conclusion or even got its basic concepts sorted out (eg what is really the place and nature of profit in a large multi-plant or multinational firm). There are, of course, positions to be defended and attitudes to be preserved, and the attempt to re-think is therefore likely to be long and hard. Nevertheless, a definition of the economic objectives of enterprise relevant to modern circumstances is clearly needed; without it the first and second levels of activity discussed above are likely to remain rudderless. This issue is much bigger than that which concerns the personnel specialist function alone, but it is one whose solution is a prerequisite for satisfactory personnel policy formation.

Important also is whether the responsibility of the personnel manager for the low productivity of British industry may be questioned. On the face of it, productivity is something which is

546

achieved through the line management, not *by* the personnel specialist. The personnel manager may in the past have been seen to split the role of the foreman, into a generalist component left with the foreman and a specialist element which the personnel manager took to himself, but in so doing the latter did not remove the responsibility for getting the production out. Similarly, if the personnel specialist is to play a role at a more senior management level in developing policies, he may choose to see himself as taking the specialist advisory stance and as leaving the general line management with the responsibility for achieving objectives.

Comforting though such conceptions may be, they probably do nothing but decrease the likelihood that the personnel manager will ever play any very effective role at the corporate level. The Fawley productivity agreements, or the Devlin proposals for the modernization of the ports, or the more recent development of planning agreements in the motor car industry, all provide examples of situations in which somebody (whether personnel specialist or not, in the event) had to look again at the objectives of the enterprise, *and* to do so in terms of forecasts of likely productivity under varying conditions, eg doing nothing, investing capital in a particular direction, changing manning ratios etc. The 'hard' objectives of an enterprise may not be the prime concern of the personnel manager as such, but clearly corporate planning decisions depend upon the predictable labour response to varying conditions of change, and the personnel manager could be expected to assist with that kind of question. Since the stakes may be extremely high, and the runners are often ones with which the personnel manager is assumed to be familiar, the justification for his contribution seems established (see for example Killingsworth, 1962).

What more directly concerns the personnel function at this level involves him in personnel policy formation in terms of aggregates rather than individual cases. Such policies are required in two broad areas. First there is the reward-contribution area as a whole, which means in effect treating all types of reward and contribution together at a policy level. For example, a simple concern with pay structure, in which the basic criteria of evaluation are related to competitive or market rates for any given class of labour, is likely to be replaced, first with a concern for compensation programmes which are judged by the performance they elicit and, secondly, with a conception of reward for labour in conjunction with rewards to all other factors and contributors—something which, incidentally becomes more feasible with open disclosure of information to employees. In effect, this implies that the notion of profit as a residual benefit which 'automatically' accrues to shareholders of private industry as its prime beneficiaries, is one which has no useful place in compensation planning in a modern large-scale company where the contributions of capital from institutions are responsive to near-contractual arrangements for the treatment of dividends. It is unlikely that we shall have an adequate foundation for an acceptable policy on rewards for contributions to efficiency, if we continue to believe that big industry's profits go mainly to individual shareholders (cf Diamond Report, 1975) or that more efficiency must mean more profit to the capitalist, to that extent there is hardly likely to be a foundation for a satisfactory and acceptable policy governing rewards for greater contributions to efficiency.

Secondly there is the area which is essentially concerned with the determination and allocation of authority or discretion: this means essentially the development of some kind of concordat between the various interest groups in enterprise—workers, managers, shareholders, customers. Here too there have been major shifts in the situation to which the policies must relate. Some have been brought about through legislation on trade union recognition and bargaining structures and processes, and will be further developed in legislation on participation. Some have been brought about as a consequence of the greater involvement of governments in managing economies characterized by oligopolistic structures in major industries and by highly structured international competition—reflected in planning agreements and incomes policies. Some are brought about by simple—if still highly significant—changes in cultural values relating to work and by the greater capacity of society to articulate problems of power in modern society in the language of the social scientists. In effect, therefore, there have been sufficient significant changes in the circumstances of enterprise decision taking to make it extremely likely that new institutional forms to contain such decision taking will be required.

It can be reasonably foreseen that:

(a) disclosure of information must develop beyond its present superficial requirement, and
(b) new structures (whether in the form of structures to contain an extension of collective bargaining or those implicit in the notion of a participation agreement) will emerge over the next few years to embrace corporate decision taking.

It will not therefore require the exhortations of the Donovan Commission, the Industrial Relations Act or the Code of Industrial Relations Practice to make industrial relations a boardroom responsibility. In the emergent ball-game, the new rules dictate the need for new corporate policies on what might be termed the cost-benefit rules of the enterprise and on the kind of representational structure which will, in Brown's early phrase, sanction managerial authority (Brown, 1951). More to the point, in the present context, both these aspects will be ones on which the personnel specialist will be required to give advice and help, because they are both traditionally in his court—even if, as Fischer argues, he has in the past been more concerned with them as activities and must now become involved with them as policies (Fischer, 1964, quoted in McFarland, 1971).

Nevertheless it remains possible, as this discussion suggests, that the future personnel manager will still be concerned with activities—at the welfare rights, individual case levels in the organization. He will also continue in the role of developer of methods and techniques for various purposes—although, to use Fischer's commentary again, it is to be hoped that this aspect of the role becomes more animated by theory and conceptual understanding and less a response to the fashionable (*ibid*). The major change, although one which is already foreshadowed, will be that which places the personnel function more firmly and requisitely within the corporate planning team as contributor to policies on communication, involvement and commitment, and on structures designed to secure sanction of managerial authority.

The composition of the task

To distinguish the nature of the personnel function of the future in terms of different levels of decision taking does not by itself change the distribution of tasks within that function. A greater involvement in the making of policy on the treatment of personnel may give the personnel function standing within the management but it does nothing necessarily to produce an integrity at the level of the activities carried on under the umbrella title of the personnel department: the trash-can might be as much in evidence as ever it was, at least from the point of view of the diversity of task elements subsumed.

A first set of related tasks is concerned with manning. In this area, the concern is with securing involvement and commitment of people. It is expressed through a sequence of separately identifiable tasks, from recruitment through selection and placement, training and development, performance and personnel appraisal to termination, all of which can be swept together under the general

549

heading of manning—or a concern to ensure that the enterprise has enough people of the right capability both now and in the foreseeable future to ensure that it will survive. The related questions of determining what work is required (a role often shared with the management services departments in large organizations), and of determining the level of reward necessary to ensure that the main manning objectives may be realized, are associated with this task sequence.

A second set of related tasks is concerned with mutual influence. In this area, the concern is to ensure that people know and accept what is expected of them at work. This is usually expressed in terms of induction, training, communications, counselling and the securing of commitment to the ends of the enterprise, where the emphasis is, in other words, upon getting across the organization's message to the workforce. This is never a completely one way flow of intended influence and, even if joint consultation may often be seen in this same framework, there is an increasing recognition of the need for organizations to secure two way communication, and for management to expose itself to possible influence from the other direction. The evolving relationships between enterprise managements and trade unions represent one part of this increasing acceptance of the need for organizations to equip themselves with appropriate receptors and it tends to fall to the lot of the personnel function to carry out this role.

Both of these sets of tasks involve the personnel specialist in intervention in the on-going organizational process. On the one hand, he deals with the organization's need to make continual adjustments to its demography; and on the other, he deals with the enterprise's need to adjust to the conditions of loyalty and commitment presented by its working population. Intervention in the first case takes him into selection, promotion, transfer and deselection activities, and in the second into informing, consulting and negotiating activities. But in addition to carrying out these activities *per se*, he must also therefore, thirdly, involve himself in interventionist activities in their own right; thus he finds himself having to establish interventionist relationships with managers and workers. Not only, for example, does the personnel specialist carry out selection activities but he does so by way of a service to some other manager or department in the enterprise, and the activities necessary to the making of that service available and availed of are separate and distinct from those indulged in in order to select a new employee.

This set of interventionist activities is not complete unless another aspect is recognized. Not only is a service (or advice) offered to the other, but that service (or advice) is founded upon

550

certain standards (whether these be standards related to the quality of labour or standards related to inter-personal conduct or whatever). Interventionist activities are therefore to be seen as including not only those which effect some adjustment to changed circumstances, but also those which contribute to the determination of the standards which will make that adjustment a good or right one. In the past, it has often been the lot of the personnel specialist to accept standards which have been determined by the other in the service relationship (eg line management simply told him what they wanted). At present, there is much more of a partnership discernible in the establishment of standards and criteria of judgement. The link between the two was essentially the welfare officer role. Thus the third set of tasks on which the personnel specialist will find himself engaged will be tasks which are concerned with developing and maintaining standards through intervention in the on-going system, in much the same fashion that, in principle, the welfare officer intervened to maintain an enterprise conscience.

Finally, the fourth set of tasks which might be discerned is that which surrounds the act of objective setting or policy making. The tasks here are essentially those of collecting and collating data necessary to the reaching of decisions, usually on a collective or team basis. This tends to mean that the personnel manager must so organize that part of the intelligence system which is his special concern as to provide his fellow managers with readily assimilable information on personnel matters. Even if the team taking these decisions in future may compulsorily or voluntarily include representatives of the workforce itself, the tasks of providing the information will remain essentially the same.

There is a clear sense in which none of these categories of tasks is new: some of them are central to personnel management no matter where it is practised, and examples of the others are certainly to be found in modern enterprises even if they are not yet universal or central. The main argument being advanced here, however, is that because it is possible to make certain forecasts as to how the situation of the personnel function will continue to change, it is also possible to predict that the work of the personnel specialist will in future tend to focus mainly upon these four broad categories of tasks.

Nevertheless, such predictions will produce no automatic consequence. A personnel manager is no different from anyone else in the particular sense that he will only acquire a role in modern enterprise if he can bring to bear the skills which are necessary to the performance of that role. The identification of task areas is not therefore of itself of great importance, but it is particularly relevant to any attempt to define the kinds of skill which the personnel specialist will be expected to possess.

From what has already been said, for example, it is possible to predict that the future personnel specialist will be expected to possess two broad types of skill, one of which might be identified as the skills of the case worker and the other which might be labelled the skills of the manager. The case worker skills are traditionally associated with three areas:

First, the skills associated with the hiring and firing sequence (recruiting, interviewing, counselling, training and advising), coupled with consequential skills required to establish universal standards of fairness in the hiring to firing sequence, of decisions which the supervisor would be expected to implement.

Secondly, and not really as a separate category of skills, the personnel officer is then liable to be built into the appeals machinery in disciplinary matters and other grievance procedures, within which the individual worker is still to be seen as the focus: the skills called for remain essentially those associated with the manning sequence, interviewing, counselling etc, together with an ability to set and maintain fair standards and secure their successful implementation.

Thirdly, the personnel officer is usually given charge of that major element in the trash-can conception—the amenities (such as sports clubs) the canteens, the pension schemes, the sickness clubs and so on—which provides him with some resources which he can deploy to help in the solution of problems. In so doing, even if the justification is the interest of the enterprise or the employer, he is still operating (using skills) within the framework of the case worker role.

The case worker skills are essentially those which enable the specialist to help individuals to identify problems, explore solutions and make apposite choices in the circumstances. The conception of the welfare worker in industry rested upon just such a characterization of the skills required. However, in social welfare work generally, very real doubts have been expressed about the paternalistic overtones in this kind of role and in personnel work these same doubts must have similar validity. It is, for example, insufficient for the case worker to seek to help a client to solve his problems by his own efforts if the problem is system generated; the question of how far the case worker should go in helping to change the system in order to help the client solve his problems is as real in

552

the industrial context as it is in the developing tension between the traditional social worker and the emerging exponents of community action approaches to social welfare.

This in itself indicates a change in the approach to welfare in industry, but it also says something both about the position of the personnel specialist in the scheme of things, and about the kinds of skill which a welfare role must command. He must have both the position and the skill to act as a change agent within the organization when the solution of personnel problems (at the 'case' level, as in disciplinary or grievance matters) requires the organization as well as the individual affected to change.

It also follows that the case worker will require two other broad types of skill, group work skills and negotiating skills.

The first category comprises skills which are by no means unknown to the personnel specialist at present; he uses them in committees or in training and he is used as a resource person for them by colleagues who need advice on these matters. It has been predicted above that in future much more communication is likely to take place in small group situations—work groups and working groups—and there is a likely demand for advice and assistance on how most effectively to communicate in such situations. Such relatively unstructured communication will tend to shade into consultation and negotiation, and comparable advice and help may well be required to facilitate these processes. In the general training field also, most communication is oriented towards small group structures, and advice will be required here even if the personnel specialist is not actually involved in the execution of the training activity. Such skills as are called in question in this context are those of the social psychologist or group dynamicist—by whatever brand name they may be known.

As a special sub-category of these skills, we might also distinguish the more structured or purposive application of communications and influence techniques. The distinction is between the group processes which might be applicable to the free group (on which much of the social psychological experimental work has been based) and those which are relevant in situations characterized by some variation on the negotiation theme, where what is sought is the intentional influence by one group (through representatives) of another group (through their representatives). In this context, the group ceases to be a free or spontaneous or natural group, and both sets of representatives must inevitably listen to their respective constituency drummers and march to their tunes, regardless of the extent to which as persons they may meet as a cohesive negotiating group. The skills involved in this constrained context may be com-

553

parable to those in the free group situation, but they acquire an added dimension of formality in the preparation and presentation of cases, and in the separation of personal predispositions from representative ones. The knowledge-support for this kind of skill is more likely to be found in role theory as developed by the sociologists.

It might also be suggested that the demands upon the personnel specialist will have both the personnel and situational connotations. The first are commonly considered in connection with leadership theories (and particularly those which focus upon action centred leadership; see Ross and Hendry, 1958) in which the skill of the person is linked to the requirement of action. The second are usually discussed in connection with structure, in which context the social, economic and technological features (ie external to the person involved) are seen to impose their own limits on what the person can do. Consequently, the personnel specialist may be expected to have identifiable social skills (perhaps even as a leader) and also such knowledge and skill as may enable him or her to effect restructuring of the situation in order to diminish the constraints upon action (ie to have knowledge and skills which, currently, are usually conceived of as adhering to interventionist strategies in OD (organizational development).

The fact that realization of standards of fair treatment is one of the ends to which personnel department skills must be devoted has led to a constant (and recently increasing) pressure to build on to the function a role in personnel policy making, which will ultimately become a corporate function. Pressure from that starting point is also supported by the pressures which arise from the other task base of the personnel manager, the structuring of relationships with collectivities, and from the skills which associate with this— the manipulation of power and information in the negotiating situation. The need for policy here, developed through what have come to be referred to as processes of intraorganizational bargaining, is just as real as the need in the other area, and the increased power acquired by or given to the trade unions in recent years adds its own extra degree of urgency to its realization.

This development, which is already well in train in many organizations, imposes a new set of skill requirements upon the personnel function, associated with the collection, interpretation and use of decision taking data which, in this context, are not bounded by the parameters of the purely inter-personal relationship. These are the skills of the corporate planner as distinct from those of the professional who deals with individual client problems. In particular, they call for skills of judgement which must now be exercised in re-

554

lation to data about persons and classes of persons, in circumstances where the opportunity to check that data against the human reality may be extremely limited. Movement of the role to this level within the enterprise increases the pressure on all organizations to develop a functional management organization, and to draw the fundamental distinction between hard and soft technologies (or between the knowledge of method applied to the physical resources and the knowledge of method applied to the human resources). As this kind of movement takes place, the personnel manager will be expected to advise on the structuring of the organization and will thus find the appropriate corporate role for his function.

By virtue of this expectation, therefore, the personnel special ist with the case worker/group dynamics orientation in his or her role, is provided with a linking bridge to that other conception of the personnel function which emphasizes the need for skills associated with management. In this second conception, the personnel manager is more concerned with the workforce as a whole and less with individual cases within it, and the major end of his endeavour is so to develop or manage the system as a whole as to reduce the number of problem cases which might be thrown up by its operation. The skills which permit successful planned intervention in organizational change will be different from those which are demanded for succcessful management of personnel, but both sets of skills are applied at the same level of organizational system.

The managerial skills required of the personnel specialist are those skills which the textbook is prone to associate with decision taking. However, everyone takes decisions about something or other and it cannot therefore be decision taking *per se* which distinguishes the manager. The manner in which the textbook distinguishes management functions provides one clue to the distinction but, rather than using concepts like planning or controlling to define this process, it is probably more useful to see management as concerned with decision taking about wholes or aggregates (whether these are in fact sections, departments, firms or economies or alternatively the production, marketing or development functions). The specialist manager (such as the personnel manager) may well be concerned with the first type of whole (eg the firm as a whole) where a production manager may be concerned with the second (eg the production function). It is *then* possible to argue that managers are essentially involved in decisions about how these wholes should be organized, steered or controlled in order to achieve definable objectives.

Decision taking at this level (as distinct, say, from decisions about cases) calls for the kinds of skills which can be associated with the elements of that process: the defining of situational needs (or of recognizing problems), discovering possible or feasible solutions to the problems identified, and the making of appropriate selections from the range of alternatives given the circumstances in which the problem occurs. Just as the social skills mentioned above involve two differentiated orientations, so too in this case the skills identifiable can be linked to two main attributes of the person, knowledge and judgement, and to two features of the situation, information and normative standards. In other words, in order to participate successfully in this process of policy formation, the person must be knowledgeable about (what above we have called) theory and be able and willing to exercise judgement in relation to the situation, and feasible changes in it; but he must also be able to acquire (or be supplied with) information about the situation and conceptions of what normative standards are to be used in making evaluative judgements (cf Vickers, 1968).

It is this which creates the major form of tension discernible in the personnel manager's role, for it immediately provides for at least two sets of criteria of judgement, one of which emanates from the enterprise/employer objectives and the other of which springs from the goals of workers or the objectives of trade unions. Thereby the man-in-the-middle assumes the hot seat.

Criteria of evaluation
The diverse origins and orientations of the personnel management role have contributed to the confusions which have certainly in the past and may still at present surround the role. Given two potential clients, the employer and the employee, the personnel manager's contribution may be subjected to evaluation against two distinct sets of criteria which stem from their different objectives and goals. An employer who seeks an agent of his interest is likely to be distrustful if he finds himself with a case worker dedicated to serving the employee interest; the employee who seeks a mediator of his interest in his dealings with the employer is equally likely to be suspicious of the manager dedicated to the protection of the employer's interest. Either might then turn elsewhere, the employer to his association and the employee to his trade union.

The personnel specialist's criteria of self-evaluation might well reflect a similar divergence, but there is some reason to suppose that the personnel management profession, as a whole, now adopts criteria for self-evaluation which are derived chiefly from the employer's interest. Although up to the 1950s, it was not uncom-

556

mon to hear personnel officers discussing their work in terms comparable to those used by social case workers (in whose training many of them had at that time shared) in the 1970s personnel managers are more likely to talk like managers.

This is perhaps not so surprising since the criteria associated with managerial roles have been more fully worked out in the industrial context. Work takes place within an economic context, and the criteria of success are efficiency oriented; personnel managers concerned with the workers but paid by the enterprise are therefore not unlikely to measure their success in terms of similar efficiency criteria. Indeed, greater sophistication—and as many would argue probably greater humanity—may be seen to lie in treating people at work in terms comparable to those used for the physical assets. As Giles and Robinson put it in the opening paragraph of *Human Asset Accounting*, which is chiefly concerned with training applications of the concept: ''Will it pay?'—the frequent cry of those concerned with the decision to do or not to do in management—usually means is it profit earning or will the end value be greater than the initial value plus the cost of our decision' (1972, p 9).

As they go on to suggest, it is only man amongst the range of resources available to management that has 'so far completely eluded financial evaluation and expression in terms of asset/liability value' (*ibid*); and they suggest how, in training activities, this omission can be rectified.

Whilst it may be generally true as these authors suggest, that such evaluations as are discussed in the literature of personnel management tend to be expressed in behavioural terms—such as the assessment of length of stay of selected employees, of quiescence of the shop stewards following the introduction of a new set of procedures or the settlement of a wage claim—this approach should not obscure the fact that the length of stay or the quiescence are assumed or believed to correlate closely with cost-savings or asset improvement. The evaluation is therefore still linked to the same efficiency criteria.

Similarly, the function as a whole will tend to be evaluated by the employer in these terms: whether a firm introduces or continues with a personnel department is a question which will be answered in terms of whether it will pay, although the costs of discontinuation may still allow an established function to persist even when the immediate cost-benefit calculation is adverse. In the past, the welfare or training functions were more prone to be switched on or switched off according to the surrounding economic climate of the enterprise; if this is less so now, possibly because of the increase in the volume of specialized administration emanating from legislation, the basis of the assessment is likely to remain firm. The alternative criteria which might be applied to the work of the personnel department are certainly different from these but they are not necessarily diametrically opposed. Certainly they must link more closely and directly to the goals of those at work but whilst they could, theoretically, elevate these in significance to the exclusion of the objectives of enterprise, to do this would be both unrealistic and incapable of realizing the end because of the nature of the false choice involved in this approach. Just as a cost conscious enterprise cannot completely ignore the goals of workers, so a socially conscious enterprise could not completely ignore the economic objectives (cf Dubin, 1958).

These alternative criteria must therefore focus upon the development of an accounting procedure which places more direct emphasis on the social costs. The kind of question which arises is the extent to which, say, additional training costs should be assessed against private (eg enterprise) benefits or against social (eg the increase in the stock of trained manpower overall or the greater development of the individuals trained) benefits. It is this incorporation of social costs and benefits into the calculation which permits an alternative set of criteria to be established. These would then emphasize efficiency in the Barnard definition of the term, but calculated on a broader base than the single enterprise, and would be more supportive of the conception of personnel management as a professional concern.

One of the significant developments in British society over the past 15 years is the development of new conditions attached to what we referred to above as the licence of the enterprise. It is perhaps difficult to say where the beginning of this process lies, but manifestations of the change are at least heralded by the Terms and Conditions of Employment Act 1959 and formally announced with the Contracts of Employment Act 1963, and since then its presence has been increasingly felt. Some of the particular implications of this change have been discussed above: here we want to draw attention to the very real possibility that this imposition of standards from outside the enterprise (in the form of statutory duties) may create the conditions for a more independent role for the personnel manager. In effect, most of these changes effected via legislation make it more expensive for the employer to treat labour in traditional ways, which could be just another way of saying that more of what were previously social costs must now pass through the accountant's books within the enterprise.

Another way of representing these changes is to see them as

redefining consideration within the context of the employment contract. In particular, some of those elements of the contract which were not readily reducible to, or compensated for, in money terms—such as dignity or security—have now been provided for in a set of rights capable of being upheld by the law and of being expressed as a cost to the employer, even if less significantly as a monetary gain to the employee. What is thus swept into the contract in this indirect fashion is the element of psychological income, which the human relations school have hitherto had much to say about but which has until relatively recently been treated as something over and above, or outside, the mainstream of what the contractual relationship was all about. Clearly, this process has not gone far and there is much more to the psychological contract than a few pieces of legislation have yet been able to underpin. But the significance of this change is perhaps that what was previously regarded as a bit of a luxury—the soft management approach—is now hardened through the device of a legally enforceable duty placed upon the employer. Given the historical association of the personnel management function with human relations or the soft management approach, these changes are likely to have their significance for the future development of the role but, more importantly in our present context, they serve to shift the balance of criteria of judgement of success.

Such influence as the personnel management profession has had upon the development of these social standards of interpersonal conduct, or of treatment of individuals and groups within modern organizations, ought to make it an ally of the trade union, on the face of things. Because it has sought to mitigate the harsher consequences of a pure economic rationality it is not possible to characterize the role of personnel management as being completely within the ambit of profit optimization in private enterprise concerns, with no qualification to that statement. There is another strand of concern with treatment or fairness and justice, and this responsibility for the development of the corporate conscience should not be discounted too heavily. Just how much influence personnel officers have had upon shaping the way in which individual enterprises treat people at work would be difficult to assess precisely. But it can be said that in the past quarter century they have clearly brought a knowledge of method and technique in the behavioural science area into the management organization. This has helped shape the responses made to changing social values and motives, often channelled through the shop stewards' movements. If Donovan could cast doubts on the influence of the employer's associations, we can at least attribute some of the responsibility for ensuring that the employer influence was not completely amateur to the development of the personnel management function as one which had both a basis in human concern and a foundation of theory.

The problem which remains, however, is that which surrounds the response of organized labour to a personnel specialist role which is also managerial in its orientation: essentially, the problem is whether there is really anything at all in the suggestion that the personnel specialist is a man-in-the-middle. In his case worker role, there may well be something of this about it; in the managerial role, there may well be nothing. The differentiating factor is the perennial problem of independence in the role, usually spoken of in terms of professional independence.

If, however, there is anything in the prediction above about the continued diminution of respect for authority—whether sapiential or bureaucratic—it may be that the personnel specialist will be denied employee sanction of his authority along with everyone else. He will then have to win his own spurs either on the basis of his wisdom (sapiential foundations of authority) or on the basis of a freshly legitimated position (comparable to the position given to an auditor under legislation). This represents something of the nature of the choice before the profession—if the predictions above hold.

The kind of problem that, in practice, arises in this situation might be illustrated by comparing the personnel specialist not so much with the favourite comparison of yesteryear, the foreman, but rather with the union officer. The shop steward and the full-time official of the union undoubtedly have the sanction of their members in most situations and they are usually expected to carry out roles which, if they were to be expressed in personnel language, could be described as oriented towards securing the welfare of those who are represented. To that extent, the role of the personnel specialist and the union officer have a good deal in common. What skills might be needed by the one might also be predicted to be desirable in the other: the personnel specialist has often developed his on the basis of formal training and the union officer on the basis of native wit allied to experience. But what can or should the relationship between the two be?

What prospects are there for parallel development (with the personnel specialist and the union officer dealing with the same areas on behalf of two separate constituencies) and what prospects of complementary development (with the personnel specialist providing expertise to both sides of the relationship of trade union to employer/enterprise)? Clearly, if the personnel specialist is an active participant in a zero-sum, win-lose game of negotiation, the

560

answer to the first of these questions is likely to be in the negative and the second does not then arise. But if the personnel specialist is able (permitted) to remain aloof from actual involvement in such processes or if zero-sum games are given up, then the first question can be answered in the affirmative and the second can be tackled by using the specialist as a resource person in the group dynamics sense. This is to state an ideal which is infrequently realized or even attempted in practice. But it does raise questions about the professional independence of the personnel specialist and therefore about the professional *role* which a personnel specialist will be enabled to take up in an employment situation.

To make these suggestions (or implicit predictions) it is not inconsistent with the development of the role on a professional foundation. The evidence suggests that the development of a profession must rest upon a recognizable and distinguishable occupational role, and upon the opportunity to structure this role in some independence from others who may yet derive benefit from its exercise. To meet the first, the personnel management role must achieve its separate identity from other roles; to meet the second it must become at least as free and independent as, say, the role of the accountant in organizations. In the second of these, the recent development of constraining legislation assumes significance in providing at least a foundation for this kind of independence, and in allowing authoritative appeal to standards other than those set by the employer in the event of conflict. Whether this means that personnel management will develop a new professional standing, or whether it implies the demise of the profession as it now exists because the opportunity to decide policy is simply taken away from the enterprise itself, is not really the open question that it may seem. Whilst organizations continue to be given freedom to decide for themselves within any framework, they will, perhaps more often than in the past, have to decide their own policies about employees.

Bibliography
and indices

Bibliography

ABELL P. *Organisations as Bargaining and Influence Systems*. Heine-mann, 1975

ADAMS A. Performance Appraisal and Counselling, in Torrington D P and Sutton D F (eds), *Handbook of Management Development*. Gower Press, 1973

ADAMS J S. Towards an Understanding of Inequity, *Journal of Abnormal and Social Psychology*, 1963

ADAMS J S. Inequity in Social Exchange, in Berkowitz L (ed), *Advances in Experimental Social Psychology*, 2. Academic Press, 1965, pp 267–300

ACAS. Industrial Relations Handbook. HMSO, 1980

ACAS. Codes of Industrial Relations Practice. ACAS, various dates

ALBRIGHT L E, GLENNON J R and SMITH W J. *The Use of Psychological Tests in Industry*. Muksgaard, Copenhagen, 1963

ALBROW M C. *Bureaucracy*. Macmillan, 1979

ALDERFER C P. *Existence, Relatedness and Growth: Human Needs in Organizational Settings*. Free Press, 1972

ALDERFER C and McCORD C. 'Personal and Situational Factors in the Recruitment Interview' in *Journal of Applied Psychology*, 54 (4), 1970, p 777

ALDERFER C. "Organisational Development" in *Annual Rev. of Psychology*, 28, 1977, pp 197–223

ALGIE J. Management and Organization in the Social Services, *British Hospital Journal*, 26 June 1970

ALLEN G C. *The Structure of Industry in Britain*. Longman, 1961

ALLEN L A. *The Management Profession*. McGraw-Hill, 1964

ALLEN L A. *Improving Line and Staff Relationships*. National Industrial Conference Board, Studies in Personnel Policy, No 153, 1956

ALLEN V L. *The Sociology of Industrial Relations*. Longmans, 1971

ALLEN V L. *Power in Trade Unions*. Longman, 1958

ALLEN V L. *Militant Trade Unionism*. Merlin Press, 1966

ALLPORT F H. 'Attitudes' in Murchison, 1935, qv pp 798–884

ALLPORT G W, VERNON P E and LINDZEY G. *Study of Values*. Houghton-Mifflin, 3rd edn 1960

ANASTASI A. *Psychological Testing*. Macmillan, 1961

ANASTASI A. *Individual Differences*. Wiley, 1965

ANDERMAN S D. *Unfair Dismissals and the Law*. IPM, 1973

565

ANDERSON N. *Work and Leisure*. Routledge and Kegan Paul, 1961
ANNETT J. "Training in Theory and Practice" in Warr (1978), pp 59–75 qv
ANSTEY E, FLETCHER C & WALKER J. *Staff Appraisal and Development*. Allen & Unwin, 1966
ANSTEY E. *Staff Reporting and Staff Development*. Allen & Unwin, 1961
ANSTEY E and MERCER E O. *Interviewing for Selection of Staff*. Allen and Unwin, 1956
ANTHONY P and CRICHTON A. *Industrial Relations and the Personnel Specialist*. Batsford, 1969
ANTHONY P D. The Coal Industry, in Balfour, Participation in industry (1973), qv pp 56–82
ANTHONY P D. *The Ideology of Work*. Tavistock, 1976
ANTHONY P D. *The Conduct of Industrial Relations*. IPM, 1977
APPLEYARD J. *Workers' Participation in Western Europe*. IPM, Information Report No 10, 1971
ARENSBERG C M and McGREGOR D. Determination of Morale in an Industrial Company, *Applied Anthropology*, 1, 1942, pp 12–34
ARGYLE M., The Concepts of Role and Status, *Sociological Review*, 44 (3) 1953
ARGYLE M. *The Psychology of Interpersonal Behaviour*. Penguin, 1967
ARGYLE M. *The Social Psychology of Work*. Allen Lane & Penguin, 1972
ARGYRIS C. *Executive Leadership*. Harper and Brothers, 1953
ARGYRIS C. Organizational Leadership in Participative Management, in Huneryager S G and Heckman I L. 1967 qv
ARGYRIS C. *Integrating the Individual and the Organization*. Wiley, 1964
ARMSTRONG E. *Industrial Relations: an Introduction*. Harrap, 1969
ARMSTRONG I. *The Crowthers of Bankdam*. Collins, 1940
ARMSTRONG M & MURLIS H. *A Handbook of Salary Administration*. Kogan Page, 1980
ARMSTRONG Sir W. *Personnel Management in the Civil Service*. HMSO, 1971
ARNFIELD R V (ed). *Technological Forecasting*. Edinburgh UP, 1969
ARNISON J. *The Million Pound Strike*. Lawrence and Wishart, 1970
ASCH S E. *Social Psychology*. Prentice Hall, 1952
ASHFORD J. *Statistics for Management*. IPM, 2nd edn, 1980
ASHTON T S. *The Industrial Revolution*, 1760–1830. Oxford University Press, 1948
ATKINSON G G M. *The Effective Negotiator*. Quest, 1975
ATKINSON J W. "Motivational Determinants of Risk-Taking Behaviour" in *Psychological Review*, 64, 1957, pp 359–372
BACHRACH P and BARATZ M S. *Poverty and Power*. Oxford University Press, 1971
BACHRACH P and BARATZ M S. Two Faces of Power, in Castles F G *et al*, 1971, pp 376–88 qv
BAIN G S. *The Growth of White Collar Unionism*. Clarendon Press, 1970

BAIN G S *et al. Social Stratification and the Trade Unions.* Crane-Russack, 1974

BAINS M A. *The New Local Authorities: Management and Structure.* HMSO, 1972

BAKER H and FRANCE K R. *Centralization and Decentralization in Industrial Relations.* Princeton University Press, 1954

BAKKE E W. *People and Organizations.* Harper, 1950

BALDAMUS W. *Efficiency and Effort.* Tavistock, 1961

BALDAMUS W. Type of Work and Motivation. *British Journal of Sociology*, 2, 1952, pp 44–58

BALES R F. *Interaction Process Analysis.* Addison-Wesley Press, Cambridge, Mass, 1951

BALFOUR C. *Participation in Industry.* Croom Helm, 1973a

BALFOUR C. *Unions and the Law.* Saxon House, 1973b

BALFOUR C. *Incomes Policy and the Public Sector.* Routledge and Kegan Paul, 1972

BANKS J A. *Marxist Sociology in Action.* Faber and Faber, 1970

BARBER D. *The Practice of Personnel Management.* IPM, 1979

BARBER J W . *Industrial Training Handbook.* Iliffe Books, 1968

BARNARD C I. *The Functions of the Executive.* Harvard University Press, 1938

BARNARD C I. Functions and Pathologies of Status Systems in Formal Organizations in Whyte W F (ed). *Industry and Society.* McGraw Hill, 1946 pp 207–43

BARNES R. *Motion and Time Study.* Wiley, 1969

BARNES L B. *Organizational Systems and Engineering Groups.* Harvard University Press, 1963

BARRETT B, RHODES E and BEISHON J. *Industrial Relations and the Wider Society.* Collier-MacMillan, 1975

BARRETT P F. *The Human Implications of Mergers and Takeovers.* IPM, 1973

BARTHOLOMEW D J (ed). *Manpower Planning: Selected Readings.* Penguin, 1976

BARTHOLOMEW D J and MORRIS B R (eds). *Aspects of Manpower Planning.* English Universities Press, 1971

BARTHOLOMEW D J and SMITH A R (eds). *Manpower and Management Science.* English Universities Press, 1971

BARTHOLOMEW D J, HOPES R F A and SMITH A R. Manpower Planning in the Face of Uncertainty, *Personnel Review*, 5(3) Summer 1976, pp 5–17; and in Smith (1980) pp 126–53

BASS B M and VAUGHAN J A. *Training in Industry: The Management of Learning.* Tavistock, 1968

BASS B M. *Leadership, Psychology and Organizational Behaviour.* Harper, 1960

BATES J and PARKINSON J R. *Business and Economics.* Kelley, 1961, 2nd edn 1969

BATSTONE E, BORASTON I & FRENKEL S. *Shop Stewards in Action.* Blackwell, 1977

567

BATSTONE E, BORASTON I & FRENKEL S. *The Social Organisation of Strikes*. (Blackwell, 1978)

BATTY J. *Industrial Administration and Management*. Macdonald & Evans, 1979

BEACH D S. *Personnel Management of People at Work*. Macmillan, 1975, 3rd edn

BEAUMONT P & GREGORY M. "The Role of Employers in Collective Bargaining in Britain" in *Industrial Relations Journal*, 11 (5) Nov/Dec, 1980, pp. 46–52

BEISHON J and PETERS G. *Systems Behaviour*. Harper and Row, 1972

BELASCO J A and ARLUTTON J A. Line and Staff Conflicts: Some Empirical Insights, *Academy of Management Journal*, 12 December 1969, pp 469–77

BELL D J. *Planning Corporate Manpower*. Longman, 1974

BELBIN R M. *The Discovery Method in Training*. HMSO, 1969

BELL J D M. *Industrial Unionism: A Critical Analysis*. (McNaughton & Gowenlock, 1949; and in McCarthy (1972) pp 109–40

BENDIX R. *Work and Authority in Industry*. Harper and Row, 1963

BENNIS W G et al. *The Planning of Change*. Holt, Rinehart and Winston, 2nd edn, 1970

BENNIS W G. *Changing Organizations*. McGraw-Hill, 1966

BENNIS W G. *Organization Development*. Addison Wesley, 1969

BERCUSSON B. *Annotations on the Employment Protection (Consolidation) Act, 1978*. Sweet & Maxwell, 1979

BERELSON S. "The Study of public opinion" in White L D (ed). *The State of the Social Sciences*. University of Chicago, 1956

BERGER J, ZELDITCH M and ANDERSON B. *Sociological Theories in Progress*. Houghton Mifflin, 1972

BERLE A A and MEANS G C. *The Modern Corporation and Private Property*. Macmillan, 1932

BEVERSTOCK A G. *Industrial Training Practices*. Classic Publications, 1969

BEYNON H. *Working for Ford*. EP Publishing/Allen Lane, 1973/1975

BINDRA D and STEWARD J. *Motivation*. Penguin, 1971

BLACKABY F. *The Future of Pay Bargaining*. Heinemann, 1980

BLAIR J. Three Studies in Improving Clerical Work. *Personnel Management*, February 1974, pp 34–37

BLAKE R R and MOUTON J S. *The Managerial Grid*. Gulf Publishing Company, 1964

BLAU P M. *Bureaucracy in Modern Society*. Random House, 1956

BLAU P M and SCOTT W R. *Formal Organizations*. Routledge, 1963

BLAUNER R. *Alienation and Freedom*. University of Chicago Press, 1964

BLOOD J W. *The Personnel Job and a Changing World*. AMA, 1964

BLOOM B S et al. *Taxonomy of Educational Objectives: Handbook I; Cognitive Domain*. David MacKay, 1956

BLOOMFIELD M and WILLITTS J H. *Personnel and Employment Problems in Industrial Management*. American Academy of Political

568

and Social Science, 1916

BLUM F H. *Work and Community*. Routledge and Kegan Paul, 1968

BLUM M L and NAYLOR J C. *Industrial Psychology*. Harper and Row, 1968

BOARD OF TRADE. *The Conduct of Company Directors*. HMSO, 1977

BOELLA M J. *Personnel Management in the Hotel and Catering Industry*. Barrie and Jenkins, 1974

BORASTON I, CLEGG H & RIMMER M. *Workplace and Union: A Study of Local Relationships in Fourteen Unions*. Heinemann, 1975, 199 pp

BOSWORTH D and EVANS G. Manpower Forecasting Techniques, *Personnel Review*, 2(4), Autumn 1973, pp 4–16

BOULDING K. General Systems Theory—the Skeleton of a Science. *Management Science*, 2, 1956, pp 197–208

BOWEN P. *Social Control in Industrial Organizations*. Routledge, 1976

BOWEY A. *Handbook of Salary and Wage Systems*. Gower, 1981

BOWEY A and LUPTON T. *Job and Pay Comparisons*. Gower Press, 1973

BOWLEY A. *Salary Structures for Management Careers*. IPM, 1971

BOYDELL T H. *A Guide to Job Analysis*. BACIE, 1970

BOYDELL T H. *Identification of Training Needs*. BACIE, 1971

BOYDELL T H. "What's it all About?" in *Industrial Training International*, 8 (7), July, 1973

BRAITHWAITE R and POLLOCK J. Analysing Response to Recruitment Advertising. *Personnel Management*, December 1974, pp 25–27

BRAMHAM J. *Practical Manpower Planning*. IPM, 1978

BRANNEN P, BATSTONE E V, FATCHETT D and WHITE P. *The Worker Directors*. Hutchinson, 1976

BRECH E F L. *The Principles and Practice of Management*. Longmans, 1975 edn

BREWSTER C & CONNOCK S. *Industrial Relations Training*. Kogan Page, 1980

BREWSTER C J & CONNOCK S L. "IR Training—A Focus on Policy" in *Personnel Management*, August, 1977, pp 28–35

BREWSTER C J, GILL C G & RICHBELL S. "Industrial Relations Policy: A Framework for Analysis" in Thurley & Wood, 1981

BRIDGE J. *Economics and Personnel Management*. IPM, 1981

BRIDGE J and DODDS J C. *Managerial Decision Making*. Croom Helm, 1975

BRITISH INSTITUTE OF MANAGEMENT. *Merit Rating—A Practical Guide*. BIM, 1954

BIM. *The Cost of Labour Turnover*. Management Publications, 1959

BIM. *Absence from Work: Incidence Cost and Control*. Management Publications, 1961

BIM. *Industrial Relations Training for Managers*. BIM, 1971

BROSNAN P. "The Ability to Predict Worker Preferences" in *Human Relations*, 28 (6), 1976, pp 519–41

BROSS I D J. *Design for Decision*. Macmillan, 1953

BROWN J A C. *The Social Psychology of Industry*. Penguin, 1954
BROWN W. *Some Problems of a Factory*. IPM, 1951
BROWN W. *Piecework Abandoned*. Heinemann, 1962
BROWN W. "A Consideration of Custom and Practice" in *British Journal of Industrial Relations*, X, 1972, pp 42–61
BROWN W. *Piecework Bargaining*. Heinemann, 1973
BROWN W. *Exploration in Management*. Heinemann, 1960
BROWNING K W. Management Succession Planning. *Personnel Management*, XLV (365), September 1963, pp 107–110
BRUNEL UNIVERSITY. *Working Papers on the Reorganization of the National Health Service*. Brunel University, 1973
BRYANT D J. Recent Developments in Manpower Research. *Personnel Review*, 1 (3), Summer 1972, pp 14–31
BRYANT D J. A Survey of the Development of Manpower Planning Policies. *British Journal of Industrial Relations*, November 1965
BUCKINGHAM G L, JEFFREY R G and THORNE B A. *Job Enrichment and Organizational Change*. Gower, 1975
BUCKLEY W. *Sociology and Modern Sytems Theory*. Prentice-Hall, 1967
BULLOCK LORD. *Report of the Committee of Inquiry on Industrial Democracy*. (Chairman: Lord Bullock), HMSO, 1977
BURGOYNE J & STUART R (eds). *Management Development Context and Strategies*. Gower, 1978
BURGOYNE J G *et al*. *A Manager's Guide to Self-Development*. McGraw Hill, 1978
BURKE W W. "A Comparison of MD & OD" in *Jnl. of App. Behavioural Science*, 7 (5) 1971, pp 569–79
BURNS T. *Industrial Man*. Penguin, 1969
BURNS T. Management in Action. *Operations Research Quarterly*, 1957
BURNS T. The Sociology of Industry, in Welford A T (ed) *Society*. Routledge and Kegan Paul, 1962
BURNS T and STALKER G M. *Management of Innovation*. Tavistock Publications, 1961
BURNS T R & BUCKLEY W (eds). *Power and Control: Social Structures and their Transformation*. Sage, 1976
BUTTERISS M. *Job Enrichment and Employee Participation—a study*. IPM, 1971
BUTTERISS M. *Techniques and Developments in Management—a selection*. IPM, 1975
CAMPBELL J P, DUNNETTE M D, LAWLER E E and WEICK K E. *Managerial Behaviour, Performance and Effectiveness*. McGraw-Hill, 1970
CANNON J. *Cost Effective Personnel Decisions*. IPM, 1979
CAPLOW T. *Principles of Organization*. Harcourt Brace, 1964
CAPLOW T. *The Sociology of Work*. McGraw-Hill, 1964
CARBY C. *Job Redesign in Practice*. IPM, 1976
CARROLL P. *Time Study for Cost Control*. McGraw-Hill, 1954
CARTWRIGHT D (ed). *Studies in Social Power*. Institute for Social Re-

search, Ann Arbor, Michigan, 1959

CARTWRIGHT D. Influence, Leadership, Control in March J G. *Handbook of Organizations*. Rand McNally, 1965, pp 1–47

CARTWRIGHT D, and ZANDER A. *Group Dynamics*. Row Peterson, 1953

CARVALHO G E. Managing a Dynamic Compensation System. *Management of Personnel Quarterly*, 1965, Quoted in *Personnel Management*, ed McFarland, 1971, qv

CASTLES F G, MURRAY D J and POTTER D C. *Decisions, Organizations and Society*. Penguin, 1971

CATTELL R C. *Personality*. McGraw-Hill, 1950

CEMACH H P. *Work Study in the Office*. McLaren, 1969

CENTRAL TRAINING COUNCIL: *Training of Training Officer: a Pattern for the Future*, HMSO, 1968

CENTRAL TRAINING COUNCIL. *Training for Commerce and the Office*. HMSO, 1966

CHADWICK-JONES J K, *Automation and Behaviour*. Wiley, 1969

CHADWICK-JONES J K, BROWN C A and NICHOLSON N. Absence from Work: Its Meaning, Measurement and Control. *International Review of Applied Psychology*, 22 (2), 1973, pp 137–55

CHAMBERLAIN N W and KUHN J W. *Collective Bargaining*. McGraw-Hill, 1965

CHAMBERLAIN N W & KUHN J W. "Conjunctive and Co-operative Bargaining" in Flanders, 1969 qv pp 317–332

CHAMBERLAIN N W. *The Union Challenge to Management Control*. Harper, 1948

CHARLESWORTH & CAIN (Cain T E (ed)). *Company Law*. Stevens, 11th edn, 1977

CHASE S. *The Proper Study of Mankind: an Inquiry into the Science of Human Relations*. Phoenix House, 1950

CHERNS A. *Using the Social Sciences*. Routledge & Kegan Paul, 1979

CHERRY C. *On Human Communication*. Chapman and Hall, 1957

CHILD J. *The Business Enterprise in Modern Industrial Society*. Collier-Macmillan, 1969

CHILD J. *British Management Thought*. Allen and Unwin, 1969

CHILD J (ed). *Man and Organization*. Allen and Unwin, 1973

CLARKE R O et al. *Workers' Participation in Management*. Heinemann, 1972

CLEGG H A. *A New Approach to Industrial Democracy*. Blackwell, 1960

CLEGG H A. *How to Run an Incomes Policy*. Heinemann, 1971

CLEGG H A. *Industrial Democracy and Nationalization*. Blackwell, 1951

CLEGG H A. *The System of Industrial Relations in Great Britain*. Blackwell, 1977

CLEGG H A. *The Changing System of Industrial Relations in Great Britain*. Blackwell, 1979

CLEGG H A "The Substance of Productivity Agreements" in Flanders, 1969, qv pp 352–65

CLEGG H A. *General Union*. Blackwell, 1954

571

CLEGG S. *Power, Rule and Domination*. Routledge and Kegan Paul, 1975

CLEGG S and DUNKERLEY D. *Critical Issues in Organizations*. Routledge and Kegan Paul, 1977

CLEGG S & DUNKERLEY D. *Organisation, Class and Control*. Routledge & Kegan Paul, 1980

CLIFF T. *The Employers' Offensive*. Pluto Press, 1970

COATES K. *Can the Workers Run Industry?* Sphere Books, 1968

COATES K and TOPHAM A. *Industrial Democracy*. Penguin 1968

COCH L and FRENCH J R P. Overcoming Resistance to Change, *Human Relations*, 1948 (1), pp 512–532 and in Cartwright & Zander, 1953, qv pp. 257–79

COCHRANE A L. *Effectiveness and Efficiency*. Nuffield Provincial Hospitals Trust, 1972

CODDINGTON A. *Theories of the Bargaining Process*. Allen and Unwin, 1968

COKER E & STUTTARD G. *Trade Union Negotiations*. Arrow, 1976

COLE G D H. *Workshop Organisation*. Clarendon Press, 1923; Oxford, 1973

COLLINGRIDGE J M and RITCHIE M. *Personnel Management: Problems of the Smaller Firm*. IPM, 1970

COMMISSION ON INDUSTRIAL RELATIONS. *Second General Report*. HMSO, 1971

CIR. *Industrial Relations Training, Reports*. Nos 33 and 33A. HMSO, 1972, 1973

CIR. *Disclosure of Information*, Report No 31. HMSO, 1972

CIR. *The Role of Management in Industrial Relations*. Report No. 34. HMSO, 1972

COMMONS J R. *Legal Foundations of Capitalism*. Macmillan, 1924

CONFEDERATION OF BRITISH INDUSTRY: *The Provision of Information to Employees: Guidelines for Action*. CBI, 1975

COOKE P J D. How to Learn from Curves. *Management Today*, November 1967, pp 72–5 and 148, 152

COOPER C L. *Theories of Group Processes*. Wiley, 1975

COPEMAN G. "Profit-Sharing in Perspective" in *Personnel Management*, 11 (1), January, 1979, pp. 36–9

COPEMAN G. *Employee Share Ownership and Industrial Stability*. IPM, 1975

COPEMAN G H. *Leaders of British Industry*. Gee and Company, 1955

CORFIELD K G. *Business Responsibilities*. Foundation for Business Responsibilities, 1972

CORLETT E N and MORECOMBE V J. Straightening out Learning Curves. *Personnel Management*, June 1970, pp 14–19

COSER L. *The Functions of Social Conflict*. Routledge and Kegan Paul, 1956

COTTON & ALLIED TEXTILES I T B. *Improving Industrial Relations: A Practical Guide*. CATITB, February, 1975

CRAIG R L and BITTEL L R. *Training and Development Handbook*.

McGraw-Hill, 1967

CRICHTON A. *Personnel Management in Context*. Batsford, 1968

CRICHTON A and COLLINS R G. Personnel Specialists—a Count by Employers. *British Journal of Industrial Relations,* July 1966

CRONBACH L J and GLESER G C. *Psychological Tests and Personnel Decisions*. University of Illinois, 1965

CROZIER M. *The Bureaucratic Phenomenon*. Tavistock, 1964

CUMING M W. *The Theory and Practice of Personnel Management,* Heinemann, 1975

CUMING M W. *Hospital Staff Management*. Heinemann, 1971

CUMMINGS L L and SCHWAB D P. *Performance in Organizations: Determinants and Appraisal*. Scott Foresman, 1973

CUNNISON S. *Wages and Work Allocation*. Tavistock, 1966

CURRIE R M. *The Measurement of Work*. Pitman, 1972

CURRIE R M and FARADAY J E. *Financial Incentives Based on Work Measurement*. BIM, rev edn 1971

CUTHBERT N H and HAWKINS K. *Company Industrial Relations Policies*. Longman, 1973

CUTHBERT N H & WHITAKER A. "IR—A Matter of Policy" in *Personnel Management*, August, 1976, pp 29–32 and 37

CYERT R M and MARCH J G. *A Behavioural Theory of the Firm*. Prentice-Hall, New York, 1963

CYRIAX G. Setting Targets for Senior Management. *Financial Times*, 12 January 1967

DAHL R. The Concept of Power. *Behavioural Sciences*, 2, 1957

DAHL R. *Who Governs? Democracy and Power in an American City*. Yale University Press, 1961

DAHRENDORF R. *Class and Conflict in an Industrial Society*. Routledge and Kegan Paul, 1959

DALE E. *Planning and Developing the Company Organization Structure*. AMA, 1952

DALTON G W. *Organizational Structure and Design*. Irwin, 1970

DALTON M. *Men Who Manage*. Wiley, 1959

DANIEL W W. *Beyond the Wage-Work Bargain*. PEP, 1970

DANIEL W W and McINTOSH N. *Incomes Policy and Collective Bargaining*. PEP, May 1973

DAVIES J L. MbO in LEAs and Educational Institutes. *Educational Administration Bulletin*, 1972 (1) pp 10–16, 2 (1) 1973, pp 38–54

DAVIES K. The Case for Participative Management, in Huneryager S G and Heckman I L, 1967, qv

DAVIS L E and CHERNS A B. *The Quality of Working Life*. Collier-Macmillan, 1975

DAWKINS R. *The Selfish Gene*. Oxford University Press, 1976

DENNIS N, HENRIQUES F and SLAUGHTER C. *Coal is our Life*. Eyre and Spottiswoode, 1956

DEPARTMENT OF EDUCATION AND SCIENCE. *Shop Steward Education and Training*. DES, 1972

DEPT OF EMPLOYMENT. *Code of Industrial Relations Practice*. DE,

1972 (a)

DEPT OF EMPLOYMENT. *Company Manpower Planning*. HMSO, 1968

DEPT OF EMPLOYMENT. *Training for the Future*. DE, 1972 (b)

DEPT OF EMPLOYMENT. *Training for the Management of Human Resources* (the Hayes Report). HMSO, 1972 (c)

DEPT OF HEALTH AND SOCIAL SECURITY: *Management Arrangements for the Reorganized NHS*. HMSO, 1972

DERBER M. "Changing Union Management Relations" in *Am. Jnl. of IR*. March, 1977

DESSLER G. *Organization and Management: A Contingency Approach*. Prentice Hall, 1976

DEUTSCH M. *The Resolution of Conflict*. Yale University Press, 1973

DEVERELL C S. *Personnel Management: Human Relations in Industry*. Gee, 1968

DOERINGER P & PIORE M. *Internal Labour Markets and Manpower Analysis*. Lexington, 1971

DOLLARD J, DOOB W, MILLER N E, MOWER O H and SHEARS R R. *Frustration and Aggression*. Yale University Press, 1939

DONALD B. *Manpower for Hospitals*. Institute of Hospital Administrators, 1966

DONALDSON L & SCANNEL E E. *Human Resources Development: The New Trainer's Guide*. Addison-Wesley, 1978

DONOVAN LORD. Royal Commission on Trade Unions and Employers' Associations Report. HMSO, 1968

DOOHER M J and MARQUIS V. *Rating Employee and Supervisory Performance: a Manual of Merit Rating Techniques*. AMA, 1950

DOUGLAS A. *Industrial Peacemaking*. Columbia University Press, 1962

DOULTON J and HAY D. *Managerial and Professional Staff Grading*. Allen and Unwin, 1962

DRUCKER P F. *The Practice of Management*. Mercury Books, 1961

DRUCKER P F. *Managing for Results*. Heinemann, 1964

DUBIN R. Industrial Workers' Worlds. *Social Problems, III*. January 1956, pp 131–42

DUBIN R. *The World of Work*. Prentice-Hall, 1958

DUBIN R. *Human Relations in Administration*. Prentice-Hall. 1974

DUNCAN C P. "Recent Research on Human Problem-Solving" in *Psychological Bulletin*, 1959, 46, pp. 397–429

DUNKERLEY D. *The Study of Organisations*. Routledge & Kegan Paul, 1972

DUNKERLEY D. *Occupations and Society*. Routledge and Kegan Paul, 1975

DUNKERLEY D. *The Foreman*. Routledge and Kegan Paul, 1975

DUNLOP J T. *Wage Determination under Trade Unions*. Kelley, 1944; revised edn 1950

DUNLOP J T. *Industrial Relations Systems*. Holt, 1958

DUNNETTE M D and BASS B M. Behavioural Scientists and Personnel Management, in *Industrial Relations*, 2(3), 1963, pp 115–30

DUNNETTE M D. *Personnel Selection and Placement*. Tavistock, 1966

DURKHEIM E. *Division of Labour in Society*. Free Press, 1947

DYER W G. *Team Building: Issues and Alternatives* Addison-Wesley, 1977

DYER B. *Personnel Systems and Records*. Gower, 1980. 3rd edn

EDWARDS C & HARPER D G. "Bargaining at the Trade Union and Management Interface" in Abell, 1975, qv pp. 41–71

EDWARDS C. "A Study of Local Union Power in the Coal Industry" in *British Journal of I R*, XVI (1) March, 1978, pp. 1–15

EDWARDS R and PAUL S. *Job Evaluation*. Association of Professional, Executive, Clerical and Computer Staff, 1977

EGOOD C. "Experiential Learning" in *Industrial and Commercial Training*, December, 1976, pp. 478–81

ELBOURNE E T. *Fundmentals of Industrial Administration*. Macdonald and Evans, 1934

ELDRIDGE J E T. *Industrial Disputes*. Routledge and Kegan Paul, 1968

ELDRIDGE J E T. *Sociology and Industrial Life*. Nelson, 1971

ELLIOTT D. *The Lucas Aerospace Workers' Campaign*. Fabian Society, 1977

ELLIOTT J. *Conflict or Cooperation*. Kogan Page, 1978

ELLIS G D, THOMPSON F F, PRATT S K and BARRACLOUGH T. Learning and the Human Resource Revolution. *Personnel*, September 1968

EMERY F E. *Systems Thinking*. Penguin, 1969

EMERY F E. *Characteristics of Socio-technical Systems*. Tavistock, 1959

EMERY F E and THORSRUD E. *Form and Content in Industrial Democracy*. Tavistock, 1969

EMERY F E and TRIST E L. Socio-Technical Systems, in *Management Sciences Models and Techniques*. Pergamon Press, 1960

ENGINEERING EMPLOYERS' FEDERATION. *Business Performance and Industrial Relations*. EEF, 1972, reprinted 1976

ENGINEERING INDUSTRY TRAINING BOARD. *Training for Engineering Craftsmen: the Module System*. EITB, 1968

ETZIONI A. *Readings on Modern Organizations*. Prentice-Hall, 1969

ETZIONI A. *A Comparative Analysis of Complex Organizations*. Free Press, 1961

EVANS G J and LINDLEY R M. *The Use of RAS and Related Models in Manpower Forecasting*. Research Paper No 22, Centre for Industrial Economic and Business Research, University of Warwick, 1972

EVELY R and LITTLE I M D. *Concentration in British Industry*. Cambridge University Press, 1960

FAGEN R E and HALL A D. Definition of Systems. *General Systems*, 1, 1956, pp 18–28

FALK R and CLARK I. Planning for Growth. *Management Today*, June 1966, pp 85–8 and 151

FARNHAM D & PIMLOTT J. *Understanding Industrial Relations*. Cassell, 1979

FAYOL H. *General and Industrial Administration*. Durod, Paris, 1915

575

FERRIS P. *The New Militants: Crisis in the Trade Unions*. Penguin, 1972, 112 pp

FESTINGER L. *A Theory of Cognitive Dissonance*. Row Peterson, 1957

FIELDS A. *Method Study*. Cassells, 1969

FINNIGAN J. *Industrial Training Management*. Business Books, 1970

FISCH G G. Line-Staff is Obsolete, in *Harvard Business Review*. 39 (5), September–October 1961

FISCHER F E. Personnel Function in Tomorrow's Company. *Personnel*, 45, 1968, pp 64–71, and in McFarland D E. 1971 qv

FISHER M R. *The Economic Analysis of Labour*. Weidenfeld and Nicolson, 1971

FLANAGAN J C. Critical Requirements: a new Approach to Employee Evaluation, *Personnel Psychology*, 2, 1949

FLANAGAN R J and WEBER A R. *Bargaining Without Boundaries*. University of Chicago Press, 1974

FLANDERS A. *Trade Unions*. Hutchinson, 1952

FLANDERS A. *Industrial Relations: What is Wrong with the System?* IPM, 1965

FLANDERS A. *Management and Unions: Theory and Reform of Industrial Relations*. Faber and Faber, 1970

FLANDERS A. *Collective Bargaining*. Penguin, 1969

FLANDERS A. *Collective Bargaining: Prescription for Change*. Faber and Faber, 1967

FLANDERS A. *The Fawley Productivity Agreements*. Faber and Faber, 1968

FLANDERS A. POMERANZ R and WOODWARD J. *Experiment in Industrial Democracy: a Study of the John Lewis Partnership*. Faber and Faber, 1964

FLEISHMAN E A. *Studies in Personnel and Industrial Psychology*. Dorsey, 1961

FLORENCE P S. *The Logic of British and American Industry*. Routledge and Kegan Paul, 2nd edn, 1961

FLORENCE P S. *Economics and Sociology of Industry*. Watts, 1964

FOGARTY M P. *Personality and Group Relations in Industry*. Longmans, 1956

FOGARTY M P. *The Just Wage*. Chapman, 1961

FOGARTY M P. *The Rule of Work*. Chapman, 1961

FOGARTY M P. *Company and Corporation—One Law?* Chapman, 1965

FOGARTY M P. *Women in Top Jobs*. PEP, 1970

FOGARTY M P. *Sex, Career and Family*, Sage, 1971

FOOD, DRINK & TOBACCO ITB. *IR Training: Methods Guide*. FDT ITB, 1976

FORBES A F, MORGAN R W and ROWNTREE J A, Manpower Planning Models in Use in the Civil Service Department. *Personnel Review*, 4 (3) Summer 1975, pp 23–35; and in Smith, (1980) pp. 89–111

FOULKES D. *Law for Managers*. Butterworths, 1971

FOWLER A. *Personnel Management in Local Government*. IPM, 1980

FOX A. *The Milton Plan*. IPM, 1965

FOX A. "Management's Frame of Reference" in Flanders (1969) pp. 390–409

FOX A. *Man Mismanagement*. Hutchinson, 1974

FOX A. *Industrial Sociology and Industrial Relations*. Research Paper No 3: RCTUEA. HMSO, 1966

FOX A. Collective Bargaining, Flanders and the Webbs. *British Journal of Industrial Relations*, 13 July 1975

FOX A. Industrial Relations: A Critique of Pluralist Ideology, in Child J. 1973, qv

FOX A. *A Sociology of Work in Industry*. Collier-Macmillan, 1971

FOX A and FLANDERS A. The Reform of Collective Bargaining: From Donovan to Durkheim. *British Journal of Industrial Relations*, 7 July 1969, pp. 151–80

FOX A. *Beyond Contract*. Faber and Faber, 1974

FOY N. *The Missing Links: British Management Education in the 1980's*. Oxford Centre for Management Studies/Foundation for Management Education, 1978

FOY N. "Management Education—Current Action and Future Needs" in *Journal of European Industrial Training*, 3 (2), 1979

FRASER J M. *Introduction to Personnel Management*. Nelson, 1971

FRASER J M. *Employment Interviewing*. Macdonald and Evans, 1966, 4th edn

FREEDMAN J L, CARLSMITH J L & SEARS D O. *Social Psychology*. Prentice Hall, 1970

FRENCH J R P and RAVEN B H. The Bases of Social Power, in Cartwright D (ed) 1959 qv

FRENCH W. *The Personnel Management Process*. Houghton-Mifflin 1974

FRENCH W & BELL C H. *Organisational Development*. Prentice Hall, 1973, 2nd edn, 1978

FRIEDMAN M. "The Social Responsibility of the Business Enterprise is to Increase its Profits" in *Issues in Business and Society,* 1977

FULTON LORD. *The Civil Service*. Vol 1, Report of the Committee. HMSO, 1968, Cmnd 3638

GAGNE R M. *The Conditions of Learning*. Holt, Rinehart and Winston, 1970

GALBRAITH J K. *The New Industrial State*. Hamish Hamilton, 1974, 2nd edn (b)

GALLIE D. *In Search of the New Working Class*. Cambridge University Press, 1978.

GARDINER G. *The Operating Executive and the Personnel Department*. AMA Personnel Series, No 121, 1948

GARDNER W and TAYLOR P. *Health at Work*. Associated Business Programmes, 1975

GARNETT J. *The Work Challenge*. Industrial Society, 1973

GENNARD J. *Financing Strikers*. Macmillan, 1977

GENTLES E M. *Training the Operator—a Practical Guide*. IPM, 1969

GEORGE C S. *The History of Management Thought*. Prentice Hall, 1972

GIBSON J L, IVANCEVICH J M and DONNELLY J H.

Organizations—Behaviour, Structure, Processes. Irwin-Dorsey, 1976, 2nd edn

GILES W J and ROBINSON D F. *Human Asset Accounting.* IPM, 1972

GILL C G & CONCANNON H. "Developing an Explanatory Framework for IR Policy within a Firm" in *Industrial Relations Journal*, Winter, 1976/7, pp. 13–20

GILL D, UNGERSON B and THAKUR M. *Performance Appraisal in Perspective: a Survey of Current Practice.* IPM, 1973

GILL J and MOLANDER C F. Beyond Management by Objectives. *Personnel Management*, August 1970

GILL R W T & TAYLOR D S. "Training Managers to Handle Discipline and Grievance Interviews" in *Journal of Education and Training*, May, 1976

GILMAN G. An Inquiry into the Nature and Use of Authority, in Haire M (ed), *Organization Theory in Industrial Practice.* Wiley, 1962

GLYNN A and SUTCLIFFE B. *British Capitalism, Workers and the Profits Squeeze.* Penguin, 1972

GOLDSMITH M and MACKAY A, *The Science of Science.* Penguin, 1964

GOLDTHORPE J H, LOCKWOOD D, BECHHOFER F and PLATT J. *The Affluent Worker: Industrial Attitudes and Behaviour.* Cambridge University Press, 1968

GOLDTHORPE J H. Industrial Relations in Great Britain: A Critique of Reformism. *Politics and Society*, 1974, pp 419–52

GOODMAN J F B and WHITTINGHAM T G. *Shop Stewards in British Industry.* McGraw-Hill, 1969

GOODMAN J F B, ARMSTRONG E G A, DAVIS J and WAGNER A. *Rule Making and Industrial Peace.* Croom Helm, 1977

GOODRICH C L. *The Frontier of Control 1920,* Penguin, 1975

GORE W J (ed). *Administrative Decision-making: A Reader.* Free Press, Glencoe, 1962

GOTTSCHALK A W. A Behavioural Analysis of Bargaining, in Warner M (ed). *The Sociology of the Workplace.* Allen and Unwin, 1973, pp 36–81

GOULDNER A W. *Patterns of Industrial Bureaucracy.* Routledge and Kegan Paul, 1955

GOULDNER A W. Organizational Analysis, in Merton R K, Broom L and Cottrell L S. *Sociology Today.* Basic Books, 1959, pp 400–28

GOWER L C B. *Principles of Modern Company Law.* Stevens, 4th edn, 1979

GOWLER D. Determinants of the Supply of Labour to the Firm. *Journal of Management Studies,* 6 (1), February 1969

GOWLER D. Values, Contracts and Job Satisfaction. *Personnel Review*, 3 (4), Autumn 1974, pp 4–14

GOWLER D and LEGGE K. *Managerial Stress.* Gower, 1975

GOYDER G. *The Responsible Worker.* Hutchinson, 1975

GRANT J V and SMITH A. *Personnel Administration and Industrial Relations.* Longman, 1969

GREENHALGH R M. *Industrial Tribunals—a Practical Guide.* IPM, 1973

GREGSON D & RUFFLE K. "Rationalising Rewards at Rogerstone" in *Personnel Management*, 12 (10), October, 1980, pp. 62–4

GRINOLD R C and MARSHALL K T. *Manpower Planning Models.* North Holland, 1977

GROSS N, MASON W S and McEACHERN A W. *Explorations in Role Analysis.* Chapman and Hall, 1958

GUEST D and FATCHETT D. *Worker Participation: Individual Control and Performance.* IPM, 1974

GUEST R H. *Organization Change—the Effect of Successful Leadership.* Tavistock Publications, 1962

GUION R M. *Personal Testing.* McGraw-Hill, New York, 1965

HABERSTROH C J. Organization and Design of Systems Analysis, in March J G,1965, qv

HACKMAN R C. *The Motivated Working Adult.* AMA, 1969

HACKMAN J R, LAWLER E E & PORTER L W. *Perspectives on Behaviour in Organisations,* McGraw Hill, 1977

HADDEN T. *Company Law and Capitalism.* Weidenfeld & Nicolson, 1972

HAGUE H. *Executive Self-Development.* Macmillan, 1974

HAGUE H. *Management Training for Real.* IPM, 1973

HAHLO H R and TREBILCOCK M J. *Casebook on Company Law.* Sweet and Maxwell, 1977, 2nd edn

HAINE M. *Organization Theory in Industrial Practice.* Wiley, 1962

HAIRE M, GHISELLI E E and PORTER L W. *Managerial Thinking.* Wiley, 1966

HALEY Sir W. The Look of Management, *The Manager,* November 1964

HALL D T and NOUGAIN K E. An Examination of Maslow's Need Hierarchy in an Organizational Setting. *Organization Behaviour and Human Performance,* (3), 1968, pp 12–35

HAMBLIN A C. *Evaluation and Control of Training.* McGraw-Hill, 1974

HANIKA F de P. *New Thinking in Management.* Hutchinson, 1965

HARRIS M (ed), *The Realities of Productivity Bargaining.* IPM, 1968

HARRISON R. "Self-Directed Learning" in *Management Education and Development,* April, 1975, pp. 19–36

HARTMANN H. Managerial Employees—New Participants in Industrial Relations, *British Journal of Industrial Relations,* XII (2), July 1974, pp 268–81

HARVEY B and MURRAY R. *Industrial Health Technology.* Butterworth, 1968

HAWKINS K. Company Bargaining Problems and Prospects. *BJIR*, July 1971

HAWKINS K. *The Management of Industrial Relations.* Pelican, 1978

HAWKINS K. *Industrial Relations Practice.* Kogan Page, 1979

HAYWOOD S C. *Managing the Health Service.* Allen and Unwin, 1974

HEALD G (ed). *Approaches in the Study of Organizational Behaviour.* Tavistock Publications, 1970

HEINRICH H W. *Industrial Accident Prevention: A Scientific Approach.* McGraw-Hill, 1959, 4th edn

HEISLER H (ed). Foundations of Social Administration, Macmillan, 1977

HEKEMAIN J S and JONES C H. Put People on Your Balance Sheet. *Harvard Business Review*, 1967

HELLER F. An Evaluation of the Personnel Management Function, in McFarland D E (ed), 1971, qv

HENEMAN H G and SCHWAB D P. An evaluation of research on expectancy theory predictions of employee performance. *Psychological Bulletin*, 1972

HEPPLE B A and O'HIGGINS P. *Employment Law.* Sweet and Maxwell, 1979, 3rd edn

HERZBERG F. *Work and the Nature of Man.* Staples, 1968

HESSELING P. *Strategy of Evaluation Research in the Field of Supervisory and Managerial Training.* Assen, Holland, 1966, Van Gorcum

HICKS J R. *The Theory of Wages.* Macmillan, 1932

HICKSON D J *et al.* A Strategic Contingencies Theory of Intra-Organizational Power. *Administrative Science Quarterly*, 16, 1971

HIGGIN G. *The Architect as Professional.* RIBA Journal, 1964

HILL J M M. A Consideration of Labour Turnover as a Resultant of a Quasi-Stationary Process. *Human Relations*, 4 (3), August 1951, pp 255–64

HINTON B L. An Empirical Investigation of the Herzberg Methodology and Two-Factor Theory. *Organization Behaviour and Human Performance* (3), 1968

HOBSBAWM E J. *Labouring Men* Weidenfeld & Nicolson, 1964

HOGGART R. *The Uses of Literacy.* Penguin, 1958

HOLDING D H. *Principles of Training.* Pergamon, 1965

HOLLOWELL P. *The Lorry Driver.* Routledge and Kegan Paul, 1968

HOMANS G C. *The Human Group.* Routledge and Kegan Paul, 1951

HONEY P. "On the Trail of the Personnel Professional" in *Personnel Management*, April, 1976, pp. 33–5

HONEY P. *Face to Face.* IPM, 1976

HOPKINS R R. *A Handbook of Industrial Welfare.* Pitman, 1955

HOPKINS T K. *The Exercise of Influence in Small Groups.* Bedminster Press, 1964

HOVLAND C I & JANIS I L (eds). *Personality and Persuadability.* Yale University Press, 1959

HOVLAND C I & WEISS W. "The Influence of Cause Credibility on Communication Effectiveness" in *Public Opinion Quarterly*, 15, 1952, pp. 635–50

HOVLAND C I & MANDELL W. "An Experimental Comparison of Conclusion Drawing by the Communicator and the Audience" in *Journal of Abnormal and Social Psychology*, 47, 1952, pp. 581–3

HOWELLS G W. A Scientific Approach to Job Specification. *Scientific Business*, August, 1964

HOWELLS R and BARRETT B. *The Manager's Guide to the Health and*

Safety at Work Act. IPM, 1976

HUGHES C L. *Goal Setting: Key to Individual and Organizational Effectiveness*. AMA, 1965

HUGHES E C. *Men and Their Work*. Free Press, 1958

HUGHES J. *Trade Union Structure and Government*. Royal Commission on Trade Unions and Employers Associations Research Paper No. 5. HMSO, 1966

HUGHES J and POLLINS J H. *Trade Unions in Great Britain*. David and Charles, 1973

HUGHES M G. *Secondary School Administration: A Management Approach*. Pergamon, 1970

HULL C L. *Principles of Behaviour*. Appleton-Century-Crofts, 1943

HULL C L. *A Behaviour System*. Yale University Press, 1943

HUMBLE J W. *Improving Management Performance*. BIM, 1965

HUMBLE J W. *Management by Objectives*. Industrial Educational and Research Foundation, 1967

HUMBLE J W. *Management by Objectives in Action*. McGraw-Hill, 1970

HUMBLE J W. *The Experienced Manager*. McGraw-Hill, 1973

HUNERYAGER S G and HECKMAN I L (eds). *Human Relations in Management*. Edward Arnold, 1967

HUNTER L C. *Labour Problems of Technological Change*. Allen and Unwin, 1970

HUNTER T D. Hierarchy or Arena? The Administrative Implications of a Socio-Therapeutic Regime, in Farndale and Freeman, *New Aspects of the Mental Health Services*. Pergamon, 1967

HUSBAND R M. Payment Structures Made to Measure. *Personnel Management*, April 1975, pp 27–9 and 39

HUSBAND T M. *Work Analysis and Pay Structure*. McGraw-Hill, 1975

HUSSEY D E. *Corporate Planning*. Pergamon, 1974

HYMAN H H. The Value Systems of Different Classes: A Social-Psychological Contribution to the Analysis of Stratification, in Bendix R and Lipset S M (eds). *Class Status and Power*. Free Press, 1953

HYMAN R. *Disputes Procedure in Action*. Heinemann, 1972

HYMAN R. *Strikes*. Fontana, 1972

HYMAN R. *Industrial Relations: A Marxist Introduction*. Macmillan, 1976

HYMAN R and FRYER B. Trade Unions in McKinlay 1975 qv, pp. 150–213

HYMAN R and BROUGH I. *Social Values and Industrial Relations*. Blackwell, 1975

INBUCON. *Survey of Executive Salaries and Fringe Benefits*. U.K. INBUCON Management Consultants, London, 1980

INDUSTRIAL SOCIETY. *Guide to the Health and Safety at Work Act*. Industrial Society, 1974

INDUSTRIAL RELATIONS TRAINING RESOURCE CENTRE. *Management Training in Industrial Relations*. IRTRC, April, 1978

INDUSTRIAL SOCIETY. *Practical Policies for Participation*. Industrial Society, 1974

INGHAM G K. *Strikes and Industrial Conflict.* Macmillan, 1974
IPM. Statement on Personnel Management and Personnel Policies. *Personnel Management*, March 1963, pp 11–15
IPM. *Personnel Management: a Bibliography.* IPM, 1975 (in six parts)
INTERNATIONAL LABOUR ORGANIZATION. *Job Evaluation.* ILO, 1960
IRON AND STEEL ITB. *Identification of Training Needs.* ISITB, 1975
IRVINE A. *Improving Industrial Communication.* Industrial Society/ Gower, 1970
JAAP T and WATSON J A. A Conceptual Approach to Training. *Personnel Management*, September 1970, pp 30–33
JACKSON D, TURNER H A and WILKINSON F. *Do Trade Unions Cause Inflation?* Cambridge University Press, 1972
JACKSON J M. The Normative Regulation of Authoritative Behaviour, in *The University of Kansas. Comparative Studies of Mental Hospital Organization*, Kansas, 1962
JACKSON J. "The Organisation and Its Communications Problems", in Karn & Gilmer, 1962, qv, pp 407–415
JAFFE A J and FROOMKIN J. *Technology and Jobs.* Praeger, 1968
JAFFE A J and STEWARD C D. *Manpower Resources and Utilization.* Chapman Hall, 1951
JAHODA M. *Current Concepts of Positive Mental Health.* Basic Books, 1958
JAQUES E. *Measurement of Responsibility.* Harvard University Press, 1956
JAQUES E. *Equitable Payment.* Heinemann, 1961
JAQUES E. *Time Span Handbook.* Heinemann, 1964
JAQUES E. *Progression Handbook.* Heinemnn, 1968
JAQUES E. *The Changing Culture of a Factory.* Tavistock, 1951
JARMAN L C. "The Nature of Management Development" in Torrington D P & Sutton D F. *Handbook of Management Development.* Gower, 1973
JENKINS LORD. *Report of the Company Law Committee* (Chairman: Lord Jenkins). HMSO, June 1962, Cmnd 1749
JENKINS C & SHERMAN B. *Collective Bargaining.* Routledge & Kegan Paul, 1977
JENSEN G E. *Dynamics of Instructional Groups.* National Society for the Study of Education, Yearbook, 1960
JOHNSON D M. *The Psychology of Thinking.* Harper & Row. 1972
JONES G N. *Planned Organizational Change.* Routledge and Kegan Paul, 1969
JONES G, BELL D, CENTER A and COLEMAN D. *Perspectives in Manpower Planning.* IPM, 1967
JONES K. *The Human Face of Change—Social Responsibility and Rationalization at British Steel.* IPM, 1974
JONES R M. *Absenteeism.* Manpower Paper No 4. HMSO, 1971
KAHN-FREUND O. *Labour and the Law.* Stevens, 1972, revised edn 1977

KAHN R L and KATZ D. Leadership Practices in Relation to Productivity and Morale, in Cartwright D and Zander A. *Group Dynamics*. qv 1953, pp. 612–28

KARN H W and GILMER B V H. *Readings in Industrial and Business Psychology*. McGraw-Hill, 1952; 2nd edn 1962

KAST F E and ROSENZWEIG J E. General Systems Theory: Applications for Organization and Management. *Academy of Management Journal*, December 1972, pp 447–65

KATZ E. The Diffusion of New Ideas and Practices. Schramm W L, 1963, pp 77–93 qv

KATZ E and LAZARSFELD P F. *Personal Influence*. Free Press, 1955

KAY H, DODD B and SIME M. *Teaching Machines and Programmed Instruction*. Penguin, 1968

KEENAN A. "Some relationships between interviewers' personal feelings about candidates and the general evaluation of them" in *Journal of Occupational Psychology*, 50, 1977, p 275

KEENAN A. "The Selection Interview: Candidates Reactions and Interviewers' Judgements" in *British Journal of Clinical Psychology*, 17, 1978, p 201

KEENAN A. "Interviewing for Graduate Recruitment" in *Personnel Management*, February, 1978, p 31

KEENOY T. *Industrial Relations: Power and Conflict*. University of Oxford. D Phil Thesis, 1977

KELLEY H H. Communication in Experimentally Created Hierarchies in *Human Relations*, 1951, 4, pp 39–56 and in Cartwright & Zander, 1953, pp. 443–61

KELLY J. *Is Scientific Management Possible?* Faber, 1966

KELLY R W. *Hiring the Worker*. Engineering Magazine Company, New York, 1918

KENNEDY G, BENSON J & McMILLAN J. *Managing Negotiations*. Business Books, 1980

KENNEY J, DONNELLY E & REID M. *Manpower Training and Development*. IPM, 2nd edn, 1979

KENNY T P. Stating the Case for Welfare. *Personnel Management*, September 1975, pp 18–21 and 35

KEPNER C H and TREGOE B B. *The Rational Manager*. McGraw-Hill. 1965

KESSLER S and WEEKES B. *Conflict at Work—Re-shaping Industrial Relations*. BBC Publications, 1971

KETTLE V. "Training in Industrial Relations" in Torrington (ed), 1972, qv, pp. 221–237

KILCOURSE T. "IR Training: What the Line Manager Needs to Know?" in *Personnel Management*, May, 1977, pp. 32–5

KIMBERLY J R, MILES R H et al. *The Organisational Life Cycle*. Jossey Bass, 1980

KING B, STREUFERT S & FIDDLER F E (eds). *Managerial Control and Organisational Democracy*. Winston, 1978

KING D. *Training Within the Organization*. Tavistock, 1968

583

KLEIN L. *Multi-products Ltd.* HMSO, 1964

KNIVETON B H & TOWERS B. *Training for Negotiating*. Business Books, 1978

KOONTZ H and O'DONNELL C. *Management: A Systems and Contingency Analysis of Managerial Functions*. McGraw Hill, 1976, 6th edn

LAIDLER H W. *History of Socialism*. Crowell, 1961

LANDY F J and TRUMBO D A. *Psychology of Work Behaviour*. Dorsey Press, 1976

LANE T and ROBERTS K. *Strike at Pilkingtons*. Fontana, 1971

LANSBURY R. "Professionalism and Unionisation among Management Service Specialists" in *British Journal of Industrial Relations*, XII (2) 1974, pp. 292–302

LARKCOM J (ed). *Personnel Management Handbook*. Business Publications, 1967

LASSWELL H D. "Communication as an Emerging Discipline" in *Audio-Visual Communication Review*, 6, 1958, pp. 245–254

LAWLER E E and SUTTLE J L. A Casual Correlational Test of the Need Hierarchy Concept. *Organizational Behaviour and Human Performance*, 7, 1972, pp 265–87

LAWLER E E. *Pay and Organizational Effectiveness*. McGraw Hill, 1971

LAWRENCE J (ed). *Company Manpower Planning in Perspective*. IPM/ IMS, 1975

LAWRENCE J. Manpower and Personnel Models in Britain. *Personnel Review*, 2 (3) Summer 1973, pp 4–26; and in Smith (1980), pp. 18–46

LAWRENCE P R and LORSCH J W. *Organization and Environment*. Harvard University Press, 1967

LAWSHE C H. *Principles of Personnel Testing*. McGraw-Hill, 1948

LEARY M. "Industrial Relations: The Training Contribution" in *Journal of European Training*, 4 (4), 1975, pp. 195–227. MCB Monograph, Bradford, 1975

LEAVITT H J. *Managerial Psychology*. Chicago, 1974

LEGGATT T W. *The Training of British Managers*. NEDO, 1972

LEGGE D E. *Skills*. Penguin, 1970

LEGGE K. *Power, Innovation and Problem-Solving in Personnel Management*. McGraw-Hill, 1978

LEICESTER C. *The National Environment for Manpower Planning* in Bosworth and Evans, qv

LEISERSON M W. "Wage Determination and the Wage Structure in the US" in Hugh-Jones E M (ed), *Wage Structure in Theory and Practice*. North Holland, 1966, pp. 1–70

LERNER S W. *Breakaway Unions and the Small Trade Union*. Allen and Unwin, 1961

LESTER R A. *Manpower Planning in Free Society*. Princeton, 1966

LEVINE J and BUTLER J. *Lecture vs Group Decision in Changing Behaviour*, in Cartwright and Zander 1953, qv pp 280–86

LEVINSON H M. *Collective Bargaining by British Local Authority Employees*. Institute of Labour and Industrial Relations, University of Michigan, 1971

584

LEVINSON H. "Management by Whose Objectives?" in *Harvard Business Review*, July/August, 1970, pp. 125–34

LEVY A B. *Private Corporations and their Control.* Routledge and Kegan Paul, 1950

LEWIN K. *Field Theory in Social Science.* Harper, 1951

LEWIN K. *Principles of Topological Psychology.* McGraw-Hill, 1936

LEWIN K. Studies in Group Decision, in Cartwright and Zander 1953, qv pp. 287–301

LEWIS R and STEWART R. *The Boss.* Phoenix House, 1958

LIKERT R. *New Patterns in Management.* McGraw-Hill, 1961

LIKERT R. *The Human Organization.* McGraw-Hill, 1967

LILLEY S. *Automation and Social Progress.* Lawrence and Wishart, 1957

LINTON R. *The Study of Man.* Appleton-Century-Crofts, 1964

LIPPITT G L. *Organization Renewal.* Meredith Corporation, 1969

LIPPIT T R and WHITE R. Leader Behaviour and Member Reaction in Three Social Climates, in Cartwright and Zander, 1953, qv pp. 585–611

LITTERER J A. *The Analysis of Organizations—Organization, Structure and Behaviour.* Wiley, 1967

LITWIN G H and STRINGER R A. *Motivation and Organizational Climate.* Harvard Business School, 1968

LIVY B. *Job Evaluation.* Allen and Unwin, 1975

LOCKE H W. *Fundamentals of Personnel Management.* IPM, 1943

LOCKYER J. *Industrial Arbitration in Great Britain.* IPM, 1979

LOCKYER K G. *Factory and Production Management.* Pitman, 1974

LOGAN H H. Line and Staff—An Obsolete Concept. *Personnel,* January-February 1966

LORIN B C & CARSTEVENS E R. *Coaching, Learning and Action.* AMA, 1971

LORSCHE J W, BAUGHMAN J, REESE J & MINTZBERG H. *Understanding Management.* Harper & Row, 1978

LOVER J. "Shop Stewards: Conflicting Objectives and Needs" in *Industrial Relations Journal, 7* (1), 1976, pp. 27–39

LOVERIDGE R. *Collective Bargaining by National Employees in the UK.* Institute of Labour and Industrial Relations, University of Michigan, 1971

LUCIUS M J. *Personnel Management.* Irwin-Dorsey, 1975

LUKES S. *Power: a Radical View.* Macmillan, 1974

LUMLEY R. *White Collar Unionism in Britain.* Methuen, 1973

LUPTON T. *Industrial Behaviour and Personnel Management.* IPM, 1964

LUPTON T. *Management and the Social Sciences.* Penguin, 1971

LUPTON T. *On the Shop Floor.* Pergamon, 1963

LUPTON T (ed). *Payment Systems.* Penguin, 1972

LUPTON T and BOWEY A M. *Wages and Salaries.* Penguin, 1974

LUPTON T and GOWLER D. *Selecting a Wage Payment System.* Kogan Page, 1969

LYMAN E L. Occupational Differences in the Values Attached to Work. *American Journal of Sociology,* 61, 1955

LYNCH J U. *Making Manpower Effective.* Pan Books. 1968

LYNCH P. Are Careers Obsolete? *Personnel*, August 1968
LYONS T P. *The Personnel Function in a Changing Environment*. Pitman, 1971
LYTLE C W. *Job Evaluation Methods*. Ronald Press, 1946
LYTLE C W. *Wage Incentive Methods*. Ronald Press, 1942
MACE M L. *Directors*. Harvard Business School, 1971
MACKENZIE DAVEY D *et al*. *Attitude Surveys in Industry*. IPM, 1970
MADDEN J M. A Review of Some Literature on Judgement with Implications for Job Evaluation, in USAF WADD, *Technical Note*, 1960, No 60–212
MAGER R F. *Preparing Instructional Objectives*. Fearon, 1962
MAHLER W R. Let's get more Scientific in Rating Employees, in Dooher and Marquis, 1950 qv
MALBERT D. *The Board Responsible to Whom?* Foundation for Business Responsibilities, 1973
MANGHAM I. *The Politics of Organisational Change*. Associated Business Publishers, 1978
MANPOWER SERVICES COMMISSION. *People at Work: Auditing Management Development*. MSC, 1979
MANSFIELD COOPER W and WOOD J C. *Outlines of Industrial Law*. Butterworth, 1974
MANT A. *The Experienced Manager*. BIM, 1969
MANT A. *The Rise and Fall of the British Manager*. Macmillan, 1977
MARCH J G (ed). *Handbook of Organizations*. Rand McNally, 1965
MARCH J G and SIMON H A. *Organizations*. Wiley, 1958
MARCHINGTON M. *Responses to Participation at Work*. Gower, 1980
MARGERISON C & LEARY M. *Managing Industrial Conflicts: The Mediator's Role*. MCB Books, 1975, 94 pp
MARGERISON C. "Action Research and Action Learning in Management Education" in *Journal of European Industrial Training*, 2 (6), 1978
MARGERISON C & ASHTON D. *Planning for Human Resources*. Longmans, 1974
MARGERISON C J and ASHTON D. *Manpower Planning*. Longman, 1974
MARGERISON C J. *Managing Effective Work Groups*. McGraw-Hill, 1973
MARGUILES N and RAIA A P. *Organizational Development*. McGraw-Hill, 1972
MARKS W. *Induction—Acclimatizing People to Work*. IPM, 1974
MARKS W. *Preparing an Employee Handbook*. IPM, 1972, revised edn 1978
MARKS W. *Politics and Personnel Management*. IPM, 1978
MARPLES D. *The Decisions of Engineering Design*. Institute of Engineering Designers. 1961
MARRIOTT R. *Incentive Payments Systems*. Staples Press, 1968
MARSH A I. The Managerial Grid. *Industrial Welfare*, October 1965
MARSH A I. *Managers and Shop Stewards—Shop Floor Revolution?*

IPM, 1973, 174 pp

MARSH A I, GILLIES J & RUSH M. *The Training of Managers in Industrial Relations*. Training Services Agency, MSC, August, 1976

MARSH A I. "Tailoring IR Training to the Manager and his Needs" in *Personnel Management*, August, 1977, pp. 26–7 and 35

MARTIN R and FRYER R H. *Redundancy and Paternalist Capitalism*. Allen and Unwin, 1973

MASLOW A H. A Theory of Human Motivation. *Psychological Review*. 50, 1943, pp 370–96

MASLOW A H. *Motivation and Personality*. Harper and Row, 1970

MATHEWSON S B. *Restriction of Output among Unorganized Workers*. Viking Press, 1951

MAURER H. *Great Enterprise*. Macmillan, 1955

MAYFIELD E. "The Selection Interview—A Re-evaluation of Published Research" in *Personnel Psychology*, 17, 1964, p 239; and in Fleishman. 1967, qv, pp. 23–39

MAYO E. *The Human Problems of an Industrial Civilization*. Macmillan, 1933

MAYO E. *The Social Problems of an Industrial Civilization*. Harvard Business School, 1949. Routledge and Kegan Paul reprint, 1975

McBEATH G. *Organization and Manpower Planning*. Business Books, 1969

McBEATH G and RANDS D N. *Salary Administration*. Business Books, 1969

McCARTHY W E J. *Trade Unions* Penguin, 1972

McCARTHY W E J. Changing Bargaining Structures, in Kessler S and Weekes B (eds), *Conflict at Work*. qv

McCARTHY W E J, O'BRIEN J F and DOWD V G. *Wage Inflation and Wage Leadership*. The Economic and Social Research Institute, Dublin, 1975

McCARTHY W E J and COLLIER A S. *Coming to Terms with Trade Unions*. IPM, 1973

McCARTHY W E J *Making Whitley Work*. Dept of Health and Social Scurity, 1977

McCARTHY W E J & ELLIS N D. *Management by Agreement*. Hutchinson, 1973

McCARTHY W E J. *The Role of Shop Stewards in British Industrial Relations*. RCTU & EA, Research Paper, No. 1, HMSO, 1966

McCLELLAND D C & WINTER D C. *Motivating Economic Achievement*. Free Press, 1969

McCLELLAND D C. *The Achieving Society*. Van Nostrand, 1961

McFARLAND D E. *Personnel Management Theory and Practice*. Macmillan, 1968

McFARLAND D E. *Personnel Management*. Penguin, 1971

McGEHEE W & THAYER P W. *Training in Business and Industry*. Wiley, 1961

McGLYNE J E. *Unfair Dismissal Cases*. Butterworth, 1976

McGREGOR D. *The Human Side of Enterprise*. McGraw-Hill, New

York, 1960
McGREGOR D. *The Professional Manager*. McGraw-Hill, 1967
McIVER R M and PAGE C H. *Society—An Introductory Analysis*. Macmillan, 1953
McIVER R M. Professional Groups and Cultural Norms, in Vollmer H M and Mills D L. *Professionalization*. Prentice-Hall, 1966
McKERSIE R B & HUNTER L C. *Pay, Productivity and Collective Bargaining*. Macmillan, 1973
McKINLAY J B. *Processing People*. Holt Rinehart, Winston, 1974
MEAD Sir C. *Report re-appraising the Aims and Organization of the British Institute of Management*. BIM, 1968
MEAD J P de C and GREIG F W. *Supervisory Training: a New Approach for Management*. HMSO, 1966
MEGGINSON D F & BOYDELL T H. *A Guide to Management Coaching*. BACIE, 1978
MEGGINSON L C. *Personnel—a Behavioural Approach to Administration*. Irwin, 1972
MENZIES I E P and ANSTEY E. *Staff Reporting*. Allen and Unwin, 1951
MEPHAM G J. *Equal Opportunity and Equal Pay*. IPM, 1974
MERRET A J and WHITE M R M. *Incentive Payments Systems for Managers*. Gower Press, 1968
MERRIE A H. Evaluation of Manual and Non-manual Jobs. *Personnel Management*, July/August 1948, pp. 174–81
MERTON R. *Social Theory and Social Structure*. The Free Press, 1948
METCALF D. "Unions, Incomes Policy and Relative Wages in Britain" in *British Journal of Industrial Relations*, 15 (2), 1977, pp. 157–75
METCALF H C and URWICK L. *Dynamic Administration*. Pitman, 1941
MILLARD G. *Personnel Management in Hospitals*. IPM, 1972
MILLER D C and FORM W H. Industrial Sociology. Harper, 1951
MILLER E J and RICE A K. *Systems of Organization: the Control of Task and Sentient Boundaries*. Tavistock, 1967
MILLER K. *Psychological Testing*. Gower, 1975
MILLERSON G. The Qualifying Associations. Routledge, 1964
MILLS H R. *Teaching and Training*. Macmillan, 1967
MILNE-BAILEY W. *Trade Union Documents*. Macmillan, 1929
MINER J B and MINER M G. *Personnel and Industrial Relations*. Macmillan, 1977, 3rd edn
MINER J B. "The O D – Management Development Conflict" in *Business Horizons,* 16 (6), 1973, pp 31–36
MINISTRY OF LABOUR. *Dismissal Procedures*. HMSO, 1967
MINISTRY OF LABOUR. *Glossary of Training Terms*. HMSO, 1967; 1971
MINTZBERG H. *The Nature of Managerial Work*. Harper & Row, 1973
MINTZBERG H B. "The Manager's Job: Folklore and Fact" in *Harvard Business Review*, July/August, 1975, pp. 49–61
MITCHELL E. *The Employer's Guide to the Law on Health, Safety and Welfare at Work*. Business Books, 1974
MITCHELL W. *Employee Relations within the Factory*. Macmillan, 1973

MOORBY E T. "The Manager as Coach" in *Personnel Management*, Nov. 1973, pp. 30–32

MOORE M R. *A Proposed Taxonomy of the Perceptual Domain and Some Suggested Applications*. Educational Testing Service, 1967

MOORE W E. *Industrial Relations and the Social Order*. Macmillan, 1951

MORGAN J G. *European Approaches to Responsibility*. Foundation for Business Responsibilities, 1975

MORLEY I and STEPHENSON G. *The Social Psychology of Bargaining*. Allen and Unwin, 1977

MORRISON R F, OWENS W A, GLENNON J R and ALBRIGHT L E. Factored Life History Antecedents of Industrial Research Performance. *Journal of Applied Psychology*, 1962

MORRISON J H & O'HEARNE J. *Practical Transactional Analysis in Management*. Addison-Wesley, 1977

MORSE N C and WEISS R S. The Function and Meaning of Work and the Job. *American Sociological Review*, 1955

MORSE N. *Satisfactions of the White Collar Job*. Michigan, 1953

MOSER C A. *Survey Methods in Social Investigation*. Heinemann, 1971

MOSS A. A Company Approach to Industry Manpower Forecasting. *Personnel Review*, 3 (2) Spring 1974, pp 8–24

MOUZELIS N P. *Organization and Bureaucracy*. RKP, 1967

MOXON G R. *The Functions of a Personnel Department*. IPM, 1966

MUKHERJEE S. *Changing Manpower Needs*. PEP, 1970

MUMFORD A. *The Manager and Training*. Pitman, 1971

MUMFORD E. *Computers, Planning and Personnel Management*. IPM, 1969

MUMFORD E. Job Satisfaction: A Method of Analysis. *Personnel Review*, 1 (3), Summer 1972, pp 48–57

MUNNS V G. *Employers' Associations*. RCTUEA Research Paper No 7, 1967

MURCHISON C (ed). *Handbook of Social Psychology*. Clark Univ. Press, 1935

MUSGROVE F. *Patterns of Power and Authority in English Education*. Methuen, 1971

MYERS C S. *Industrial Psychology in Great Britain*. Jonathan Cape, 1933

MYERS M S. *Managing Without Unions*. Addison-Wesley Press, 1976

NATIONAL ADVISORY COUNCIL ON EDUCATION FOR INDUSTRY AND COMMERCE. *Committee on Technician Courses and Examinations Report* (Haslegrave). HMSO, 1969

NATIONAL BOARD FOR PRICES AND INCOMES. *Payment by Results Systems*. HMSO, 1968

NBPI. *Top Salaries in the Private Sector and Nationalized Industries*. HMSO, 1969

NBPI. *General Problems of Low Pay*. HMSO, 1971

NBPI. *Job Evaluation*. HMSO, 1968

NBPI. *Productivity Agreements*. HMSO, 1968

NBPI. *Salary Structures*. HMSO, 1969

NATIONAL ECONOMIC DEVELOPMENT OFFICE. *Management*

Training in Industrial Relations. NEDO, 1975

NATIONAL INSTITUTE OF INDUSTRIAL PSYCHOLOGY. *Statistical Records about People at Work*. NIIP, July, 1964

NAYLOR R and TORRINGTON D. *Administration of Personnel Policies*. Gower, 1974

NEWCOMB T M. *Social Psychology*. Tavistock, 1952

NEWELL A and SIMON H A. Heuristic Problem Solving. *Operations Research*, 6, Jan/Feb 1958, and May/June, 1958

NEWPORT AND GWENT INDUSTRIAL MISSION. *Redundant? A Personal Survival Kit*. Newport and Gwent Industrial Mission, 24, Old Hill Crescent, Christchurch, Newport, 1975

NEWSHAM D B. *The Challenge of Change to the Adult Trainee*. HMSO, 1969

NEWSTRON J W *et al*. *A Contingency Approach to Management: Readings*. McGraw-Hill, 1975

NICHOLS T H and BEYNON H. *Living With Capitalism*. Routledge and Kegan Paul, 1977

NICHOLS T. *Ownership, Control and Ideology*. Allen and Unwin, 1969

NIVEN M M. *Personnel Management, 1913–1963*. IPM, 1967

NORSTEDT J P and AGUREN S. *The Saab-Scania Report*. Swedish Employers' Confederation, Stockholm, 1973

NORTH D T B and BUCKINGHAM G L. *Productivity Agreements and Wage Systems*. Gower, 1969

NORTHCOTT C H. *Personnel Management, Principles and Practice*. Pitman, 1955

ODIORNE G S. *Management by Objectives*. Pitman, 1965

ODIORNE G S. *Personnel Administration by Objectives*. Irwin, 1971

ODIORNE G. *Management Decisions by Objectives*. Prentice-Hall, 1968

ODIORNE G. *Personnel Policy: Incomes and Practices*. Merrill, 1963

ODIORNE G S. *Training by Objectives: An Economic Approach to Management Training*. Macmillan, 1970

OECD. *Job Re-design and Occupational Training for Older Workers*. OECD, Paris, 1965

OGDEN Sir G. *The New Water Industry: Management and Structure*. HMSO, 1973

O'HIGGINS P. *Workers' Rights*. Hutchinson, Arrow Books, 1976

OLDFIELD F E. *New Look Industrial Relations*. Mason Reed, 1966

OLSEN K. Suggestions Schemes Seventies Style. *Personnel Management*, April 1976, pp 36–39

OPSAHL R L and DUNNETT M D. The Role of Financial Compensation in Industrial Motivation. *Psychological Bulletin*, 66, 1966, pp. 94–118; and in Fleishman, 1967, pp. 288–97

ORTH C D *et al*. *Administering Research and Development*. Irwin, 1964

ORZACK L H. Work as a Central Life Interest of Professionals. *Social Problems*, 7, 1959

PADFIELD C F. *British Constitution Made Simple*. Allen and Unwin, 1972

PAHL R E and WINKLER J T. Corporatism in Britain: why protecting industry need not mean more bureaucracy. *The Times*, 26 March 1976

590

Palmers' Company Law. Stevens, 22nd edn

PALMER R. A Participative Approach to Attitude Surveys. *Personnel Management*, 9 (12) December 1977, pp 26–7 and 37

PAPER & PAPER PRODUCTS ITB. *An Approach to IR Training within a Company*. PAPPITB, 1973

PARKER S. *Workplace Industrial Relations, 1972*. HMSO, 1974

PARKER S, BROWN R K & SMITH M A. *The Sociology of Industry*. Allen & Unwin, 1967

PARKINSON C N *The Rise of Big Business*. Weidenfeld and Nicolson, 1977

PARSON T. The Social System. Free Press, 1951

PARSONS T. Suggestions for a Sociological Theory of Organization. *Administrative Science Quarterly*, 1, 1956

PARSONS T. A Sociological Approach to the Theory of Organizations in Etzioni A, *Complex Organizations: A Sociological Reader*. Holt Rinehart and Winston, 1964

PARSONS T. *Professional Groups and Social Structure*. Prentice-Hall, 1939

PARTRIDGE B E. "The Process of Leadership on the Shop Floor" in King, Streufert & Fiddler, 1978, qv pp. 187–200

PATERSON T T. *Job Evaluation*. Business Books, 1972

PATTEN T H. *Manpower Planning and the Development of Human Resources*. Interscience, 1971

PAUL W J and ROBERTSON K B. *Learning from Job Enrichment*. Imperial Chemical Industries, 1970

PEACH D A and LIVERNASH E R. *Grievance Challenge and Resolution*. Harvard Business School, 1974

PEACH L. Personnel Management by Objectives. *Personnel Management*, March 1975, pp 20–23 and 39

PEDLAR M. "Industrial Relations: The Implications for Training Officers" in *Training Officer*, February, 1975

PEDLAR M. "The Training Implications of the Shop Steward's Leadership Role" in *Industrial Relations Journal*, 5 (1), 1974, pp. 57–70

PEN J. A General Theory of Bargaining, in *American Economic Review*, March 1952

PERLMAN H. Social Work Method: A Review of the Past Decade. *Social Work*, October 1975

PETTMAN B O. Some Factors Influencing Labour Turnover: A Review of Research Literature. *Industrial Relations Journal*, 4 (3) Autumn, 1973, pp 43–61

PHELPS-BROWN E H. *Collective Bargaining Reconsidered*. Athlone Press, 1971

PHELPS-BROWN E H. *Pay and Profits*. Manchester University Press, 1968

PHELPS-BROWN E H. *The Economics of Labour*. Yale University Press, 1962

PHILLIPS M H. Merit Rating for Skilled and Semi-skilled Workers. *Personnel Management*, June 1962, pp. 120–28

PIGORS P. *Effective Communication in Industry.* National Association of Manufacturers, New York, 1949

PIGORS P and MYERS C A. *Management of Human Resources.* McGraw-Hill, 1973

PIGORS P and MYERS C A. *Personnel Administration.* McGraw-Hill, 1977, 8th edn

PILDITCH J. *Communication by Design: a Study in Corporate Identity.* McGraw-Hill, 1970

PLUMBLEY P R. *Recruitment and Selection.* IPM, 1968, revised 1976

POLLARD H R. *Developments in Management Thought.* Heinemann, 1973

POLLARD S. *The Genesis of Modern Management.* Edward Arnold, 1965

PORTER L W. Job Attitudes in Management: Perceived Deficiencies in Need Fulfilment as a Function of Job Level. *Journal of Applied Psychology* (46), 1962

PORTER L W. A Study of Perceived Need Satisfactions in Bottom and Middle Management Jobs. *Journal of Applied Psychology* (45), 1961

PORTER L W. Job Attitudes in Management: Perceived Importance of Needs as a Function of Job Level. *Journal of Applied Psychology* (47), 1963 (a), pp 141–8

PORTER L W. Job Attitudes in Management: Perceived Deficiencies in Need Fulfilment as a Function of Line Versus Staff Type of Jobs. *Journal of Applied Psychology*, 47(4), 1963(b), pp 267–75

PORTER L W, Job Attitudes in Management: Perceived Deficiencies in Need Fulfilment as a Function of the Size of Company, *Journal of Applied Psychology,* 47 (6), 1963 (c), pp 386–97

PORTER L W, LAWLER E E and HACKMAN J R. *Behaviour in Organizations.* McGraw-Hill, 1975

PORTER L W and LAWLER E E. *Managerial Attitudes and Performance.* Irwin-Dorsey, 1968

POWELL L S. *Communication and Learning.* Pitman, 1969

PRANDY K. *Professional Employees.* Faber and Faber, 1965

PRICE N. Personnel: Human Resources Management, in Brech EFL, 1975, qv

PRITCHARD R D. Equity Theory: A Review and Critique. *Organizational Behaviour and Human Performance*, 4, 1969, pp 176–211

PROHANSKY H and SEIDENBERG B. *Basic Studies in Social Psychology.* Holt, Rinehart and Winston, 1969

PUGH D S (ed). *Organization Theory.* Penguin, 1971

PURCELL J & EARL M. "Control Systems and Industrial Relations" in *Journal of Industrial Relations,* 8 (2), 1977

PURCELL J & SMITH R (eds). *The Control of Work.* Macmillan, 1979

PURKISS C J. Manpower Planning Literature: Manpower Demand. *Department of Employment Gazette*, November 1976, pp 1–4

PYM D. Technical Change and the Misuse of Professional Manpower. *Occupational Psychology*, January 1967

PYM D. *Industrial Society: Social Sickness in Management.* Penguin, 1968

RACKHAM N & MORGAN T. *Behaviour Analysis in Training.* McGraw-Hill, 1977

RACKMAN N & HONEY P. *Developing Interactive Skills.* Wellens, 1971

RAIA A P. *Managing by Objectives.* Scott, Foresman, 1974

RAIA A P. Goal Setting and Self Control, *Journal of Management Studies,* February, 1965

RAIMON R L. The Indeterminateness of Wages of Semi-Skilled Workers. *Industrial and Labour Relations Review,* 1953

RAMSAY J C. Negotiating in Multi-Plant Company. *Industrial Relations Journal,* Summer 1971

RAMSAY J C and HILL J M. *Collective Agreements—a Guide to their Content and Drafting.* IPM, 1974

RANDALL P E. *Introduction to Work Study and Organization and Methods.* Butterworths, 1969

RANDELL G A et al. *Staff Appraisal.* IPM, 1972, revised 1974

RANDLE C W and WORTMAN M S. *Collective Bargaining.* Houghton-Mifflin, 1966

RAY M E. *Recruitment Advertising.* IPM, 1980

REDDIN W J. *Managerial Effectiveness.* McGraw-Hill, 1970

REDGRAVES. *Factories Acts.* Butterworths, 1966

RENOLD G C. *Joint Consultation Over Thirty Years.* Allen and Unwin, 1950

RENOLD, Sir C. *The Organizational Structure of Large Undertakings—Management Problems.* BIM, 1950

REVANS R W. The Education of Managers: 1 The Theory of Practice. *Universities Quarterly,* September 1962

REVANS R W. *Developing Effective Managers.* Longmans, 1971

REVANS R W. *Action Learning.* Blond & Briggs, 1980

RHEINSTEIN M (ed). *Max Weber on Law in Economy and Society.* Simon and Schuster, 1954

RHENMAN E. *Industrial Democracy and Industrial Management.* Tavistock, 1968

RICE A K *The Enterprise and its Environment.* Tavistock, 1963

RICE A K. *Productivity and Social Organization: the Ahmedabad Experiment.* Tavistock, 1958

RICE A K et al. The Representation of Labour Turnover as a Social Process. *Human Relations,* 3 (4), 1950, pp 349–72

RICE G H and BISHOPRICK D W. *Conceptual Models of Organizations.* Appleton-Century-Crofts, 1971

RICHBELL S. Participation and Perceptions of Control. *Personnel Review,* 5 (2), Spring 1976, pp 13–19

RICHTER I. *Political Purpose in Trade Unions.* Allen and Unwin, 1973

RIDEOUT R W. *Reforming the Redundancy Payments Act.* IPM. 1969

RIDEOUT R W. *Principles of Labour Law.* Sweet and Maxwell, 1979, 3rd edn

RIESMAN D. *The Lonely Crowd.* Doubleday, 1955

RITZER G and TRICE H M. *An Occupation in Conflict: A Study of the Personnel Manager.* Cornell, 1969

ROBERTS T J. *Developing Effective Managers*. IPM, 1967, revised 1974

ROBERTS B C. *Trade Union Government and Administration*. Bell, 1956

ROBERTS B C & GENARD J. "Trends in Plant and Company Bargaining" in *British Journal of Industrial Relations*, 1970

ROBERTS B C and LOVERIDGE R. *Reluctant Militants*. Heinemann, 1972

ROBERTS B C and SMITH J H. *Manpower Policy and Employment Trends*. Bell and Sons, 1966

ROBERTSON K. Managing People and Jobs. *Personnel Management*, September 1969, pp 20–24

ROBINSON D. *Local Labour Markets and Wage Structures*. Gower, 1970

ROBINSON D. "Future Trends in the Labour Market" in Cuthbert & Hawkins (1973), qv, pp. 157–72

ROBINSON J and BARNES N. *New Media and Methods in Industrial Training*. BBC, 1968

ROBINSON O and WALLACE J. *Pay and Employment in Retailing*. Saxon House, 1976

ROCK M L. Wage and Salary Administration. McGraw Hill, 1972

RODGER A. *The Seven Point Plan*. NIIP, 1952

ROETHLISBERGER F J. *Man-in-Organization*. Harvard University Press, 1968

ROETHLISBERGER F J and DICKSON W J. *Management and the Worker*. Harvard University Press, 1939

ROFF H E and WATSON T E. *Job Analysis*. IPM, 1961

RONISZOWSKI A J. *The Selection and Use of Teaching Aids*. International Text Book Company, 1968

RONKEN H O and LAWRENCE P R. *Administering Changes*. Harvard University Press, 1952

ROSE A M. *Human Behaviour and Social Processes*. Routledge and Kegan Paul, 1962

ROSS A M. *Trade Union Wage Policy*. University of California Press, 1948

ROSS J. Predicting Practical Skill in Engineering Apprentices. *Occupational Psychology*, 36 (1 and 2), 1962

ROSS M G and HENDRY C E. *New Understandings of Leadership*. Association Press, 1957

ROTHE H F. "Does Higher Pay Bring Higher Productivity?" in *Personnel*, 37, 1980, pp. 20–38 and in Fleishman (1961), pp. 251–9

ROTHWELL S. *Labour Turnover: Its Costs, Causes and Control*. Gower, 1980

ROWBOTTOM R. *Hospital Organization*. Heinemann, 1973

ROWE K H. An Appraisal of Appraisals. *Journal of Management Studies*, 1 (1) March 1964, pp 1–24

ROWNTREE J A and STEWART P A. Estimating manpower needs—II: Statistical Methods. *Manpower planning in the Civil Service*. HMSO. 1976, pp 36–53

ROY D. "Efficiency and the Fix" in *Am. Journal of Sociology*, LX (3), November, 1954

RUBENSTEIN A H and HABERSTROH C J (eds). *Some Theories of Organization*. Irwin-Dorsey, 1960
RUBIN J Z & BROWN B R. *The Social Psychology of Bargaining and Negotiation*. Academic Press, 1975
RUDDICK R. *Roles and Relationships*. Routledge and Kegan Paul, 1969
RUNCIMAN W G. *Relative Deprivation and Social Justice*. Routledge and Kegan Paul, 1966
RUSSELL B. *History of Western Philosophy*. Allen & Unwin, 1946
SABINE G H *A History of Political Theory*. Harrap, 1963
SADLER P J and BARRY B A. *Organizational Development*. Longman, 1970
SALAMAN G and BRISTOW J. Why Appraisals Fail. *Management Today*, October 1970, pp 37–46
SALAMAN G. Community and Occupation. Cambridge UP, 1974
SAMPSON R C. *The Staff Role and Management: Its Creative Uses*. Harper, 1955
SAMUEL P J. *Labour Turnover: Towards a Solution*. IPM, 1971
SAUNDERS N F T. *Factory Organisation and Management*. Pitman, 1952, 3rd edn
SAVAGE I and SMALL J R. *Introduction to Managerial Economics*. Hutchinson, 1967
SAYLES L. *Behaviour in Industrial Work Groups*. Wiley, 1958
SAYLES L. *Managerial Behaviour*. McGraw-Hill, 1964
SAYLES L R and STRAUSS G. *Personnel: Human Problems of Management* Prentice-Hall, 1967, 2nd edn
SAYLES L R and STRAUSS G. *Human Behaviour in Organizations*. Prentice-Hall, 1966
SCHAFFER R H. *Managing by Total Objectives*. AMA, 1964
SCHATTSCHNEIDER E E. *The Semi-Sovereign People*. Dryden Press, 1960, 1975
SCHEIN E H. *Organizational Psychology*. Prentice-Hall, 1970
SCHEIN E H. The Individual, the Organization and the Career. *Journal of Applied Behavioural Sciences*, 7, 1971, pp 401–26
SCHLECH E C. *Managing for Results*. McGraw-Hill, 1961
SCHMITT N & COYLE B. "Applicant Decisions in the Employment Interview" in *Journal of Applied Psychology*, 61, 1976, pp. 184
SCHNEIDER A et al. *Organizational Communications*. McGraw-Hill, 1973
SCHRAMM W L (ed). *The Science of Human Communication*. Basic Books. 1963
SCHULTZ T. *Investment in Human Capital*. Free Press, Glencoe, 1971
SCHUSTER J R, CLARK B, ROGERS M. Testing Portions of the Porter Lawler Model Regarding the Motivational Role of Pay, *Journal of Applied Psychology*, 55, 1971, pp 187–195
SCHWITTER J P. Computer Effect upon Managerial Jobs. *Academy of Management Journal*, September 1965
SCOTT Sir B. *Inquiry into the Value of Pensions*, Report HMSO Cmnd 8147, February 1981

SCOTT W E and CUMMINGS L L. *Readings in Organizational Behaviour and Human Performance*. Irwin-Dorsey, 1973

SCOTT W H (ed). *Office Automation, Administrative and Human Problems*. OECD, 1965

SCOTT W H *et al. Technical Change and Industrial Relations*. Liverpool University Press, 1956

SEEAR N. *The Position of Women in Industry*. HMSO, 1968

SEEAR N. *The Re-entry of Women into Employment*. OECD, 1971

SEEAR N *et al. Married Women Working*. Allen and Unwin, 1962

SEEAR N. *A Career for Women in Industry*. Oliver and Boyd, 1964

SEEBOHM Sir F. *Report of the Committee on Local Authority and Allied Personal Social Services* (Chairman: Sir F Seebohm). HMSO, 1968

SELEKMAN B M. *A Moral Philosophy for Management*. McGraw Hill, 1959

Selwyn's Law of Employment. Butterworth, 1976

SELZNICK P. Foundations of the Theory of Organization. *American Sociology Review*, 13, 1948

SELZNICK P. *Leadership in Administration*. Harper and Row, 1957

SELZNICK P. Towards a Theory of Bureaucracy, in Coser L and Rosenberg M (eds) *Sociological Theory—a Reader*. Collier Macmillan, 1969

SEMEONOFF B. *Personality Assessment*. Penguin, 1966

SEYMOUR W D. *Industrial Skills*. Pitmans, 1966

SEYMOUR W D. Recent Developments in Operative Training. *Personnel Management*, July–August 1949 pp. 169–80

SEYMOUR W D. *Skills Analysis Training*. Pitman, 1968

SHACKLE G L S. *Expectation, Enterprise and Profit: The Theory of the Firm*. Allen & Unwin, 1970

SHACKLETON V and DAVIES J. The Unionized Manager. *Management Today*, June 1976

SHAFTO T A C. *Introducing Economics*. Nelson, 1971

SHALLENBERGER J B. Are European Managers Better Organized? *The Manager*, November 1961, pp 855–58

SHANKS M. *The Stagnant Society*. Penguin Books, 1961

SHANNON C E and WEAVER W. *The Mathematical Theory of Communication*. University of Illinois Press, 1949

SHEPARD H A. The Duel Hierarchy in Research, in Orth C D *et al*, 1964, qv

SHIBUTANI T. Reference Groups and Social Control, in Rose A, 1962, pp 128–47, qv

SHIMMIN S. Case Studies in Measured Daywork. *Personnel Magazine*, October 1966

SHONE K J and PATERSON R G. *Analysis of Controls and Design of Production Planning Control Systems*. Sawell Publications, 1963

SIDNEY E and BROWN M. *The Skills of Interviewing*. Tavistock, 1961

SILLS P A. *The Behavioural Sciences: Techniques of Application*. IPM, 1973

SILVERMAN D. *The Theory of Organizations*. Heinemann, 1970

SIMON H A. *Administrative Behaviour*. Macmillan, New York, 1953

SIMON H A. *The Shape of Automation*. Harper and Row, 1965

SIMON H A. Comments on the Theory of Organizations. *American Political Science Review*, December 1952, and in Rubenstein A H and Haberstroh C J, qv

SINGER E J. *Training in Industry and Commerce*. IPM, 1978

SINGER E J and MACDONALD I D. *Is Apprenticeship Outdated?* IPM, 1970

SINGER E J and RAMSDEN J. *Human Resources*. McGraw-Hill, 1972

SINGER E J and RAMSDEN J. *The Practical Approach to Skills Analysis*. McGraw-Hill, 1969

SINGLETON N. *Industrial Relations Procedures* (DE Manpower Paper, No. 14). HMSO, 1975

SINGLETON W T. "Acquisition of Skill: The Theory Behind Training Design" in Robinson & Barnes (1968), qv

SISSON K. *Negotiating in Practice*. IPM, 1977

SMELSER N J. Social Change, in Smelser N J (ed), *Sociology: An Introduction*. Wiley, 1967

SMITH A R (ed). *Models of Manpower Systems*, English Universities Press, 1970

SMITH A R. Developments in Manpower Planning. *Personnel Review*, 1 (1) Autumn 1971, pp 44–54

SMITH A R (ed). *Manpower Planning in the Civil Service*. Civil Service Studies No. 3. HMSO, 1976

SMITH A R (ed). *Corporate Manpower Planning*. Gower, 1980

SMITH B & DELF G A J. "Strategies for Promoting Self-Development" in *Industrial and Commercial Training*, November, 1978, pp 494–501

SMITH C G and TANNENBAUM A S. Organizational Control Structure, *Human Relations*, November 1963

SMITH I G. *The Measurement of Productivity*. Gower Press, 1973

SMITH W J, ALLBRIGHT L E and GLENNON J R. The Prediction of Research Competence and Creativity from Personal History. *Journal of Applied Psychology*, 45, 1961

SOMERS G G (ed). *The Next Twenty-Five Years of Industrial Relations*. IR Research Association, Madison, 1973

SOMERS G G (ed). *Essays in Industrial Relations Theory*. Iowa State UP, 1969

SOUTHGATE G W. *English Economic History*. Dent, 1970 rev. edn

SPROTT W J H. *Human Groups*. Pelican, 1958

STAINER G. *Manpower Planning*. Heinemann, 1971

STAMMERS R & PATRICK J. *The Psychology of Training*. Methuen, 1975

STARK W. *Social Theory and Christian Thought*. Routledge and Kegan Paul, 1958

STEERS C E B. *Clarifying Objectives in Supervisory Training*. BACIE, 1966

STEWART A & V. "Selection and Appraisal: The Pick of Recent Research" in *Personnel Management*, January, 1976, p 20

STEWART J D. *Management in Local Government: a Viewpoint*. Charles

Knight and Company, 1974

STINCHCOMBE A L. Formal Organizations, in Smelser N T. *Sociology*. Wiley, 1967

STOKES P M. *Total Job Training: A Manual for the Working Manager*. AMA, 1966

STONE C H and KENDALL W E. *Effective Personnel Selection Procedures*. Staples Press, 1957

STOUFFER S A *et al. The American Soldier*. Princeton University, 1949

STRAUSS A. *Negotiations*. Jossey-Bass, 1978

STUTARD G. *Learning from Industrial Relations*. Longmans, 1975

SULLIVAN G R. The Relationship Between the Board of Directors and the General Meeting in Limited Companies. *Law Quarterly Review*, 93, October 1977, pp 569–40

SWANNACK A R and SAMUEL P J. The Added Value of Men and Materials. *Personnel Management*, February 1974, pp 26–29 and 41

SWANNACK A R. Small Firm Salary Structures. *Personnel Management*, January 1975, pp 31–34

SWEDISH EMPLOYERS' CONFEDERATION. *Job Reform in Sweden*. SEF, 1975

SYKES A J. "The Effects of a Supervisory Training Course in Changing Supervisors' Perceptions and Expectations of the Role of Management" in *Human Relations*, XV, 1962, pp. 227–43

SYKES A J M. "The Ideological Basis of Industrial Relations in GB" in *International Management,* 1965–6

TAFT R. The Ability to Judge People, in Whisler T L and Harper S F, 1962, qv

TAGIURI R. Value Orientations of Managers and Scientists, in Orth C D *et al*, 1964, qv

TALBOT J R and ELLIS C D. *Analysis and Costing of Company Training*. Gower Press, 1969

TANNENBAUM A S. *Control in Organizations*. McGraw-Hill, 1968

TANNENBAUM R. The Manager Concept: A Rational Synthesis. *Journal of Business*, 1948, and in Tannenbaum R, Weschler I R & Massarik F. *Leadership and Organisation*. McGraw-Hill, 1961, pp. 243–64

TAVERNIER G. *Industrial Training Systems and Records*. Gower, 1971

TAVERNIER G. *Design of Personnel Systems and Records*. Industrial Society, 1973

TAYLOR F W. *Shop Management*. Harper & Brothers, 1910

TAYLOR F W. *Scientific Management*. Harper and Brothers, 1947

TAYLOR P J. *Absenteeism—Causes and Control*. Industrial Society, Notes for Managers, No 15, 1973

TAYLOR G W, SMITH W R, GHISELIN B and ELLISON R. *Explorations in the Measurement and Prediction of Contributions of One Sample of Scientists*. Report No ASD-TR-61-96, Personnel Laboratory, ASD, Lackland, AFB, Texas, 1961

TERRY M. "The Inevitable Growth of Informality" in *British Journal of Industrial Relations*. XV (1), 1977, pp. 76–88

THAKUR M. *OD: the Search for Identity*. IPM, 1974

THIBAUT J. An Experimental Study of the Cohesiveness of Under-privileged Groups. *Human Relations*, 3, 1950 and in Cartwright & Zander, 1953, qv pp. 102–20

THOMAS K. *Attitudes and Behaviour*. Penguin, 1971

THOMAS J. Group Capacity Assessment. *DATA Journal*, May 1967

THOMAS B, MOXAM J and JONES J A G. A Cost-Benefit Analysis of Industrial Training. *British Journal of Industrial Relations*, VII (2), 1969 pp. 231–64

THOMAS R E. *The Government of Business*. Phillip Allen, 1976

THOMAS R E. *Business Policy*. Phillip Allen, 1977

THOMASON G F. *Job Evaluation: Objectives and Methods*. IPM, 1980

THOMASON G F. "Corporate Control and the Professional Association" in Poole, MJF & Mansfield R. *Managerial Roles and Industrial Relations*. Gower, 1980, pp. 26–37

THOMASON G F. *The Professional Approach to Community Work*. Sands, London, 1969

THOMASON G F. *The Management of Research and Development*. Batsford, 1970

THOMASON G F. *Experiments in Participation*. IPM, 1971

THOMASON G F. *Improving the Quality of Organization*. IPM, 1973

THOMASON G F, DOUGHTY G H and SPEAR H C. *Industrial Relations in the London Fire Service*. ACAS, 1977

THOMASON G F. *The Individual, The Trade Union and the State: Some Contemporary Issues*. Irish Association for Industrial Relations, 1978

THOMPSON J and ROGERS II R. *Redgrave's Factories, Truck and Shops Acts*. Butterworth, 1956, 19th edn

THOMPSON J D (ed). *Approaches to Organizational Design*. University of Pittsburgh Press, Pittsburgh, 1966

THOMSON A W J & BEAUMONT P B. *Public Sector Bargaining: A Study of Relative Gain*. Saxon House, 1978

THOMSON A W J & HUNTER L. "The Level of Bargaining in a Multi-plant Company" in *Industrial Relations Journal*, 6 (2), 1975, pp. 23–40

THURLEY K E and HAMBLIN A C. *The Supervisor and His Job*. HMSO, 1963

THURLEY K and WIRDENIUS H. *Approaches to Supervisory Development*. IPM, 1973

THURLEY K and WIRDENIUS H. *Supervision: a Re-appraisal*. Heinemann, 1973

THURLEY K E & WOOD S J (eds). *Management Strategy and Industrial Relations*. Cambridge UP, 1981

THURLEY K E, GRAVES D & HULT M. "An Evaluation Strategy for Management Development" in Training Research Bulletin, 6 (2), ATT ITB, Staines, 1975

TIFFIN J and McCORMICK E J. *Industrial Psychology*. Prentice-Hall, 1965

TOMLINSON R C. Operational Research in the Coal Industry: 2, Study of Manpower Problems. *Colliery Guardian*, December 1964, pp 789–92

TORRINGTON D & CHAPMAN J. *Personnel Management,* Prentice

Hall, 1979

TORRINGTON D. *Encyclopaedia of Personnel Management*. Gower Press, 1977

TORRINGTON D. *Handbook of Industrial Relations*. Gower Press, 1972

TORRINGTON D. *Face to Face*. Gower Press, 1972

TOSI H L and CARROLL S. Some Factors Affecting the Success of Management by Objectives. *Journal of Management Studies*, 7 (2), May 1970

TOWERS B, WHITTINGHAM T G and GOTTSCHALK A W (eds). *Bargaining for Change*. Allen and Unwin, 1972

TRADES UNION CONGRESS. *Automation and Technological Change*. TUC, 1965

TUC. *Costs and Profits: Financial Information for Trade Unionists*. TUC, 1970

TUC. *In the Automated Office*. TUC, 1964

TUC. *Job Evaluation and Merit Rating*. TUC, 1974

TUC. *Training Shop Stewards*. TUC, 1968

TUC. *A Review of Trade Union Education Services*. TUC, 1975

TUC. *Paid Release for Union Training*. TUC, 1977

TRAINING SERVICES AGENCY. *A Five Year Plan*. HMSO, 1974

TREITEL G H. *The Law of Contract*. Stevens, 1975

TRIANDIS H C. *Attitudes and Attitude Change*. Wiley, 1971

TRIST E L, HIGGIN G W, MURRAY H and POLLOCK A B. *Organizational Choice*. Tavistock Publications, 1963

TURNER H A *et al*. *Is Britain Really Strike Prone?* Cambridge University Press, 1969

TURNER H. *Management Characteristics and Labour Conflict*. Cambridge UP, 1977

TURNER H A. *Trade Union Growth, Structure and Policy*. Allen & Unwin, 1962 and in McCarthy (1972) qv, pp. 80–108

ULRICH L & TRUMBO D. "The Selection Interview since 1949" in *Psychological Bulletin*, 63 (2) 1965, pp. 100–16

UNGERSON B (ed). *Recruitment Handbook*. Gower Press, 1970

URWICK L. *Personnel Management in Perspective*. IPM, 1959

URWICK L. *Problems of Growth in Industrial Undertakings*. BIM, 1949

URWICK L and BRECH E F L. *The Making of Scientific Management, Volumes I, II, III*. Management Publications, 1945–1948

URWICK L. *The Elements of Administration*. Harper and Brothers, 1943

VAN BEEK H G. The Influence of Assembly Line Organization on Output, Quality and Morale. *Occupational Psychology*, 38, 1964, pp 161–72

VARNEY G H. Group Goal-Setting in MbO, *Management by Objectives*, 5 (3), 1976

VEBLEN T. *Imperial Germany and the Industrial Revolution*. University of Michigan Press, 1966

VEBLEN T. *The Theory of Business Enterprise* (1904). Mentor Books, 1958

VEBLEN T. *The Theory of the Leisure Class* (1899). Mentor Books, 1953

VERNON P E. *Personality Assessment: a Critical Survey*. Methuen, 1964

600

VERNON-HARCOURT T. *Rewarding Top Management.* Gower, 1980

VETTER E W. *Manpower Planning for High Talent Personnel.* University of Michigan, 1967

VICKERS Sir G. *Towards a Sociology of Management.* Chapman and Hall, 1967

VICKERS Sir G. *The Art of Judgement.* Chapman and Hall, 1965

VICKERS Sir G. *Value Systems and Social Process.* Tavistock, 1968

VITELES M S. *Industrial Psychology.* Norton, 1932

VOLLMER H M and MILLS D S (eds). *Professionalization.* Prentice Hall, 1966

VROOM V H. *Work and Motivation.* Wiley, 1964

VROOM V H and DECI E L. *Management and Motivation.* Penguin, 1970

VROOM V H & YETTON P W. *Leadership and Decision-Making.* University of Pittsburgh Press, 1973

WAGNER R. "The Employment Interview: A Critical Summary" in *Personnel Psychology,* 1949, 2, pp. 17–46

WAINWRIGHT D. *Race and Employment.* IPM, 1970

WALKER J. *British Economic and Social History, 1700–1977.* MacDonald & Evans, 1979

WALL T D & LISCHERON J A. *Worker Participation.* McGraw Hill, 1977

WALLINGTON P. Discrimination, Equal Pay, and the Living Changing Law. *Personnel Management,* January 1978, pp 28–31

WALSH W. Enrichment in the Office. *Personnel Management,* 1 (6), October 1969, pp 42–4

WALTON C B. *Corporate Social Responsibilities.* Wadsworth, 1967

WALTON R E and McKERSIE R B. *A Behavioural Theory of Labour Negotiations.* McGraw-Hill, 1965

WARD P B and BIRD M W. *Identifying Supervisory Training Needs.* HMSO, 1968

WARR P. *The Psychology of Collective Bargaining.* Hutchinson, 1973

WARR P & WALL T. *Work and Well-Being.* Penguin, 1975

WARR P (ed). *Psychology at Work.* Penguin, 1971, 2nd edn, 1978

WARR P, BIRD M, RACKHAM N. *Evaluation of Management Training.* Gower, 1970

WARREN A. "The Aims and Methods of the Education and Training of Shop Stewards: A Case Study" in *Industrial Relations Journal,* 2 (1), 1971a

WARREN A. "The Challenge from Below: An Analysis of the Role of the Shop Steward in Industrial Relations" in *Industrial Relations Journal,* 2 (3), 1971b

WARREN N and JAHODA M. *Attitudes.* Penguin, 1969

WATSON T J. *The Personnel Managers.* Routledge and Kegan Paul, 1977

WEBB S and B. *History of Trade Unionism.* Longman, 1894

WEBB S and B. *Industrial Democracy.* Longman Green and Company, 1920

WEBER M. *The Theory of Social and Economic Organization.* Free

601

Press, Glencoe, 1947

WEBSTER B. Participation—Power Shift or Power Sharing. *Personnel Management*, November 1975, pp 20–22 and 34

WEDDERBURN A. Waking Up To Shiftwork. *Personnel Management*, February 1975, pp 32–35 and 47

WEDDERBURN K. *The Worker and Law*. Penguin, 1971

WEEKES B, MELLISH M, DICKENS L and LLOYD J. *Industrial Relations and the Limits of Law*. Blackwell, 1975

WEIR D. Radical Managerialism: Middle Managers' Perceptions of Collective Bargaining. *British Journal of Industrial Relations*, XIV (3), November 1976, pp 324–338

WEIR D. *Men and Work in Modern Britain*. Fontana, 1973

WEITZ J. "Job Expectancy and Survival" in Fleishman, 1961, qv, pp 26–9

WELLENS J. *The Training Revolution*. Evans Bros. 1963

WELLMAN G. Practical Obstacles to Effective Manpower Planning. *Personnel Review*, 1 (3), Summer 1972, pp 32–47

WEXLEY K N and YUKL G A (eds), *Organizational Behaviour and Industrial Psychology*. OUP, 1975

WHISLER T L and HARPER S F. *Performance Appraisal*. Holt, Rinehart and Winston, 1962

WHITEHEAD R. Communications and Control, in Wells G and Yearsley R (eds), *Handbook of Management Technology*. Heinemann, 1967

WHITELAW M. *The Evaluation of Management Training*. IPM, 1972

WHITLEY R D. Concepts of Organization and Power in the Study of Organizations. *Personnel Review*, 6 (1), Winter 1977, pp 54–9

WHITMORE D A. *Measurement and Control of Indirect Work*. Heinemann, 1971

WHITTINGHAM T G and GOTTSCHALK A W. *Bargaining for Change*. Allen and Unwin, 1972

WHYTE W F et al. *Money and Motivation*. Harper, 1955

WHYTE W H. *The Organization Man*. Penguin, 1960

WILD R. *Work Organization*. Wiley, 1975

WILENSKY H L. The Dynamics of Professionalism. *Hospital Administration*, Spring 1972

WILLIAMS G L. "The Validity of Methods of Evaluating Learning" in *Journal of European Training*, 5 (1), 1976

WILLIAMS Sir B R. Pyramids of Disillusion, *Management Decision*, Winter 1967

WILLIAMS D J. *Capitalist Combination in the Coal Industry*. Labour Publishing Company, London 1924

WILLIAMS W M. *Occupational Choice*. Allen and Unwin, 1974

WILLE E. *The Computer in Personnel Work*. IPM, 1966

WILLS G. *Technological Forecasting*. Penguin, 1972

WILSON B. The Added Value of Pay, *Management Today,* November 1977, pp 101–4

WILSON K. Social Responsibility: A Management Perspective, in Poole M J F and Mansfield R: Managerial Roles in Industrial Relations.

Gower, 1980, pp 50–62

WILSON N A B (ed). *Manpower Research*. English Universities Press, 1969

WINKLER J T. Law, State and Economy: The Industry Act. *British Journal of Law and Society*, Winter 1975

WILSON K. "Social Responsibility and Management Perspectives" Poole, M & Mansfield R. *Managerial Roles in IR*. Gower, 1980

WITHNALL A. "Education and Training for Shop Stewards; A Reassessment" in *Industrial Relations Journal*. 4 (2), 1973

WITHNALL A. "Education and Training for Shop Stewards" in *Journal of Industrial Relations*, Spring, 1972, pp. 40–50

WOLF M G. "Need Gratification Theory: A Theoretical Reformulation of Job Satisfaction and Job Motivation" in *Journal of Applied Psychology*, 1970, 54 (1), pp. 87–94

WOOD S J *et al*. The Industrial Relations System Concept. *British Journal of Industrial Relations*, XIII (3) November 1975, pp 291–308

WOODWARD J. *Industrial Organization: Theory and Practice*. Oxford University Press, 1965

WOODWARD J. *Industrial Organization: Behaviour and Control*. Oxford University Press, 1970

WOODWARD J. *Management and Technology*. HMSO, 1958

WORTMAN M S Jr. *Creative Personnel Management*. Allwyn, 1967

WORTMAN M S and RANDLE C W. *Collective Bargaining: Principles and Practices*. Houghton Mifflin, 1966

WRAY S. "Marginal Men in Industry: The Foreman" in *American Journal of Sociology*, 1949

WRIGHT O. "Summary of Research on the Selection Interview since 1964" in *Personnel Psychology*, 1969, 22, p 391

YODER D. *Personnel Management and Industrial Relations*. Prentice Hall, 1970, 6th edn

YODER D. Personnel Administration, in Somers G G, 1973, pp 141–56, qv

YORK D and DOOLEY C. Checking the Manpower Costs. *Personnel Management*, June 1970, pp 34–5

YOUNG A. Models for Planning Recruitment and Promotion of Staff. *British Journal of Industrial Relations*. III, 1965, pp. 301–10

YOUNG A and ALMOND G. Predicting Distributions of Staff. *Computer Journal*, 3, 1961

YOUNG A F. *Social Services in British Industry*. Routledge and Kegan Paul, 1968

YOUNG D E & FINDLATER J E. "Training and Industrial Relations" in *Industrial Relations Journal*, 2, 1972, pp. 3–22

YUKL G A and WEXLEY K N. *Readings in Organizational and Industrial Psychology*. Oxford University Press, 1971

ZEIST N L and LIEVEGOED B J. *Developing Organizations*. Nederlands Pedagogise Institute, 1972

Author Index

Index